Edward M. Kennedy

Edward M. Kennedy

An Oral History

BARBARA A. PERRY

OXFORD
UNIVERSITY PRESS

Oxford University Press is a department of the University of Oxford. It furthers the University's objective of excellence in research, scholarship, and education by publishing worldwide. Oxford is a registered trademark of Oxford University Press in the UK and certain other countries.

Published in the United States of America by Oxford University Press
198 Madison Avenue, New York, NY 10016, United States of America.

Library of Congress Cataloging-in-Publication Data
Names: Perry, Barbara A. (Barbara Ann), 1956– compiler. |
Kennedy, Edward M. (Edward Moore), 1932–2009, interviewee.
Title: Edward M. Kennedy : an oral history / Barbara A. Perry.
Description: New York, NY : Oxford University Press, 2019. |
Series: Oxford oral history series | Includes bibliographical references and index.
Identifiers: LCCN 2018027757 (print) | LCCN 2018029313 (ebook) |
ISBN 9780190644857 (updf) | ISBN 9780190644864 (epub) |
ISBN 9780190644840 (hardback)
Subjects: LCSH: Kennedy, Edward M. (Edward Moore), 1932–2009—Interviews. |
Kennedy, Edward M. (Edward Moore), 1932–2009—Friends and associates—
Interviews. | Kennedy, Edward M. (Edward Moore), 1932–2009. | Legislators—United
States—Interviews. | United States. Congress. Senate—Interviews. | United States—
Politics and government—1945–1989. | United States—Politics and government—1989– |
Oral history. | BISAC: HISTORY / United States / 20th Century. |
POLITICAL SCIENCE / History & Theory.Classification: LCC E840.8.K35 (ebook) |
LCC E840.8.K35 P47 2019 (print) | DDC 973.92092 [B]—dc23
LC record available at https://lccn.loc.gov/2018027757

9 8 7 6 5 4 3 2 1

Printed by Sheridan Books, Inc., United States of America

To Suzy Joy Brill, Debra Tabb DeCamillis, and Julia McDonough—
my loyal friends and supporters

Contents

Preface

Marking the fortieth year of his US Senate tenure in 2002, Edward Kennedy met with a group of family and friends over dinner to discuss how he might begin to capture and solidify his legacy. Edwin Schlossberg, husband of the senator's niece, Caroline Kennedy, suggested the idea for what would become the Edward M. Kennedy Institute for the United States Senate. Dedicated in March 2015 and located next to the John F. Kennedy Presidential Library and Museum in Boston, the institute features a full-scale model of the US Senate chamber, where visitors participate in congressional simulations. For generations to come, students of democracy will learn through interactive exercises the complex task of crafting and passing legislation, a process at which Senator Kennedy excelled.

But how would Ted Kennedy portray his remarkable life and the lessons he and his colleagues absorbed through their toil in the *real* Senate? At the 2002 dinner, Kennedy's wife, Victoria (Vicki) Reggie Kennedy, raised the possibility of an oral history project to focus on the senator, his Senate colleagues, staffers, foreign leaders, journalists, and his family. The renowned historian and presidential advisor Arthur Schlesinger Jr., also present at the dinner, immediately seconded the idea. Schlesinger, a special assistant to Presidents Kennedy and Johnson, had organized and conducted interviews for the John F. Kennedy Library's Oral History Project and had produced Jacqueline Kennedy's oral history. A Pulitzer Prize winner for his book on JFK's administration, *A Thousand Days*, Schlesinger was a staunch advocate for capturing unique historical insights through the art and science of oral interviews.

Senator Kennedy turned to his fellow University of Virginia Law School alumnus Lee Fentress to search for an appropriate institution to execute the Edward M. Kennedy Oral History Project. Although UVA's Miller Center focused primarily on presidential oral histories, starting with the Gerald Ford administration in the late 1970s, Professor James Sterling Young, who headed the program, convinced the Kennedys that the Miller Center would be the logical institution to produce the spoken record of the senator's biography and career. The Edward M. Kennedy Oral History Project would eventually comprise more than twice as many interviews as the largest Miller Center presidential project.

Before his death from brain cancer in August 2009, Edward Kennedy recorded 29 conversations, with some 250 added by a host of colleagues, friends, and family members over a ten-year period. This book is based on the 23 Kennedy interviews cleared for release by the senator's estate in 2015. They are generally arranged here in the chronological order of Kennedy's life, starting with biographical conversations, followed by discussions of historical events involving the senator and his family, interspersed with key policies that Kennedy addressed over his long career. To augment Senator Kennedy's own stories, each chapter contains "Perspectives," with pertinent quotations from the rich interviews provided by those who knew him best professionally and personally. Because the biographies of the senator and his family are so well known, the reader may find insights from the supplementary interviews even more revelatory.

What distinguishes this vast interview archive from the voluminous secondary works published on Edward Kennedy and from his own memoir is the nuanced detail that emerges from the senator's fulsome, never-before-published descriptions of his life and work, juxtaposed with the observations of his associates. *Edward M. Kennedy: An Oral History* weaves material from the more than seven hundred typescript pages of the senator's interview transcripts, which his staff fact-checked and the Miller Center's Oral History Program lightly edited for readability, into a compelling narrative of his remarkable life. Professor Stephen F. Knott initially directed the project before departing the Miller Center for the US Naval War College. He and Professor James Sterling Young, founder of the Miller Center's Presidential Oral History Program, collaborated on several Kennedy interviews, but Young became the solo questioner for most of the senator's interviews and directed the project until ill health intervened. Janet E. Heininger and Knott interviewed most of the other participants. No questions or topics were placed off limits in the project. The interviewers' italicized queries, along with author's notes and annotations, guide readers through the senator's life, the cast of characters he encountered, and the political events, historic landmarks, and legislative processes that he shaped and that, in turn, molded him. Given the Kennedys' well-known penchant for image creation, what the senator does not say or how he articulates what he chooses to include is often more enlightening than a simple declarative statement. *Edward M. Kennedy: An Oral History* reveals in the senator's own voice his unexpurgated story about the epic Kennedy tragedies and how he attempted to play his part in the family's commitment to public service on the domestic and world stages. Addressing his Irish Catholic immigrant roots, his political DNA, his work with ten presidents (JFK to Obama), his legislative accomplishments and failures, his unsuccessful run for the presidency, his impact on the Supreme Court, his observations on Washington gridlock, and his epic personal weaknesses, Edward Kennedy spoke on the record, as did allies and adversaries alike, creating an unsurpassed and illuminating compendium for historians, political scientists, policymakers, journalists, teachers, students, and other readers of history. His thorough explanations and mastery of congressional intricacies serve as a user's manual for prioritizing, crafting, and creating public policy. A man of complexity and paradox, Edward Kennedy could launch partisan salvos on the Senate floor but work across the aisle with the opposing party to find common ground. Testimonies abound of his care and concern for others, but his personal failings are also legendary. A master of compelling rhetoric, he could sometimes wander into puzzling syntactical cul-de-sacs or utter confounding malaprops. This oral history archive is replete with examples of his multifaceted personality—marked by an infectious joie de vivre, a profound humanity, and, sadly, feet of clay.

Senator Kennedy titled his 2009 memoir *True Compass* because, as he said in its opening pages, "Sailing, for me, has always been a metaphor for life." With that historic life ebbing, the senator concluded, "[Y]ou might not reach your goal right away. But if you do your best and keep a true compass, you'll get there." He would not reach the distant shore of seeing his oral history project through to completion, nor would his trusted navigator, the late Jim Young. It was my honor and privilege to steer the project into port.

Launching this endeavor in December 2004, Senator Kennedy remarked, "I've always loved history, and I've long believed that scholars, politicians, and private citizens and the country as a whole, would benefit from a fuller examination of what we do as senators, and that's the purpose of this oral history project."

A cooperative endeavor of the Edward M. Kennedy Institute for the United States Senate in Boston and the Miller Center at the University of Virginia, the Edward M. Kennedy Oral History Project comprises nearly three hundred interviews, ranging from hour-long conversations to multi-day discussions.

Most of Senator Kennedy's interviews, which ended with his cancer diagnosis in May 2008, along with nearly two hundred of his associates' transcripts, are available online at the Miller Center (www.millercenter.org) and the Edward Kennedy Institute for the United States Senate (www.emkinstitute. org). Consistent with the Miller Center's ongoing obligation to protect confidentiality, according to the protocols of oral history, some parts of these interviews remain closed until future dates, as requested by the interviewees in their deeds of gift.

While a PhD candidate at the University of Virginia in the 1980s, I occasionally spotted Senator Edward Kennedy at commencement exercises, which he would attend with his sister-in-law, Ethel Kennedy, when one of her eleven children graduated from the UVA Law School. Despite his hectic schedule in the US Senate, where he served for almost half a century, Senator Kennedy never ceased serving as a surrogate for his fallen brothers, Senator Robert

F. Kennedy and President John F. Kennedy. It was a homecoming of sorts for Teddy Kennedy, who had earned his law degree from Mr. Jefferson's university. How appropriate, then, that he and his friend, fellow alumnus Lee Fentress, would choose their alma mater to produce this unprecedented archive of his oral history.

The Miller Center's first foray into a comprehensive presidential oral history began in the early 1980s when Jim Young persuaded another native Georgian, President Jimmy Carter, and members of his administration to participate in a project of recorded conversations about the thirty-ninth presidency. Through the leadership of then–Miller Center director Philip Zelikow and Jim Young, a continuing oral history program emerged when the George H. W. Bush Foundation financially supported an oral history of his administration. The program subsequently conducted oral histories of Presidents Ronald Reagan and Bill Clinton, and it has since completed George W. Bush's Presidential Oral History Project.

In addition to these "POTUS" projects and Senator Kennedy's oral history, the Center has produced a project on Lloyd Cutler, White House counsel for Carter and Clinton, as well as recorded group sessions examining the Falklands War, White House congressional relations, presidential speechwriting, and the presidency and domestic policymaking.

Jim Young, Steve Knott, and Jan Heininger could not have conducted hundreds of interviews for the Edward Kennedy project without the support of first-rate Miller Center faculty and staff, including Jim's successor Russell Riley, Marc Selverstone, Rob Martin, Jane Wilson, Beatriz Lee Swerdlow, Bonnie Burns, and Bryan Craig, along with our superb consultants.

The senator's wife, Vicki, was crucial to the enterprise, and I have had the honor of knowing firsthand how meaningful this project is to her. Senator Paul G. Kirk (D-MA), Senator Kennedy's special assistant, advisor, friend, executor, and replacement in the Senate, could not have been more gracious in facilitating the release of the senator's interviews. As I have come to know Vicki and Paul, I can see why Edward Kennedy felt so fortunate to have them in his life.

Jean MacCormack and Nell Breyer, of the Edward Kennedy Institute, provided superlative assistance as the Miller Center processed interviews, through the tireless efforts of my colleagues Mike Greco, Sheila Blackford, and Amber Reichert. The Center's director from 2006 to 2014, Governor Gerald L. Baliles, remained committed to the project throughout his tenure, and the chair of the Miller Center Governing Council, Eugene V. Fife, offered expert guidance to acquire and execute the project. William J. Antholis, the Miller Center's current director, made one of his first goals the timely release of the Kennedy project, and he supported my need to disappear during a summer hiatus, as I devoted several months required to bring this compendium to fruition.

I am especially grateful to my colleague and friend Russell Riley, who set the gold standard for such volumes with his superb Oxford University Press publication *Inside the Clinton White House: An Oral History*. Oxford's Vice President and Executive Editor Nancy Toff first suggested that we undertake these products of our oral histories several years ago, and we are most appreciative of her inspiration, guidance, and confidence in our work. OUP Assistant Editor Elizabeth Vaziri could not have been more helpful in facilitating the many details of the publishing process. The Miller Center's Alfred Reaves IV provided expert research in tracking down photographs, and Rob Martin's vast knowledge of the Edward Kennedy Oral History Project contributed to my drafting of introductions to chapters 4, 5, 11, 13, and 14.

I will always regret that I arrived at the Miller Center just after the Kennedy interviews were completed, so I had no opportunity to participate in them. But I will forever be grateful that Governor Baliles placed his faith in me to finalize the endeavor. Those who had assisted Jim Young so loyally and expertly, Rob Martin, Bonnie Burns, and Jane Wilson, generously lent their knowledge, experience, and talents to me. When Jane retired, Gail Hyder Wiley seamlessly continued the work of processing interviews and, along with Shirley Burke, updated and reviewed the list of Kennedy project transcripts, included in this book's appendix.

The last two lines of what would be the final interview between Senator Kennedy and Professor Young, in March 2008, convey an accurate assessment of their journey together:

> **Kennedy:** I think we got a lot of material down.
> **Young:** Yes, we did.

It was a "good sail," gentlemen.

Editorial Note

The beauty of oral history is its ability to capture authentic expression, whether it is smooth and eloquent or marked by verbal tics and non-fluencies. Authenticity, however, does not necessarily lend itself to artful narrative. Occasionally, the quotations contained in this book contain ellipses to note deleted phrases. To maintain more readable passages, however, ellipses at the end of sentences have been removed. Bracketed wording indicates the author's prerogative of adding information to clarify references to dates, events, or identities. Longer explanations have been included in footnotes.

To focus on the speakers, rather than the interviewers, in these conversations (except in the Epilogue on approaches to oral history), questions or comments begin with a simple Q. Some interview segments have been rearranged for chronological sequencing, thematic consistency, or removal of repetition. Readers who wish to see the full transcripts of each released interview in this project (minus occasional respondent-requested redactions), along with the names of all interviewers, should consult the interview archives at the Miller Center or the Edward Kennedy Institute.

1

Growing Up Kennedy: Lessons from a Political Dynasty

The last of Joseph and Rose Kennedy's nine children arrived on February 22, 1932, when his mother was forty-one years old. Well-meaning friends thought her foolish to have a ninth baby at her age. She was determined, however, to remain cheerful about her ongoing maternity, both for her own peace of mind and for the baby's welfare. Because the child was born on George Washington's birthday, Jack, his waggish fifteen-year-old brother, lobbied to name him for the first president, but his parents resisted and christened him Edward Moore Kennedy, after his father's faithful secretary. The family dubbed the chubby tot "Teddy." Although the Kennedys had moved to New York in 1926 to escape anti-Irish parochialism and to be closer to Joe's Wall Street concerns, Rose returned to her beloved hometown for the birth, ensuring that Teddy would always be a Bostonian.

He was only six when the Kennedys pulled up stakes from their New York estate and sailed to London, settling into the American embassy for Joe Kennedy's ambassadorship in 1938. There young Teddy reveled in the attention lavished on the charismatic clan. They were the toast of London, with Teddy pictured in newspaper and magazine stories about the American ambassador's large and boisterous family. He learned at a tender age to smile and be gracious in public settings. When a baby elephant attempted to snatch a peanut from Teddy's hand as he and his brother Bobby opened the Children's Zoo in London, the youngster maintained his poise and giggled with delight. When the Kennedys attended the coronation of their friend Pope Pius XII at the Vatican in 1939, Teddy received his First Communion from the new head of the Roman Catholic Church at a private Mass.

Later that year, however, with World War II's outbreak, the Kennedy adventure came to an abrupt end when Joe shipped the family home and out of harm's way. Thus began a challenging period for the youngest Kennedy. His parents sold their New York home in 1941 and annually followed the sun from Cape Cod to Palm Beach, uprooting Teddy from a string of day schools. Ultimately, he became a boarder and faced bullying and abuse from older students, an experience that imbued him with a lifelong empathy for the underdog.

Kennedy's maternal grandfather, John F. (Honey Fitz) Fitzgerald, provided a respite from boarding school misery for young Teddy. Each Sunday he traveled from Fessenden School in the Boston suburbs to visit Grandpa Fitzgerald, absorbing the lessons in grassroots politics that Teddy carried with him throughout his career. Honey Fitz was a colorful, leprechaunish figure and former Boston mayor and congressman. His moniker derived from a sweet-talking patter and mellifluous voice that he revealed in warbling his theme song, "Sweet Adeline." As they explored Boston's historic sights and visited favorite restaurants, Teddy observed how his grandfather never met a stranger and spoke to diners, waiters, cooks, and busboys alike. Of the four Kennedy brothers, Teddy emerged as the most gregarious and effervescent. Whereas Joe Jr. and Jack thought their grandfather too corny, brother Teddy admired his genuine knack for connecting with the public. Years later he would keep a photo of Honey Fitz's Ferry Street birthplace in Boston's North End in his Senate office. It represented Kennedy's humble roots, his concern for immigrant experiences, and how the characteristics of a traditional Irish pol can serve a legislator well in the modern polarized Congress.

After attending ten primary and secondary schools, Teddy followed his brothers and father to Harvard but was suspended after his freshman year for cheating on a final exam in Spanish by enlisting a friend to take the test for him. Harvard readmitted Kennedy upon completion of his two-year army enlistment, spent primarily on a NATO base near Paris. Teddy had wanted to volunteer for the Korean conflict, but his brothers begged him not to, out of deference to their parents' grief suffered at the loss of Joe Kennedy Jr. in World War II. Despite the plum assignment in France, the army exposed young Kennedy to strata he had not known as a son of privilege. The experience would also make him a leading advocate for military veterans throughout his Senate career.

Following his Harvard graduation, Teddy enrolled in the University of Virginia Law School, as had his older brother Bobby, and served as Jack's campaign chairman for his 1958 Senate re-election. Now Teddy could begin applying the informal tutorials in Massachusetts politics that master teacher Honey Fitz had led for his grandson. Just after Jack's successful 1958 campaign, Teddy married Joan Bennett, whom he had met at his sister Jean's alma mater, Manhattanville College. They would have three children, Kara (1960), Edward Jr. (1961), and Patrick (1967). Teddy graduated from UVA Law School in 1959, with mediocre grades but an impressive victory in the school's moot court contest, where he partnered with future California senator John V. Tunney.

EMK: I think the one sort of overarching sense that we [the Kennedy family] all had is we were enormously happy together. Our best friends were our brothers and sisters. We enjoyed doing things together. There may have been times when my father and mother weren't present, but we really were never conscious of it. One thing that has struck me over the time that I've become older and realize the political activities of our whole family. I don't remember ever, a single political event taking place in our home, either Cape Cod or in Florida. On rare occasions, my father would have people up to lunch when he was down in Florida, more often when we weren't around, and very rare occasions when we were around. But I don't ever remember a dinner, never remember a cocktail party, never a fundraiser. Home was always a place where we gathered and it was sort of our space and time. That was just the atmosphere and the climate that we grew up in. My brothers used to joke that my sisters would never get married, because they were having such a good time with my brothers, and I remember them talking about it. And of course, they went on in that period of time, they all got married somewhat older than most of their colleagues.

Even with the disruptions and the losses that took place in the course of the family, people had a great time together, they enjoyed each other, were very close to each other and close to our parents. And it was a house of activity. [T]he people who had read books would be talking at the table, the people who had gone on trips, went to interesting places, they would be able to talk and people would ask questions. It was a sort of continuing educational process, and a lively process. And there was always a good deal of sports activity wrapped into all of that, the games we played together, with a few close friends around the community, but there always seemed to be enough of us to make it interesting and fun. So that's sort of a background.

And we took trips with our mother at very early ages, to visit historic places in Massachusetts: Plymouth, Walden Pond, the historic sites in Boston, Paul Revere's home. This sort of fit in to what my grandfather [John F. "Honey Fitz" Fitzgerald] had done with me, I mean this was sort of a continuum.

I can look out my window next to my desk [in Boston] and see where my grandfather was born on Ferry Street and where my mother was born on Garden Court Street. My father was born on Meridian Street in East Boston; that's fairly blocked. I can also see the Old North Church and St. Stephen's Church, the Bunker Hill Monument, the *Constitution*. And if you lean out a little bit and look to the right, you can see Faneuil Hall.

This is the whole birthplace of America, and down the sweep of the harbor, I can see the building where eight of my forebears came in in 1848, out of one window, which is absolutely unique and special. That's a very inspiring location.

Where all of the ships, all the immigrant ships, came in and passed to the docks. The docks are still there, where my great-grandparents came in, in 1848. Eight of them came in, and the steps are still there, where they walked on [to American soil]. They're called the golden steps, because it was the golden steps into opportunity, into the United States.

The *Constitution*, the USS *Constitution* of course.[1] Grandpa Fitzgerald had saved the *Constitution* in 1896. He went up to Portsmouth, New Hampshire, before he got elected to Congress and saw that it was sinking up there. His first appropriations effort was to get enough money to bring it to Boston and get it repaired. It was saved again in the '30s by pennies. We've been very much involved in the development of the museum and a training program about the *Constitution* now.

EMK: As I think back on the times of politics . . . the presence of my grandfather emerges as a larger and larger figure, because I did spend a good deal of time at a very impressionable age, and I had a very close, warm personal relationship where he was sort of my father, a member of my family when I was first off at boarding school. I saw him and observed him and observed his relationship with people and the joy he had from relating to people, and how he related. He was outgoing and warm, and he was able to break through people's barriers and reticence, and do it in an expansive, warm, lovely way. These were my first observations of what you really talk about in politics, and what is most important—how you're going to relate to people.

Q: Was 1958 your first experience campaigning? It was for your brother for the Senate. Was that a relevant first introduction to campaigning in Massachusetts?

EMK: I would say yes. The '58 campaign certainly was intense. I had dabbled. I'd hardly call it campaigning. I'd gone to appearances and events with my brother. I remember going to the old Copley Plaza and hearing [James Michael] Curley[2] speak with my brother when I was very young. I wouldn't call that campaigning, but he would take me along with him to different events. I remember even going to a few events with my grandfather and my brother, but those were sporadic—That was very early, forties, mid- and late-forties. But for all intents and purposes, '58 was the first major involvement in a campaign. I . . . learned a lot, traveled all over Massachusetts. Enormously educational and very interesting and you learn so much. I traveled around at that time, with Larry O'Brien.[3] It was very important that [JFK] do well, because that was sort of the launch of the '60 [presidential bid]. It was both interesting and

---

1. Named by President George Washington and launched in 1797, the USS *Constitution* was among the first frigates in the new US Navy. It saw action in the Quasi-War with France, the First Barbary War, and the War of 1812. During the Civil War, it served as a training vessel for the US Naval Academy. The ship was retired from military service in 1881.

2. James Michael Curley was among the most colorful Democratic politicians in early twentieth-century Massachusetts, serving as Boston mayor, governor, congressman, and jail terms for corruption. He sabotaged John F. Fitzgerald's career, and Honey Fitz's namesake, JFK, happily succeeded Curley in Congress and refused to sign a petition to pardon his grandfather's nemesis.

3. Lawrence F. O'Brien Jr., a Massachusetts political strategist, directed John F. Kennedy's 1952 and 1958 US Senate campaigns, as well as his 1960 run for the presidency. JFK appointed him congressional liaison, and O'Brien served as part of the president's most trusted inner circle in the White House.

a learning experience. You learned not only the state, but also that politics is about people, and you get a real feel for also, about whether this is something you wanted to do, or at least I certainly did from that kind of life experience.

The one time I campaigned with Bobby and Jack in Massachusetts was in 1958. Bobby was up towards the end of the campaign. It was a rather interesting phenomenon. My brother ran against a fellow named Vinny Celeste,[4] who was not a very notorious figure. He [Jack] had gone abroad for ten days in the summer, and when he came back, it was just after the primary, and he had gotten more blanks than Foster Furcolo.[5] More people in the Democratic primary had blanked him than Furcolo. This was a real concern to my father. It never really got reported, but my father was very concerned.

We went over and had a meeting in New York, just when my brother got back from Europe, with Bobby and my father and me. We were going to have to intensify the campaign because there was an apparent backlash out there. Either the Italians were upset or some other people were upset. Bobby took an interest. He didn't campaign much himself, but he followed it more closely for the last few weeks. The primary was in mid-September. The night before the election, they used to have this famous rally at the G&G Delicatessen out on Blue Hill Avenue.

It was a hundred-year-old tradition. You'd speak from the top of the roof of the delicatessen. They'd have big speakers and lights and balloons and everything. They always got a very good turnout. That night my brother said he had made all the speeches in the campaign, but this night we were going to sing. So instead of making a speech, my brother, Bobby, and I, we all sang. We sang three songs for the crowd. And then my brother just talked—

Q: *What were the songs?*

EMK: "Heart of My Heart" and "That Old Gang of Mine." "Wedding bells are breaking up that old gang of mine." I'd sing it for you but, I'm—

Q: *Sure. Do it! Do it!*

EMK: Well, it's (singing): "Heart of my heart, how I love that melody. Heart of my heart keeps that melody. When we were kids on the corner of the square, Boylston, Tremont Street, we were rough and ready guys, but oh how we could harmonize to heart of my heart, oh my friends were dearer then. You could borrow ten. Too bad we had to part. I know a tear would glisten, if once more I could listen, to that gang that sang heart of my heart.

"Now there's no one on the corner. It's a pretty certain sign, those wedding bells are breaking up that old gang of mine. Now don't you get that lonesome feeling every time you hear those chimes? Those wedding bells are breaking up that old gang of mine. There goes Jack, there goes Jackie down through

---

4. Vincent J. Celeste, a Boston lawyer who, as the Republican candidate for the US House of Representatives in 1950 and the US Senate in 1958, lost to John F. Kennedy.

5. Foster Furcolo, Democratic governor of Massachusetts from 1957 to 1961.

lovers' lane. Now and then we meet again, but it never seems the same. Now don't you get that lonesome feeling every time you hear those chimes? Those wedding bells are breaking up that old gang of mine."

And then there's "Bill Bailey, won't you please come home?" [Jack] didn't know the words to it very well. I knew the words to it.

Q: Bill Bailey?

EMK: (singing): "Bill Bailey won't you please come home?" Um, let's see. "Knock, knock, knock. Who's there? You've gone and I hear you, darlin'. I hear you down there"—something—"home for me. Oh, won't you come home, Bill Bailey? Won't you come home? I prayed the whole night long. I'll do the cookin', honey. I'll pay the rent. I know I've done you wrong. Oh, no, there's a rainy evening. I put you out with nothing but a fine tooth comb. I know I'm to blame. But ain't it a shame, Bill Bailey won't you please come home? Come on home, Bill Bailey. Bill Bailey won't you please come home?"

I remembered the words a little better then. But that was a time that we all three had actually a lot of fun. It was one time we were all together [campaigning]. . . .

Kennedy recalls meeting Richard Nixon:

EMK: In the Russell [Senate Office] Building, on the fourth floor, way down this corridor, I had an office at one time, and I think my brother [Jack] was down on the second floor. [As a senator] I never [used] his office. But right opposite my brother's office was Richard Nixon's office. I remember coming down here [to Washington] to visit my brother one time when I was in law school. I took the overnight train, and I came on up [from Charlottesville]. The office was closed, and I was sitting on my suitcase reading, and this single figure came down. Who was it but Richard Nixon? He said, "Come on in my office." I don't think he had Secret Service or anything. It was just unbelievable. I went in there and talked to him for thirty minutes, waited until my brother's office [opened] up. I thought he was the nicest person. He was interested in what I was doing in school and liked my brother, and it was just an amazing half-hour. This was before anything zoned in in terms of Richard Nixon.

Q: To back up again, what I'm trying to get at here is how you learned about Massachusetts politics and campaigning. It seems to me that your visits with your grandfather [John F. Fitzgerald] were your first exposure, even as a kid, to something about politics. And then you begin to hear Curley and so forth.

EMK: Oh, very definitely. As I think back on the times of politics, looking reflectively back, the presence of my grandfather emerges as a larger and larger figure, because I did spend a good deal of time [with him] at a very impressionable age, and I had a very close, warm personal relationship. . . . I saw him and observed him and observed his relationship with people and the joy he had from relating to people, and how he related. . . . I had a unique entry, or observation, into that. And I must say I saw that it was different in my brother [Jack], who was much more reserved. I saw his evolution and development from his hesitancy in the beginning, his remarkable ability to be insightful and precise, but still have a hesitancy, which eventually in the buildup from '56 to '60 he overcame.

Q: You mentioned this was unique in your experience. You were the only child in the family who had this exposure in this way.

EMK: Really the only one.

Q: So that's quite important as a first—

EMK: That's true. I think my brother interacted with him, but in an entirely different kind of relationship. When my brother was running, Grandpa was a figure, and I think he didn't know whether he did or didn't want Grandpa there. But for me, he was an ideal, and extraordinarily unique. I had not seen those qualities in my own family, and the more I observed it, the more I learned about him, he was just an incredible phenomenon, a character. His inquisitiveness into life and people and events, and the joy he got out of knowing everything was enormously instructive. I think he had a similar impact in terms of my brother Jack, who spent more time; my brother Bob [Robert F. Kennedy], some. He was always inquisitive, but Grandpa's inquisitiveness and thirst for knowledge were very contagious. My parents had that, but at a different pace. He had that, and the ultimate sense that there were interesting qualities and a sense of humor in people and a sense of joy and happiness if you just touched the nerve. He always was able to get there in a unique and special way. I don't think any of us could ever get to the point that he did. It came naturally to him, and I think part of it was growing up at that time, and his own personal experience and evolution and development as well.

Q: Right. Somebody's going to ask, "Was Grandpa your first role model?" I don't like those terms, but it's—

EMK: Oh, I always thought that Grandpa knew how to do it. If politics was going to be your game, he was the name. I was struck more by the personal association and contact and the joy he had in it. Obviously, to a child, the issues were somewhat blurred, but the idea that he would sing and get people aroused and interested and enthusiastic and be able to identify and attract people to him was the incredible ingredient. And my reading of the period tied into this. I can't remember now whether it was my reading or whether Grandpa told me about how when he was first in public office, the Irish were too poor to buy newspapers. So they'd say to him, "How do you stand, Honey Fitz? How do you stand?" And he'd effectively tell them his position on whatever it was, and that was good enough for them. I think the people at that time made their judgments and decisions about politicians from the heart more than from the mind. And I think, looking back over history, it's probably that they'll continue to make some mistakes in doing it, but they'll be more right than wrong, even today. But it was the way that people identified politics—

Q: Do you think it's still true that people—

EMK: I think it is true.

Q: Do you find that in your own contemporary—

EMK: I still do. People have a sense of you and your inner qualities and strengths. They may differ with me, as frequently they do, but they have a sense that I'm standing up for things that I believe, which is most important. Stand for what you believe in is always a good indicator.

My grandfather used to take me around Boston. We'd always have lunch up at the Belleview Hotel, and then he'd take me for a walk in Boston and show me Milk Street, where the cows used to walk, or Water Street, where there used to be wells for the early settlers, and then over to the Old North Church and the *Constitution*. So it was a continuing sort of educational seminar on the one hand, and then there was also the religious seminar on another hand, that was never far behind. As I mentioned, my brothers were all altar boys, I was trained in that. That was a big force and factor. So that was sort of the climate and atmosphere everyone grew up in, which was very natural.

Some of my earliest impressions were about discrimination in our society, rather than just the issue as we think about it today, in terms of civil rights. And I believe those earliest impressions really started from my relationship with my grandfather. [I]n those walks that we'd have around Boston, he'd talk about the discrimination that took place against the Irish, and about the different sections of the city. In some sections, the Italians lived; in other sections, the Irish lived; and others lived in other communities. Jews lived in other parts of the city, Negroes lived in other communities, and some of these communities moved and shifted as the immigrations came on. He talked about how, in some places, the last people who came in, who would get the jobs, would be of a different party. He talked about the French up in Lowell and Lawrence. They came in and they got the jobs and replaced the Irish. The people who gave them the jobs were Republicans, and so they were much more inclined to be Republican.

Grandpa talked about the unfairness of the immigration rules—I remember that, long before everybody got into the immigration—how the immigration worked, discriminated against people about where they were born. He was very strongly against that. He was a mender, and he was looking for ways to try to mend the different kinds of groups together as a politician, and he saw that this was something that was very strongly held in terms of the different ethnic groups. I can remember him talking about that at a very early age. There had been a good deal of discrimination. I mean, Catholics in Massachusetts in 1780 couldn't even vote, and you had discrimination in these schools—the Lord's Prayer in the public schools, so the Catholics all wanted the private schools. They were sort of evident around in Boston, and the reasons you hear why is because the Protestant schools made Catholics say Protestant prayers and things like that. When I went to Protestant schools, I always had to have a separate time out to go to Catholic instructions with the other boys. It was always made possible, because my mother made such a deal out of it, but it was always, you were very much aware that there was tension between the Protestant and the Catholic.

I think there are complicated ethical issues and questions that always need focus and attention, and we all need guidance in areas. But my sense is that on the one hand you have your basic moral and spiritual religious motivation, which helps to define your philosophy. You can go back and say, well, can you be agnostic and have values? A non-believer and have values? Many of them do. They say that that is part of the human gene—goodness and evil.

Others believe that the basic moral values comes from religious traditions, and great religions have common values of fairness and caring about the poor, others. My religion has the precepts which are laid out in its teachings, and which I find very powerful, and that motivated me—[St.] Matthew['s Gospel], about the hungry and the thirsty and clothing the naked, welcoming the stranger and visiting the prisoner, and the provisions of [St.] John['s Gospel]— when you have done it to the least of these, you have done it for me. The very powerful [scriptural] passages that exist, which are uplifting, inspiring, and pretty clear as to the purpose of life.

I grew up in a family where religion was very much a part of our own iden- tity. I mean it was as much a part of our identity as the large family was, the Irish tradition was, the fact that brothers and sisters were members of the family. It was an inherent defining aspect of who we were. Now, I had parents who approached it in a somewhat different way. My mother was very accepting, rarely doubting, although she did doubt, particularly the loss of Bobby [Robert F. Kennedy]. She doubted, how could the Lord take away the father of ten children? That was a very powerful question that she had to live with.

My father questioned the hierarchal aspects of the church, although many of those that were in the hierarchy were his best friends. Father [John] Cavanaugh who was the president of Notre Dame, was one of his four or five best friends. Every time he stayed here he said Mass at seven in the morning, my father was there. Every single morning he did that. Or wherever we were, if we were down in Florida or someplace and [Father Cavanaugh] was saying [Mass], my father was there. Plus my father—in this house [at Hyannis Port] every person went to church on Sundays, even a candidate for president of the United States—he can't get in very late. No one showed up for lunch if they hadn't been to church, or dinner.

[My father] was very close to Cardinal Cushing,[6] and he was very close to a fellow named Count Galeazzi, who was the architect of the Vatican and the personal advisor to the popes. Galeazzi used to come visit my father in France,

---

6. Richard Cardinal Cushing served as Boston's archbishop from 1944 to 1970. The Kennedy family's prelate, he presided over JFK's wedding and funeral masses and gave the benediction at President Kennedy's inauguration.

and my father went down to Rome to talk with him. And so he was very interested and he was a very strong believer, but he couldn't—there were aspects of authority that he was not accepting, although he was very internally spiritual, and a very strong believer.

So in any event, religion was very enormously influential and very powerful, and continuing. I went to a Protestant school—every year my mother asked me to go, I had to go on a [religious] retreat, and more often than not she would go with me. The idea that you crank out a couple of days down at Cape Cod and drive on up to Lawrence, [Massachusetts] which we did, or—I guess it was outside, between Lawrence and Lowell, a wonderful retreat house up there.

Vicki Kennedy:[7] You can tell that story about your going to that sailing—that's always struck me. On your way to go sail.

EMK: Well, we were going off to—loved to sail, loved to race, and we had our crew all set, and we were going to this kind of regatta, and my mother called out the window, "Teddy, dear, this is the weekend you're going on the retreat." And I said, "Well, I think I'm going on the race." "Oh, no, you're going on the retreat, Teddy dear." [*Laughter.*]

Q: How old were you?

EMK: Uh, probably sixteen, fifteen, sixteen.

Q: And you went on the retreat.

EMK: And off I went on the retreat. So I never—always getting to the retreat was the problem. Once I got to the retreat, I kind of enjoyed it, liked it, but the getting there was onerous.

Q: It was a large Catholic family, and there were no priests among the children, no one who went into the priesthood, and nobody went into the sisterhood and became a nun. Is that something that needs to be explained, because it was very common in earlier times at least for each family to have one of the sons go into the church?

EMK: I really don't think so. So much of the circumstances were so dramatic at the time that the older members of the family were growing up, I mean the war [World War II] was upon us before the very crucial, critical time when people are thinking about what they might have been doing. This was something that was all-encompassing, and I think all-compelling, and I think the question—Joe[8] might have, my older brother Joe was very religious. He was

---

7. Victoria (Vicki) Reggie Kennedy, a Washington corporate lawyer and daughter of Edmund (a Louisiana judge) and Doris Reggie, who supported JFK, starting with his brief run for the 1956 Democratic vice-presidential nomination. Vicki knew the Kennedy family throughout her life. In 1992, she and Edward Kennedy married at his home in McLean, Virginia. Mrs. Kennedy is credited with setting his life back on course and partnering with him for the last seventeen years of his life in the Senate. She participated in several of his oral history interviews.

8. Joseph P. Kennedy Jr., the eldest of Edward Kennedy's siblings and apple of his parents' eye, was a hero to his youngest brothers and sisters. A graduate of Choate and Harvard University, he left Harvard Law School to become a naval officer and aviator in 1940. Joe

very devoted and very religious, and he left law school to get in the service. Jack [John F. Kennedy], after Joe had gone in, felt that he had to go. Bobby was eighteen and went in the navy. Suddenly they had three or four years out of their lives, and I think the quieter time and that kind of an aspect when you're spending more thoughtful times, I think was a very tumultuous kind of a time. My mother always used to talk about, "Maybe it'll be this one," looking at me as someone who would go into the church [as a priest].

You know I think my mother thought that Bobby was sort of on his way, and I think Bobby probably could have gone in very easily. Moral righteousness, belief, and he was a very strong practicing Catholic. The Newman Club up at Harvard, he was the one—it's an extraordinary story. Came down and told my father, said, "You know, they're teaching, I have a . . . priest up there, Father Feeney,[9] teaching that there's no salvation outside of the church." My father said, "Bobby, you must have it wrong." "No, no, I got it right." So over my father went and said, "Why don't you drive right up and talk to Cardinal Cushing. He'll see you right now about this."

So we went up and talked to Cardinal Cushing. Cardinal Cushing said, "Well, let me think about it and send somebody over there to listen to this person." And this was just about the time of, later, it was [Pope] John's meeting and gathering [the Second Vatican Council], and when the issue came up of whether there was salvation outside of the church, they thought Bishop [John] Wright was going to make the presentation. Cardinal Cushing said he wanted to make it because he had gotten so interested in this. And he made the presentation, which was accepted, which was the basis of the ecumenical movement.

And that's where it all opened up, in terms of all the other religions. The Catholics said there is salvation outside of the Catholic Church, and that—eventually they took Father Feeney and told him he could not teach any more religion in a sacramental place. He went back to try and teach, and they had to defrock him. He was on the front page of *Life* magazine. And it really all started with Bobby. It's an amazing story, and I remember it just as clear as a bell. My father just sort of challenged him, you know, "Get back in your car and go drive back to Boston. Come on, I'm calling Cardinal Cushing right now. If you feel so strongly about it." And this was something that was very strong with Bobby, and I think under other circumstances he might have gone [into the priesthood].

---

perished in August 1944 when his plane exploded over the coast of England on his volunteer mission to destroy Nazi artillery emplacements in France.

9. Father Leonard E. Feeney was a Jesuit priest, sometimes known as Massachusetts's "Father Coughlin" for his conservative theology and anti-Semitism. Opposed to modernizing the Catholic Church, he preached that only Catholics could acquire eternal salvation.

Vicki Kennedy: But he met Ethel.

EMK: But he met Ethel. But he could have [gone into the priesthood]—my sisters were all very strong [Catholics].

Vicki Kennedy: They went to Catholic schools all the way through.

EMK: And the next generation, they thought that [my nephew] Timmy Shriver was going to be [a priest]—because he reads everything, he's almost—

Vicki Kennedy: But then he met [his future wife] Linda [Potter].

EMK: But he was really on his way [to considering the priesthood].

Vicki Kennedy: Still, a very spiritual person, very—

EMK: Very, underneath. Does all the readings, writes so much like my sister Eunice [Kennedy Shriver], thinks about the retarded being in the image of God, he's got these marvelous lines. He reads all these Catholic philosophers and theologians.

We had in the Fitzgeralds . . . my mother's brother—their son Father Jack Fitzgerald who was a priest, we were first cousins. I think one other too—

Q: It's noteworthy that I heard you say your mother thought that maybe Bobby might be [a priest], or maybe you might be a [religious] brother. In other words, there was no shaping a child, one of the children, to be that. You were on your own. And your parents were waiting to see, or just interested to see who might choose that. Or you might have the qualities that—

Vicki Kennedy: This is a vocation, you're called to a vocation, but your mother certainly gave you total exposure to the faith. To see if you were called.

EMK: I think that's true. We mentioned earlier, every year that I went to a Protestant school I was off at a retreat, and when I was off at a Protestant school, I had religious instruction during the week. My mother would find out who the other Catholic boys were in the class and get a hold of their mothers and ask them if they wanted to go. When I went to Milton Academy every Wednesday or whatever it was, study hour, we met over at the cathedral and the Catholic priests from St. Sebastian's taught—and some were better than others.

But in college, when I was at Harvard I used to—John Droney, who was a friend of my brother's, and a fellow named [John] Zamparelli, who's still around—he's obviously old, but he was—they used to go to church every morning, and at Lent time I went every morning. They would call my mother, and my mother was so pleased. They were smart enough. You know, they ran *against* each other for district attorney and Droney won. Hated each other. They ended up being best friends. And they went to church all the time, and they were both very strong supporters of my brother Jack's. And they didn't know my mother, campaigned with her, and they were smart enough, they'd call up, "Well, your boy's at church over here. Good boy." [*Laughter.*]

But in any event—when we were growing up, there were always three basic tenets that were non-public. One was the family, this house [in Hyannis Port] was always a very sacred place for all of us. [H]e had that wonderful saying that home holds no fear for me. You go out and do the best you can, and you can always come home.

He had this family, religion, and patriotism, they were all assumed, and you didn't have to wear those on your sleeve. Which was very important. Everybody went in the service, my brothers went in the service, everyone went in the service. My brother Jack would have done anything for anybody who was wounded, but didn't—in the beginning until he ran for president he didn't support the GI Bill. He said everybody, his generation, we're all called in there. Anything for the wounded, but there's no—then when he ran he supported it. Religion was assumed in the family, respected in the family, and the patriotism was all assumed.

Now the politics has changed. Now people who are not involved in that outwardly flaunt it. We've been run over, our side has been run over on this thing [patriotism and service] because we didn't flaunt them. I think that's a political reality. We've got to be clever. If you want to stay in the game you've got to be clever enough to win. Obviously there are ways of being able to do it without flaunting it. But this is certainly true about it.

George Bush, Cheney, deferments, John Tower—biggest hawks in the Senate are people that never went to war. Biggest dove, George McGovern,[10] was a [war] hero, an authentic hero, and he got pilloried. So it's—but to get back to the other aspects of it, that was something that was never explained, no one ever explained that to us. The family, religion, and patriotism was something that you were born into, and it became a part of us. My father never said, "Boys, look, we've gotten through the summer and didn't have a political event down here. Isn't it wonderful?" But at the end of the day you just knew it. We have some [events] now, try to keep it, obviously, in the summer.

Q: So nobody would think of not going to Mass.

EMK: No one. Everybody went. My mother, right up to the end, everybody went. And more often than not, they wanted to go when she went to Mass. "What time are you going to Mass tomorrow?" I mean it was either eight o'clock or nine o'clock, there wasn't really much—if her stomach had bothered her she said, "I'm going at nine o'clock." Otherwise at eight. Everyone, all my sisters, up to the time that she left when she was ninety, ninety-five down there, then was here [Hyannis Port] the last nine years of her life. Whenever, everybody wanted to go with her, wanted to be with her, to chat with her, talk with her. Everybody wanted to go now.

They didn't—there were exceptions. My brother was two years away from getting the Democratic nomination and was going to miss the eleven o'clock

---

10. Kennedy is referring to President George W. Bush's stateside service in the Texas Air National Guard and Vice President Richard Cheney's five deferments from the Vietnam War draft. John Tower was a Republican senator from Texas; George McGovern, a Democrat, served in the Senate from South Dakota.

Mass. My father pulled in down here, trying to get across the fence over on the other side, sent me out there with a car to pick him up and make sure he could get to Mass.

There's that wonderful story . . . about my father and President Kennedy, just about the family, and that is that when my brother was president, and we were coming over here for dinner, and I'd gone over to visit him at his house, and actually we were playing checkers. He liked to play checkers, my brother played checkers, but he talked with you when you played. You'd chat, and— seven o'clock was when the cocktail hour started here, and at 7:29 we went in there for dinner. It was a Friday night, and you'd been out working, but only since probably '56, you know we never had liquor or wine served in the house until about '55 or '56. My brother was elected to the Senate and then my father would—I don't ever remember hard liquor, he'd have daiquiris, never wine. Friday night, there was a little glass—if you hung out, you could have one. Two of them on Saturday night. And there weren't any daiquiris served on Sunday night because you were leaving for work, if you hadn't left for work, which you should have. But if you stayed over Sunday night, to leave for work on Monday, there were no daiquiris served.

Q: This was when your brother was in the Senate?

EMK: Senate. And we'd come home on a weekend for something like that, law school, and he'd be there, my father here. On the weekends. I mean there was nothing served during the week. But on weekends. So we came over to his house at 7:00 and walked across, and as the story is told, he and I were walking through that little gate that's over on the side here by the Robert Kennedys' [house], that faces our house on what would be the west side. Caroline[11] came around the front, my father came around from the front of the house, and Mac Bundy[12] said, "Mr. President, they want you—the White House wants you in here." My brother said, "Teddy, take Caroline. I've got to go in there and take the call." And he went in by the kitchen, and my father saw this, and I talked to Caroline. We turned around. We walked on in. My father walked into the dining room and sat down. He was just teed off.

So my brother finished and came out, saw everyone in the dining room, sat down. My father said—he would start the conversation depending on what he wanted to talk about. My brother was on his way to Vienna to meet Khrushchev.[13] My father said, "Jack, I know you're thinking about meeting Khrushchev. Let me just tell you something. Nothing you do as president is going to be more important than how your daughter turns out. And don't ever forget it." Wonderful line. This was from a person who did everything to elect

---

11. Caroline Kennedy is JFK's daughter.

12. McGeorge (Mac) Bundy, a professor of government at Harvard, was the dean of its Faculty of Arts and Sciences when JFK asked him to serve as National Security Advisor.

13. Nikita Khrushchev was the Soviet premier, with whom JFK met in June 1961.

him president and had this wonderful line. You didn't really have to tell him that. My brother was a great father. But in a way it was just sort of reflective of this fundamental atmosphere and climate that existed here from the very beginning. He had the priorities straight.

Q: But as a kid, this [religion] *was something that was a given and something that you had to do. It was part of life here, it was part of the family, it was a given. When you leave the sacred place and you go out on your own, it's nothing you have to do anymore, is it?*

EMK: Well, probably something other than that. For us it was as meaningful as breathing or loving our parents or relationships with members of our family. It was all intertwined, all intertwined, it was all part of—sure, you drive to church on Sunday, but it was all intertwined, all part of this whole package, as much as love of the sea and you walk to the beach, it's the love of a faith and following the rituals of it. And I think, what of course happens is very quickly, and maybe it's more ritualistic when you're very small, because you get people bundling off, but what happens is that at the time when you're sort of leaving the nest, so to speak, it is at some point fixed in your heart and soul and your being in terms of its source of inspiration, its source of hope, its source of solace, and its source of strength. I mean it fits into this. The teachings become inspiring, you find out, do some of the things that these parables [teach], you find out that this is enriching to your life, it adds an additional dimension to it. This compounds itself, becomes even more of a factor or force.

There are obvious dramatic events that shake those foundations. You certainly face those. In the '70s my son lost his leg with the cancer, and others which are dramatic. But I always found that at the end of the day this was a wonderfully constructive and positive force in my life. And I think it's part of the eternal optimism, that makes me sort of an optimistic person. I think it's the hopeful aspects of the belief. Leave it to others to do the analysis, but for me those teachings and that uplifting aspect of faith is the one that gives a great deal of hope and optimism to me.

Perspectives

Ann Gargan, Edward Kennedy's cousin: Jack always used to say, "You know, if I walked across the stage, slipped on a banana peel, and went sliding, if I called, Dad would say, 'That was so graceful! You looked in charge of the whole thing!'"

They had that faith in God Almighty, and it was transformed into their home. They knew, no matter what they did, they had a support system. And I think that that has been so strong in him—well, really, in everyone—but being the youngest, because everybody looked out for Ted. Not looked out for, but he was the youngest in the family, especially among the boys. He knew he had that support system. No matter what else happened in the whole world, he had faith not only in God, but in his family unit. No matter how things went, he had his mother and father 100 percent behind him. They might tell him, "That wasn't too bright," but they never let him down. I think that's what everybody wants, and he had it, and he knew he had it, which is another thing.

But as I said, when things would go wrong, he'd say, "Oh, boy," like any of us. And you might think you were going to get a real blast, and maybe you got a real blast. But that was the end of it. Whatever you did, you could come home and have great support. I think that kind of support sustained him too, because God knows he's had more than his share.

Q: Some people have told us that he's probably closest to Jean[14] *among his sisters because they grew up fairly close together. I think they were four years apart or so.*

Gargan: Yes, because you see, they were very young when the family was in England. As years go by, as we all know, the years don't become as important. He was close with Bobby, but he did a lot more things with my brother, Joe. Of the boys, the older ones were eligible to be in the service, and even Bob joined the navy. But you see, these two, Ted was still at home. And my uncle [Joseph Kennedy Sr.] got all sorts of projects for the two of them: cutting the bridle paths over in Osterville and that kind of thing. Jean was home, but even Kick [Kathleen Kennedy] had joined the Red Cross, so she was in England. But it's like any family: different age groups do different things. And I would think probably Jean was around the most.

Vicki Kennedy: And I think that's why he loved the Cape so much, because that was home. The Cape for him—oh, it's the beautiful view, it's the sea, but it's home because it's the place he associated with his parents and his siblings. It's the place he associated with his family being whole in his childhood, it's the last place they were all together, when everybody was alive. It's the place he had the happiest memories, it was the place of joy in the summer, when he had that nomadic school lifestyle. It was the place he would find joy, it's the place he learned to sail, it's the place he was with his older brothers and his sisters. It's home. And then later, the place with his kids. He just loved home, and he I think longed for a stable home.

I think something very positive happened there. I think there's something extraordinary about the family, his parents and the children, the bond that they all developed. It's something that I continue to just be amazed by. The extraordinary accomplishment of all of his siblings, his parents, the bond they had with each other, the incredible love they had for each other, it's really

---

14. Jean Kennedy Smith is Edward's youngest sister and eighth of Joe and Rose Kennedy's nine children. She married businessman Stephen E. Smith in 1956, who managed the Kennedy family finances and served John, Robert, and Edward as a skilled political strategist. She served as US ambassador to Ireland from 1993 to 1998, under President Bill Clinton.

extraordinary. Something happened in that family that his parents instilled in them, and the love their parents encouraged them to have for each other, the bond their parents encouraged them to have for each other. I feel like a lot of it happened at the Cape. I just feel that something happened there.

Q: It's kind of mysterious, isn't it?

Vicki Kennedy: It *is* mysterious. It's almost like magical properties, whether it's the water or the sailing, or whether it was the joy of just being there. Teddy was a little boy. The last time they were all together was 1941, and that's a long time ago. He was nine.

But it still was special to him, and then even when they weren't all together, because they lost Joe [Jr.] and then Rosemary was away, and then they lost Kick.[15] Still, the remaining siblings were there and would come together. They were so much older than he was, we forget that. Teddy was so much younger than the rest of them and then at some point, the age difference doesn't make a difference any longer. It still was—the Cape was that unifying place. It was the place they came together.

William J. vanden Heuvel, Attorney General Robert Kennedy's special assistant, deputy US permanent representative to the United Nations: It was an interesting combination because they retained the provincial quality that strong family ties cause. Their first relationships were with each other, and that was the primary relationship and nothing broke that. Whatever went on between them or among them, others may see fragments of or have a sense of it, but it was an enormously close bond that had been forged, in large part by the father, who, although frequently absent, was a very real presence in their lives all of the years of his life.

I saw Mrs. Joseph P. Kennedy quite often. I went to Palm Beach with Teddy once, I think it was for New Year's of 1965–66. He had just come back from Vietnam. He and I think John Tunney had been over on a briefing tour. I stayed at the family home in Palm Beach. It was wonderful to see Rose Kennedy in action. She was such a methodical person. At breakfast, she'd come down and would direct the conversation, questions and talks about current events and attitudes and opinions. There was no idle chatter.

Elizabeth Shannon,[16] wife of US Ambassador to Ireland William Shannon, Edward Kennedy's friend: Ted told me a funny story too. You know, they all were in some ways afraid of their mother, afraid of her wrath, because she was tough on them all. They mostly just wanted to keep the peace with her. One

---

15. Rosemary, Teddy's eldest sister, had to be institutionalized after a failed lobotomy in 1941; Kathleen Kennedy Cavendish, Teddy's second-eldest sister, died in a 1948 plane crash.

16. After Ambassador Shannon died in 1988, Edward Kennedy courted Elizabeth for several years.

time, when John was president, he was home in Hyannis and Mrs. Kennedy said, "Now you boys will all have to go to Mass today." They said, "We will. You go to the early [Mass], and we'll go to the late," or, "You go to the late and we'll go to the earlier." Anyway, they wanted to get out of it and in some way they did.

They were playing ping-pong in the garage when they were supposed to have been at Mass, and she unexpectedly came back. They heard her car coming up the drive and John hid under the ping-pong table. Teddy said, "He's president of the United States, and he's hiding under the ping-pong table because he wasn't at Mass and his mother's going to give him hell for it." So in those ways she ruled the roost, but then in other ways she just let her husband run roughshod.

Laurence Tribe, Harvard Law School professor and Edward Kennedy's advisor: Because I had gotten to know the family really well through that trip [with them to the Soviet Union in the mid-1970s], my ex-wife and I were invited to go to Hyannis Port just to hang out. We didn't quite know what to expect. We thought it would be kind of cool. We would meet Ted. Somebody said we might meet Rose.

We arrived, and I remember not really having seen the senator before in any setting other than on television, and he was mixing drinks or something and we walked into this place and there he was. It was very interesting. He was a charismatic and compelling character. We had dinner with him and with his mom and with various other members of the family. Jackie[17] was there.

From the very beginning, I was struck by what a complicated role he played in that family. Rose was merciless with him, joking in various ways, making fun of him. Although Carolyn[18] [Kreye Tribe] and I were the only non-family members there, we faded into the background quite quickly, and we just saw the family dynamic to the point where, after a few drinks he would say, "Mom, you always left me behind, or you did this or you did that." It was really remarkable to watch the family tensions.

By the end of a very long evening of having dinner with them, and there was some touch football and other stuff, we really had the sense that this was a very complicated family. I had the sense that this was a guy I would love to get to know. There was warmth, and there was vulnerability, and there was seriousness at the same time. From that point on I always thought, if there's anything he wants, I'm there for him. And he wanted lots of things. He called me from time to time and asked for advice. But it was in that context that I first met him, at this family gathering in Hyannis Port.

---

17. Jacqueline Bouvier Kennedy Onassis married John F. Kennedy in 1953 and Aristotle Onassis in 1968.

18. Carolyn Kreve Tribe was Laurence's wife.

John Kenneth Galbraith, founder of Americans for Democratic Action, President Kennedy's advisor and ambassador to India, Harvard professor of economics:

Q: *If you could just tell us if you have any early memories of meeting Ted Kennedy, as opposed to Jack or Bobby.*

Galbraith: Well, I met him many times over the years. I have no particular memory of any first meeting. That was rarely explained. I had a certain association with the Kennedy family, and I first met him when it was a family occasion, and he was one of the family. My distinctive memory of this young man, by my standards, was not particularly great. My memory was of the family rather than of Ted himself, and that, to some extent, has been true of his life.

It was a very important factor in Ted Kennedy's career that he followed four people. He followed a father who was very active in politics, and there was nothing restrained about him, as an ambassador, as a figure in Massachusetts. And then, of course, his two brothers. He was, in Massachusetts history, the fourth in line. Only gradually over the years did he have his recognition of his full role, which was that of being the premier senator of his time.

Q: *Let me ask you a speculative question. Do you think he would have made a great president?*

Galbraith: Oh sure, no question about that. Being the fourth in the Kennedy hierarchy was definitely a handicap. There was his father, his two brothers, and then in age came Ted. But Ted was, in my view and in the common view, a top-notch senator, and he would have been a top-notch president. I hold the somewhat outdated view that to be a good president you need (1) to be intelligent, and (2) to have a basic understanding of the social and economic structure of the country—and he had both. That, in my case, began when he was still a student at Harvard.

G: *You knew him then?*

Galbraith: I knew him then, yes. I knew all three—the oldest brother, who was shockingly killed during the war and was a really talented figure, and the two brothers who also inhabited . . . rooms at Winthrop House when they were undergraduates.[19]

Q: *Would you feel comfortable making comparisons among the brothers, the things you noticed, since you knew them all fairly well?*

Galbraith: I wouldn't have any embarrassment on that. They were all equally bright. It's possible that the oldest brother who was killed had a range of effort and knowledge that was greater than the other two as undergraduates. That was my impression. But I regarded them as ideal students, all three of them.

---

19. Joe Jr., Jack, and Teddy Kennedy all lived in Harvard's Winthrop House as undergraduates.

Senator John Culver (D-IA), Edward Kennedy's Harvard classmate and friend:

Q: What kind of a football player was Ted Kennedy?

Culver: He was very tenacious and tough. He really, as evidenced in his professional career, worked harder than anybody else. He didn't have the most athletic gifts, was not very fast, but was very good defensively and he worked hard on his weaknesses. For example, he worked with another player after practice, and with no pads, to improve his tackling, which none of the rest of us did.

I think Ted's [military] experience was every bit as important to him, though, and valuable to him. I really do. I remember later talking about experiences he had. Going through boot camp or whatever the equivalent is in the army, he didn't receive any favoritism. And he ran into some tough characters. I think it was a formidable and formative experience in his life. Now, when he went to Paris, he was an MP. I think that year was a very meaningful experience for him.

Q: Did you notice the big change in him when he returned to Harvard?

Culver: Yes. Even though he always enjoyed having a good time, he was really quite serious about his studies. I think the influences—his father looking at those report cards, and he had Joe as an example and Jack as an example, and Jack talked to him. I remember Jack saying to him, "You should never be without a book. You should always be reading something, all the time." He was serious about doing well academically. I think undoubtedly when he came back, he was even more focused.

The one thing about him that I would mention that is really significant, Ted always had a real magnetic personality and he was always fun to be around. I remember in Winthrop House in the dining room, when he came back in '53, which, again, would have been my senior year, there was a table up front that he often sat at with seven or eight people. He was always the center of fun. I think that's a quality that he's always continued to have. Ted was very extroverted and fun-loving, warm and friendly. People greatly enjoyed his company. I don't think as undergraduates we took an active interest in the political clubs or related to them at that time. We were interested in sports.

Q: John Kennedy was quoted once as saying that Edward Kennedy was the best politician in the family. Would you comment on that assessment?

Culver: Yes. I think the warmth, openness, and fun contributed to President Kennedy's special affection for Ted. Ted, being the ninth child, was always looking for attention. He would be the clown at the family gatherings; even today I just find it amazing how much he enjoys a birthday party. His own children, his own grandchildren, his birthday party. Those things mean so much to him. I think that's wonderful.

He's always the life of the party in the best way. I mean, getting the party going and getting everybody to have fun and relax and enjoy it. Jack also really loved to have Ted tell him stories about what he was doing, who he was dating, etc.

Senator John V. Tunney (D-CA), Edward Kennedy's University of Virginia Law School classmate and friend:[20] I met Ted Kennedy for the first time on the first day of law school. I came into the classroom, which was in Clark Hall, and there were a bunch of students milling outside. Somebody pointed him out to me. This was in 1956, and it was shortly after his brother had tried to win the nomination for the vice presidency. So John Kennedy was a big name in the country, in the law school, and I was introduced to Ted. The first thing he said to me was, "Your father arranged to have a sauna built up at our place at the Cape." And I said, "Really? We have one of those saunas in our home." So we had a short conversation about that.

The thing that happened to me during that conversation was that I felt that this was a person that I was really going to like, just the way he carried himself when he talked, a smile. I thought, "This is a person that I'm really going to enjoy knowing." So that night, I came back to my room and I called my father and said, "There's a classmate down here called Ted Kennedy, and he says his father knows you." Dad said, "Well, I know a lot of Kennedys. Who?" And I said that apparently his father was ambassador to England. Frankly, I didn't really know that at the time. I said, "But his brother is a senator." And Dad said, "Oh, Joe Kennedy. Oh, yes, he's a wonderful man, a great man. Yes, I did arrange to have the person who put our sauna in put it in for them up there." So the next day I told Teddy that I'd spoken to Dad, and he was extolling his father. Teddy said, "Well, that's great."

During the next week or two, all of us were working extremely hard. The subject matter was new to us, we had tons of homework. We didn't have much time to do anything. We were spending a lot of time in the library. Gradually we would ask one another to go out to lunch, or we'd go out and have dinner together. It became clear very quickly that we were going to be really good friends. I started a friendship that has lasted until today. Ted became an intimate friend, I mean a *really, really* close friend, to the point that I think it's fair to say that I treated him more like my brother than I did as my friend. I would share everything with him: thoughts about my life and my family, my girlfriends, things of that kind. And I think it's fair to say that he did very much the same thing with me. I have maintained a veil of privacy around all of those conversations and thoughts because I felt that the friendship was much more

---

20. Tunney's father was the 1926–28 world heavyweight boxing champion, John J. (Gene) Tunney.

important than any temporary type of satisfaction I'd get by talking about him or members of the family and having it be reported. Whatever little celebrity I might have gained, I would have lost tremendously by the lack of the guarantee of intimacy.

So we became really close pals. We began spending all of our vacations with each other. We would travel together. That was back in the days of Virginia [Law School], too. Not that we shut other people out, because we didn't; we had many friends in the law school, but we did have that bond that we were living together. Not the first year. It was the second year and the third years that we did. But the fact was that we were always together and doing things together and talking together made that relationship a very rewarding one for me and it helped me, I think, in my feelings about law school.

I must say that at times I was very unhappy with the amount of energy that I was putting into my studies, when I didn't really believe I was ever going to be a lawyer. It wasn't that I disliked the law, but it was just such an incredible and rigorous regimen that we were under. I have to tell you, those early days in law school the first year, say, up to Thanksgiving, I think that I was studying fifteen hours a day. I think that probably Teddy was too. You'd go out for lunch, have a quick lunch, and have a quick supper. The rest of the time you're studying. Then you go back and go to bed for maybe seven hours or something. There was no real fun, as I recall. Then, maybe gradually, as we got further along towards the fall, we would take Saturday afternoons off and play touch football. That was the big reward for the work that we'd been doing during the course of the week, a couple of hours of touch football.

But there was such anxiety. You knew that everybody in the school was pretty smart. They wouldn't be there if they weren't. And you also knew that not everybody was going to make it, and you didn't want to be one of the ones who failed. Teddy felt the same way that I did about it, and so we worked our heads off. I think that during that period, as our friendship ripened, we had camaraderie, having been tested by fire, and we got through. I mean, it's that first year, that first semester, when maybe both of us thought that we might be left behind, but we made it. After that, law school was much better. We didn't have to work quite as hard because we were old hands, so to speak. That time, I think because our fathers knew each other well and because we had a similar family culture, was very important in bringing us together.

I got to meet John Kennedy through Teddy very quickly in late 1956. In '57 and '58 we saw much more of him and much more of Bobby too. As a young guy who had progressive instincts, I couldn't help but be dazzled by John Kennedy. He was so articulate. He had such a *great* sense of humor. He was witty in the way he approached issues, and his skepticism about people and places and times was always, I found, charming and instructive and enlightening. So I became a real fan of his brother, and of course Jackie was so beautiful, you couldn't help but be a fan of her.

I was around the Kennedy family a great deal then because Teddy and I did everything together at that point in our lives, so I was always there. We'd go up to see Bobby and we'd stay at Bobby's house in McLean[, Virginia]. We'd go over to John Kennedy's house for dinner, and I was always accepted as a friend and as a person who they perhaps had heard of.

You asked me to give you some impressions of what I thought of Jack Kennedy and what I thought of Bobby Kennedy when I first met them. I was awed by Jack Kennedy. I mean, I just was awed by him. You couldn't help but be. At least I couldn't help but be. I thought he was so smart and so quick and clever, and he just seemed to have everything going for him.

When I first met Bobby, I didn't have an opinion much one way or the other, except that he had a great sense of humor. The first weekend we spent with Bobby—I think it might have been during the fall of '56—we went up and spent the night and the day and then came back down. We played touch football. Teddy threw me a pass and I went up to catch the pass, and it was touch, and Bobby *nailed* me from behind and I went head over heels. I was infuriated. I got up and said, "What the hell are you doing?" He gave me this smile and said, "What's wrong, can't you take it?" I remember thinking that this guy is just a punk. I couldn't abide him, if you want to know the truth. [*Laughter.*] I was so angry. I was his guest, so I had to be polite, but I was just infuriated by him.

The interesting thing is that over the years, my impressions of Bobby not only changed, but towards the end of his life, I looked upon him as one of the most extraordinary men that this country has ever produced. I thought he was just a brilliant, marvelous man of tremendous passion and feeling, and I think he would have been a great, great president. I think that part of it was that Bobby softened too. I think Bobby's compassion for people, which was always there in his heart, but because he was so competitive with other members of his family, he never really had a chance to express it the way he did towards the end of his life, particularly after his brother's assassination. He was always a great family man, right in the very beginning. But he was also a person who, I think, didn't suffer fools kindly, nor did he suffer whiners or complainers kindly, especially on the athletic field. So I had a real metamorphosis with Bobby. With Jack, I always had a feeling of extraordinary appreciation for his skills, his character, and things of that nature. With Bobby it came slower, but it became very intense at the end. He was truly a giant among men.

So there it was. Teddy and I used to suffer, probably, from similar feelings of, "Are we going to be up to the mark? Are we going to be adequate?" In my case I had my father, who was sort of an icon. There had never been a professional fighter like him, actually, if you want to know the truth. I mean, here was a guy who had been heavyweight champion. He lost one fight, retired undefeated.[21] He was great friends with George Bernard Shaw, Ernest Hemingway. We used to have musical directors, like Eugene Ormandy, at our house. His associations were with people in politics, people in music, people in the arts, and they all admired him, liked him. Dad was very smart, even though he had a very limited education. He had lectured at Yale, in Shakespeare, back in the time he was heavyweight champion, and not only didn't make a fool of himself but had done extremely well, and people really appreciated his personality. And so I was fighting *that* image, and I think Teddy was fighting the image of his father and his brothers. But we shared some of those same feelings. Are we going to be adequate to live up to our family's names?

Q: You both talked about this openly?

Tunney: Oh, yes, we sure did. Not as though we were sitting on a psychiatrist's couch, but just two buddies talking about things. You got the impression that he had a big burden. His father was a major figure in his life in those days. I mean a *major* figure. You could just tell when he was talking to his father on the phone, that his father played a huge role in his life, in his thinking. The thing that impressed me getting to know Teddy at that time was what an extraordinary family man he was. His family was critically important. Of course, every book that's ever been written about the Kennedys keeps proving that point over and over again. I can tell you from the inside, it was that way. They were just bound to each other.

Q: You were both in the same situation in many ways, measuring up, establishing your mark, and so is that one of the reasons you were working so bloody hard, both of you?

Tunney: I think that's right. No, I don't think there's any question. Also, I think that both of us realized that we had others looking over our shoulders. The others in my case were my father and my mother. I didn't care so much about my brothers' opinions. I'm very fond of my brothers, but I didn't really care so much about their opinions. I cared much more about my father and mother's opinions, and I guess Teddy probably cared equally about his father—no. His father's opinion was most important, and then his brothers after that. He carried perhaps a larger weight family-wise than I did. Numbers are not really what count, it's the intensity of the feeling that counts. I felt very intense feelings about whether or not I was going to measure up, and he did too.

An interesting thing happened in our second year of law school. Teddy said to me, "How would you like to be partners in the moot court competition?" I had never really thought about the moot court. He said, "Really, I think it's

---

21. Gene Tunney lost only one fight as a light heavyweight and was undefeated as a heavyweight.

something that we should do." I said, "Do you really think so? And he said, "Yes." I said, "OK, let's do it then, I'll be happy to do it." As you recall, or maybe you don't know, at Virginia in those days, practically the entire class did end up in the moot court. It was something that was expected that you would do, even though it was an extracurricular activity. You had to do moot court in your class activities, and I think you had to have two arguments, but the extra was joining the competition, which was a two-year competition, in your second and your third years.

We had our first argument and we won by a split decision. Afterwards, one of the judges—I guess there were third-year students that were our judges in that first competition, and one of the judges came to me and said, "You won 2 to 1. But the only reason that you won was because of Kennedy's argument. Your presentation fell short." I said, "Really, why?" And he said, "You didn't have a positive way of speaking, you didn't exert yourself." I said, "Wow. Thank you very much for that."

So the next time, I had done some training on my own, and it was much better. At that point I think we became really good partners with each other. But Teddy always did have, right from the very beginning, that very forceful presentation, whereas in my case, I had to learn it. And I think I learned it from him, to be really honest about it. I saw the way that he was presenting himself and so I became more that way, but I kept my own style. As you can see, I have a different way of talking than he does. But allowing the energy within to flow out through the mouth, the vocal cords, through the eyes, through the presentation, that came from him. I'm learning from him.

Then we went on, and as you know, we won the moot court competition, and it was really a terrific thing for both of us because it was an intellectual pursuit. It was something that—neither one of us was going to be in the top ten of the class, so we were very pleased to have been able to achieve something intellectual, that was understood to be intellectual in that group of people, many of whom were quite brilliant. The other thing was, it was a distinguishing mark because we had the final argument on Law Day. There were probably three or four hundred people in the audience. We had a Supreme Court justice there. The chancellor of England was on the court. Haynsworth, who was on the Court of Appeals,[22] was there. I got two job offers from Wall Street firms after that argument, from people who were in the audience; they asked me if I would consider coming up to their firm. It couldn't have been a better thing for us, and I think, to a very considerable extent, it helped bring us even closer together. On a friendship basis we were always very close, but this was something that we were able to do together in a way that gave us

22. The lord chancellor of England was Sir David Maxwell Fyfe, Viscount Kilmuir. Judge Clement F. Haynsworth served on the US Fourth Circuit Court of Appeals.

confidence about the future and what our future potential was, whatever it might be.

Now by this time, this was 1959, John Kennedy was campaigning. I should go back. In 1958, John Kennedy was running for re-election to the Senate, and Teddy was going to spend the summer doing his campaign work. I guess he was chairman of his campaign. And then I came back [from Holland] and spent the last month of our vacation with Ted up in Massachusetts, on the campaign trail. So I had that experience of being with him and being with Larry O'Brien and the other people involved in the campaign. I don't think that there's any question that at that point Ted was seriously thinking about a political career for himself. I'm not so sure about when we first got to law school, but certainly by '58 he had thought about a political career, not necessarily in Massachusetts. I think he was thinking of going west, going out to maybe California and putting his roots down. He even talked about having part ownership of a football team, an NFL team or something of that kind, anything to get his roots down, but his idea was politics.

Obviously, Larry O'Brien was a very important figure in that campaign. We all know that Larry O'Brien was a brilliant political strategist. At that point, Teddy was still very young, and he was learning. He learned very well, but he was learning at that point. He hadn't reached the maturity that he achieved later on.

Q: *Was Kenny O'Donnell*[23] *around?*

Tunney: Yes, he was involved. Kenny was there too, sure. He [Teddy] was learning the ropes. They [O'Donnell and O'Brien] were the ones who were close to the senator. Teddy was in a family way, but they were the ones in a political and strategic way. It's not that he was pushed aside or walked over. He played a very active role, and they would consult with Teddy on things. I don't mean to suggest that he was just pushed off. But he was a novice obviously, and they were the pros and they were there close to the candidate. But Teddy learned fast and everybody adored him. It was clear that he had a magic with crowds; the way he spoke, the way he looked, he was very handsome. It's hard to know what it is in the brain and the heart of a candidate that enables him to catch whatever fire there is as background music in the community, that allows that candidate to synthesize hopes and aspirations and needs, and get it out there in a way that that person then becomes an image of what people want in the way of leadership. You can't describe that very easily, but there is a connection between the brain and the heart. There's a fire that develops in a really successful candidate, and I'm not saying that all of them have it. Some don't have it but they still get elected. But every now and then you do see that

---

23. Kenneth P. O'Donnell, a Harvard roommate and football teammate of Robert Kennedy, was a Massachusetts political consultant and became a special assistant and appointments secretary to President Kennedy.

combination of fire in the heart and the articulation of the need through the brain that allows people to be willing to follow. And that is what John Kennedy had. Bobby, later on, got it. He didn't have it at first, but he got it. Teddy had it very naturally. He was a great politician. He just had it, and his family used to say that he was the most natural politician in the family. I mean, he just had it. He had a great sense of humor, great buoyancy, and was very positive about things. It was not a question of why can't you do it, it's always how are we going to do it, how are we going to get it done? Now let's go, let's do it. And he had that on the athletic field. He was the president of the Student Legal Council down there [UVA Law School], and he was able to get some of the better speakers from the Senate and other places to come and be with us. He had that thing, that magic. It's ineffable. You can't describe it really, but it is something between the brain and the heart. And he's always had that.

2

The Making of a President: Campaigning for JFK

Fresh from law school, Teddy plunged into presidential politics when Jack asked him to campaign in the western United States during his 1960 campaign for the presidency. Teddy also appeared with Jack in the crucial state of West Virginia, where the Kennedys' Catholicism was a key issue in that overwhelming Protestant state. With Honey Fitz's flair for grassroots politicking and a natural exuberance, the candidate's kid brother was an enthusiastic stand-in for Jack.

Nothing deterred the youngest Kennedy sibling. In Wisconsin, he hurtled down a ski jump, and in Montana, he accepted the dare of riding a bucking bronco. In typical Kennedy fashion, Teddy jumped atop the unbroken colt, and the wire services flashed his photo around the country as the horse made its first buck. Wearing a cowboy hat and holding one hand in the air, the New Englander looked surprisingly at home—until the wild horse tossed him off after a few more kicks. But Kennedy, who came up limping with a pulled muscle, noted wryly that his dad would have fired him if he had avoided the dare. Circulating on the floor of the 1960 Democratic National Convention, Teddy stood with the Wyoming delegation as their votes put JFK over the top for the party's presidential nomination.

In western states, where Democrats were more likely to support party stalwarts like Senate Majority Leader Lyndon Johnson of Texas and Senator Hubert Humphrey of Minnesota, young Teddy's force of personality and winning arguments for JFK converted many delegates and voters to the Kennedy campaign. More important for his future career in the Senate and as a campaigner, Teddy's experiences in the 1960 race paired him both with old pols in the Democratic Party, such as Hyman Raskin of Chicago, and with rising stars, such as Senator Frank Church of Idaho, whom Kennedy would join on Capitol Hill. He also witnessed firsthand JFK's skill at political hardball, as when Jack Kennedy pressured Ohio governor Michael DiSalle to run as a "favorite son"¹ committed to JFK in the Buckeye State's presidential primary. Once Jack secured the top spot on the ticket, his younger brother watched the nominee reach out to his former rivals, Johnson and Humphrey, to win over their teams and mend party fences. Yet Teddy saw that his brother, once in the Oval Office, encountered major obstacles posed by southern Democrats on Capitol Hill, especially involving civil rights. LBJ, now the vice president, had lost his power base as the former Senate majority leader and faced a personality conflict with the new attorney general, Robert Kennedy.

EMK: I think it's pretty well developed through my own life experience, in college, observing my brothers, being part of this family, hearing them, the level of discussion, reading the books, being interested in the historical period of the New Deal that my father had been a part of. I was interested in all of that. The general challenges we were facing as a nation and how we came through that period were enormously interesting, and I had the opportunity to meet some of the figures who had been a part of that whole New Deal period.²

I had just enough exposure to think that I would—both by nature and disposition—embrace that philosophical view, basically international and anti-communist. Having gone through the campaigns in '58, and hearing my brother and being exposed to that side of the political philosophy, it came very natural to me to be both a Democrat and to be concerned about working people and their interests. A basic sense of fairness and opportunity was always evident in our house, emphasized and stressed. The exposure I had at a very early age, going back to my grandfather, about the discrimination against the Irish, stuck with me.

I remember Grandpa showing me the signs that had been in windows. I think they were kept there, probably as keepsakes—I never saw them. They said, "No Irish Need Apply." It's difficult to believe that in the immediate postwar period those kinds of signs were still evident. In my house down in Washington, I have a sign my grandfather had with a little frame—"No Irish Need Apply." It was an authentic sign. I got it either from him or from my mother. I can't quite remember, but I've had it for a long time. Grandpa was both a philosopher and a politician, and he talked about the persecution in

---

1. A "favorite son" is "an aspirant to the presidential nomination of his party whose principal source of support lies in the backing of his home state delegation. [H]is candidacy serves chiefly to permit his delegation [to the national party convention] to delay committing itself until the prospects of the major contenders for the nomination can be gauged, thus improving its bargaining position." Joseph Dunner, ed., *Dictionary of Political Science* (Totowa, NJ: Littlefield, Adams, 1970), 180.

2. These included John Kenneth Galbraith, Harvard professor of economics, who authored *The Affluent Society* (1958), supported JFK in 1960, and served as his ambassador to India from 1961 to 1963.

Ireland, the persecution in this country against the Irish, and the very significant ethnic tensions.

Even in my time in Massachusetts, the tension between the Irish and the Italians was very intense. Learning about the discrimination against the Irish, and seeing for myself the ethnic tensions, made a very powerful impression upon me. I'll give you an example. In the 1958 campaign, my brother had a slogan, "Make your vote count. Vote Kennedy."[3] A group of Italian leaders from the state came in and wanted to see me at my brother's headquarters. They sat down and said, "This is an insult to the Italians."

I said, "I don't understand. What we're trying to do is say, 'Make your vote count. Your vote counts for President Kennedy in '58, and it's a vote really for 1960. Your vote is important. Make your vote count.' The idea is to get them to vote because your vote will count, and it'll count towards 1960"—even though he didn't have a strong opponent, a fellow named Vinny Celeste, at this time.

They said, "No, no. The way we interpret it is the vote counts if it's for an Irishman, but it doesn't count if it's for an Italian. Your vote is counting for Kennedy, but it isn't counting for the Italians. So therefore it's directed at us, and we resent it." They had the head of every Italian organization in this. We had to tear up all the literature and change the slogan. I mentioned this thing to my brother: "I don't know. I'll work it out." My father was at the Cape; he came up, and they sat down with a fellow named Don Dowd, who was a friend of my father's and was in advertising. And he stayed there all day long, trying out slogans, like you see in the movies.

He was in this pinstriped suit, I remember, with white checks on it, and he had suspenders and a moustache that moved, and dark, very groomed hair. He had five different pencils and pads of paper, and he'd write out slogans and show them to my father. My father would say, "No, that doesn't work, Don. That's not good. You can do better than that. That's not good." And he [Joe Kennedy] went over to Bailey's, which was right across the street, and he had his lunch, a chocolate soda. That's all he'd eat. He loved ice cream, but he didn't want to gain weight, so that's just what he'd have. He'd come back in half an hour; that was his lunch break.

"How are you doing now, Dowd?" Dowd would just sit there, beginning to perspire, and the dye would begin to run in his hair a little bit—he was just under such pressure. Finally he came up with, "He has served Massachusetts with distinction," which is like a Schenley's ad, a liquor ad, but my father thought that would do. So that became the slogan: "Kennedy: He has served Massachusetts with distinction."

---

3. JFK's speechwriter, Ted Sorensen, maintained that the 1958 Kennedy slogan that Italian Americans complained about was, "Be Proud of Your Vote!" See Ted Sorensen, *Counselor: A Life at The Edge of History* (New York: Harper, 2008), 260.

But the sensitivity from that time has been dampened, because Italians married *Irish*. Coming back to 1958, the overall strategy of that campaign was for my brother to do well in Massachusetts but to continue to use '58 as a springboard into 1960. And I was very surprised how little time he spent in the state, even during the '58 campaign. He'd stop in Worcester for an hour and a half in the morning, and then go to New Hampshire and spend the day. He'd come on back to an event in the evening in Lowell or Lawrence, but he'd be gone all the rest of the time. He was very well scheduled—. . . But the aspect of the campaign that got me started is I traveled with Larry O'Brien. . . .

Larry was the most important. In different communities we had Kennedy secretaries or coordinators, but we had two or three a night, and we did it every single night in different parts of the state. And so I got to both listen to him and listen to people. Larry O'Brien was a very skilled organizer and a skilled behind-the-scenes person—not strong on issues, but strong on organization and campaign technique. He had written what they called the Larry O'Brien Manual, which was very important in the 1952 campaign and updated in '58, and was really the basis of '60, although they used some very different techniques in '60—more so probably later in '68, Bobby's campaign.

In any event, I traveled and learned a lot from Larry, learned and traveled the state intensively. The basic aspects of that campaign were where Senator John Kennedy was going to go and spend the time, and the field organization, and the fundraising aspects, and then the communications—television and radio. Basically, I did some fundraising events with my brother. But I spent a great deal of time in the organization until probably the last two or three months, and then I went around myself speaking for him. I got so I knew the issues he was talking about, and I could go to events and speak for him. I did a lot of campaigning for him around the state.

Q: *Except for the events, were most of the people you were talking to in this campaign politicians, organizers, or people in the factories? Did you do much of that?*

EMK: It was the Democratic constituency. I wasn't out talking to the League of Women Voters. It was limited in terms of chambers of commerce. I did the historic Democratic constituents.

Q: *He was also seeking independent votes, though.*

EMK: Independents. He had separate organizational structures; that was different, different secretaries. He always tried to get people in the independent areas who would be strongly supportive, and he had very substantial success with that, very substantial success. That was my primary experience during that period of time.

Q: *It was, again, learning about and learning by doing campaigning. I had started out talking about your early experiences in campaigning and what you brought, what you learned and from whom, your grandfather and so on.*

EMK: Well, I did a lot in the '60 campaign. I finished law school in the spring of '59 and was away for part of the summer. Then we had the [campaign strategy] meeting down here [at Hyannis Port] . . . over at Bobby's house.

My brother said, "What part of the country are you interested in?" I said the West, because I hadn't been out there. And he said, "Well, all right. We'll give Teddy the western states." And I left after that for six weeks. And with mostly Ted Sorensen's memoranda, because my brother had been out to these states, and there were these series of memoranda. He had a handful of contacts in each of these states, people he had picked up, and those became the principal operatives. I can still remember Skeff Sheehy in Montana. He eventually ended up being on the state supreme court, and he's retired now.

I can remember these people very well; that's such an important period. That was organization and the state conventions, because that was all for delegates. I went up to Alaska two or three times. I got to Hawaii only once, I think, but I traveled extensively in those other states. That was a second campaigning experience.

Q: *Was that also a case of people skills, rather than issues, being very important?*

EMK: Yes. It was conventions, delegates, state conventions, who was going to go, what they cared about, what the contacts were, who influenced them. I traveled around out [West] a good deal with a fellow named Hy Raskin, who was a great old Chicago pol, white hair. I was challenged to get them stirred up about my brother, and then Hy would sit them down and talk about what was happening in the real world—where Daley was going to go. These old pros wanted to know where Daley was going and what Lawrence[4] was doing and all the rest, and Hy would spin this stuff. It was a one-two punch. At the end, I became very good friends with this fellow who was forty years older than I was and completely different. He came up through the Chicago political life. I learned a lot.

Q: *But here's a guy from Massachusetts and pol from Chicago going out West.*

EMK: That's it.

Q: *New territory.*

EMK: New territory, but it's much more open. There's a much more open society where all the people who had gone out there had been—Teno Roncalio[5] from Wyoming who had been on the beaches of Normandy and had a great affinity with my brother Jack just because of the shared war experience. And this was true of a lot of these people. Frank Church[6] has been out there, and

---

4. Richard J. Daley was Chicago's mayor, and David L. Lawrence was mayor of Pittsburgh. Both were bosses of powerful Democratic political machines.

5. Teno Roncalio led the Wyoming delegates supporting JFK at the 1960 Democratic convention and cast the deciding votes for John Kennedy's nomination. He would represent the Cowboy State in the US House of Representatives from 1965 to 1967 and 1971 to 1978.

6. Frank Church was a Democratic senator from Idaho.

had a similar war experience. An awful lot of people who were involved in the Democratic Party were all younger. A lot of them had associations or history back in the East.

Q: You observed earlier that you'd learned a lot and you had changed over these many years concerning campaigning, what you learned. How accomplished do you feel you were with this background in [the Senate race of] '62? Would you rate yourself as—besides a very hard worker—a pretty astute campaigner? Or was it still very much of a learning curve for you?

EMK: Well, I think it was very much learning, but I enjoyed people. I liked political people, I liked the characters. The whole ethnic aspect of politics at that time was still very strong. And that was very colorful.

It was interesting, and one reason it was able to work for me is that I get along well with the different kinds of ethnic groups. I'd come into the [1962] campaign after we'd gone to Italy with that group to celebrate the centennial of Italian unification in 1961. We had taken a whole group of Italian leaders over there. I arrived in Turin, and Gianni Agnelli, who had been a friend of my brother's and who was a leading industrialist, owned the leading newspapers there, gave a reception at his house. And once the newspaper ran that—it was a terrific picture—once we started with Agnelli, and Agnelli thought it was important, everybody in Italy thought it was important.

So I got a sense of the importance and the humor and the fun aspects of ethnic politics and the liveliness and the interest in the history of the relationships with the United States, and I learned a lot from it. It was fun. I enjoyed it. I enjoyed the people.

[T]he time I really spent in California was in the [1960] presidential campaign. I was in California, but that wasn't one of my states. I spent time at the very end there, going around and speaking, because it was so close. They had a fellow named Jesse Unruh,[7] and he wanted to run the whole thing. He wasn't interested in any help from anybody and never got an absentee ballot out, and we lost [California's electoral vote to Richard Nixon, who was from the Golden State].

But Unruh was a very significant political figure, and I wasn't going to be able to make much progress there, I didn't think. I'd looked at the western states. I thought that if I didn't live along the coast, I'd want to live along the Rocky Mountain spine from Montana down to the Southwest. The states in the Southwest were more interesting because they had a Hispanic population, and they were Democratic—New Mexico was. I was rather struck with that. But I never got much further than that. I remember talking to some people just generally out there—Colorado, and I think maybe Arizona. In New Mexico,

---

7. Jesse M. Unruh was a member of the California State Assembly, who would become its speaker and California state treasurer. He was an early supporter of Robert Kennedy's 1968 run for the presidency.

I talked to a few people about it. But it was never very serious. We were all focused on the election, and I didn't really spend a lot of time thinking about it. But it passed through my head.

Q: You said that your brother Robert got wholly immersed in something and didn't really plan or think ahead. Were you different in that way?

EMK: I think so, yes. I was thinking about what I was going to do afterwards. I mentioned I talked to my brother about doing some things. I was interested in arms control, even at that time. I thought of getting some experience. It was the Cold War, a lot of tension between East and West, and the escalation of the arms race was one of the more obvious areas. I thought of getting a good understanding of that, because that was something that was going to be with us—learning a lot about it, being involved in it—

Q: But not as an alternative to an elective political career on the way?

EMK: In 1961 I thought I'd do that before going back. I didn't have it very well thought out in Massachusetts. My brother Jack's advice, of course, was absolutely on target and made a lot of sense: being at the district attorney's, which I enjoyed. I learned a lot. I had fun doing it. It was great experience.[8]

It would have made no sense to have done [arms control]. That was just good judgment and good sense on Jack's part, and once I listened to him, it made sense.

Going for your supper, Splash?[9] Is it quarter of four?

Q: Twenty of four.

EMK: You want to go out for your supper? [Sound of dog running]

Q: I think that's a yes.

EMK: Isn't that something? That dog understands English.

Q: He has a good clock, too, a very good clock.

EMK: I campaigned a good deal with my brother in West Virginia and to some extent in Wisconsin, but very little. When he lost his voice, I campaigned with him for three days in West Virginia, but generally we were in different locations.

I traveled with him to Youngstown, Ohio, in '57, '58 when they met Governor DiSalle, and he got the ultimatum: either he was going to support my brother, or my brother was going to run in the Ohio primary. That was the night all the waiters in there were lifers. They all had been convicted of murder, all the people who tended the governor's mansion. This made a big impression on me. I think DiSalle was against the death penalty; I believe he

---

8. After JFK's presidential election, Edward Kennedy served as an assistant prosecutor in the Suffolk County District Attorney's Office in Boston from 1961 to 1962.

9. Senator Kennedy adored his and Vicki's two Portuguese water dogs, Splash and Sunny, to whom he refers throughout his oral history. The senator even wrote a children's book with Splash, *My Senator and Me: A Dog's-Eye View of Washington, DC* (New York: Scholastic Press, 2006).

was. But in any event, whether he was or wasn't, everyone in there who was associated with the governor's mansion was a lifer. That was as impressive to me as the fact that he was supporting my brother for president. We had gone to a great rally in Youngstown, which was still then a major manufacturing area. And there was just tens of thousands of—Extraordinary. That's one of the few times I traveled with [Jack]. But that was very early in the campaign.

My brother Jack got along [with Lyndon Johnson], but Bobby had tensions with him. Most of it was later on. I just don't think Kenny and those other people used him. What happens is, every single time a president is elected, they bring their whole crowd in here, and they never use the people here. And 95 percent of them would be glad to work with a new president and would be loyal to him.

You saw that in the Justice Department with my brother Bobby. He had never worked with Nick Katzenbach,[10] but he was absolutely loyal to him. Never worked with Burke Marshall,[11] absolutely loyal to him. Jack Miller,[12] who was a Republican, absolutely. John Nolan.[13] He had a group in there who were just super tens, super tens. And every one of them, after six weeks, would have lain down under a freight train for him.

And Democrats who are interested in using government would have worked with Johnson in the new administration. But everybody comes in and they have their own people, and they won't use the other people, won't work with them. They're suspicious of them, they have an agenda. Everyone makes the same mistake. Carter made the mistake. Clinton made the mistake.

My brother understood this, and one of the smart things he did after he got the nomination, after his speech at the [Los Angeles] Coliseum, he went up to the Cape. He brought up a plane full of all of his supporters, and they had a cookout, and they played volleyball and took a swim. They had drinks that night, and everybody was all set to go.

The next day, the Johnson people came up. And they were at one half of the football field, and the other half were the Kennedys. Finally, they went in swimming. The others wouldn't talk, but finally they had a cookout, and they finally had the drinks. And then the next day, my brother brought up about

---

10. Nicholas deB. Katzenbach served as Attorney General Robert Kennedy's deputy attorney general and succeeded him as attorney general in 1964. In 1966, President Lyndon Johnson named him undersecretary of state.

11. Burke Marshall was Robert Kennedy's assistant attorney general for the Justice Department's Civil Rights Division.

12. Herbert J. (Jack) Miller Jr. was appointed by Robert Kennedy as assistant attorney general of the Justice Department's Criminal Division.

13. John E. Nolan Jr., a Washington lawyer, who had worked as an advance man in JFK's 1960 campaign, served as an administrative assistant for Attorney General Kennedy in 1963 and participated in his 1964 Senate campaign and his 1968 run for the Democratic presidential nomination.

half a plane of Humphrey people. By this time, the Johnson people and the Kennedy people considered it was their territory. The Humphrey people were outsiders, and then the same kind of thing. Everybody needed a couple of days off, at any rate. Then there were some other people like Symington and Stevenson[14] who came in last, at the very end.

At the end of four days, he had a good political group to work on the campaign from all of those candidates. They were all set to go. He understood it. But when you're the candidate, you can't keep that thing cooking. And he couldn't do it as the new president to ensure that everything was being done around here with Lyndon. My own sense is that [the Kennedy administration] probably could have used him a lot more.

The real tough thing was getting [legislation] through the Rules Committee over at the House. You had the mental health bill, three or four of those different things. Basically, you were being cascaded with foreign policy. You had the civil rights issue and the economic issue. You had a tough time getting the tax cuts because the Republicans wouldn't support any expenditures over a hundred billion dollars, which was the budget the first year. Doug Dillon[15] said we had to go back and keep cutting, because otherwise the Republicans wouldn't cut taxes. They didn't want to be out of balance. What a change in the Republicans now. That was one aspect of it. You had Berlin,[16] which was red-hot at the time. You had the beginning of the Vietnam War, and you had the whole civil rights movement.

Q: I'm not sure Lyndon Johnson's influence in the Senate carried when he left.

EMK: No, this was built on a power structure.

Q: And it was built on the leverage he had on procedure and the process and the people.

Kennedy: That's right.

Q: You don't have that if you're not in the Senate.

Kennedy: That's right.

Senator Kennedy described his brother's use of the presidential yacht for political gatherings.

---

14. Stuart Symington was a Democratic senator from Missouri who ran for the party's presidential nomination in 1960. JFK briefly considered him for the vice-presidential slot before ultimately selecting Texas senator Lyndon Johnson. Adlai Stevenson, the former governor of Illinois, had run unsuccessfully for president in 1952 and 1956. Some Democrats, including Eleanor Roosevelt, continued to support him for the nomination in 1960. He served in the Kennedy administration as US ambassador to the United Nations.

15. C. Douglas Dillon served as secretary of treasury in the Kennedy administration.

16. Divided among the four allied countries that defeated the Nazis in World War II (the United States, France, England, and the USSR), Berlin lay deep inside Soviet satellite, Communist East Germany. In August 1961 Berlin became a flashpoint, as it had in 1948, between the Western Allies and the Communists, who constructed a wall to separate West and East Berlin. It prevented East Berliners from crossing into free West Berlin.

Q: Did your brother use the Sequoia[17] *much?*

EMK: Yes. It was very interesting, the *Sequoia*. We would go on the *Sequoia*, I imagine, once in the fall and once in the spring. We went with the secretary of labor. I remember going with the Republicans one time and just the Democrats another. We'd go at quarter to seven, and be back in at nine. That boat was moving every single evening. He turned it over to another Cabinet official. It was terrific, lovely. It was a great treat, and the [Potomac] river is spectacular. In thirty-five minutes, you can get down to Mount Vernon. It was lovely, and people really enjoyed it. The [cabinet] secretaries thought the president was doing something for them. A great, great kind of thing. It was the silliest thing in the world [for President Jimmy Carter] to get rid of.

The silliest thing. I've been on it. I still have the pictures of a birthday party when I was on it with my brother in the spring of '63. He has all the pictures inside. I don't know how the hell they ever got them, but they have them from the time of the birthday party. He used to enjoy that a lot, and I don't remember him over-using it. It was moving every evening—

There was a different Cabinet member each night all the spring and summer. We were here [in Washington] all summer, so they used it all through the summertime. When he had the *Honey Fitz*[18] up at the Cape, he was out on that every day. [H]e'd go to the beach and set little John Jr.'s sails. They had this wonderful [toy] sailboat the Italians had given him, and he [JFK] was a very good sailor. He'd set it so it would go out to sea. And then they'd go back over to his house and get his bathing suit. They'd get lunch, and then they'd walk down to the pier and get on the big boat. They'd go out, and the challenge was finding the sailboat. It became a great game. "Where'd it go? Where's the sailboat? Oh, we have to find it." They'd swim over to it and bring it back. That was always great fun. They'd give that sailboat about an hour. It would take an hour to find it. He wouldn't do it in choppy weather, but on most days, it was just marvelous. He probably had some maid up there keeping an eye out for it so it wasn't going to get completely lost. But at least all of us thought it was on the level.

---

17. *Sequoia* was the official presidential yacht from Herbert Hoover to Jimmy Carter, who sold it in 1977 as an austerity measure. President Kennedy loved boating, the only time he could truly relax, without phone disruptions, according to his wife. He held secret meetings on the *Sequoia* during the Cuban Missile Crisis in 1962 and celebrated his last birthday aboard the yacht, May 29, 1963. His brother Edward attended the party.

18. Named for John Kennedy's maternal grandfather and namesake, Boston Mayor John F. (Honey Fitz) Fitzgerald, the *Honey Fitz* was another presidential yacht, slightly smaller than the *Sequoia*. With various names, it was used by Presidents Truman through Nixon. JFK had the boat sailed to his parents' home in Palm Beach, Florida, during the winter and spring, and to Cape Cod in the summer and fall, so that he could enjoy excursions on it over Christmas, Easter, and summer/autumn holidays.

And he had a very cute little game like Blind Man's Bluff he'd play with the children. He'd put a wastepaper basket over their head, and then he'd call them, and they'd have to guess where he was. He'd make up games. He was very good at that kind of thing.

I'm not really sure that a lot has been written about President Kennedy and his children, but he was incredibly attentive, and he had a lot of contact with them when he was around. It was a joyous time, the little games that he used to play.

He was always thinking up games. He'd have what he called "floaties." They'd take scallop shells that he'd just find on the beach when there was an offshore breeze. He'd pick one up and little John and Caroline picked them up and see whose would float out the furthest. And then after they floated to a certain place, you could take a stone and throw it out, to see if you could sink the other person's, but it had to get out to a certain place. So it was whose got out there first, and then whose was sunk first. So it was all made up at the time in familiar circumstances, climate, and atmosphere. It was a very happy, joyous kind of circumstance. There are pictures of Bobby and all of his children out at Hickory Hill and sailing and swimming all the kinds of activities— a legion. He was just a very devoted and involved parent.

On Sundays, one of [President Kennedy's] favorite pastimes was to visit the Civil War battlefields. He did that as often as he could. He'd invite Bobby and myself to go with him. Occasionally he would drive up to Camp David, although I only stayed up there one weekend when he was president, but he didn't use it very much. On the weekends he stayed down in the White House and worked most of the time. But on Sundays he'd helicopter out to these battlefields and always took a historian with him. This was supposed to be a learning experience, continuing education.

One of the wonderful things that my brother would do on the weekends, he'd talk about presents for heads of state. He'd say, "Now the State Department says we can give five different kinds of presents. Which presents do you think we ought to give someone?" And everyone at the table, little children, grandchildren, could talk about it. He'd involve them. He'd say, "Now we have the head of such-and-such a country coming, and I can give him one of four of these things. Which one would you like to give to him?" He was just an incredible conversationalist about bringing all of them in. They'd say, "No, no, no. Don't do that. Don't give him that!"

[Irish prime minister] Sean Lemass[19] did come over and was at a dinner. It was the only [state] dinner I went to at the White House. Sean Lemass was fascinated by George Washington. He was a great devotee of Washington. My

---

19. The state dinner for Sean Lemass was the only one Edward Kennedy attended during his brother's presidency.

brother had the exact replica of George Washington's sword forged with identical ivory and colors and all the rest, but he had to have two of them because they were scared that the metal used in the blades would break. He gave me the second one because I had gone to the dinner. I still have it.

But one thing that [JFK] had is a wonderful carved boat, and he told my father, "If I don't get along with Khrushchev, I'm not going to give him the boat." He didn't get along with him, but he still gave him the boat. I think he understood that Khrushchev was a bully and, like most bullies, was more bark and bluff than real determination—

Q: *That was the only time he had an opportunity to take Khrushchev's measure? In Vienna?*

EMK: That was the one time and the only time.

Q: *Was the Bay of Pigs anything that affected you in any way?*

EMK: No, it was some distance, obviously, from where I was [in Boston]. I hadn't been involved in it, and I was as surprised as anyone else about it. [M]y brother . . . accepted the responsibility for it, and then Bobby said, "Let's call Dad. He can always find something good about anything." They went back and called my father, and he said, "It was the best thing you ever did. People understand people can make mistakes, and you're willing to take responsibility for that. They'll admire and respect you." And boom! The polls all went up. It was something he believed, even though he was, obviously, enormously disappointed as well. I heard a good deal afterwards. My brother felt enormous responsibility about getting the prisoners out—and he got most of them out. I got probably the last one out some years ago.[20]

They had a colonel who was the last one. Probably now it's ten or twelve years ago. Greg Craig[21] helped me work this. The last message that Castro said, "I have to keep ten human rights people in jail, or Kennedy won't come down here. The only way he'll come down here is if I let human rights people out of jail." There was some truth to it. This fellow was the last one. He had been with Castro in the mountains, highly decorated, very close to Castro, but he was against the dictator. He was not the zealot Communist, and he split with Castro. He had been in the army, and very close to Castro, and then he was in jail for twenty-five years. He was probably the last one, a very elegant person.

My brother [Bobby] was very involved. I can remember meetings they had down on the Cape on weekends about what Castro needed: "What were

20. Some 1,100 Cuban freedom fighters, trained by the CIA, were captured by Fidel Castro's forces at the failed Bay of Pigs invasion in April 1961, a US-backed effort to overthrow Castro's Soviet-allied Communist regime, ninety miles off the coast of Florida. The next year, most of the prisoners were released in a deal brokered through Robert Kennedy, in exchange for millions of dollars' worth of American pharmaceuticals and baby food.

21. Gregory B. Craig, a Washington lawyer, served as a senior advisor to Senator Edward Kennedy on foreign and defense policy from 1984 to 1988. A decade later he was special counsel for President Bill Clinton during his impeachment trial.

Castro's needs? How can we possibly get it? We have to be careful on this." And it was all medicines; it was all pharmaceuticals. So they made a swap of pharmaceuticals for prisoners over a period of time. It's very interesting. There's a fellow here in Washington, John Nolan, who was the go-between. John remembered the whole thing, and he's written it up. All of that was Bobby. I can remember his strong, strong commitment to not let those people rot in jail. We had to get them out. They got probably three-quarters of the people out. Castro kept twenty of them, but he gradually let them out over a period of time. But it was very instructive, the follow-through. [Nolan] was a very bright, solid, smart, tough guy.

Castro had always been so fascinated with Jack and Bobby. He's always trying to get me down there. It's a very interesting story. We've been very active and involved in terms of the Cubans, the refugees. All of them are real right-wingers.

Senator Kennedy described the Senate at the time his brother was president.

EMK: When I first got to the Senate, we had one administrative assistant and one legislative assistant who covered everything. So if the administration sent over community mental health centers to the committee, which President Kennedy did; he had Lister Hill chairing that committee,[22] and he had this proposal. He explained it to you. The staff explained it to you. You either had to know something about community mental health, or your staff had to know something about it, because if they don't, he's moving it through. He's the chairman of the committee, he has a Democratic majority, and that thing moves on through. It moves to the floor; it's out of that committee.

Other people had their one staffer covering all of their parts, so it was almost a parliamentary system. If it came through the system—the House had the Rules Committee—but at least in the Senate, if, as president, you had something to propose, and you were able to work it out with the chairman. The chair had an enhanced capacity. Lister Hill was from Alabama, and he had to have some idea what you were saying about mental health; he had to have some interest. You had your people, your Cabinet secretary came over to talk to him and convince him. You were able to get reaction and response to these issues, because the other members of the committee were very limited.

Now we have so much staff that they have to justify their presence; they have to come up with five amendments on these issues. So this whole process gets worked out. And if they're smart staff, they call up the mental health groups and find out what's happening. They get to the meeting and they say, "Oh, my gosh. You're talking about that bill!" The groups have become much more active.

---

22. Senator Lister Hill, an Alabama Democrat, chaired the Labor and Public Welfare Committee.

Now whether the final product is all that much better is a question. If you had the administration, you had the secretaries, you had a president who was interested in community mental health. You had a secretary who was a highly competent person with a very good staff, and they would have done all of that work before. But now we have so much staff, and they have to justify themselves. Every one of them has an opinion about it. So it takes different skills, because you have to have a staff that's brighter and smarter than the rest of them, and who have their own political skills to be able to pull it all together.

[Before large staffs, y]ou'd have to take the time to find out about this stuff. If you were interested in it, you'd find out about it. You'd go down to the agency and get briefed. You'd get more involved in it. That isn't the way it's done now. The staff goes down, maybe moves ahead.

And that's so completely in contrast to how it was. I was obviously spoiled, being down there at the time my brother was down there [in the White House]. We had people come into the departments who were just superstars. The greatest example, of course, was Bobby [as attorney general], who took in the top six people, none of whom he knew before: Jack Miller, who was a Republican, criminal division, and ended up being probably one of the top, not only in the criminal division, but afterwards as a criminal lawyer. He was just breathtaking. You had Katzenbach, whom he never knew before, who ended up being attorney general. He had Burke Marshall, who went back up to Yale as the outstanding civil rights authority of the time. John Douglas in the civil division was absolutely brilliant.

None of them knew who Bobby was, but every one of them was brilliant in his own area and could help lead that department and ensure that in each of these aspects of justice, the American people were getting the best. And that standard, which is what this democracy expects and should expect, has just been constantly deteriorated and diminished and lowered in a way that's a tragedy, just in terms of the structure of government.

Perspectives

Robert Healy, Washington bureau chief and executive editor for the *Boston Globe*:

Q: When does Edward Kennedy appear on your radar?

Healy: I had met him in Wisconsin. I met him on the ski trip. It was the one where he jumped off the—he was in the gin mill one night and somebody challenged him and—Teddy was a really bold figure, you know. I mean you really have to understand he was—first of all, he was unlike the Kennedys. Bobby was kind of a tough guy, but Teddy was a big physical presence too. He was strong as hell, and he was a pretty fair football player although he didn't— he got screwed up in Harvard. And of course we'll get to that, but he was big and he was daring and he went off—that's where I met him. I can't think of the town, either, but I'm sure it's in somebody's notes. I met him the night that he was challenged. I was with him and I think there were a couple of other news guys there but I don't—I may have been alone, I don't know.

Anyway, he did the jump. He went off the damn thing [ski jump]. I thought he'd kill himself. He wasn't a jumper. At the time, I was a pretty good skier because I skied with the mountain troops out in Aspen, the Tenth Mountain Division. I wasn't in the division but I was—He was not a bad skier, but he had more guts than he had brains, you know. He survived the jump and he took the—yes, there it is. The guy said to him, "You won't do the jump," and he said, "Yes I will, if you'll vote for my brother."

So that's how it was. The same night he was getting bitten by dogs. Instead of putting the Kennedy stickers on the back of cars, he would put them on the windows inside, and a dog attacked him. Then, I really didn't see much of him during the campaign. And I wouldn't, because he went west. Yes, he went west and he delivered Wyoming, if you remember, which was the big casino in '60 [because its votes put JFK over the top at the convention].

Vicki Kennedy: Also, I hope that at some future date, that people looking at his whole history look at his role in the 1960 campaign, and his going out to the western states for his brother during the primary. I think a couple of things of what he did really showed—and he was a kid. I mean, he was really a young kid, but if you look at the states that Teddy went to, his personal skills—I'm talking about getting the nomination.

First of all, they were pretty tough states. There weren't that many primary states to begin with at that period of time, and you're dealing with states that looked like they were going to be for Johnson, looked like they were going to be for Humphrey. They were not places that were pro-Kennedy country, and here this young man goes out to these states and is making the case for his brother. Look at how many delegates he peeled off in those states, and because of his personal relationships, was able to get Wyoming in the final analysis, to agree that they would throw all their delegates to his brother if they would be the one that would tip it over. That alone, the difference that his personal relationships and all that hard campaigning did in making a first ballot victory for JFK—again it's so often just said like, "Oh, yes, well, he went out there and how did he do?" There's that—I'm sorry for the [Boston] *Globe*, I'm sorry they're not going to be happy with me, but that *Globe* book, which really made it seem like he went out there and he wasn't successful.

The Last Lion.[23] "He went out there and he wasn't successful." It's phenomenal. Look at what he did in all the states he went to, not just the western states. President Kennedy, then Senator Kennedy, had him come out to West Virginia

---

23. Peter S. Canellos, ed., *Last Lion: The Fall and Rise of Ted Kennedy* (New York: Simon and Schuster, 2009).

because he was so successful. He was in Wisconsin. He knew that Teddy was a campaigner, he could make a speech. Now, remember the time in West Virginia when President Kennedy lost his voice and he said, "Get Teddy," so Teddy could make the speeches for his brother. Well, Teddy was doing so well. He said, "Teddy, you can't run for president until you're thirty-five." Kind of kicked him out and said, "I can speak now, go back and go do something else."

He . . . was so focused and so disciplined in getting his brother elected. He gave it everything he had, in states that were really difficult, and he got enough delegates to be able to add to the pile enough to get his brother the nomination on the first ballot.

Q: *And he was this stranger from back East.*

Vicki Kennedy: Exactly, stranger from back East who had no connection. No connection, and he flew his own airplane and rode bucking broncos and did ski jumps. And he said the only thing he refused to do was to have the cigarette shot out of his mouth. He thought about that one and said, "No, I think I'm just going to pass on that one." But he would do these things to get attention for his brother. He had a natural way with people and a natural political ability, but a discipline, and during that time he was taking notes. I have the handwritten notes. In those days he wasn't dictating. I have his notes in longhand that he wrote, from that 1960 campaign. It's incredible, the discipline that he was showing. This isn't some wacky kid who is just barely getting by. You know, that storyline about some ne'er-do-well, it just doesn't mesh. You know? He was a complicated guy, I mean he was very complex, very—that's what made him so interesting, I think, but hard work and discipline were very much a part of who he was. And this innate political ability.

Senator John Culver (D-IA), Edward Kennedy's Harvard classmate and friend:

Q: *With a brother in the White House, did that help him? I mean, did he turn to the president often to help him with problems, even issues related to Massachusetts?*

Culver: I think he may have called once or twice. I saw some reference in one of those books about how Jack said, "You're on your own." I found that hard to believe because Jack couldn't have been more interested or desirous of helping in every proper way. But he sure loved Ted and wanted him to succeed.

More often than not, it seems to me it would be something lower down the food chain, and he [Ted] would call over there—to Kenny O'Donnell or Larry O'Brien. And it was just the same as talking to the president because they would talk to the president and get back to him, or on their own authority say, "Yes, I'll take care of it."

Q: *Do you know if he had a good relationship with Vice President Johnson? Of course, there was this reputed tension between Bobby Kennedy and LBJ. I'm just wondering about Edward Kennedy.*

Culver: Yes. My sense is that Ted missed most of that flak, even in 1968, at the time of the convention. Ted, in the midst of that chaos, Ted was still acceptable to all factions. I mean, roughly speaking. He hadn't been as outspoken on the war. He hadn't been as polarizing.

So in relation to LBJ. I remember the first time I met LBJ. I went with Ted to a cocktail reception in the Capitol hosted by Democratic administrative assistants. I suppose it may have been in December of '62. I saw Ted shake hands with Johnson.

Ted was talking to somebody, and Johnson came over to me and said, "Why don't you come over and see me some day? I'm over at the Capitol. I'd love to meet you and talk to you more." I said, "Fine, Mr. Vice President." Of course, I never did, but it was interesting. He wanted to learn more about Ted through me. He was interested in the people around Ted, what are they like, because he was such a consummate politician. And he had this tension going with other elements of the Kennedy family.

Edward Martin, Edward Kennedy's staffer:

Martin: I think he [President Kennedy] came to Boston twice, and both times I did see him. But there was one time, and this is true, when he came up to Boston, and he had talked to Steve Smith, who was running the [1962 Senate] campaign, and his [JFK's] plans were to fly up to Boston, then take a helicopter and arrive at the Public Garden. He was going to stop at Locke-Ober's for his favorite soup, lobster stew, I guess, and then he could come around the corner and go into our headquarters, which is right on Tremont Street.

We were concerned that the senator didn't have too much in the way of background, and we were always complaining that he was running because he was brother of the president. And I didn't think that the president's arrival in Boston would help us any, so I passed word that he should come into Boston with his wife and land on Boston Common and go up to vote, which is up near the State House, and then leave immediately, which he did. Others probably agreed the same thing. Later on, Steve Smith told me the president was rather concerned. He said, "Tell Martin, the next time I come home I'll be wearing a clown suit." [*Laughter.*] Apparently it had bothered him. Then I had stayed with the senator during that first campaign, all the way through.

During Teddy's 1962 Senate campaign, President Kennedy intervened to manage release of the story of Teddy's 1951 expulsion from Harvard for cheating on a final exam.

Robert Healy, Washington bureau chief and executive editor, *Boston Globe*: We knew about the story about Teddy being bounced out of Harvard.

Q: Were his opponents spreading this story [in the 1962 campaign]?

Healy: No. We always had pretty good connections at Harvard, you know what I mean? I ran a study group over there for eight years, too, so you'd have faculty, and the faculty guys knew about it. But you couldn't get them to talk about it and these were days when you didn't run a story just because somebody told you. You had to get some evidence, and we made a rule that until Harvard gave us a shot at what happened, which they would not give us until they got permission from the Kennedys to do it—I'm sorry. I'm a little obscure there. What I meant was you had to get—Teddy had to—the Kennedys had to call Harvard and say, "Look, give him the story."

I got a call from Dick Maguire. He was the treasurer of the Democratic National Committee. He said to me, "I'd like to talk to you." I always got stories from him and so it wasn't unusual, and I said, "I'm up here doing some business now. I'll give you a ring." He said, "No, I'm in Boston." And I said, "Where are you?" And he said, "I'm at the Parker House." So I said, "Well, we'll do it." He said, "No. Why don't you come down? You might be—I want to talk to you if you've got time." So I said, "Sure."

Anyway, I finished my business and went down there and Dick was kind of uncomfortable, you know. You could tell he wasn't giving me anything—nothing that I was interested in—and then all of a sudden he said to me, "What do you know about Teddy?" It came just like that, right out, changed the subject, and I said, "What do you mean? The cheating story?" And he said, "Yes. What do you know about it?" And I said, "Not a whole lot. We know there was an exam involved. Someone took it for him and we don't know—we know that much but we can't confirm it. Harvard won't confirm it. Our guys aren't going to run it." And he said, "OK."

Then he left and the next thing I know, he came back to the room. He excused himself. I thought he was going to the bathroom. He came back and he said to me, "I got a phone call for you." Like I said before, Jack would get on the phone with you, and he never introduced himself. I mean he just began talking, and so it was the president on the phone and he said to me, "So you just told Maguire about how much you knew about the cheating story." And I told him what I just told Maguire. And he said, "Well, we could sit on this thing." And I said, "Yes, and Eddie McCormack [Ted Kennedy's primary opponent] will blow you out of the water in the first debate." He laughed and he said, "Yes, you've got it."

Anyway, he said, "Come on over to see me," and I said, "Hey, I'm in Boston. I'm negotiating my future." He said, "When are you coming back?" I said tomorrow morning, and he said, "Come over to see me." I went over and he has in the room—well, I met with him first, and we just went over the details.

Q: The two of you one-on-one?

Healy: One-on-one, yes. And then he invites in Kenny O'Donnell and Mac Bundy. I got a great line here for you. Jack is going over this whole thing about the play, and of course initially he wants—this is just the two of us. He wants it in a biographical sketch of Teddy. I said, "Christ, you've got to be kidding. I'd write that story, put it in the tenth paragraph and the AP would lead with it all over the country that Teddy got caught cheating at Harvard. No way am I going to do that." Then Jack got involved with the play of the story and so forth.

Q: Did he get irritated with you at all during that meeting?

Healy: No. I mean the Oval Office is still the Oval Office, but I had been there enough, and I had known him well enough so that—I've watched guys go in that Oval Office, you know, and they're shaking. But I wasn't shaking. I mean, not that I was so bold, but I was accustomed to him.

And also, he knew I was telling him the truth. I wasn't the first one to think about the debate, I'm sure. The only reason they did it was for that reason, you know, to blunt the possibility of McCormack. I said McCormack is coming out, and he's going to be tough.

Jack then brings in Bundy, and somebody else was in there too but I can't remember who. But Bundy was there, and O'Donnell. I remember when Jack brings them in. I knew Mac Bundy pretty well, and I knew Kenny, a pal. Jack could swear like a pirate, as you probably know. He says, "We're talking about the cheating story at Harvard." And he said, "I'm having more fucking trouble with this than I had with the Bay of Pigs." And Bundy, I'll never forget Bundy. Bundy says, "And with about the same results."

So that was the way—so I got the deal that I wanted, basically. They opened the gates. Bundy was instructed at that meeting to call Harvard. He had been the dean at Harvard and he called somebody and when I called, they knew exactly what they had to—they gave me the whole record. And I told them, I told Jack—and he wanted to know what day it would run, too. Kind of interesting. I hadn't even thought of that. They were going to hold up the Harvard transmission so that the news magazines would be out for the week. Are you following me?

We got the story on Monday so that by next Friday—

Q: It was old news.

Healy: It was kind of old news and you've got to consider that the news magazines in those days were terribly important—*Life* magazine, *Newsweek*, and *Time*, and particularly out in the Middle West. It was a big story. And I wrote it pretty straight. You've got copies of it so there's no point—It led with the cheating. I mean there was no question about—and they didn't have—I had a guy then who was sort of our executive editor. [H]e was smart as hell. He was very watchful of my copy on this thing and properly so. You know, I welcomed it because I didn't want to—

Q: What were the concerns?

Healy: Well, he didn't want me to go in the tank for the Kennedys. That was the main concern and that it be straight and that it be complete. And they also gave me—they also threw into the package Teddy's record at the University of Virginia, which was a plus of course for him because he had done his work pretty well. It was good. It was as close as you could come to a one-day-wonder story as you could have. It ran quite lengthy, and it was pretty complete with comments on—the only thing they didn't give me—Harvard would not give me the name of the other student—who was from Connecticut.

Q: *The person who took the exam* [for Teddy]?

Healy: Yes. But that's how it happened. There's nine versions of it but, you know, everybody gets the idea that Healy was a Kennedy guy in private, and obviously I was, but the stuff that I wrote was pretty straight, if you read the stuff. And pretty complete.

Theodore Sorensen, President Kennedy's speechwriter and special counsel:

Sorensen: My impression, though, was that sometime later—one of my duties that I remember most about was writing jokes for the president. There was a dinner for Ted up in Boston. Do you know about this joke?

Q: *No, I don't think so.*

Sorensen: The president said, "Well, Teddy came to me and he said people were saying that he was getting his job just on his name. And he wanted to change his name. I said to him, 'Fine, Teddy. What do you want to change it to?' He said, 'I don't want to be Teddy Kennedy anymore. People are saying I'm trading on a famous name. I want to change it to Teddy Roosevelt.'" Just totally fiction, you understand. Anyway, it showed the great Kennedy trait, the ability to poke fun at themselves.

3

Joining the Family Business: Teddy Goes to the Senate

With JFK in the White House and Bobby settled in the cabinet, their father began planning a strategy to maintain Jack's Senate seat for the family. It was the last political machination that Joe Kennedy would perform before suffering a debilitating stroke, just prior to Christmas 1961. When Teddy was asked whether the Kennedys were creating a political dynasty, he offered a bemused retort, "[I]f you are talking about too many Kennedys, you should have talked to my mother and father at the time they were getting started."[1]

After serving as an assistant prosecutor in Boston, Teddy claimed JFK's Senate seat in a special 1962 election. The president and First Lady had flown to Boston to vote, and after the victory, JFK gleefully introduced himself as "Teddy Kennedy's brother."[2] Teddy was now on Capitol Hill, and the Kennedy dynasty had reached its apogee.

Only a few weeks beyond the constitutionally mandated age of thirty for assuming a Senate seat, Edward Kennedy maintained due deference toward his senior colleagues and tried to keep a low profile, despite Life *magazine's feature story about his arrival on Capitol Hill. As the youngest of nine children, Teddy had an instinctive knack for relating to his elders, which served him well in a chamber of aging senators. He happily accepted appointments to the Judiciary Committee's Immigration and Constitutional Rights Subcommittees. Diligently performing his legislative homework each night, he also made sure to attend meetings for his other assignment on the Labor and Public Welfare Committee. He won friends among fellow senators for giving them primary credit when co-sponsoring bills, understanding that his surname would distract from their efforts. A natural extrovert, Teddy got to know Senate colleagues in the steam room, where they could talk shop in an informal atmosphere.*

---

1. James MacGregor Burns, *Edward Kennedy and the Camelot Legacy* (W. W. Norton, 1976), 80.
2. Ibid., 91.

Kennedy hoped that having a brother in the Oval Office would provide special attention to Massachusetts's problems. Yet when Senator Kennedy told President Kennedy of increasing unemployment in their home state, JFK reportedly responded, "Tough shit."[3] The president, however, appreciated his kid brother's reports on what senators were thinking about difficult issues facing the chief executive in the summer of 1963, especially civil rights, Khrushchev, the space race, legislative bottlenecks, and military advisors in Vietnam.

As a junior senator, Teddy was presiding over the chamber during a routine debate on November 22, 1963, when an aide dashed in to tell him that the president had been shot while riding in a Dallas motorcade. It fell to the youngest son, and his sister, Eunice Kennedy Shriver, to inform their invalid father that Jack had died of his wounds.

The next November, Teddy ran in the regularly scheduled 1964 Senate election, at the same time that Bobby, who had resigned as attorney general, was vying for a Senate seat from the family's adopted home in New York. Having suffered a broken back in a private plane crash on the way to the Massachusetts Democratic convention that past summer, Teddy had to campaign from his hospital bed through surrogates, especially his wife and mother. He returned to the Senate, walking with a cane, just in time to welcome the new junior senator from New York, Robert F. Kennedy, in January 1965.

EMK: I went back up to Massachusetts [after the 1960 election], and this is when I really became much, much closer to my father. I went to my brother [Jack] and said I was interested in elected office, and he said, "Don't waste your time any further." Earlier he'd given me other advice—going to Africa for five weeks and things like that. But he said, "Go back up to Massachusetts. Every day you're up there, you'll meet people and you'll find out—we'll find out how people react to you and whether you're able to inspire them to your ideas and your viewpoints. I'd go right back up and start going to work up there." I went up and talked to my father about it, then went to Boston and signed on as [Suffolk County] assistant district attorney.

Q: You said this is a period when you're very close to your father.

EMK: To my father, because my brothers now were gone, they'd gone. Jack was the president and Bobby . . . had been appointed attorney general, and I was up in Boston. When my father came back up there, particularly that summer of 1961, I spent a lot of time with him. He'd go out on his boat and I'd go out with him, and it was really a very enormously interesting, exciting for me, because he had been so involved with my older brothers Joe, Jack, Bobby, and now was sort of focused.

Q: Is that it? You were finally getting the attention.

---

3. Adam Clymer, *Edward Kennedy: A Biography* (New York: William Morrow, 1999), 47.

EMK: "Who's left around here? It's Teddy over here; oh well, now."

I was just looking and going around Massachusetts now and speaking, in 1961, and we were getting a pretty good reaction. I had traveled to different places. I went to Latin America and Africa, and I'd go around speaking to different chambers of commerce about those things. I was chairman of the Cancer Crusade, and I'd go out and talk about cancer.

But he [my father] had this wonderful expression that he'd mention to all of the boys and the girls too, and that was, "Home holds no fear for me." That is, you ought to go out and do the best you can. If it doesn't work, you can always come home. There's always a place here. We embrace you and love you and will be a source of strength and inspiration so you can go on out and try again. So you would take on the tough challenges, take on the difficult battles and do what you believe is right, because you can always come back here. This is always going to be a place that's going to be supportive, and we will always support you.

Q: Were you hearing in part, not only that home holds no fear, there's a safe place to come back to?

EMK: A safe place.

Q: For recovery or renewal. But were you also hearing a message about, expect some rough times?

EMK: Rough times?

Q: Some rough times out there. He's not bringing any of you up to be like himself, in the sense of his being a businessman, a financier, or something like that.

EMK: No. Two points. One is that we didn't really understand—at least I didn't at the time—the nature of the challenges both personally and emotionally, as well as professionally, that you would be facing. No, but you knew that he would be very much in your corner.

So we went on through the fall of '61 and at that time, I had gotten around a little bit [in the state], and was getting a good reception. That's what my brother Jack was hearing—he'd talked to a lot of his pals in different places—that we were getting good receptions. Then, the concept of running in '62 was beginning to emerge. Of course my father was very much in my corner. My brother Jack's political people were questioning the wisdom of this, and Bobby's political—he was fine, Bobby was really sort of fine with it. He thought if it was going to—

Q: Was he ever thinking about running for the Senate, and then when Jack—

EMK: I think after my brother was elected [president], I think Bobby wanted to do something sort of separate.

Q: And your father wanted Bobby to be there with Jack, too.

EMK: My father wanted—generally wanted him to be there too. I don't think it took a lot of persuasion to get him there. Obviously, if he had been running for the Senate, I'm not sure quite where we'd all have fitted in. But I wasn't thinking about that at the time. My father was sort of my strongest advocate, and he was great fun. I remember my brothers calling him when they were facing challenges, and he always had some good advice for them. And here I was, talking to him on the same kind of plane. So it was a very exhilarating time. And then the end of that year, he had a stroke, December of that year, and that was a major kind of blow.

This would have been in December of '61, so it was just prior to the time that I announced [for the Senate race]; everything was kind of in place. By this time they were fine, my brother Jack and Bobby were fine on it. They took sort of their own soundings and found out that we were doing pretty well up there, and they were fine on it. But he, my father, was very much involved. I got closer and closer to him over this whole period of time, then suddenly this person who had been my kind of right hand and principal figure was struck down. He was down in Florida, I remember going down there with Jack and Bobby, at the time he first had his first stroke, and the terribly difficult time he had. And he had a very difficult time from then on through to the end in 1969. So that was a very—

Q: Whom did you turn to? Did you have anybody to turn to?

EMK: Well, it was very hard, because at that time, you didn't know how bad all of this was. I went down frequently to visit him. They thought he was going to get better, you know this thing was going to be temporary, it was all going to get better, but it just never, it just never did. Parents are sort of obviously, the irreplaceable people, and your wife and children. This was a very powerful blow to me. My mother was still strong and she was very—she was energetic. It was very important to keep her spirits up and going.

Q: Her spirits up, but what about yours?

EMK: She was great.

Q: How did you keep your spirits up?

EMK: Well, this was a difficult kind of a time. We were just in the midst of the beginning of everything—our family, the race, this. It was just a very challenging time. There was no going back or really changing direction. We didn't heed—because my father, he wanted me to do well. This is still important to him. I knew it was. He'd want to hear about what was going on, that was a source of inspiration, because he was still alive, and I always thought could understand. So I still felt he was in our corner and felt he was more frustrated than I was, and it was important to keep moving and going on.

Q: So he was with you in spirit.

EMK: In spirit, I felt.

Q: But he was a different person. That must have been a pretty hard thing to take.

EMK: So, I won't spend time really going through the election. We had the success in the campaign, but 1962 was also a time when I was really very moved or concerned. At the beginning of the campaign, I noticed that my wife[4] drank. It hadn't—all the time that we'd been at law school, I never noticed,

---

4. Teddy's first wife was Joan Bennett Kennedy.

it never really affected her. I remember the first time. We were supposed to go to the State [Democratic] Committee meeting, and I asked her if she was ready, and walked in the room and saw that she was unsteady. I thought that's strange, because it was sort of the first time that she hadn't been able to make it to an event. This was the start of '62, and that kind of thing sort of picked up during the period of '62. That was a difficult thing to cope with and deal with. I'm not sure that I dealt with it very well in terms of how do you get through it, get through it until the election. This was becoming increasingly a problem that was gnawing at me.

Q: *It was soon after Teddy* [Jr.] *was born* [in September 1961].

EMK: Just about after that. So we get through the '62 campaign, and we're down here in Washington. It's an exciting, interesting time to arrive down here. But there was still concern about these other issues.

Q: *That summer* [of 1963], *Joan was spending on the Cape, at Hyannis Port, I think.*

EMK: Yes.

Q: *And you were in Washington.*

EMK: Yes.

Q: *So, were you seeing a lot of your brothers?*

EMK: I saw a lot of them. He acquired a great—he was always inquisitive about everything, Jack. He was always inquisitive. He asked me about being in the army, asked me about the different people and their backgrounds and where they came from, about the training programs and what was going on, about the weapons and everything. He was always asking questions and inquisitive. He was inquisitive about what was going on in the Senate. Of course, the senators assumed that I was going down there to the White House and talking about them every night, which I didn't. But if he wasn't tied up, he'd ask me to come down [to the White House] for a swim. He'd come down [to the White House pool] about 6:30. I'd go down and take a swim with him, and he'd have some daiquiris, and we'd go up the elevator to his own place on the second floor. More often than not, he had creamed chicken and rice, that's what he liked, and peas. That's what he had for dinner, and the plates were served, and you sit down. He was interested in what was going on, and, then by dessert time, he had found out, and he was interested in going in and reading.

He was great fun, interested in the personalities. I'd tell him stories about what's going on in the steam room, how Jennings Randolph[5] was about to pass out because he'd been in the steam room so long, and, when I came in, he sat in there and talked to me about a postmastership down in Charleston, West Virginia. I thought Jennings was going to die if we stayed in there any longer.

---

5. Jennings Randolph was a Democratic senator from West Virginia.

[M]y first impressions of the different people, the personalities. He was interested in political characters and sort of the rhythm and the—

Q: Well you were too, weren't you?

EMK: Yes, yes. And then once in a while, we'd sit out on the porch, and I'd smoke a cigar. Once in a while we would go out on the boat. Cabinet members used to take their different committee members, and they'd get more business done out on those boat trips in just a couple of hours. It was a great way to relax. The times we went out on the boat, he'd always have some other people that he was trying to sort of do business with. I saw a good deal of him. We'd fly with him up to the Cape, and we'd have a chat on the plane.

Q: He was interested in the characters and interested about finding out what's going on in the Senate. Did you have conversations about his own work, the characters that he was meeting, or did he not talk about this?

EMK: It was more—well, he talked about his trip to see Khrushchev. This was up at the Cape when he was just leaving from there to see him in Vienna.

Senator Kennedy recalled the assassination of President Kennedy.

EMK: And then we have 1963. I had been presiding in the Senate on the 22nd of November, and at 11:30, our time, and this fellow Stan Kimmitt or someone came over and said, "Your brother has been shot, and I'll get you relief from presiding over the Senate." I remember leaving the Senate and going over to the—they used to have two big boxes; one had the AP and the other had the UPI news ticker, you could watch the ticker. I was seeing the words coming through and thinking I better try and get ahold of my brother Bobby, to find out. I remember getting back over to my office. It was still really uncertain you know, there was disbelief that this thing was going to be real, you know, terribly serious. But it was ominous. I hadn't really thought that it could be more than something that would not be fatal. I remember getting to my office and talking to Bobby. He told me that it was very serious, and you ought to go on home.

At that time, I went home to Georgetown and you couldn't—there weren't any communications, all the communications were down. You couldn't call anybody or get ahold of anybody, that kind of thing. And then I remember talking to Bobby sometime in the afternoon and he said, "You know, he was not going to"—it was a hopeless situation. So, I went up [to Hyannis Port] and talked to my father.

Q: I've got some tears too.

EMK: So we got on a plane and went and told my father, which was a difficult thing. So we got through that period.

Q: After the funeral and all of that, how was it?

EMK: Well, this was enormous personal devastation. He was always close to all the members of the family, and I always felt close to each of my brothers in different ways. So, you know, it's an extraordinary personal loss of the most powerful and searing kind. But I don't think I prayed a lot at that time. I think we were very conscious about the importance of Jackie's well-being and John and Caroline. I knew that Bobby was enormously upset, and I was close to him, and it was just very important that—there were important things to do. It made a difference in doing them, too, for the members of the family at that time. It was an enormously difficult time, inspired by people's reaction and their feelings for Jack.

Q: *But the personal grief is yours.*

EMK: Yes, it was hard to deal with.

Q: *People were grieving in their own way, alone, is that it?*

EMK: A lot of that.

Q: *As it was earlier?*[6]

EMK: They were all—yes. They're not good at—you know, they're rather quiet and very—it's an exuberant family when it's together, and it's enthusiastic and hopeful and joyous and fun, but it doesn't—I'm not sure that we handle all the grief and the sadness exceedingly well. This is a much more— you know, we were getting caught up with it now, with increasing sort of frequency, but it was very devastating. And you would think, "Is this a reaction against my father and my mother?" It's a very—

Q: *This was perhaps the first time you had encountered the violence, or the hatred was it, that's "out there," as they say, and that caused this terrible murder of your brother. I could easily imagine your thinking this is part of—is this part of America, or is it an aberration? There was all sorts of talk at the time about a conspiracy.*

EMK: That whole thing, it was—the loss was overpowering and overarching. Bobby asked me to go and visit with Justice Warren,[7] and I went over and listened to him, talked with him for a couple of hours, and then after I did that, made some notes about some things, questions I had. Warren came over and talked with Bobby and me together, but you know it was the loss that was overpowering. We never really got wrapped up about other people or other—

Q: *I didn't mean that. I meant, it was—did it make you wonder about your country, that these things could happen here?*

EMK: I had seen the kind of bigotry and the hatred myself. I had seen it when I went down South for Martin Luther King, you know the nails in the road and the bitterness and hatred, and I'd seen some in the '60 campaign, and read about it. This was obviously the—I was really much more consumed by the emotions and the feelings of it. To put it in some kind of perspective, I didn't associate this—I mean, I didn't know the motives and background and all of this. I never really—

---

6. The interviewer is referring to the tragic deaths of Teddy's brother Joe Jr. in World War II and their sister Kathleen in a 1948 plane crash.

7. Earl Warren was chief justice of the United States from 1953 to 1969 and was asked by President Lyndon Johnson to direct the Warren Commission's investigation of JFK's assassination, which concluded that Lee Harvey Oswald was the sole perpetrator of the murder.

Q: It was the loss itself.

EMK: The loss itself was overwhelming, and that was the paramount overwhelming, overarching kind of issue for us.

Q: Did you have anybody that you particularly turned to at that time?

EMK: Well, in '63, we were very—it was really very much a family kind of time. I spent time up with my father, I spent two or three days up there, with my mother. I had that part and then came back down with my sisters. And then there were all the events surrounding the thing which were so powerful.

Q: You were looking out for your mother, being supportive of your mother, of your father, and I guess my question is, who was being supportive of Ted Kennedy?

EMK: Yes. Well, there was a lot of concern, you know you were close to my sisters and all.

A lot of things happened subsequently, but I think the next traumatic moment was my plane crash in 1964, . . . going to the Democratic convention in Springfield, Massachusetts. We landed at the—or tried to land at Barnes Airport, and we crashed just short of the runway, in an apple orchard, probably to the north of the airport. I was with Marvella and Senator Bayh,[8] who was going to be the keynote speaker, and myself. I was with an aide named Ed Moss, who actually worked for the telephone company—he was flying back up to the convention with me, he was a good personal friend—and the pilot, there was only one pilot. The Aero Commander has the two seats that face forward and then the four seats right—and then there's two seats facing the rear, in back of the pilot and copilot, and I guess there's three seats that go across. So there were the four of us in the back part of it and the pilot. He had waited some period of time, because we had the civil rights bill, an important civil rights bill that got passed in late, late afternoon, and then we took off and left.

Q: That was your brother's bill.

EMK: In '63.

Q: Well, it was passed under Johnson but it was his [JFK's], too.

EMK: It was the '64 Act, public accommodations. I remember—I am a pilot, or I was when I was in law school—saying that we're getting close to Springfield, and Birch started writing some notes, and I took my papers out and started writing some notes. Ed Moss said, "It would probably give you people more room if I sat up in the copilot seat." So he got up just before we landed and went to the copilot seat. I think that probably cost him his life. I turned just as he said, "We're just landing now, we'll be landing in three or four minutes."

I had my seatbelt loose, so I could turn to watch the approach, and I remember looking down at what I thought was going to be the approach, and

8. Birch Bayh was a Democratic senator from Indiana. He and his wife, Marvella, were friends of Senator Kennedy.

suddenly seeing rocks and a field almost directly in front of us, and trees sort of beyond that. It looked like we were coming right on down in sort of a rocky bluff, that kind of thing. He put the gas on and we rode—the plane sort of came up and rode 166 feet along the tops of these trees, across the tops of these trees, the landing gear was down. Then the left wing hit a big, tall tree and it spun the plane off to the left, which was fortunate, because these were all tall pine trees. If we crashed, I'm sure we all would have been killed, but this one tipped it over to the left and put it into an apple orchard. The plane went down and it went 166 feet—not long, it was 30 yards or so, but that was enough to slow it down and it just opened up the front of it like this, right at the face, in the apple trees. I can remember being hit in the head, hanging between what was the pilot and Moss. I remember mosquitoes coming in and absolute silence, nothing going on, absolute silence.

Then I heard Birch Bayh and Marvella, she was chattering. Bayh said, "Are you all right up there, are you all right up there?" I couldn't answer. I couldn't answer, but I was conscious of it. So they got out of the plane, and then he went a little ways away, sort of helping her and strained his back, and she was very nervous. And then he said, "The plane might catch on fire." Then he went back to find if anybody was alive. He said, "The plane's going to catch on fire, so I better go down the hill and get some help."

Q: Yes, but he went back to the plane.

EMK: He came back to the plane, and I think when I heard that the plane might catch on fire, I thought I'd better start moving. So I said to Birch, "I'm still alive." I was really paralyzed sort of from the waist down, but I turned myself around and got my arm out around him, and he dragged me out.

Q: Through the window?

EMK: Through the window. Most of it was gone, I mean I still have cuts on my knees and all the rest, from where—some of the plastic was still there. Then I said, "I'll just let go—"he couldn't bend over—"when we're far enough away." He said, "We're far enough away," and I just let go and dropped to the ground. And then he went back to look and tried to get Moss out, but he couldn't get him out. So then he went down to the road; Marvella went down to the road, and eight cars went by. Finally, they got a nice driver that stopped after twenty minutes or so. Now, the airport had radar, had seen it coming down, and finally the ambulance comes out. It comes up some distance, and people come with a stretcher, and they ask me if I'm all right. I said, "Yes. Why don't you look at the other people in the plane." And then I hear them talking, and they get Moss out, and they run back out. But I thought then that I was going to die. It was sort of pain but it was more numb, but you could just sort of feel everything going out of you, I mean you could just feel it, just sort of conscious that my head was on the grass. It wasn't enormously painful, but I felt that the tide was just going out.

And then about ten or fifteen minutes later they came back up and picked me up and brought me down to the ambulance. Now, it's really beginning to hurt—my back—so I asked them for sodium pentothal, which really had worked the one time I'd had it for a dislocated shoulder. But they said they couldn't give me sodium pentothal because I had massive bleeding.

Internal bleeding. So you know just then, I passed out, I passed out. I had one collapsed lung, and they got that worked out. I stayed at the hospital there for two or three weeks, and then went into Boston. But I remember being with the doctors, when first I got to the New England Baptist Hospital. The first day they came in and said, "You're never going to walk again," which was a sobering thought.

Q: Well, had you thought you wouldn't walk again?

EMK: I had thought I would, I thought I would. I worked my toes and thought I had a bad back and legs, but I'll still be able to walk.

Q: It was worse than you thought?

EMK: It was worse than I thought. Well particularly, they said that if they operated I'd be there for six months. My back was broken in six places, and several ribs broken. What saved my back is the vertebrae kind of exploded, they all broke into a lot of pieces, so that they didn't sever my spinal column. But they said that we'd do what they call bridging between the vertebrae, and even though they're displaced, with the bridging, they could be weight-bearing. And you could either have an operation, and they can try to put the pieces back, or you can try it without the operation and see if it will come back. But if it doesn't, then you have to have the operation after that, and you're going to be in there for six more months.

Q: What did you decide?

EMK: Well, I decided not to have it, and the person that was the most decisive was my father. He had gone through the back operation with my brother Jack, which almost killed him, in the '50s. That's when he went down to Florida, you know he did the book down there, the *Profiles [in Courage]* book, but he had a terrible, terrible experience, and it almost killed him. My father was very strong. When I dislocated my shoulder, and I had three or four of the doctors in for a meeting, my father listened to each one's advice, and one of them said he wouldn't operate on it. My father said, "Well, Teddy, he's got as good degrees as any of the others, and if you were asking me, I'd follow his advice." And he got up and walked out and left me there with these doctors. I said to them that I'd follow it. My father came up very clear: "No, no, no, no, no, no." Though he couldn't speak, you could understand when he was decisive and definitive.

Q: And did he come to the hospital?

EMK: He came to visit me, yes, he'd come up and visit me—I've got great pictures of the first day I stood. I stood with him. That was five months later, but he'd drive up mostly with Ann Gargan.

Q: And this was at New England Baptist?

EMK: New England Baptist Hospital. Let me go back just a minute. After I got into the hospital, Ed Moss lived for seven hours. For me, it was always something on my mind about, you know, if he hadn't moved and gone up to the copilot's seat. If he had stayed in the back there, if he hadn't said, "Let me give you more room back there," and we had said, "No, no, you sit here," or whatever, he probably would have survived. I maintained very close contact with Mrs. Moss and their three children. We were very close to all of those children. I spoke at each of their graduations from schools, and they came to work in my office, and I got involved when Mrs. Moss died, probably eight, nine years ago now. The girls are still alive, married, have children, live in Massachusetts. They still come to rallies and events and that sort of thing, and the children are all doing pretty well. And, of course, the pilot's family felt terrible. His wife came on in to see me. I felt bad enough about her husband, and she felt so bad that it looked like it was a pilot error. The FAA was going to do a big report. The head of the FAA was—I'll remember his name, the father of Queen Noor.

Q: Halaby?

EMK: Halaby. He was the first person that came in to see me. I said, "What the hell am I doing talking to Jeeb Halaby, even though I can hardly breathe." He's asking me what happened. But I remember [the pilot's wife] coming in and inquiring about me, and I said that we didn't need the report out about whether it was pilot error or whether to have an investigation that could destroy how he'd be remembered. And she was a terribly nice woman; I felt terrible about her. But the Moss children were very special, and Mrs. Moss was lovely, gracious, and, of course, I felt terrible about her. Now, you've got sort of these flashbacks in terms of the loss again, of 1963.

One of the positive aspects of my being laid up after the plane crash, when I was at the New England Baptist Hospital, I used to have issue days, where people would come in and brief me on different subject matters. I first met Ken Galbraith at Harvard, but now I was getting a crash course on Ec[onomics] 1. He remembered coming, and he also remembered a number of other people who had come there to brief me on different policy issues. During that period of time, I also had people who came in and briefed me on civil rights, in a number of different areas.

Q: Were these intellectuals or activists?

Kennedy: By and large, they were academics. And I certainly kept that up after I got out, in '64, trying to do what they would call an issue night.

Q: I'd like to hear a little bit more about that, those issue nights. Was this something you thought up?

Kennedy: I grew up in a house where we always had interesting people, on interesting subjects, talking about interesting things. My father had made that happen, and that was true of my brothers as well. They brought, by and large, friends who were doing interesting things. We had always been encouraged, if we traveled, to go to useful places and learn things. I mean, Bobby went to Central Asia with Supreme Court justice Bill Douglas in, I think, the '50s, and after he graduated from Harvard, he went over to the Middle East and wrote a series of articles.

After the '52 election campaign, my brother Jack had recommended that I travel to North Africa, in 1954 and '55, when these countries were just emerging independents, Morocco and Tunisia, in the midst of the Algerian battle. I went actually with JFK staffer and Harvard tutor Fred Holborn. My father always thought if you take someone who's bright and smart with you that can sort of be sort of a continued tutorial, which we did. That was really the basis of that speech that Jack gave in 1957, on independent Algeria, on the basis of a lot of the observations and conclusions and conversations that I had with him.

When Bobby was attorney general, he had meetings at his house probably every six, seven weeks, where people would read a book, or they'd have an interesting person who came out and talked to him about interesting subjects. So this concept or idea was certainly one that I was familiar with. I adopted it and have followed it really closely, probably up to the last few years.

Q: But this wasn't entertainment or edification so much for its own sake, as it was about issues that concerned you, is that right?

EMK: That's right, in the committee. One that was very memorable was one that Ken Feinberg[9] had about sentencing reform, where we had Judge Weinstein, who came down from New York, and made the recommendations about sentencing reform. We took that up and eventually passed legislation, but it was an idea that came out of one of these evenings. I had always gotten doctors together every year to talk about—you know, Patrick's a chronic asthmatic—and got doctors together on Teddy's cancer,[10] sort of the same thing, the idea of getting people together who were gifted and talented, and know their subject matter. That was all a part of our climate and atmosphere growing up.

So I followed that while I was in the hospital, on different subject matters during this period of time. And then I get out in December, and I go down South for three or four weeks, and I come back at the start of '65.

---

9. Kenneth Feinberg is an attorney from Massachusetts who specializes in mediation and alternative dispute resolution and is well known for determining compensation for victims' families after the 9/11 terror attacks. He serves as chair of the board of the John F. Kennedy Library Foundation.

10. Kennedy's two sons are Edward M. Kennedy Jr. and Patrick J. Kennedy.

Perspectives

Senator Paul Kirk (D-MA), Edward Kennedy's special assistant, attorney, and friend:

Q: Paul, can I ask you a question about Kenny O'Donnell and Ted Kennedy? We've heard stories that it was not a great relationship. Could you comment on that? Some people have suggested O'Donnell opposed Ted Kennedy's run in '62.

Kirk: I don't know that it was actual opposition, but I do know that Kenny didn't think Ted's running for the US Senate in 1962 was a good idea; that it was too much Kennedy, too much dynasty, and not helpful to the president. And that's what I mean, i.e., anything that Kenny thought might, in any way, dilute John Kennedy's strengths, interests, advantages, Kenny would question. As a result, I don't think Ted ever felt all that warmly toward Kenny. I remember during the '66 [Massachusetts] gubernatorial campaign there was the question of whether Ted would endorse Kenny, and it never came to be. I think they respected each other all right, but what Kenny viewed as a conflict with JFK's interest caused a little bit of a breach that never quite knitted together the way I would have hoped. So I think that was the genesis of it, I don't think there was anything more than that. It was just that Kenny was calling it the way he saw it, and Ted probably felt—you know, "What the hell is this?"

Dan H. Fenn Jr., President John F. Kennedy's staff assistant:

The Doug Cater story, I really got burned. Doug Cater, who was then with *The Reporter* magazine, Max Ascoli's magazine, a great little publication, liberal Democratic publication. Doug and I were in college together and we were in the *Harvard Crimson* together. As a matter of fact I was the president of *Crimson*, welcomed him onto the board. I'd arranged for him to go to some youth festival in Prague. We had a pretty good relationship. When I went down there [to Washington], I went over to his house, and we'd talk fairly regularly. One time he called and asked about Teddy's 1962 campaign. I told him I was just up there in Boston working on the thing, and then it occurred to me, he's wearing two hats here. So I called him back right away and I said, "Doug, that stuff about my being in Massachusetts was just between us old *Crimson* editors, right? You understand that?"

"Oh yes," he said, "oh yes." So I'm watching the [president's] press conference a few days later. Cater stands up and says, "Mr. President, what's the involvement of the White House in your brother's campaign for the Senate in Massachusetts?" Kennedy gave him that technical assistance stuff. Then Doug asked a follow-up question, which you didn't do in those days. He said, "I understand that a member of your White House staff was in Massachusetts working on the campaign in the last week or two." The president was quite taken aback. I didn't think he knew I was there. I've forgotten how he worked his way out of that one. But I think it's just a piece of evidence, it was sort of like the Bay of Pigs. I mean, this is our enterprise, but we don't want our fingerprints on it. I never gave Cater the time of day or the weather after that.

Milton Gwirtzman, attorney, speechwriter, Robert and Edward Kennedy's advisor:

I met Ted Kennedy in March of 1962, when he had already decided to run for the Senate and when he'd come to Washington to appear on *Meet the Press.* I think he announced around the middle of March. I met him in the office of Senator Ben Smith, who was then a senator from Massachusetts, and for whom I was then working as a legislative assistant, what they now call legislative director, but at that time Senate offices only had one.

I had not known him at college because, of course, two of the years I was there he wasn't, and we didn't travel in the same circles. I really had not followed his career, although I did travel through Massachusetts with Ben Smith after the Senate had recessed in 1961. Ben didn't do a political tour then; no one knew what Ted was going to do. They said he might run for attorney general, he might go out to Wyoming and run for office there. So Ben decided he would act as if he might run himself until he knew what Ted was going to do. He was certainly loyal to the Kennedys. He had been John Kennedy's roommate in college and stayed close to the family. His was a prominent Catholic family in Gloucester.

So we did the sort of tour that a sitting senator does, going to factories and meeting with public officials and things like that, all pointing to the possibility that he, Ben, might run. Then, as soon as Ted decided to run, he came down to see Ben and also to be briefed at the White House by Ted Sorensen and others for his *Meet the Press* appearance. He went in to see Ben and he was probably in there for an hour, and it was at that point that Ben offered Ted, me, and a couple other people in his office to help him. I was called in, I met him, and we talked about what I could do, which was to stay as a legislative assistant but be in close touch on the issues. He had a speechwriter, Hal Clancy, who was a former editor of the *Boston Traveler,* who had written some early speeches for Ted. Hal took a tour to Europe and the Middle East, and had written some articles for him. Hal was the one who came up with the idea that he should call himself Edward (Ted) Kennedy on the Democratic primary ballot. Hal reasoned that because of Ted Williams, the name Ted had a very good connotation in Massachusetts.

Q: How interesting. Was that not how he was known by friends?

Gwirtzman: Family and friends knew him as Ted, but you usually occasionally, not often, someone runs for office and they put their nickname, but he wanted to really pound that nickname home.

Q: That's interesting. I have not heard that. So a very political decision from the very beginning.

Gwirtzman: Oh, sure. We decided that I should send copies of any speeches that I had written on issues to him, and keep him current on what was going on in the Senate, and then go up there once a week on weekends, to Hyannis Port. Once he started campaigning, he'd campaign Monday through Friday and most of Sunday, but spent Friday night and Saturday and Sunday morning at his home, which was on Squaw Island, but not that far from the president's home [at Hyannis Port].

Q: When he made the decision to run, was he still working as an assistant district attorney?

Gwirtzman: Yes, but he resigned. He had done a number of cases, but it became fewer cases and more luncheon appearances and such things as that. I don't know who set up his schedule, but it was a typical Massachusetts schedule. Sundays, lots of communion breakfasts and lots of Brotherhood, Jewish breakfasts and things, and then during the week a lot of lunches and meeting with political leaders because there was a convention coming up in June and he wanted to be endorsed by that convention. He knew that Eddie McCormack[11] was going to run, Speaker John McCormack's nephew, and Eddie had been a factor in many conventions there, was very well liked by the politicians, and had been a good attorney general. He had been a good attorney general even for civil liberties and the things that the academics in Massachusetts are concerned about. So Ted knew he was going to have a fight and he didn't want to bypass the convention. That is what some of them do. Usually, the person who loses in the delegate fight at the convention says, "I will go to the people." Well, Ted was going to do both. He was going to win that fight and go to the people.

Q: What was the press response at this point?

Gwirtzman: At that point it was the same as it would be now if someone his age, he had just turned thirty, and who was the brother of the president though our current president has no brother, let's say [Jeb] Bush decided to run for senator. The public didn't follow it as closely as the press, but they loved John F. Kennedy in Massachusetts, and they loved the family, going all the way back to Honey Fitz. So the public reaction was not negative. The press had a generally negative reaction: too young and not as bright as his brothers. The Kennedy dynasty. The joke was that John Kennedy would serve until 1968 and then Bobby would be elected for eight years, and then it would be Ted in

---

11. Edward J. McCormack Jr. was the Massachusetts attorney general when he ran against Edward Kennedy for the Democratic nomination for Senate in 1962. His uncle John W. McCormack was Speaker of the US House of Representatives from 1962 to 1971, and his father, Edward Sr., was a prominent Irish pol in the Bay State. Edward Jr. criticized Teddy's youth and inexperience in the campaign.

1984,[12] which was the title of the book about the fascist dictatorship. George Orwell.

And then some very important people in the academic community were very strongly opposed. First of all, they were impressed by McCormack. They had worked with him on issues they were concerned with, and even someone as prestigious as Mark Dewolfe Howe, who was a professor of law at Harvard Law School and a leading liberal, sent a letter saying that Ted had no qualifications, a public letter, saying he was completely unqualified. It didn't help that he had had to leave Harvard for having had someone take a test for him.

Q: *Did that come up immediately in the press?*

Gwirtzman: Almost immediately, and it was deliberately planted by the Kennedy camp. They decided that with something like that, which was really the only big skeleton in his closet that anybody knew about, it would be better that they get their version of it. They weren't going to justify it.

And so they got Bobby Healy, who was a political reporter for the *Boston Globe*, which was by far and still is a dominant newspaper in the state. They got him to write the first story. It was as nice a story as it could be, given the fact that Ted had been suspended for two years from Harvard for having someone take an exam for him, which at Harvard was about the worst thing that you could do, worse than what just happened there, when a drug dealer was shot in one of the Harvard houses. So that certainly was on people's minds.

To go a little farther into the campaign, I was in Harvard Yard with him; we were going to a meeting during his campaign, I think after he had won the primary. The meeting had something to do with our Harvard class, the class of 1954. One member of the class came up to him and said, "Ted, you are a disgrace to the class of 1954." And Ted said, "I'm sure there are others who probably agree with you." So yes, that was a problem and it continued to be with that group for quite a while, maybe twenty years.

[Ted] Kennedy had the organization of Kennedy secretaries, which had been formed by his brother when he first ran for the Senate in 1952, and it had been involved in the presidential campaign and was right there for Ted to use. The liaison to that was a very fine man named Eddie King, who was the father of Jimmy King, who used to be head of OPM here, under Carter. He just went through the state, activating what was called the Kennedy secretaries, with a Kennedy secretary in each city and town of the 190 cities and towns in Massachusetts, and they started to work.

Q: *That's a very powerful way of organizing the campaign.*

---

12. If the brothers had served three consecutive sets of two presidential terms, Ted would have been president until 1985.

Gwirtzman: However, Eddie McCormack had a very strong organization in Boston, which is where maybe not the majority, but a large part of the vote in a Democratic primary would be cast, more so than now, since the suburbs are much larger than the city. So he had a good source of strength there and his uncle was the Speaker and could dispense patronage. There were charges right up to the convention and afterward about whether either the White House or the Speaker's office offering jobs in return for delegate votes and things like that. Now, I have no idea whether knowledge of that is true, but there was bad blood between the two camps. But as far as I know, there was nothing personal between Kennedy and McCormack until the first debate in south Boston in June.

JFK didn't know whether Teddy was going to run, although he wanted Ted to have some career in Massachusetts politics, eventually. The strongest person for Teddy within the Kennedy family was Joseph Kennedy. He kept pushing and finally, as I understand it, he said to his other two sons, "You've got your places, now I want Ted to have his." They deferred to that. And of course he financed the entire campaign.

Q: Did you get any sense about what JFK or RFK thought about Ted's running?

Gwirtzman: Yes. They wanted him to run, but they wanted him to do it in a way that would not affect their prestige if in fact he wasn't successful. John Kennedy did not take any part, aside from his own personal discussions with Ted, which we can get into later. He did not take any part in the campaign. He instructed everyone in the White House not to interfere in the campaign. He wanted to make it look like he was doing nothing, but he certainly wasn't opposed to it. Kennedys love to do things indirectly and not have fingerprints to show.

And so he [JFK] didn't want any fingerprints. Every time we went to Hyannis, we saw him informally. We didn't have long discussions. We would go to the cocktail parties. Very often John Culver and I would meet up at Logan Airport, and John would drive us down to Hyannis. As we were going into the [Kennedy] compound, the president's motorcade would be coming out from the airport, to the compound. We'd all stop, and President Kennedy and Ted would have a little talk. "Would you do this event?" "Oh, you went to Fitchburg?" "Oh, God, I remember—Did you see so and so?" John Kennedy had lived the life of a Massachusetts senator for eight years and had just campaigned himself two years before, so he knew the people. They were his people. Ted would give him a little tickle with it. After the primary, where Ted did very well, he loved to say, "Jack, you know, in Leominster, I got more votes in the primary than you got in the general." [*Laughter.*] But it was a relationship between brothers many years apart, not anywhere near as close and intense as between RFK and JFK.

Now as to RFK, I don't know anything directly because he was busy being attorney general of the United States. The one time I know it came up was prior to Ted's debate with George Lodge[13] in the general election. It happened to be just as the Cuban Missile Crisis was ending, but they weren't sure it was ending, and he just wanted to make sure that Ted knew enough of what was going on so that he wouldn't say something that the Russians could interpret as, "The president's brother said. . . ." So they were very careful and he was very careful.

If I could tell just one story. He [Ted] had started the breakfasts, Sunday breakfasts at churches and synagogues and things, quite early in the previous fall. He would start out by saying, "When the emcee got up and said, 'Now it's my privilege to present the president of the Brotherhood,' I jumped up, thinking he had said 'the brother of the president.' "

Q: Now was Joan traveling at all with him?

Gwirtzman: Joan went to appearances, yes. She went to numerous appearances, especially those teas that Ted's sisters put on for his brother. They did teas, they did other women's groups, and she of course had a major role at a fundraiser or something. She did not put in the same full day that he did, but she traveled a lot and was very good.

One story. Within the family, Ted was the youngest and was never considered the intellectual, brightest of all of them, and he suffered from that, and she knew that he suffered from that. But she would go out and there would be a receiving line, and the women would come through and they had heard Ted speak and answer questions. And Joan said, "The women would say, 'He's so smart.' " She was amazed and delighted. She had never gotten that from her sisters-in-law or others.

Q: Did she enjoy the campaigning?

Gwirtzman: Not as much as Ethel did. And the other thing is—Was she pregnant during that?[14] She may have been pregnant during part of that, so it would have made it a little more difficult for her. I would always see her in Hyannis, and she fully participated and went out on the boat, did all that stuff.

Q: Was she consulted? Did you get a sense that he consulted her on political matters?

Gwirtzman: No.

Q: So he had his own network and that didn't include her, for the politics.

Gwirtzman: Yes, well, she never professed to be a politician or someone who knew about politics. And he was away. He would get up early in the morning. He had gotten his routine down that he could shower, shave, and dress in twelve minutes, before the car came to take him to his—He'd be out

---

13. George Cabot Lodge, the son of former Massachusetts Republican senator Henry Cabot Lodge Jr., lost to Edward Kennedy in the 1962 special election to fill the Senate seat John F. Kennedy vacated for the presidency. JFK won the seat by defeating George's father in 1952.

14. Kara Kennedy was born in February 1960 and Teddy Kennedy Jr. in September 1961.

shaking hands at factory gates at 6 in the morning. He had enormous stamina. He went through until 9 at night, one thing after another. *Time* magazine had an article that went through a day of his, which I'm sure you have in your—

Q: Was he energized by it?

Gwirtzman: Oh, he loved it. He had limitless energy and was young, very young. In a sense, at least my own opinion of him was, that sort of political campaign, the old kind of person-to-person, shake as many hands as you can, meet as many people as you can, that's what people wanted. They wanted that connection and especially with him, because he was the closest connection they had with the president of the United States, who was a co-religionist and from Massachusetts, and they were just so proud, the people who voted for him. But to him it was not unlike an athletic event. He would get his guys together and they'd go as fast and as hard as they could, and it was exhausting. It was sort of like a football game.

To me, who is not an athlete, I saw them do this, and it was sort of like it was the team, it was athletic, it was very physical. It was a bunch of big guys engaged in a common enterprise.

Then, the next thing is, is there going to be a debate? McCormack wanted fifteen debates. [*Laughter.*] He must have known he was behind. Ted said, "I will do three debates, but the first one can be in South Boston, in your backyard, at South Boston High School." And so we spent lots of time, lots of briefing papers.

Wait, excuse me. He made a major speech in maybe May. The underlying issue in Massachusetts at the time was corruption. The State House was full of corruption. They had just built a garage underneath the Boston Common, and it was rife with payoffs to politicians from developers and contractors. Massachusetts had a very bad reputation and people were sick of it. That was the overriding issue. Ted made a speech about why he was running for the Senate, and the main point of the speech was people who seek public office for money or for power have had their day in Massachusetts. Now we want people who want to serve. That was the code word for get rid of the old-line politicians; here is a clean-cut young guy who wants to be in the Senate, who is not in it for the money, and he will be good, honest.

Q: Was McCormack tainted with any of the corruption?

Gwirtzman: He was not, but he had been in Massachusetts and in politics for a long time, and his family had been in politics, not just his uncle, who was the Speaker, but his father, Knocko McCormack,[15] who had no organization. He put up his own signs. It really was the old politics against the new in that sense. So this speech was about why Ted was running. It wasn't a knock on McCormack.

---

15. Knocko McCormack was Edward J. McCormack Sr.

Despite advice from his brother, the president, who, after the first debate, said maybe you should try to say that the crime has increased in Massachusetts since Eddie McCormack had been attorney general. Ted refused to do that. He said, "No, no, no. I'm not going to say a bad word against him." Even though by that time he hated him because of what McCormack had done in the debate, before an enormous, nationwide audience, just ripped him apart.

Q: Well, tell me about the debate.

Gwirtzman: We prepared him very well for this debate. The theme of the debate was, "This is a very difficult time for the United States. Last week, an American convoy was stopped at the wall in Berlin. There were very delicate trade negotiations going on, and this has immediate effects in our state. At the bakery in Lynn, which I visited last week, there was an increase in the price of grain, and that was going to mean an increase of the price of bread." We took these national things and drove them right home as individual examples and made them local. That's the way he tried to say, "I want to be a United States senator because national issues have enormous impact on your daily life."

His opening statement and his closing statement were written out so he could memorize them. In between, he answered questions, and very well, because by that time he had been doing it for several months and so he knew. He had been briefed on all the issues.

So anyway, we get to the debate, and how he prepared for the debate. He was very careful. He prepared for a high-level debate, and McCormack just picked him up and slammed him down to the ground and said, "This man is running on the most disgusting slogan I've ever heard, 'He can do more for Massachusetts.' What does that mean? It means he has connections, he has relations, and that's not what this—This campaign should be based on who has had accomplishments. I have." And he'd list all the things, and they were considerable, that he had done as attorney general. And then, which was the worst mistake he ever made, McCormack looked at Kennedy and he said, "If your name was Edward Moore, your candidacy would be a joke. But it's not, it's Edward Moore Kennedy, and you have no qualifications of your own." We were not expecting that.

How did Kennedy react? Kennedy was shocked; he turned white and he bit his lip, but he did not respond in kind. He said, and this was something that we had prepared for the conclusion statement: "We shouldn't be talking about personalities; we should be talking about the people's destiny here in Massachusetts." Nobody knew the attack would be so vicious because he [McCormack] was running on his record.

And this was televised nationally, and everybody watched in Massachusetts. Afterward, the first thing he did was to call Mary Moore. Edward Moore was Joseph Kennedy's longtime personal secretary and assistant. The first thing that came to Ted's mind was Mary Moore had to watch on national television her husband being belittled. This is the wonderful personal quality that

Ted has with the personal things. "I've got to call her and apologize for this guy saying that about her late husband." He's very classy. "I will be the nice guy. . . ."

Q: *What was the media response?*

Gwirtzman: Well, none. So he calls Mary Moore, then he calls his father, and then he gets a call from the president saying how did you do? I don't know whether the president saw it or not. Ted handed me the phone and said, "Would you tell him how things went?" He had just been kicked in the you-know-what by this guy. He had never been through anything like that, and he just didn't feel that he could give a dispassionate account. So I gave a dispassionate analysis. I said, "Look, on points, if people just look at the pros and cons, McCormack did pretty well, but I think Ted's demeanor was the right sort of demeanor." President Kennedy said, "Don't give him an objective analysis. He has to go out tomorrow morning and shake hands at the docks. Tell him he was great." I learned something. At times like that you just buck up the candidate. Don't just be objective.

Q: *But I'm assuming that Jack did want the dispassionate analysis, so he could actually know how it went, even though there was a difference between what he would say.*

Gwirtzman: He was upset and he'd been through enough of these himself. When he in effect lost in Wisconsin, he wasn't able to do well enough in the Protestant areas. So he had to do it all over again in West Virginia. He went through some tough times in his own campaigning.

Then we turn on the radio, to the talk shows, and all these Irish ladies are calling in saying, "Oh, that Ted, he was such a fine boy, and that McCormack, that dirty politician." Over and over again. And he said, "That's the campaign." The two of them were never going to get the same huge audience, never going to be so dramatic. And clearly, at the gut level, Ted had won, and McCormack had killed himself. We just listened to those wonderful ladies, and we all felt much better after that. And sure enough, he won like 70 percent of the vote. He got a larger vote in the primary than candidates for the Senate in Massachusetts get in the general election, when your entire state can vote. He got more votes in the Democratic primary than in the statewide election for the Senate. There was a huge turnout. Everyone voted.

Q: *He did what he thought was the right way to respond. Was there ever any discussion subsequently with McCormack about it that you know of?*

Gwirtzman: Shortly before McCormack passed away [in 1997], I think they had a couple of meetings. I'm not sure what transpired, but I think if you look at what Ted said in his own interview about Eddie, he said, "I made peace with him," and Eddie really said he was never proud of the things that he'd done. So he did, but apparently not at that time.

[During the general election campaign in October 1962, a] car comes in, and out of the car gets Robert Kennedy and Ted Sorensen. Robert Kennedy said, "Have no fear, we are here." And they had been dispatched just after the height of the Cuban Missile Crisis. There was an exchange of letters between JFK and Khrushchev, and then JFK sent a second letter. The ships bearing the missiles had not turned around yet, and they just wanted to make sure that Ted didn't say anything . . . that could be interpreted. The newspapermen were obviously going to ask him about the Cuban Missile Crisis, which was the only thing people were thinking about, since the world could have come to an end. Without getting him involved and telling security information, they put him through paces on exactly what to say to questions on that subject.

But there was one other thing that happened between him and Bobby. Bobby was out on the lawn. There's the house and a big lawn that overlooks a little beach. It's very dramatic because the beach is a cliff that goes down. Bobby was talking about what to talk about, about why he's running for the Senate, in his opening statement. Bobby said, "Tell them why you're interested in public life. Tell them why you don't want to be sitting on your ass in an office in New York." And that said it all about the three of them. That's how their father had made lots and lots of money, but they wanted to serve. In other words, he was saying just talk from the heart about why you want to serve the public. And this was coming from Robert Kennedy. It was unforgettable to hear that.

Lodge was campaigning, and Stuart Hughes, the grandson of the chief justice of the United States, who was running as an Independent, antiwar. He was a professor at Harvard; he was very much opposed to war generally; antiwar, anti–nuclear program. And that drew interest not just because it was Ted Kennedy, the brother of the president, and George Lodge, the son and grandson of senators whose father had beaten Ted's grandfather. No, his grandfather beat Ted's grandfather. There was a lot of dynastic things about that in the news magazines, which many more people read then than now. It had pictures of the three of them, with the dynastic implications, on the cover of *Time* magazine. They used to say you were successful when you get on the cover of *Time*. They were all on the cover of *Time*.

The thing that happened was the Cuban Missile Crisis, which really locked it in for Ted, because by the time of the election, the Cuban Missile Crisis had been successfully resolved and [President] Kennedy was at the height of his popularity.

Q: Did you get the sense that it would have been any different had that not happened? Would it have been a closer election with Lodge?

Gwirtzman: A little bit, yes. . . . Are we going to cast a vote of no confidence in the Kennedy family after the way JFK resolved that? . . . He came to Washington, and they very carefully choreographed his first days, because he just was not some other senator. He was the president's brother, in the Senate. . . . So can you imagine having the brother of the president in the Senate? They didn't know quite what to do. But Ted's great advantage is that he was the youngest of a large family, so he had learned instinctively through his family how to deal with older people. He was thirty. There were senators who were sixty, seventy, eighty, but he knew how a young person should deal with the old people and when to be deferential.

He had the best manners I've ever seen. He would always open the door. It could be a man or woman, he'd open the door. He just had a natural grace and good manners. But aside from that, he knew how to—And remember, these were senators, all of whom had clawed their way up to get to the Senate. They clawed their way up, and here he's coming in because he's the president's brother, so there was at least some resentment. But it changed quickly. I remember going up in an elevator with Stuart Symington, who had two sons Ted's age. And he said, "I didn't know what he was going to be like; but he's so attractive." I could just see the two of them together, and Ted just knew when to defer. He said, "sir," and the whole thing. It was natural with him.

There was a lot of attention paid to him, but the first thing he says is, "I'm not going to take any speaking engagements or anything outside of Massachusetts for the first six months." He wanted to be the senator from Massachusetts, no matter who his brother was. He wanted to batten that down. He got involved with the fishing industry.

And the other thing is that he knew that if he attached his name to a bill or got involved with something, the press would play him up, and he always made sure to share the credit, in fact give the other, if there was a colleague who was co-sponsoring, give him more credit, because he knew that the natural inclination of the press would be to give it to him because he was a Kennedy.

Even before he broke his back, everyday he'd go to the steam room. They had a Swedish masseur there named Olaf, and of course, that's where they [the senators] socialize, in that steam room. He made a lot of friends in there. I think he saw that as a way to—because he had to—get on a basis with these people who had been in the Senate for a long time and who were much older than he.

Q: So he expected there was going to be skepticism about him.

Gwirtzman: Oh, of course. These people read the national press. He didn't get any good national press during his campaign. The national press was, "this thirty-year-old guy, the Kennedy dynasty will go to 1984 and what's he done?" And so that's what they knew about him. Then they'd be with him in the steam room a couple of times, and they began to like him because he was such a very attractive person. And you forget how—We've seen him now, for many years, as sort of an old man, but how rigorous and energetic, personable, he was.

Along with being deferential. He didn't do it the way Lyndon did it. I mean, he didn't know everybody's birthday and call them, and he wasn't in a position to do deals with them because he didn't really have much power, and he was basically born with the administration. While his brother's first speeches had been on the economy of Massachusetts, his was on the civil rights bill, and that's because of what happened in—Remember, in early '62 was Birmingham, all that stuff, ending with Kennedy's [June 11, 1963] speech to the nation where he put forward a civil rights bill. He worked on that.

I don't know whose idea it was, but he's always had a great interest in foreign policy, especially in arms control. Somehow, he wanted to give a speech on relations with China. We had no relations with China. No recognition. No contact.

I don't think that the administration was giving much thought to this, but he didn't want to just be a lackey for his brothers. So he thought if he could take a long view, we've got to live with China. He didn't recommend diplomatic relations with them, and he didn't even go into Taiwan. I forget what the substantive parts of the speech were, but I know I worked on it. But that got him some attention, except not in Massachusetts. The wags there said Kennedy has a policy toward China but not toward Massachusetts. They're very parochial up there. [*Laughs.*]

George Lodge, Edward Kennedy's Republican opponent in 1962 Senate election:

Now, when Ted was nominated in September, he and I—both of us, I think—had much the most difficult time with our primaries. When we confronted one another, I can't remember anything on which we disagreed. Of course, I was trying to get him to debate. I remember we had a kind of a debate in October at a Temple Brotherhood in Worcester. At least we were both going to answer questions—kind of a debate; not really a debate.

This was the evening that President Kennedy went on national television to disclose the presence of Soviet missiles in Cuba, and the whole hall was lined with television sets so that everybody could hear President Kennedy talking about what might have been World War III. That was over the fruit cup. Over the dessert, Ted and I were supposed to be debating. So, needless to say, I was at a slight disadvantage.

It was not easy campaigning against the brother of the president in Massachusetts, especially where the president was so popular, understandably. I liked him. So it was hard to get an edge. I remember Ted, after the campaign, I think I remember now—all these things I'm saying, I may be dead wrong—but to the best of my memory, I remember meeting him in Washington after the campaign somewhere, at somebody's house, maybe it was at Bobby's. But anyway, he invited me to come home with him. So I went to his house, which, as I remember, was in Georgetown, and he spread out his polls on the floor. He made a poll every week or something. He pointed out that the gap between us was closing. He was ahead but it was closing until the Cuban Missile Crisis, and then it widened.

Q: I was going to ask you about the significance of the missile crisis, if that took some of the steam out of your campaign.

Lodge: Oh, yes, it sure did.

Q: In those so-called debates, or exchanges that you had with the senator, did you find that he was good at that kind of an exchange, or was he still kind of learning at that point?

Lodge: The only exchange we had was at a Temple Brotherhood in Worcester, and he, as I remember it, he did perfectly all right. But it wasn't an exchange; it was both of us answering questions against the backdrop of the Cuban Missile Crisis. But he did fine.

Q: When election night came and the results came in, do you have any vivid memories of that evening, of what that was like and whether you heard from Senator Kennedy that night or the next day? Did you contact him to concede?

Lodge: I just conceded. Since then he asked me to join the Senior Advisory Committee of the Kennedy School, the Institute of Politics. That was about thirty years ago. So I saw him two or three times a year at those meetings, regularly. I've had the good fortune of knowing him over the years in that way, and as I say, I like him very much.

I just have admired so much what he's done, particularly in healthcare, education, minimum wage. There hasn't been a stand he's taken that I haven't admired. And standing up to Bush on Iraq—I wish there were more Democrats like him. They pussyfoot around too much. So I really admire him. I think we're very lucky to have him.

Senator John Culver:

Q: Could you give us more of a sense of what you did in 1962, what your role was in the '62 Senate campaign?

Culver: I traveled with him. Got some law school classmates together to work on issues and background books for the various towns in the state, as well as occasional speech writing. I commented on his appearances before and after, ideas and suggestions on what to say, and occasionally what not to say. I am reminded of the exchange I had with Ambassador [Joseph] Kennedy at Hyannis about having someone with Ted that he trusts, and that loyalty and judgment were more important than brains. Ambassador Kennedy said, "Brains are a dime a dozen. I can always buy those. What you can't buy is judgment and loyalty. And how important it is that Ted, at his age, have someone that he was comfortable with in that regard." He further said, "But this is a great opportunity for you too!"

The one thing that I mentioned in my Kennedy Library oral history that I remember very well was that on Saturday we'd go out on the boat, on the *Honey Fitz*, with the ambassador and the president and Bobby, Ted, and myself. I would just try to make myself as inconspicuous as possible and hide in the woodwork. They would talk about the campaign and how Ted is doing, even though the official line of the White House was that people in Massachusetts must decide, but obviously the whole family was understandably concerned.

Early on, some White House advisors were very much against Ted running because they were interested, of course, primarily in Jack being re-elected. That was a very interesting time. Other than that, I don't think the president was involved.

Q: Senator, before we started the tape, you talked about organizing the academics in Massachusetts.

Culver: Yes. One of the assignments I got somewhere along the line in the course of the campaign, probably in the primary, was to organize academics. McCormack enjoyed widespread support among academics in Massachusetts, particularly at Harvard and Harvard Law School.

Ted was tagged early on as someone who really had no business, based on his record, running for the Senate. And that was a theme in McCormack's campaign—that Ted never held a job.

I might mention, as an aside here, I remember one time we were at a plant gate. McCormack had made much of the fact that Ted had never held a job, that he didn't know anything about working people. So we were at the plant gate with Ted, and this workman comes by with a lunch bucket and he yells, "Hey, Teddy, I hear you never had a job in your life." Ted laughed and said, "Yeah, that's right." The plant worker said, "Let me tell you something. You never missed a thing." [*Laughs.*] That's what the guy said. So anyway, academics were all on top of him for never having—

McCormack had a pretty impressive record. Very Boston, city council, head of the city council, I think. Elected attorney general twice. Naval Academy. And a very liberal record on civil rights, civil liberties. He was hammering Ted on that. I was given the task of organizing a TV program of academics for Kennedy. I tell you, that was like looking for the Hope diamond. I finally asked my favorite Harvard Law professor, Charlie Harr, and I asked Sam Beer, who headed the ADA [Americans for Democratic Action]; James McGregor Burns, who I knew had been sympathetic to Ted; and John Plank, and Robert Wood from MIT. Robert Wood later was at HUD with Charlie Harr once the president was elected.

That exhausted the list of academics that I could find, by making every effort. We had a coffee table set up, and the whole theme of this half-hour program was why academics, plural, are for Kennedy. It didn't really emphasize the fact that the only ones for him were the five in the room [*Laughs*], and so we had this conversation. Each of them, in turn, would say why they saw his candidacy to be attractive or positive. I've often wished that somebody like Mark DeWolfe Howe and some of those critics who were really very cruel to him had lived to see his accomplishments.

Q: Why do you think there was that sort of distance, or even animosity in some cases, among academics in Massachusetts? Any thoughts on that?

Culver: Well, on the facts, it wasn't hard to understand. If you had an opponent that really had very strong credentials, in their eyes—McCormack—on the issues they were concerned most about at that time, and then you had someone that really was taking the place of a seat-warmer, and not even constitutional age when he announced, it was just too presumptuous. The only qualification he had was a brother as president. What does that entitle you to? What are your qualifications? What have you done in terms of life's achievement?

[Ted] had a remarkable sophistication. I noted a number of times when others would ride with us in the car, or we'd be in a meeting, and I would be privy to people complaining to him about someone else working in the campaign. Ted just never would say anything. He might occasionally, if I was alone with him later, say something. I always was impressed by that, because he just wouldn't lend himself to gossip about the individuals in the campaign. He would make his own private judgment as to how valuable this person is or isn't, and how well they're doing their job for him. He might know something that this other critic doesn't know. But the maturity of that, because all political campaigns are fraught with all kinds of backbiting and fighting; it's endemic to the nature of the beast. He was mature that way, I thought. Sometimes, as well as I knew him, I thought, where'd you learn that, where'd you get that kind of perspective on something like this?

Theodore Sorensen, President Kennedy's speechwriter and special counsel:

Ted Sorensen: I was remotely connected to the [1962] campaign. You should, of course, understand, first, I was very young myself at that time. I was not a power in the White House, much less in the family, and given the extent to which I was at all times over-scheduled, overworked, overcommitted, there was no way that I could keep track of everything going on in the White House. So lots of JFK's discussions, decisions went on without my being present or knowing about them. Nevertheless, as I have recorded in my book *Kennedy*, I do know that the president was in a ticklish position for more than one reason.

Number one, it was ticklish because he was already accused of nepotism for having appointed his other brother, surviving brother, as attorney general. And if he then looked as though he were absolutely bent on getting still one more brother into high office in Washington, the nepotism charge would become possibly a serious criticism, to say nothing of a subject for late night comedians. Number two, he was in a ticklish position because John McCormack had—well, he was the majority leader—had he become the Speaker yet? I think he was. And, of course, the Speaker is next in line after the vice president. He's a power in his own right. John McCormack was a veteran of the House, highly regarded, highly respected, highly influential, including with some of the older Democrats who were pretty skeptical of the young, inexperienced-in-their-view president, so he didn't want to offend John. And Eddie McCormack, Ted's principal opponent in the primary, was the apple of Uncle John's eye, and how to proceed and not offend John and start a family feud, that caused the president concern as to whether Ted should even run, much less expect or receive help from the White House. And third—but this I have no firsthand information about—is I assume that Ted's decision to run was influenced by their father, and their father had plenty of disagreements with John F. on matters of policy as well as personality and almost everything else. And so very likely, as was the case with the appointment of Bobby as attorney general, if the father said, "Ted is going to be the new senator." That's it, Jack was not—he had enough disagreements with his father on policy not to pick any new arguments on family matters. So for all those reasons, he was in a spot and said publicly, made quite clear publicly, that he was neutral. He was keeping hands off, and that the White House would not be involved.

Despite all of that, I can recall only two interventions on my part. And when I say interventions, neither one of them, you can be sure, was at my initiative; both of them were at the direction of the president. One was that Bobby and I flew unannounced, I think to Cape Cod, and had a long session with Ted to talk about the campaign and particularly about the debate, the first debate. I gather from the materials your staff prepared that there was more than one.

But Bobby and I took part in that, a little bit like the way I would prepare the president for a press conference, that is, I would have had a list of possible questions and issues. I would fire them at Ted, see if he was prepared to respond to them or how accurate and complete his response was, possibly make suggestions where it needed to be filled out, rounded out, improved, or whatever. And then I went to that debate and sat in the audience without any announcement or disclosure of any kind.

And the other intervention, if you want to call it that, came in very late October when Ted was scheduled to go on *Meet the Press.* The president had two reasons for sending me up. One was, in general, just to help Ted prepare, advise on that appearance. But the second was that we had just completed what your profession calls the most dangerous thirteen days in the history of the world, and the president was wise enough to know that whatever Ted said on the subject of the Cuban Missile Crisis would be interpreted around the world as the policy and words and views of the president.

He wanted to make sure that, therefore, Ted was well briefed on what he could and should not say. I should add that in between, on October 22nd, which is the midpoint in the crisis, after we had formulated a response, on the evening of October 22nd the president was going to go on nationwide television and declare that the missiles had been spotted, which at that time was not public information, and that the United States was determined upon their removal, and what our policy was going to be. It was an impossibly busy time for me, and I accepted only two or three phone calls all day, one of which was from Ted. His question was: "Should I give my usual speech on Cuba?" And the answer was no, wait until you hear the president's speech.

As you also know, just from the calendar, Ted was really a different part of the family than Jack and Bob. Jack and Bob were close, both had a lot of experience, and Ted was distant in every sense of the word—

4

Striving for Equality: The Civil Rights Work Begins

Civil rights was Edward Kennedy's defining legislative issue. From the outset of his Senate career, fighting for equality took precedence on Kennedy's agenda. Democrats held a massive majority over Republicans when he arrived in the Senate. But a bloc of powerful southern segregationists, with seniority, constituted nearly one-third of the Democrats in the upper house. Across the Hill in the House of Representatives, an equally obstructive Virginia congressman chaired the omnipotent Rules Committee, bottling up President Kennedy's New Frontier legislative agenda. In fact, JFK delayed sending a meaningful civil rights bill to Congress until June 1963.

The legislation's centerpiece would allow Congress to ban racial segregation in privately owned businesses through its power to regulate interstate commerce. As a freshman senator, Edward Kennedy participated in a closed-door meeting of the Judiciary Committee and the assistant attorney general to preserve the bill's heart, while allowing amendments to its other provisions. In a historical anomaly, three brothers—as president, attorney general, and senator—moved forward what would become, through Lyndon Johnson's subsequent leadership, the 1964 Civil Rights Act.

For his maiden speech on the Senate floor, Kennedy chose to speak in support of the historic civil rights bill. Kennedy had become increasingly engaged in the civil rights debate and delivered a carefully crafted speech in the spring of 1964, as southern Democrats and conservative Republicans maneuvered to thwart the legislation. Many colleagues gathered to hear the young Massachusetts senator give his debut performance, and they offered positive reviews. The oration launched more than four decades of Kennedy's rousing speeches and debates in one of the world's most historic parliamentary chambers. His 1969 election to the Democratic whip's position gave him a formal platform for legislative leadership. Lawmaking was a full-time job, with members working in Washington throughout the week and very few recesses. Kennedy noted in his oral history that votes were sometimes taken even during the week between Christmas and New Year's, and he bemoaned the contemporary Senate's

Tuesday-through-Thursday schedule, which truncates debates but allows members to fundraise at home over long weekends.

In the wake of the 1964 Civil Rights Act, Kennedy turned his efforts to his first legislative initiative—a bold attempt in 1965 to abolish the discriminatory poll tax that prevented thousands of African Americans in the South from exercising their right to vote. The Twenty-Fourth Amendment, ratified in 1964, banned the poll tax in federal elections, but it remained valid in state elections. The issue was legally complex, and Kennedy turned for guidance to Harvard Law School professor Charles Haar, who remembered that the young senator was "quick to absorb ideas, novel as they may be, and draw his own implications and conclusions." Policy makers differed over whether to include poll tax abolition in the 1965 Voting Rights Act. Ultimately, the US Supreme Court, in Harper v. Virginia State Board of Elections (1966), voided such taxes in state elections as a violation of the Fourteenth Amendment's Equal Protection Clause.

Nevertheless, the poll tax debate served as a training ground for how Senator Kennedy would prepare for future legislative contests—by calling on experts, mastering issues, working with interest groups, collaborating with the executive branch, shepherding bills through committees, and building alliances among colleagues. He applied these lessons to his leadership of securing the vote for eighteen-year-olds, via the Twenty-Sixth Amendment, ratified in 1971. He reasoned that, if men that age could be drafted and sent into combat in Vietnam, they deserved the right to vote and have an impact on policy.

Kennedy's commitment to civil rights was shaped by his Catholic faith, his experiences in school and the army, and his family's Irish immigrant roots. His grandfather, John F. Fitzgerald, taught him early lessons about discrimination based on religion and national origin, and his brothers Jack and Bobby eventually became ardent supporters of the civil rights movement. All these influences broadened Teddy's definition of civil rights. Discrimination on the basis of race, religion, national origin, language, gender, sexual orientation, mental illness, and physical and mental disabilities all fell under Kennedy's civil rights rubric. Nothing captured his heart and mind like the need to help any disadvantaged group whose rights were systematically denied.

Kennedy particularly embraced the cause of individuals denied healthcare, education, jobs, and housing. When Robert Kennedy joined the Senate in 1965, the three brothers worked together on these issues, but they also pursued their respective policy preferences, which allowed them to double their impact. After Bobby's assassination in 1968, Teddy continued laboring on those policies as the last Kennedy brother, championing traditional civil rights and expanding them to encompass more contemporary causes, such as equality in marriage and military service.

Yet the years after Bobby's death revealed additional rifts in American politics, including among blue-collar Catholics who had supported all three Kennedy brothers as part of the New Deal Democratic coalition. In 1974, when a federal judge ordered busing to achieve racial integration of Boston's public schools, Edward Kennedy found himself literally set upon by mobs of angry white working-class parents who *vehemently, and sometimes violently, opposed the policy. He would sit for hours listening to distraught parents pour out their frustrations and anger. Kennedy viewed such constituent interaction as much a part of his senatorial role as tracking down a missing Social Security check or drafting legislation.*

Q: *You had mentioned that this discrimination against the Irish—the "No Irish Need Apply" kind of thing—was the beginning of your concern about civil rights.*

EMK: Civil rights, it was.

Q: *You learned about that discrimination through experience, but also through stories.*

EMK: Through stories and observation at the time. In 1962, we had a number of people in my campaign, although it wasn't a big state issue. Of course, Bobby's help in getting Dr. King out of jail [in 1960] was enormously important. We were aware of this as a national issue, but it wasn't so much a state issue, and it wasn't an issue in the campaign against Eddie McCormack. We both wanted civil rights laws.

And it wasn't against George Lodge. We had young people, students from Boston University, going down to the lunch counters in Georgia. We had that fellow who was the party boss in Louisiana,[1] a notorious figure, who was sending blacks up here. He'd send blacks from the South up to the Cape to see what we were going to do with them, if you can believe it.

Wallace[2] was trying to prevent the integration and then in 1963, Jack made that extraordinary speech about asserting the morality of the issue and what was really at stake in terms of the country, in terms of our society, in terms of values. I think it was one of his greatest and moving speeches, about who would want to change places [with a black American]. He had a word picture of the life of blacks in the country that was just enormously powerful, and I think it made a real impact on the country.

And then you had coming up, still now it's August '63—we're just in the Senate—we had that Civil Rights March on Washington. It was the issue at that time, about going to that march or not going, local people who had asked me to join them. I was just in the beginning stages of understanding, you know, where this issue was going and what was happening, and the emotion around it, and aroused by it. But I was also understanding that a lot of this was targeted [at] both my brothers, President Kennedy and Bobby. I talked to

---

1. Leander Perez was a segregationist political boss in Louisiana, who taunted the Kennedys in 1962 by busing poor blacks from the South to the family compound on Cape Cod. Perez viewed this act as payback for the "Freedom Rides," in which white and black activists rode buses from northern cities to the South, to desegregate interstate travel.

2. George Wallace was governor of Alabama when he attempted to thwart federal court orders to integrate the state's flagship university in June 1963.

the White House just about going on down there, and I was urged not to go. I watched it on the television at the time.

Q: You were urged not to go because it was hard to know what was going to happen?

EMK: Well, they didn't know what was going to happen down there, and somehow my presence as being the representative of the family on this, President Kennedy and Robert Kennedy would have some impact on that, that was really unpredictable. And it did seem to me that they were sufficiently engaged, particularly after the JFK speech in June of '63, they were sufficiently engaged in this that I ought to listen to their recommendations. They gave thought to it, but it was explained to me that it would be wise not to go.

Q: And that very next morning [after JFK's speech], early, Medgar Evers[3] was killed.

EMK: Yes.

Q: Right after your brother gave his speech. Quite a reaction. Did you have any chance to hear from either of your brothers about their experiences in Mississippi or Alabama during the run-up to that speech? I mean, that was pretty powerful stuff in Alabama and Mississippi. Did you have any chance, or did you have a sense from other senators, of how they reacted to that presidential commitment in that speech, and how the chances were assessed for getting it through, because it seemed to me to be very chancy at that time. It was a very high-risk policy also for your brother to take this moral stand and push it.

EMK: I think on the speech, it got very wide attention on television and in the print media. The people who were allies in Washington were very reassured and very uplifted, I mean, people we worked with very closely, Senator Mathias, Senator Hart, at that time, and Javits.[4] We were very moved by it and uplifted by it. I don't know of the other side, you had a very important and significant opposition, because you really had the deans of the Senate. We had a big Democratic majority in the Senate, but a big chunk of those Democrats in the Senate were from the South, and they had some very formidable leaders.

They had the old guard, Richard Russell, who was a very talented and highly regarded senator under other circumstances, very knowledgeable about the rules. Besides him you had Ellender, who was from the Deep South, and Spess Holland, who had been around a long time in the South, and Talmadge, who was very gifted and a smart, tough person. Senator Byrd—the two Byrds,

---

3. Medgar Evers was field secretary of the National Association for the Advancement of Colored People in Mississippi when he was ambushed and murdered by a Ku Klux Klansman outside his home in Jackson. President Kennedy invited Mrs. Evers, her children, and her brother-in-law to the White House shortly after the tragedy. A World War II veteran, Evers was buried with full military honors at Arlington National Cemetery.

4. Charles Mathias (R-MD), Philip Hart (D-MI), and Jacob Javits (R-NY) were Kennedy's Senate colleagues.

Harry Byrd and Bob Byrd.[5] You had a very active, committed, determined, tough, knowledgeable group of people who were very resolute, and so how this was going to play out certainly didn't appear to me to be a clear path towards victory. I don't think I saw it at that time, and it took a good deal of time to be aware of it. Certainly it appeared to me that the opponents seemed to have the horses on this, and the—

Q: That was true in the House too, wasn't it?

EMK: Well, Howard Smith[6] controlled the Rules Committee and controlled through that all of President Kennedy's legislative agenda. That certainly was the feeling. I mean, the country had to move ahead, and the Senate was the place to move ahead, but you had a very strenuous, vigorous, determined opposition on this. And it continued through the early fall [of 1963], until . . . you have the young girls at the Birmingham church who got killed.[7] So that startled the nation.

You had the incidents during this period, I think, that just aroused the country; the police dogs and the beatings. I remember very clearly Bobby coming up and testifying in the Senate Judiciary Committee. Senator Sam Ervin questioned Bobby at least three days. My sense is it was five days. I never knew when I was going to be able to come on up to question, because you didn't know when Sam Ervin was going to stop, and he went on and on and on and on.

Q: So this was questioning Bobby on—?

EMK: This was really the beginning of the debate on public accommodations,[8] and that had been recommended by President Kennedy in the early part of the year, and that takes you on to the—you know, there had been different discussions that were going on between all of these people, President Kennedy and Dirksen[9] and others over in the House. And then we run into [President Kennedy's assassination in] November of 1963. We were effectively out of there for some period of time, until probably January of '64. I have heard that of the sixty-seven Democrats, twenty-one came from southern states, twenty of them vigorously opposed the bill, and Republicans were split too. So you

---

5. Senators Richard Russell (D-GA), Allen Ellender (D-LA), Spessard Holland (D-FL), Herman Talmadge (D-GA), Harry Byrd (D-VA), and Robert Byrd (D-WVA) were all southern conservatives.

6. Congressman Howard Smith was a conservative Democrat from Virginia.

7. Four young black girls, attending Sunday services, were killed when a bomb planted by white supremacists exploded at Birmingham's Sixteenth Street Baptist Church on September 15, 1963.

8. The public accommodations provision of the civil rights bill allowed Congress under its interstate commerce regulatory power to ban racial discrimination in privately owned accommodations that served the public, e.g., restaurants, hotels, motels, department stores, and movie theaters.

9. Senator Everett Dirksen was the Republican Senate minority leader from Illinois.

had a major chunk of the Democratic Party opposed to it, and a very important part of the Republicans opposed to it.

This was the issue in question now, whether we're going to have to try and change the rules to be able to get the bill [to a vote], change the cloture rules [to cut off debate]. So then we had those kinds of battles going on, on the side, and then you had President Johnson speaking about these issues now, after 1963, and bringing a new sense of urgency to all of this, giving it additional new energy. The tragedy, the loss of President Kennedy, and debates and roll call votes to try to change the rules, which were unsuccessful. Eventually, they had a conversation, Johnson did, with Dirksen, who said he'd make some adjustments on the public accommodations.

The most interesting part of this for me was the meeting that we had in 1964 in what is now called the Howard Baker Office. It's the room right opposite the Old Senate Chamber, which is the room where the British soldiers lit their torches when they went down and burned the White House [during the War of 1812], and it's the Republican leader's room. It was Frist's[10] room when he became leader. In that room—which at that time was a regular office room, and now it's extended into a series of rooms to become a suite for the Republican leader—but in that room, Nick Katzenbach came, and we had about eight or nine senators. All the members of the Judiciary Committee were invited, and you could bring one staffer. We sat in there for probably seven hours, and went over this particular provision, this public accommodations provision, the part that was the heart of the bill.

At the end of it, there were still areas where there was not agreement, but the basic core of the agreement was that we would not—no one would attempt to alter or change the heart, the framework, of the public accommodations. You could have amendments on other different parts of it, but we would not change or alter the basic core framework of the legislation. Everyone signed off on that, and that was really the basis of the provision, and it was the fact that the senators stayed in the room—they didn't let staff do a rough draft, then come back. They stayed in that room, and just stayed there until they got that thing worked out, all of them.

With Katzenbach, and I think Burke Marshall was in for a good period of the time. Katzenbach would go out a little bit and come back on in, but all the others worked it out. Dirksen was in and out. He didn't stay the whole time. That was what I thought was *the* meeting on the '64 Act, that he—Dirksen finally signed off and the rest of it began to make sense. That happened a little later in the year.

In the spring of that year, I made my maiden speech on civil rights. Up to that time, newer members rarely spoke the first two years they were in. Now

---

10. Senator William Frist was a Republican from Tennessee.

they all speak fairly soon, but at that time, they waited a couple of years to be able to speak. It seemed to me that this was the issue, this was the time. We were increasingly involved in both the substance of the discussion and the debate, and I felt it was very important to speak. I think it was an important speech—we spent a lot of time on it—and afterwards, we were very appreciated.

We got a lot of nice comments from Paul Douglas,[11] who was sort of the dean of the issue on civil rights at that time, economics, and a number of others made very good comments about it. And a number of them had come over, sat around there. All the senators had sat around me. They didn't have the electronics then as we have now, so if it was a speech that was important, they would come over and listen, and get other chairs and turn them around, and people would come. If you got a gathering, that was the high sign that you were making some sense. It was a good speech.

Q: *Did you notify people in advance that you wanted to give it?*

EMK: Yes, the leadership, I told them, and that was in April. In March, the filibuster is sort of going on. You have a lot of negotiations, you have a lot of amendments being introduced. There are offers of different numbers of amendments and different types of amendments, and finally in June—From March, April, May, finally June 10th, the filibuster was effectively broken.

Q: *It wasn't a first, but it was pretty nearly a first, wasn't it?*

EMK: Yes. We had twenty-three Democrats and six Republicans opposed. Those Democrats were southern Democrats. And I think what was very evident is a recognition that this was going to have a very significant and dramatic impact in terms of the election, for prospects in terms of the future. I mean, this is separate from obviously, the substance of the issue and the importance of the issue. This issue, which had been enshrined in the Constitution, where our Founding Fathers failed, and they effectively wrote slavery into the Constitution, and then we failed with the Civil War.

What happened, I think, is that you had Dr. King, who really prepared the ground in the late 1950s and into the early '60s on this whole movement towards nonviolence, which was a very difficult and trying time, when you look back and read those stories about his strong commitment and how he had been influenced by Gandhi and others on nonviolence.

And then you had a political leadership that had fought in World War II, and who assumed the powers in the Congress, the president and in the Congress, many who fought in World War II. They had seen that they had contained the communists for a while, and they looked back. They also had the [1963 Nuclear Test Ban Treaty], so they sort of looked at this as though they had a holding ground, and then they said, "What do we have to do at home?" And

---

11. Senator Paul Douglas was an Illinois Democrat.

it was the race issue. They said, "We have to do it, this is our generation," and they took that on, and I think they all felt that this was absolutely important. They had seen, from World War II, how people had been treated, and the value of the individual, and they understand it intuitively, knew about it intuitively and instinctively, and from observations, and they were very committed to it. They had been on the battlefields and understood what this country had to deal with.

I think that the Democrats also recognized that this was going to be just incredibly costly politically—Lyndon Johnson was the one who said, "We may win this legislation, but we're going to lose the South for a generation." I mean, he understood it. Others understood that as well, but they thought that that was important, and it was right, and it was important for the nation to do it. That's been a consequence of all of this, no question. I mean, it was the right thing to do, and it will take time to build back the party structure in that region of the country to try to gain confidence of the voters, but there's no question in that generation's mind, basically the ones who had gone to war, that this was the right thing to do and they were going to do it.

And I think it was that atmosphere and that climate and that spirit, and King's nonviolence and the reminder to the American people about the way [blacks] were all treated with dogs and clubbings and beatings, that this was intolerable, that moved the country into doing this. And really, from this part of the progress that was made, I mean it was public accommodations in '64, and we moved on into voting in '65 and eventually into housing in '68, but it also opened it up on the '65 immigration legislation and knocking down walls of discrimination on national origin quotas, and about Asian Pacific triangles, non-discrimination, race, religion and employment, and using federal funds.[12]

Q: Getting back to what you were saying earlier about the new generation of American leadership, understanding that this was something we had to do and there were going to be costs from it. I think part of that context maybe was that the United States was now fully engaged in the affairs of the world, for the first time in history, and what went on internally became a subject of public consumption. I think that's where the media coverage of the beatings and all that was just ruinous: "The Americans say this, but look what they do." And the Soviets were playing on that in their propaganda more, and off of that.

EMK: I think that's true but you know . . . I certainly sensed that listening to my brothers, and the people that were committed in the Senate, that this was really a decisive moment in terms of America's destiny, and we're in this

---

12. Here Senator Kennedy was referring to the 1964 Civil Rights Act, the 1965 Voting Rights Act, the 1968 Fair Housing Act, and the 1965 Immigration Act.

place and this is the time. We've got to be able to do it, and I think that that's what had to be done.

There's no question that the '64 Act opened up the whole movement for knocking down discrimination, as I mentioned, in immigration and national origin, which discriminated against large areas of the world. You were admitted here based upon the place of your birth and your family's birth, instead of the merits of individuals.

And also the elimination of the Asian Pacific triangle, which had limited the number of visas to Asians to one hundred a year, and that was eliminated in the '65 immigration law. Then we saw the eventual march towards knocking down walls of discrimination of women, which is Title IX [of the 1972 Education Amendments Act], and eventually disability, in the Americans with Disabilities Act, and some of the disability legislation just before it, and I think we're seeing a continuing of that, knocking down some of the walls of discrimination on terms of the issue of sexual preference, gay or lesbian issues, which we're obviously not there yet. I think it's sort of a continuum.

When Robert Kennedy entered the Senate from New York in 1965, he and Teddy worked together on civil rights legislation but also chose different areas to focus on in order to expand their influence.

EMK: My brother Bobby is elected, and he is in the Senate as well. We're both on the Labor Committee. You know, it wasn't usual to have people from the same states or having, I suppose, brothers—not that there have been that many brothers—but we were on the—and I worked on the education and health, and he did the community development programs, focused on the Bedford-Stuyvesant Program and also on housing, and it was great fun.

He was the one who got me interested in the injustice on the draft, and I started offering amendments to eliminate the inequities in the draft, which began later on in '66. The summer of '65 is the summer of the immigration reform, and the dramatic event of the early part of '65 was the Edmund Pettus Bridge, the Bloody Sunday, and the Selma to Montgomery march for voting rights. We had done public accommodations, but the issue now that began to emerge is voting rights. Johnson had asked for the voting rights in '65, and I had met with a number of the civil rights groups, as I had been active in support of the civil rights issues, and the issue about the poll tax that came up. I became very immersed and engaged in it, and spent a good deal of time on it and eventually offered it. There are a number of different phases of the poll tax that we can talk about.

Q: So how did you get [to the] poll tax?

EMK: Well, this was another civil rights bill, and we had a close relationship now with the civil rights leaders. They had raised this issue with me, and I had indicated that I wanted to press forward with it, to a number of people that I talked to about it. I then went about trying to get this worked through, and I talked to a lot of people. We were in constant contact with civil rights leaders during this whole period of time.

There were a number of different features of the Voting Rights Act, registrars, and a number of different parts of it. One of them was on the issue of [the] poll tax, were we going to continue to have the poll tax? Johnson's legislation didn't include the state and local election poll tax, although the federal election poll tax had effectively been eliminated by the Twenty-Fourth Amendment. I think it was Joe Rauh[13] who was particularly worked up about this issue about the poll tax, and I became very much involved with it and offered it later on.

I'm on the Judiciary Committee. That's the committee that's going to be dealing with these issues, and we had already had a good relationship [with Rauh], and I'm sure Bobby spent a lot of time with him, but this certainly was something that I was interested in and followed up on. I mean, there were a number of features in the voting rights area, but this was one that was of particular interest. You have the literacy issues and literacy tests, you have the poll tax.[14] There are a number of other questions, the registrars. There's half a dozen different kinds of features of it, and this was one that was left out [of the 1965 Voting Rights Act]. Lyndon Johnson wasn't—I can't remember whether people thought it was going to be in or not in, but it was glaring that it was out.

Joe Rauh spoke to me about it and I spent a lot of time on it, and I spent a lot of time with him. I talked to Thurgood Marshall, who had been on the Second Circuit, about this. I talked to people at Howard Law School, Clarence Ferguson was the dean, and I guess it's Jeanus Parks, from Howard Law School, and Professor Reid, who was [at] Howard. And then I have Charlie Haar from Harvard, who had been an early supporter of mine, and up at the end, Mark DeWolfe Howe[15] and Paul Freund. Freund was sort of the grand old man in terms of constitutional law at Harvard. And they were all very positive in terms of what should be done and the importance of getting this done.

Q: So they came to your house?

EMK: Oh, they came out frequently. We had sessions on the weekends. We had a lot of questions and answers, and dry runs and debates on it. We spent a lot of time on this. They were very good and very helpful, very informed, and generous in terms of time and the willingness to spend that time.

---

13. Joseph L. Rauh Jr., founder of the liberal advocacy group Americans for Democratic Action, was among the nation's foremost civil rights attorneys. He lobbied for passage of all the major civil rights legislation in the latter half of the twentieth century.

14. Although the Fifteenth Amendment, ratified in 1869, technically enfranchised black men, even as late as the 1960s, the Jim Crow South excluded them and their female counterparts from the ballot box via poll taxes, literacy tests, and an array of obstacles to voter registration for otherwise eligible African American citizens.

15. Herbert O. Reid was a Howard University law professor; Mark DeWolfe Howe taught law at Harvard.

Q: So this was you and the experts sitting down together, and you're mastering the subject or mastering the constitutional issues here. The activists weren't at these affairs, were they?

EMK: No. I think Rauh was probably an academic and an activist. He and Clarence Mitchell[16] were the two principal figures in any of these kinds of undertakings. In any event, we spent some time, and I spent a lot of time on it. Then we offered it in the [Judiciary] committee and were able to carry it on the committee, and then I made a strong pitch on the floor in April of '65, and had, I think, a very strong statement on it. The one line that I think always had a lot of resonance was that not only was the poll tax conceived in discrimination, not only has it operated in discrimination, but its effect is obviously effectively discriminatory. But we had opposition from the Justice Department, Katzenbach. There was the issue about whether we put that in, what would this do to the rest of the Voting Rights Act.

Q: Was that the real reason, do you think? You know, the ostensible reason was that this will screw it all up, so to speak, and we'll lose the more important issues if you insist on going ahead with this. So it was kind of a strange situation, and it seems to me a notable one, in which you and the administration were at odds on this question, and the civil rights activists were on your side of this issue.

EMK: Well, I think you've got it. I think you said it. The question was how much could this train take, in terms of getting the votes. That was the judgment that was made on their part, that this might be enough to sort of tip it over, and there were differences within the civil rights community, and there were differences in the administration.

I thought the case was a very compelling one. I mean, you have part of the Constitution that says the time, manner, and place for these elections will be decided by the state, and then you have to have that in an explicit, constitutional framework, versus the fact that it is being used in a discriminatory way. So it presented itself in that context, that it had been used as a way of discriminating extensively. There had been some court holdings and in certain circumstances it could be permitted, but it seemed to me at that time that it was a very strong case.

So we kept at it. We had letters from Katzenbach saying that although he agreed with the purpose, he didn't agree with the strategy. We had different meetings to see whether there could be some other kind of compromise, and what eventually took place is the idea that this would get challenged early in the courts to find out its constitutionality, which was probably what we all wanted to get. Another question is whether you ban it or whether you void

---

16. Clarence M. Mitchell Jr. was a civil rights activist and the principal lobbyist for the NAACP for nearly three decades.

it, and there were constitutional scholars who thought by voiding it, by challenging it in court, you had a stronger case than banning it. I mean, that was sort of a drill on it. In any event, we went ahead and we did very well with it.

Q: That was a great surprise to a lot of people. There's a lot of interest in this among the people who have written about you and about civil rights, and this poll tax, for several reasons. One is that it's seen as your own first measure, initiative. So there's a lot of interest in why you chose it, why it was important to you, as your way of getting into a civil rights issue. Up to now, after your brother's death, it was Lyndon Johnson's show—he was running it. And second because of Clymer, Jim Burns,[17] a lot have seen this as very important, and I think they're right because it shows you first, your way of preparing, your way of preparing for the floor, your way of mastering the issues, your way of working with outside groups and carrying the water for this. You were very good on the floor with this, it was really amazing, and I think that was recognized by the attention and the praise it got, and it was always, you did a heck of a lot of work on this, didn't you?

EMK: Yes.

Q: One-to-one work with other senators, outside work, inside work. Mary McGrory[18] said it was your bar mitzvah in the Senate. Is that all right?

EMK: Well, it did seem to me that if you're talking about voting, and that was the issue and that was the key, that this was a notorious device used for discriminatory purposes, and if we're coming to deal with the issues on voting, we ought to address it and not duck it. That was a rather powerful, powerful—I mean, there were two tests. One was the literacy and the other one was the poll [tax]. They were both out there, and we did it with regard to the literacy, and it did seem odd to me to be wondering why we're not doing the rest of it with regard to the poll tax. I mean, there didn't seem to be an—there were complicated constitutional issues, but I thought the case was sufficiently compelling that it ought to be presented. We had what I thought were very gifted, talented, knowledgeable people in strong support of it. So I thought we were probably on pretty strong grounds on it, although there was obviously a case to be made the other way, as I mentioned, about banning it [by law] or challenging it [in the courts].

Q: Do you feel that Mansfield[19] and Dirksen had made an agreement not to proceed with this bill, without the poll tax provision? Was Mansfield's support of the administration on this and this turndown of your request to include it a surprise to you, or did it not sit well with you?

EMK: Well, they didn't have it in their proposal on it. You know, it's difficult for me to think what kind of emotion or feeling that I had. I had a pretty good sense about where I was going with it, and you want to work with them when you can, but I had a sufficient sense that we were on the right track on it and

17. Adam Clymer and James MacGregor Burns were Kennedy biographers.
18. Mary McGrory was a *Washington Post* columnist.
19. Mike Mansfield was the Democratic Senate majority leader from Montana.

they were off. It didn't bother me then and it doesn't bother me now, in terms of Senate leadership on these issues, but I think that they're not focused on it.

Q: Well, it's pretty feisty for a young senator to do this, and to do it so well.

EMK: It was a major undertaking. We had good colleagues, they were good support on it, in support of it. I think you know, as the history points out, the civil rights groups were prepared to make some adjustment, even at the end, on it. History shows Mansfield wasn't ready to do it, and we ended up having to vote on it, and almost won on it.

The two votes on it that were the most troublesome were the fact that Gene McCarthy, who had opposed the poll tax previously, voted against us, and Vance Hartke[20] voted against it, and I think those were the two that were very difficult trying to explain. McCarthy never gave a clear explanation on why he was that way, but those two were very difficult to explain.

Q: You came within four or five votes [of success].

EMK: Yes, it was 45 to 49. Now we're into July, I guess, of '65. The House passed a slightly different version that kept in the poll tax ban, and we compromised on the poll tax. We have final passage of the Voting Rights Act in August of '65.

Q: I think word came from Martin Luther King that he'd rather have a bill without the poll tax ban than no bill, when it was in conference, or about the time it was going to go into conference. There's nothing that I found, in any of the writings, that mentions what your brother Robert's feelings about the poll tax were. You said he was doing other things, more concerned with community issues, and there were some Vietnam issues he was also concerned with. It's noticeable, so I wonder what he was doing, if anything, in the poll tax area.

EMK: I think we were very supportive of each other, but if one got into it and was off and going on it, the other kind of—we found that there was an awful lot that needed doing, and we wouldn't duplicate. I mean, I think he was very supportive of what I was doing. I'm sure I talked to him during that time, and I'm sure I got encouragement to keep on moving from him. He was deferential when I had something like this, when he was working on some particular things. We kind of let him move ahead on some of the issues that he was most involved in.

Q: So the two of you, during that time in the Senate together, had your own projects. He had his and you had yours. Supportive, but there's a question that arises here that's important historically. Some people have written that you were working hand in glove on everything, and that was not my impression, that it wasn't a two-man thing, but it was your things and his things, and you supported each other but it was not a team effort. Is that generally correct?

---

20. Senators Gene McCarthy and Vance Hartke were Democrats from Minnesota and Indiana, respectively.

EMK: Yes, I think that's an accurate description.

Q: You did co-sponsor some things, but that's different.

EMK: No, I think that's . . . accurate. Bobby got me into the draft and about the inequities of the draft, but he didn't really participate. I offered the amendments, but he didn't participate. I mean, he really didn't have to. He was involved in some other things. So we knew what each other was doing and were supportive, but I think you've described it. We sort of did our own things on it.

So when we basically had this flap about the poll tax, and lost it narrowly, the final language that came out of the conference was going to permit the attorney general to move ahead and challenge it in court, and then effectively, when they did that, they found out that the courts struck down the poll tax. We haven't seen the end of it. We've had it in the most recent times, the Georgia case, and now we're talking about spring of 2007, where we have a Georgia registration case with a $20 fee in order to be able to register to vote in Georgia. That was struck down by the career people in the Justice Department, and overridden by the Bush political people in the Justice Department. We had a similar situation on the restructuring of the congressional districts in Texas, and that Texas plan, that was developed in Texas, was struck down by the career people, but it was overridden by the political people.

In August 1966, I was invited by Dr. King to go down to Mississippi, the Southern [Christian] Leadership Conference convention in Jackson, Mississippi, which I did with Mrs. King.[21] If we had thought that all of the problems had been over about the racism and the tension on this issue about knocking down walls of discrimination, you wouldn't know it at that particular convention, since we had demonstrators outside, and we had people who threw nails under the car to try and halt the automobile. We were kind of rushed out, after we finished the speech, out of the back way to the airport, to get back to Washington.

We were beginning to see the beginning of a backlash and more violence in the country. We had the Watts riots, where thirty-four people had been killed—that was in August 1965, and we had the increasing tensions taking place in the country. In that same year, you had Stokely Carmichael, the head of SNCC and Black Power, raise a more militant tone than before, in October of '66. Huey Newton, Bobby Seale, Black Panthers.[22] Amazing, in the end of November of '66, Ed Brooke, my colleague, was elected as the first black

---

21. Coretta Scott King was Martin Luther King Jr.'s wife.

22. Stokely Carmichael became head of SNCC (Student Nonviolent Coordinating Committee) the year after the 1965 Watts riots in Los Angeles and encouraged the organization to become more militant in embracing black nationalism. In its most violent form, that movement was represented by the Black Panthers Party, cofounded by activists Huey Newton and Bobby Seale.

senator by popular vote in Massachusetts, virtually free from any kind of race connotation whatsoever in that state. Unlike the most recent election, which was 2006, where Deval Patrick[23] ran, and Kerry Healey had ads that showed a woman in a darkened garage, saying that Deval Patrick defended rapists, defended pornographers, defended felons. These defendants are entitled to a defense, but is Massachusetts entitled to a governor who campaigns like that? I came out with strong statements and comments condemning that activity, and said we've seen this type of "swift boating"[24] before. We've heard this, seen this play, heard this music, and we don't need it in Massachusetts, and Massachusetts rejected it. But Ed Brooke was elected in '66, without any problem.

As we come into '67, we have Thurgood Marshall being nominated to the Supreme Court, and he has a long, difficult fight but gets there by October of '67, makes it, but the tone of the questioning is a lot different for Thurgood Marshall than sometimes we had seen with regards to other nominees, which was positive. Cassius Clay[25] had had his title taken away, being opposed to Vietnam and refusing to join the army, and you had Dr. King speaking against the war and encouraging civil rights and antiwar people to get together.

Q: *Is your impression that the antiwar movement was overtaking the civil rights movement in importance at this time?*

EMK: Well, I think you had a sense that we had taken major steps now in the civil rights, with the public accommodations and the voting. You had some way still to go in the housing, but these were major, major achievements, and you're getting a big backlash. You had all kinds of other things that were taking place at the time on civil rights, and the war issue was clearly rising in '66, '67. In '68 the Tet Offensive and the draft. Key issues on this. They had the Kerner Commission that had been set up to look at the [urban race] riots. They came to the conclusions that we were moving towards two societies—one black and one white. So you had these dramatic steps of inclusiveness in our society that were taken, and you have the backlash that's coming up in response and reaction to it, and you also had the increasing focus and attention on the war.

Senator Kennedy spoke about the advantages of spending a long career in the Senate.

EMK: I always felt I was very lucky to get here, and at that time I thought I had the luxury of some time. The institution moves in a very slow process.

---

23. Deval Patrick, an African American, won the governorship of Massachusetts.

24. Democratic senator John Kerry's 2004 run for president was opposed in ads that questioned his Vietnam service aboard navy swift boats. Kerry was a decorated war veteran who renounced his service medals in protests against the Vietnam War.

25. Cassius Clay converted to Islam and changed his name to Muhammed Ali, shortly after winning the world heavyweight boxing title in 1964. For draft evasion, he was stripped of the title.

But I've been able to look at things over a longer period of time. We had the '68 Housing Act[26] that didn't really do very much.

And then it came back in 1980 and missed cloture by two votes. Senator Howard Baker just wouldn't work hard enough to get the two votes, and Senator Bayh got defeated [in 1980]. Then I took over the Banking, Housing, and Urban Affairs Committee, and eventually we passed the housing [bill] in '88. And we included in the Housing Act in '88—this is twenty years later—not only discrimination on race, but we had discrimination on disability and also discrimination on women and children, families, and it was a big deal. Three more things we got. It took twenty years to get it. I was always at the barricades in terms of moving it, but you can keep coming back to these things, and I was prepared to do it.

We've got '69, when I become whip. I get elected in '69 and I take over Bobby's subcommittee on Indian education, and go around Alaska. The Republicans all leave because they say it's part of a presidential campaign, with the exception of Ted Stevens,[27] who stays there. But at the end, the Interior Department is able to talk all the old Indian chiefs into saying that they want to remain within Interior, where the whole Indian education had been. So our focus and attention had to be for the Indians who lived off the reservation, where the greatest problem was, than the Indians who were on the base. We got basically sidetracked on those recommendations.

So I don't know whether we want to do the eighteen-year-old vote.

Q: I'm just wondering, to what extent this could be compared with your initiative on the poll tax, because some of the politics apparently was the same again. You found yourself sort of going against the leadership. Again, you had some powerful expert support for the position. Again, there was a constitutional issue raised, and again, the saying was, "Oh, let's not do that because it will wreck the rest of the Voting Rights Act." On this one, I think, maybe some of the civil rights community was of two minds on it.

EMK: I think this whole eighteen-year-old vote issue that came up in '70 was really the result of the Vietnam War, clearly. It was tied in the back end of this, that we had had a draft system that worked to the disadvantage of the poor and minorities, and that had been highlighted as really a civil rights issue, and the country changed and went to random selection so that everybody would serve. That was 1968. Nixon wins but the war continues, even though Congress had taken action to try to cut off the funding. There was still a lot of turmoil about who was serving and what their rights were.

---

26. The Civil Rights Act of 1968, known as the Fair Housing Act, banned discrimination in the sale, rental, and financing of housing based on race, religion, national origin, and gender.

27. Ted Stevens was Alaska's Republican senator.

The issue that came forward in February of '70 was the issue of whether we shouldn't extend the eighteen-year-old vote to people who were going to go fight in Vietnam. The general emotional as well as the political argument was if they're old enough to fight, they're old enough to vote. So there was really the question about did it meet muster in terms of the Congress being able to lower the age by statute instead of having to amend the Constitution. I again went and talked to people who—Archie Cox[28] and Paul Freund—who were knowledgeable obviously, in terms of the Constitution. They said it could be done. This was going to be my amendment. This was going to be my [1970] amendment to the '65 Voting Rights Act. So the question was whether this amendment would do damage to the '65 Act, rather than just having an extension.

And so we have Congressman Celler,[29] who was the chairman of the House [Judiciary] Committee, who felt very strongly that we shouldn't go ahead and do it. We had Nixon, who asked that we have a separate legislation to try and do this. Barry Goldwater[30] and I testified before the Senate Judiciary Committee, saying that Congress has the authority. State and local leaders aren't happy. We had notified our leadership about this, at that time Senator Mansfield, and I found out, when I came back from making a speech over in Ireland, which was in March, Trinity College, that Mansfield and Magnuson[31] were putting the eighteen-year-old amendment on the legislation, and I ended up being a co-sponsor on it.

Q: *But it was your issue, wasn't it?*

EMK: It was, but that happens at times, as we have seen.

Q: *Especially when you're away in Ireland.*

EMK: In February, I had given the leadership the memo. I had given a memo, in February, to Celler, who was opposed to it. In any event, it eventually got included in the House bill, even though Celler had been opposed to it, and we called to get a test on this at the district court. Then I argued this issue, as a friend of the court, in the district court in Washington, and the district court agreed. And then eventually, in December of that year, the Supreme Court ruled on it and Hugo Black[32] broke the tie by saying the eighteen-year-old vote was OK for the federal elections, but not for state and local elections. By March of the next year, a constitutional amendment [the Twenty-Sixth] passed to extend the eighteen-year-old vote to all elections.

So all of those elements worked together, in terms of the preservation and the integrity of the right to vote: stopping the poll tax and its ability to interfere

---

28. Archibald Cox, a Harvard-trained lawyer and constitutional law professor at Harvard Law School, was an expert in labor law, who collaborated on labor legislation with Senator John F. Kennedy, and was appointed solicitor general by JFK in 1961.

29. Congressman Emanuel Celler was a Democrat from New York.

30. Barry Goldwater was a Republican senator from Arizona.

31. Senator Warren Magnuson was a Democrat from Washington.

32. Hugo Black was an associate justice of the US Supreme Court.

with the vote, the eighteen-year-old vote in terms of the expansion of the vote to people who could make judgments that were responsible judgments in terms of the democracy, and having the vote count because it hadn't been effectively gerrymandered, so that it was a true, meaningful vote.[33] In a period of seven or eight years, these were probably the three most important decisions made by the Congress and the courts in terms of the sanctity to vote for future generations.

We see, even now, on the redistricting, the efforts that were made by the Justice Department and the restructuring of the Congressional districts, which was a Texas reconstruction under this Justice Department of Gonzales,[34] in this year of 2007, and how that was rejected by the career people, based upon and back to those judgments and decisions that were made in the '60s, and how that was overturned by the Bush political personnel. So these issues, even though you think they're resolved and decided at that particular time, come back again, and if we hadn't gotten it right at that particular time, we wouldn't be getting it right today.

Q: Because you certainly couldn't do now what you were able to do in the '60s.

EMK: No.

Q: Even with all the old southern opposition. Was that period a hopeful period, the '60s?

EMK: Oh yes. So the forces of change were coming, but the most obvious and dramatic was on the issues of schools and race. During that period of the '60s, when I was involved as the United States senator, at that time we met eleven and a half months of the year—there was no August recess. We got the Fourth of July, Lincoln's [birthday] week, and Thanksgiving weekend, and in several of those times, we were voting between Christmas and New Year's, because we had civil rights and the war. We never got up here to Cape Cod until Friday night, until well after dinner. We were voting, busy all Friday afternoons, and we'd have to leave Sunday night because Monday morning is when everything started. It wasn't this Tuesday through Thursday kind of routine we have now, in which the Senate has followed the House, with weeks off in between. We were completely involved and engaged in the life of what was happening in the nation's capital.

The Boston School Committee was being challenged in courts from the early '60s until the mid- to late '60s, about the school system. The school system basically had been established years before by the school committees. The schools in the black communities had grades from kindergarten to four

---

33. In 1967 Edward Kennedy worked across the aisle with Republican senator Howard Baker from Tennessee to pass legislation that would implement the Supreme Court's view that legislative districts should be relatively equal in population. See Edward M. Kennedy, *True Compass: A Memoir* (New York: Twelve, 2009), 253–54.

34. Alberto Gonzales was US attorney general in the George W. Bush presidency.

and then they stopped. Then they had black schools that started from fifth grade to ninth grade, while the white schools went from kindergarten to the sixth grade and started at seventh grade. So for a black child to go to a white school, they would have to get out in the fourth grade, then go to a white school for two years, then get out of that and get on the white school track. It was framed in such a way that the grades—when children graduated and when the middle schools and the high schools started—were all completely out of sync. So it was virtually impossible for black children to go to a white school, and the other way around.

The Boston School Committee was responsible for this, elected local officials. The committee had the real power, and they were basically following what had been established previously. What we were finding out, what we saw during that period of time, is the school teachers who went to the black schools were not nearly of the quality that were going to the white schools. The turnover of schoolteachers was much more dramatic than it was in the white schools. You had vast overcrowding of white schools and black schools, but you had schools that were in between, that were under capacity and yet there was no desire to move either the overcrowded whites into some of those schools or the blacks into any of these schools. They kept them either crowded or in these communities.

If there was any kind of anxiety in the white school system about the public schools, they had the option to go the parochial schools, which served as an outlet for them during this period of time, the '60s, '70s, earlier and certainly continued on. So the facts that were laid out in these legal arguments were just irrefutable in terms of how these schools had been set up and what the results were. It was clear or even clearer after *Brown v. Board of Education* that they were completely separate and unequal, and violating the Supreme Court [ruling].[35] So the question was, How are you going to deal with these and how are you going to remedy this problem?

At this time, you had busing in Boston. You had a certain number, eighteen thousand or so out of ninety thousand. You had eighteen thousand children who were being bused through the Boston School System already and the issue and question that came on down is how are you going to deal with this situation? Arthur Garrity was appointed by the court to work out a system to do this. His proposal included increased busing.[36] The total amount certainly wasn't even—I mean, most estimates stated from eighteen thousand

---

35. In *Brown v. Board of Education*, 347 U.S. 483 (1954), Chief Justice Earl Warren, writing for a unanimous Supreme Court, ruled that public schools, segregated by law on the basis of race, were inherently unequal, and therefore violated the Fourteenth Amendment's Equal Protection Clause.

36. In 1974 the federal district court in Boston ordered racial desegregation of the city's public schools through compulsory busing between white and black sections of the city. US District Court judge Garrity imposed the busing plan. Protests and riots erupted, especially among conservative white residents, who turned their wrath on Senator Edward Kennedy.

to twenty-five thousand, twenty-eight thousand maybe. It wasn't this overall massive movement, but it was significant.

It operated in such a way that it moved children from these particular communities that I described earlier, into other communities, all of which were very isolated, individualistic, and had a separate life and culture and view and attitude, and it caused unshirted hell. The 1971 Supreme Court decision on the *Swann*[37] case indicated that [busing for racial integration was constitutional].

I think the real issue for me was what was my role going to be in this period of time. We tried, through a variety of different undertakings, to play a positive and constructive role in this whole process, I think with probably marginal kinds of effect. But we were very much engaged in trying to find ways that we could be positive and constructive and noninflammatory, and hands-on in the sense of being personally involved.

I think once Garrity got involved in this and once they started to draft the [busing] programs, we had the emergence of a number of local political leaders who were extremely demagogic in some instances. In some instances racist, not all of them, but in a number of them. Racism was a factor and a force with some, but not all. My own sense was I could have no influence on the racists but some influence on people who were concerned and bewildered and troubled and filled with anxiety and wondering what was happening to their children.

They were concerned about the safety of their children and they were concerned about the distance in case their children got ill or sick. People, I can understand, moved to different districts so they could be near schools that were good. People in that group didn't have a lot of that kind of option and opportunity, but increasingly they understood what was happening. So there were a lot of very legitimate concerns. There were individuals like Louise Day Hicks, who was a very tough, shrewd, confrontational, and bellicose figure, and Pixie Palladino, from East Boston, who followed me around and hassled me, who was small, short. I can see the pictures of these people in my mind just like you're there, Jim [Young], I can see them. You're much better looking. This Pixie Palladino—short, pitch-black hair, and flaming eyes.

She confronted, and always came out of nowhere. Louise Day Hicks, you could spot her a half a mile away, but Pixie Palladino, you walked into some hotel lobby and boom, she was there with all of her people and standing in front of you, not letting you move, wanting you to push her or do something.

Q: She was stalking you politically?

They even firebombed JFK's birthplace, a national historic site, in the nearby Boston suburb of Brookline.

37. The US Supreme Court's 1971 unanimous ruling in *Swann v. Charlotte-Mecklenberg Board of Education* (401 U.S. 1) upheld forced busing to integrate schools.

EMK: Yes, yes, any place, any public place. Any place it was announced that I was going. In any hotel, inside or outside. If she could get into the hotel, she got into the hotel. The lobby, top of her lungs. Make a scene.

We now have to look at where are the leaders in the community, where are the leaders on it? The most important leadership was the Catholic Church or Catholic communities. This was at a time when Cardinal Cushing was in the last waning days of his life. He had been at full force during the '60s but after the mid-'60s and into the '70s, he became very frail. He was still the cardinal, but increasingly inactive and separated from the figure he was, and this just arrived at full force on the scene. In very general terms, the Church was missing in action. The local monsignors and the church groups all played the game with the local parish groups. You had some of the younger priests, but they were not effective, and the older ones played along. Some of them even went on the marches for the anti-busers.

So the moral issue of equity and fairness, and also the support for the courts and court decisions, the institutions, was completely lacking. We were basically an institutionless society. The business community was isolated. They did not become involved. They didn't really become involved and engaged as you would, for example, in our healthcare bill that was just passed, where you had the whole business community completely involved, and as they are today engaged and involved in the life of these communities.

This was the beginning of the end for the old Brahmins. They weren't getting their hands—they went to the Boston Symphony and the Museum of Fine Arts, but this wasn't their business. They weren't involved and engaged in the life of the community. They never were a part of this whole process, and they resented the people in this. So there was a complete separation. This is the cultural history.

We didn't have people . . . like Lenny Zakim, who emerged in the '80s as a person for reconciliation in different communities. He was a very important and significant force between the Jewish community and the black churches and the business community. He was an extraordinary figure and a force, and it was just the force of personalities.

There were some very important black leaders: the Snowdens, Otto and Muriel Snowden, and they were great supporters of my brothers and good supporters of mine, friends. Ruth Batson, who was very tough but reasonable, not unreasonable, and very highly regarded in the community. A woman named Ellen Jackson,[38] who played a very constructive and positive role and

---

38. Otto and Muriel Snowden were influential leaders and activists in Boston's African American community. They founded Freedom House, a community improvement center in Boston's black suburb of Roxbury. Ruth M. Batson advocated for equal educational opportunities in Boston, serving on the Public Education Committee of Boston's NAACP branch. Ellen Jackson, a Boston civil rights activist, founded a grassroots organization in 1965 that bused inner-city students to less crowded, predominantly white schools.

endured enormous hostility and tremendous vituperation, just scalding, as she tried to help develop a program that would help solve these issues, by looking at whether communities and colleges would take some of the students. This was a good program, and we might as well talk about it for a minute here. We're getting away from the general into the more particular, and what they called the METCO[39] program.

Now you had places like Stonington College, an hour outside of Boston, eager to participate. It's a Catholic school out there, eager to participate and working with other schools and colleges to bring some of the children out there and work out a program of education. We had a number of high schools, some of our first-rate schools, in Newton and Brookline, that really reached out, I mean very courageously, in a very important way. They brought children in, and we were able to—I was—to get funding for this program, eventually get funding for it. Eventually, President Ford and President Reagan killed it, but at this time we were able to get funding for it.

What was always lost in the Garrity proposal is that they developed these magnet schools, which were going to be schools with a great capacity for training in the sciences, in electronics, in other kinds of skills. The idea was to try and attract white and black children, and get the parents to understand that if their kids went to these schools, they would get advanced education. So all of that was out there, which was very constructive and very positive and very unique to Boston, but no one focused on it. All they focused on was the issue of busing. That's all they focused on.

So in 1974 the tensions are extraordinarily high. We have the Garrity plan, which is the court-ordered busing. In the summer, just incredibly tense. There were incidents taking place all over the city of Boston. There were a series of public rallies and the emergence of this group called ROAR.[40] It was an appropriate name for them. In August I did a television spot urging calm. I think others did similar kinds of television spots, urging calm, and talking about support for the courts, which we began the conversation about. At that time, there was enormous animosity in many parts of the country and I think probably even in Massachusetts. There was no respect for institutions and institutional leaders and for court judgments and court decisions.

Then I issued a statement and comment in September, just before school. On September 9, school was opening and there was a question in my mind about what's the role for that particular day. There was a lot of focus, a lot of attention obviously; the whole city and the state and parts of the country were watching what was going to happen, and particularly in South Boston. I mentioned about how I had a staff member—Bob Bates, who is black—go

---

39. Metropolitan Council for Educational Opportunity.
40. Restore Our Alienated Rights.

down on the school buses and into South Boston, where they were having the children attend school for the first time. There were swarms of police down there and metal detectors, and a lot of people yelling insults at these kids, and I think they hit the buses that went on down to South Boston.

I went over to South Boston to see this, and it was just a nasty, nasty situation. It wasn't going to do me any good to walk in and walk out of the school, but I just went over to observe it. Then we knew that there was this big rally at City Hall opening day of school. It was in my mind whether to go to that or not go to that. I mean, I was really unsure of what to do on that. I felt that I should go and that I had a responsibility to go, it was my city and this is the issue that we care about, and there are good people who are trying to find out what this whole struggle is about, and maybe they would be willing to listen, that this was the focal point of this whole city's turmoil and that it was better to face this issue. I'd issued the statement, I'd done television, and done that aspect of it. I always felt that that was somewhat distant, and it wasn't engaging them. I met with leaders, but it was a small group of leaders. It seemed to me that when you met with leaders, you got the worst of it because they'd come on out and they'd all talk, and you'd come out and talk, and you weren't able to—you just saw the ones whose minds were made up in any event, and you weren't able to reach the others who might be willing to listen for a while.

In any event, we pulled up to City Hall and there was a crowd, several hundred, outside the JFK Building, not far from in the middle of that red brick area between City Hall and the JFK Building. There were several hundred there, and they had bullhorns, and there were speakers going on. I don't remember being necessarily invited to it. I don't know whether they invited all of us to it. I kind of think they didn't. I think they just were having this rally against [busing].

So I thought I ought to go over there, but I thought I ought to go by myself. I didn't want it to look like I was coming over there with a group—that would be a different feel for it. So I just walked across the mall there, towards the crowd, and as I got closer I heard them say, "There he is, there he is, there he is." Then they started yelling insults, and they had their own security. They kind of opened it up, a way for me to get on the podium. I think it was a fellow named Kerrigan,[41] who told me, "What do you want to do, speak? You're not going to speak. You've taken away our rights, we're going to take away your rights, how do you like that?" Then they sang "God Bless America" and all turned their backs to me. Then they turned around and they had some more insults.

---

41. John J. Kerrigan was a member of the Boston School Committee from 1968 to 1976. He was one of the leading opponents of the court-ordered busing plan to integrate the Boston public schools.

So then after [Kerrigan] spoke, another person got up and gave a fire and brimstone speech on this thing. After he spoke, I went over towards the mic, and they put their hands on the mic and wouldn't let me talk. Then they all turned their backs and sang another song. So I had a feeling that this isn't going to work; this thing isn't going to work.

After that they were still yelling insults, and the people on the stand started yelling insults and being nasty and saying, "Why are you being nice to him?" "Well, we're not going to let him talk. You shouldn't." It was an increasing rise of hostility, so I thought it was better just to—there was nothing more I could do confrontationally. I mean, there wasn't any ability to confront them because they weren't going to let me talk. So I started down. There was another stairs on the other side, and I started down. They opened it up a little bit but not too much. They opened it up, and then they raged insults to me and my family and blacks and all kinds of things. "One-legged son,[42] send him to Roxbury" and stuff like that. It was just a very nasty day. Then I can remember there were some things being thrown, and then there was some pushing and shoving.

I remember stopping on the way because I always intuitively know that crowds like these are cowards, basically they're cowardly, and they don't—if you're facing them, they're much more reluctant. If you wait around awhile, they'll get emboldened, but they don't. So I'd stop and they would stop. They'd yell, but the stuff wouldn't start. I stopped a couple of times, and they sort of stopped and continued to yell. Others began to come on out at the top, but the front ones coming at me just stopped. They didn't continue to come out.

Q: Were they coming at you?

EMK: Yes, following me. I mean coming around and going to the sides, but not in front of me. They didn't get in front of me. I saw the doors of the JFK Building, and then I stopped a couple of times, but each time I stopped, they kept getting closer and closer, and finally there was about thirty yards to go [to the JFK Building]. That's when I went towards the doors, and they opened those doors and then boom, they threw rocks and everything, crashed through those windows. I went in, and they didn't get in the building.

Q: Did they try to get in?

EMK: They came up to the edge. They had police inside the building, and they didn't come in, they just yelled and broke the windows.

Q: But you didn't have a police escort.

EMK: I didn't. Not there, no. So I was headed back and I thought, "Hell, I might as well go back to Washington." Then I got in the elevator and was going down to go back to Washington and then I thought, "Well, they'll say

---

42. Kennedy's son, Teddy Jr., at age twelve, had lost his right leg to cancer in 1973.

they ran me out of town." So I thought I'd better stay around for a while, so I rode upstairs.

Q: *That must have shaken you terribly.*

EMK: Well, that was a really nasty crowd.

Q: *Was that the first time you had ever encountered that kind of nastiness?*

EMK: Yes, I suppose. Yes, yes.

Q: *And it just erupted. There wasn't a cheerleader there.*

EMK: No. It all fed on itself. Then I had a situation that I always thought was more dangerous, and that was when we were in Quincy at an event out there. It was something in the mid-morning. I can't remember what the particular event was. There were several hundred people on something else, some domestic issue. At the end of it, we had heard that ROAR was out there demonstrating, and there were a few hundred of them outside. They were picketing. So I thought, "Well, we still have to go outside." There was a fellow named Jack Crimmins, who used to drive for me during this time. We walked out, and Jack usually stayed with the car, but he came into the back of the meeting hall, and then we went back out.

They were yelling and had signs, and there were several hundred and I thought, "Well, we'll get in the car." We came over to the car and all the tires were flat, and they had put dog [excrement] under all of the handles and on the windshield, so you couldn't move the car. Now they are around, and there's very little security around there. I don't think we had any at this time, and there were several hundred of them. So I start to walk, and I don't know where the hell I'm walking. I have no idea where I'm walking. I'm talking to whoever was the aide at that time saying, "Do we have a friend around here, do they have a house? There must be somebody around here who's got a house. I could just walk on in and stay in his house until we can get out of here." They said, "Let's see, which street are we on?" They didn't know, so we walked and they all started walking behind. There was no one else in the streets, and they were taunting and yelling, and I didn't have the slightest idea of where to go. I just knew we had to get moving. I didn't know if I could see a house or didn't know where the hell I was going to go.

Q: *Was this a residential area?*

EMK: A residential area. We walked, and then the crowd was beginning to build and was getting nastier. Then, out of the corner of my eye I saw the subway station. I looked at Jimmy King,[43] who was with me then, and I said, "Jimmy, we've got to get in there." But of course I thought, "My God, I'll be in the subway, and I'll be waiting seven minutes for the subway to come." I knew if I walked and indicated it, they'd all go over and block it. So I had to walk

---

43. Jimmy King was Kennedy's staffer.

in sort of a different direction but fairly close to it, and then they kept going, and Jimmy King went on over to the door, and when I got about fifty yards I turned and they said, "He's headed to the subway station!" So then I ran into the subway, and they all ran after me. I got in the door, and Jimmy King kept that door shut. They were all trying to come through the one door, the only door that they could get in. I get downstairs, and he held that door closed. The subway came and I got in it, and they've got rocks and everything, hitting the subway cars all the way back into Boston—

Q: *So they had the rocks with them.*

EMK: Yes, they had the rocks with them on that day. Those were the two times when I felt that there might be—I mean, I was thinking. I wasn't as worried about security as I was thinking about how I was going to try and get out of this situation.

We had a third event in my office that wasn't physically threatening, where this Pixie Palladino and this woman from South Boston, Rita Graul, I'll never forget her name. I've tried in preparation for this to find out if she's still alive. I mean, it isn't difficult to believe that she is still alive, because I'm still alive.[44] If they could ever get her, she'd be—we ought to write down that name, because if she's still around, from South Boston, she is something else. Rita Graul, and she was a member—she had three children in school, and two of them were going to be moved, bused. She did not say a word.

We went into this room in my Boston office, and there must have been seventy of them. Seventy of them came in to my office, so I was sitting in the seat, and the whole room was just surrounded, and each of them spoke one at a time, for seven hours. Seven hours it went on, until I realized, I'm not leaving here until the last one leaves. The last person out of that room was Rita Graul, and she never even talked. I thought if I was going to be against the German lines, I wanted Rita Graul to be in that foxhole with me; she's the toughest cookie I've ever seen. "Oh golly," she said, "now we'll hear from Mary over here. Mary O'Sullivan. You know the O'Sullivans used to be a great source—" She introduced everybody, knew who they were, where they came from, where they came from in Ireland you know, just to rub everything in. "Why are you torturing her kids," you know, "she's got two nice children, Megan and Sean. Sean was on the baseball—he can't play baseball any more, Senator. Do your kids play baseball?" Saying it in a quivering voice and talking, "Why are you doing this to us, and why are you doing this to me?" Seven hours of it.

Q: *And vent? Was it mainly venting?*

EMK: To vent, venting.

Q: *It wasn't threatening?*

---

44. Rita B. Graul outlived Senator Kennedy by two years, passing away in 2011.

EMK: No. That wasn't physically threatening. I always thought I'd get some begrudging respect from the fact that I was meeting with them. Having gone through this process for a long time, I mean, this was more intense than others.

Q: You're not hiding.

EMK: I'm not hiding. I've gone up in Gloucester, when they were closing the fishing place, and gone up and walked in that hall of five hundred fishermen, and they're booing you, just booing you. And they get up and speak, and you stay there two-and-a-half hours. Remember that, Vicki [Kennedy]? We went into this hall and they were just booing and hissing, and "why haven't you done this and why don't you do that." At the end you get a standing ovation. You can turn it around; "well, he's going to stand with us. He should have done it but he didn't," but there's a sort of begrudging—it was hard to feel that sense, which I've seen as a politician. Hard to get that sense with any of these [anti-busing] groups. It was just too deep, too intense.

Q: Your brothers never had this kind of experience.

EMK: Not that I know of. I was down with my brother in West Virginia [in the 1960 presidential primary], and we had people individually yell at us and things like that.

Q: Heckling and all that, but this is something very different.

EMK: This was very nasty, very nasty.

Perspectives

Charles Haar, Harvard law professor and Edward Kennedy's advisor: We decided, and I don't know exactly who made that decision, that we would go over the poll tax most carefully so that he would fully understand the situation, and that when he made a speech in the Senate it would be to the point, be impressive, and it would make the various arguments.

I remember sitting with him, not here, on the other side of Langdell Hall, and we went over the poll tax history, the early cases, the different policies. I worried about how well I discharged my function. I hadn't had any experience in dealing with the fascinating issue of how do you take the law and the precedents and go on to present the picture that you have in your mind to somebody who either doesn't have that perception or has a totally different picture? What words can you use, and how do you make it clear, and straightforward— what was the purpose of the whole property requirement? We went back to *The Federalist Papers* to what Alexander Hamilton was writing about, the suffrage requirement. Or the requirement in many state constitutions when our Constitution was written, and the general understanding of the requirement that you had to have property to vote.

I mean, you didn't have the impression that the senator was looking for some buzzwords to give to a reporter. He wanted to understand the issue and what the poll tax meant, why Congress should act; then we went into questions like, well, if Congress doesn't act, what is the likelihood of the Supreme Court, in the case that's wending its way up there, what it's going to find? You know, it seemed pretty clear to me that it would find it unconstitutional. So if you didn't get the bill through the Congress, you'd get the end result anyway of eliminating this barrier to equality. The senator thought as he worked there, that it would be better to have Congress act, rather than raise the whole business of a non-elected judiciary, a small elite group doing it. It was time for a statement. America has decided it's time that equality before the law meant that voting should not be done on the basis of prejudice, or wealth status or social status.

Does his diary have any of this, because I don't have any idea how many days were spent on the poll tax issue. It was a long period, many hours we spent. I remember talking to my colleagues here, reading old cases and texts. Trying to understand fully the different viewpoints. I don't know why we worked out of doors; I still have the feeling of sitting on the stones of Langdell Hall. Ask the senator if he remembers that aspect. Why didn't people come around and say what the heck are these guys doing? It seems strange now, but nobody paid particular attention, and we just sat there and we talked and argued. Maybe it was on a weekend when there weren't many students around. But I do remember those discussions and how good I felt about them because sometimes when you teach, you feel you're—and possibly it's your own fault—that you're talking to yourself, not communicating to the students. The senator wanted to learn, and he did. So that was the feeling I had about him.

Of course, I think the senator is a very smart man. Intellectuals tend to emphasize certain aspects of the personality. I guess to some degree it's truer of natural science than of social science, but I think Kennedy has a brilliant mind. He hasn't been trained in certain ways of analysis and thinking, but he's made up for it in others, by far, with decision-making power and excellent judgment.

Q: Well, his brother, certainly President Kennedy, had the reputation for being very smart, and perhaps Bobby as well. Sometimes that word is not always applied to Senator Kennedy, but you would disagree?

Haar: I would most certainly disagree with that appraisal. I think, as raw talent, he's very, very bright; with time and experience he has become extraordinarily competent in appraising people and in evaluating their positions and advice. He's quick to absorb ideas, novel as they may be, and draw his own implications and conclusions. I remember I was very impressed because I couldn't skim on the surface of the poll tax. He would not let me. He really was after me, and he'd ask me things and I'd say, "That's a damn good question." I would be honest enough to say, "Gee, I don't know the answer to that. Let me think about it and look it up some more."

Representative John Lewis (D-GA): Teddy, on a stop, I'm talking about when he's at a rally—it's the best. He reminds me of the fire and the passion that

Hubert Humphrey had. You talk about the politics of hope, optimism, and when Teddy gets wound up, he's really at his best. When you see him speaking to a hall full of union members, human rights, civil rights types, he'd come there with fire. From time to time in the early years, he would have a manuscript. Now you see him from time to time, it's two or three cards. Sometimes he puts those cards away and just goes for it, and he's good.

Robert Bates, Kennedy staffer: I get to Memphis, all alone [in April 1969]. My job was to be in touch with the chief of police and the city officials. The senator was coming in on a private plane [to speak on the one-year anniversary of Dr. Martin Luther King Jr.'s death], and I was supposed to be in contact and let him know when to come into downtown Memphis. There were street demonstrations. Kennedy's address was outdoors, in the street, and so there were folks out in the street waiting for his appearance. I get this phone call, and he's at the airport. I'm in the street with the crowds, and there are gunshots. Folks start shooting. I don't know who was shooting or who were the targets. Not only that, there was a black person who took me around, and this person introduced me to the chief of police. The chief refused to shake my hand. I thought to myself, "Wow, this is a nice how-do-you-do."

Q: Was he a white chief?

Bates: White chief of police, right. But there was so much energy and so much electricity and so much excitement that I didn't have time to be afraid. I just had to go along with what was going on. And it was my job to let the senator know when to come in town. "You should be here now," or "They're expecting you at such-and-such time, and so come on in," or, "I think you should—" So there I am trying to make these judgments in the midst of this chaotic stuff that was going on. But I finally said, "Hey, look, come on; bring it on. If we're going to do this, if you're here, let's do it." And he came in. The big concern, of course, once Dave Burke[45] and the other guys showed up, was his safety, having heard these gunshots. Who the hell had guns? Here we are dealing with a police force that wasn't happy about having this thing going on anyway. Would they do their job in trying to protect him?

Of course, as it happened he gave a rousing speech. The crowd was overwhelmed. They just loved him. It was terrific, and everybody loved it. He got through, we left, and we got on the airplane and came back home.

---

45. David Burke was a Kennedy staffer.

5

Striving for Equality: The Civil Rights Cause Continues

The 1980s ushered in new challenges for Senator Kennedy in the area of civil rights. Although he saw progress in his hometown of Boston, after turmoil over busing in the 1970s, the Reagan-Bush presidencies (1981–93) and loss of the Senate's Democratic majority (1981–87) created obstacles to maintaining and expanding equality at home and abroad.

In addition to his work in promoting civil rights domestically, Kennedy also fought to protect those rights overseas. Nowhere was Kennedy's work defending equality internationally more visible and effective than in South Africa. Continuing Robert Kennedy's work from the 1960s, Kennedy traveled to the racially divided African nation in 1985, at the invitation of Archbishop Desmond Tutu, and returned home to lead the fight to pass, and then overturn President Reagan's veto of the Anti-Apartheid Act. It took a bipartisan effort to do so, which Kennedy helped to forge through dinner seminars at his home with Senate colleagues and leading opponents of apartheid.

Kennedy understood all too well that crafting and passing legislation took time. He tried no fewer than four times in the 1980s to pass the Civil Rights Restoration Act, succeeding only after overriding another Reagan veto. Kennedy also understood the importance of reaching across the aisle to work for compromise reform. His first collaboration came in the 1960s in working with Tennessee senator Howard Baker on "one man, one vote," to ensure equally apportioned voting districts. Over the years he would toil with many other prominent Republicans on civil rights legislation, including Senators Robert Dole of Kansas, Orrin Hatch of Utah, John Danforth of Missouri, Charles Mathias of Maryland, and Jacob Javits of New York. The 1982 Voting Rights Act extension, the 1988 Fair Housing Amendments, the 1990 Americans with Disabilities Act, the 1991 Civil Rights Act, and the 1993 Religious Freedom Restoration Act serve as testaments to these bipartisan alliances. Cooperating with Republican colleagues to pass landmark legislation would, in fact, become one of the hallmarks of Edward Kennedy's Senate career.

On women's rights, Kennedy worked closely with this friend Birch Bayh in supporting Title IX of the 1972 Education Amendments Act to ban gender discrimination in universities. The Equal Rights Amendment to the Constitution, which Kennedy introduced in multiple Congresses, was never ratified by the states. Breaking from his church's doctrine on abortion and his sister Eunice Kennedy Shriver's staunch pro-life position, he saluted the Supreme Court's 1973 Roe v. Wade *ruling as a major step in guaranteeing reproductive rights for women. He never wavered in searching for judicial nominees to uphold the* Roe *precedent.*

Again departing from Roman Catholicism's dogma, Senator Kennedy took up the cause of gay rights and expanded his concerns to cover military service, AIDS treatment, bans on discrimination against those with HIV, anti-gay hate crimes, and marriage equality. He parted ways with New Democrat president Bill Clinton in opposing his ill-considered "don't ask, don't tell" policy on gays in the military and the Defense of Marriage Act, which Clinton signed into law in 1996. The latter allowed states not to recognize gay marriages sanctioned in other states.

By 2007, Kennedy offered mixed reviews for his country's record in civil rights. He praised its inexorable march toward progress but feared setbacks he witnessed in the George W. Bush administration, especially on voting rights. The Massachusetts senator was simply unable to heed Justice Antonin Scalia's admonition to critics of the Supreme Court's Bush v. Gore *decision to "get over it."*

EMK: I think one of the real dilemmas I felt during this whole period of time is on the one hand, the leadership that had been provided by my brothers in the whole area of civil rights, and the involvement of my brother Jack and obviously Bobby. The principal reasons of his [Bobby's] candidacy [in 1968] were the poverty issue and the war, there were always those two. So much of his life had been the deterioration of the quality of life in the inner cities, particularly among poor blacks and poor whites. People had commented during his candidacy that he's the candidate who could bring poor whites and poor blacks together in a rather unique and special way, which I think was very true, and that had always been impressive.

My service had been on the focus of opportunity for people in the areas of education, health, jobs, housing. Those issues, and knocking down the walls of discrimination—I spent a lot of time on that issue in the Senate, and I think the overarching issue for our country and society is how we are going to deal with the forms of bigotry and discrimination. I think we were and are the revolutionary society. No country, no culture, no history has ever made the progress that we've made on race and religion, on ethnicity, on women, on disability, and also now I think in terms of gay rights. If you look at what's happening in so many different parts of the world, it is so incremental in any of these areas, and we have made enormous progress. There's still incredible problems to go, but we start off with that.

Still, there are no political forces that are alive in our country that want to go back, but I always call this the march of progress, which is this period of time in American history. There's no politician saying let's go back. They'll come along the edges about courts and let's have strict constructionists, and they will try and limit the possibilities of voting, and then they'll play up emotions and tensions in terms of race. I mean, I see that even now as we're dealing with the immigration bill, the idea that Jeff Sessions[1] will offer an amendment saying we're not going to permit the earned income tax credit for people that are undocumented, even if they are in good standing the rest of their lives, although we don't do it to murderers and rapists and pornographers or child molesters or anything else. So you still have elements of that kind of attitude alive and well, and people willing to exploit it. But there is no political process to try and reverse these major elements of progress that we've made in our country and society. Enormously important, and President Kennedy and Robert Kennedy were very much involved. I certainly worked on them while I was in the Senate and here you have internally these two factors and forces that are in contrast here. As one who has tried, in the Senate, to find common ground in different areas, and I've had some ability to do so, you couldn't find common ground on these.

Q: *You couldn't.*

EMK: And that conflict was very real and very significant and very powerful, and was something that was obviously perplexing and distressing as life went on. Eventually this part of my career, I could still work on both of these areas, and we have strong support from both communities again. But for that time and for that period of time, when the country was in turmoil with the [Vietnam] war, we had cities that were burning, and then both the tragedies, not only in my family, the loss of Dr. King, all of this turmoil and conflict were so close to the surface during this. It was a time of enormous convulsion just in terms of how I looked at the scene during that period and how we looked at the future.

Q: *Were you discouraged?*

EMK: Discouraged, yes. I mean I basically had felt that everything was going to get—a person is basically hopeful. I just saw things getting worse. There was a conflict of what I felt in terms of in the Senate—if you're there for a period of time, you understand what you believe better, you understand how to get things done better. You're able to prioritize what you want to do, even though you're drawn into a lot of different tensions. So you have more of a handle in terms of what you're doing professionally. Tied into this was a good

---

1. At the time of the Kennedy oral history, Jeff Sessions was a Republican senator from Alabama.

deal of personal anxiety as well with what was happening to my family and other issues of that period.

Q: It could make you feel kind of helpless in this situation, when they turn their backs on you and start doing that. That's why I say it must have been very discouraging [during the busing crisis].

EMK: And in a very disciplined—they just knew exactly how to—I've been in the army, and they had a coordination and a discipline that the Marines would have envied. They'd all turn their back, they'd all listen to their people, they'd all be responsive, they'd all fall in line. They all knew how to get to me, and did it very well. It wasn't hard for them because they saw it—I mean I had some appreciation of how they viewed this. I'm sure you know that my children were going to private schools at this time. I'd gone to private schools. My parents always thought that members of the family ought to go to public schools. They went and moved to Bronxville, New York, which had good public schools, and my brothers and sisters all went to public schools. My sisters went to convents, but they also went to public schools for part of the time, and my older brother Joe did and Jack did.

Q: So it was perhaps an upsurge of class antagonism?

EMK: I was such a target. The fact is, I understood it. I mean, at least I understood it. I didn't like getting targeted, and I knew what I believed in and what I thought was the right course, but I had a very clear awareness, a very clear understanding, and a good deal of empathy because the white schools were bad and the black schools were bad. We were viewed as trying to do something about education and trying to find ways that we could deal with those issues, and this other—I can't call it a diversion, but it wasn't about trying to elevate poor white schools and poor black schools, it was this other factor and force about trying to—never to get to that point to talking about what are we going to do to really strengthen education, all of it. You could never get to that point, you couldn't reach that because of the emotion that was involved in the question of busing.

Our [poll] numbers just dropped in Boston. Then, about four years later in similar areas—still, I never got back to where I was in terms of a lot of the different wards—the numbers for "stands for what he believes in" went up, both in the state and in Boston. "Stands for what he believes in" always went up, and then, correspondingly, my other [poll] numbers inched on up.

I always remember my brother Jack telling me, "If you get over 54 or 55 percent [approval ratings] you're not doing your job. You're not standing up on issues. You have to take tough positions, and you shouldn't expect to have more. If you go for those upper parts, you're not doing what you should." This was when we were first talking just after I got elected to the Senate.

Senator Kennedy recalled the aftermath of busing in Boston.

EMK: Finally in '84, [Judge] Garrity gives—we have a different school board, school committee in Boston, and a black had even gotten elected to it, and Garrity gives the planning back to the control of the school committee. Then in '85 there are polls in Boston and black parents favoring the freedom of choice of schools was 74 percent, which is exactly what the whites were saying at the start of this whole process.

Q: *Did any good come of* [busing]?

EMK: I think today, the Massachusetts schools are the best in the country in the fourth and eighth grade, under the NAVE[2] test, and more progress has been made reducing the disparity between black and white in Boston than any other major city in the country, and generally in Massachusetts we've reduced the disparity more than any other state. I was looking at those NAVE tests yesterday in one of the newspapers, and we're still at the very top. Our disparity between our state test, which is the national test, is very little, and we still do the best on it. What happened was there was such focus on it in the Boston schools that subsequently, the enlightened business community came together and said, "We have to do something about our school system."

They got started on education reform in Boston before the No Child Left Behind [Act of 2002], but having gotten started, with the No Child coming in after it, the results have been that we've done better than other places. I don't think it's any question that that turmoil took the next generation of business leaders and legislative leaders, black leaders, city leaders. Mayor Menino, who has been mayor now for ten years, when this Tom Payzant, who was superintendent of Boston Public Schools and President Clinton's secretary of education, Secretary Riley, were looking for a different way. I mentioned this to Tom Menino, and he had already put in play an outreach program to get it. When we talked about who was the best educator, superintendent in the country, boom, he went and got him and kept him for seven years, and gave more help and support. They've given a lot of focus and attention. It isn't that they haven't still got a lot of problems up there, but they've done a lot better than most urban areas.

In that immediate post[-busing] period, we had the usual amount of youth violence that took place up there. We had the Morning Star Baptist Church, where they were having a funeral, and some kids came in during the funeral and killed other kids. Menino set up this group. Now we had the Lenny Zakims, these conciliators, people who were in the business, religious community who, with the mayor, developed what they called the Ten Point Coalition, which were black ministers, and the COPS[3] program, local police, the schools with the truant officers and the superintendent of schools, the district attorneys, and we went for a period of fifteen months without a youth

2. National Assessment of Vocational Education.
3. Community Oriented Policing Services.

homicide, fifteen months. I mean, there's a hundred of them in Washington, DC, already this year. It was unbelievable, and all of that was the residue. People just said we don't ever want to go through this again. Boston's still got a lot of problems, but we have this dinner that Vicki and I went to, which is called—the dinner, One Boston, and it's a thousand people there, and they're all the new immigrants who have begun to make it in Boston. It is spectacular. They've had it for several years, but it's probably the only city in the country that's got it, and it is extraordinary. There are people from every different culture, country, and everything, and all doing very interesting things, and all interested in keeping Boston together. They understand that. We're the only city in the country that has worked on that and done that. I think so much of that comes in the aftermath of what happened.

A new generation that has come in there, people who want this thing to happen and to go on. They've been very clever. They've got the Gates Foundation, they've developed an institute for training teachers, and now they've got teachers who are staying longer, twice, three times the national average, twice the academic achievement, going into underserved areas and things like that. They've really attempted to do some things. As I say, it's certainly not out of the woods, but there's a very deep desire never to go back.

We had this marvelous basketball player, Bill Russell, who was a superstar, and he just won national championship after national championship [with the Boston Celtics]. At the end of his career he left Boston, which is just about this period, the '70s. We were with him the other day and he said, "What a difference in the life and the atmosphere in this city. It's a big change." This person was revered by black, white, every community. He was a superstar athlete, and he just said he felt this pressure, that he could never live here [as an African American]. He comes back now and says it's a new city. You know, you certainly hope so.

Q: *Some of those dark days, when you were so discouraged, in the '70s it wasn't—*

EMK: Well, those dark days in the '70s in Boston have been transferred to the dark days in this century on Iraq. [*Laughter.*] But I know you're right.

Q: *Each set of dark days, so that whatever you could do in Washington had—there was something to work with here. There was a self-effort, and Boston was redeeming itself, I guess.*

EMK: There's that.

Q: *Where are the Louise Day Hickses of this era? Are they gone?*

EMK: She has gone on to her reward.

Getting back to civil rights, it was a very difficult time, and we had a president in the form of Ronald Reagan, who started off with education cuts in the beginning. He was willing to defend Bob Jones, giving tax breaks to Bob Jones even though Bob Jones University banned interracial dating. [Reagan] was also in opposition to the efforts many of us made in 1983 to create a holiday for Martin Luther King. He had used derogatory remarks about Dr. King—saying we'd find out in thirty-five years whether he was a communist.

We had important Supreme Court decisions being made then. In 1984 the *Grove City*[4] case, which was really the architecture of the Reagan Justice Department, said that American taxpayer funds could be used at a university, in different departments of the university, as long as the financial office of that university did not practice discrimination. That meant there could be discrimination in the dormitories, there could be discrimination among the faculty, there could be discrimination in sports, there could be discrimination in other aspects of the life of the college and university. That was decided by the Supreme Court in a 7–2 decision, which is absolutely extraordinary because one of the underlying tenets of the Civil Rights Acts of '64, '65, '68, and others, was that we would not permit taxpayer money to be used in any way to support segregation, in whatever the form or shape that it would be. This was in complete conflict with that decision.

Q: That was in 1984, the Grove City *case. That same year, you tried first the Civil Rights Restoration Act. Failed. In 1985, you tried it again. In 1987, you tried again, but that was the Bork[5] year. Then in 1998, you tried still again, and you won. That's an extraordinary event. Reagan vetoed it, and the Senate overrode the veto. That tells you something about how much energy and time it took, but it's still an amazing story. Reagan was in his second term then.*

EMK: It was a very long, time-consuming effort, because it was a complex case.

So there was very clever opposition to it, and it was a very long and complicated struggle. This was going on at the same time—'83—when we had completed the Dr. King holiday. I was the principal supporter of it, and it was a bitter, bitter debate with the southerners, Jesse Helms and Jim Eastland,[6] and even though the votes were overwhelming, there was a nasty floor debate and discussion.

Dr. King, of course, had died in '68, and it took us all the way until '83 to get into a situation where we could move this as a holiday. We had talked about it during that time, but for one reason or another the time wasn't right. We decided we would move ahead on it, and the arguments were very controversial.

"Why are we having another national holiday? There are many national heroes we don't have holidays for," [opponents argued.] The business community was strongly against it. They said we were going to lose x billions of dollars

---

4. *Grove City College v. Bell* (465 U.S. 555).

5. U.S. Court of Appeals judge Robert Bork was Reagan's 1987 nominee to fill the US Supreme Court seat of retired associate justice Lewis Powell Jr. The Senate denied his confirmation.

6. Senators Jesse Helms, a Republican from North Carolina, and James Eastland, a Democrat from Mississippi, were both conservatives.

with another holiday. There was the question of whether this was the best way to honor his life, because people would just take a holiday and wouldn't focus on it. There were a thousand different arguments at the time, but it came together at the very end, and it passed.

It was a very nasty debate, with a lot of very vicious attacks on Dr. King. But we went on, and the next year was the speech at the United Nations, in the spring of that year, about apartheid in South Africa. All of us know about the stains of apartheid: the cruelty, the exploitation, the viciousness, the brutality of it all, the killings that took place, the murders. It had been emerging, but it was emerging more and more as a matter of international importance. I spoke at the United Nations, and I made a very strong speech about that issue. Then at the end of that year, Archbishop Tutu and Boesak[7] came to visit me in my Washington office and invited me to come to South Africa in November of that year.

Nineteen eighty-four. I was reluctant to go down there. Bob [Kennedy] had gone down there in 1966 and had an incredibly powerful visit. He gave some wonderful talks and speeches; he had such credibility emerging from his battles on civil rights issues here in the United States. He was warmly received by the heroes of the anti-apartheid movement and very significantly condemned by the supporters of apartheid. He had a great impact in South Africa and handled it, typically, very well.

Pope Paul VI said [in a 1976 meeting at the Vatican] that he remembered Bobby Kennedy coming up and seeing him, after my brother Bobby's trip to South Africa, and telling him at that time that the church was on the wrong side on apartheid. And Bobby gave him the names and the people and the things that they had very specifically on it. The pope told us that this made such a powerful impression and really altered his mind on it. It was really very powerful to hear that, for Joe[8] to hear it.

Yes, from the pope. It was just extraordinary, what he said about apartheid, and my brother Bob's enormous interest in it. That was basically the theme, that he had remembered that trip that Bob had taken. After he went to South Africa, Bob wanted to come up and tell the pope, because he had seen what the Catholic bishops were failing to do in South Africa.

Q: You were reluctant to go [to South Africa]?

EMK: At that time, I was interested. There had been violence—what they call the Soweto riots—where people had been brutally killed. They estimated there were ten people killed, then a hundred people killed, and then a thousand people killed. Ronald Reagan was asked about it, and he said the government forces were protecting themselves. He wouldn't condemn the violence.

---

7. Archbishop Desmond Tutu and the Reverend Allan Boesak were anti-apartheid activists in South Africa.

8. Joseph P. Kennedy II was Bobby's oldest son.

Q: And this was an internal matter?

EMK: Yes. So this had made an impression on me. I made a tentative decision to go. Afterwards, when Tutu got the [1984] Nobel [Peace] Prize and called me, he said he still wanted me to go.

Q: Bishop Tutu talked about that meeting you referred to. He and Boesak were explaining the realities of the situation to you, among other things, and Tutu says you said, "What can I do to help?" It was not something to indicate any reluctance on your part. That was a very powerful moment for Bishop Tutu, when you asked what you could do to help. So you were ready.

EMK: Yes. I was ready to help. We spelled this out up at the United Nations. I didn't quite know where it would be best to do this, and that was really the reluctance. Once Tutu said this is important—not that he needed more credibility or authority—but it just seemed to me that if he thinks it's important, it's important.

Q: And the government of the United States was not about to apply sanctions.

EMK: No, no. We were engaged in "constructive engagement" on it, but it was not effective. So in '85 we travel to South Africa; we're back in South Africa, and have an incredible trip. I don't know if we want to go through it. There were certain parts of it that were particularly memorable. One was meeting Winnie Mandela.[9] At this time, she was in good standing. She had been isolated and kept in a rather barren part of South Africa. We went by to see her in the place where she was living, a very small, simple little house. I went in to talk with her, and her first words were, "How can you bring up children without a father?"

She was very empathetic, very sympathetic, very appealing. I was rather startled later on when I read all the stories about her, but she was certainly a very dramatic personality at that time, before she got involved in a lot of these other activities. I think I've told the story about one of the rallies where they weren't going to let me speak. It was in Cape Town. There were several thousand people at the Cape Town rally. I was supposed to speak, and Allan Boesak was introducing me. There were some ANC[10] people in the crowd, a group of Buthelezi[11] people who weren't sympathetic to my trip down there. They were only probably a hundred people, and they were clustered in the center of the crowd.

---

9. Winnie Mandela was Nelson Mandela's wife.

10. African National Congress.

11. Mangosuthu Buthelezi is a South African politician and Zulu tribal chief who in 1975 founded the Inkatha Freedom Party (IFP), which eventually diverged from the African National Congress. He became minister of home affairs in the post-apartheid government of South Africa, from 1994 to 2004.

After Boesak introduced me and I got up to speak, they all stood up and started to chant, so I couldn't speak. Boesak said, "Let me handle this." And I said, "No, no. I know how to handle demonstrators. I'll deal with this."

But he said, "No, you can't. You don't know how to deal with it here." Then they had this enormously interesting and profoundly impressive dance, which Boesak started and led. He started chanting the names of the heroes of the anti-apartheid movement and the heroes of Soweto, the names of the people at Sharpsville, I guess, where they had the killings years before.

He started, and the crowd started to repeat them, and they all got up and started to chant and move and dance. It was sort of a dance, a kind of shuffle. In the beginning, maybe a thousand people picked it up and started to do this and go around, but this created a climate and atmosphere where their voices and the noise overrode everything else that was happening. And then he stopped and said, "Now we'll hear from Senator Kennedy."

Up get the hundred again, and they start to chant louder. So he starts in again, with more intensity, and then he did it a third time and a fourth time and a fifth time. You could feel this incredible—they had danced themselves into a rage. And by this time, you had five thousand people, and the whole stadium was shaking, and when they stopped, they all reached over to this crowd of one hundred, and I thought they were going to tear them limb from limb, and they thought so, too. They shut up and didn't say a word. Boesak said, "Now Senator Kennedy will speak," and they just kept quiet.

The government provided transportation for the demonstrators. They had our schedule. We'd get on a plane and fly to someplace, get out, and there were our demonstrators. The government had flown them in on a plane. Wherever we went, we had demonstrators.

Q: *You had a police escort, too, when you went out to Soweto, and they discouraged you.*

EMK: The point coming back—this enormously moving, dramatic point. We met these incredible miners and looked into the mines where they worked, just horrific conditions. Soweto was a positively devastating kind of life for these people: the separations of the family, separations of the women from the men. It was really barbaric.

The question came up then about the [US economic] sanctions, and virtually every one of them said, "We have suffered so long, go ahead and put the sanctions on. We don't mind suffering so our children won't." Every one of them said that—the miners, the leaders of the miners, all the people who were going to be hurt most by it. All the government officials said, "You don't want it. The sanctions won't bother us; they will bother the people you're trying to represent, the miners."

This was an example where the sanctions worked dramatically. Eighteen months after those sanctions were put in, Mandela was out of jail. Eighteen months. Pik Botha, the foreign minister at that time, just effectively threw in the towel, because of what was happening to their economy because the sanctions had been put on by the Europeans. Margaret Thatcher[12] was strongly against it, but the Europeans had put it on, the Swedes. Other countries had put it on, so when the United States entered, it was really effective. Sanctions don't work unless everybody's going to be on board. If everybody was on board on this, they were going to work, and they worked in South Africa. It's an incredible story.

When we got back, I remember appearing at the Foreign Relations Committee with Weicker.[13] He hadn't gone, but he had been very active and involved before, and I worked easily with him and made the presentation on this. Then we had a long, long battle. The House acted independently and had a very strong bill dealing with Krugerrands and investments, and with a number of trade issues. Theirs was stronger and tougher and probably wouldn't have passed, and we were having difficulty at that time, even with Lugar and Nancy Kassebaum.[14]

I had dinners at my home with a number of people. There was Malcolm Fraser,[15] an Australian who had been very involved in apartheid, and I sat them next to each other. We had some very prominent African leaders. We had a series of different meetings and dinners, particularly with Lugar and Kassebaum. Towards the end of the session, I went over and spoke at the Black Caucus and told them where we were going, and that we really had strong legislation, although not as strong as theirs.

President Reagan indicated he would veto it. Reagan had put out an executive order to undermine us previously, to take the wind out of the sails on this thing, which was what you would consider an unfriendly act. Then he vetoed it, and we overrode the veto, which was a big deal.

Q: *Dole was with you on the first vote, but he didn't vote to override, I think.*

EMK: Yes.

Q: *Was this bipartisan?*

EMK: Yes, bipartisan. We were still not in control. We got control over the Senate later in the year. That was a big battle in '86. Rehnquist[16] was up for chief justice at the time, and I led the fight against him. We had also traveled down to Chile. We were working on the restoration of democracy in Chile and the Soviet Union on arms control. So it was a busy year.

---

12. Margaret Thatcher was British prime minister.
13. Lowell Weicker was a Republican senator from Connecticut.
14. Senators Richard Lugar and Nancy Kassebaum were Republicans from Indiana and Kansas, respectively.
15. Malcolm Fraser was former prime minister of Australia.
16. Reagan promoted Associate Justice William Rehnquist to chief justice in 1986.

[W]e also had an opportunity to knock down the walls of discrimination against women. This was an evolving process. When I was talking about this issue with Adam Clymer, I recalled very clearly during my first campaign going out to talk to a women's group and talking to my brother Jack, who happened to be up at the apartment at 122 Bowdoin Street [in Boston].

He wrote out for me three or four pages about the role of women in the Soviet Union. He had traveled to the Soviet Union, where so many of the men had been lost, and he remarked about how women in Soviet society were taking every important position and every responsibility and doing it with great skill. He still obviously differed with the system, but, in his visits to the Soviet Union and in talking with representatives, he noted that they had found women playing very important and significant roles. He suggested that it was something that was going to be forthcoming in the United States.

It made an impression on me, and I always remembered it. This whole movement in the country of knocking down the walls of discrimination really started over extensions of the Fourteenth Amendment and the existing constitutional provisions that had been passed as a result of the Civil War and how they applied to women. That took a period of time in the early and mid-'70s, before there was a recognition that the [Supreme] Court interpretation—even though the courts were interpreting some of these other areas dealing with civil rights positively, even though they were beginning to turn about this time—wasn't going to finally do what was going to be necessary to free women to have full equality and recognize that there were Founding Mothers as well as Founding Fathers.

That was really the origin of the Equal Rights Amendment, which I welcomed the opportunity to sponsor and support. That effort continued for some time. But as that constitutional amendment was moving through—and it was going to face major dissention—there was also continued movement in our committee on what we called Title IX, which was developed as an extension of the Civil Rights Act.

Title VII[17] knocked down walls of discrimination on employment. Title IX was to knock down the walls of discrimination against women in sports and also at universities, and that's its great significance today. There's no question it had a dramatic impact in terms of full equality for women in sports.

I worked in the Senate with others. Senator Bayh was a lead figure on it, but I was active and involved and was very supportive. We were good friends and worked very closely in that area. Of course, we had the decision in the *Roe v. Wade* case in '73, a defining issue in terms of reproductive rights and a major force in terms of the whole movement for equality that was moving ahead.

---

17. Title IX of the 1972 Education Amendments Act extended the 1964 Civil Rights Act to cover women's rights in education. Title VII of the Civil Rights Act protected women from discrimination in employment.

Just a final point on the Equal Rights Amendment: this goes back to the early '70s. I was reminded that Birch Bayh was the first one to introduce the Equal Rights Amendment. After he introduced it, I've been the one who has introduced it. Paul Tsongas[18] introduced it, but I've been the one to introduce it for the last number of years in the 97th, 98th, 99th, 100th, 101st Congress. The Equal Rights Amendment also importantly dealt with the extraordinary discrimination against women in pay.[19]

We had not only the issues of employment, health, and other aspects of life, but also in pay. Even though President Kennedy had signed the pay bill for equality of pay, it had been interpreted in the courts as not insisting on equal pay for equal work. Everyone believed the Equal Rights Amendment and the Title IX provisions that were added to the higher ed bill would help, but that has not been achieved in terms of the Equal Rights Amendment, although Title IX has obviously made an extraordinary difference.

About this same time [early 1979], my colleague Paul Tsongas introduced the first legislation to knock down walls of discrimination on the basis of employment for gays, and I was one of five co-sponsors of that attempt. It never got a hearing, never moved at all, but it was a place-marker in the movement. I would say, from my own personal evolution in terms of the full understanding of both of these areas, that the '80 [presidential] campaign was where we first had strong, strong support from the gay and lesbian community and strong support from the women's community. They were very much involved in the campaigns in California and New York and otherwise. At the end of those campaigns, I was very much in their corner in terms of being a spokesperson and leader in the Senate, working with others to try to continue to make progress in these areas.

Q: Was that campaign a defining moment for you [on gay rights?]

EMK: I think it was. I think there was a marvelous—I believe his name was Forrest, in San Francisco, who was a terrific Kennedy supporter, happened to be gay, and was a uniformly highly regarded, respected worker. I can remember flying down to Southern California one time to have a meeting with some of the gay leaders down there. I had some staff people briefing me on gay issues, and I said, "Where is Forrest, the leading politician?" And then he came up and gave—I can't remember the exact briefing on it, but I said, "This is the real thing."

His first advice was, "You have to be comfortable talking about these issues. The community will understand if you're nervous about talking about them,

---

18. Paul Tsongas was a Democratic senator from Massachusetts.
19. In 1972 both houses of Congress passed the Equal Rights Amendment to the US Constitution, which would have banned gender discrimination. The ERA went to the states for ratification, but it failed to attract the constitutionally mandated three-fourths of states to approve.

if you're uncomfortable talking about them." At this time it was just meeting and shaking hands and being with them, and how they react, whether they shake hands or slap you on the shoulder. "The community will understand if you twinge, if you don't—" This was then. It's unbelievable now. Just in talking about it, I remember that this was the most important aspect of the briefing. It was very interesting.

We went to an event in Los Angeles, and there were about twenty-six cameras up there, because it was unusual to have one of the first major events. I supported change in the immigration law to permit gays to be able to bring their lovers in. The question was, "They're prohibited now. Would you support it?"

Of course, I hadn't been briefed; I didn't know about it. I couldn't believe it. All the cameras, the little bright lights went on, and I could feel this lump in my throat. I thought, "I can't wait to see what I have to say on this one." So I said, "Of course I am. We can't have discrimination in immigration." They all cheered, and it was all over. From that time on, they were all on my side. They thought, "This is the real thing."

Q: When did hate crimes become an important issue in your mind?

EMK: In the '80s. We had hate crime legislation, but we had a number of instances of hate crimes that had taken place against blacks and gays. We even had some against women in one of the national parks. I remember the women campers.[20] The Southern Poverty Law Center founder, what is his name?

Q: Morris Dees.

EMK: Morris Dees. On the issues of hate crimes, he came up—he has the whole record of this. There's hate crime legislation that was initially passed after Dr. King was lost. That was the first hate crime, but it was limited in jurisdiction. A hate crime had to be done in a federal jurisdiction and involve interstate commerce, and was limited to blacks. So it was a very restricted definition, and so many of these other crimes were taking place outside of it.

The question was whether you were going to fight hate crimes with one arm tied behind your back or with the full power of the federal government in terms of the FBI. The argument on the other side is, isn't any murder a hate crime? And if that's true, aren't we federalizing all of this? So it had to be clarified, and we had procedures whereby local authorities would consult with the Justice Department. We wouldn't give them a complete blank check, but we had ways of proceeding.

[African American] church burnings increased dramatically during this period, the early '90s. I worked with Lauch Faircloth, a very conservative senator from North Carolina. We passed church burning legislation that brought the

---

20. Julianne Williams and Laura Winans, a lesbian couple, were murdered in Shenandoah National Park.

FBI into it, and almost overnight they stopped. They just didn't want to fuss with the FBI, even though the FBI in a lot of the southern counties had been playing footsie with a lot of bad people. This was one that had a remarkable effect. Lauch Faircloth was looking for something to get himself re-elected, and I wanted to do this and get it done, and we got this thing passed. He was still defeated. I think John Edwards defeated him. [Church burning] was another type of expression of the hatred going on.

Q: *What accounts for that surge in hate crimes?*

EMK: Well, words and actions have results. I don't think there's any question that recently there was an enormous amount of hatred and poison built up in the wake of the immigration debate. I was talking with Lindsey Graham[21] two or three days ago, and he said, "You can't believe the mail I'm still getting at my house." He said the degree of nastiness and hatred is very surprising. I think we get a good deal of it—not so much in this state, although there is stuff from this state as well.

To continue with the issues of discrimination against gays and lesbians, ENDA[22] was one issue, hate crimes a second. We had the "don't ask, don't tell" policy in the first year of the Clinton administration. But they made a major, major mistake because they had about seventy-five executive orders in place when they took over, and they eliminated or restructured all seventy-five. Some dealt with labor and . . . contracts. Others dealt with environmental issues. Their administration changed all seventy-five of them, and one of them led to "don't ask, don't tell." It was part of a whole series of actions they took that caused ripples in the water, besides just this issue.

What was startling about it is that there was absolutely no preparation for it whatsoever. None of the military leaders knew about it, none of the members of Congress knew about it. Nobody who had been supportive of gay rights knew about it. It landed like a ton of bricks and caused an incredible stir in Congress. We on the Armed Services Committee know that if you work with the military for a period of time, you understand the officers are going to do what they're told to do, and you can find out who are going to be the leaders and which ones you want. They're the easiest of all political problems to work through because they do what they're told, by and large. But no effort was made, and so there were a lot of them complaining, and it caused a real backlash.

We had the hearings in the Armed Services Committee, and I remember them very well. They went back into wartime, when they court-martialed people for being gay. What they found out in Vietnam is when the fighting was

---

21. Senator Lindsey Graham is a Republican from South Carolina.

22. The Employment Non-Discrimination Act is proposed legislation in Congress that would ban discrimination in hiring and employment on the basis of sexual orientation or gender identity by employers with fifteen or more employees.

the most severe, they had the fewest court-martials. At the Tet Offensive, the number went down, and in other battles in Vietnam, they went down.

In World War II, they all went down, and they found that there were no complaints about the performance under fire of any of these individuals, virtually none. You look back at the court-martials, and there are none that alleged that the three people, all who were gay, were leaving the field of battle. There were virtually none. But the numbers in the reports indicated that when there was the least amount of conflict and the least amount of tension in the military service, the numbers all went up.

It was completely inconsistent because the arguments: we have to have jointness [among the service branches], we have to have training, we have to have people with confidence in each other, people who trust each other. This is an action that will bring distrust, disharmony, conflict, and confusion, and you'll have a unit that will not be able to function in the line of fire. That was the argument, but all the statistics and figures showed it wasn't true. It was just dramatic, but it didn't make any difference.

I always admire Chuck Robb,[23] who had a lot of military service. He stood up and said, "I've been in combat, I've been in Vietnam, and I know the truth of this, and this is not the problem." He stood up on it, and we had the vote in the Armed Services Committee. I think it was an executive order, and the committee disapproved it, but it was still an executive order, and I voted against the majority and filed minority reports on it.

One interesting story is that we had a hearing on this when the whole issue was coming to a head. President Clinton invited the members of the Armed Services Committee down to the White House to hear from each member. He wanted to hear himself, and the meeting went on for two-and-a-half hours. It started at 6 and went 'til 8:30. Baryshnikov was dancing at 8:15, and I was supposed to go with Vicki, and I could see the clock ticking. Finally we got out at 8:30, and I went over. She couldn't understand how a meeting with the president could last two-and-a-half hours.

[Clinton] went around the room, and different people spoke. The last person who spoke was Bob Byrd. He's a member of the Armed Services Committee. He doesn't come very much. He came on this particular occasion and talked at great length and with great passion about how he was a great supporter of the military; West Virginia is a great supporter of the military. He had grandsons who were thinking of going in, but if this went into effect, he was going to insist and do everything he could to make sure his grandsons didn't go into a military that had this rule, that permitted this kind of rule. There had to be an absolute, complete ban [on gays in the military].

---

23. Senator Charles Robb was a Democrat from Virginia and Vietnam War marine veteran.

Then he talked about how Julius Caesar had been a sex slave when he was a young general, and when he escaped, he came back and got more divisions and went back and captured and killed the man who had made him a sex slave. And Marcus Aurelius was kept as a sex slave, and then finally he escaped and they had conflict.

Then he said the worst example of all was Tiberius. I had little notes. I know I have these notes someplace, because I wrote this down. I said, "This is too good, I have to write this down. Tiberius." I didn't want Byrd to catch me, which would be like being caught in school reading a book you shouldn't read with a false paper cover on it.

So I had Tiberius (I can remember Tiberius, because it was the name of a good restaurant in Washington). He had a story about Tiberius that just didn't stop. I'd never heard of the kinds of things that happened to this poor guy, and this went on and on, and now it's 8:20.

Finally, they'd given about five notes to President Clinton, and he said, "Well, Bob, I'm very glad to get your views, and I'm very glad to get the views of everybody else here. But Moses went up to the mountain and came back with Ten Commandments, and discriminating against gays wasn't one of them. I'll take it under consideration, but this is the end of the meeting." And he walked out, and everybody else walked out. As I went over to see Vicki, I said, "Just remember these names: Tiberius, Marcus Aurelius, Julius Caesar. I'll fill in the blanks later."

Q: And then you went to the ballet?

EMK: Then I went to Baryshnikov. ["Don't ask, don't tell"] went into effect, it was challenged, and we participated in filing briefs in some of the legal cases. Now it's being re-challenged. We won't get to it, I don't think, before the 2008 election, primarily because of the order of different amendments that I think the community feels should be prioritized.

At the time, we were firing 1,100 gay servicemen—some translators—at a time we don't have Arabic translators. This illustrated the ridiculousness of this issue at this particular time. We're letting in people with general problems of moral turpitude. We've dropped the standards for recruitment, but we're still firing these individuals, and this is, I think, a powerful issue.

But we're now coming into the fall of '07 and the '08 election. What the community is most interested in is the hate crimes legislation, which we're going to put on the Defense Appropriations Bill, and then we will do the "don't ask, don't tell."

Q: In the end, how would you assess the effect of the "don't ask, don't tell"?

EMK: It's really varied: there are a lot of places where they're not dismissing people, while in other narrower areas they are dismissing. For a while, servicemen were testing it; they would provoke a situation to challenge it. There are a large number of units where they don't have any incidents at all because people aren't challenging it, nobody's looking for it, and they're just going ahead with the situation. We had that meeting at the White House on January 27, seven days after Clinton took office.[24] I think it's fair to say it was probably the opening of the antagonism towards Clinton.

Q: It was his most publicized, earliest action, and even today people are saying, "Why in the world did he pick that as the first thing?"

EMK: People couldn't understand it.

Q: Do you have any clue why that was?

EMK: When I saw all the other actions they took, there was somebody there who said, "Look, we have all these other things working against workers . . . [in existing executive orders]. Let's knock all of that stuff out and stick this thing in there."

Q: So it wasn't established as a priority.

EMK: No, it wasn't.

Q: —which is how it came out in the press.

EMK: [Clinton] told Vicki and me in a conversation that he didn't anticipate the ferocity of opposition he received. He really felt he didn't have any alternative but to back down and change his position.

We had on this issue a major Supreme Court decision in Massachusetts, about eight months before the Kerry [2004 presidential] election, where the Massachusetts courts, interpreting the Massachusetts Constitution, permitted gay marriage. The chief justice was Margie Marshall who, interestingly, was head of the students at one of the universities in South Africa who invited Bobby Kennedy to go there, which he did in the '60s. She married Tony Lewis, a very distinguished writer for the *New York Times*.

She drew on the part of the Massachusetts State Constitution, written by John Adams in 1780, that referred to the protections of rights and liberties. She issued a finding that permitted gay marriage in Massachusetts. Now that was against a background of what we call the DOMA, that had been passed probably five years before—we're talking about the late 1990s—that said that a state did not have to recognize a gay marriage in another state. Bill Clinton signed that. I was one of, I think, thirteen who voted against it.

Q: This was the Defense of Marriage Act. What was the motivation for it?

EMK: The act that triggered or stimulated it was individuals moving into states and communities to test whether they prevented them from getting married. We faced that in the United States Senate. . . . But in the '60s you had states decriminalizing homosexual acts: Illinois and Wisconsin, the first state to outlaw discrimination on the basis of sexual orientation. And then you had a Supreme Court decision in the '80s that denied gays and lesbians protections against discrimination, calling them special rights. This was always the issue.

---

24. See Russell L. Riley, *Inside the Clinton White House: An Oral History* (New York: Oxford University Press, 2016), 172–75, for a description of how the issue rose to the top of Clinton's agenda.

Q: That was the Bowers *case, which was overruled in a* Texas[25] *case more recently, that* [recognized sexual] *privacy between consenting adults.*

EMK: So you had this taking place in the states, and the Supreme Court making judgments about some of these actions. In 2004, same-sex marriages became legal in Massachusetts. I was the only public official who supported it, the only one. In Massachusetts, I'm the only one today who supports it.

Vicki Kennedy: Barney.

EMK: Barney Frank,[26] yes. Barney Frank supported it. I made the point in Massachusetts that this doesn't require the churches to do anything. This doesn't require the Catholic Church to marry somebody. They have a right, but it doesn't say to any Catholic Church, to any Protestant minister or Jewish rabbi, it doesn't say to any of them that they are required to perform a marriage. There's nothing in this that sanctions any member of the religious community to take any action, none. This ruling goes back to what is basically the contractual aspect of marriage. I found that although people differed with me on this, if you explained it, they were relieved. They felt, when this first came out, that it was going to require Catholic priests to marry and Protestants to marry [gay couples]. Once they understood, you could feel the air come out of it.

This issue is completely generational in terms of the politics, not the morality. You will find in Massachusetts and some other states, people over forty strongly condemn this while people under forty couldn't care less. That's not true about the death penalty, that's not true about most other issues. It's all across the borders with different age groups, different communities, different educational experiences, all that. Not on gay marriage; it's absolutely generational. I'm aware of this now, but I wasn't aware of this when we got involved in it.

Q: Is this generational divide true nationally?

EMK: Nationally, too. It's very interesting. There's no other issue like this, and so the politicians are trying to figure out where to land on it. Most of them have landed with both feet against it.

I don't think there's any question that this had a profound impact on John Kerry in the election. He had a different position than I had, but he was still asked about Massachusetts. He comes from Massachusetts. This led to McGovern,[27] antiwar, permissiveness, and it all added to the aura of the state and tied to some of the other issues. You know, "He goes windsurfing—does

---

25. In *Bowers v. Hardwick*, 478 U.S. 186 (1986), the US Supreme Court found no constitutional right to homosexual privacy; the court overturned this ruling in 2003's *Lawrence v. Texas*, 539 U.S. 558.

26. Barney Frank was a Democratic congressman from Massachusetts.

27. George McGovern was a liberal senator from South Dakota and the unsuccessful Democratic presidential nominee in 1972, losing in a landslide to President Richard Nixon.

he really understand me?" and the rest of that kind of thing. It added a dimension.

Just an additional point on the gay marriage decision in Massachusetts, the Margie Marshall decision. There wasn't any question in 2004 when she issued the ruling that Republicans saw the opening this was going to provide for them. They were very active in getting the gay marriage issue on a number of state ballots in order to motivate evangelicals and the anti-gay community. They did that in a number of states and did it very successfully. I don't think there's any question it had an impact; we're not prepared to go over this state by state to see how that would have altered or changed it, but there's no question that the antigay group within the Republicans was very active and involved in exploiting the Massachusetts decision to the disadvantage of John Kerry.

A very important public policy related again to the whole discrimination against gays was the issue of AIDS, and how that was going to be handled. My first real association with this and understanding of it, other than in a general way, was thanks to Mathilde Krim, who was the wife of Arthur Krim. Arthur Krim was a very successful Hollywood producer and Democrat. He was very close to President Johnson but was a very strong supporter of my brother Bob. It was always interesting because he was probably the most prominent of all the people from that period who supported President Kennedy.

Mathilde Krim was a foreigner by birth and just a brilliant, intelligent, caring person, a great partner for him. She got started very early in terms of the AIDS issue and asked me to come up to New York so she could give me a briefing, which I did, and which was enormously informative. She was incredibly helpful.

That was in 1983, just after the virus had been identified. She wanted our Health Committee to do a good deal on this issue. I told her that we had a full health agenda, and I didn't have personnel who understood the issue or had the time and all the rest. She said she would provide the personnel. She provided a fellow named Terry Beirn, who eventually died from AIDS, and Mike Iskowitz, who's still around. She said she would pay them, and, if I found that they were valuable and this was the issue, I ought to pick it up, but she would start it off. They were two superstars. They made an extraordinary contribution in terms of my understanding and in terms of the nation's focus on AIDS.

The next thing I did was talk to Everett Koop, who had been pilloried as the surgeon general for being very doctrinaire, but who was enormously courageous in recommending a preventive program. He talked about condoms and the public health issues. I also talked to Tony Fauci, who was a top researcher at NIH.[28]

---

28. National Institutes of Health.

When I first became aware of this, Mathilde had an organization called AmFAR[29] that she had developed, which was a very important organization. I knew of it, but I had not been as much aware of it, obviously, before I went up and talked with her about it. They were the principal organization dealing with all of this. She was very involved.

Right after '83, I started getting briefed. This issue looked like it was getting absolutely out of control. Dr. Fauci from NIH predicted that three to five million Americans would be HIV-positive, and a million would die of AIDS. This was in '86, and by '87, two-thirds of the public said it was a serious health threat. And the cultural issue: the right wing said it's God's punishment, and we had a lot of actions to isolate gay people in states. In '87 Koop tried to quiet the issue down.

In the '86 elections, the Democrats won the Senate, and I recaptured the Health Committee, and we started right off trying to get help and assistance in this area. But the kind of discrimination against gays during this period, and the vehemence and the vitriol directed towards them, was just extraordinary. The disease was obviously the result of gay sexual behavior, but it was also the result of the use of needles and of the blood supply being contaminated.

People who were hemophiliacs were getting AIDS and were suffering this extraordinary discrimination. In school, parents would be yelling at children not to play with other children. It was a very volatile, hate-filled moment, and although we were able to get additional funding for this in the '80s, it took until 1990 for us to actually pass legislation, the Ryan White Bill, which is the framework for helping to deal with the care and treatment of those who test HIV-positive.

We had a series of amendments by Helms. I remember going up to his office and asking, "Do you have to offer all of them?" He said he'd still offer five or six. Nobody with AIDS could work in a salad bar, for example, and so everybody had to be tested who worked in a restaurant. We heard long passages from the Bible, the Old Testament, and things like that on the floor of the United States Senate. It's well worth going back and looking at that debate. I can't capture it here today, but it was just a mean, nasty time.

At this time, I had [Orrin] Hatch as a co-sponsor. Hatch stayed with us most of the time, and we all agreed that the bill that came out of the committee would be the bill that stayed. But the thing that held Hatch and that really permitted it to pass, with all due respect, was the fact that Ryan White was a hemophiliac who died of AIDS, and the Ricky Ray family had three sons with the disease, and they all got it from the blood supply. So there was a recognition that we had to do something. But these voices that had been out there in

---

29. American Foundation for AIDS Research.

opposition to civil rights, out there in terms of antigay, out there in terms of AIDS, were all the same.

Q: You didn't talk very much about what you were trying to do about AIDS; that is, what this bill was about.

EMK: Basically, the legislation as I remember it had a research component that told the NIH that they had to give a priority to opportunities for this research. It also put a coordinator in the NIH to look at breakthroughs within the various agencies that might be related to AIDS. That was one thing, and the funding for it.

Secondly, it gave funding to communities with high incidence of HIV. So it targeted various communities to help with protection and caring for these people. One section of it worked with the pharmaceutical industry to help them develop additional kinds of drugs. It has moved up into several billion dollars a year now. It started off with a couple of hundred million.

We had a formula that those communities where HIV was being detected as the key aspect of the formula, and then the [medical care]. But that shifts the emphasis to areas like New York and San Francisco, older communities, where they have been able to develop the caring process and the support systems and the types of drugs to care for those people, and they're living longer and longer lives. The newer places aren't able to get the funds because of the formula, but recently we've seen the expansion of the formula to parts of the rural South and the rural Midwest and rural West.

So there's now a lot of tension, and we almost didn't get the Ryan White Bill reauthorized the last time because of the fight for funding. The only way we got it is we used some of the CHIP[30] money from Texas that was not being used. They had three or four hundred million dollars that they were not going to use to look after children, which was going to come back into the federal government. So we recaptured that money. That's a resourceful staff that knows these bills.[31] We recaptured that money, distributed it to the new areas, and the bill was passed. Otherwise, the money just would have gone to reduce the debt.

We came within a hair of having enormous conflict on the basis of formulas. That's another issue, but there's no question that this whole massive effort has had a very important impact. So much of that research is being used in Third World countries to benefit these children. Terry Beirn died of AIDS. Mike Iskowitz is still alive, but they were two enormously creative, active, involved individuals who made an extraordinary difference.

As an interesting sidebar, I had a sickness in '85 or '86. I don't know whether they ever figured it out.

Vicki Kennedy: Eating oysters or something; it was seafood.

---

30. Children's Health Insurance Program.

31. Senator Kennedy's office and committee staffs were legendary for their vast policy expertise and understanding of the legislative process.

EMK: My blood count went way down. I went out West with my children. I skied, and I was just getting weaker and weaker. I thought it was the flu. The doctors said they didn't know. Larry Horowitz[32] said, "You'd better go back," so I came back and went to Georgetown, and my red blood count was down. I must have had four or five liters of blood, and they found at Georgetown that the blood was contaminated.

As a member of the Senate, I was scared to death to go in to have a test, even when they were all blind tests, because, my God, what the outcry would be. They found contamination in the Georgetown blood, so the fear was legitimate: you had the growing danger. It was a very nasty and dangerous time.

I always said I was very lucky that my blood was okay, needless to say. When I got that, I had no idea that this was—it was years afterwards when I knew that this thing was happening. I think Elizabeth Dole eventually took over the Red Cross. She got into this, but it was a major challenge. She had her hands full.

Q: The presidents didn't give you much support on this or come out front, or did they?

EMK: It was the Reagan period, and we didn't get support other than Koop and Fauci, the medical community. We didn't get any other support. But we didn't get a veto, which was good.

Kennedy recalled his work on behalf of Washington, DC, residents.

EMK: [JFK] felt very strongly that the federal government had a very important responsibility to the people of the District of Columbia, and his administration was going to respond to that. My brother Bob was very involved in helping local schools and school districts get athletic facilities.

I can remember playing [tennis] with Arthur Ashe,[33] who then was the national champion, down in the inner city in Washington, raising funds for some projects there. He was very engaged and very involved. For the last twelve years, I've read with a second grader once a week at the Brent School in a program called "Everyone Wins." I read with her for about fifty minutes; we alternate reading pages. She'll read one page, and I'll read the next. I try to get books that are somewhat challenging so on each page there's one word she doesn't know. We write down the word she doesn't know, and then we look it up in the dictionary, and when I come back, I ask her about the words she didn't know.

We play little games about who's going to read the first page, the odds or evens. You throw out one finger or two fingers. I know exactly what she's going to throw out because if she says odd, she's going to throw out one finger, and if she says evens, two fingers. So whenever she says evens, I know she's going

---

32. Dr. Larry Horowitz was a longtime Kennedy advisor.
33. Arthur Ashe was the first black man to win a Wimbledon championship.

to throw out two fingers, so I throw out two, and so she wins all the time. She can't understand why. She's this cute little thing.

Another little game we play is rock, paper, scissors. The paper can wrap up the rock, but the scissors can't cut the rock. We play that to get started, and it keeps her lively and interested, and she's reading very well. I met with her mother after they finished up. She's in the second grade and is reading very well. She's taken all the tests, and she's right up at the top of her class and doing well.

Q: Is this one particular person you're responsible—

EMK: One person I read with each year. It's called the "Everyone Wins" program. Jim Jeffords got me interested years ago. Harkin[34] and I are probably the last two senators [to participate]. We had probably ten or twelve senators, probably twenty-five House members, and a number of staff from the Capitol who did it. Tuesday at twelve always worked for me because the caucus was at a quarter of one, ten of one, and if you're going to a hearing, you can always make sure you're out of there by five of twelve. It was a time that worked for them and for me. They juggled it around a little bit to make it in the middle of the afternoon to make it possible for me. If they keep it like this, it's going to continue.

One of the issues that had been languishing [in Congress] for some time was voting rights for the District of Columbia. That had been an issue, I think, as long as the District of Columbia had been there. There are 870,000 people there with effectively no voting rights in the House and Senate. They do now for the presidential election, but they don't for the House or Senate.

It was during this period, after 1976, after President Carter was elected, and their administration made some recommendations dealing with the capital's problems. One of them was to give voting representation in the House and Senate to the District. So we had Judiciary Committee hearings about the constitutionality. What did the Founding Fathers want when the land was initially donated? Was the District intended? What are the various juridical issues surrounding the District and the people and all the rest of this? We eventually passed legislation, a constitutional amendment, to give the District of Columbia two seats in the United States Senate and a House seat. That passed in the Senate and passed in the House.

It was part of the whole civil rights issue because this was in the nation's capital, and we're talking about voting rights. We had the '65 Act. We're talking about public accommodations, fair housing. Fair housing is the other issue. The people in the District raised this and said, "Why aren't you doing something about this?"

---

34. Senator Jim Jeffords was a Republican senator from Vermont who became an Independent and began caucusing with the Democrats in 2001; Tom Harkin was a Democratic senator from Iowa.

So we had to do something about it, and eventually, that constitutional amendment got eighteen votes. Eighteen states ratified it, but that was not enough. We needed thirty-eight states, so under the procedures of a constitutional amendment, it died. Now we're looking at getting one voting delegate in the House, representing the District, no Senate, and adding a vote to Utah. That's the proposal now. I'm supporting it because I like to support what people want in the District, but it certainly seems to me we could do a lot better. I'm not sure this is the best time to do it, but the people in the community want it, and that's their desire.

Q: What was the source of the opposition in the states?

EMK: The opposition said, "Look, the District has representation. They have the senators from Maryland representing them, because a chunk of that land was from Maryland." Others said, "No, they have the senators from Virginia because part of that land is from Virginia. So they're better off than a lot of other places because they have four senators representing them, from Virginia and from Maryland. We meet all the requirements, and the only part that isn't is the exact federal track, the House and Senate." Others said, "Let's carve out just the Capitol and the monuments."

Q: Did the fact of the large black population [in DC make a difference?]—

EMK: There's no question. The Republicans knew the senators were going to be Democrats, and that was primarily the reason for it. It was very clear, even though, as I remember it, there were thirteen states with smaller populations than the District of Columbia at that time. They're being taxed, and they're serving in the armed forces abroad. So they have the burdens of citizenship without the privileges or the guarantees. That was the overwhelming issue.

Another cause that Senator Kennedy championed in civil rights was banning discrimination in housing.

EMK: One other issue I think we ought to talk about that's related to this is the Fair Housing Act. In 1964, we did public accommodations. In 1965, we did the Voting Rights Act. Those carried with them enormous authority and power, and we also did Medicare and higher education. Discrimination in housing came in last, so to speak.

When we got to the issues on busing later on, people were thinking that we should have done more on housing, because where people reside indicates where their schools are. And if you have the redlining of districts and discrimination in housing, one of the principal problems you'll end up with is the schools, let alone what the school boards are going to do. In '68, if you read back through the history of it, you'll see that not a lot of consideration was given. We passed a law, and everyone understands it was a very weak law.

Q: It was a very weak law, and it was defeated twice. In '68 it passed, but one wonders why so much opposition to it?

EMK: They exempted homeowners who rented part of their house to other families. You had what they call the—when you have the duplex and the three-story house. They had "Mrs. O'Leary's house," [which was] exempted from the law. Are we going to say that if you own one level of the house, the second level, and you have family members, can you rent to other people who are neighbors? So the focus of this argument was all around very local kind of housing, which had a lot of appeal to people in a lot of different communities.[35]

Q: I'm sure it was racial.

EMK: It was unquestionably racial.

Senator Kennedy spoke about how a more conservative federal judiciary, during and after the Reagan presidency, created obstacles for broader interpretations of civil rights.

EMK: We have talked in the last day or so about the series of cases that the courts moved towards in the '80s and '90s that really threatened, in a very important way, what we call the march towards progress. There have been a number of decisions since that time, but let me mention two that reflect, I think, the disintegration of reverence for the courts and reverence for the institution of the Justice Department. That's what we're basically talking about: the fact that we had . . . distinguished individuals who were highly regarded and respected and were working through the protections and rights that have been guaranteed in the Constitutions. Now, there might have been some differences, but the country finally recognized those, and we are, as I think most all agree, a fairer, stronger, better nation because of it.

Then we saw the actions that were taken by Republican administrations to change the makeup of the courts, and we saw some of their attempts to diminish those rights and liberties, and efforts by Congress to resist those. We did that successfully.

Now what phase are we in? I'll just take a moment to talk about this phase because it's a different phase, and I think it's illustrated in 2007 by two very important decisions. One was the Georgia automobile licensing case in which career members of the civil rights division voted virtually unanimously that the decision by the Georgia legislature to require a [voter] identification card that could be used as a driver's license, and that could be obtained only in certain locations, and that voters would have to pay for, would be in effect a poll tax on the voters of Georgia. This was in spite of the fact that there were some provisions in the legislation that said that if the individuals could demonstrate financial hardship, there would be a program to help them.

The career attorneys in the Justice Department stated that this was illegal because it would re-establish a poll tax, and the ruling was virtually unanimous. But the political operatives in the Justice Department overrode that and

---

35. The question in the debate over the public accommodations provision of the 1964 Civil Rights Act was would the owner of a private home, who took in renters, be covered by the anti-discrimination law in the same way as a hotel or motel would be? The answer was no. The shorthand reference to such a private home was "Mrs. O'Leary's house."

stamped their approval on it, and sent it out as approved. That Georgia position was rejected by the [Fifth] Circuit [US Court of Appeals].

In a similar case, Tom DeLay,[36] who has been dismissed from his office in the Congress for [election law] irregularities, was very much involved in drafting a redistricting of Congressional districts in Texas. Again, the career officers in the Justice Department's Civil Rights Division unanimously rejected that as violating the Equal Protection clause—and, I imagine, the one man, one vote . . . decisions—and it was virtually unanimous. The political operatives said it was satisfactory.

I want to get this correct. There's no question that the career attorneys in the civil rights division of the Justice Department were overturned in the Georgia case and in the Texas case. In the Texas case, the Supreme Court, in a 5-4 decision, upheld a good part of the redistricting but struck down one area dealing with the representation of Hispanics in the western part of the state, Congressman Bonilla's[37] district. The basic issue is the fact that it isn't the career jurists who are making the judgments. It's the political operatives in the Justice Department, and in some instances, it's the courts that are upholding.

I think, finally, as we leave this area, the one issue that still resonates in my ear—and I think the country's ear—is what happened in Florida in the [2000] presidential campaign and *Bush v. Gore*. I think history, when the final chapter is written on the 5-4 Supreme Court decision, will find that the politics of the Supreme Court, rather than the legal issues, held sway, and I think that's going to be reflected in the final history as written. Clearly, in the Florida situation, unfortunately Jim Baker was a stronger figure than Warren Christopher in terms of the internal fighting and discussion of the Florida case.[38]

As we wind up this section, we now have come full circle. [T]he noble aspirations and work of those extraordinary men of the Fifth Circuit[39] opened up the pathway for progress for this country by interpreting the Constitution. The courts were the backbone of this whole march for progress, up to the example, I suppose, reflected in the Supreme Court decision in the *Bush v. Gore*. Today in the Justice Department politics has taken over regarding judgments, decisions, and interpretations of law. The courts themselves have been so programmed that politics has emerged as the dominant force, rather than the true

---

36. Congressman Tom DeLay, a Texas Republican, was the majority leader in the House of Representatives.

37. Henry Bonilla was a Republican congressman from Texas.

38. Former secretary of state James Baker III led the George W. Bush legal team to victory over Vice President Al Gore's attorneys, directed by former secretary of state Warren Christopher.

39. The Fifth Circuit US Court of Appeals was located in the southern states during the civil rights movement, and many of its heroic judges issued rulings expanding civil rights and liberties.

meaning of the Constitution, and that is something that this country is going to have to deal with.

The bigger picture is something that most of the people aren't thinking about. They don't realize how much we have done. I think we were the revolutionary society. You look at—India has been a democracy. They still have the Dalits.[40] That's 140 million people there who still are cleaning sewers, and they've never emerged out. I mean, we've done it on race; we've done it on gender; we've done it on disability. We're halfway there in terms of people who are gay—you know, that's a generational thing the next generation's going to do. We did it on immigration. It's been remarkable, historical. There won't be a country in the world that has ever made the progress that we've made in nonviolent ways on that part. We had to confront it at some time and we did, but then the question is, are we going to deal with the new challenge, which is globalization?

Perspectives

Archbishop Desmond Tutu, South African anti-apartheid activist and 1984 Nobel Peace Prize winner: At a lunch [in 1984], I think we talked about Robert Kennedy's 1966 visit [to South Africa] and the incredible impact that had made. One of the major newspapers—it doesn't exist any longer, it was killed off by apartheid—the *Rand Daily Mail* characterized it as a gust of fresh air into a room that is closed and dank. I think I was with the members of the family, Ted's family, probably Ethel, and said it would be a good thing for a return visit of the Kennedys to South Africa because it was so crucial to keep the apartheid situation on the agenda of the world, and especially the United States because the Reagan administration had this policy of constructive engagement and they were very firmly set against the sanctions.

Of course I did this on my own lonesome, not having consulted anybody. When I went back home, Dr. Allan Boesak, who, as you know, was in the forefront of the struggle, concurred with me, but I wasn't smart then and didn't maybe consult sufficiently around. So when [Senator Kennedy] arrived in January, AZAPO, the Azanian People's Organization, which at the time was very virulently anti-American and anti-capitalism, were opposed to this visit. They had this demonstration at the airport, about forty of them, but there was clearly a kind of collusion between them and the apartheid authorities because this was grist to their mill that there should be these differences between us.

Of course Ted was not exactly a blue-eyed boy with them and so any embarrassment that happened to him would be one in the eye for him and something that they could celebrate. So they would allow—generally you were not allowed to have demonstrations in the airport, but they would allow it, and

---

40. Dalits are the "untouchable" castes in India.

the media had a field day. [*Laughter*] There was a wonderful contrast because his first night in South Africa he spent in a black township, as they were in Soweto. Quite unusual and in fact it was breaking the law for him to do that. There was a very warm reception for him. There were about five hundred or so people with candlelight.

Q: *Father, could you talk a little bit about the impact that the visit had, both within South Africa and perhaps in the international community?*

Tutu: Well, there was a lot of coverage, especially I think the sort of negative aspect of having a group that was opposing him. But there was no question at all about the fact that it kept the South African issue alive in the international community. The fact that so many of the blacks received him warmly was saying that for us it was a crucial symbol of the fact that the world had not forgotten us, and that we had significant allies such as he. One can't obviously compute what effect it had on our morale. I mean, I couldn't say to you that we were at that level and then after his visit—but it was a very significant boost for our morale, especially at a time when there was President Reagan, there was Mrs. Thatcher, who were very clearly firmly set against sanctions. They were supporting the apartheid dispensation, and many of the foreign companies were as well.

Robert Bates, Edward Kennedy's staffer: I also went on a trip with Bob Hunter, who was Kennedy's foreign policy guy. He and I went on a trip, just the two of us, to South Africa. We were met at the airport, and we had a little press conference. I was the militant one. Bob was scholarly and diplomatic. I was going to change apartheid. He was educated at the London School of Economics, PhD, very erudite, a very smooth guy. After this interview, he said, "Now, Bob, when you're in a host country, you must be courteous. You don't go into a country and talk about their policies like that. You have to recognize—" So we were there maybe four days. When we got ready to leave, they had another press conference at the airport. I had to tone *him* down. After having been there for four days and his seeing what the conditions actually were, he became the militant one. He said he had been to Russia and had seen conditions there, and he complained that South Africa was much worse than Russia.

Carolyn Osolinik, Edward Kennedy's staffer:
Q: *What was the biggest disappointment you think he had?*

Osolinik: The amount of time it took to overturn the *Grove City College* decision was a very big disappointment. He was disappointed about some of the compromises that were made with respect to gender discrimination in the Civil Rights Act of 1990. It was something that had the potential to divide the civil rights community, because that was something of an omnibus bill. There was, of course, a concern that it was in some ways a zero-sum game, and if

Senator Kennedy held fast on one issue, he was going to have to find somewhere else to compromise. It was those kinds of things.

Sheila Burke, Senator Robert Dole (R-KS)'s chief of staff: [Regarding the Americans with Disabilities Act,] Dole's view is you have to give people the right tools, and you have to give them an environment in which they can function. Most people want to become productive human beings. I think that's how he approached that question. His was perhaps a little more skeptical view of these issues but at the end of the day, he wanted to do the right thing. So it was a combination of Kennedy instinctively wanting to help the population and Dole's somewhat more jaded view of some of these issues that combined to find a middle ground.

Q: Kennedy didn't start out with a track record—and you didn't either—with the disability community. . . . At what point did he get to the point of being their main person?

Osolinik: By the time the new Congress started. Very quickly . . . [h]e was recruited by the disability community to become part of the leadership of this. The reason he was recruited was because he was so effective—so effective in the arena of civil rights. Although this was a very different subject, and a very complicated subject, he had an outstanding, proven track record, he had the seniority, and he had the passion. The disability community was not . . . nearly as sophisticated as the other civil rights communities at that point. There was an education process going on within that community about what was doable and what made sense and was why Kennedy's judgment was so valuable. You could take it to the bank. If he thought he could do it, he'd do it. The decisions he was making were strategic and tactical decisions to get this done.

Anthony S. Fauci, AIDS researcher and director of the National Institute of Allergy and Infectious Diseases: So [AIDS] started to become a social issue in the United States, because gay men were frightened. They didn't feel anyone cared about them. They felt that the government wasn't doing enough. I think that was the theme that brought Kennedy in, that the government needs to be doing more. What are we doing? Are we doing everything that we possibly can do? And that was in two arenas. One was getting enough resources for research and health-associated issues. Then as the first drugs started to come about, with AZT,[41] which was the first approved drug, back in 1987, I believe that's when the Kennedy connection was starting to really be felt, because he wanted fair and equitable treatment for people who could not have access to clinical trials. Clinical trials were very restricted.

---

41. The AIDS drug azidothymidine.

Laurence Tribe, Harvard law professor and Edward Kennedy's advisor:

Q: Have you seen an evolution in him, in these core values?

Tribe: I don't know for sure. I've sensed more constancy than evolution. For example, on some issue like gay rights—I imagine but I don't know for sure that he had a harder time with that earlier and probably is much more comfortable with it now, but I simply extrapolate that from what I know of his character. I can't say that I've observed it myself over time.

Q: But I'd say there are a couple of them on which that observation might be relevant. One of them is equality for women, because he came later to a support for the ERA.

Tribe: That's right, but it was clear that the support was absolutely deep. And reproductive rights as well. . . . He fought with Eunice enormously over that. I was there during a lot of their fights. He would humor her in various ways, and he would turn it into a source of some kind of family joke. "Oh, Euni, you're always saying that," or something like that. She was very much against *Roe v. Wade* fundamentally, and he was always for it. I say always for it, but I don't know how he felt in '73. I hadn't met him yet.

Q: There are those who would say that was one that, as a Catholic, he had to—

Tribe: Struggle with.

Q: Struggle with, yes, but once he got to the point that he did, then, as you described it, it fit within that core constitutional value.

Tribe: Right. And it wasn't an awkward fit when you think about it. Pushing against the grain of family is a hard thing for him, and certainly his mother and his sister. Sarge [Shriver] actually was pretty helpful in that respect, because he also had a difficult time, to some extent, with things like *Roe v. Wade*. He concluded it really should be up to the woman, and when he did he was very strong about that.

6

From Hawk to Dove: The Vietnam Dilemma

Like many Americans, Senator Edward Kennedy initially did not oppose the war in Vietnam. He supported President Kennedy's policies to increase the flow of aid and military advisors to the region. Following his brother's lead, and the consensus among both Democrats and Republicans during the Cold War, the senator believed it was necessary to take a strong stand against communism's spread. He continued to support such policies when Lyndon Johnson assumed the presidency upon JFK's assassination. Senator Kennedy agreed with the 1964 Tonkin Gulf resolution, which escalated America's role in the conflict. (Recovering from his near fatal plane crash that summer, however, he was not present to cast a vote on the measure. Yet in a recorded phone conversation, Kennedy told LBJ that he supported the resolution.)

Returning to Capitol Hill in early 1965, he began to focus on refugee issues, arguing that neither the US nor Vietnamese governments had a plan to deal with the people displaced by the war. As chairman of the subcommittee on refugees, in 1965 Kennedy participated in an inspection tour of Vietnam organized by the US military, where he received encouraging reports on refugee issues.

Kennedy subsequently learned that the US military had intentionally misled him during his refugee tour. In 1966, he wrote his first critical statement on Vietnam, marking the beginning of his transition from hawk to dove. One of Kennedy's main concerns regarding Vietnam dealt with the war's impact on the American people. Kennedy knew firsthand the high costs of war, having lost his oldest brother, Joseph P. Kennedy Jr., in World War II. He was particularly troubled by the unfairness of the draft system, which drew disproportionately from the poor and the African American community. In addition to refugee issues, Kennedy began to fight for draft reform and, later, to lower the voting age so that those subject to the draft at age eighteen could also vote on the very policies affecting their lives.

Kennedy's opposition to the war increased after he organized his own inspection tour in January 1968, where he witnessed rampant corruption within the South Vietnamese government. He grew increasingly disillusioned with President Johnson's reports on the war and questioned their accuracy. As Senator Robert Kennedy was moving closer to challenging President Johnson for the 1968 Democratic presidential

nomination, Edward Kennedy became a national leader in the antiwar movement.
After Bobby's death, in June 1968, Teddy continued their work, calling on the Johnson
and then the Nixon administrations to stop the bombing campaign and to refocus the
peace talks on US withdrawal from South Vietnam.

EMK: We had an evening with the French writer who wrote the books on Vietnam, Bernard Fall. He was a very important French writer. And he asked me to come over for dinner at his place because he had been over. I went over [to Vietnam in 1965]. He asked about my impressions, and I said, "I think it's going reasonably well. Inflation is getting under control." "Oh," he said, "inflation is getting under control? Well, where did you go?" "We went to Hue." "Oh, you did. And inflation is getting under control?" "Yes." "Where in Hue?" "Well, I have my notes right here. Let me tell you where."

He said, "Well, let me just"— and he'd go up to the shelf and pull out a book, which was the USAID[1] book. He'd open it up to Hue, and you'd get the pounds of rice and what the rice was in Hue, and what the rice was in this town. It showed that it had gone up 600 percent in the last seven months. So he said, "So do you think they're pacifying that road? Do you think they're getting through? Why do you think it's gone up 600 percent?"

He did that just using American information from American documents that undermined all of the part about inflation and about what was happening, the indicators we had had and all the rest. I was saying "my goodness" to this, but this really happened.

I think one of the people thinking a lot about that had been Frank Church.[2] He had been one of the real early doubters [about American Vietnam policy]. But whoom! That really took me—I read everything after that with a great deal more care and concern.

I believe it was 1966 when I went to the University of Wisconsin to speak for both Gaylord Nelson—who was moving towards an antiwar position but hadn't declared it—and Pat Lucey,[3] who had been very involved with my brother's [1960 presidential] campaign. We were at the University of Wisconsin. We went into this big hall, and in the back of the hall were these white sheets with skeletons drawn, dead people, all done in charcoal, graphic—almost ghoulish, but not ghoulish. There were also marks of explosions—big white sheets with black charcoal or black paint on them all across this back wall, and probably three thousand students. We had Gaylord Nelson, who was a very eloquent and capable speaker, a very knowledgeable person, especially on the

---

1. United States Agency for International Development.
2. Senator Frank Church was an Idaho Democrat.
3. Senator Gaylord Nelson and Lieutenant Governor Pat Lucey were Wisconsin Democrats.

environment, a very tough, smart person. And Pat Lucey was an extraordinary politician and a former state chairman. He was good on his feet.

I was the first one to get up and speak, and there was a roar in the crowd as I started speaking. There was a lot of disturbance, disturbance, disturbance. I asked if they were going to let me speak. "No, no." Then a lot of chanting started against the war, and it just intensified. I finally said, "I'll let one of you come up. I'll listen to you speak, and then you listen to me." One of them finally said okay. Up comes this fellow named Schultz. I can still remember. He was from New York City, and he got up at that podium, and he gave a talk and a half for about seven minutes about the war, antiwar. The place just cheered and went bananas for this fellow—emotion and feeling ran high in that place. Then he stopped, and he got the roaring, roaring, roaring approval of the students.

So I said, "You can keep going. Keep going." He mentioned a couple of other facts, and then he stopped. I said, "Keep going. This is a major issue. Keep going." And he said, "I don't have anything more to say." "You don't have anything more to say? That's all you had to say?" Then the crowd started getting mad at me for trying to keep after this guy. But he just ran flat out of gas. He went on dead empty.

So he left, and then they let me talk for the same period of time, eight minutes I think it was. I talked generally about Vietnam—I was critical. We hadn't gotten to the point of the exit strategy at that time; it was the following year. I was looking around for Nelson and Lucey to come on up—their home state—and take over, which they never did. At the end of my talk, the authorities and the police came in and took us all out. They never let them speak because they were worried about violence on the campus.

Now Madison, Wisconsin, is known to be a very high-powered place. I went up there in 1980 and tried to finish a speech. Because we had re-codified the criminal code and restated what the Supreme Court had said—that you can have demonstrations up to within five hundred feet of the courthouse, but you can have only *silent* demonstrations between five hundred feet and the courthouse—they thought that I was taking away the First Amendment right to demonstrate. They thought this was a limitation on the right to gather. They wouldn't let me finish speaking up there. When I was campaigning for John Kerry [in 2004], I said that the first time [in 1966] they let me finish. [*Laughter*] It's a lot quieter on campus now.

We'd seen this in Illinois. We saw it in Wisconsin and other communities, but not with the intensity and not as dramatically as in those meetings. What they were saying, the message that we brought back, is that there was something very important happening in the country in 1966.

Q: *What was your public position at that time, and why were they going after you?*

EMK: They were going after anybody who wasn't for getting out of Vietnam and getting out then. There probably were a couple of members of Congress like Charlie Porter[4] from Oregon, and one or two others. In 1962 Stuart Hughes ran for the Senate [as an Independent against Kennedy], and we had lost thirteen people, and he was against going into the war [in Vietnam]. So there had been this latent group, and I think the '66 [midterm congressional] campaign showed its power, certainly to me. It was evident, and it was out there. We were for stopping the bombing [of North Vietnam], which was considered to be a major step forward, to see if we could get some corresponding action.

We'll have to get the series of speeches out to look at the progress and movement—but we were as far out as any—with the exception of Morse and Gruening,[5] who had been against the war. I don't know whether they were talking about solutions to it, but the halting of the bombing was probably the most out there. But as far out as we were—and we were considered to be far out—the population, the people, had gone right by us.

I think '67 was the year when a number of politicians, including my brother [Bobby] and me, made that transition. So the seeds of doubt had been planted in my mind during that time. I think Frank Church was a prominent antiwar activist, even in the early, mid-sixties. And he was a good friend, particularly to me. I traveled with him in West Africa before I came to the Senate. He had been a supporter of my brother's [Jack]. He befriended me when I came in. He was a very able, gifted person. And he'd been working with me and others on the war issue. So that had been going on for a period of years before.

The people who were showing up at these rallies [in 1966] were making it clear with their demonstrations about war policy. They were raising it with banners, shouts, petitions, whatever. I don't remember them stopping us from speaking, but that was the first place that I saw, in a very determined way, the fissures and divisions that existed in the crowd. Many people in Illinois provided the traditional Democratic support, historic support, the great respect they had for Paul.[6] But there was another group out there that might have—probably did—shout at him or heckle him about the war. Me less so, but I certainly was a part of the whole thing. I picked up the vibes, certainly, during that time. And Douglas lost [his 1966 re-election race]. I think a good part of that loss was because of the Democrats who stayed home. There were other complicating factors in this, but that was certainly a major contributor.

Senator Kennedy commented on the impact of what were known as the Fulbright hearings, named for William Fulbright, the Democratic chairman of the Senate Foreign Relations Committee. The hearings, which ran between 1966 and 1971,

---

4. Charlie Porter was a Democratic congressman.
5. Senators Wayne Morse and Ernest Gruening were Democrats from Oregon and Alaska, respectively.
6. Senator Paul Douglas was a Democrat from Illinois.

investigated the Vietnam War and turned many senators against American involvement in Southeast Asia.

EMK: I think those hearings had started at some time, and they were continuing and playing along. I can't put an exact date on this, but they were having, clearly, some impact. I believe they started just after the '66 elections. Maybe they had them before; I don't remember. But they clearly had an impact here in the Senate. One of the people who moved rather dramatically—this is an interesting story, . . . Stu Symington, who had been a successful businessman, a successful politician, the secretary of the Air Force. He started as a strong hawk and then transitioned into strong antiwar, but that was later.

There were a series of senators and a series of changes [in their positions on Vietnam] over the historical timeframe. I know that for Bobby it was '67, and I did something after that. I spent a good deal of my time and effort with regard to refugees and the humanitarian aspects of the war. Most of my speeches were about what was happening to the people, and the failure to take care of the refugees, the creation of the war refugees and the free-fire zones, the bombings of villages where people had no idea they were going to be bombed.

Q: You went [to Vietnam] *again in January of '68?*

EMK: That's right. That one was completely on refugees. Five or six people went over beforehand and set it up, advanced it, so that we weren't going to be dependent upon the military to do it. The first time I went over there, I became acquainted with a fellow named Dr. Durant, who eventually went back to Mass General Hospital and organized all of their humanitarian programs. Mass General sends out these medical teams. They did it in Vietnam, they've done it in Darfur, and they've done it in Iraq. They organize a very highly specialized group who go for eighteen days, and they work twenty hours a day until they're exhausted; then they ship them back. Durant was the one who got me interested in the refugees and what was happening to the people over there. I stayed in very close contact during the first trip, all the way through the second trip, and I did subsequently on other humanitarian issues. He was the one who really got me interested in the human aspects of this terrible tragedy, and the extraordinary loss in human life and the suffering that was taking place in the population.

Q: When you came back in January of '68 from your trip to Vietnam, you gave a very strong speech or statement. It was on Face the Nation, *and you were speaking not just about the refugee problem, the killing and the human cost to the Vietnamese, but you were also talking about the corruption of the regime. You were quoted as saying, "Our message to them ought to be 'Shape up, or we'll ship out.'" Was that in your mind when you went to Vietnam? Did you see evidence of that corruption there or was it in the general knowledge of the situation?*

EMK: I think it was general knowledge, as you learn, but once you see it and experience it, it has real meaning. I was always concerned that an awful lot of the refugees—not all, but a lot of the refugees who got out—were people who had the contacts and had the money. And the people who had been the most loyal to the CIA and to the military got left there. I was for the refugees coming here, but I was not one waving the flag on that. I was following when those people were getting out of those forced camps. I don't know what they called them. They were effectively concentration camps.

A lot of them wanted to come here, but we had gotten tired of taking in Vietnamese, and I made special efforts to look after those individuals who had been great friends to the United States and had been working and had risked the most and didn't take part in the corruption and who were the ones at greatest risk. That's an incidental aspect of it, but that was something we followed closely for a long, long time because of this problem.

Senator Kennedy turned to the story of his brother Bobby's evolution on the Vietnam War policy.

EMK: I think history—and reality—would show that through '67, with the increase in losses and the increased futility of a military solution, there were increasing questions about how we were going to change the policy. Even with the Fulbright hearings, it didn't appear that there were going to be the votes in the Congress to change it. The only place it was going to be changed was the executive branch. It was about this time, '67 or so, that there were a series of polls taken by different national organizations that showed Bobby in a strong position, even ahead of LBJ for the Democratic nomination, which is very heady stuff. He made his speech, I believe, in February of '67, his tough speech about getting out, and Hubert[7] responded, "That's like putting a fox in the chicken coop," almost questioning [Bobby's] patriotism [for his suggestion that a coalition government in South Vietnam include the Viet Cong].

So [Bobby] was increasingly campaigning on that issue and about the withdrawal, and that became something central in terms of his life and his politics. At the same time, it was becoming increasingly apparent that President Johnson was wounded by this war, and the political landscape was very unsettled. Around this time, my brother Bob used to go over on Saturday mornings and meet with Bob McNamara.[8] He had a long series of meetings with McNamara, and McNamara was very candid and very honest and very frank. There's no question that Bobby had a very important impact on McNamara, and McNamara, on the other hand, had a very important impact on Bobby.

---

7. Hubert Humphrey was now vice president in the Johnson administration and supported LBJ's Vietnam policy.

8. Robert McNamara had been secretary of defense in the Kennedy administration and remained in the Johnson cabinet after JFK's assassination. He became head of the World Bank in November 1967.

And these were never really reported. Subsequently, LBJ moved McNamara over to the World Bank.

[Bobby] began to pick up these wisps directly from McNamara and the generals. McNamara was beginning to have very serious second thoughts [about Vietnam], but was unwilling or unable—or both—to be able to change it. I think talking to McNamara deepened Bobby's concern.

Q: *Would that have been as early as '67?*

EMK: Yes, because he was removed in '67.

Q: *They had known each other, of course. He was in Kennedy's administration.*

EMK: Yes.

Q: *So they had a relationship?*

EMK: They had a very strong relationship. Bobby was very high on McNamara and liked him, and liked Maggie.[9] They skied together out West; they had social contact. He was a friend and somebody Bobby had a strong relationship with and had, as I mentioned, these conversations. During this period—now we're talking '67, mid- to late '67—he had made the talk in February about an exit strategy over there, and he had been criticized by Humphrey and labor. They were strongly supportive of the war, very strong. Meany[10] was very strong, and this caused tensions between labor and Bobby. They already had some tensions from past investigations.

Perspectives

Senator Kennedy's friend, John Culver, commented on their initial support of US involvement in Vietnam.

Senator John Culver (D-IA): I think we were all of a persuasion that we weren't the French; we weren't there [in Vietnam] for the same reasons the French were there. We were there for the right reasons. We were there to give these people a choice and a hope. Also, with our power at that time—massive, overwhelming military strength and power—it was inconceivable to appreciate the limitations of America. But in that environment, that context, as we've all learned, you're a crippled giant in many ways.

David Burke, Edward Kennedy's staffer: When I first met [Edward Kennedy] in 1965, in the office around me, there was really no discussion of Vietnam. He was—hawk is too strong a word. Disinterest may be a more appropriate one, because when you think, in his lifetime there had been World War II and Korea, where no one said a word of opposition to anything. The experience of

---

9. Maggie was Robert McNamara's wife.
10. George Meany was president of the AFL-CIO.

people of that generation was if you are opposed to your government when American soldiers are at war, that's pretty cuckoo.

Senator John Tunney (D-CA), Edward Kennedy's University of Virginia Law School classmate and friend: The first trip [with Kennedy to Vietnam in 1965] was when we were surrounded by officialdom. We were constantly being fed information by these officials, and they gave us input that we took back home, which was just dead wrong. Dead wrong. I mean, it was what I guess they hoped that they would accomplish. But it didn't take us all that long, after we had gotten back home, before some fissures began to show up in the edifice of propaganda that they had surrounded us with. So we began, tentatively at first, but gradually over a period of time, a period of months, we began to move away from that position.

Kennedy came to change his position toward US involvement in Vietnam.
    Burke: [Kennedy's advance man during his second 1968 inspection tour] would take us right up to the head of the hospital and right to the nun who was running the infirmary for the kids and so forth. And it was awful. It was an awful trip because we saw things that you shouldn't see. Napalm burns on a child. Bones—arms frozen to the side of the body by the melted skin. Just horrible things that you don't want to see and we are dropping tons—Bernard was right, Bernard Fall—tons of technology on human beings in diapers who had done nothing to us. . . . When [Kennedy] came back, his mind was clearly made up and he had no fear about stating it because "I've been there and you haven't," and it was a wonderful underwriting insurance policy. "I've been there and I've seen it. . . ." So he wasn't just a fresh senator any longer. He was rather an expert in this.

The Vietnam War draft prompted Bobby and Teddy Kennedy to advocate changing the voting age to eighteen.
    Carey Parker, Kennedy staffer: The Vietnam debate was at the heart of the issue. The argument was, "Old enough to fight, old enough to vote. If we can send your son to Vietnam, why can't he vote on what our policy should be?" That argument was resonating particularly with Democrats and even with a lot of Republicans. But it turned out that as we were beginning to make headway on the issue, resistance was developing among key House Democrats who were worried about adding eighteen-year-old voters to their constituencies, and it became a serious political issue, a serious problem.

One of the enduring "what ifs" in American history is how things might have been different, particularly on Vietnam policy, had President Kennedy not been assassinated.

Senator George McGovern (D-SD): Jack made a speech[11] in September before he died and said, "In the final analysis it's their war. They're the ones
who will win or lose it. We can send our men out there, we can send advisors,
but only Vietnam can resolve this conflict." That was an indication, I thought,
that he might put the brakes on if he had been re-elected [in 1964] and try
to see if something could be worked out to justify our disengagement. That's
about the only concrete thing. If he had seen that every time the army asked
him for more troops, he granted it, and we were getting nowhere, I think that
he would have had more confidence in his own judgment and would have
balked at some point. And he might even have balked on the bombing of
North Vietnam after the My Lai massacre, things like that. By then, you know,
Bob and Ted were dissenting from the war. Whether they would have if Jack
were in the White House, I don't know.

---

11. Actually McGovern is referring to an interview that President Kennedy gave to CBS
news anchorman Walter Cronkite, on Labor Day weekend of 1963, to mark expansion of the
network's evening news program from fifteen to thirty minutes.

7

Trying to Restore Camelot: Bobby's Last Campaign and Its Aftermath

As both brothers anguished about Vietnam, Bobby wrestled with his conscience over whether to toss his hat into the presidential ring for the 1968 Democratic nomination. His brother thought 1972—after President Johnson completed a presumed second term—would be a more propitious year for RFK to unite the Democratic Party and reclaim the White House for the Kennedy family. But by March 1968, Senator Eugene McCarthy, with his antiwar platform, had revealed President Johnson's vulnerability in the New Hampshire primary, coming within seven points of defeating the incumbent.

The Kennedys and their faithful advisors gathered for strategy sessions at Bobby's fabled estate, Hickory Hill, in northern Virginia, and at the home of Jean and Steve Smith in New York. In addition to his growing opposition to the Vietnam War, Robert Kennedy wanted to make urban and rural poverty a centerpiece of his platform. In the "guns vs. butter" debate, guns to fight the war were winning, and the Kennedy brothers believed that JFK's legacy and Johnson's Great Society were the losers. Bobby sent Teddy to Wisconsin on a mission to ask McCarthy to include poverty issues in his candidacy. If McCarthy would agree to do so, RFK would reconsider joining the race. But the Minnesota senator was "completely uninterested," according to Teddy. Believing he could delay no longer, on March 16, 1968, Robert Kennedy announced his candidacy in the Old Senate Office Building Caucus Room, where JFK had made his announcement eight years earlier.[1]

The Kennedy clan once again dispersed across the country to campaign for the presidency, this time focusing on primaries in Indiana, Nebraska, Oregon, South Dakota,

---

1. After Edward Kennedy's 2009 death, the Senate named the historic chamber the Kennedy Caucus Room in honor of Jack, Bobby, and Teddy—the only three brothers to serve in Congress's upper house.

and California. Teddy worked especially hard for his brother in the Hoosier state, to get the campaign rolling, and then moved on to California, where the Democrats' winner-take-all delegate rule made it a crucial state, especially after Bobby suffered the first-ever Kennedy election defeat, at the hands of Oregon voters.

Bobby's assassination, after he declared victory in Los Angeles that June, devastated the sole surviving son of Joe and Rose Kennedy. As the family matriarch later wrote, "It seemed impossible that the same kind of disaster could befall our family twice in five years. If I had read it in fiction, I would have said it was incredible."² Teddy pondered the unimaginable scenario that at the very time he had become close to his father, Jack, and Bobby, as a full-fledged member of the quartet, each had disappeared from his life, leaving him utterly isolated.

New burdens now descended on Teddy. He became a surrogate father to Jack's and Bobby's thirteen children, in addition to looking after his own three, Kara, Teddy Jr., and Patrick. The senator buckled under the strain. He had always been the family jester and foil, not the keeper of the family image. He tried to brighten his parents' lives but disappeared into his own grief when he was not with them. Nighttime sailing trips from Hyannis Port to Maine, guided by the North Star, salved his torment. Yet an assassination nightmare haunted him, and he drowned his sorrows in alcohol. Rumors of his womanizing circulated in the tabloids.

In July 1969 Teddy retreated to Martha's Vineyard for the annual Edgartown sailing regatta and a nostalgic party for several women who had labored in Bobby's ill-fated 1968 campaign. They gathered in a cottage on Chappaquiddick, the tiny island across a narrow channel from the Vineyard. Teddy contributed a trunkful of spirits and beer to the summer feast. He was genuinely grateful to the women for their loyal support in past Kennedy campaigns and knew that they would follow him into battle for the 1972 Democratic presidential nomination, should he run. Yet these gatherings were bittersweet, evoking memories of his departed brother.

Late in the evening, Teddy left the party with one of the women, Mary Jo Kopechne. No one will ever know the exact circumstances surrounding the accident at Chappaquiddick's narrow Dike Bridge. With no guardrails to guide the senator's sedan, his car plunged over the side, into a swirling inlet, landing on its roof in pitch-black water. Teddy testified that he managed somehow to escape the submerged car and tried unsuccessfully to rescue Mary Jo. The official cause of death was drowning, but the diver who recovered her body the next morning believed she suffocated after depleting an air pocket. With her went Kennedy's presidential aspirations. Even worse, he failed to report the accident to authorities. Attempting to wish away the horror as he swam back to Edgartown, Teddy testified, he collapsed in his hotel room and did not tell police until the next morning, after consulting with family advisors.

---

2. As quoted in Barbara A. Perry, *Rose Kennedy: The Life and Times of a Political Matriarch* (New York: W. W. Norton, 2013), 295.

"Chappaquiddick," the one-word code for Edward Kennedy's personal and polit-
ical fall from grace, haunted him for the rest of his life. Still, he clung to his Senate
seat, after Massachusetts voters responded 10-to-1 in favor of keeping him in office.
Nevertheless, in 1971 he lost his Senate leadership position, as majority whip, which
he had held for two years.

Senator Kennedy sat out the 1972 presidential race. Chappaquiddick remained
too close in time, and his family worried about his safety. In 1973, twelve-year-old
Teddy Jr. underwent surgery to remove his cancerous right leg and endured two years
of debilitating chemotherapy. His father stayed by the boy's side during much of the
ordeal—an experience that prompted the public policy battle of his life to expand
health coverage for all Americans.

In contemplating the lead-up to the tragedies of 1968 and 1969, Senator Kennedy
remembered how he seemed to be recovering from the shock of JFK's assassination four
years after the terrible events in Dallas.

EMK: I think this was a very hopeful period for me. Patrick was born in 1967, and I remember this as being a positive period, a more hopeful period. We were sort of trying to get 1963 further behind. Things were coming together, our lives. I think I talked with you earlier about the course of my faith during this period of time. It was still present, expansive to some degree, and grew.

You had the polls going up, the polls going down [for Bobby]. There was the Manchester affair, the book written by Bill Manchester, and Bobby's interventions on behalf of Jackie, which was very public and costly to him. People viewed him as trying to censor the work of a distinguished writer.[3] Nonetheless, by the end of the year he was moving back up again.

And then you have somewhere in the middle of the year—I don't know, maybe it was earlier—the idea from other people of a challenge to LBJ, a series of different people who would come in and talk to Bobby about the possibility of running. Al Lowenstein[4] was one. And some others.

---

3. Bobby and Jackie Kennedy enlisted historian William Manchester, who had published a glowing account of JFK's early presidency (*Portrait of a President*), to write the authorized account of the assassination. Mrs. Kennedy subsequently disapproved of some passages in the manuscript for *Death of a President*, believing that they violated her and her children's privacy and revealed too much about the Kennedy family's conflicts with President Johnson. When Manchester refused to delete the segments she found objectionable, Mrs. Kennedy sued him. Ultimately, she dropped the suit when the author agreed in a settlement to delete portions of the manuscript and to turn over to the Kennedy Presidential Library most of the considerable revenue earned through serialization of the book.

4. Allard K. Lowenstein was a Democratic lawyer, politician, and activist, who helped Robert Kennedy write one of his most notable speeches, advocating an end to apartheid, delivered in South African during RFK's 1966 visit there. As a vehement opponent of the Vietnam War, Lowenstein started urging Bobby in 1967 to oppose Lyndon Johnson and run for president.

Q: And Jesse Unruh,[5] apparently, about the same time as Lowenstein, was in talking with him about that. When do you think these feelings about policy began to gel—in your mind or in your observation or in your brother's mind—into a view of a political movement or a political move to unseat LBJ or to run against him?

EMK: It's difficult to put a time. There was the obvious background on Bobby and LBJ. It was tense right from the beginning. To my knowledge, he never spent a lot of time worrying about the relationship. He just didn't have it, and he had other things to do. President Johnson wanted to have a good working relationship. He worked at it with President Kennedy, and he did with me. He was always attentive, willing to talk or having meetings on a lot of the things that we were working on, textiles and shoes. I'd go down with other people, and he'd always pull me aside and ask about the family.

As this whole war issue developed both in intensity and emotion, my brother Bob, probably earlier than '67, took a trip over to France. He had a meeting with some dissidents and came back and had a meeting with President Johnson. There was a lot of hostile reporting about those meetings. Both of them were very edgy about it and looking out after their own positions.

But when he came back, Bobby said to Lyndon, "Look, if you want to appoint me to be the ambassador over there, I'd be glad to do that," which was extraordinary. All of us were very surprised that he would do it. But he felt that intensely about it, and he thought that that might have one attraction: you get rid of Bobby. John Kennedy had been involved in getting into the war; let Bobby get us out. You could, after a period of time, cut some slack on that kind of thing. Gets rid of him before the other—

I never understood the creative thinking that Bobby had as a political leader. That was an ingenious thought. I think I mentioned before that he was the one who—when he saw the ambassador from Algeria among a lot of ambassadors—asked the Algerians to help get Gary Powers out.[6] He was a very creative political thinker. He thought in very large terms. President Johnson thought [Bobby's idea to become ambassador to France] was some kind of a trap. They hadn't really gotten started on this [idea].

Q: There was no talk about Paris negotiating—

EMK: No, there wasn't, although Bobby had met over in Paris with French diplomats who were in touch with the North Vietnamese. He thought that there might have been some possibilities, but the negotiations that we were used to were the Kissinger negotiations that came much later.[7] [Bobby] thought

---

5. Jesse Unruh was a Democratic political leader in California.

6. Francis Gary Powers was an American CIA pilot shot down by the Soviets while flying a spy mission over the USSR in 1960. The international incident sparked increased Cold War tensions. In 1962 the United States exchanged a captured KGB spy for Powers.

7. Under the Nixon administration, National Security Advisor and Secretary of State Henry Kissinger led peace negotiations with the North Vietnamese in Paris.

that there were some possibilities [earlier]. I don't know whether he was right. But in any event, this is intensifying now [in 1967]. He's not running [for president]—we've had meetings about it, and there are conversations about it.

Q: *There was a meeting on October 8, 1967. If I remember correctly, Pierre Salinger[8] had suggested this.*

EMK: Yes.

Q: *And this is the first evidence we have in the record of a meeting with a number of different people about what to do.*

EMK: Prior to that, individuals had talked to him, but this was really the first meeting of people that reflected the thinking of some of those who had talked to him, plus very close political supporters. Pierre Salinger obviously had worked with Bob. Chuck Daly and Ted Sorensen had been in the White House. Dick Goodwin had been in the White House and had started in the '60 campaign. Kenny was very close to Bobby. Bobby knew Ivan Nestigan[9] from the '60 campaign in Wisconsin. He'd been a very strong mayor for Jack. Steve Smith, my brother-in-law. Joe Dolan, who was his administrative assistant, from Colorado. Fred Dutton, who spent a lot of time on Bobby's campaign, had been in the White House, and was a very shrewd, good, political person. And [William] vanden Heuvel had been in Bobby's Justice Department as a deputy and a friend.

So this was at the Regency Hotel in room 212. As we look through some of Bobby's notes, Pierre opened the meeting, and we thought we'd lay out some different alternatives. One was a confrontation with Johnson, with a decision to confront him, how would we lead up to the confrontation?

Q: *What was meant by that word, confrontation?*

EMK: Well, running against him. I think that's probably another way of saying running against him. You'd be taking him on issues with the idea that you'd run against him. And then a second one was if LBJ did not run, what should we be doing in the meantime in anticipation so that we'd be able to take advantage of the situation? Which I think was rather prophetic, obviously, when we found out what did happen. And then, third, if something happened to LBJ, and the vice president took over, what would we do? There was a thought that he might get out, and if the vice president took over, then what would we do? Then, finally, should we make any effort to try to secure the vice presidency for Bobby in '68? Those were at least the four subject matters that were talked about at that time. And the follow-on from those was that different people had different ideas about things that ought to be done.

Q: *I'm looking at your notes of the meeting. We have this in front of us, October 8. I notice you say, "I then suggested what some of the alternatives would be." It seems*

---

8. Pierre Salinger had been President Kennedy's press secretary.
9. Nestigan was the former mayor of Madison.

to me that this suggests that the thinking in the meeting was to push for this, and you were putting a cool hand of restraint on it, saying we need to think. Is that a right interpretation of these notes?

EMK: I think so. There were varying degrees of intensity about him running. I had reservations about it, because I thought it was very important that Bobby be president, and I thought it was inevitable that he would be president. And it seemed to me that, if that were so, we ought to think about how he could be president and would be president, and it was going to be high risk in terms of '68, high risk in terms of challenging the president. If the president lost, he was going to be blamed.

It was going to be not only the party leaders, but members of Congress and the Senate, and history would do that, and you wouldn't advance the cause that you were most interested in—ending the war. So I was very cautious all the way through. I thought he'd be a slam-dunk, really, the next time around, and I thought—That would have been '72. We could have worked on the war in the Senate and tried to do it. So that was one side. Then the other sides were the obvious ones—that he felt so intensely about the war. And the other part that's missing in this, he felt also extremely concerned about what was happening to the cities, the deterioration of the cities.

Because you don't see that. This is all about running. And we've all talked about what was happening in terms of the war. He was very bothered by the general deterioration in the cities, the growth of violence in the cities. And he didn't see anything that Gene McCarthy was doing about it, which we'll come to, because it was the subject matter of my conversation with McCarthy and why I went out to see him.

I'm convinced that if McCarthy had begun to talk about the cities and what was happening, then Bobby still wouldn't have run. He would not have run. But McCarthy had no interest whatsoever—by nature, disposition, he had none, and demonstrated none. For the war, yes, but that was pretty—You look back historically, his interest in the war came pretty late, too.

Q: Referring to the October 8th meeting and the various questions or considerations you had suggested—the four here—there isn't any mention specifically of who the Republican candidate would be. Did that figure at all in these calculations?

EMK: Not that I really remember, no. I think there was some discussion about Nixon, and I think there was some discussion at that time about Rockefeller.[10]

Q: Rockefeller got in. Romney had put his name in early; withdrew early. Reagan[11]—

EMK: I think there was casual interest in this. It's interesting that you mention Reagan because I think Bobby had two appearances with him. One was

---

10. Nelson Rockefeller was governor of New York.
11. In 1968 George Romney and Ronald Reagan were Republican governors of Michigan and California, respectively.

on this global television that I remember about American power, whatever it was. I remember we all watched this thing, and we were impressed that Reagan was able to get his points across as well as he could.[12] And then he had one other time. I don't remember quite where it was. It might have been out in California, and Reagan, I thought, did surprisingly well. I think there were low expectations about him, but I think he handled himself rather well. That made an impression on me very early. But I don't think any of us were thinking about what the opposition on that side was going to be.

Q: But wouldn't there be a logic to thinking that, if there was a buildup of antiwar sentiment or anti-Johnson sentiment, the beneficiary of that might be a Republican candidate, not another Democrat?

EMK: Well, it would, and certainly Nixon understood that, because he very early on talked about a secret plan [to end the war]. So he understood that, and that was the way he made an appeal to this group. I would have to go back in history. I don't think that had very much of an appeal to the antiwar group, that Nixon had this secret plan. I don't think that had much juice to it. I don't have the details, but I think there was the sense that Rockefeller was moving, and I don't know where Goldwater was at this time.

There was the beginning of stirrings against the eastern establishment. It looked like it was going to be a rather raucous Republican convention as well. In thinking about whether Bobby ought to run or not, I don't think it really was that he would run if so-and-so looked like he was going to get it, or not if somebody else was going to get it. But there was an awareness that there might very well be turmoil within the Republican Party.

Q: You mentioned earlier that there was this history of personal antagonism between LBJ and your brother. Several times in these materials, in these notes, it appears that it was a real matter of concern that, whatever your brother did, there was always a risk that it might be interpreted as a personal antagonism against him, or revenge or something.

EMK: Yes.

Q: You know the story that went around. Was this one of your concerns about his entry in the camp against Johnson, that it might be seen—?

EMK: Well, yes, very much so. It was going to be blind personal ambition for power and using the war as a lever to try to steal away the nomination because the Kennedys felt that they were entitled to it. And, secondly, it was going to reaffirm a view about Bobby being particularly aggressive and ruthless and letting nothing get in his way. Those were some of the characteristics

---

12. On May 15, 1967, RFK debated California's new Republican governor on the Vietnam War. CBS produced the debate, entitled "The Image of America and the Youth of the World," and labeled it a "Town Meeting of the World" because international university students in Britain posed the questions. Veteran correspondent Charles Collingwood moderated the debate that 15 million Americans watched.

that he had, and this played into that. He understood that very well. Bobby understood that. But there was no question that that was the real danger, that enemies would play that up, and if you have a series of facts that lend themselves to that kind of explanation, it's a pretty dangerous potion you're serving up. Because this would fall into that definition of ruthless, ambitious, power-hungry, trying to seize power in a war which his brother had gotten started, and he's not giving the support.

So you have that versus how in the world can we continue as a country failing to understand that we're not going to get a military solution to a political problem [in Vietnam], and that it's costing this country both lives and treasure over there, and we're failing to deal with the problems here at home, and we have an absolute abdication, really, of presidential leadership. These are dramatic poles. And these aren't easy differences. These are big-time differences. And some of us thought they could very well be the destruction of Bobby, should he pursue it.

Q: Yes. You know, he's quoted in here himself as being concerned that, "If I do this, they'll say I'm ruthless and all of these things."

EMK: That's right.

Q: All the more reason, it seems, why what we might call the moral issue or the policy issue, the reason for running, has to be very clear, very dramatized, in order for him to move.

EMK: I think that's right. You see in these notes that he's also concerned that he would become in the future too much of a lightning rod in terms of the politics of the time. That's what happens around here, there's a general kind of swing. When you arrive here, you're inexperienced, you're not knowledgeable, you ought to stay around here and learn. Then you stay around here and learn a bit, and you take some votes—on guns or the death penalty or privacy in abortion or healthcare—and you're labeled in terms of national political—He was a smart enough political leader to understand that, as someone who was at the cutting edge in domestic and foreign policy, time was not necessarily going to work on his side the longer he stayed in here. Because he wasn't going to duck issues, and it was going to be costly.

Q: So from his thinking, there wasn't a clear case for waiting until '72?

EMK: That's right. No, no. He had seen what had happened with the Manchester book where he dropped a good deal in terms of public support. And he certainly had seen Lyndon Johnson drop in public support. And he was well schooled in the vicissitudes of life and politics, and he had an appreciation of his own role as a cutting-edge politician. He realized that these opportunities were going to be limited.

But it wasn't just blind ambition. Bobby never had this drive for power. His whole life experience was really quite different. I mean, my father—as we've gone over—wanted him to move to Maryland, to get in line to be a senator. And he just didn't, this was not his bag. He'd take these things as they came.

But he also believed in the use of power, political power, and he wanted to have a chance to have a use for it.

Q: Senator, you mentioned earlier that President Johnson at times seemed very focused on your brother and concerned about your brother and why he didn't seem to like him. But your perception was that your brother didn't spend a lot of time thinking about President Johnson. I was wondering if you'd elaborate on that a little more, because this perception is still out there that there was a blood feud between your brother and Lyndon Johnson.

EMK: Well, it goes back really to the vice president nomination where my brother had favored Senator Scoop Jackson,[13] and my brother Jack selected Lyndon. Then by nature of their personalities, they were not easy allies or friends. They had entirely different kinds of personalities, entirely different friends, entirely different interests, entirely different approaches to problems.

Their worlds were really somewhat different, and the more Jack relied on Bobby to be involved in crucial decisions like the Cuban Missile Crisis and civil rights, the more it isolated Vice President Johnson. He was not the one my brother listened to on those issues. So I think Johnson wondered, "What, really, am I doing here?" and "Why are they excluding me?" I think so much of this is explainable. Lyndon Johnson was not Bobby's type of guy, basically. I think it was really as simple as that. It happens around here, it happens in life, and it just happened in those two.

People who observed it, political writers and all the rest, made a good deal of it, and then it all developed during the time of the antiwar movement, where it appeared to be a threat to him, going back even to '64, the apparent threat of Bobby trying to get the nomination in Atlantic City. I learned recently that Lyndon had FBI agents up there checking people out. In the wake of this Felt decision,[14] there was an FBI agent I talked to who had been up in Atlantic City for Lyndon Johnson, checking out. They had 150 agents up there, because Lyndon was worried that Bobby might try to get hold of the FBI, so he had his loyal people there, trying—

Q: Checking out what?

EMK: Checking out the delegates, checking out communications, checking that nobody else was coming around, there were no other movements, that everything was the way it was presented, checking out all the security, that there wasn't going to be a rush on the building, all the rest of these things they were asked to do. I think that's how it developed.

---

13. Senator Henry Jackson was a Democrat from Washington.

14. Former FBI associate director Mark Felt confirmed in 2005 that he was the "Deep Throat" source for *Washington Post* reporters Bob Woodward and Carl Bernstein in their Watergate investigation.

Bobby was disappointed that they didn't fund the OEO[15] and poverty programs, so those things didn't work well for the basic relationship. The rest, then, is history in terms of the war.

We had one other meeting—I have the notes—in later October, with EMK, Joe Dolan, and Dave Burke in my office. That's on Tuesday, October 17th. We met with Congressmen Culver, Boland, and Dave Burke,[16] and we went through some cards. We had agreed at the earlier meeting that we were going to have a laidback strategy. We were going to do some soundings with people in different states to find out who were the likely political supporters should he go. We got that much of a green light from Bobby. So we had subsequent meetings down here that I mentioned in terms of the members of Congress we knew and knew well, to sound out some of the leaders, and also some of the governors. We were going to try to see if they were handy, if they were around. Bobby ought to have a chance to visit with them, maybe go to some of their fundraising efforts. We thought there may be a few governors—I mentioned here Ken Curtis of Maine, whom I was going to talk to, who came aboard—who would come aboard (even though Bobby hadn't announced), and would be a helper on this. The bottom part of the meeting shows that we decided to do some polling, and we were going to try to frame some of the questions about Vietnam, about personality. Here are the words, again, Vietnam and personality, which are the kinds of things we've been talking about.

Then we went out and reviewed Iowa, California, Montana, and I got the names, loosely, of people in probably twenty-five of the different states, the principal states. It was sort of a soft organization. We were sounding people out, talking to people, what did they think, what did they have—People had been urging him to run, he's certainly not made the decision, he's not running at this time. What are you hearing? What are you doing? Who are those people who might be—? . . . Then we have a December 10 meeting in New York at the home of Bill vanden Heuvel.

So now we've gone through these meetings, and we're talking about these general subjects that keep coming up. We're going to have LBJ for four years. He's just going over these points again. They've talked to some of these people. Arthur Schlesinger has his comments here that if Bobby didn't run in '68 it was going to be the end of the party, and he thought there was a good chance of winning. And Dutton, who was very politically shrewd, said the longer we wait, the more difficult it is to assume that McCarthy's supporters would go for Bobby. Now McCarthy had just announced.

He had come down and talked to me on a couple of different occasions prior to that, saying that he was going to get into the race. It was fine with

---

15. Office of Economic Opportunity.

16. Congressmen John Culver and Edward Boland were Democrats from Iowa and Massachusetts, respectively; David Burke was Kennedy's chief of staff.

me, and I indicated I might have to preserve running as a favorite son in Massachusetts. It was more of a notice. It wasn't asking. It was a courtesy and a notice, those meetings, looking back on it. But he was in now, and the point at the December 10th meeting was that Dutton was saying, the longer you stay [out], the harder it is for Bobby to win over some of the people who are supporting McCarthy but would have supported Bobby. And we had other ideas, vanden Heuvel talking about the vice president and other thoughts.

Sorensen said that he assumed everyone there wanted to see RFK president, which of course led him to the second point, what would be the best way to proceed, that it might be better to try in '72 when he had greater things going for him than in '68. That was basically my position. This stimulated discussion as to what shape RFK would be in in '72; whether he'd be more controversial then than he is now; whether, by the fact that he does not challenge, he will have lost the support of many young people and liberals who are looking to him for leadership. Would they now be looking for another candidate in '72?

That's the other side of the coin. We generally considered that we'd take a look at the situation after the first of the year and see what kind of impression McCarthy was making and continue the contacts.

Q: That was a real tough one, wasn't it? Seventy-two or—

EMK: Yes, that's a very tough one. Those are the arguments, and they can be made with a good deal of passion on both sides. And that was a very troublesome one. So we go on through a couple of meetings I had with Gene McCarthy on November 28th of '67 and December 6th.

Q: Senator, he would tend to use you? You were the conduit between McCarthy and your brother?

EMK: I had the best relationship with him, yes, having served in the Senate with him. Bobby had, too, but I'd been in for a longer period, and it was easier for me to do that with him. In that December 6th meeting, I have that funny little part about me asking McCarthy who's running his campaign in Massachusetts, and he mentioned Professor Fluks. I asked if he was talking about Fuchs.[17] He said, "Yes, he's from Boston University." I said, "Isn't he the professor at Brandeis?" He said, "Yes, that's right." But as one who has trouble with names myself [*Laughter*], I don't—

Q: I bet you don't have trouble with the names of those who are running your campaign!

EMK: I think I have that pretty well set. Now we have the December 10 meetings. You can see now where we have the eighth, the seventeenth. These meetings are now every two weeks. And New York, there's a slight change. Milt Gwirtzman[18]

17. Professor Lawrence H. Fuchs taught at Brandeis University.
18. Milton Gwirtzman, a Harvard and Yale graduate, advised all three Kennedy brothers in their political careers and served as speechwriter for them. He wrote one of the most moving passages of Teddy's eulogy for Bobby: "My brother need not be idealized or enlarged

is at this, Jerry Bruno,[19] Dave Burke. Well, this was get in touch with the fifteen or twenty leading figures of the convention of '68 through third parties. See RFK assessments. Dolan and Burke had a list of key people, and that had been worked through at our previous meetings. We'd gone through those meetings on October 17, and we were going to go through—and contacts: Unruh and Ned Breathett and Terry Sanford.[20] They would get back after the first of the year and report the results. And then there was general discussion about LBJ's strengths and weaknesses.

In January 1968, Senator Kennedy made a fact-finding tour of Vietnam.

EMK: At this time, Christmastime, when I went over to Vietnam, I was to be over there seven days. I had planned to stay in Hawaii for two or three days. I remember getting off the plane and going into the hotel and getting undressed, getting ready to go to bed, and being really tired, and the phone rang. It was Bobby, and he said, "Come on back now. We're going to meet out at McLean, either tomorrow or the next day." I remember getting dressed and going to find out about getting a plane and coming back. I've seen the pictures of that meeting out there. I know Bill vanden Heuvel was at it, and a number of other people.

At Hickory Hill. I don't have any notes on it, but I remember that. It was when I felt [Bobby] had moved—just from the conversations he had with me, something had moved in his mind. There was an intensity.

Q: Yes. One of the things that tends to get omitted in the documents we have here is precisely the urban violence, the unrest, what was happening to blacks and to whites and—as the Kerner Commission put it, the movement toward a divided society of blacks and whites. And it's historically very important, I think, your mention that into this mix was not just the Vietnam War and the developments in that war and the development of sentiment about it, the escalation of the war, the body bags. But there was, on the domestic side, an important factor here, which tends to get lost. And I think you're saying your brother Robert—and probably yourself—were very much concerned about that. It wasn't just the Vietnam War.

EMK: I remember walking into Bobby's house, probably '65, '66, and he mentioned the draft and who was fighting the war. It was all the poor and the blacks—and the people who were getting the education deferment, the marriage deferment, the skill deferments. He said, "I can't take that on." I had an

---

in death beyond what he was in life; to be remembered simply as a good and decent man, who saw wrong and tried to right it, saw suffering and tried to heal it, saw war and tried to stop it." Douglas Martin, "Milton Gwirtzman, Adviser to Kennedys, Dies at 78," *New York Times*, July 26, 2011, http://www.nytimes.com/2011/07/26/us/politics/26gwirtzman. html. Gwirtzman joined this interview with Senator Kennedy and commented later in the conversation.

19. Jerry Bruno was an advance man.

20. Edward Breathett was governor of Kentucky, and Terry Sandford was the former governor of North Carolina.

interest in that, so I started offering these amendments, which we were getting beaten on. But we had very good debates on them. It was all of '66 and '67. And finally, at the end of '67, we got a commission to study random selection, and that turned into the random selection system.

Woolsey told me the other afternoon that Stennis[21] thought that I had conducted these debates in a very constructive and positive manner, and very straightforward. There was a great effort to try to drop it in the conference, and he said, "No, out of a personal respect I've developed for Senator Kennedy, I'm going to keep that in." And McNamara . . . came up with the random selection system. Kay Graham's[22] son was drafted. The Tet Offensive came, and the war ended. It's not quite that sharp, but I'll tell you, there's a scenario there, the Tet Offensive and the random selection. Bobby was involved in it. I offered the amendments and worked on that part, but probably the inspiration for me was from the conversations with him. He said, "Look at what's happening to these people."[23] We spent a lot of time on that. It was reflective and indicative of, one, the injustice about the war, but also what was happening to our people, and who was paying the price. It was people from the inner cities, the poor. And this was something that Bobby was very strongly committed to.

You have to take his trip down through Mississippi[24] and his work in hunger also in that period. His interest in Indian education. I succeeded him. He was chairman of the Indian Education Committee. He had hearings on Indian education and about the boarding school abuses that were taking place. After '68 I filled in as the chairman of the committee, and we had our report. But he had had hearings all over on what was happening to Indians, the working poor, the people in the inner cities, and what was happening on the issues of race. They were all out there, and then the war.

But you're absolutely right. These other forces were pushing him and driving him, but people weren't talking about that. It's an accumulation of things, the war and this lack of attention to urban issues. It was definitely cumulative, definitely cumulative.

Q: Yes. I think it may be worth us spending a little time . . . talking about what was concerning you and him in the Senate, because history, Vietnam, tends to just obliterate everything else—

---

21. R. James Woolsey Jr. was an anti–Vietnam War activist and future CIA director; Senator John Stennis was a Democrat from Mississippi.

22. Katharine Graham was the publisher of the *Washington Post*.

23. Bobby and Teddy Kennedy worked to change the draft law to a lottery system, so that such a random selection process would eliminate the preferential deferment process, based on education status, that disadvantaged the poor and minorities, who were less likely to be enrolled in higher education or have connections that would allow them to avoid the draft.

24. Bobby made a trip to the poverty-stricken Mississippi Delta in 1967 and was appalled by the substandard housing and hunger that he witnessed there.

EMK: That's right. You see, he got started the Bedford-Stuyvesant program[25] in the Senate.

And this was all Bobby's idea. It was made up of locals and high-powered people. He had Tom Watson on it, and Frank Thomas, who eventually became president of Ford.[26]

Q: Yes. Was Benno Schmidt?[27]

EMK: Yes, Benno Schmidt was on that. He had a crowd on there that was just unbelievable. He thought the local people should say what they needed, and the other people would help them get this thing developed. That whole area had almost a million people. And one of the parts of it was . . . the restoration of the neighborhood streets.

Jake Javits heard about it, got in, and he found all kinds of problems until he had a part. I mean it was so typical. I like Jake and I respected him and I always will, but this thing was Bobby's, Bobby's, Bobby's, and he nosed into it.

This was interesting, the sequence to this thing. They got that thing started, and then Kemp[28] eventually came in, Republicans, and they reshaped the concept of it and really got away from what Bobby—although there was still a whisper of what Bobby wanted to do. It was a reflection, again, of his interest in the cities and in people and in getting people in those local communities to be involved in their community and their streets.

But we're just back to the point that, for the underprivileged, the underserved, issues on civil rights, what was happening to them in our country and society, what was happening to the cities, the injustices there, the inflaming of the cities, the failure to really deal with all of these kinds of issues, the cutting back on the appropriations, on the OEO programs—President Johnson just would not back those up because the money was all being expended on the war. Bobby felt, and legitimately so, that that was such a key part of President Kennedy's legacy. He was certainly enormously impressed—as all of us were—in the very early years with the passage of the '64 Act, the '65 Act—those were the heydays of that. But after that, it deteriorated—the '68 Act on housing was actually meaningless. We had to pass one in '88 that dealt with it.

Q: So the escalation of the war was not only itself having an impact on people's lives through the draft and things like that, but it was also siphoning money away from the remedial programs and the attention to them, siphoning it into the war. Again, I think

---

25. The Bedford-Stuyvesant Restoration Corporation, a public-private partnership to revitalize the blighted neighborhood in Central Brooklyn, was created in 1967 through Senator Robert Kennedy's amendment to the Economic Development Act of 1964. It was the first nonprofit community development corporation in the nation and became a much-replicated model in poor urban areas across the country.

26. Tom Watson Jr. was president of IBM, and Frank Thomas became president of the Ford Foundation.

27. Benno Schmidt Sr. was a venture capitalist.

28. Jack Kemp was a Republican congressman from New York.

it's very important that the historical record here show that those things are proceeding in tandem. This is with respect to Robert's decision to run and your own thinking about the war during this time.

EMK: Absolutely.

Q: It was more than just the war. It was what the war signified.

EMK: That's right. In terms of the whole society, in terms of the direction of the country, why we were in public life, what was happening in terms of the legacy of President Kennedy, all of this wrapped in together. The question was, when people came here and said, "You can change this. You can do it, it's possible, it's feasible, and we're prepared to help you do it." It's very heady stuff.

[At] Steve Smith's house the evening that Bobby had the interview with Walter Cronkite.[29] We were watching the interview, and all decided afterward that Bobby had decided he was going to run. The meeting changed from, "Should he?" to "What are we going to do?" That was very important. I remember the meeting very clearly. A lot of these others are less clear. When Bobby came back, everybody cheered when he walked into my sister's room. We ended up then getting assignments for different places.

I can remember the meeting. The basic point was the uncertainty, and then the fact that the ultimate decision was really made by Bobby himself on the basis of his own instincts after a lot of anguish. When it came down to it, he knew what was in his soul on this.

Really, the important part of it was the Walter Cronkite interview in which Bobby talked rather freely, and there was no listening to that and not knowing that he was going to run. When he came, everybody recognized it, and I think it clicked in his mind that he was then the candidate. That's the important part of it, and that part I'm very sure of.

Q: Were you surprised, Senator, that in the midst of all of this, McCarthy did quite well in the New Hampshire primary?

EMK: After March 12, I went out to Wisconsin to see him. That's when I ran into Dave Schoumacher. March 15, and my brother was now 90 percent of the way in, and he asked me to go out to see whether there was anything that could be worked out. He had two messages. One was if McCarthy was going to talk about the cities and urban policies as much as about the war, he wouldn't get in. And, secondly, if that wasn't going to be his choice, could there be a possible joint way of defeating Lyndon Johnson. If he wasn't going to do that, my brother would get in. Those were the two points to find out. I went out. It was nighttime, and for security I came up the back stairs of this hotel in Wisconsin. And as I went up in the hotel to the floor, like the eighth floor, there standing in the stairwell is David Schoumacher, who was the principal reporter covering

---

29. This was March 13, 1968, the day after the New Hampshire primary in which Gene McCarthy came within 7 percentage points of President Johnson. The Kennedy family gathered to consider whether Bobby should seek the nomination.

Gene McCarthy, at nighttime, with his camera. He said, "What are you doing here?" It probably didn't make a lot of sense in any event, by that time, but it was a last chance. We had a very difficult meeting. It says in here I just talked to Abigail;[30] I talked to him. I waited about an hour, hour and a half. He came in and just was basically completely uninterested.

Q: Had he been told by this time—by you or anybody other than his own people—that your brother was going to run?

EMK: Well, he probably had seen the Cronkite interview. There was a lot of ripple after that. I think he had a pretty good sense that Bobby was going to get in it. And he certainly got from me that he was going to get in it unless they were going to talk about urban issues, poverty. This was really my brother's last way of closing the door on this aspect: I've done everything I could have. I tried. If they'd talk about the cities and what's happening there, I'll still hold. But once he didn't, it cleared in his mind that he could. It was a green light to go ahead. And McCarthy was just basically tired, uninterested, rather disdainful. He was on a big high. It had all moved for him. He was pretty much in the catbird seat, wondering why in the world he was being disturbed. Then he gave the whole story, flipped in his way, to Schoumacher.

I had a decent relationship with him [McCarthy], although he voted against me with Vance Hartke on the poll tax. I thought he always had a little edge for the Kennedys. I inherited a lot of these things. He had an edge for me, or always had that thing: he was more Catholic, more liberal, more intellectual than John Kennedy.

I campaigned with my brother Bobby . . . when he announced for the presidency, and he came up for the St. Patrick's Day speech. I have the picture up there on the wall. That was in the St. Patrick's Day parade in Boston in March of 1968.

I was walking in the parade, and I heard a lot of stir, and rather than coming back with me, he had gotten in the parade way up in the front. So I went up to join him, and you can see from his arm, "I'm doing all right, Teddy. You don't have to come up." You can see him sort of pushing me away from the fun. He said, "You don't have to. I'm doing fine by myself. I'll see you later on." That's that picture—you see, he has his hand pushing me away. We walked though in the parade, and it was a great, great reception. He got an extraordinary reception up there. It was a wonderful time. But we rarely campaigned together.

Q: Events were moving fast, too. You asked very early on what would happen if LBJ should pull out of the race.

EMK: Yes. I don't think we ever looked at that. It was rather prophetic, but I don't think we ever gave it any consideration. The first thing we did was

---

30. Abigail was Gene McCarthy's wife.

decide about the primary, back at Bobby's house. He'd been out campaigning. The whole question then was whether to go into the Indiana primary.

There were long, long discussions about that because it was so difficult: the home of the Ku Klux Klan; a tough governor;[31] the Teamsters, who were a very big union—one of the two biggest unions—and were strongly against it; and a big agricultural community. There were blacks, but they were in pockets, not a great population, and basically very conservative. So if you announced that you were going in, and you got licked right away before you ever got to the other states, this would be a major, major setback. I effectively moved out to Indiana for three or four weeks.

Q: How was that decision made, to go into Indiana?

EMK: We didn't have an alternative. You had to go if you were going to announce. The focus and attention was on whether to get in, the circumstances were going to be uncomfortable getting into this thing with all the implications, and there were efforts to reach out into different states and all the rest. But it hadn't been thought through that the first primary would be Indiana, and he had a very good chance of getting licked there. I don't remember that subject ever being discussed until after. Which primaries now are you going to have to go into, looked at globally? Jesse Unruh has 250 [delegate] votes there, and you're going to get the ones in New York. You look around at different pieces that you may be able to get, but suddenly you're confronted with this. And the early polls did not look terribly good. They show that he was somewhat behind in the very beginning.

Q: So the pre-decision thinking did not really connect with the question of where he'd have to go first and what he'd have to do.

EMK: It did not.

Q: It was only March 16th or 15th or somewhere around there that that began to be thought of, and I guess you were the person who put that into the mix.

EMK: Yes, I was looking through these notes from that night, and it says, "Indiana, TK, and South Dakota, Ted Kennedy."

Q: But the interesting thing is the date. It's 3/16. That's the date your brother announced.

EMK: And if you look back at the other meetings, the meetings we had had here in Washington at this time—the rundown of the states is California, Montana, Wyoming, New Mexico, Colorado, Nevada, South Dakota, Nebraska, Minnesota, Wisconsin, Illinois, Indiana. There's a very thin list on this. "Gordon St. Angelo,[32] not to be trusted."

Birch Bayh, I was a good friend of his, but it says, "RFK uneasy with him. Should try to be more friendly," which he should have. Bob Keefe was a very

---

31. Indiana governor Roger Branigan was running in the May 7 Democratic presidential primary as a "favorite son."

32. St. Angelo was Indiana Democratic state chairman.

good fellow, but just an attorney. Andy Jacobs was a big supporter. Bob Nix. But it was very thin.

Senator Kennedy explained how the nomination process in 1960 and 1968 differed from the contemporary system when candidates have to run in virtually every state, which has either a primary or caucus.

EMK: Well, the important difference between the primaries, even in my brother Jack's day and Bobby's day, is that they had a small number of primaries. President Kennedy had ten primaries, but Wisconsin and West Virginia were the decisive battles, for all intents and purposes. They had Oregon, but that wasn't really very much; it was all over, really. He had those two. Bobby had Indiana—which he won narrowly, but we said it was a big, big win—a loss in Oregon, and then the blowout in California, the big win out there. That would have given him enormous impetus.

But you can stay in these states for a period of time, five or seven weeks. You say it [Indiana primary] was May 7, so we were out there for close to two months, and we *stayed* there for two months. He would come in for two or three days at a time. But everybody we had, friends we had, just stayed, lived in that state. And in that period of time, you can get around in the state, and people begin to form impressions. You can have some impact.

In the 1980 campaign, there were thirty-one different primaries. The most you do in most of these states is land at the airport and take off again. Your supporters come out, you greet them, and boom, you're gone to another place. But in 1968 they could get a different feeling—and they did, because of the dramatic moments. You had the death of Dr. King.[33] These were momentous moments, where people were transfixed. And they were transfixed by the beginning of this, the wild enthusiasm for Bobby. Then he could see that that was scaring people, and the whole change in his appeal, all softer television, which made a big, big difference. Well, for Bobby it was a transition from being a super-hot candidate, which he was, with a lot of emotion and feeling and crowds, to sitting around and finding out that watching this sort of thing on television was turning people off, that Indiana didn't like that. What does it in New York and Massachusetts—we have an exciting candidate, a hot candidate, one I can see, understand, hear, who gets me worked up—that isn't what they were looking at. It was a whole transitioning of the campaign—which Bobby did, and you can see it in the course, changing the schedule and

---

33. As Robert Kennedy arrived in Indianapolis on April 4, 1968, to begin campaigning for the primary, he heard that Martin Luther King Jr. had been assassinated in Memphis. RFK's eloquent, heartfelt, extemporaneous remarks to a black audience, after he announced King's death to them, are considered among the finest American speeches ever delivered. A transcription and recording of this speech can be found at https://www.jfklibrary.org/Research/Research-Aids/Ready-Reference/RFK-Speeches/Statement-on-the-Assassination-of-Martin-Luther-King.aspx.

the time he spent with people and all the rest. But the other part was—most important—the beginning of the changing of the press.

Every night, after the events, he would sit down and have a drink with members of the press. They would talk until 2 in the morning, and then he'd go to bed. He could last three days, and he was exhausted. It was a very interesting thing. But he had a compulsion of wanting to be a straight talker, a kind of John McCain. By natural disposition, he would sit down and talk to them. And at the end of that campaign, those press people had an entirely different view of him. I always thought that was probably the most interesting aspect of it. And you look, after his loss, the press formed this group that stayed together and created the [Robert F. Kennedy] press awards in which Dick Harwood, who died [in 2001], was very much involved—Sandy Vanocur, there's a whole group.[34]

They formed a group that each year gives a press award for a high school essay or editorial on the subject of poverty or civil rights—the television programs, the books that are coming out, radio broadcasts. They do it down here [in Washington] one evening, and it's very moving. They were the ones who structured, organized, and raised the money to do it. And at the end of that campaign, he [Bobby] had them absolutely locked in. They all wanted to maintain their journalistic independence and declared it and all the rest, but they became so emotionally involved because they really had a chance to sit with him.

But it was at an incredible cost. I always looked at it like an athletic contest. You have to get to bed at 10:30 if you're going to get up at 6 or 6:30. You have to go to bed. It's a training course. You can't go out; at least I couldn't, and I was young then. But [Bobby] would stay down.[35] I'd tell him, "This thing is crazy." He'd get up at 7:30 in the morning and go on through, still could do two or three days; then he'd have to come back [home] for a day and a half to get rested and then get back at it. But this was a major transformation that took place from the press [who had seen him as] this cynical, arrogant figure.

He came out of Indiana [with a victory], and he was involved in a national movement. And then in Oregon—they say it's only suburbs out there—he had difficulty getting started, and he spent a relatively short period of time. Then California—that thing was moving so rapidly, he didn't really have the chance. But Indiana, in those evenings downstairs at the Sheraton bar, those guys would sit around, and they'd be after him, talking about it. He'd talk about Camus and poetry and books that he had read. And they just got blown away.

---

34. *Washington Post* reporter Richard Harwood and NBC correspondent Sander Vanocur created a press award in Robert Kennedy's name.

35. Bobby would stay in the hotel bar chatting with reporters until the wee hours of the morning.

Q: *Senator, you were given responsibility to handle the non-primary states as well, which I would have thought was probably a pretty tough task since you're dealing more with party leaders. I was wondering if you might share with us how that task unfolded and how well it went.*

EMK: We stayed in Indiana the whole time. I might have come out and made some calls on different people, but I was in Indiana. I did a very light touch-over in Oregon. And then I was in California for the most part. I can remember going to Iowa and seeing the caucuses there, and just being amazed. You had a thousand people at that time. Now, it's three thousand or so—or bigger in some communities—where they all go in, they hang out, and people have a chance to talk to them. Then they all divide in the different parts of the room and select their own people. There's a big blackboard, and people put the numbers up, and that's the number of delegates. That was really the startling thing about how the process worked, so different in so many different areas.

I went to South Dakota briefly, where we had some good contacts, and Iowa, which was important. Humphrey was making major inroads because of his very strong stand with labor and on the war. And this was true in Indiana as well as in some of the other states. We didn't have very much in terms of the agricultural appeal. Most of the party people were still for President Johnson, and increasingly antagonistic that other people were going to divide the party.

So it wasn't a rush to sign up or join up. I went to the selected states or areas or conventions where it looked like we might have some opportunity for delegates, but after that, I went to the primary states. I think in our notes we have the talk I gave out there in Los Angeles. . . . I talked about the challenges that we were facing, about how if Bobby could appeal in Indiana, which was conservative, fighting the state organization, and with the possibility of Republicans potentially crossing over—which I think had an adverse impact, but not enough to change the outcome. And then the organization, how they tampered around with the levers of the voting machines and the ballot machines, and how the newspapers had been very tough on Bobby, and still he had done extraordinarily well. . . . I don't have them here, but I believe the polls would show that he started out behind and was able, even against a lot of this kind of opposition, to be successful.

There was one wonderful story. There was a Teamster official in Charlestown, Massachusetts. I'd see Bobby and talk to him usually in the late afternoon when he took a tub [bath]. I'd come in and give him a report of what was happening in the state. And this fellow who was a member of the Teamsters, from Charlestown, [Massachusetts,] Irish, came in to see me and said, "Look, if Bobby Kennedy tells me that he will take the parole board report on Jimmy Hoffa[36] when it comes up—" This assumes he's going to be elected, and it's

---

36. James R. Hoffa was president of the International Brotherhood of Teamsters union from 1958 until 1971. In 1968 he was serving a prison term for jury tampering, fraud,

going to be some time during his term that the parole will make a recommendation. "And if you tell me that he will accept that parole, the Teamsters are prepared to support Robert Kennedy in Indiana, and we will make a contribution of a million dollars to you."

I said, "Well, I don't think that's going to fly, but I'll run it by the candidate." Bobby was in [the bathtub], putting the soap on, and he said, "What's going on?" I said, "Well, we heard from so-and-so up in Charlestown. He was absolutely clean, but very close to Hoffa. He used to go home every day and take care of his disabled wife, and he had an incredible work ethic. He was crazy about Hoffa because of what he did for the Teamsters."

Anyway, I mentioned this to Bobby, who was sitting in the tub. And he said, "You tell so-and-so—I know him and I like him—if I get to be president of the United States, Jimmy Hoffa is never going to get out of jail, and there are going to be a lot more of them in jail. Do I make myself clear?" I said, "Okay, okay. Let's go to the second item." [*Laughter*]

I never took the chance of giving the report back to the guy. You know what's interesting is that I think Nixon took it, took the money and took the endorsement. And I wouldn't be surprised to find out that McCarthy made that pledge to them, too, because we saw this money come into both these campaigns at the time. I'll never forget the story. Bobby didn't flinch about any of these kinds of things.

Q: Going into California, what was the assessment of his chances for the convention?

EMK: We had some important assets in that state. Unruh was an important figure there and knew the political leaders, and we had family members out there who were supporters. It was much more of an imbalanced state than it probably is today. Bobby was by this time a hot campaigner, and he had that message down well. He felt the surge that was moving for him. He identified with the people who were going out and supporting him. He enjoyed the enthusiasm that was building and developing there, and it was just a fit between Bobby and California. That whole momentum, all of it, just took off, and we could feel it, see it, and it caught him up.

One of the reasons for Bobby Kennedy's strength in California was his support for the farmer workers' movement led by Cesar Chavez.

---

and attempted bribery. As counsel to the Senate Labor Subcommittee in the late 1950s, Robert Kennedy had unsuccessfully pursued criminal charges against Hoffa. While attorney general, RFK continued his pursuit of organized crime, especially its influence on labor unions. His team of investigators and prosecutors, known as the "Get Hoffa" squad, succeeded in obtaining the union boss's conviction and incarceration. Released in 1971, per a pardon agreement with the Nixon administration, he vanished in late July 1975, probably the victim of an organized crime murder. See journalist Larry Tye's excellent biography, *Bobby Kennedy: The Making of a Liberal Icon* (New York: Random House, 2016), for the most recent analysis of RFK's crusade against Hoffa.

EMK: [They] developed a personal relationship because Cesar saw what a leader he was in terms of these kinds of things. And Bobby kept that. I had a relationship, but not nearly like Bobby did. And then in, I think it was '67[37]—you'd have to check the dates on it—he went through this fast about organizing, about the unwillingness of the farm owners to give him the opportunity for organizing. He had this long twenty-day or thirty-day fast, a very serious one. When he announced he was going to break it—I think it was on an Easter Sunday or something like that, Ascension Thursday, one of the holy days—it was a big deal.

Bobby went out there and spent the whole day, went to the Mass with him. He was very weakened and enfeebled, and it was an event that just electrified California, the Hispanics generally and in California in particular. I don't remember it being at the time of the campaign. I think it was before this campaign.

[Chavez] was a real visionary. He talked in philosophical and theological terms. He was a very simple person, but he had an eloquence that was very deep and breathtaking. I listened to him a couple of times, and you didn't want to follow Cesar [as a speaker]. He was very powerful.

So the campaign itself was very uplifting and moving. Bobby left it a few times and went up—I think there was about an eight-day difference between Oregon and California or so. So when he was out there, he did a couple of stops up in Oregon and came back and might have gone to the state of Washington. But it was just basically California.

McCarthy spent a lot of time out there. The money wasn't flowing in at this time. Bobby's campaign was ten weeks and cost $10 million. And at the end, after California, he had a probably a $6.5 million debt.

This thing was the big enchilada, whether you were going to look like you were moving towards it, which would have brought in the dough or the resources. Everything was laid out on the line in California, and it was a great response. It had this enormous emotional buildup because this was where it was. You couldn't keep roaring at this pace. The campaign couldn't have kept it up unless we were going to have a breakthrough, and of course, that night we got the breakthrough. I think he had a good opportunity to win the nomination.

I never was one who thought, even with California, that it was going to be a slam-dunk. I think that thing would have been a tough slog all the way down the rest of the trip. Humphrey and the others had reached in too deep by then. I forget what the numbers were. Even at the end of California, Humphrey still

---

37. 1968.

had a big chunk of delegates.[38] Bobby had a good chunk, but I don't know where—who would have known? Who could tell?

Q: Well, at that time, it was still, to a certain extent, an open convention. You still had favorite sons, didn't you? You have very little of that anymore; you already know the result ahead of time.

EMK: Yes, that's it.

Q: It's a big if that will never be answered [about whether RFK could have won the Democratic nomination].

EMK: Yes, that's right. It's a big, big if, a big if.

Q: I know your brother when he was out there on Sunday—the festival day or whatever it was—was giving a speech [with Cesar Chavez], *and he had learned Spanish phrases to use. And there was a very interesting, funny little byplay to hear Spanish spoken with a Massachusetts accent and a little bit of nice joking between him and—*

EMK: He had a great, great sense of humor, and he could play with the crowd. Once he got started on a roll of what he was talking about, it was a different pace. He had a very easy, very good sense of humor, and he could see the humor in just about everything.

Senator Kennedy described how he heard that his brother had been shot in Los Angeles just after declaring victory in the California primary.

EMK: I was up campaigning for Bobby in northern California when I heard the news, and then went down.

Q: You were in San Francisco.

EMK: San Francisco.

Q: You were with John Siegenthaler.[39]

EMK: Siegenthaler.

Q: And Dave Burke.

EMK: Burke.

Q: What were you doing in San Francisco?

EMK: At that time, I was out speaking in different places. I had been in Indiana for three weeks or so, kind of getting the campaign going as I did in other states and when I first went out to California as well. But at the end of the campaigns, it's always much more effective for me to be out in public speaking to different groups. The last week, five days, I'd go out and speak. I'd been speaking around San Francisco when I'd gotten the news and of course it's—that evening time, when everyone was quite euphoric that the campaign was going so well and looked good. I mean, it was still going to be a slog in terms of the nomination, but this was a big, big win. I think particularly after

---

38. Even after winning the California primary, RFK was still trailing Vice President Humphrey in the delegate count. Humphrey, supported by the Democratic old guard, had amassed 561 delegates, Robert Kennedy 393, and Eugene McCarthy 258.

39. John Siegenthaler was a journalist from Tennessee who had worked with Robert Kennedy as his administrative assistant at the Justice Department.

what happened in Oregon, we had gotten—it hadn't gone well, so this really was a big, big boost.

I had sort of set my mind, when flying down to Los Angeles, I remember—he'd been wounded but he's still alive at this time, and it was very serious. You know, you didn't want to believe the worst. I didn't want to believe the worst and wouldn't believe the worst. Then you're confronted with the reality of his presence and my presence in the [hospital] room. Then it's the reality and, you know, you have a difficult time letting him go. That was a very tough time, difficult time. I spoke at the funeral up in New York. We can come back to that, and going out to Arlington [Cemetery] as well.

Looking at it in this broader perspective, which you asked about at the initial conversation, that's when I really—I think I probably kind of checked out [after Bobby's death]. That was going to be it for me. Shortly after that, I spent the time—my father was still alive, but I spent a good deal of time, about three months, in a boat up in Maine, the coast of Maine. I'd come back periodically to see him, but I turned around and went back out there for the summer. My mother was still alive. At other times I always felt that I owed it to them to come back and see them. But at that time, I felt that whatever justice there was, whatever the meaning of life in terms of spirituality and reliance and source of strength that would come from my faith—I found it was pretty empty, pretty empty. I mean . . . the losses, his loss. All these children growing up without the kind of extraordinary human beings that both of my brothers were. All the things they'd been involved in.

Dr. King had been a loss, been kind of a punch, a body blow, but you never translated that into thinking how anything could happen again. It just underlined the importance of what Bobby was all about—ending the war, getting the country back into a new direction, doing the things that you believe in philosophically and spiritually, and in every other kind of way, all of those things. The bottom just dropped out, and I just sort of checked out. It was a spectacular area up there, wonderful, the Maine coast, just breathtakingly lovely, beautiful, and you could—I stayed there.

Q: *Were you a lot by yourself at this time?*

EMK: Yes, a lot of time by myself.

Q: *Wondering. It was very hard to let go, wasn't it?*

EMK: Yes, and it was very hard to get going again. It seemed to me that you had to get, to get—you know, an opportunity to try and maybe do something in terms of the things that Bobby had been interested in, we all worked on. I thought probably Humphrey could get back on into it.

Q: *That's why you're going to get back into it? You spent a lot of time out on the water.*

EMK: Yes, all during—from whatever time in June, until I think almost early August.

What was always sort of—what I was beginning to think in my mind is, "Here, I was sort of close to my father and suddenly he was lost [after his 1961 stroke]. I had a great summer with my brother Jack, this personal relationship, and suddenly he was lost. And then Bobby arrived in the Senate and even though you're moved and troubled by what was happening in the society, in terms of the war and all the rest of it, suddenly he's, in personal terms, lost."

Q: *Efforts were made to get you to enter the race* [after Robert Kennedy's assassination on June 6, 1968].

EMK: Well, prior to the convention in [Chicago], I had had a meeting with Humphrey. He came out to the house in McLean, and I spent half an hour, forty-five minutes with him. It was clear that he was going to get the nomination. We have a very warm and touching conversation. It was about the vice presidential nomination and about how he understood the difficulties, personally, and how strongly we all felt about the issue. He was going to try and work that issue through. We never had any real specifics about how that was going to be done, but he understood that this was something that was absolutely—

Milton Gwirtzman: Vietnam?

EMK: Vietnam. We had always had a good relationship, even though Humphrey had run against my brother Jack. . . . He and I worked easily in the Senate. Because of the competition, there's a lot of blood boiling in these circumstances, but underneath it all, it was a very strong friendship. I think I mentioned that he asked me out to speak at his final dinner before he passed [in 1978]. So at this time, I liked him, but I wasn't prepared to sign on. The basic feeling was that it was too much too soon. I was going to be putting my family through all this. I was uncertain about where he was going to go. This was a cause that people had been so worked up in support of my brother, felt so strongly about, and I was a part of that. Humphrey hadn't separated from Johnson on Vietnam and didn't see clearly where he could. This would be betraying this whole effort and movement. So it really wasn't a close choice or decision.

Q: *But people kept coming after you.*

EMK: Yes.

Q: *Not only for vice president but then, later on, a draft* [for president].

EMK: I had some other conversations along that line. I felt also that if I was going to make a run for the presidency, I wanted to do it on my own. I didn't want to have it in the wake of all these other circumstances and tragedies. I always felt that if I was going to have that opportunity, I wanted a free and clear time for it, and not to be into this.

Secondly, I remember very clearly that, even though my brother sought [the vice presidential nomination] in '56, it's a real holding operation. And at this time, with the involvement in the issues I had already started in the Senate, I didn't see a holding pattern for eight years with possibilities then of getting a good crack at the presidency. It just didn't seem to me to be worth the wait and the time with everything else that was happening.

The Democrats had sixty-five or sixty-six senators at that time. And in the Senate, things were happening. It just didn't make a great deal of sense. I guess we had the convention going on now, and the great focus was going to be the peace plank. We had an interest in it. I personally had an interest in it. People—the delegates, our supporters, whom I'd worked in a relationship with all during the course of the campaign—cared very deeply about it. This was their cause now. And I couldn't not have at least some kind of a presence, although I wasn't going to go to Chicago. So Steve Smith went out there, and I think he was puttering around to see what the mood was and the sense of the convention itself, where the plank was going, what was developing. There's one story about that issue, about the peace plank and the modifications and the changes. You had another part of the convention, which was the violence out there.

Ribicoff and the group of demonstrators,[40] about which I don't have any special things to add, other than the general observations. Then as the nomination was being thought about, I talked again to Daley. And one other. I talked to them from a phone booth in Stonington, Maine. By this time I had sailed up there. But I really had not had an interest. And the other thing that was very clear to me was if I indicated an interest in going for the number-one job, I couldn't then turn the party down for the number-two job. If I was able to, willing to, risk my family and risk the kind of violence and other possibilities in running for the first one and going for it—and not get it because Humphrey was there—it's a very dicey situation. If you're willing to do that, you couldn't very well say no to number two, I didn't think.

And to be honest about it, I never was really quite sure what some of the—I had very good supporters, and people who wanted me to run and thought we could have maybe gotten the convention on it. But I also thought that there were other people who wanted me to go in, and—if I didn't get it—would have insisted that I be number two, and that I didn't want. That would have been the worst, to have made a stab—not that you mind taking a chance and trying to run at it—but if you were in for that part, you were in for number two, I thought. I didn't feel that I could separate those. And that really was a matter of concern for the reasons I mentioned earlier.

So it was a combination and not really clear—the personal equation was very weighty and heavy, and I think I felt I could do something myself later on. There were a number of both emotional and political concerns—I think the

---

40. While giving the nominating speech for draft candidate Senator George McGovern, Senator Abraham Ribicoff of Connecticut referred to the "Gestapo tactics" of Chicago police toward protestors amassed in the Windy City. From the convention floor, Mayor Daley reportedly shouted an anti-Semitic slur at the Jewish senator.

emotional was probably the right calculation. The political might have been different when you're looking back historically. But I don't have any regrets, and certainly didn't at the time.

After they got the nomination—now Humphrey had the nomination—they made some adjustments on the plank.[41]

Q: By the way, where was McCarthy in all of this at the last minute?

EMK: I think he was in Chicago, but I can't remember—

Gwirtzman: In a hotel room watching—he was concerned about his kids [supporters], who were getting beaten up. You're asking whether he said he would throw to Kennedy—There's a story about that.

EMK: It was very hard. It was very murky, who the messenger was and what exactly the message was. It didn't have a ring to it. Humphrey had given me assurances on some things. I think it was probably too raw with McCarthy to think that—

Q: Did you have the feeling—this wasn't the point of the game—that Daley and the rest were trying to play you into a strategy of their own?

EMK: I wasn't sure they weren't. And it wasn't even definite assurance. I'm not as cynical as most politicians, quite frankly, or skeptical about that. But it was too much of a risk. He'd [McCarthy] be the kind of politician who would say, "Well, we did the best we could for that part, now the party really needs you. You've said yes, you would do this, and now you can't let us down." And you were in. You were in on this thing. From the beginning, I never really moved off my position on it.

Gwirtzman: Also, didn't he say you'd have to go out there, and the security people said that it really wasn't—

EMK: You'd have to come here [to Chicago].

Gwirtzman: The Johnson Secret Service said you shouldn't.

EMK: There were security issues and questions of concern. I didn't feel that was something that was bothering me.

Q: But you probably would not have gone anyway?

EMK: I wouldn't have gone, no. What's your purpose out there? We were monitoring the [peace] plank, and the plank was moving. They were changing words, and people were having some impact on it. I can't describe what that plank was at the present time, but it ended up being fairly reasonable from the antiwar groups. But Humphrey still wasn't there. After he got the nomination, he called and asked me if I'd reconsider [for vice president]. And we had a similar conversation. He called. I talked to him personally.

Gwirtzman: Then he asked you about Muskie.

---

41. This refers to the segment of the Democratic platform calling for an end to the Vietnam War.

EMK: He asked me about Muskie, and—was it Fred Harris? Or was it Mondale?[42]

Gwirtzman: Fred Harris.

EMK: Fred Harris. Yes. He said he thought he was trustworthy and logical, prefers Muskie to Hughes, although Hughes was a good governor [of Iowa]. I knew Fred Harris was working on it. The other names that were in were Terry Sanford and John Gardner.[43] I asked him whether he would consider McCarthy, and he said he might have McCarthy forced upon him. He thought McCarthy had a cynicism about life that he could not tolerate. He felt if he was vice president, McCarthy would go away and sulk. [*Laughter*] He said he could not conceive a circumstance where he would take McCarthy. He said he would be in touch on the vice presidency, and again, RFK got into the campaign because of the Vietnam issue, and he felt strongly about it, as Bobby had. Whatever the dilemma was, he hoped it could be resolved.

Q: Humphrey wasn't moving strongly toward the peace plank, or at all, was he?

EMK: No, [Not until] . . . the Salt Lake City speech.[44] And then history shows he was gaining a point a day. From that time on, he was gaining a point a day. If that speech had been made four days earlier, or if the election had been three days later, he would have been elected. It's most extraordinary to see that thing moving. But, you know, those were all the complicated issues between him and Lyndon.

Kennedy occasionally read from his notes that he had taken in 1968.

EMK: [Humphrey] "called last night and told me that he thinks the campaign is—Said he had the biggest crowds in Tennessee, feels his speech was a breakthrough." See, this is October 2nd and I was the first person he heard from [after the September 30 speech]. "He said that my support has made a difference in the campaign, and he'll never forget it . . . keeping our fingers crossed. I mentioned that we were going to cut [video] tapes for him sometime soon." He said, "You've done enough for me, but obviously, this will be very helpful."

Gwirtzman: You didn't do a lot of campaigning. You made a lot of TV with candidates.

Q: You had the one public appearance with Humphrey in late September.

EMK: Yes, at Tremont Street [in Boston] and the other park, which was a real—There was a demonstration against us. I think it's reasonably into the campaign. And the interesting thing was, we drove down the street earlier

---

42. Vice President Hubert Humphrey, the Democratic presidential candidate, consulted with Kennedy about possible vice presidential nominees: Senators Edmund Muskie of Maine, Fred Harris of Idaho, and Walter Mondale of Minnesota. Humphrey eventually chose Muskie as his running mate.

43. John Gardner was former secretary of health, education, and welfare.

44. On September 30, 1968, Humphrey gave a speech in Salt Lake City, calling for a halt to bombing North Vietnam and a ceasefire.

to go to the Parker House, and we saw these same people who were the demonstrators. You know what they were doing? They were practicing how to get on one another's shoulders, and what they were going to do.

We said, "Isn't that interesting?" What they were doing on the corner of the Commons. And when we went up and came in through Filene's, I looked out there and I saw them all, and they did the exact thing that they had been practicing over there, to hassle us. They got on each other's shoulders so they could rise up and spread out a big banner and hassle us.

Q: Did the course of the campaign on the Republican side after Nixon's nomination surprise you at all?

EMK: I don't think so. Nixon was a talented campaigner, a bright, smart person, and I certainly had seen that previously. But I thought the whole effort about "I have a secret plan to end the war" was so phony, all of it. But it was so difficult getting started with Humphrey. That was a real dilemma; that was the enormous tragedy of it, getting that going and started.

And then Muskie had done very well in the campaign. He was getting a lot of recognition, acceptance; he was a real addition to him. I don't know whether I had any predisposition about what the outcome was going to be. I was certainly pulling for Humphrey, and enthusiastically so at the end when it became apparent that he had altered and changed his position on Vietnam and would have done something important.

The last people [American troops] out of there were in '75. This is '68. This is halfway. [Nixon] went all the way from '68 to '72, and you still had people in there later on. Half the people we lost, we lost after the '68 election. So an awful lot of people were killed after this. And then, you know, you had the whole Cambodian situation,[45] which was a disaster. He gets credit, obviously, for the opening of China. Historically, it was certainly moving in that direction in any event, and he gets some credit. But Southeast Asia, the rest of it was just so bad.

Q: The Humphrey campaign after the convention was a disappointment. It was too little and too late.

EMK: Too little too late. I'm sure he would have won. That drive at the very end was so powerful and so uplifting, and it ended so narrowly.[46] I don't think there was any real question in people's minds that, if this had gone on for another day or two, or if he had changed his position a week or ten days before, it really would have had a dramatic impact and change.

Q: As an observer, what do you think accounted for it? Was it LBJ's pressure?

---

45. In spring 1970, Nixon expanded the war in Southeast Asia to Cambodia in an effort to eliminate North Vietnamese army and Viet Cong forces amassed on the border with South Vietnam. A total of 58,220 Americans were killed in the Vietnam War.

46. Nixon won the popular vote by only 0.7 percent, but garnered 310 electoral votes, to Humphrey's 191. Third-party candidate George Wallace mustered 46.

EMK: Oh, clearly. But it's always a question, once you have the nomination. Of course, I suppose he thought that President Johnson could undermine him in some important ways. But he had a lot of supporters and constituents. Labor was very anti–peace movement. Very strong. George Meany was around here all the time. I remember that. They were really upset with Bobby. Just strong, strong. He was a rabid anti-communist. He was just rabid about this. So you still had a very divided country and society. And his [Humphrey's] whole base was very hawkish, a lot of hawks around in military, labor. And he was reluctant to leave his base, not knowing where he was going to go. He just didn't see it. He didn't see it, feel it, was not willing to taking a chance on it. So we now are in the—back into it through the late fall. We lost the campaign and now we start 1969. In 1969, it seemed to me that there were a number of things that Bobby was interested in and I thought I ought to try and sort of pick up on, and one of them was Indian education. He had done a lot on housing, which was still unfinished, but Indian education was, I thought, manageable. I said this was something I could do.

Q: He'd been on the [Indian Education Sub]committee.

EMK: He had chaired the committee. He had hearings about Indian schools. [He was moved by] the great tragedy of the Indians, and he traveled out to these places where it seemed that the poorest of the poor and the dispossessed lived. It's an area he hadn't completed, but a lot of the hearings had been done and we could complete this, which we did eventually. So we went up to Alaska and we traveled around [to Indian and Eskimo schools]. But we had the—I had that trip back where alcohol was consumed, and it became a national story.[47] So I'm back but sort of wasn't back. I never really thought that I was back. I never quite thought that it was—obviously, I had made a mistake.

We come to the time in the summer of '69 when I was up at the Cape to sail in the Edgartown races, which I had done in previous years. At that time, the group called the "boiler room" got together there. They had all worked in Bobby's campaign in '68, the year before. They had worked not only in the campaign but they also worked at the funeral, the same group of people, mostly from Massachusetts but not exclusively. They went over to this—over to the place up there [a cottage on Chappaquiddick Island], which they rented over the weekend. I made mistakes, but one of them was going by there and going to their event. But I had sort of thought, "Well, if Bobby had been around here, he would have gone." You know, I can't go through the—the series of events,[48]

---

47. The senator became intoxicated on one of the flights home from Alaska, and the press reported his rowdy behavior.

48. See Kennedy's memoir, *True Compass* (New York: Twelve, 2009), 287–93, for the last rendition he provided of Mary Jo Kopechne's death in the car that the senator drove off a bridge into a pond on Chappaquiddick.

they've been out there and I've spoken about them in public, when I had a much clearer memory—

Q: You don't have to go through that.

EMK: —than I have now. I think the power of the accident and the tragedy in this, is that this, unlike the other times, when people that were very much a part of my life were sort of taken from me, you had a person that was taken from *her* family life, and which I had a responsibility for. This was a person that I had no—hadn't any relationship with previously, and hadn't really— may have met but that didn't know—but who now becomes a part of my life and will be until my death because of this incident where she lost her life. I knew the extraordinary loss that those that were close in my family were to me, so I could understand, really, something of the loss that she was to her parents and her family, and . . . the loss of a life that she could have lived. The loss of my brothers and what they meant to my family and me—I could see this now replicated, duplicated, in the loss of her life, and what it would mean to her family. This was something that has always remained with me, from that time.

I had tried, over the period of time, with their family, you know to mend the broken hearts of her parents. It always seemed that my presence brought more pain to them, which was both saddening to my point of view but sort of realistic, you know, something that I could sort of understand. So I made up my mind that the best I could do was my prayers for her, my prayers for that family, and my recognition that this was an individual who could have had a joyous and wonderful life, and that I bear the responsibility. It was a tragic, tragic accident, but I certainly have understood that my actions were the principal cause, to blame for this.

The thing that was very apparent to me, looking back at that time, was sort of the disbelief of the whole event. I had a great deal of difficulty, as I remember back now, in believing that these series of events really happened, at the time when they were happening. I mean, it was like you were sort of living in a nightmare. You'd wake up and this would not have happened. It was really sort of too much for me to take in and absorb and try and think through. I kept thinking, this isn't [real]—I'm going to wake up, and we're going to be headed down to the dock for the next day's race. There was a whole series of different actions that obviously, you'd handle differently, but this [unreality] was something that stayed with me for a real considerable period of time. I don't know when it sort of finally ended and what ended it. I should have had a different kind of frame of mind . . . from the time of the accident on, instead of a state of almost disbelief that this was all going on, even happening. But that doesn't, certainly, excuse any of my actions or activities . . . in the immediate aftermath of the accident, and I don't offer it as any kind of excuse. I am trying to understand my own thought process and my own actions. This was something that was a factor in my own actions.

Q: *Well, that's all very human. I've looked at what you were doing in that year between Bobby's death and the race event and the party. I'm trying to track some of your activities and my impression is, once you got back into the Senate—Clymer writes that you tried to go back to the Senate soon and you just couldn't face it, you had to have some more time away. But then I think it was by September, you're back in the harness. It seems to me that you were just driving yourself very hard. You were doing so much, so active, and a lot of it looks to me like it was Bobby's causes. You mentioned Indian education. You went to Memphis for the Martin Luther King tribute. You went out to the place where he died, in California, for a [Cesar] Chavez event. You went to the Indian reservations; you went to Alaska. It's just a very intense period of throwing yourself back and picking up the fallen standard. And then the way it ended—the tragedy at Chappaquiddick, when you were standing in for Bobby at that event—I don't see how any human being could have taken that. The fact that you were in a period of disbelief—how could this happen, it was a nightmare, I'll wake up—when it comes on top of everything else I think is very understandable. And also, as you mentioned it's the first time, in this accident, that you had caused harm to another, and you're by nature so supportive of others, so feeling of others. I'm talking too much, it's your story.*

EMK: No, well that's—

Q: *That's what I'm seeing.*

EMK: My feelings about her loss and having the responsibility was something that always has stayed with me, does stay with me.

I think also—this is less important—about going back into the Senate. Here, you're going back, wondering how you're going to be received, bearing the shame of that incident, and wondering whether you could ever be effective again. Here you are living to try and make a difference in other people's lives, carry forward the unfulfilled missions of your brothers and other family members. And that's part of your motivation. Now you've lost the ability to have an impact, carry on a tradition. Would the people of the state continue to support you in this? I'd been around long enough to know that in the initial kinds of reactions, they always support somebody. But then when things settle on in, will they stay with you? So you know, everything that you've tried to do . . . your whole reason for—your public life, your pathway of life depends on [the trust and support of] others. So this was something that was—you were thinking about when you're coming on back in. And then of course I came back to the Senate and got beaten in the leadership fight [for Democratic whip], by Senator Robert Byrd, which is the message that was going to be sent.

Q: *And you were wondering if this might mean the end of your career.*

EMK: Yes, sure.

Q: *Or your purpose in your career.*

EMK: Purpose, I think it's the—

Q: *Because you couldn't fulfill the purpose anymore?*

EMK: You had lost some of the opportunity. People aren't going to pay attention to your viewpoint, people aren't going to care very much what you think. You lose so much of your political leadership, people's confidence, people's trust, people's belief. You know?

You speak for them, are you on their side? Are they going to be able to trust that you'll be on their side? Will they believe in your integrity in the political process, which has been your power in terms of your public life? So that was in my mind coming back.

Q: *And also the destructive part, the character destruction that follows.*

EMK: Yes, that's right.

Q: *So you get stereotyped as—*

EMK: Absolutely. Being a public figure, you're getting the assaults on this, people are exploiting all of this to your disadvantage. You're conscious of what this means to the Kopechne family and what it means to your family. I mean, I think you may be able to sort of get through this yourself, in terms of being able to carve out what you want to do, and face the music in that way. But it's obviously impacting and affecting other people. Those are body blows that come up sort of underneath the rib cage, I mean those can get at you. It's one thing as a politician, to deal with what people are going to say about your position on a particular issue, which you can deal with. But these kinds of body blows are particularly cruel and difficult and painful. And that was going to continue—and has continued on through in this last election.

Q: *It never goes away but it ceases to be determinative.*

EMK: No, it never goes away, but it makes you mindful of other parts— And then, just as we were coming through this period, my father dies [in November 1969]. And even though he had been ill and sick, he still had. . . . He was devastated with the loss of Bobby and the rest, and basically sort of gave up living. That was a great loss.

There had been a sort of upswing in '64, when Bobby was coming into the Senate, and I was coming back, a hopeful kind of time. Then all of this happened, which sort of closes out that decade.

Q: *Can we go back?*

EMK: Sure.

Q: *Could you talk about—or do you want to talk about after the accident. There was a much publicized gathering of the friends and advisors at the house in Hyannis Port, and there are sort of different interpretations of where you were in this process of making a public statement and so forth. I mean, I'm talking about Clymer and the others who have written about this.*

EMK: Yes.

Q: *I'm assuming that that was a period of time in which you were maybe still having the nightmare, and still in the period of denial, and you weren't in charge of planning the public response to this. Would that be a correct reading?*

EMK: Well, I had that one—you know, to speak to the people of Massachusetts. I think people, you know friends came there, there was sort of a gathering aspect of a plan. Something happens and everybody sort of comes. That was certainly true. People from my brothers' campaigns, everybody came.[49] I think they felt that they ought to come to reassure me and to try and give some. . . . There was always the speculation of some grand design down there. I never heard it if there was one. There were people that cared deeply about me, cared about our family, cared about—were very close to Bobby and my brother Jack.

Q: *Steve Smith came didn't he?*

EMK: And Steve came, he was very—

Q: *Dave Burke was there, I think.*

EMK: Dave Burke was there.

Q: *Among others, Bob McNamara.*

EMK: Dave had been my administrative assistant and Steve, my brother-in-law. We're getting ahead of ourselves now.

Q: *There was one other thing.*

EMK: Yes?

Q: *You didn't know how you'd be received in the Senate. So if you could go back to your re-entry into the Senate. What happened first, before the whip fight.*

EMK: What first happened, I think I had talked—I don't have the exact memory of it, but I believe Mansfield had called me, and I think some of the other senators had called me before I went back, and I remember Mansfield being very kind and gracious when I returned. We had some good friends there at the time. I felt that one of the things about the Senate is that at times when people are under the most intense pressure, there's a pretty good sense of collegiality, at least in terms of receiving you back. You don't know quite what's on their minds, but at least in appearance they were decent about having you come on back. That didn't answer the questions about whether you were going to be effective, whether people were going to follow you, whether they were going to let you lead on different issues, whether you could really be a force or a factor, but at least in superficial aspects, there was—I think people and members of the Senate also had—this is 1969—an awful lot of them had gone through the '63 and '68 [assassinations]. I think there was some empathy and some sympathy probably from people that had been either involved or cared

---

49. Friends and advisors gathered at Hyannis Port to discuss how to deal with the tragedy. Among them were Richard Goodwin, Ted Sorensen, Milton Gwirtzman, David Burke, John Culver, and John Tunney, according to Peter Canellos, ed., in *Last Lion: The Fall and Rise of Ted Kennedy* (New York: Simon and Schuster, 2009), 161. They decided that Kennedy should speak to the people of Massachusetts in a televised address, explain the accident, and ask his constituents whether he should stay in the Senate.

or who were friends during that period of time. So I think that was obviously a force or a factor in getting back.

Q: Were you still thinking in your mind, after you went back to the Senate, let's see how this works out, how effective I can be, what I can do, and reserving judgment on whether you would stick with it? Or you were already determined to stick with it and make something of it?

EMK: Well in my mind, I thought that it was going to be—in my mind, I thought that I had to work to earn the confidence and trust of people back, I knew that. But I thought I could, because this had been—all of them said it had been an accident. I mean, it was a terrible one and I was at the wheel, and I had made some mistakes which I admitted at the time, so it was a devastating event. But I thought that it wasn't—I mean, I accepted all that. I thought that there still was the possibility to regain confidence and regain trust and regain support. I believed that, but I wasn't absolutely sure. I knew that the only way you're going to do it is a lot of, *lot* of hard work, a lot of slogging away and a lot of working with colleagues and deference to them, you know, re-earning your stripes, so to speak, in there. So that's what I did. I think that was compelling. I never thought of turning away from it, but I was very conscious that there was a lot of work to do.

Q: When you look back on this, would you think this was a turning point for you? Were you different after that and after it was sort of over and you're back to work in the Senate, than you were before that or before Bobby's [death]?

EMK: I think so. You know, when I first arrived in the Senate, I knew I was very lucky to be there and I knew there was a lot to learn, and I know that I was going to—I was afforded the luxury of spending a lot of time. I just sort of worked as—I mean, I got started on the poll tax, but it was—I think the life experience. Then you suddenly realize where you are and what you can do and what is possible to get done and you try to do it right. I think I sort of reached that point then. I certainly wanted—was prepared to be an important senator. I had sort of a glimmer of thought about the possible future. I mean, I wasn't thinking this at the time I first came back, but I knew I wanted to work hard and do something of importance and consequence. That's sort of where I was, and that's what we tried to do.

Q: Did you have a sense at this time of the dangers of being a public figure?

EMK: Well, I think so, I think so.

Q: I guess your family certainly was.

EMK: I certainly did. At some events subsequently you wear a bulletproof vest and other kinds of things like that. I mean, I knew there were dangers out there, but there were some that. . . . I was very involved in the '68 Gun Act. I knew that was going to tee-off people, but I didn't really care. I didn't really care. I felt that you had to have some prudence in this case, you had some responsibility. But on the other hand, you don't want your life's work to be conditioned on that kind of constraint either.

Q: I am thinking about the various ways people deal with tragedy. I remember my wife[50] telling me about something that I think anthropologists have called grief work. I think this may have been a term that Margaret Mead used. Survivors respond to the death of someone important to them by doing work instead of dwelling on their loss. The work can be pretty crazy and exhausting. But this is a way some people grieve, instead of withdrawing to mourn or turning inward. I was thinking of how you threw yourself back into Senate work, working even harder, after the tragedies. It brought this idea of grief work to mind. I thought I would just throw that out.

EMK: No, I think there's a lot to it.

Q: When you lost Bobby, you picked up his work.

EMK: No, I think there's a lot to it. I think you also have a lot of periods of loneliness during this period and seeking solace. I was bothered by my back at times. In other words, there were times where—

Q: You were experiencing constant pain weren't you?

EMK: I felt that, yes, it's with you all the time, more sometimes than others, but it's very much there. So I mean, you had those kinds of times.

Q: What was your immediate family situation, Joan's situation, during all of this?

EMK: This was a difficult time with her. I mean she tried and tried hard to get help during this time, and she went to different places. It looked like it was OK for a while, and then she had a tough period. I think the disease is not completely inherited, but an awful lot of that thing is inherited. I mean her parents, unfortunately, both died of alcoholism. You could see in your living family the dangers that people can have in these things. I think there's a lot we've still got to learn about it, but boy it is devastating, a devastating disease. I think she's tried nobly to deal with it. It's just been devastating, I think over her entire life, really.

Q: But again, there was nobody at home that you could turn to.

EMK: No, no. Well, now you have the—we have Teddy [Jr.]'s time and his recovery from cancer [1973–75]. Patrick now is a chronic asthmatic, and we spent a lot of time with him in hospitals. He had a lot of difficulty. He's so incredible. These dogs [Sunny and Splash] are not allergenic, and yet he reacts. He's the one person I was trying to think of. Who else, Vicki, reacts to the dogs? He'll get a reaction.

Q: Breathing problems.

EMK: He's had it since childhood, and he's had a very tough time, where— you know, playing sports, not being able to do these things, and that's been a big, you know a major challenge.

---

50. Professor Jim Young's wife, Virginia, was an anthropologist.

Perspectives

Senator Paul G. Kirk (D-MA), Robert Kennedy's presidential campaign staffer, Edward Kennedy's special assistant, attorney, and friend: The thing that was interesting, which was sort of an eye-opener for me, was that at the RFK headquarters, not unlike what happens in a lot of campaigns, you had three different levels of Kennedys. You had the John Kennedy group: Ted Sorensen, Kenny [O'Donnell]—and sometimes they'd work together and sometimes they didn't, so there was a little tension there. Then you had the Robert Kennedy group: This is *our* candidate, screw the *John* Kennedy people, and who do the *Ted* people think they are? Then you had the Ted Kennedy people. I'm in there looking at this from the outside and thinking, "Jesus, if the American people knew what was really going on." But it happens in every campaign, there's always internal friction going on. But it's sort of the normal—well, I shouldn't say normal, because it's such a different chapter of history and all. But there were those tensions within. It was nothing that impeded the progress of the campaign, but I wondered, why is all this necessary?

Q: Then there were other family members as well, right? Sisters and—

Kirk: Oh, yes. And none of them shy, and none of them without an opinion, and all of them smart—as is true of all aspects of the Kennedy family and life. To me it's so remarkable that each and every one of them is, in one way or another, working for the public good—the Special Olympics, the Very Special Arts, you can go down the line. As I say, no shrinking violets in the garden. All fun and all constructive. That's probably the best I can do with that question.

Q: Do you recall what your impressions were of Ted Kennedy during that campaign?

Kirk: By that time, this was a serious senator who had basically, in everything I had seen and observed, made up his mind that he was going to be a good senator, was going to learn the ropes. There wasn't anything else out there. Obviously, he had lost one brother in the war, and the president was gone. If Bobby chose to run, fine. Ted's role was to be an active, working legislator. Marty Nolan of the *Boston Globe* wrote something early on about the difference between a workhorse and a show horse, and how everyone expected Senator Edward Kennedy to live off the name. Quite to the contrary. He engaged early with Richard Russell and all these guys who were two generations older than he, and he learned the ropes, and he kept his head down. So my impression of him was that here's a guy you like to see and you're glad to meet, and that he's serious-minded about what he's going to do. Though, obviously, a member of an important family.

At the same time—although I didn't see that much of this aspect of him then, because it was schedules and so forth, but it's almost the same way today—when he walks into a room, he just fills it. Vroom, sucks all the oxygen out. He's always got a story.

David Burke, Edward Kennedy's chief of staff: It's very hard for me to put it into words the feelings that I had in '68 while Bobby was alive and before Bobby announced. We've talked before about how Ted was opposed to Bobby's running for the presidency, because he had a feeling of dread. But Ted is also a good politician. He would look around the universe and come to his own conclusions as to whether Bobby would succeed. I think he felt that Bobby wouldn't succeed. I think that it was an intense time, and you're together all the time, and things are said or left unsaid during those times that have meaning.

He and I went to the states that held conventions, which was the majority of states in those years, as opposed to primaries. To win a convention, of course, you have to do well with the leaders in that state—the head of the local legislature, the House and Senate in the state, union leaders, and so on. It was quite clear that Bobby was not close to them. Other people were close to them, such as Hubert Humphrey and others, who had spent a lifetime working that side of the street. Bobby had no real interest in doing that, and he never did that.

I think it is possible—and I don't know since I didn't reside inside his brain—that Ted may have been of the mind that besides the dread he had that someone was going to hurt Bob, which was quite real, that Bobby might lose badly and that that would not be good for Ted as he went forward with his life. Why put everything at risk, including the life of my brother? I sensed that. Now, I never had a conversation with him about that, but if you threaten me with my life, I'd have to confess that I had a sense that it would have been better in his mind if Bobby just hadn't run and had instead stayed in the Senate for a while and had then figured out what else he was going to do in his life, having already accomplished some rather wonderful things. That was the first sense I had that underneath a ton of baggage—and underneath the horrors of the '60s—was a yearning on his part to someday have his shot for the presidency of the United States of America.

I used to talk with other members of the staff. We were very proud. We would go into a state when Bobby was running for the presidency, and people would say to us, "You're not like Bobby's people." Well, we weren't. We were a reflection of Ted Kennedy. Bobby's people were slash-and-burn and run riots through a city or a state, whereas the Teddy Kennedy people got Christmas cards for years after from people they had met on the campaign trail. They liked Teddy's people, and they liked Teddy. He was comfortable to them, and he carried a magic. He had to sense that; he had to know that. As we've described before, he is not a fool. You may think he's not paying attention, but he knows things, and he knew that. So I watched him.

I remember, on the day of Bobby's announcement, we were out at Bobby's house picking out neckties, and Ethel was all nervous energy and running around and doing very competent work, I would say. Bobby was getting annoyed at all of the fuss and bother. Bobby was not a patient person in those kinds of situations. "Any tie will do," he would say. Well, that wasn't the answer for Ethel. She wanted the right tie. Finally Teddy said to me, "Come on, David. Let's go outside and take a walk," which we did. The grounds at Hickory Hill were pretty extensive, and we could walk around, so we did.

During that walk he made it clear again how much he didn't like this, and he left me with the impression of, "We have to take care of ourselves, Dave. We have to conduct ourselves in a way that's right." This may have been my hopeful thinking, because naturally, as a person associated with him and who had come to admire and respect him on substantive matters and on the kinds of things he was attracted to in the legislative area, I wanted him to be successful one day. We didn't have to have long, drawn-out conversations about what "We have to take care of ourselves" meant.

It could have meant that we had to take care of ourselves physically. You will recall, in those days, that there was no Secret Service protection for people running for office. There is today only because of what happened that year. So that could have been what "take care of ourselves" meant. It also could have meant, "Remember, wherever you go, I want to make sure the Christmas cards keep coming next year. We have to watch ourselves on issues so that we don't get locked into a position on this, that, or the other thing." So my first instinct was that Bobby's running for president was not attractive to him at all. And then when the worst thing that could have happened happened, he was quite crushed by it. He might even have been hurt by the fact that he may have not been as supportive as he could have been when his brother made the choice.

After all of that happened, inexorably the convention time was coming around in Chicago in '68, and some people, especially those led by Mayor Daley of Chicago, were not going to let this thing go. They wanted a Kennedy on the ticket, and they wanted Ted Kennedy on the ticket—not clearly thought out and not open to argument. It was just, "We're going to ram this thing." While the convention was underway, he was under an onslaught of phone calls from politicians around the country. He was buoyed by the phone calls, but I cannot say that he wasn't carried away by them. I think it became the thought of going to Chicago, standing for the nomination, getting it by acclamation.

All of this was promised by Daley and the others: motorcades into town, motorcades out of town, security all over the place. "Don't you worry. We'll take care of everything. We'll have cops in everyone's bedroom. Nothing bad can happen here." He was afraid because all of a sudden, there it was, right in front of him. It could possibly happen. There had been no preparatory work. You know, from talking to him, that when he prepares for something, he prepares for something. He has books; he has endless documentation, papers. Because he's never, ever sure that he has it all. By that definition, he never has it all. He's just never sure of that.

But in Chicago, Mayor Daley said, "If you want to have the nomination for president of the United States, you could have it tomorrow morning if you want. You come into town, and Chicago will be stood on its ear, and you will, by acclamation to the whole nation, you will—" Ted said, "But I don't know what I stand for. I don't know where I am. I don't know what my preparation is. I haven't looked at it. I haven't thought about it. I haven't talked to enough people. We should get some people and talk about it." There was no time to talk to people. This was underway. The momentum was there, and the madness was in the air. He wasn't coy about it in any way, but he was not easy to convince. It was easy to convince him to disregard the phone calls.

Suddenly the presidency, besides being something that may have been in the back of his mind, was now staring him in the face, or the potential of running for the presidency, and he wasn't ready and he knew it, and people close to him also knew he wasn't ready. It wasn't that he wasn't ready because he was not capable of getting ready. It was because his brother had just been murdered, and he was a hurt person. In that kind of situation, you can't ask a person to run for the presidency of the United States and guarantee to that person that you will launch him into a campaign that was going to be madness for the next couple of months. It would have been horrible. So that was that. That's my remembrance of '68.

He might not remember, but there's a Robert Frost book, the title of which is, *Hard Not to Be King*. It's difficult not to be king when it's in you and in the situation. This is what he had. It was in him and in the situation—in him because his name was Kennedy, in the situation because he was growing in strength in the Senate. He was gaining a reputation of his own, and the tragic deaths of his brothers placed him in an historic setting. Someone writing a play for Broadway couldn't figure out a series of events that would place someone in that. Therefore, from '68 on, it was a governing factor in his mind. He wanted to someday be the president of the United States of America. There's no doubt in my mind about that. And as long as he took care of himself, he could do it rather easily. To me, strangely enough, '68 was the only spontaneous activity surrounding him and the presidency of the United States. Everything else was supposedly "planned," and those plans were stiff and not good, and it didn't work.

Q: Talk about 1980. Carter was now president.

Burke: Carter was president, and he's going to have a revolution here. Eighty was ten long years after '70, which was when I left. Over the course of the '70s, I was involved with him not often but in some serious matters, such as the Paris peace talks, and should he go to Hanoi, and that sort of thing, which I enjoyed. He had plucked me to do things like that, and I enjoyed that. But he had a whole new staff and all sorts of things that I had not been privy to and so on, and I distanced myself. Then in '77, when I went to work for ABC News, that's when I made the decision that if he were to run for president, I would have absolutely nothing to do with it.

Q: How did you come to leave?

Burke: Leave him in the first place?

Q: Yes.

Burke: It was a mixture of all sorts of things. Chappaquiddick was a bad event for me, and it tore a lot of foundations away that had been holding me up. His behavior had been on and off, errant on many occasions, and I heard, "That's all right. We'll always see our way through it." After that I left. Other people in the office left after that event too. I didn't because he was running again in 1970, and if I was going to be the last man in the office, I was going to be the last man. I didn't care.

Q: You were in that campaign?

Burke: Oh, yes. I wouldn't leave until that was over, but I knew I was going to leave. It wasn't a big surprise to a lot of people that I was going to leave. You have your whole life controlled by another person, so you live by what they do or don't do.

Q: Was the 1970 campaign a tough one for him or for you?

Burke: It should have been, but it wasn't. No, it wasn't.

Q: Why not?

Burke: That's interesting. In Massachusetts, so close to '68, Massachusetts being Massachusetts, to throw a Kennedy out of office, no matter how much you disapproved of his behavior, it would have been a large event, and not one that people would have wanted to do. Everyone, I believe, was shocked and hurt by what they considered to be his bad behavior, but that didn't mean that they were going to throw him out. They weren't guaranteeing him anything for the future, but just two years after his brother's death and seven years after another brother's death and then this situation, it is astonishing that other Democrats didn't rise up to challenge him. In the atmosphere of the times, strangely enough, that would have been a heretical act. You don't do that to Jack's brother, to Bobby's brother. Bobby wasn't that popular in Massachusetts all the time, but still, you don't do that.

So it wasn't a tough campaign. I don't think it was tough. I spent most of the campaign in Boston. The campaign was Steve Smith in New York, myself in Boston, and the Boston folks, who were wonderful—Gerry Doherty and those kinds of people. It was clear that this was not going to be a bad campaign, and the vote was what, 64 [62] percent or something like that? It was an extraordinary vote. Sixty-four percent is not the kind of vote you get after a hard-fought campaign; 52 percent is what you get after a hard-fought campaign. When that was over, I left.

Burke: Mike Mansfield, for example, he loved Mike Mansfield, but you had to be careful that you didn't show that too much because Mike Mansfield was an upright, straight guy, and he didn't have anyone fawning around him.

I remember campaigning with the senator. He and I went out to Montana, not that you had to, to campaign for Mike Mansfield when he was running for re-election at one time. Who has to campaign for Mike Mansfield? He learned all the stories about Mike Mansfield: how many languages he could speak, how he had been a high school dropout, how he married as a very young man to a wonderful woman who straightened him out and made sure he went to college.

Mike was a miner. He put the dynamite in the holes in the rocks, and his working buddies used to call him "Tap her light Mike," because Mike was the one who had to tap the dynamite into the hole in the rock ever so gently. I don't know how the senator [Kennedy] found that out. Good staff work? I remember in one of the last speeches he gave for Mike Mansfield in Montana, he turned back on the podium, and he looked back at Mike, and he said, "Tap her light, Mike." I thought Mansfield would dissolve. Where did that come from? He hadn't heard it for years. That was the endearing quality. After the accident in Chappaquiddick, when Ted came back, Mansfield wouldn't let him stand alone in the Senate. He said, "I'll come right down by my desk here. Stand with me while I talk to the press."

With the old guys, especially the southern old guys, he [Kennedy] was very courteous. He brought everything his mother ever taught him to bear, because they wouldn't have liked his father but they would have liked his mother, because she was a very elegant woman. There were other senators in the Senate you could clown around with, but you would never do that with the older southerners.

Milton Gwirtzman, Edward Kennedy's speechwriter and advisor:
Q: Let's talk about Bobby's eulogy.
Gwirtzman: OK. Ted was in San Francisco when he heard that his brother had been shot, and he came down to Los Angeles. By the time he got to Los Angeles, the specialist who had been flown in from Boston was saying, and I heard him say, "eight to eighteen hours," which was how long it would physically take before everything would shut down because of the trauma of the brain injury. In other words, some time in that period he would die. So that's about when Ted got there. . . . Now, in whatever suite of rooms that had been assigned to Robert Kennedy, there was an outside room where people like me would be just waiting. Remember, this was—We had had this win in California, and then he was shot, so there were enormous grief and trauma at the time. There was a surreal aspect to it. Mrs. Martin Luther King felt that she had to be there, because the same thing had happened to her husband. And she really felt that she had to be there. Ethel had never met her. Ethel was in no shape to receive anybody, so how do you deal with Mrs. King? And it's not as if someone's great-aunt is coming in. Mrs. King had just had her own tragedy. That's the sort of thing that people like me were thinking about: What do you say to Mrs. King?

But inside, where he [Bobby] was dying, it was just the family, and that's where Ted was.

So we get to the hotel [in New York City] and Ted's in the room with John Tunney and they're trying to decide about the eulogies. Adam Walinsky[51] had given them some of Bobby's sayings, some of his speeches, to include. Ted wanted to include some material from Bobby's speeches. Tunney and Teddy felt very strongly that Ted should say some things of his own. Tunney was, I would have to say, Ted's best friend. Ted had not slept in three days. You could just look at his eyes; they were puffy and red, and he was sort of reacting. The two of them instructed me to write something about love and use some of RFK's quotes. Ted and Tunney felt very deeply that they wanted the eulogy to be about love, and the love that Ted had for his brother and the love that his brother had for people. Love would be the theme.

So I went back to my room and I wrote something. I wouldn't say it was suffused with love, because there were some other things that I thought should be in there. I had just read a column by Tom Wicker, in the *New York Times*, that John Kennedy would not have been so beloved a figure had he not been assassinated. It wasn't a criticism, it just said this is the way we always put our assassinated heroes up on a bigger pedestal than the ones who died natural deaths. Lincoln.

Anyway, Wicker had written this, and that's why I used the words "Let us not make of him something more in death, than he was in life," and that he should be known just as a simple man who put three things together, which I thought encompassed his life: that he saw wrong and tried to right it, which was his career as a prosecutor and then attorney general; that he saw suffering and tried to heal it, which referred to his interest in the Indians and the people in Mississippi, the people in Bedford-Stuyvesant, and poor people in general; and that he saw war and tried to stop it, which was his opposition to the war in Vietnam. But then I said, "Those of us who loved him—" and that's where I used their theme—"and who take him to his rest today, pray that what he was to us and what he wished for others will somehow come to pass for all the world." And so Ted read that. He read it beautifully, but his voice cracked right at the end, when he said the things I just said.

I was just trying to express, for someone who was in such shock and grief he was not in a position to compose something himself, what he would have said had he been in the position to compose something. Ted had just lost his greatest friend, the closest brother he had ever had; he had had no sleep. He was really in very difficult shape. You try to help someone like that. He had to appear before the whole world on live TV. Sure, he could have said, "I'm

---

51. Adam Walinsky was a speechwriter for Robert Kennedy.

not going to say anything at this funeral," but that's not the way the family operated. He wanted to say something.

Q: Did you write the whole thing?

Gwirtzman: Yes.

Q: Did he make any changes?

Gwirtzman: No. I think it's the best piece of writing I have ever done. And it came out of my own feelings for Ted.

Q: Well, let's skip ahead to another period of real involvement with Ted, and that was on Chappaquiddick.

Gwirtzman: Well, I can only talk—He's been interviewed on Chappaquiddick.

Q: Right, but I want you to talk about what was your role in the writing of a speech.

Gwirtzman: Let me put these things in order here. This is 1969 and at that time, I was still writing his speeches, but not all of them, because even by 1969, his staff had expanded. One thing he always made sure was that when he was taking on any new personnel that they could write, so in case they had to write a speech about their area, they could do it. So I did not have to do all the writing. So I was not as involved, but would drop in his office frequently.

One Saturday I dropped in. The drowning had taken place on a Friday, it was a holiday. But I dropped in on a Saturday, and Dave Burke was there, and he calls me into his office and told me what had happened and showed me the statement that Ted had given the police. Ted had called him about it. I think he had also called Burke Marshall. No one else, except Steve Smith. Dave could see this was going to be very difficult, especially since he knew that Scotty [James] Reston was on the island because his son, at that time, edited at the *Vineyard Gazette*. So Scotty Reston, the main political columnist for the *New York Times*, was on the island.

Then there was a period of a few days when it became a huge national story, but nothing emanated from Hyannis at all. A number of us, not just me but other people, were saying this can't keep going. Not only did he not tell what he did and why he didn't do some things, but there's all these rumors that he did all sorts of other things, for example, that young Joe had been driving, and he was taking the rap for Joe. Or that he tried to get Gargan to take the rap for him. Drew Pearson[52] was writing; he had been on the island several times and knew the island of Chappaquiddick very well. In reality, Chappaquiddick is just a beach off of Martha's Vineyard. It's not very wide, but there is a very deep and strong current between the two. A ferry goes back and forth, but it was only like five hundred feet.

---

52. "Young Joe" was Bobby's eldest son; Joseph Gargan was Kennedy's cousin; Drew Pearson was a syndicated *Washington Post* columnist and national radio personality.

So Wednesday came and I said, "I've got to go up there. They are not aware of what is going on in the country." I have some notes that I wrote on the plane. "He's got to talk to the public about this. He's got to say something." I had been talking to Angelique Lee,[53] who was there, who said Ted was talking about issuing something saying little more than, "I'm very sorry that she's dead," nothing about how and why. I said that's not going to get you anywhere. I did not know Mary Jo. I fear I looked at it as primarily a political problem, even though it was an intensely personal one, a young woman dead at the prime of life. I looked at it from his point of view, not hers or her family's. I did it because my entire career and a lot of my life had been invested with him over the past ten years. I couldn't believe someone who was that fine a person and that concerned about everybody would let this girl drown. There must be some reason for it, and he should tell what his reasons were.

So I just went up there. Angelique arranged for me to come, and I saw Steve. Steve Smith and I had been working very closely on a lot of stuff at that time and he said, "Okay, you're going to be one of our lawyers." He said that because he could talk to somebody who he had taken on as a lawyer. And he probably said that to every lawyer who went up there, because I wasn't the only person. Some people were already there. I think they all went up on their own. They were not called or summoned. I think they all went up on their own because of their love of Ted, their desire to help him, and they just couldn't understand why there was silence coming from Hyannis Port, as days went by and the public mood about this became worse.

Well, when I got there, I could see why there was silence, because the lawyers he had retained in the negligence case (leaving the scene of the accident) were telling him that if he said anything prior to being sentenced for leaving the scene of the accident, the judge would just throw the book at him. So he said, "I can't say anything. My lawyer is saying I can't say anything." That happens. Nowadays, your lawyer speaks for you, which is okay, but then—

Sorensen was there, and then I saw Ted [Kennedy]. First of all, he was in a brace. You could see that he was in terrible shape. I don't know whether he was under medication for pain or what. It was before he went to her funeral, and what he was saying was basically, "I willed her alive." I thought maybe this was something in his religion. He could not believe she was dead. He thought that she had escaped from the car just as he had, but it was a matter of will, that he willed it, and that's why he—Well, he'd dived several times and couldn't get anywhere because of the current. He didn't continue because after he dove several times and saw nothing, he thought she had gotten away. That's the main thing I remember about my conversations with him. From then on I worked with Sorensen and we divided—

---

53. Angelique Lee was Kennedy's secretary.

The strategy I suggested at that point was that for Ted to save his career he had to rely on the people who made it possible. These were the people of Massachusetts. He had to put to them the question of whether he should continue in office. If they said no, he should get out, and if they said yes, he could stay in office. They were his base and they would support him because they knew him. The people in the rest of the country just knew him as the dead president's brother. This was 1969; he didn't have a big Senate career because he had only been in there six years. They knew him from the funeral, and they knew him from his eulogy at Bobby's funeral, but they didn't know him as a person. All they knew is this guy ran away from an accident where a girl had drowned, and that he was responsible for her going over the bridge. That's very bad. He had to deal with his own people in Massachusetts, and therefore he had to speak to them and tell them, as he said in the speech, it may be, because he had admitted to leaving the scene of this tragic accident, he should retire from public life.

I also suggested saying, "And I know that because of this, I will never be able to seek the presidency." Eunice took that out. But Ted did the narrative, and I did the end, which was referred to as the send in your box tops or the Nixon Checkers speech thing. It was generally decried as tasteless and out of place, but it worked. He got 100,000 letters, not e-mails, 100,000 written letters from people in Massachusetts, urging him to stay in office despite this, because they knew him, and they knew what he had done for them. He had been a part of their lives for the last seven years. It's the difference between someone you just read about in the paper a couple of times and someone you feel you've known personally for years.

Q: So clearly, the Chappaquiddick speech resonated in Massachusetts.

Gwirtzman: It did what I hoped it would do. Let me just say that, at the time, Dave Burke was much more involved with helping him decide whether to stay in office, personally. I was not really involved with that. At one time he was talking about leaving public life. He was serious about it, and Dave Burke said, "What are you going to be, the Duke of Windsor?"[54]

Paul Kirk: So I met a lot of people in the political world [during Robert Kennedy's 1968 presidential campaign], and that may have been a reason why later I ended up being asked to join Ted Kennedy's staff. But then it ended; it was perhaps two-and-a-half months, because I went to DC in mid-March, right after RFK's announcement in '68, and of course, it was over in June. We went up to New York, helped in planning the funeral, and returned to DC on the funeral train. I can still remember young Joe; he was just a kid, walking

---

54. The Duke of Windsor was a reference to Britain's King Edward VIII, who abdicated the British throne in 1936 to marry a twice-divorced American.

through that train. I will tell you, personally, I was destroyed. The best way I can describe it—it was the end of hope. We'd already lost President Kennedy by assassination, then Martin Luther King, now RFK, and I decided, this is it for me. I'm not doing this any more. My emotions were wrung out. I couldn't get far enough away; I went to Hawaii for about a week, just to be away and get some perspective on life. I came back and I said, "That's it, it's too much. John and Robert Kennedy both inspired the nation. They tried to do the right and good thing—committing themselves to public life, and then they're blown away. So to hell with it."

For the next year I was back practicing law in Boston. And then for close to a year Dave Burke, Ted Kennedy's administrative assistant, and others were saying, "Why don't you come down and join Ted's staff?" I said, "I'm not coming." Then finally I thought to myself, "Jesus, if the fourth and last surviving brother somehow can suck it up after the losses that he's endured and continue the struggle, who the hell am I to be wallowing in the grief?" So without Senator Ted Kennedy even saying a word, it was like, "Okay, Paul, get a life. You've got to get out of this." It was Ted Kennedy's own example that inspired me to get involved again.

Partly it was Senator Kennedy's office per se—compared to other offices. I'm willing to bet it's the same today; the interest and attention that was visited on him as a human being and as a public figure, plus his work ethic, plus the kinds of issues that he chose to get involved in, and the reasons for those choices. It was like, this is as good as it gets. You are right in the firestorm there. His staff, I'm sure, still have to run like hell just to keep up with him. Enormous endurance and intellectual and physical energy. You've met him enough to understand all that.

Thomas Oliphant, *Boston Globe* reporter and columnist:

Q: How would you explain to somebody who might be reading this interview fifty years from now, or a hundred years from now, how Senator Kennedy politically survived Chappaquiddick? It probably would have destroyed other politicians.

Oliphant: Maybe. The thing that I've always said that I felt at the time covering it—I was on rewrite that weekend.

Q: The moon-landing weekend.

Oliphant: Yes. Extra people were pulled in. It was a Saturday, and so everything was just coming in over the transom. A week or so later, as he was getting ready to make the speech, I thought that his own description of his own conduct was so damning and so thorough that it almost cut off the discussion. In other words, if you list the adjectives that he lists—"not understandable," "terrible," "unforgivable," "inexcusable"; there's this long list of adjectives—no one's ever topped it. It's funny, the story hasn't changed either, interestingly enough, and I think that's basically what happened. What is forgotten is the harshness of his own judgment of himself. As I say, I don't think anybody talking about that accident in public has ever exceeded the ferocity of those adjectives that Kennedy himself applied to himself.

So one reason that he survived—"prevailed" actually is the correct word—is that there was a feeling that he'd not confessed, but that he had been harsher on himself than most people wanted to be if they were grounded in the facts of what happened. Also there was a long time to get ready for 1970, and the Republicans, bless their heart, obliged with a really ugly primary.

They had a right-winger, I don't remember his name—anyway, an early example of a hard-right politician—and then a Yankee.

Q: Spaulding.

Oliphant: Cy Spaulding. And Cy won it [the GOP primary], and it was a cakewalk after that. He was a gentleman. That was his own image of himself. He really was. The guy he ran against had wanted to use this, but it became clear, I think, in the primary that he could characterize Chappaquiddick differently, but he didn't have anything; the story didn't move. People forget, I think, how much Kennedy said in that initial period, in those first few weeks, not that he'd confessed, but that there had been a degree of candor and self-judgment that was enough. And this idea that somebody else might not have survived it, I don't know. It's conjectural.

Q: Sure. Were you assigned to cover any aspect of that story?

Oliphant: I had a piece of the speech—not the case in the court, as such—one weekend in Wilkes-Barre at the time of the [Kopechne] funeral. Everyone knew her. Again, this is lost to history. The idea that there was something between them is so obscene. Mary Jo Kopechne was, God, I want to say "altar girl." Is there such a thing in that church? No, they wouldn't let that happen, would they? But I mean, an intensely—

Q: Convent student.

Oliphant: Well, borderline. The "boiler room" in 1968 [Robert Kennedy's campaign], it wasn't like a frat house.

Q: It was a real working—

Oliphant: In a boiler room, you're on the phone nineteen hours a day. She was about as straight an arrow as you could imagine. Sadly, the public-at-large never got to know her, but that part of the conjecture is really ridiculous. She was very quiet, unassuming. I guess we all know girls who went to Catholic school, right? And she was central casting.

Nance Lyons, Robert Kennedy and Edward Kennedy staffer:
Nance Lyons wrote this passage as an addendum to her oral history transcript.

Lyons: I have never discussed the tragedy at Chappaquiddick. The events of that weekend were tragic. Mary Jo was my roommate. I knew her parents. Chappaquiddick changed my life. First, the women who had had significant responsibility in the national campaign for Bobby Kennedy were portrayed as girls of no significance—even as party girls. It was humiliating—but no one bothered to set the record straight. Then, for the next ten to twelve years on each anniversary, we were pursued by the press, subjected to hate mail, and demeaning descriptions of our work and those veiled accusations about our moral rectitude.

Even though I returned to work within ten feet of his office, he never, never, never asked how I was doing; or said how sorry he was that I and the other women were subjected to such scrutiny. And, I certainly didn't feel welcomed back by this staff. Still, he never mentioned Mary Jo to me. No call during each year's anniversary scrutiny. No thank you for supporting him during these trying times. To me this was unbelievable and I have not forgiven him for that insensitivity. The women from Chappaquiddick suffered greatly both personally and professionally. Some lost jobs, some didn't get jobs, no judgeships in Massachusetts for Maryellen or me, etc. Frankly, I believe he set my departure up. He knew I wanted to leave. I was offered a job in New York through one of his associates. It took me a while to understand the ploy, but I did move on to New York.

Many years later, Joey Gargan is quoted in a book accusing me of being the one who suggested that we come up with a story that someone else was driving the car. In fact, it was the women who derailed that brilliant idea. We refused to go along—not that I think the senator was aware of that proposal. It was Joey and some of the other men. I was outraged by the book.

And then, in his last and final words on the subject, in his book *True Compass*, the Senator says that he really didn't want to go to Chappaquiddick that weekend, but that I insisted. Who knew I had such power!

Kilvert Dun Gifford, friend and staffer of Robert and Edward Kennedy:

Gifford: Whatever happened there [Chappaquiddick] happened. I wasn't there. I didn't witness it. I was there early the next morning. I flew over—you probably know all this, right? I chartered a little plane. I flew over with a friend of mine. He flew me over. I really didn't know much when I got there, just the bare story. I went down to the bridge and looked at what was going on there. Went to the—actually, my first stop was to go see the chief of police, Dominick J. Arena. I thought that was the right thing to do and it was. I said, "I'm here. I don't have an agenda—whatever I can do to help you."

He said, "Really?" I said, "Really. Just try me. I'm his legislative assistant. I work in Washington. I have a house in Nantucket. I've been around these waters a lot. I know what's going on. I'm a big boy and I went to law school." I think he just didn't trust me at first. So that was my first stop. Then I went to see the medical examiner because I knew there was an issue about identifying the body legally. I was looking around to see if any of the boiler room girls or anybody else was still around. They were getting the ferry to the Cape and so I only saw them for a few minutes. There were no state policemen around to talk to. There was no prosecutor around to talk to. I sort of went down a mental checklist that anybody else would do if thrust into that situation.

I went back to see the chief again. I told him what I was doing. We got to be friends over the years; he worked up here outside Boston afterwards. But anyway, I satisfied the medical examiner that anything he wanted he'd get and he was happy with that. I said, "Just ask me, and I will go to the people involved and I'll get whatever I can get if you have any questions." A couple of hours later I went back to him again. I kept going back to these people because I just didn't want to leave anything hanging. He said, "You know, I don't have any questions. She's ready to go to the funeral home." I said, "Then release her to the funeral home. That's the right thing to do." So he did. Then I went back and told the chief and then I went over to the funeral home because I was the only one who could actually make the ID of her body, of her. So I did.

Q: *You'd known her from the boiler room?*

Gifford: She worked for me in the boiler room, and we'd been friends. I mean friends, not just acquaintances. She was one of the best of them. I identified her body. I looked at her clothes that had been put in a bag. I had some instinct about wanting to see whether she was cut or anything. So I asked—I didn't have to ask. This is a naked person lying on a table, right? You don't have to ask much. I looked closely to see—and I'll come back to this in a minute. I said, "I need to see the other side." Okay, fine. She's who she is reported to be. I worked out getting them in touch with the family's choice of a funeral home down in Pennsylvania. I made that connection with Bill vanden Heuvel.

Then, you might say I was volunteered to accompany her down to Pennsylvania, which I was happy to do because I liked her and there wasn't much left to do, nothing left to do. The medical examiner, funeral home, police department, had all done everything that needed to be done. So I said, "Okay, let's make the plans to leave from here to go down to Pennsylvania tomorrow morning." I made one more set of rounds to everybody, the chief, the medical examiner, just to make sure nothing was hanging. It was late afternoon by the time I got back to Nantucket.

I had talked to Senator Kennedy regularly during the day, which was his and my agreement, so that he knew what I was doing and if I had any questions, I asked him and he answered them. There was never any problem with that. It was clear she was dead. It was clear that she died from being in the car and I didn't know, I didn't ask, I have never asked Teddy for any other version of the story than the one he has told. I don't think he ever lied to me about anything I asked him. Quite the opposite. We had come to trust each other for all the reasons I've already talked about, going back a long way together. Then I went back to Nantucket for the night.

The next morning, I flew back to the Vineyard from Nantucket with my suitcase. I met the hearse at the airport, and then the plane flew in. It's a small airport and you can't fly in in secret, so it was all known almost immediately by the airport people what was happening. Everybody was buzzing about it, all standing around. It was late morning by the time we took off with all the paperwork done. She was in a body bag, a normal funeral home body bag. It was a twin-engine plane and the only place to put her was in the aisle where you walked between the seats. The plane had about ten seats, and two pilots. I sat in the back with the body bag. Off we went. It was a miserable day. Thunderstorms. Not one smooth ten-minute period in that whole entire flight. God is smiting me down for being involved in this, I kept on thinking. We landed in a downpour in Wilkes-Barre, Pennsylvania, transferred the bag to the hearse, and I went to the funeral home in the hearse, too.

Then the funeral home director and his wife had to get a dress for Mary Jo and do the makeup, because her mother and father wanted an open-casket funeral. The funeral home people had never seen Mary Jo before, or a picture of her. So I said, "Get her dressed and made up and we'll work from there." So they did, but with the worst hairdo you can imagine and with lipstick like this, almost like a baby-doll hooker. I looked down and they showed me and I said, "No, no. She never wore her hair that way. She always wore it straight and she barely wore lipstick. We're going to fix this up." They said, "No, this is how we always do it here in Pennsylvania." I said, "Well, it's not how we're doing this one." So we got her all fixed up and she looked really terrific when they had her redone. They put a simpler dress on, not a frilly thing. Then we had the moment when her parents came in and saw Mary Jo for the first time. That was awful. It was me and them and the open casket. That really was the worst part of it for me, with her parents, and as a parent myself.

Then the second worst part, I had to go outside—I knew I had to do this— I had to go out and talk to the press about what was going to happen. I'd never before been pinned against the wall, and it was the first time I'd ever been the object of a mob. But I didn't anticipate it somehow, I wasn't thinking straight I guess. That was very difficult. There was nothing to say except, "Her family has been here and now they've gone away. You won't get a picture of them today. You can't talk to them. They are very upset and don't want to be bothered. Yes, the funeral will take place in a day or two and Senator Kennedy will be here with his wife and others," and so on, over and over.

The funeral itself was fully covered—very fully covered—by print and electronic media, of course. But the fascinating thing for me was the quick emergence that Mary Jo was alive right after the accident, and if Ted had dived down he could have saved her from drowning. This became a staple of the scandal sheets and sensationalist TV programs.

I haven't spoken about this publicly and I'm doing it here because of the confidentiality arrangements you've just explained to me.

If you look at the pictures of the car after it was pulled from the water, you'll clearly see that the windows were broken. There was broken glass inside the car, and on the windows. If a person had been alive in the car after it crashed, that person would have struggled to get out, not just lie there. The instinct for survival takes over, I don't care who you are. The only way to get out of that car would have been to try and find a window that was open and squeeze out, the way Ted did. There would have been severe cuts from the broken glass, inevitably.

Mary Jo had no cuts on her hands, and none of her fingernails were broken. I saw her clearly when I identified her in the funeral home on the Vineyard. So I am fully persuaded that she was unconscious. Alive? Who knows? But for certain not conscious. There never was the kind of autopsy that would have determined whether she had contusions from being hit in the neck, or whether in fact she had a broken neck. But I'm persuaded myself that because her hands and fingernails were pristine, that she never struggled. Had she struggled, she would have struggled with cut glass, window glass, and her hands would have been severely cut.

Teddy knows I know this and he's said, "It's your story. It's over for me, and that's it." I always thought he might want to have me say it, but he didn't. The aftermath of it was difficult for everybody. I was never called as a witness at the inquest, which sure was fine with me. I didn't care one way or another. If I had been called, I'd have told under oath what I know.

I think it truly was an accident, and a very sad one. I think it's pretty clear where they were headed. They never got there. I don't think there's any doubt about that. Again, that could have been innocent or not, depending on your point of view.

So that's the Chappaquiddick piece. The aftermath of it, the Nixon presidency—politics were turning nasty by then. Ted would have been president but for that. That's really it.

Senator John Tunney (D-CA), Edward Kennedy's University of Virginia Law School classmate and friend:

I happen to believe that Chappaquiddick was a direct result of what happened to Bobby a year earlier. To me, it's so obvious. I was very worried about Teddy when I saw him shortly before Chappaquiddick. I could tell that there was a wildness in his brain and although he was still performing very well as a senator, getting legislation introduced and legislation heard and legislation passed, but there was kind of a wildness there that was almost a flaunting of rules of the game, so to speak, because he was so angry. There was an anger that he felt about the unfairness of the way his brothers had been gunned down. I think that the Chappaquiddick thing added colossally to this sense that not only was he on the wrong side of destiny, but he began to question where he was in this world, where he had set out to achieve such wonderful things, bold, courageous things in public life, and all of a sudden he is looked upon as being something quite different from that.

Senator George McGovern (D-SD), 1972 Democratic presidential candidate:

Q: How did he overcome Chappaquiddick inside the Senate?

McGovern: That was tough. I don't know how he overcame it in himself. Most of the senators I know would have just resigned, would just think, "Oh, hell, I've screwed this thing up, and I'm going to get out of there." He never did. He was at his office early and late, I think, from the day after that tragedy. Obviously it tore him up inside, but he never quit. And while he mishandled it at the time—as he and everybody else knows—he never let it get him down. It never slowed his work in the Senate that I could see, and I knew him pretty well.

I think he just decided, "I'm not going to let this one tragic incident—I can't bring this girl back. I can't erase what's done. I'm going to continue to be a good senator." And he pulled it off. It took, I think, more personal and inner strength and integrity than I thought was possible. And he did it. So I think senators who at first were shocked by the incident and by the way he handled it gradually came around to the view, "Here's a strong man who's handled this well."

On asking Kennedy to be his vice-presidential running mate in 1972:

McGovern: I knew that the Kennedy name was magic. I knew that any Kennedy was going to be more charismatic than anybody else, but I never had any fear about appearing inadequate to handle the responsibility. I thought he would help bring big crowds and excitement. He's a charismatic figure, and I thought that would help the ticket, too. As I told you, I always thought it would help clear the air on Chappaquiddick for him if we won and he were vice president for four years—maybe eight years. By the end of that, nobody would think he was unqualified to be president of the United States. I still feel that to this day.

Edmund and Doris Reggie, Edward Kennedy's parents-in-law:

Doris Reggie: I think Teddy assumed the family leadership position, naturally, when his brothers died. I think that role is a very important one to him, and he takes it very seriously. I think he is living up to what he knows his brothers would want, and he's giving them his all, with their children, with all of the family responsibility, with the strength. I mean, he is the example. He knows he has to be the one, and he is.

Edmund Reggie: I think that's a source of great strength to him.

Doris Reggie: And he is so devoted to his brothers and misses them so much. I think it's tremendous. One day—maybe this is too personal, but we were in Washington, and Edmund and I were with him in the car, and he said, "Do you mind?" He went to Arlington, and we went there, and had tears, you know? Then that was it. Got back in the car. It really affected us.

Edmund Reggie: It's a no-show deal.

Doris Reggie: Oh no, there was no camera. It was no special holiday—nobody was there. He just had this need to go. He says, "Do you mind?"

You know? It was so touching. I remember when we were in New Orleans at a restaurant, and the waitress came after we finished eating, and she said, "I just want to tell you, Senator, that my son served and knew your brother when he was the hero, and my son died—" the son or the brother, whatever the family relationship was. Teddy got teary, and the woman just wanted to thank him for what his brother had done and what he does for the poor people, for his fellow man. We saw it over and over, how he welcomes people, how he's gracious to people. They want to take a picture with him. He's always very aware of the other person. He's not one of these standoff people.

Edmund Reggie: You know, he's told me on two different occasions—we were out sailing here in the [Nantucket] Sound—he said, "You know, the first time I saw Nantucket, Jack sailed me here." He just remembers that.

Doris Reggie: He feels close to them with the sea.

Edmund Reggie: Yes.

Doris Reggie: They're with him always.

8

Challenging a President: The Quest for the 1980 Nomination

Chappaquiddick meant that Camelot's restoration might never happen, certainly not in the 1972 presidential election. Jimmy Carter's improbable success in 1976 made a draft-Kennedy movement moot, and Teddy bided his time for another four years until the 1980 race. Initially, the senator supported President Carter's policies, voting with him on tax reform, arms control, human rights, energy independence, airline deregulation, and the Panama Canal Treaty. But their collaboration broke down over health-care reform. Kennedy and Carter also parted ways when the president refused to back Teddy's friend Archibald Cox for a judicial appointment to the First Circuit Court of Appeals. In addition, Carter's puritanical lifestyle (no liquor at the White House) and propensity to lecture legislators rankled Kennedy.

By late 1979, Senator Kennedy, discouraged over Carter's direction for the country and, bowing to pressure from the Democrats' liberal wing to challenge the president for the party's nomination, tossed his hat into the fray. A sour economy, soaring mortgage rates, the Iranian hostage crisis, and energy shortages weakened the incumbent, yet a sitting president maintains numerous advantages. Kennedy's candidacy never gained sustained momentum after an overwhelming loss to Carter in the Iowa caucuses.

The senator pursued his presidential quest all the way to the convention, but won only a third of the delegates. Nevertheless, he dominated the quadrennial meeting with his eloquent concession speech, concluding to thunderous applause, "For me, a few hours ago, this campaign came to an end. For all those whose cares have been our concerns, the work goes on, the cause endures, the hope still lives, and the dream shall never die." It ended his run for the White House but launched the next, and most consequential, phase of his career. He would never become president, but that reality liberated him to become the most influential senator of the late twentieth and early twenty-first centuries. As Kennedy's wife Vicki observed after his passing, he accomplished more in his nearly half-century in the Senate than he could have ever achieved even with two terms as president. "I just think legislation, bringing people together, crafting the compromises, the personalities, the personal interactions, the chemistry of the Senate, the chemistry of the whole legislative process, was something he understood so well and was so adept at making work," she commented. Or as one of Teddy's friends told him, "[T]he best thing that ever happened to the United States of America is that you lost in 1980."

Kennedy's marriage to Joan ended in divorce one year later, the victim of alcohol abuse by both parties and Teddy's infidelity. Kennedy toyed with the idea of running for the 1984 presidential nomination, but his children begged him not to do so, and their opposition was decisive. Aware of the toll his personal transgressions had taken, in 1991 the senator delivered a public mea culpa at Harvard. In the audience as Teddy's special guest was Victoria Reggie, a successful Washington attorney, who would become the senator's wife in 1992. She is accurately credited with his subsequent redemption and making the last seventeen years of his life the happiest he had known.

EMK: We're talking this morning basically about the judgments and decisions that went into the consideration of running in '72, '76, and 1980 and 1984, with the greatest emphasis on the '80 campaign. After the '68 campaign, I ran for assistant majority leader in the Senate against Russell Long. Over Christmas, we were out West skiing, and I decided to make the run at that time. I came back early and won by several votes, and it was a new opportunity for leadership in the Senate.

So we were off to a pretty fast start as we went through the early part of 1969. And then in July of that year, we had the Chappaquiddick tragedy, which effectively stopped the national aspirations. I made the judgment then about running for the Senate in 1970 and indicated that was my only ambition, and that I would not run [for president] in 1972. We had the follow-on campaigns, which resulted in 1972 with George McGovern.

In the early part of '69, we had taken steps to start to build some organization, some outreach, but, as I mentioned, all of that really stopped. I thought about running in 1972. I had been in the Senate for ten years, national politics for sixteen years, and had been inspired in terms of political judgments by my brothers, President Kennedy and Bob. I had worked on all the national issues in the Senate, had met a good many of the leaders internationally, had developed a good staff who were very effective, and had developed more understanding and awareness about the workings of the institutions. And at least in the beginning part of the year, I thought that we were set to—

Q: Can I interrupt with a question? You referred to your election by the Democratic caucus as assistant leader or whip. Russell Long had left.

EMK: I beat Russell Long in 1969.

Q: You beat him?

EMK: Yes.

Q: *Since you've brought it up, were you thinking at that time about Democratic Party leadership, and eventually majority leadership in the Senate? Were you thinking of a ladder up and a career in the Senate?*

EMK: No. I think I saw an opening for advancement. Russell Long was vulnerable at this time. We had great numbers of Democrats in the Senate. I think we were up to—I would have to check. In '64 or '65, we had a big majority [66 to 34]. Mansfield was the majority leader, and I thought he'd be there. I had a lot of respect for Mansfield. He was very close to my brother. And so I never really thought very much about following along Mansfield.

But it did seem to be an opening and a good opportunity to move up in the party and in influence. It turned out that with the exception of the losing part, it was good to get out of the whip's job, because you get absorbed in the knickknacks of the Senate process and procedure. It draws away from being more heavily involved in the issues, even in terms of the policy issues and questions you have. With my position in history, I had more ability to have an impact and influence in the Senate than from the position as whip. And since I was a target at that time of the Republicans, they had an opportunity to make life more difficult for me. If they knew that I had to go someplace, make a speech, they would delay the recessing of the Senate, and all those games were being played during that period.

Q: *I'm glad to have that on the record, because that was the purpose of my question.*

EMK: The high point of that was winning the [whip] election in 1969, and the second high point was losing the election in 1971. Although that's an interesting race. We may come back to that. I had Magnuson and Scoop Jackson, and I had Bill Fulbright with me. But the next time I ran, I lost both Magnuson and Jackson because I had been against the SST, and Byrd[1] went very strongly for the SST, and in the appropriations "Maggie" (Magnuson) actually helped him to get some additional money for the SST. So I lost both of those.

Then during this period of time—probably '69–'70 —the Vietnamese sent me a communication that they would release the names of the prisoners [of war] to a representative of mine. I spoke to Bill Fulbright and told him what they had offered, but I immediately sent John Nolan, who had been the negotiator for my brother Bobby to get the prisoners out of Cuba after the Bay of Pigs. He had been in the Justice Department and was highly regarded and respected. He went over and got the names of the prisoners and immediately gave them to the American embassy there so they could let families know, and they could try to find out whether those were accurate names. He came back immediately and gave them to the State Department.

---

1. Senator Robert Byrd was the new whip and supported the supersonic transport aircraft.

I sat next to Fulbright on the following Tuesday—this was over a period of a weekend on the floor—and I said, "Bill, remember I called you last week about getting the names?" And he said, "Yes, that's right, and we're going to have a committee meeting this afternoon to decide what we're going to do." I said, "I've already sent someone over there, and we have the names." He said, "That's a matter for the Foreign Relations Committee." And I said, "Well, that's what happened."

He had an edge from that point on. He thought I'd interfered with his committee's jurisdiction, so he voted against me when I was up [for whip]. And then four new senators were coming in (whose names I don't have now, but history will have them).[2] They had said they were going to be for me, and when they came to counting the ballots, Byrd was not going to run against me if Russell died. Russell was very sick, and he had given him a proxy. If Russell died, Byrd wasn't sure enough of the vote to challenge me.

But Talmadge was still alive. So Byrd ran and beat me by three or four votes—more than he thought. The four new senators who were coming up were all pledged to me, but when they looked at the ballot, two senators spelled "Byrd" B-i-r-d instead of B-y-r-d, so we knew that they were two of the new senators, and we figured out who they were. [*Laughter*] Anyway, it went on, and actually Byrd did a good job and became the majority leader.

In '69, when I was just back there, I had been very involved in the criticism of the administration in January/February. I had a speech on Hamburger Hill. That's the incident where the Marines marched up and suffered heavy casualties [in Vietnam]. Then at nighttime, they marched back down again, and the Viet Cong went right back up. So in the morning, they were right back where they had been. This was a senseless and irresponsible operation—those were the words I used: "senseless and irresponsible." I was labeling the South Vietnamese government as corrupt, and I called for a significant reduction in American force levels in Vietnam.

I also had taken strong positions on reducing the space and defense programs, was very much involved in the tax reform that was still out there and a lively issue, and also on changing the draft to random selection. I offered a number of amendments on that, and eventually we got the [Burke] Marshall Commission set up. They made a recommendation that they have random selection, which I believe was about '71. And that and the Tet Offensive, I think, ended the war. I also introduced legislation in the neighborhood health centers that year. So I had been very active and very much involved.

Q: This was '69 you're talking about?

EMK: Yes. This is in the winter of '69.

---

2. Actually five new Democrats joined the Senate in 1971: Lawton Chiles (FL), Hubert Humphrey (MN), Lloyd Bentsen (TX), John Tunney (CA), and Adlai Stevenson III (IL).

Q: The first health center was at Columbia Point [in South Boston]?

EMK: There were two of them in the War on Poverty: one at Columbia Point, and one in Mound Bayou in Mississippi. They were initiated by fellows named Jack Geiger and Count Gibson, who were at Tufts Medical School. I had seen them here and talked with both of them at very substantial length, and took that concept and put it into broad legislation, and we passed it in the Senate—about $35 million for the first one.

We had a conference with Adam Clayton Powell,[3] and in the conference he said, "Teddy Kennedy, you want these neighborhood health centers?" "Yes." "How many are you going to have for $38 million?" I said, "Well, we're going to maybe get three or four." He said, "You write in there that one of them is going to be in my district, and you've got it in here." I said, "That's fine with me." One of them was going to be in his district, and that was the beginning of the neighborhood health centers.

In the spring of that year, Paul Kirk[4] was drawing up lists by states, very low-key, and the "Draft Kennedy" programs were beginning [for the 1972 presidential nomination]. All of that ended with the tragedy at Chappaquiddick, which I was personally enormously both moved and saddened by, and accepted responsibility for. But even having done all that, it was a very heavy emotional burden for me and has been for my whole life. I know we're going to come back to that. That effectively ended all of the activities in terms of the national campaign, and I focused on the state, running in 1970 in Massachusetts.

So we had the development of the presidential campaign. And the final part of it was that in '72, when McGovern got the nomination, he asked me if I was interested in the vice presidential nomination. I wasn't interested. At that time, I was still very much troubled and anxious about the tragedy, and also very concerned about the children and responsibilities to them. I didn't feel that I was ready in terms of the vice presidency.

Q: The vice presidency wouldn't have interested you very much under any circumstances, would it?

EMK: I think that's right. In '68, when Hubert [Humphrey] mentioned it and offered it to me, I was just really too close to all the events of 1968, and I wasn't prepared at that time even to try for the nomination. I never felt that that was something real. I know there was a lot of positioning by some political leaders on it, but the serious issue was the vice presidency, and I wasn't interested. I didn't feel that it was appropriate then. In '72, I always felt that there

---

3. Congressman Adam Clayton Powell Jr. was a New York Democrat.

4. Paul G. Kirk Jr., a Harvard-trained Massachusetts attorney, was a special assistant to Senator Kennedy from 1979 to 1987. He eventually became chairman of the Democratic National Committee and ultimately was appointed to Edward Kennedy's Senate seat when he died in 2009. He has also served as the chairman of the John F. Kennedy Presidential Library Foundation Board and as a founding member of the Edward M. Kennedy Institute for the United States Senate Board.

would be a time when I could run and would run, but I always felt that I had much more opportunity to affect public policy in the Senate. If you're going to really do the vice presidency, you're there for eight years, then you have a leg up with regard to the nomination.

Although it was during that time, I think, that Ted Sorensen gave me a memorandum that said it was possible for me to be a vice president and also be a Cabinet member. So that sort of opened up a little interest—that I could serve as a Cabinet member, rather than just being the vice president. There's nothing prohibiting that, historically and constitutionally, but it still didn't have an appeal for me.

When Humphrey asked me who I preferred after 1968, Fred Harris or Muskie, I indicated Muskie. First of all, I liked Muskie. I like Fred Harris, too. He was a very impressive figure in the Senate. He was a Rhodes scholar, could talk like the wind, and took on powerful interests—and lost because he did. So he had a lot going for him. I found him attractive and appealing. And I liked Muskie. I'd known him a long time. He had a relationship with my brother. But even though I edged toward Muskie, I always thought that if I was ever going to run in the future, I'd rather have someone from my region, because this is where I was going to be stronger in the mix than somebody from outside, where I wouldn't be as strong. And I just thought it probably made more sense with Muskie, as he was going to be strong.

So now we go through the campaign. There were a lot of intervening steps. They had the Eagleton situation[5] and eventually Sarge on the ticket. I campaigned a good deal for George. I'd say I spent half of the last ten days with him. I went to Philadelphia; I went to all the major big cities with him. And it was incredible, because he got crowds that just were mind-boggling, so much bigger than Nixon.

McGovern, yes. He got just incredible crowds, even two or three times what [John] Kerry got this time [in 2004]. Down in Philadelphia, there were 250,000 people. Kerry had 70,000 down there. Just unbelievable! And it began to feel a little bit—although the people in the back of the bus had the polls that showed that he wasn't going to win—if you were out there campaigning with him, you got a real sense that all of this was possible. But then, of course, he got beaten, and he got beaten badly [by Richard Nixon].

Q: Could you talk a bit about how Sargent Shriver emerged as the choice?

EMK: Well, the best information I have, really, is [from] Pierre Salinger. Shriver was in the running early on. After Eagleton got out, when they had

---

5. After Democrats gave Senator Thomas Eagleton (D-MO) the vice presidential nomination in 1972, his previous treatment for depression, including electroshock therapy, became public, and he had to leave the ticket. Kennedy's brother-in-law, R. Sargent Shriver Jr., founding director of the Peace Corps during JFK's presidency, and US ambassador to France in the Johnson administration, replaced him.

the first meeting the next morning after George McGovern got in at 8 o'clock, they had probably—

This is the Pierre Salinger article about this. I think he was involved in most of this. [Initially] [t]hey looked at Father Hesburgh. He called, evidently, Gaylord Nelson first, and Nelson said no. Then he talked to Ribicoff, and Ribicoff turned them down. They had Woodcock of the UAW, and Cronkite was on the list. Hesburgh was on the list, White was on the list, Wilbur Mills was on the list, Sissy Farenthold from Texas was on the list, Pat Lucey was on the list. But Pat Lucey got off the list when they found out that his wife had locked him out of his room in a hotel. That was the story, and they pulled that.[6]

They showed the polling of the various candidates, and then they decided on Shriver. They called Shriver, and he was in Moscow, or, according to Pierre, he would have gotten it. So when they couldn't get Shriver, they went to Eagleton. That's their sequence. And then when Eagleton got off, they came back to Shriver.

There's all the historic speculation about whether I was for Sarge or whether I was against Sarge or whatever. There was a general sense among the Kennedy people that Sarge hadn't come back from France in 1968 to help Bobby. So there was a good deal of anxiety about that. I personally hadn't gotten into it, but you find these things in terms of the people who are the operatives. Many of the people in the Robert Kennedy campaign were really the ones who had some resentment over the fact that he hadn't come back in Bobby's campaign. But it didn't bother me. I was delighted to have him. I think the world of Sarge. So he came back.

But that was the backwater stuff on it, and some of it's written in Sarge's book. I always had a very good relationship with him and did then. I didn't have a lot to do at that time campaigning. No one thought it made a lot of sense for me to go out and campaign with Sarge. It was always with McGovern, and that's what we did. But I thought Sarge did very well.

I'm going to leave this [article] with you. You want to take a look at it. Quite frankly, I think it's more about Pierre and his being offered the national chairmanship and not getting it, and also going to Paris and talking to the North Vietnamese—and then McGovern denying that—and his tension with McGovern, but it's interesting.

Now we start off in '73, and we have a similar kind of effort. I had asked Paul Kirk and Dave Burke if they could make soundings among political leaders about the future. And we had drawn up a list of candidates who we had helped with fundraising and personal appearances in '72, a list that covered thirty-nine states. [Frank] Mankiewicz, the campaign manager for McGovern,

---

6. Father Theodore Hesburgh was the president of Notre Dame, Leonard Woodcock was the head of the United Auto Workers, Congressman Wilber Mills was an Arkansas Democrat, and Frances Farenthold was a state representative from Texas.

sent a private memo on the lessons drawn from the experience along with the names of the best operatives and fundraisers. And we increased foreign travel during that time. That year, '73, in July, I even went down to Alabama and spoke with George Wallace in the Spirit of America [July 4th celebration].

Then toward the end of the year, in November, Teddy [Jr.] was diagnosed with cancer. His leg had cancer. And that changed the mix to a very substantial degree. He ended up having his leg amputated in Washington within a couple of days after it was diagnosed. It was a very dangerous type of cancer, and there was a real question about his survival.

He went up to Boston to do a treatment that had been approved by the NIH. Just a handful of children had gone through it. They had had some success, but still, only a handful had gone through it. That treatment was to last two years, every three weeks for three days. Teddy would go up after school on a Friday and begin to get the treatment on Friday night, which made him just incredibly, incredibly ill and sick to his stomach all night long. Then on Saturday, he was weak—still sick, just absolutely wiped out. By Saturday night he would feel a little bit better, and then Sunday noontime he would leave and come on back. It wiped him out for school and everything else.

Every three weeks, and that's when we saw these families in the waiting room who had mortgaged their house or sold their house, and said, "Look, we can have our treatments for a year." It had been taken off the NIH list of research because it had been approved to be satisfactory. So each treatment was $3,000. Our insurance covered it—the United States Congress/Senate covered it. But others didn't, and so the families were wondering, after they could have nine months or ten months, what the chances were of those children surviving. Again, this was a very powerful message for me in terms of national health insurance coverage.

I made up my mind that I was going to be at all of those [chemotherapy treatments], which I was. The only one that they had to shift around was the one when I went down to Georgia.

But that [Teddy's treatment] took a lot of emotion and attention and absorption of energy and focus. After '74, in July, there was a fifth anniversary article by Robert Sherrill about the tragedy at Chappaquiddick. It raised all the issues and questions again, and by the fall, I had really made up my mind that I wouldn't be running for the president/vice president in '76, and I announced it during that period of time.

Q: That was a very unequivocal statement, as I recall.

EMK: That's right. There were numbers of factors: the well-being of the children—mine and also the other children. If something happened to me, what was going to happen to the family? The family considerations. I had also the consideration of the impact on Joan, who was having a difficult, challenging time. If I was going to get into this in a serious way, what was going to happen to her on this? And in '76, I was supposed to run for the Senate, so I'd be giving up a Senate seat.

So for all those reasons, I was out of the '76 race. And then, as this went along, it became clear—this was just after Watergate, too, and the mood changed with the Carter campaign—about morality, and playing against Washington and against the politics of the Congress and Senate, an outside sort of view. You could feel that this had a powerful appeal among the electorate. It was a time when the outsider had a real opportunity. It just was the wrong time.

Anyway, I made my statement on Labor Day of '74. There's this story about Tip O'Neill,[7] and we were joking about "Keep me alive, Tip." He'd go around and say good things about me, and I was still showing up decently in all the polls. But there was never serious thought on my part, any reconsideration of any of that.

Of course, one of the issues during this was health insurance, and all the candidates took a strong position in favor of it—sort of the single-payer system—except Carter, who wanted to maintain his independence on that issue, which was one of the areas of strong difference I had with him. I never had a relationship with him, nor did he reach out at all, even at the convention. As a matter of fact, it's sort of the contrary. We weren't really included in the '76 convention at all.

Q: *Did he consider you an adversary or a rival at that time even though you weren't running?*

EMK: I think he just felt that he was going to do it his way. I wasn't part of that. I was part of the institutional process, and he didn't have to deal with that. He was an outsider, and he was going to do it much more from an outsider's point of view and didn't think that we could add much to it. So he never made any overtures.

Q: *Was that generally true of his dealings with the Senate in the Carter years?*

EMK: Yes. It *was* true. This is one of the principal reasons that he didn't get along. I asked Dale Bumpers[8] at one time why Carter and Byrd didn't get along, because they both came from small towns in the South. And he said, "You have to understand southern politics. They both came from small towns in the South, but they came from different sides of the tracks. As much as Byrd is suspicious of liberals, they're much more hostile to the people who came from the other side of the tracks." And that was the inherent conflict between Byrd and Carter. It was just real personal and subsequently played out.

Although we had had a lot of tension with Byrd, I spent time with him and used to keep him informed. Now we're jumping ahead to 1980, but he never,

---

7. Congressman Thomas O'Neill was a Massachusetts Democrat and Speaker of the US House of Representatives from 1977 to 1987.
8. Senator Dale Bumpers was an Arkansas Democrat.

even in the midst of all these races, made a statement that I ought to withdraw or get out of the race as a result of the primaries. And neither did O'Neill, although he had a somewhat different kind of position. But Byrd was enormously important. If he had said it and O'Neill said it and the party people said it, it would have been much more difficult to stay in.

I don't know if there's anything else in that '75–'76 period. I think there was always the question of whether I should have endorsed somebody else. Would that have made a difference to them? Whether if I'd endorsed Mondale or someone else I had gotten along with, he might have been able to get it. I didn't do it, and I don't think I really thought that much about it at the time.

There were several people we had had a good relationship with and had worked on it: Glenn, who had worked hard for Bobby in the '68 campaign. And we had a lot of people in these areas who had been—Udall[9] had been a terrific supporter of my brother Jack. So I think that more than anything else—more than my beginning suspicions about Carter—outweighed the consideration to endorse anyone.

Q: This was the first presidential nomination process under the new rules of the parties after—

EMK: That's right.

Q: And Carter really studied up on those rules.

EMK: Those were in the wake of the reforms under McGovern, and the '64 convention, where they kept Mississippi out, Aaron Henry[10] and—They established a process for changing the rules to make sure that people were going to be included in it, and Mondale was very involved in that. We were helpful, too, but he was really the architect of a lot of the changes in the rules subsequently. Carter certainly understood them. But in order to get the party together, we all committed to trying to do something on that.

So now we are in 1977. We have Carter in the White House. On the issue of healthcare, he said that first he had to do energy. He told us that the first issue that he was going to do was health, but he said he had to do energy. That took a long time, and it was not very well done. It was basically deregulation. We had a lot of tension, Metzenbaum and I, and I think Abourezk,[11] who had the filibuster. We had a lot of difficulty with the Carter programs. Eventually, an energy bill went on through.

---

9. Senator John Glenn was a Democrat from Ohio; Congressman Morris Udall was a Democrat from Arizona.

10. Aaron Henry, a civil rights leader and head of the Mississippi branch of the NAACP, was a founder of the Mississippi Freedom Democratic Party, which attempted to persuade the national Democratic Party to seat its delegation at the 1964 Democratic National Convention.

11. Howard Metzenbaum and James Abourezk were Democratic senators from Ohio and South Dakota, respectively.

Q: Could you talk a little bit more about before 1980 how Carter was in office, and your views, or your work, or the degree of cooperation or opposition to other things beside health, energy—the Panama Canal treaties, the opening to China and so forth? Were there areas in which you and the other Democrats were in agreement with him, or was there constant tension on these matters?

EMK: In the early period, '77, our relationship was really correct enough. I was with him on 75 percent of all the votes in the first year, and eighteen out of the twenty-one or something in '78. We had started then on airline deregulation, tax reform. I was a strong supporter of tax reform, arms control, human rights, energy independence, the Panama Canal Treaty. I was supportive in all those areas.

The overarching issue was health insurance, and that's where it really broke down. We had to work hard, because when they were not going to go to the single-payer but to another plan, we had to get labor. So we were out working and spending a great deal of time on this. People within with the administration believed that they shouldn't go ahead with this.

Q: So you were having to push this almost on your own, without help from the executive.

EMK: And then, as I mentioned, he wanted to do a series of small bills, and how much it would cost and the economic situation. We went down [to the White House] in July of '78 and had a conversation with him about the importance of a single piece of legislation, particularly if we were going to be able to get anything done at the grassroots level and bring people aboard, make it a political issue and have it effective as a political issue in the future. But that didn't work.

And then we went to the midterm convention in Memphis, and laid out that health insurance. We got a terrific response from all the Democrats on that. And it took on his position versus what had been the historic Democratic position.

At this time, I hadn't really considered running against him. I think we actually had indicated to Carter at some time in the early part of the year, in '79 or whatever, that I thought I would be supporting him.

Q: Senator, you mentioned yesterday the Archibald Cox nomination. Could you talk a little bit about that?

EMK: Yes. We had a vacancy on the First Circuit,[12] and I nominated Archibald Cox. Griffin Bell called me and said, "The president isn't going to do it." Griffin Bell was the attorney general. I said, "Well, I want to talk to the president about it." He said, "It won't do you any good." I said I still wanted to talk to him.

---

12. The vacancy occurred on the First Circuit US Court of Appeals in March 1979.

I went down and I talked to the president. We have to get the exact date. I remember it very clearly. I think I took notes on it. I spent close to an hour with Carter. I thought it was going to be a fifteen-minute conversation. He wanted to talk about other things, but it was primarily the Cox nomination. He told me that Cox had supported Morris Udall in New Hampshire [against Carter in the 1976 primary], and he could never, never support Archibald Cox for the First Circuit because of that.

I said, "Well, that was a long time ago; we were all together," and so on. And he said he knew he was close to our family and to John Kennedy, and that made some difference, but not enough. And he wasn't going to do it.

And then I told him the politics of it: He's [Cox] the most respected person in the country. It would be a "ten" for him—it would be a "nine" for me recommending him, but it would be a "ten" for him. He said, "Even that isn't going to override my strong, strong feelings against Archibald Cox for supporting Udall." It had a ring to it. I always remember that conversation very clearly, about him almost having a sense of pleasure telling me that he wasn't—

Q: Was this really about Cox or about something else?

EMK: Well, it was stated about Cox, but I didn't know if he was just doing it to jam me, or just whatever pleasure he was getting out of it. We talked about some other matters—some health issues, some questions. I always felt that he didn't rush. He wanted credit for talking to me for an hour, rather than just fifteen or twenty minutes. He delayed the conversation so he could get some credit for spending a lot of time with me. That's what I felt afterwards. That's what I felt more than anything else: he wasn't really interested very much in what my views were.

President Carter made efforts to bring people down in the summer to the White House. You'd get a couple of invitations. You'd get down there 6–6:30. You know, he canceled all liquor in the White House. There was never liquor served when President Carter came. It was interesting. And he sold the boat, the *Sequoia*. He didn't want any kind of luxuries or anything.

So you'd get down there, and you'd mill around; you'd go through the line and eat quickly. And then for three hours, he'd conduct a seminar, like on Africa. He'd let you know that he knew every country in Africa, the name of every president of Africa, and he'd have the secretaries of state and defense talk about what was happening globally in these regions. And they'd do it generally on the Middle East. They were personal *tours de force*, and he had about a third of the Senate every time, and about thirty members of the House.

It was well worth going down there. It was informational. But it was so broad-gauged, you know? Every one of my colleagues thought it was a *tour de force*, but to impress you that he knew so much about the minutiae. In contrast, you read history about Franklin Roosevelt. He was the master of the situation he had to know about. And it wasn't that he knew every place, but he knew everything, and he knew all the people and knew what moved them and why they were doing this. That's the sense you always have with the great leaders: Wilson, Roosevelt.

Q: I will probably take this off the tape, but I'll tell you a story.[13]

EMK: Oh, listen to him! "I'm taking this off the tape!" Mark that, Mr. Historian!

Q: Well, the interviewer's not supposed to tell stories. You are supposed to tell them.

It's about these meetings that Carter would have on the Middle East or Africa or whatever. There was some issue about which he brought some of the congressional leaders to the White House, and the point was to try to bring them aboard. But he didn't succeed in doing that. He lectured them about the subject. I don't know what it was about—energy or something. He was telling what he knew and how he understood it; he had done his homework, and he knew—

When it was all over, one of his senior advisors said, "Do you know what you just did to those people? You're supposed to be persuading them. You're supposed to bring them aboard. What you did was let every person in that room know that you knew more than he did! That you knew more than any of them did about the subject! These are senior people in Congress!"

EMK: That's exactly it.

Q: I'll take it off.

EMK: No, no. It's just a reaffirmation of this. That's what he wanted to get across.

Q: Well, some people have thought that maybe his own experience in the Georgia legislature gave him not very much respect for the legislative and institutional processes.

EMK: Yes.

Q: Also, he was a navy officer by profession.

EMK: Yes. They feel that they have to do it, but he missed it.

Going into '79 now, I think we had polls that were going along and showed us being in a strong position. And I think the time when I was the most struck about really thinking about running in '80 was when I listened to the speech he gave in July of that year on the "national malaise." I thought that this was contrary and in conflict with all the things I believed in terms of the Democratic Party, in terms of what I thought the country was about. I thought this was a direction of the country that needed change. And with that kind of attitude and mood, I couldn't see how we were really going to address the central problems we were facing, both in the economy and foreign policy.

And so after that, later that summer, we began to get the people together down here to talk about the pros and cons of running. I met September 7 at

---

13. Professor James Sterling Young, who conducted most of the interviews with Edward Kennedy contained in this book, had also led the Jimmy Carter Oral History Project at the University of Virginia's Miller Center.

the White House and indicated to Carter that I was giving consideration to running against him, and that the family had given their blessing.

Now, I had decided that I was going to make up my mind in the summertime, and I did, just before Labor Day, down here, that I was going to run. But I was also conscious that Carter was coming up to the Kennedy Library and speaking. So I thought I would have to wait to announce until after that. This was one of the real challenges I was facing. I had it in my mind. I didn't talk to people about it, and I wasn't going to talk because I didn't want to have it leak out at the time. And so I waited until November 7. He spoke on October 20, and we had the [Iranian] hostage crisis on November 4[, 1979]. And then I announced on November 7.

I mentioned just yesterday one of the searing events was this Roger Mudd interview [on CBS]. The background on that was that Roger Mudd and Dan Rather were in a contest to see who was going to be the anchor on CBS. Roger Mudd had been a social friend, particularly to the Robert Kennedys. I knew him, but he was not a personal friend of mine. I'd see him out at the Robert Kennedys'.

At the time—we think it was in June of that year—when the president of Mexico was in New York, I had the chance to meet him about ten at night at the Waldorf-Astoria. After I met him and walked out, Roger Mudd was there. He said, "I'm in this contest with Dan Rather, and I'd love to get an interview with your mother." I said, "Well, my mother doesn't do interviews. She's older; she just doesn't do interviews. But let me think about it, and I'll get back to you." He said, "It would make a big, big difference if I could ever do that interview down at Cape Cod. Everybody's always wanted that interview with your mother."

So I talked to my mother and my sisters about it, and decided that he could do the interview with Mother walking, but I'd have to be with her. He could talk with her a bit, she could chat and talk a bit, but we just didn't want to have a sit-down or only Mother. He said that was fine. I said, "Our children are going to be there, so that's going to be the setting." He said, "That's fine."

Now, just before the time, in September, my mother got sick and went to Boston. Then my daughter got an invitation to the Hopi Indian tribe in Arizona. That is the only matriarchal tribe in the country, and they wanted the oldest daughter to come there and be a part of their big, big ceremony. Kara wanted to go, so she was out. For some reason, Teddy couldn't go. So it's only Patrick and me.

So I said to Roger, "This interview isn't going to work, because my mother's not here, the others aren't here." "Oh, no," he said. "That'll be all right. I'll come on down. We'll do you and the sea and Cape Cod, and what the sea has meant." I could talk about that, and my brother [Jack] learning to swim, and then fighting in the water [during World War II] and coming back, and using the sea as a place of repose and thought and rest, and what this place all meant to him and the family.

So down he comes and sets up at Squaw Island [near Hyannis Port], and the only two people there are Patrick and me. I have no staff, no nothing, because we're just going to talk about the sea. We talk about the sea, and we look at the time. I say, "That's about it." And he says, "Yes, just about." And I say, "Patrick, why don't you go down and get the boat and pick me up, and I'll just get these people out of the house."

So then he [Mudd] said, "Can we do one more film?" I said, "Well, I'd really like to go. I think we've done it." "No," he said. I had to do one more. And then we got into whether you're going to run for president, and what's your view about all this. I had made up my mind. I sensed that Patrick's down there by himself. He's twelve years old; he's bringing the boat in, saying, "What in the world is this all about?" knowing that I'm not prepared.

It was a disaster. I remember getting on the boat afterwards with Patrick and telling him it was a disaster, and calling Mudd and saying, "Look, if we're going to do this thing, I ought to get another crack at that thing." [14]

Q: There was considerably more to that interview, wasn't there, than was actually broadcast?

EMK: Oh, there was a lot. Yes, I had talked to him for forty minutes just about the sea, and about how we learned to swim here, and the sailing here, and it was because of that he [JFK] was able to save people's lives, and he came back here, and how the sea is sort of a metaphor of life, and my life—You know, all of these things I had thought through, and knew what my brother said. But it was this last part that he was in for. . . .

It suited their interests. I was a hot item at that time, and he was going to have the jump. They knew by that time I was going to announce for president. "Here's Kennedy. He wants to be president. This is what he had to say." But I didn't have much to say.

You have to be smart enough if you're going to do an interview. I certainly am now. You have things all worked out with your professional staff, and you have a very clear idea. They can ask whatever questions, but what is the purpose of the interview, and what is it going to be about? Then you can go on. We go with Tim Russert [15] and do all the Sunday programs, and they can ask

---

14. At the Squaw Island interview, Kennedy offered what he later characterized as "halting answers" to Mudd's unexpected questions about Chappaquiddick and his marriage. Even worse, at a second interview in Kennedy's Senate office, on October 12, Teddy gave an infamously rambling, unfocused, and inarticulate response to Mudd's question of why he wanted to be president. Kennedy subsequently observed that he had not declared his candidacy at that time; thus, he wasn't certain how specific to be in answering Mudd's query. Edward M. Kennedy, *True Compass: A Memoir* (New York: Twelve, 2009), 368–71.

15. Russert was the host of NBC's *Meet the Press*.

whatever the hell they want and we're ready for it, but you know at least the framework and where these things are going.

But now, this is the situation. We get off to a start, and as I'm the first one to recognize, having been a candidate any number of times, I find getting started in the course of a campaign always takes time. There are good campaigners who can leave the Senate this afternoon and be red-hot on the campaign tonight. It takes me a couple of days, two or three days, to get warmed up and into the mood. Less time than it used to, but it takes me a day or two. You could see even when we were down here last week, I talked twice in the noontime and the evening, but by the evening time, this part is much more sharpened up. It has always been like that. And it took longer in 1980 for me to get going.

So I thought the statement for running was strong, but we were right out. We left Faneuil Hall [in Boston, site of the announcement] and went up to New Hampshire, and we had this strong national press following by then. But the presentation was not crisp and tight, with a strong message as a candidate. I think eventually it got there. It was a lot stronger after January, and it got stronger during the course of the campaign. Our organization—rather than building up and their all knowing that we're going to get in—had to jumpstart. We had very good people, just superb people, but they hadn't had a long lead time getting in. And they had to get moved up and started in a very jumpstart way. And I think they did. They're remarkable people who have worked in subsequent campaigns and have been recognized generally among the very best. Even today, there are a number of them who have done all that and are still doing it.

So that was a deficiency. My brother-in-law, Steve Smith, who is like a brother to me, was very influential. In '60, Bobby was the campaign manager and Steve was right underneath him, and then he did Bobby's campaign in '64, and Bobby's campaign in '68. Steve had really gone through it, and he wanted to work on it, but he had a lot of angst about my safety and security and all the rest of those things.

So this was getting started. And you had the [Iranian] hostage situation. It changed the whole atmosphere, where the president obviously became stronger and stronger as a national leader, and we had the foot-faults in the beginning. It took time to get our feet underneath us.

Q: Can we go into a little bit more on that general subject? You had made up your mind sometime during the summer. Did you have a concept at that time of what your theme or your platform would be? The reason I'm asking this is that when the hostage crisis came, that changed the circumstances. Was it healthcare, or was it leadership, or was it the direction of the Democratic Party, or all of those things? Did you have a concept about what you would attempt to accomplish, and the message you'd try to get across, when you decided in the summer?

EMK: My core sense is the economy is the makeweight. President Kennedy said the greatest social program is a good job. And the strong economy, which is going to be an expanding, growing economy, is going to be a key. We had now gone through these extraordinary [high] interest rates, high unemployment—and there just seemed to me a complete unwillingness to deal with those issues. And then the health insurance was—

Q: *Double-digit inflation at that time.*

EMK: Inflation, and a real abdication or unwillingness to deal with this issue. And the health issues. He [Carter] had four years of getting through it, and effectively had either misrepresented or misstated what his own commitment on that would be, and I felt strongly about that issue.

And I thought just the general leadership issue—what the Democratic Party historically stood for, what I had *seen* it stand for. We had seen this party that had ended the war, the party that had fought for civil rights, the march towards progress. All of that was on the move, and all of that was at risk. And President Carter had said that he believed that the spirit of America was the spirit of malaise, which is so in conflict with the inherent view that I have about what this country is about, what I think the party is about, and what I'm about. I think that's about where it is. We had those platform issues, and other kinds of issues—jobs, programs, and other kinds of things—but that was the inherent sense we had.

Now before going into '80, I had spent a lot of time (I don't know how you want to get into this—probably with Larry [Horowitz[16]]) about my wife [Joan] to find out whether she would medically be able to sustain this. It was very extensive. We spent a lot of time on this. I had to get the green light—which we got that summer, in the early summer—that this was going to be all right, because the last thing I wanted to get into was to tip things over. Larry can get you great, great detail. I wasn't going to get into it unless this was going to be something that people who reviewed all of the medical conditions were satisfied could work. Not just that it was dicey, but that they thought there was a much better chance than not that she would make it through and be satisfactory.

Now, another one of the important themes in all of this besides our own origination of the course of the campaign is that power of the presidency. I'd seen the power of the presidency, but until you see it really work on you, you get very little sense of what it's about.

Example: Jesse Jackson asked me to go out and speak for him on a Sunday at the operation in Chicago. So I went out there with Steve [Smith]. His service out there is incredible. While the service is going on, which lasts about three

---

16. Lawrence C. Horowitz, a graduate of Yale Medical School, became the Kennedy family's consulting physician, in addition to a member of Edward Kennedy's staff from 1972 to 1986. He directed the Senate Subcommittee on Health staff from 1977 to 1981, while Kennedy chaired the subcommittee. Horowitz served as Kennedy's chief of staff from 1981 to 1986.

hours, you're out there for a while, and then you come back in and have coffee in his office—the service is still going on—and you talk shop.

He had indicated that he wanted to support me, but he was going to need his own campaign. It was going to have to be independently funded and do its own thing because we didn't have any money at the time. I said, "Well, that's great. Steve will handle that. He'll make sure that you're going to have this thing funded and supported." We all embraced and shook hands, and we all went back out there, and he's saying, "God Bless America" ten more times. I left, and I said, "Well, we're going to get Jesse on this."

The next Sunday, Fritz Mondale was out there, and I got the report that they went back in that room, and all the rest of it. Then, about the next Wednesday, Jesse got about $10 million in training grants, and we never got a return call from him. We could see this with mayors, with governors.

I didn't mention here some of those who had urged me to run. I was up at the Special Olympics in New York State, and Moynihan[17] made a big point of pulling me over and saying I had to run. He said he'd do anything for me, that I had to run. In a New York meeting, Hugh Carey[18] said I had to run. He'd do anything for me. But once this campaign got started, I never heard from either of them again. We had a number of people who had—

Q: You mentioned Dan Rostenkowski[19] yesterday.

EMK: Oh, yes. The Rostenkowski story. When I was in Washington just after I announced, Rostenkowski came over and said, "We're going to do the same for you in Chicago that we did for John Kennedy. You can relax. You can depend on me to do it." About ten days later, there's a gathering of congressional leaders down at the White House, and I see Rostenkowski down there. I called him up the next day, but I couldn't get him. And four days later, he announced for Carter. They had pushed in a whole new kind of transit up there in Chicago. I mean, [Carter] just picked off these [supporters]—

We had Joe Brennan up in Maine and John Durkin in New Hampshire, but we didn't see much of John. Barbara Mikulski was a big, big supporter. She introduced me at the convention, and she was there the whole time, was just very enormously strong as were Paul Simon, who is a very thoughtful person, and Dick Durbin.[20] And there are several others we could mention here, but it was a thin group.

Q: Did it surprise you—or were you not thinking of this in advance, that Carter would use that power? Had that figured—

---

17. Senator Daniel Patrick Moynihan was a New York Democrat.
18. Carey was the Democratic governor of New York.
19. Rostenkowski was an Illinois Democratic congressman.
20. Brennan was governor of Maine; Durkin was a New Hampshire senator; Mikulski was a Maryland congresswoman and then senator; Simon was an Illinois senator; and Durbin was a future senator from that state. All were Democrats.

EMK: No. I don't think so. There had been a Florida straw poll, and we did very well down there. They did it with the people who were voting, people who had been involved in work programs, and we found out in the latter part of it the Carter people told these people in the work programs that if they wanted to stay in, they had to go in and vote for Carter, since Carter was funding these programs. It was a whole segment who all came in and voted 99 percent for Carter. I remember hearing that that kind of activity was going on.

But what they were able to do with mayors and local leaders in these different towns and cities that looked important was very significant and very powerful—and very important and very effective. They just called in all of their political people—in each one of these agencies, they have a political shop—and said, "What does so-and-so need? What's he asking for?" That just made a big, big difference.

Q: *And your financial resources were not good.*

EMK: No. No. It was effectively ended at the end of Iowa.[21] Yes, we didn't have resources. The one thing that kept our campaign going was the artists. We had strong support from artists.

Q: *Warhol?*

EMK: Yes, Andy Warhol.

Vicki Kennedy: [James] Rosenquist.

EMK: And Rosenquist. Andy Warhol would take a picture of me, and sprinkle some dust or things. He did two very—

Vicki Kennedy: Wyeth.

EMK: Yes, Jamie Wyeth. But Warhol sprinkled some dust on this thing, and we'd sell those for a big chunk of change—$1,000, I think. They got a whole string of other painters, and even though we couldn't sell them, we could mortgage them, and we got money for that. We got probably a couple of million dollars, which was enough to keep the pace going along, which was very good. And then at the end of it, they sold a lot of the things. I still ended up two or three million dollars in debt that I had to pay off, but it got us through.

We didn't have any real money, but at least people were able to travel around. We had very creative—Ron Brown[22] was very creative in taking a one-spot, for example, and having a news conference in California, and they'd show the spot, and show it in the news. "Ron Brown was in Fresno today, announcing the Kennedy spot," and then they'd run the spot a little bit, and

---

21. President Carter defeated Kennedy 59 to 31 percent in the Iowa caucuses.

22. Ronald Brown was on the cusp of a successful political and legal career when he left his position at the National Urban League to become deputy campaign manager for Edward Kennedy's presidential run in 1979. He would serve as chair of the Democratic National Committee from 1989 until President Clinton named him commerce secretary in 1993, the first African American to serve in that position. He died in a plane crash while on a trade mission in Croatia in 1996.

then Ron Brown would go to Sacramento and have the press conference. And we carried California.

Q: Senator, you mentioned yesterday you thought you were going to carry Iowa. Could you tell us a little about that?

EMK: Yes. When I went to Iowa the one person who sensed that Iowa was going to be a bigger-than-life state was actually my nephew Joe, who at that time I don't think was even in Congress yet. He said, "This isn't a caucus; this is a primary state. There's so much activity and involvement."

No one really paid any attention to him. We did it the old way, which is getting the number of Democrats that were going to be with you and locate and organize. And on election eve, we had more Dems than had shown up in all of the caucuses in either of the previous two presidential races. More. In Ames, we would have 4,000 Dems, and the people who showed up in Ames previously would be 3,500 representing all the candidates. We had 4,000 Dems! I said, "I'm going to win this thing. I'm going to win it."

But Carter had forty thousand Dems. He got that thing going, and we lost. It was an interesting thing in Iowa: the more I went to these towns— I can always remember Ottumwa, Iowa. The more I went to Ottumwa, the more I fell behind. It was absolutely incredible. The more I went to these smaller towns, the more I lost. And Harold Hughes,[23] who was a supporter and enormously highly regarded, was unable to really get as involved as he was for—he was the head of a national drug rehabilitation program and he couldn't get involved. But he said, "I'll tell you: the reason is, [the way] you arrive."

I would have twenty Secret Service. I'd arrive, and there'd be a hundred people in this little town, at the church or whatever. I'd arrive, and there'd be twenty-five Secret Service people in there, pushing people around and telling them to sit over here. And then there'd be thirty cameras, because the cameras were always around in case something would happen to me. They had to follow me the whole time. So there'd be more cameras and more Secret Service. Harold Hughes said when he'd drive up into Ames, he'd drive up in a car or truck, and he'd get out himself, and he'd go into that place himself, shake everybody's hand and introduce himself. Then he'd write the names down and things, and get back in his car, and at nighttime, he'd go over the things with an aide and write the people notes. He said, "That's what you have to do in Iowa."

So we did it with me speaking; I did it with me sitting; I did it with me at a panel. I tried to change the format in every possible way. You couldn't do it. The only place you could do it was in the big cities where they didn't care quite as much. But that state is so much small towns, and we just couldn't get—

---

23. Harold Hughes was the former Democratic governor and senator from Iowa.

The other thing was, we had all the UAW people in the beginning, and I started to lose them. And they called it Chappaquiddick, but it was really the gun issue. They did a terrific job on me on guns. You know: Kennedy and gun control. The gun issue was a very powerful—and is powerful. Actually, I have a very strong position that I'm very strongly committed to, but that was a very powerful factor. By the end of that campaign, in terms of the UAW—I had it 90/10 when I went there, and it was probably 55/45 by the time the election was held. Very interesting.

After that, after I went home and listened to the results in McLean, that night I had to call my mother. I was the first Kennedy who had lost an election.[24] So I called my mother to tell her that I'd lost. And she said, "Oh, that's all right, Teddy dear. I'm sure you'll work hard, and it'll get better," and was very upbeat and hopeful.

And then, she was so sweet. She said, "Teddy, you know that nice blue sweater I gave you at Christmastime? Do you remember that?" And I did. I remembered it, yes. She said, "Have you worn it?" I said, "Well, I'm not sure that I've worn it." She said, "Is there something special about it? Because I just got the bill for it, and it was $220." It had a turtleneck, and it had a little pocket in the front. It was a sweater that had been made in France that she'd got on Worth Avenue down there [in Palm Beach]. It was wonderful material; it just felt so good. So she said, "Well, Teddy, will you check it out? And if you haven't worn it, will you send it back, because I've got another blue one here that I think is just as nice and is not nearly as expensive." [*Laughter.*] It was kind of a reality check after all this.

But I can remember that night very clearly, and Steve Smith had told me, "Look, no money now. We're in debt. If you get out now, no one really— You took a crack, but don't worry. Your career is still intact. You go back to the Senate, and it's not a real knock. But if you stay in, I have the poll here in Massachusetts, and you're getting beaten by twenty-five points in Massachusetts. And if he beats you in Massachusetts, your career is gone. Finished. That's what you're looking at. And that's in another seven weeks. You have no money, and I don't know what's going to turn this thing around."

That was a very tough conversation. I remember walking around the field for a while. I said, "I think I'll think about it." So I went up and walked around a little bit. And I said, "I think I'll just wait a couple of days. I'll just make my mind up. I think I'll just go around a little bit, a couple of days, and see what—" And then I went around a couple days, and I said, "I'm staying in it." Fine. The people were worked up about these issues and did care about them. I certainly was worked up about it.

---

24. Actually it was brother Bobby who had lost the 1968 Oregon primary.

So we tried to reconstruct it with that speech at Georgetown in January after Iowa to try and tighten it up, get the real focus and attention on what the things were that we wanted to emphasize and press. And that really stepped up the whole thing.

Q: *Were you thinking you could turn this around within those two days?*

EMK: No, I didn't think I could turn it around. I just had to run this thing through my own senses.

Q: *But he told you to give up.*

EMK: That's right. Are you going to give up? Go back to the Senate? That wasn't really the question.

Q: *Did you really think you would give up the Senate?*

EMK: I wasn't planning to give up the Senate. If I quit the presidential, I'd be going back to the Senate. I wasn't going to give up, but if I continued, I had a pretty good shot at Carter beating me in Massachusetts in a primary, and that was not a good message for me in Massachusetts.

That would be the end of my career.

Q: *You might even be ineffective in the Senate.*

EMK: Might be ineffective in the Senate, and any number of things could happen. I hadn't thought about all those things. The day before, I thought we had more people in Ames, Iowa, than anybody else had and we were going to win it, and then—

Q: *And Steve talked to you, and you saw the results in Iowa. And then you spent those two days, and you stuck with it.*

EMK: Yes.

Q: *Risk it all.*

EMK: Yes.

Q: *You were willing to risk—*

EMK: Yes. I thought it was worth the effort. We'd gotten started, gotten in it, and believed in it, and I thought there were enough other people out there who shared in that belief, and we could go on.

Q: *Sort of do or die?*

EMK: Well, you just do it. I didn't think about the other part.

Q: *About the die part?*

EMK: I thought we'd better just keep on doing it.

Q: *The determination.*

EMK: Yes. You're looking on down, your potential loss in terms of the Senate, and you're going to be spending the rest of your life paying off the debt. Are you going to run into big, big debt? How are you going to do that as a defeated candidate? There were a lot of downsides.

Q: *Senator, you talked a little bit yesterday about Illinois and the parade in Chicago, and the Daleys and Jane Byrne. Could you talk a little bit about that?*

EMK: The principal power brokers in Illinois, the Daleys, were going to be with Carter and Rostenkowski; but there was a new mayor out there, Jane

Byrne, who was going to be with me. But she didn't have the power levers. And there was a lot of resentment about her, and that then spilled over on me. The old party people were upset with me because Byrne was with me, and they thought I should have been with Daley, and they didn't quite understand what all of this was about.

Q: Why were the old party leaders not with you?

EMK: Because Rostenkowski and Daley made their deal with Carter. And so we didn't have a lot going on, and not much time in Illinois. It came very rapidly. We had the big Irish parade there where we got egged. It was a very tough, mean, nasty reception, and all of that was shown on national television, which was not useful and helpful. The corresponding primary came very soon after that, and we got hammered. Hammered [51 to 37 percent].

There's one on the Carter saga here. A headline from May 15, '79 issue of the *New York Daily News*: "Ted Unveils Health Plan, Rips Carter." And a second headline reads: "Performs Eight-Hour Surgery on Self." On the photo, President Carter wrote in longhand, "I think this is going too far." Signed, "Jimmy Carter." It was one of the few little indicators of a sense of humor. We were trying to figure out whether I had sent it originally to him, and he sent it back with that comment, or how that came about.

We've now gone through 'til the end of the convention.

Q: You talked a little bit about turning it around in New York [primary], particularly. You were down by twenty-seven points with three days to go.

EMK: In the '80 campaign, the polls were sometimes moving ten or twelve or fifteen points a night, which was such a contrast to what it was in 1960, where President Kennedy was nip and tuck with Nixon and would go two or three months within a point or two. But it seems now that the poll is much more volatile, and they certainly were in '80. In New York we were twenty-four or twenty-five points down with three or four days to go. And I thought that if we got beaten that badly in New York, I would probably have to give very serious consideration to getting out of the race.

But we were able to be successful in New York and win it by eighteen points, so there was a big shift, a thirty-to-thirty-five-point shift. I think it was a combination of different elements. We also saw that take place in Connecticut. It was beginning to move in other places as well, California, or even—we lost Ohio, but only by five points, and we really didn't mount much of a campaign there at all. So I think the campaigns for some reason were moving in our favor. And in New York, there was a particular vote on the Middle East at the UN where the Carter administration upset some of the Jewish voters. It's difficult to think that maybe a vote at the UN would have had that dramatic an impact, but it certainly was a factor.[25]

---

25. A few days before the New York primary, the United States cast its vote in the UN's Security Council for a resolution calling on Israel to dismantle its settlements in occupied

As we were looking toward the end of the campaign, there was a vote in New Jersey, in Ohio, and I think South Dakota and California. And probably several of the last ten days, we'd usually start with a New York appearance because the television would go over to New Jersey. Then we'd stop in Ohio, occasionally in South Dakota, not often. And then on to California and do probably one or two stops, leave there around eleven o'clock at night, and get back into Newark at six or so—stay on the plane. Then we'd go in to do the early morning shows. We did that probably six of the last eleven days or so of the campaign, and we had a good result.

I think going into the convention, the focus was on what they call "the faithful delegate." We had been doing better across the country, and the Democrats seemed to be increasingly interested in our candidacy. One of the things was that some of the delegates selected and pledged to Carter early appeared to have been willing to support my candidacy later in the process, but there had been a change in the rules put in by Carter that said that once a delegate was selected as pledged, they had to stay that way. They call it the "faithful delegate rule," which means that if they pledged, they couldn't change their mind. That caused resentment with the delegates, just generally was not popular. So we made that our principal target: the platform on issues of the economy and health and other domestic and foreign policy issues, and to change the faithful delegate rule.

We had an outside chance of changing the faithful delegate rule, and it needed to have the combination of—I remember Cyril Wecht[26] having fifteen or twenty votes, and then there were some blacks in South Carolina who were prepared to go. Others were prepared to go—Louisiana and some of the others—but all of them wanted to be the ones who put us over. They didn't want to be the base group. We couldn't get some to be willing to be the base group to start the vote to change the rule. All of them wanted to be the ones to put them over. And so finally Paul Kirk just said, "We can't do it. We can't put those numbers together." Even though I'd gone around and spoken in a lot of these caucuses, even in the caucuses that had not had overwhelming Kennedy support, and we got a great reception in those caucuses.

I had a meeting with Carter before the convention. We had challenged him to a debate and indicated that if we had the debate, I might be willing to withdraw. He was giving that consideration, and then he said that we'd express our views through the platform committees.

Q: In other words, the debate that you had in mind would have been a regular debate?

EMK: A regular debate.

Arab territories.

26. Wecht was a Democratic Party official in Pittsburgh.

Q: National debate, in public?

EMK: Yes.

Q: And he was saying put the debate before the platform committee if it's on the issues. Is that the way it was?

EMK: Yes. I think I've read subsequently that he gave thought to debating me at the platform committee . . . and then discarded that. We were looking for a freewheeling kind of debate on the issues. And we were giving consideration: if we got that, then we would withdraw, or if we got that and lost California, we would withdraw. It was something like that. But it wasn't really terribly clear in my mind exactly what I was going to do if he did debate me. Maybe I had a position then. I can't remember now what it was. But I think we thought that if we debated and I lost California, I'd get out.

Q: Did John Culver keep his distance in Iowa?

EMK: Yes. He was in a very tough race.[27] We had a long conversation about it in the very beginning, and I understood the challenges he was facing. So we had an agreement that he would let me know who the good people were, and he'd let them know about his sentiments, but he wasn't going to take a public position on it.

Q: I don't know whether you remember Drummond Ayres.

EMK: Yes.

Q: He was a writer for the New York Times at the time. This is in some of the briefing materials that maybe Milton and maybe Brian[28] put together. He made a statement that kind of struck me. He was following you through the campaign, and he said you seemed almost more contented after Iowa and after Illinois. Indeed, he said, almost more purposeful, and more contented than earlier. I don't know what to make of that, but it's something that at some point I'd like to talk to you about.

You ended up with a kind of triumph, it seems to me, in your speech at the Democratic Convention, and that was the justifying moment for your campaign. You kept going. You kept going even when everybody was telling you to get out. And then you turned it around to give that wonderful speech at the convention, which in a sense, it seems to me, was a triumph in defeat. Was that what kept you going? Was your eye on that speech, and on that end? "How do we end this? How do I end this?"

EMK: I don't really think I was thinking about how it was going to end. I still had it in my mind that it was going better, and we were getting stronger, and it was going to be really an uphill battle, but—

Q: But you hit your stride.

EMK: —many things are going, anything can happen. And you don't let your mind go in those directions in the course of the campaign. You certainly have to have gone through the doldrums or worse after Iowa and Illinois, and

---

27. Senator Culver lost his reelection bid to Republican Charles Grassley.
28. Milton Gwirtzman and Brian Hanafin were Kennedy staffers.

you're peering down into the grave as far as your political career and the hall of judgment and everything else. And then it gradually begins to come back and come around to what you'd believed and what you'd hoped. And obviously, that is uplifting and strengthening.

I wanted to give a good talk, but I didn't have any sense that the speech itself was going to be more than a good speech. In retrospect, I could give that speech at another time, and it would be a good speech, not a great speech. What made it a great speech was the fact that I had gone through all of this and had lost. It's the drama of the moment as much as the words, the resonating words. The words have enormous impact because you've carried those words and they've had meaning during the course of campaign. So that's more than rhetoric in people's minds or the delegates' minds. When you talk about those, they had real meaning and real resonance because you've gone through it. And I think that's it, rather than if you just went on out there and made that speech in Hyannis this afternoon.

Q: So the context was important. You had lost, but you were not defeated.

EMK: Yes. I think that's true. . . . Things about the speech that were very important are that every night when I got back to the hotel at 10:30, my sisters were there. All of my sisters: Jean, Pat, and Eunice were there. And they would come in the room, and they would work for a couple of hours on the talk. The beginning part was authored and suggested, and other parts were done by Shrum,[29] but the part that bothers me and troubles me is the box that had all of these changes is gone. Someone stole it out of my office. So I don't have the record from the very earliest copies to the very end.

That speech was completely altered and completely changed. We laid it out on the floor, put all of it out on the floor, and I can always remember being upstairs, and all my sisters were reading different parts of it, saying, "Look, Teddy, you have this part here. . . ." They have very good judgment and very good political sense and are really good editors. Pat reads it, and used to read everything, and is very good, and Jean as well, and Eunice has a lot of common sense. And they all were very sharp. They're still sharp, but they were particularly sharp then, and they had all been a part of the campaign. They had a very important impact. I remember that, and that's never gotten out, but every night from about ten to one—we weren't doing anything in the evenings, but every night we came back there and worked on it and made changes. They'd redraft that part in the second, and incorporate that thing, and it would be there again the next night.

Oh, yes! This thing is important! Carter insisted they have a roll call. I'm not sure that's Wednesday. Or maybe it's Thursday. I'll have to check. Take the platform win, and then they had the roll call. It wasn't necessary to have

29. Robert Shrum was a political consultant.

the roll call because I had conceded, but they insisted, which many of my supporters thought was an unfriendly act, to rub it in.

They came to Louisiana—and a lot of the states had asked to be unanimous, even in the places where we'd—and we didn't object. They came to Louisiana, and what was it? Seventy-four to one, or—Vicki?

Vicki Kennedy: Whatever the number of electoral [delegate] votes was, to one.

EMK: To one. And who was the one? None other than Vicki's mom. She just said, "I couldn't vote against my Teddy."

Vicki Kennedy: Long-range marital plan.

Q: And nobody knew about the future.

Vicki Kennedy: She took on the head of the delegation, who said, "No, we're going to be unanimous." I'm sure she told you that story. She said, "We're going to say it in French. We're going to say ours in French, so I'll tell you how to say it in French." It was one for Kennedy. She was not going to vote against him.

EMK: So that's kind of cute.

Q: We really should get on the record the handshake lore [about Carter and Kennedy on the convention stage together].

EMK: Well, after my speech, there was a wonderful reaction and a great reception for it. We stayed there for some time, and then went back to the hotel. I was there the next day. The next day, actually, at lunch, I went with my sisters to P. J. Clarke's. I remember having hamburgers and stuff like that coming back.

I couldn't believe that we were still battling and fighting over the platform. We were getting calls all afternoon and through the evening about, "We will take this; we won't take that. . . ." And someone said, "Well, they have the votes to vote it, but we could have minority reports," so the people were going to be able to still speak about these things, which drove the Carter people crazy, too.

We had all of this tension going all the way through, and I had a very substantial group of supporters who said they would be very offended after all of this battle on the platform if I even went on the stage with Carter. There was a very substantial group. And then there was another group who said, "You should." But I think it was very disputed—very good people, too.

The Carter people weren't really sure whether I was going to stay, but they didn't make any effort. I was there all day Wednesday and all day Thursday, as I mentioned. He could have said, "Well, you come down; I'd love to see you, and bring your family down. Rosalynn [Carter] would love to thank you." They could have gotten all the pictures in the world at that place, and, "I'd like to ask you if you can come on up." I'd have to say yes, or done it on Thursday. Or come up to my place! That would have been gracious, to come up and say,

"Can I come by and congratulate you?" That's what I thought probably he'd do. You think in your own mind that's probably what you'd do.

But they were continuing to fight on these things. We were still fighting with them on it. And then there was a question whether we would go, but I had told them that we felt that I would go, and that's when I told the Secret Service we'd leave at night afterwards. I had to go back, because that's when Secret Service leaves you. They leave you off at home that night, and boom, they're gone. And so, I said, "Well, where will we be?" And they said, "You can stay in a hotel, because your reception will run twenty-five minutes, and his will go twenty-five to thirty." I said, "That's fine."

So, boom! His speech ended; down we went. We had an escort down there. For fifteen minutes, seventeen minutes, it was silent in that place. The whole thing was all over. And so, instead of going to the holding room, all I heard was, "Come on up! You've got to run up! Everybody's worrying, wondering, 'Where the hell have you been?'" They were bitching because I was late. It's unbelievable because when I said I'd stay there, it was fine with me. I didn't care. "No, no. You don't have to."

And then, as you saw, when I went on the platform, they had a whole series of other people who went on. I shook his hand, shook Rosalynn's hand. And right behind me was Tip O'Neill, and right behind him was the party—Bob Strauss,[30] and a whole series of party leaders all crowding in there. You look at the picture of that podium, there are thirty people there, and not just me and him, and me over on the side. You could see all the other people who were going there. Mondale was on that. Joan Mondale was there. We had the one picture facing the crowd where Carter was on the one side, and I think it's Bob Strauss and Mondale, and then me, and then next to me is, I think, Mrs. Carter. I think she came over, pulled me on in.

I must have shaken hands with him two or three times. But I didn't elevate his hand; he made no effort to elevate mine! I thought it was proper enough. But, as the press pointed out, there wouldn't be any pictures of me raising his hand, which I had not expected to do, but if he had raised both of our hands, I would not have resisted it, certainly.

We had a conversation some time afterward. I'm amazed that we don't have the notes, because I always remember writing notes every time I've sat down with a president about what we were going to do, or what I was going to do in the campaign. I asked him for some help on a couple of [fundraising] dinners, and he said he would help, and he asked me to go to some of the places, and I said I would.

---

30. Bob Strauss was chair of the Democratic National Committee.

And then I also spoke to him about Steve Breyer,[31] if he would give support to Steve Breyer to be on the circuit court. The way that works is there are a number of judicial nominees. The Senate generally doesn't confirm them after the date of the first national convention, what they call "the Thurmond Rule." Why are we approving anybody with a lame duck or any president after the first convention? We never used to do it. And then they passed some out after the first convention; the second, they passed out about forty or fifty, and then there's sort of an agreement that they'll do eight or ten. They'll sort of divide them up: the Republicans will get some they want; Democrats get a few they want. Breyer got in that mix. And he went on through for the circuit court. He was opposed for a while by a fellow named Morgan[32] from North Carolina because Morgan was upset that I was getting my judge, and he wasn't getting his.

But eventually, Breyer got through. I went to Texas and around. They [the Carter campaign] asked me to go. They seemed to want me to go someplace, but I don't really even recall campaigning with him. I think I did with him in Massachusetts in maybe one or two places, but I don't think they ever asked me to campaign with him at all, which I think, if it was going to be somewhat effective like it was with John Kerry, it's going into places and yukking it up and trying to joke it up. We did that with Kerry in Iowa this last time. People like that kind of thing, and they think it's on the level if they see you laughing with each other. They'll listen, because they think it's for real. If you're down in some other place and say he's a nice guy, they're not buying that.

Q: *Were you surprised by the extent to which he was defeated that fall by Ronald Reagan?*

EMK: Yes, because Reagan was not all that strong. He was not all that strong at the start of that year. I had first seen Reagan debate my brother Bobby ten years before and was caught. I thought he was impressive. People had disparaged him out in California, but I always thought he was a guy who was on-message. He looks great. Whether he could take the give and take on it—but he did it well enough.

I thought Carter did pretty well in the first debate, but Reagan just had a couple of those cute little lines that seemed to get him off the hook. "There you go again," or whatever it was. I don't think Carter could dig his way out of the other kinds of problems he had.

Q: *Have you had any contact with him in the ensuing years?*

EMK: Yes. Didn't we see him at the Clinton Library? He was there. I don't know whether I talked to him at lunchtime. Did I go by, or did I say hello to him? I talked to him on the phone about Northern Ireland. He was up in Boston at some event, and I went in just to say hello to him.

---

31. Breyer became a judge on the US Court of Appeals for the First Circuit and then a US Supreme Court associate justice, appointed by President Bill Clinton in 1994.

32. Robert Morgan was a North Carolina senator.

Vicki Kennedy: He spoke at that Democratic retreat at some place up in maybe Pennsylvania or Maryland.

EMK: Anyway, I guess he was upset we were leaving.

Vicki Kennedy: Yes.

EMK: I don't have any edge with regard to him. I know he has with regard to me, but I think he's done very well in the years since that time. And the start of it, you know—the Kennedy wing of the party. It was there almost right from the very beginning, and it was rather unnecessary.

Q: He talked about how he was going to "whip your ass."

EMK: Yes, well, that was afterwards.

Vicki Kennedy: Can you talk about not running in '84?

EMK: Yes. So now, after the '80 campaign, and looking down the line for the '84, we geared up. I asked Larry Horowitz to gear up for the possibility of a candidacy, and Bill Carrick and Ranny Cooper.[33] And our Fund for a Democratic Majority actually spent millions in '81–'82 to distribute to Democratic candidates, and also pay for our own political activity. We revised the party's nomination procedures to eliminate the rule that required delegates to vote for the candidate they were pledged to in the primary. We had a couple of sympathetic five-minute ads produced by Michael Kaye about Luella Hennessy,[34] and told how I slept in a chair next to Teddy's bedside in the hospital, and Frank Manning, who was a senior citizen, admitted that I was no plaster saint, but I devoted my entire life to helping people less privileged. They had been effective in the '82 campaign, and we thought they might be—

I had spent time with my children in that summer of '82, and I actually have a very detailed memorandum of the conversations I had with my children on three or four different occasions about running or not running. They made it very clear that they'd much prefer that I not run. Teddy [Jr.] was the principal spokesman, but I spoke with them on several occasions together and also individually. And about the time when Patrick came into my bedroom at night and spoke to me about it, he was all sort of teary-eyed about that possibility.

Q: Was that decisive for you?

EMK: That was very decisive. Probably three or four meetings with them all together that lasted a couple of hours at a time, and then Patrick's time that summer. And then on election night, Thanksgiving weekend in '82, we talked again, and I indicated that I wouldn't run. I made an announcement shortly after that in Boston.

Q: There was considerable disappointment, wasn't there, among some of your friends and supporters?

---

33. Carrick was a Democratic strategist and Cooper a public affairs consultant.
34. Hennessy was the Kennedy family's longtime nurse.

EMK: Yes. We had been through the process, and we had a good organization, message. And I was a stronger and better candidate, and there was a lot going for us at that time. But the power of the children was overwhelming. They would all have supported it, but they were very strong in their views about it, that I could still play a very important role in the Senate, and I didn't have to run for president. They felt very strongly about it. And it seemed to me they probably spoke for a lot of the other children in the family, too.

After the '80s, I probably in my mind felt that whatever time I had left in terms of public service, I ought to be involved in Senate activities. We had a very ambitious program then. It was the beginning of the '82 Voting Rights Act. I was the principal sponsor of that. I'd gone to South Africa for the anti-apartheid legislation. So I had a full agenda in terms of Senate activities.

The presidency is still *the* position where you can have the maximum kind of impact, but I think probably, after New York [1980 primary] and after making that judgment/decision at the end of it, I said—in my mind at least— that I wasn't going to run. Although it pops up, you let your mind drift off on it. But it wasn't really a very hard decision in terms of '84.

Vicki Kennedy: Yes.

EMK: During the '82 election cycle, the numbers at the end of '82, the Fund for a Democratic Majority had contacted three million voters with direct mail, contributed $2.3 million to campaigns across the country, supported four hundred candidates, 70 percent of them successful. So you know, the Fund was still moving and going around. We kept that going for elections of Democrats, and to keep the political presence.

So we had a viable political organization, but it always seemed to me that after '80, you have all of that set up, always ready to go, and then you make the decision not to go. In 1980 you didn't say you decide to go and then organize. You have to have all of that and then make the decision. But you can't have all of that and then yield to it as a reason for going. I learned that lesson early, and it's an important one to learn, because it basically will control the outcome if you're not careful.

Perspectives

Thomas Oliphant, *Boston Globe* reporter and columnist:

From a journalist's vantage point, Thomas Oliphant covered Senator Kennedy's 1980 presidential campaign and offered his conclusions on why Kennedy lost.

Oliphant: I mean, that one didn't come out of nowhere. You bet it was surprising and shocking and all the rest of it. I had been around Kennedy at this point for ten years, more than that, and I had come to have very high expectations on the little things logistically, and above all, on the big things where substance was involved. I didn't think that he was, in any sense, all glitter or all sizzle and no hamburger. So, in a way, my surprise may have been even greater than others' because I had very high expectations and very low tolerance at the beginning.

Of course that's where Roger [Mudd]'s interview fits in, because it became a metaphor. The worst thing that can happen in a presidential campaign is that something that's a little off becomes like a metaphor. The interview was important because it was a metaphor, not because it was a lousy taping session at Cape Cod, but because in the context of a campaign that it wasn't about nothing, but it was pretty content-free. Anyone who studies the tapes and transcripts of that initial period will see that.

Plus, the guy [Teddy] couldn't get five words out of his mouth without screwing up. He used the most hilarious malaprops as a presidential candidate that I have ever seen. The replaying of tapes in the back of the—because by then videotape had replaced film in 1976. So we were almost in the twentieth century now. Also the networks didn't travel with a correspondent, a crew. They also had a producer, which meant you had relay equipment, playback machines, and so you could see these things almost in real time. Not only was Kennedy a horrible speaker off the cuff as a rookie presidential campaigner, he was hilariously so. He was fall-down funny. We'd play them and then write about them, of course.

There are compendiums, but when he got to Iowa on the first day, a little agriculture, in addition to the famous story about 80 percent parity on wheat. He began shaking his fist, and at the top of his lungs, talking about a distressed situation that every "fam farmily knows about."

And the first time he said "fam farmily," of course, it didn't register in his brain, and for nine months, all the way to New York City at the end of this campaign, he could not get that phrase going without saying "fam farmily." He gave an entire speech decrying the "rising prices in inflation." And then would repeat the mistake so that, "Why aren't they doing more about the rising prices of inflation?" There was a succession of these, all the more dangerous with political writers on your tail because, among other things, we're sitting there waiting to cover mistakes, not to cover things that are going well. He demanded assistance for a railroad in South Carolina that had gone bankrupt seventy years previously. Over and over and over again.

Q: Apart from the malapropism, was it bad staffing, or he was just not—To what do you attribute this, psychological?

Oliphant: Yes. I had seen him a zillion times. He could mangle words, but I had always had a minority view about that, that it was intentional, it was to put people off, that when he needed to communicate, he was clear as a bell, that he was being reined in by himself, but that he wasn't communicating anything that was close to his heart, and he wasn't talking about ideas that he was really deeply committed to. The exception always will be when the speech got around to healthcare, and then you could tell that was what he really cared about. But it was a memorably miserable launch, and within a week, we were—and of course, for a beginning, the impact of that was greatly exacerbated by the final thing that occurred: the hostages [crisis in Iran]. So the context was awful.

Q Were you ever asked by any of the Kennedy circle to go easy on Joan? Was she asked to be off limits?

Oliphant: This had been tested in various ways, particularly when we were on that little DC-3, or whatever the heck it was, in September and October before the formal announcement. Her health was quite good at that point. She, more than he, once this thing got going, came back to chat. A lot of us would see her coming and be very careful to hide the drink or whatever. She was very personable, very warm, very conversationally at ease. We kind of evolved a little idea about ground rules so that basically, off the record, no political. If all we wanted to do was quiz about Chappaquiddick, that could have been clear from a couple of questions, at which point there would have been a partition on the front of the plane, and we would have never seen her again for nine months. To get to know each other better, and I already knew her fairly well, there had to be some way to converse without working, and it was a lot easier with her than with him at first. She was very curious about—she hadn't really had that much traveling experience in 1980. But there were two or three testing occasions. Now as I say, she was in good health in this period. She enjoyed herself immensely. She was a big hit, and beginning right away, there she was. In light of everything that's happened since then, it's hard to get this across, but she really was in good shape then.

It was a hopeful period, particularly because of her son. Patrick was the worry then. He was just a little drink of water, very asthmatic, thin as a rail, not really healthy, but people just adored him because, as often happens with moderately asthmatic kids, they're just adorable, right? So the female reporters and everything were drawn to him instantly. This was a good period in her life, actually. If you wanted to get Freudian about it, it's pretty easy to figure out why: because he needed her.

And she spoke a little bit. Off camera she spoke a lot. I mean, she was very musical, extremely well educated, delightful to talk to. Actually there was some tension in this thing in the beginning, the security reasons, because it was a Kennedy. Taking on a sitting president is not such a big deal, but the first two really were and the atmosphere could sometimes—it was tense.

Among the things that loosened it up was her.

Oliphant met his future wife, Susan Spencer, while covering the campaign. Kennedy's toast at their wedding is revealing.

Oliphant: However, the CBS correspondent covering Kennedy, I married her at the end. And Kennedy shows, of course, and as he raises his champagne *bottle*, by the way, not glass, he says, "This is the only good thing that came out of this goddamn campaign."

Q: That's great.

Oliphant: He was not a sore loser either.

Q: He was not.

Oliphant: No. In that period the whole thing was lost, and the amazing thing was that it kept going.

Kennedy's 1980 convention speech, in which he conceded the nomination to President Carter, is considered among the most eloquent and inspiring of his long career.

Oliphant: Well, but that there was stimulus and response, that it was two-way communication. I always say, in the conventions, there are moments—still, by the way—when you can literally feel the almost visceral reaction to something that excites such a large group of people. And that's all it was with this thing for forty-five minutes. It was the experience of it; it wasn't the content of it. In fact, when I went back to write the story, it was hard, because the two-dimensional aspects of print journalism didn't touch this thing with a ten-foot pole. I mean, yes, he was still for wage and price controls. That didn't matter. It was more of whose side are you on? What are you about? How hard are you going to fight?—that kind of thing.

Senator Paul Kirk (D-MA), Senator Kennedy's special assistant, attorney, and friend:

Q: Can you tell us how you enlisted for the 1980 presidential campaign? You were practicing law again, you'd only been out [of Kennedy's staff] a year or two, and all of a sudden the talk comes up that he may be challenging President Carter.

Kirk: I think there was an honest-to-God draft that started. There must have been a lot of people who were disappointed about '76, when young Teddy was ill and his father had all these other personal factors. And with respect to the other issues, I think the security issue was always in everybody's mind. But the draft started with people in different states talking to each other and putting a little fuel on it. Mark Siegel, a guy who was in Washington, used to work at the Democratic National Committee and knew a lot of the players around. He was sort of ginning things up. Anyway, the draft basically did take on a life of its own. I think the senator probably wanted to disavow all this and distance himself, but at the same time, I think there was an interest in seeing, well, what's going on here.

So they said, "Maybe Paul will help—" keep the book. So just as you say, I never did get that far away. A lot of people would call and take my temperature, see what was going on, and so forth. I basically didn't discourage, and I didn't do a lot to encourage. I just said, "If you want to mark time, mark time." I think Siegel and a couple of other guys wanted more time to keep a file, and keep the names, and the rest of it. Then I think what really happened—I was against Senator Kennedy running in 1980.

Q: You were?

Kirk: Yes, I thought it was a bad idea.

Q: Why was that?

Kirk: It wasn't that if he didn't run this time there wouldn't be another opportunity. The senator had passed on '76. But I always felt that the time for a Kennedy to run was not the way Robert Kennedy did it in '68, but to run when the seat is open. Then you could pull the party together on your own because of what you did in your own campaign, and then take on the Republican nominee. But to take on an incumbent president is an enormous responsibility and a very tough challenge in any event. I just thought that with all of that, it was not the time to go. But things moved along.

Basically I think what spurred it on was that all the things that the Kennedys, now Ted Kennedy particularly, stood for, were being abrogated by the incumbent. You had the misery index, you had the interest rates, you had inflation, you had a non-energy situation, you had the Iran hostage crisis. You had a sense, if not spoken outright by Carter or his people, that this job is too big for anyone. You had the whole malaise attitude. It was counter to everything that any real Democrat, or certainly any Kennedy, believed in. If anybody believed in the politics of hope, and opportunity, and challenge, and we could do better it was the Kennedys. It was why they got involved, and had stayed involved. This whole Carter message was counter to all of that. It was enormously frustrating to Senator Kennedy. Plus, as much as anything else, the fact that there was not any love lost between him and President Carter, this sort of got the juices running.

And the polls were showing pretty good support. No internal polls, because we didn't have any, but the public polls and what you'd get from conversations and opinions.

Q: He had fellow senators urging him to run.

Kirk: Yes, this was thought to be a doable situation. So things moved forward. I don't have to tell you, it was brutal. First of all, the challenges came pretty early because you had Iowa and New Hampshire. The campaign was not really well structured. If you had to do it over again, and you knew you were really going to plan a campaign, this would not be the way to go. It was a jump off and a hope to get a couple of quick wins and then "moving on up." Of course, that didn't happen. We had this former Cadillac dealership down on 22nd Street in DC that was the campaign headquarters. I don't think it's there anymore. Guys came in, and we worked out of plywood office structures. I had this little cubicle; it didn't span from here to the chimney and no windows. The map is up there and—it got to the point where I dreaded Tuesdays, because it was Jesus, here we go again. How are we going to explain that we lost another one? It was brutal.

Everything that you might have anticipated came back tenfold. There was Chappaquiddick and every goddamn thing. Ninety percent of the time campaigns are crisis management, but this was constant. We were in the bunker from the beginning. The poor candidate was out working hard, and he wasn't having a good time either. You have to understand, he never got space and serious coverage because of other news. The news was dominated by the Iran hostage crisis. The Carter approach was perfect because they didn't have to go out and engage. They used a "Rose Garden" strategy because of this enormous crisis. So you had no megaphone on the Kennedy side, and you had all this other crisis news on the other side. If Kennedy got on the news it was because he said "fam farmily" rather than "farm family," and they'd talk about how he screwed up the syntax. Please, spare us.

Then in the meantime we're getting drubbed, I mean, we're getting drubbed like two to one in caucuses. So any sense that there might be an early liftoff was gone. And you're working against a White House that is using every bit of apparatus they can possibly use. The grants are going out to the mayors, and they're getting locked in. The mayor is saying, "I've got to be for Carter. I just got $400,000 in block grants. What the hell am I going to do?" So you've got all this apparatus coming at you and nothing at an early stage in the win-loss column to give you anything to feel good about. So it was punishing for everybody, and money is drying up. We've got no budget, we've got no money, and we're trying to do this piecemeal media strategy. It was not a lot of fun.

Then you get to the point—the rationale for getting in that I mentioned has never been articulated because you can't get the coverage. You reminded me about the Georgetown speech, and that was going back to the core rationale, if you will, of feeling he needed to say it again to get some attention. So that worked for a little while; then events took over again. Then you get to the middle of the campaign and the arguments became, "Where we began was sincere and real, and we are going nowhere. Working people in this country are taking it right in the chops. There's no response from the White House to help them. Nobody is making a case for these people." So how do we get a dialogue going? And can we get a debate with Carter?

That basically became the second rationale for the campaign. Even if we're not going to win, we can't just fold up and go away without finally letting the national audience know why we're here in the first place, right? So then, how were we going to get Carter in a debate—

Q: What was your take on that, on whether the debate was a legitimate—?

Kirk: My take was yes, this is irresponsible that we have no administration policy, no serious dialogue except a wringing of the hands about woe is me, and oh, this is so tough. So is life! So for me it was, this is not a good deal. A debate would be important, win or lose, at least you have a platform. But that wasn't going to happen. So gradually—there were some wins along the way. I will say that when it came to New York—I had spoken to the senator and to Eddie Martin and said, "Look, this is crazy. If we don't win New York we have to get out of this thing." He agreed. So we hired a room at the Parker

House in Boston. I think Barbara Souliotis[35] went to the point of chartering a plane to fly us to Boston after a New York loss. I had the script written—

Q: *The concession speech?*

Kirk: Yes, this is the exit strategy. I thought, "Thank God, we're out of here!" Wrong. So of course then you had this UN issue about how the US voted in the UN on settlements in Israel, and, of course, the Jewish community went nuts. New York, with its large Jewish constituency, said basically that Carter was selling them out. That, plus whatever other reasons, the senator wins New York, and here we go again, right? So we're off and going. I think down the line he wins Pennsylvania and New Jersey. Then the next situation occurs after California and we don't have the delegates to win the nomination and, of course, the enormous pressure to get out.

Q: *Did you ever think there was a point where it was destructive to the party for the senator to stay in?*

Kirk: Yes. First of all, I thought if we didn't win New York, this is crazy. Then at the end, at California, I thought, this doesn't make any sense, and I argued to get out. So back to the earlier point, you're going against an incumbent president who is on his way to win the convention. But, having said that, now I can look back and think maybe they were right, I don't know, because Senator Kennedy never had an opportunity to explain what it was that inspired him to run. The whole campaign had been muffled except for the fact that there had been more losses than wins. Then there was a lot of pressure from the party establishment. Obviously, Tip was going to chair the convention, and there were a lot of different things along the way. I remember asking Party Chairman John White to resign because he hadn't been neutral. They were doing all the things that I suppose you'd normally do to say, "This is over."

The thing that I think really had some justification to it was this whole rules fight. So a combination of things happened. One of them was—this was a negotiating tactic—we had some twenty minority planks in the platform, all of which related to health insurance and energy and wage and price controls, and all the different things that would impact upon working America. The key rules question was an innovation of the Carter people. They wanted to be sure that the delegates who had voted, for instance, in Iowa back in January, were still bound when they came to New York in August. The Kennedy people were making the opposite argument—that the highest convening body in authority in the Democratic Party is its national convention. It ought to be deliberative, it ought to be current, it ought to be topical, it ought to be timely. To think that the situation is the same in August as when the guy in Davenport voted in January is nonsense. So we're going to oppose the Carter rule and argue that delegates ought to be free to vote for the guy they had in January if they want,

---

35. Souliotis ran Kennedy's Boston office for decades.

but if they want to be free and open-minded, they can vote in August as they think the circumstances in August dictate.

In the meantime, I'd been visited by Edward Bennett Williams and some of the folks who were for an "open" convention. They were pushing for, "Let everybody release their delegates and we'll get rid of Carter, we'll get rid of Kennedy, and we'll nominate somebody else." So you had all this intrigue going on. We were headquartered at the Waldorf-Astoria. I had had a lot of conversations with Dick Moe,[36] whom I had known from Senate days. Then when it came time for New York, I remember the girls in our staff had this big, big suite. They had made a dormitory room. They had to vacate that so Hamilton Jordan[37] and I could spend two days negotiating and hammering out this agreement, some sort of a peace agreement, with Tip calling in and all. It was wild. In any event, we make a compromise on the platform after we lost the rule battle.

I'll never forget this, in terms of what happens to people's juices in a campaign. When I made the deal on the platform, you would think I was Benedict Arnold. I walked into this room where the Kennedy folks were working—this was like a war room—where the guys were working the delegates. To a person, man and woman, by now they are in this until the scorched earth. They don't give a goddamn about the party or anything else. They are going forward. So it collapsed their whole game plan. You would think I sold Ted Kennedy down the river. It was like, "You took all the fun out of the fair." It was a painful, crazy time.

Then the senator withdrew, and we went through this crazy game—will he raise Carter's hand in victory or not raise his hand. I can remember going down in the car with him. There wasn't any talk about it. It was just let's just get this thing over with. He went in. They went up on the podium and I was thinking, "He's not going to do it." And, of course, he didn't. Maybe even to this day, he still harbors some resentment toward President Carter, who while he didn't have to be true to the Kennedy ideals, wasn't even close to their spirit. They are all about hope, and they are all about confidence, and they are all about opportunity, and it means they have to challenge the best instincts of the American people, but we have got to get there. So that rubbed the wrong way, and then, obviously, there were a lot of things said in the campaign.

Q: *Carter said he was going to "whip his ass."*

Kirk: Then there was one point, I remember Mondale questioned Kennedy's patriotism. It was like, whoa! This is from a former colleague? Things were not fun. They were getting really bad, maybe on both sides. So that was that.

---

36. Moe was Vice President Walter Mondale's chief of staff.
37. Jordan was President Carter's chief of staff.

Q: Do you think his heart was in it, Paul? We've had some people tell us they weren't sure whether Senator Kennedy really wanted this or whether he was sort of almost fulfilling an obligation that was expected of him, that he'd have to run for president someday. I know I'm asking you to speculate.

Kirk: Yes, that's a question for him. What do I think? I think this—that he is a pragmatic politician, in the very best sense of the word. I would say that I subscribe somewhat to what you're suggesting in your question because if I were Ted Kennedy and knew that this was the one—my first opportunity, maybe my last, to run for president—I believe I would have planned it differently. This was undertaken without having taken a poll, just going from a draft movement to a campaign, and that whole transition is by definition sloppy. Then sort of putting a structure together with a campaign, and you're getting into it late, and you have an incumbent president. So from that point of view, I would say maybe that's right. Now once he's in it, he's got competitive juices just like we do, maybe more so. So once he's in it, it was, "We're going to do this." So I would say, there may have been some of that now that we're in it, we'll give it all we've got!

Q: Do you remember what the early sense about Carter's re-electability was within the campaign, had Kennedy not jumped in? Were there discussions about whether Carter was going to lose anyway in 1980?

Kirk: I think there was a real sense that Carter was in trouble. I think to this day if you ask Rosalynn Carter why Jimmy Carter lost against Ronald Reagan, she'd blame Ted Kennedy. Having said that, I'm not sure that's true at all. It probably didn't help him. So that was a factor. But I think the early public polls probably indicated no good news for Carter in the end anyway.

Q: Do you recall at all if he was surprised by the Reagan victory that fall? The Carter folks were—for a while they were hoping to run against Reagan, they thought he'd be an easy mark. I'm wondering if you have any recollections about what the senator's take was as that election approached. Did he see Reagan as a formidable candidate or somebody who—

Kirk: I think, yes, over the course of time. Obviously, you could see the gifts that Reagan had. Just the skill with which he was able to communicate dispelled a lot of early stuff about he's just an old actor. He did very well. The other thing was, he looked at the office the way a Kennedy might look at the office. He looked at that as if we're supposed to lift people up, for Christ's sake, that's what this job is about. This was before "Morning in America"[38] and all that, but, nevertheless, this guy was coming at it with a positive, uplifting point of view.

---

38. Reagan's re-election campaign in 1984 ran upbeat ads proclaiming that it was "morning again in America."

So I assume there was some of that. You could see it kind of evolve through the campaign. But that's more through my eyes, I think, than Ted's.

Q: Paul, do you have anything else from the '80 campaign?[39]

Martin: No.

Kirk: Good, thank God!

Q: I take it that it was one of the worst experiences of your life, is that an accurate—

Kirk: I would say yes.

Theodore Sorensen, John F. Kennedy's speechwriter and special counsel: Then of course came his second try for the presidency in 1980. I was again involved in those meetings, debating whether to run, what the strategy should be, and so on, and there were quite a few of those. Dave Burke and I collaborated on some strategy memos and advice.

Q: Did you think that was a good idea, for him to run?

Sorensen: No. I thought that it was not. I thought that Chappaquiddick still hung in the air, and that running against an incumbent Democrat, as I had learned with Bobby, is always a challenge. It's difficult. There might be better years to wait for. Steve and I, I believe, agreed that '80 was not the best year, until we went down to his Virginia home for a meeting one night, and some of his other advisors were there already. I've forgotten who. He said, "Well, I've decided to run." Oh. That's what we thought we'd come down there to discuss, and we said, "All right. If that's your decision, great. We'll do what we can to help."

I tried to help him a little bit in New York and so on, but I wasn't asked really to help on message or strategy or anything of that sort, including his not very helpful interview by Roger Mudd. I helped sell some tickets for a big fundraising dinner he had here, and then he asked me to represent him on the platform committee, with the convention. The platform committee actually met the week or two before the convention, in Washington. I don't think there was anybody else in the race seriously, was there, besides him and Carter?

Q: No.

Sorensen: So we had the more liberal banner, and I did my best, although I think Carter had control of the votes in the committee and in the convention. Then, I believe I attended the convention in—where was it, here [New York City]? I think so—1980?

Q: Yes, it was.

Sorensen: I attended that convention and at least on the occasion when he delivered his very wonderful speech about the dream that will never die—so

---

39. Paul Martin, a University of Virginia political scientist, was a member of the team from the Miller Center that interviewed Paul Kirk. Professor Steve Knott, who chaired the interview panel, asked if Paul Martin had any more questions for Paul Kirk.

obviously somewhere between 1970 and 1980 he became the senator and not just Teddy.

Q: Why would he want to run in 1980 and having decided and started in with it, why would he want to persist, even after it was clear that Carter had the votes in the convention? Do you have any thoughts on that subject?

Sorensen: Well, when you say persist, he's a Kennedy. Kennedys are fighters in politics, they don't give up. And he was, after all, seeking personal vindication, having let down his supporters and his family and himself in the combination of Chappaquiddick and not being able to prevail in earlier presidential nominations. So I understand him doing everything he could to wrest one last opportunity to show what he had.

The support for Carter was not that deep in 1980, and I think Ted may very well have thought that he could, if it were managed right in terms of ballots, still get that nomination in a fashion dramatic enough to take him all the way to the election, although nobody knew then how tough Ronald Reagan would be as an opponent.

Melody Miller, Edward Kennedy's senior aide and spokesperson: Senator Kennedy wasn't like others, deciding *when* they were going to run. For him it was *whether* he should even run at all. He had to go talk with Joan, and I think she said yes, it was okay, and that they would try for a reconciliation. They made a good-faith effort. I once was talking to him before he announced, and he turned his head, looked out the window, and was lost in thought, and I said, "Where are you? What are you thinking?" He said, "I'm somewhere between happiness and sadness, and life and death." I've always remembered that, somewhere between happiness and sadness, and life and death. This was his mindset before he announced for the presidency in 1980. He knew what was expected of him. He knew, reluctantly, that he probably had to go forward and do this, but he knew too it was dangerous. He loved the Senate and would have much preferred to be able to stay in the Senate, I believe.

Vicki Kennedy:
Q: Did he ever talk about his presidential aspirations to you?
Vicki Kennedy: Yes.
Q: It will be a never-ending subject of interpretation.
Vicki Kennedy: Yes.
Q: So I think you ought to weigh in on that.
Vicki Kennedy: I asked him if he really wanted to be president, because everybody assumes he really *didn't* want to be president. He said, "Oh, no, I wanted to be president." He really wanted to be president, and I believe that, I believe that. I think he feels that the time was wrong. That's why it's interesting, he said that when Barack Obama mentioned to him that he was interested—and he wasn't supporting Obama at that point at all—that he was considering it, he said

go for it. He said, "The brass ring doesn't come around that often and you'll end up taking votes that you wish you hadn't taken the longer you stay here, you'll just get yourself into other positions." And he said, "And the brass ring doesn't come around that often, go for it." And I think that was the case with Teddy. There were times that it wouldn't have been him running, it would have been standing in for his brothers. There were times that it wouldn't have been safe or fair to his family. You know, there were other times.

I don't think anybody can really reflect and look back and say '80 was the right time. I think it was a decision that almost got made for him by circumstances. You know, he was upset about the "malaise" speech, he was upset about healthcare. He just didn't think it was his vision of—the vision of America and the optimism and challenge to our people, to think that Carter met those tests. You know, he wasn't dreaming of challenging a sitting president, and I guess people can go rehash that forever.

But he did want to be president. I think that in truth, from where I sit, that it's much better that he wasn't, that what he achieved as a senator is so far superior to what a president, even in two terms, could have done. I think he was just a consummate legislator, and the way he had of bringing people together and bringing people along was just incredible. And I don't know if those same skills would have allowed him to achieve as much in a term or two as president.

So many of the battles he fought as a legislator took so long. Healthcare took forty years, and he wasn't even here to see the end of that. So many others. Mental Health Parity, ten years. That wouldn't have been a term. How long they fought for Family and Medical Leave, some of the civil rights battles. I just think legislation, bringing people together, crafting the compromises, the personalities, the personal interactions, the chemistry of the Senate, the chemistry of the whole legislative process, was something that he understood so well and was so adept at making work. I think it was good that he was in the Senate. I think the Senate was a better place, was a good place. I think his colleagues feel that way. I think he was a great asset for presidents, Republicans and Democrats, so I think his role was pretty important.

State Senator Edward M. Kennedy Jr. (D-CT) and Representative Patrick J. Kennedy (D-RI), Senator Kennedy's sons:

Q.: A lot has been written about—not a lot, but it's been frequently mentioned—his presidential aspirations and his decisions. You were very much involved, at least according to what the stories are, in the 1982 decision of his not to run in '84. We know the statements that he made about deciding not to run in '84, but I'd like your perspectives on what—this is a question of how you might have affected his decisions, because he said there were family feelings, feelings that the children were very important to this decision. I'd like you to talk about that a bit, if you can. And do you think he really wanted to run in that campaign? Was that your impression?

Patrick Kennedy: I think he was exhausted. I think he ran a couple years out beforehand. He got to run a couple of years ahead of time, when running—preparing a presidential run. So he'd been running there. Then after the '80, he had to keep running for his '82 campaign, for re-election for Massachusetts.

Q: Right.

Patrick Kennedy: And then he had to crank it up and keep it going for his '84 campaign, if he was to do that. So he had been running for, literally, six years hard, eight years in total, because he was going before then. That's break-neck. That would be enough to bury even the strongest soul, and my dad was the strongest of anybody. He could outdo anybody. There isn't a person in this world that had a stronger constitution than my dad, in terms of being able to put up and keep it going. That would pretty much bury anybody. . . .

Q: I'm trying to get the sense of—he had also run against, as you say, it was very precedent-breaking, to run against Carter for the nomination.

Patrick Kennedy: I think he ran again, so to speak, when he kept running in '80, because in a sense, most people would have packed it up after the beginning of the campaign, after he had had a series of losses in the caucuses, and yet he—

Q: The primary campaign.

Patrick Kennedy: The primary campaign. But he kept it going and then ended up wrapping up that campaign, really, on a very strong note, with a number of victories under his belt, and going into the convention very powerfully. And then, of course, he wrapped up his whole campaign very strong. But at the end he had had to really carry that whole campaign for a long—that campaign was not self-sustaining. It depended on him to carry the load.

Q: I don't think this was the end of his thinking about running for the presidency, his defeat for the nomination, but maybe I'm wrong.

Edward M. Kennedy Jr.: I disagree with you.

Q: You do?

Edward M. Kennedy Jr.: Yes. This is how I remember viewing it. You see, I was not crazy about him running for the presidency to begin with. I didn't think he needed to be president. I thought he could accomplish a lot in the Senate. I think he always felt like, well in 1968 or '72, he could have had it. So I could tell that in the back of his mind, he had always felt he should run for president.

Q: Should run.

Edward M. Kennedy Jr.: Yes. In 1980, I didn't really want to be the one who denied him. I wasn't crazy about him for running for president in 1980, I've got to tell you. I didn't want to be the one who said no to him—because there were very few people who ever get the chance to even run for president. He ran, he gave it his best shot, and my attitude was, "Why are you doing this? You tried, it didn't work out, but look, you've got a lot going on." Do you see what I'm saying? I think it was a relief to him actually, don't you guys?

Patrick Kennedy: Yes, I do.

Edward M. Kennedy Jr.: I think it was a relief to him when we said, "Why do you want to do this? You tried, you can go the rest of your life." I didn't want him to go the rest of his life thinking he could have been president but he never gave it a shot, because I think that that would have been—I think he would have, because I think in '68 he could have probably, but it was all too close after Bobby. But I think he probably could have—or in '72 even, I think he could have probably gotten the nomination in '72. I don't know how it all would have worked out, of course. That's what I think.

Patrick Kennedy: And the fact that he had a triumphant wrapping up at the convention.

Edward M. Kennedy Jr.: Being at the convention, yes.

Patrick Kennedy: And then he got really—he found his voice in the Senate. I mean, it really started taking off for him there. I think he exorcised that angst to try to do this, and then he settled back into what he really was good at.

Edward M. Kennedy Jr.: Wanted to do, yes, exactly. So I think it was, he did it, he gave it his best shot.

Q: I think these perspectives are important, because there are commentaries all over the map about this issue in his life, and there was a lot of pressure on him always.

Edward M. Kennedy Jr.: There was always political pressure.

Q: They were always on him.

Edward M. Kennedy Jr.: The pollsters and this and all that.

Q: Some staffers, everybody.

Edward M. Kennedy Jr.: They were all saying let's go, and they'd show up. But you know what? I saw the polls in 1979, and those same pollsters were saying he was going to be the next president, no question about it. I mean, I read these polls. They showed him up against Carter and up against the potential Republicans, and they showed him basically walking into the White House, OK? That's what those poll numbers showed. I think it would be good for the Institute[40] to maybe—I don't know where all that polling material is.

Patrick Kennedy: It would be very good.

Edward M. Kennedy Jr.: I think for the Institute to get copies of these polls, don't you think, Patrick? It would be very—to show the information that he had at the time.

Q: I have seen some of the—

Edward M. Kennedy Jr.: I remember it was considered a slam dunk, OK? And then suddenly it was like, "Why do you even need to do this?" And I knew he could be effective without being president. In fact, he almost was, if you really think about it.

---

40. The Edward M. Kennedy Institute for the United States Senate opened in 2015 next to the John F. Kennedy Presidential Library in Boston.

Q: Yes.

Edward M. Kennedy Jr.: The bully pulpit that he had and the persona, and his ability to raise awareness about a particular issue. For a guy who was in the Senate, I think he probably had one of the highest profiles of any political leaders in the United States. And I was thinking, "What more are you going to get out of it?" Aside from being able to live in the White House and that kind of thing.

Patrick Kennedy: The irony and the real reason why, again, this was so vital to his being a political figure, is that his strength as a person, his strength in his abilities, made him ideally suited as a legislator. I mean, he is perfect at working the back rooms, at working people, bringing together compromise. I saw Karen Ignagni[41] the other night, who said it's true. She said, "I know you probably hate hearing this, you've heard it before, but if your father was here, this deal on healthcare would have been passed by now [December 2009]—there's no one else who can call everybody together and get them all to say this is going to be the way it's going down, and it would be done." But it's true, and I heard it from Judd Gregg[42] last week. I mean, the number of people who acknowledge his political prowess as a legislator. And over and above anything else, he was—as far as the old style, like a Lyndon Johnson—a master of this, to the point where he could accomplish more than most ordinary legislators, because of his political acumen in this field. I mean as a historic figure, to study the way he operated, because he's not just a senator. He is a senator who was enormously successful because of who he was, combining everything he had to bring to the mix.

Q: I find this very useful, particularly your comment about the fit between his skills and the vocation, the Senate as a vocation, for getting things done.

Patrick Kennedy: This is the thing, our family was about presidency, and yet for him, it was ideally suited that he ended up in the Senate, until he was nearly five decades in the Senate, because through all that extra time, if he had gone into the White House, served, then he would have been out, unless he had been like an Adams[43] and gone back into the Congress, which may or may not have happened. His breadth of experience and what he gave to the country would never have been paralleled in terms of his sheer success and accomplishment. It just is amazing.

David Burke, Edward Kennedy's chief of staff:

Over that period [the 1970s], I got very intense about my own career and my own family, and about taking care of them and myself, so I didn't focus

---

41. Ignagni was a healthcare reform lobbyist.

42. Senator Gregg was a Republican senator from New Hampshire.

43. John Quincy Adams served in the House of Representatives for seventeen years after his presidency. He had been a senator and secretary of state prior to becoming president.

much on what he [Teddy] was doing. I thought if he wants to run for president, that's his business. Something clearly had been lost in the end of '68, '69, and '70. I wasn't heavily involved. People always ask, "Who's around?" and yes, he may have said one summer day, "Why don't you come over? We'll talk about this and talk about that," but that's not serious huddling. He had great people to rely on: Paul Kirk, Eddie Martin.

Q: *There is a reference to a meeting at his house in McLean in about 1980. Everybody was there. You are listed as being there.*

Burke: I was. I listened.

Q: *Paul [Kirk] was there. Jean and Steve were there.*

Burke: Yes, that's right. Everyone was there.

Q: *Was his mind made up?*

Burke: He was looking for reassurance, I believe. I was new to this thing of how can you be in the news business and also be advising someone to do something in public life that you certainly will be covering? I was unsure of how to behave, so I was silent most of the time. I thought, "I have to get out of here because I live in another world now and I can't do this. People will always say that I may have done things in journalism that were favorable to him, and I won't be able to deny that credibly if I can't believe it myself."

I'm just an observer on that. That's what I mean when I say I think he was looking for reassurance. "That's all right, Ted. Go." The planning for it, how to get ready for it. I'm not being critical of anybody, but when you think of the Roger Mudd question, "Why do you want to be president?" and there's no answer for it, that's not planning. Does the campaign—as Churchill would say, "Does this pudding have a theme?"

Q: *You had said earlier, when he's not prepared for something, he gets prepared, and that is not present here, is it?*

Burke: No.

Q: *In 1980, he's doing it, but he's not preparing for it.*

Burke: That's right. It's very strange.

Q: *Was somebody pushing him into it, or was he following their lead? Was he leading them?*

Burke: Was he pushing himself into it? If running for the presidency of the United States was like a hearing on the death penalty, and if the witnesses were going to be the dean of the Harvard Law School and so on, he'd prepare for that because he would have to prove something, that substantively he's on par with so and so. But when it came to politics, I think he was getting the feeling that he could handle many things. "Oh that's not a tough question," and, "I can do this," and, "I can do that," maybe. But the preparation wasn't there, and I don't know why.

Q: *He was also running for the nomination against a sitting president.*

Burke: Yes, that's right.

Q: *Of your own party.*

Burke: I know. It's an astonishing thing. I don't know why someone wasn't telling him, "You're not ready." I never asked him, nor have I ever asked people who were around him at the time, because I would hear, "Who are you to ask? Where were you when we needed you?" kind of thing. I didn't want any of that.

The Roger Mudd question, when I heard that, it was over. It was over if you can't do that. It's almost as though someone advised him, "They won't be bad with you. They won't ask you something like that."

Q: He had a falling out with Carter over healthcare, which is also a bit hard to evaluate.

Burke: Who knows the pressures that were on him? It may have been that he, I think, was rapidly getting better known to many special-interest groups because of the positions that he took in the Senate, which were very strong and in many cases fearless. He became a great advocate. Those groups, if they think you're their guy, they're on you in a million different ways. "Let me tell you what we can do for you." Who knows? It certainly wasn't a bunch of staffers who were advising him. I don't know where Steve Smith was on the issue, but people age and things change.

Q: So from this point on, his presidential ambitions were—

Burke: Were in tatters, I think, after the Roger Mudd question. That was symbolic of anything he wanted to do after that. I don't recall that any serious attention—I may be wrong—was given to his ambitions after the '80. Every presidential year it would come up. Of course it was worth kicking around and talking about if you're in the news business, unless I'm wrong. Am I wrong, in '84 and '88?

Q: It depends on who you talk to, I think. I believe he gave some instructions to some staff to assume, unless told otherwise, that he was going to run in '84. Then he decided not to in '88.

Burke: Well, I can understand that. You wouldn't give instructions to your staff, "I'm never going to run for president again." Because remember, a lot of smart people wanted to join your staff because they thought you were going to run for president, and they wanted to be associated with you. So you have to keep the motor running.

Q: So much is made, in the biographies, of the family's feelings, of the children, who have to be what was holding him back. It's hard to figure why he would have that discussion. The king dies hard. Maybe that's it.

Burke: Yes, maybe that's it.

Q: And there's this great game of, when did it die? [Laughter.] There's speculation about that, that this is when he became a legislator, some people say.

Burke: That's right. I don't think there was one day. I think it was happening over time, a *long* time. You can't just become a true legislator, an historic legislator, which he is. It's hard to keep from being king, but it takes a long time for it to drain away. You still think you can be king sometime, and you see that the potential promise of being a king is beneficial to you in terms of attracting interest and staff, and people come to you with good ideas.

Q: You get a lot of followers.

Burke: That's right. It was draining away, though, and his comfort level was going up with the fact that he didn't have to be president to be famous—historically famous, I mean, not cosmetically famous. And he is that. He has made an extraordinary career for himself, and who would have believed it?

Q: But even after the presidential ambition goes away, does this affect his connections, the lobbies, the interests who can do something for him, as you put it? Do they fall away too?

Burke: No, they don't.

Q: Does it make his legislative self, his legislative accomplishments more difficult or easier?

Burke: In the Senate, I think it made it easier, because it was, "If I'm a senator and you're a senator, and you're always going to run for president, and you want me to cosponsor a bill with you, I have to watch out because you're using me. But if I'm a senator and you're a senator, and you're going to be a senator for forty, fifty years and I am too, we can work together all the time." It's a collegial body. It's been the transition from the guy of "when it's in you and in the situation" to the Ted Kennedy of today.

There was a crazy little dinner party for his birthday a couple of weeks ago, a month or two ago, and a Massachusetts congressman was there, Bill Delahunt, who is a pal of his. He's a nice fellow and a straight shooter. It was just eight or nine of us around the table having a nice night, and Delahunt stood up to make a toast to Teddy on his birthday. He said, "I want to make a toast and tell you that the best thing that ever happened to the United States of America is that you lost in 1980. That's just the best thing that ever happened to this country." And he was beaming. So it's a long way from Roger Mudd's question to Delahunt at the birthday party, but it's true: God works in mysterious ways.

9

Shaping the Supreme Court: Judicial Appointment Battles

Senator Edward Kennedy's direct impact on public policy is usually measured by his crafting of legislation and a tallying of his yea and nay votes over his long Senate career. Yet his indirect influence on American law was also shaped by his participation in the Senate's constitutional role to advise and consent on the president's judicial nominations. By facilitating or blocking a series of US Supreme Court nominees, Senator Kennedy helped to mold the high tribunal and its decisions for decades.

Kennedy missed by only several months the opportunity to vote on his brother Jack's two Supreme Court nominees: Byron White and Arthur Goldberg. In Kennedy's forty-six-year Senate career, he cast votes on twenty nominations to the nation's highest court.[1] His first major contribution to a nominee's defeat occurred in 1969 after Richard Nixon named US appeals court judge Clement Haynsworth to the Supreme Court seat vacated by Justice Abe Fortas. Conservatives had blocked LBJ's promotion of his friend Fortas to the chief justiceship. Subsequently, Fortas resigned amid controversy over his ties to an indicted financier. Senator Kennedy maintained an affinity for Haynsworth, who had judged his University of Virginia Law School moot court competition a decade earlier, but the southern jurist's views on labor and civil rights were unacceptable to liberal Democrats. The confirmation vote failed 55 to 45.

About G. Harrold Carswell, Nixon's next nominee, Kennedy had no doubts. He was patently unqualified, by virtue of his lackluster résumé and racist opinions, to sit on the nation's highest court. White supremacist statements made as a state candidate in 1948 doomed Carswell's nomination. President Nixon abandoned his effort to place a southerner on the court and, instead, named federal appellate judge Harry

---

1. Abe Fortas, Thurgood Marshall, Warren Burger, Clement Haynsworth, Harrold Carswell, Harry Blackmun, Lewis Powell, William Rehnquist (associate justice), John Paul Stevens, Sandra Day O'Connor, Rehnquist (chief justice), Antonin Scalia, Robert Bork, Anthony Kennedy, David Souter, Clarence Thomas, Ruth Bader Ginsburg, Stephen Breyer, John Roberts, Samuel Alito.

Blackmun of Minnesota. "Old #3" Blackmun would call himself, after his unanimous confirmation vote placed him on the Supreme Court in the wake of two failed nominations. He would become one of the court's liberal votes, notably as the author of the majority opinion in Roe v. Wade, legalizing abortion.

Senator Kennedy opposed Nixon's final nomination to an associate justice's seat, William Rehnquist, in 1971. Though he had been a top student at Stanford Law School, Rehnquist had no judicial experience and was serving in the Nixon Justice Department. The ACLU condemned his law-and-order conservatism, but Rehnquist's confirmation succeeded.

Fifteen years later, Kennedy believed that Rehnquist, labeled the "Lone Ranger" by his clerks for his frequent solo dissents supporting conservative causes, should not be promoted to the court's center chair by President Ronald Reagan. In the Judiciary Committee hearings, Senator Kennedy proclaimed, "The framers of the Constitution envisioned a major role for the Senate in the appointment of judges. It is historical nonsense to suggest that all the Senate has to do is check the nominee's IQ, make sure he has a law degree and no arrests, and rubber-stamp the president's choice."[2] Kennedy zeroed in on evidence from Rehnquist's past that raised the specter of racial bias. The thirty-three Senate votes cast against Rehnquist were the most ever recorded for a successful nominee to the court's center chair.

Senator Kennedy prepared for Reagan's next nomination, which would come in 1987, to fill the crucial swing seat held by retiring justice Lewis Powell. A moderate, Powell cast the deciding votes, sometimes on the liberal side, sometimes with the conservatives, in a host of civil rights and liberties decisions that mattered most to Kennedy. When Reagan announced the nominee to succeed Powell, conservative federal appellate court judge Robert Bork, the Massachusetts senator immediately denounced him on the Senate floor. Recalling that Bork, as solicitor general, had executed Nixon's order to fire Watergate special prosecutor Archibald Cox, Senator Kennedy sought to preempt Bork's supporters, who saw the intellectually gifted jurist as the perfect conservative antidote for Powell's liberal votes.

Senator Kennedy described "Bork's America" as one where "women would be forced into back-alley abortions, blacks would sit at segregated lunch counters, rogue police could break down citizens' doors in midnight raids, school children could not be taught about evolution, writers and artists could be censored at the whim of government, and the doors of the federal courts would be shut on the fingers of millions of citizens for whom the judiciary is—and is often the only—protector of the individual rights that are at the heart of our democracy."[3]

---

2. Stuart Taylor Jr., "Senate Opens Rehnquist Hearing, and the Lines of Battle Are Drawn," *New York Times*, July 30, 1986, http://www.nytimes.com/1986/07/30/us/senate-opens-rehnquist-hearing-and-the-lines-of-battle-are-drawn.html.

3. James Reston, "Kennedy and Bork," *New York Times*, July 5, 1987, http://www.nytimes.com/1987/07/05/opinion/washington-kennedy-and-bork.html.

But Bork was his own worst enemy. His lengthy trail of conservative scholarly publications, recorded lectures, and judicial opinions, along with his Senate testimony that bolstered this record, sealed his defeat in the full Senate by a vote of 58–42. Ultimately, Anthony Kennedy (no relation to the senator) filled the Powell seat and became another swing voter. In all of the cases in which Justice Kennedy voted with his liberal colleagues, it is more than likely that Bork would have been on the opposite side. Senator Kennedy had the clearest judicial impact on American law through his namesake's votes in civil rights and liberties case.

More indirectly, the senator's successful strategy to defeat Bork, using his massive paper and audio trail, shaped future Supreme Court nominations and, therefore, the tribunal's decisions. For example, President George H. W. Bush's first nominee to the Supreme Court, David Souter, became known as the "stealth nominee," for his sparse record in political and judicial circles. Bush 41 thought he and Souter shared a moderate brand of New England conservatism that would offer a correction to Justice William Brennan's leadership of the court's liberal wing. Yet Justice Souter proved to be a generally reliable liberal vote in his nearly two decades on the Supreme Court.

Senator Kennedy opposed both Bush 41 Supreme Court appointees, but it was the second, Clarence Thomas, that sparked the more hotly contested confirmation battle on Capitol Hill. Believing that Thomas was simply unqualified to assume Justice Thurgood Marshall's historic place on the nation's highest court, and pondering Thomas's conservative ideology, the senator found this nomination an easy call. As a member of the Senate Judiciary Committee, he voted against Thomas. The committee's verdict was evenly split, sending Thomas's nomination to the full Senate without recommendation. Before the upper house could vote, however, Anita Hill's accusation of Thomas's alleged sexual harassment of her when he headed the Department of Education's Office of Civil Rights a decade earlier became public. Back to the committee went Thomas for another round of hearings on Hill's claim. No irrefutable evidence emerged to prove either Thomas's innocence or guilt. By the narrow margin of four votes (52–48), he emerged victorious to take his seat on the Supreme Court.

In 1993 Kennedy was delighted to vote for gender equity pioneer Ruth Bader Ginsburg, President Bill Clinton's first Supreme Court nominee. She joined Reagan appointee Sandra Day O'Connor, becoming only the second female justice to serve in the court's history. Kennedy was doubly proud to see his protégé and former Judiciary Committee staffer, Stephen Breyer, ascend to the high court one year later. President George W. Bush's two nominees, John Roberts to chief justice in 2005 and Samuel Alito as an associate justice in 2006, forced the senator back into opposition. Although Roberts had an unassailable reputation as the leading legal mind of his Baby Boom generation, complete with Harvard undergraduate and law degrees, and a clerkship for Associate Justice Rehnquist, Senator Kennedy questioned Roberts's self-proclaimed neutrality. He had worked in the Reagan administration, producing conservative memos on a variety of policy issues. Yet merit overcame ideology, placing Roberts in the chief's chair, vacated by his mentor's death in September 2005.

Alito had a fifteen-year tenure on the Third US Circuit Court of Appeals to demonstrate his conservative judicial philosophy, and Senator Kennedy joined efforts to filibuster the nomination. Visions of Bork's confirmation now returned, as Alito would replace O'Connor, a moderate conservative and swing voter. Most obviously, O'Connor nearly always voted in favor of women's rights. What would happen to such cases if Alito took her seat? Yet Kennedy and his liberal colleagues could not sustain a procedural obstacle to Alito's confirmation. The Republican-controlled Senate confirmed him by a vote of 58–42.

EMK: Just to give some focus to the alteration and change in the courts, because we've come around to talking about the importance of the courts, *Brown v. Board of Education*, the Fifth Circuit.[4] What we now see, as we're moving on into the late '60s, with all the alterations and changes that take place, a whole schedule, a whole program, a whole strategy to alter and change the courts. There was always the thought that Ed Meese[5] had written this out; there was some information that he was the grand architect of the plan to make the courts more sympathetic to the conservative philosophy.[6]

There's no question that they made this effort and have been and are successful. The first one was Judge Haynsworth. There's an interesting irony, a little tidbit on this. When I was in law school, in the moot court competition, I was in the finals with my friend and roommate, John Tunney. We argued the *Durham* case about mental health, the "right from wrong case," whether you have to have the capacity to know right from wrong. Do you just make a judgment if you can tell right and wrong, or do you have to have the capacity to tell right and wrong before you can be convicted? Bazelon[7] said that prosecutors have to demonstrate that you had the ability to tell in order to be—

Haynsworth cast the deciding vote in favor of John Tunney and me, and we won the moot court. My brothers were down there to see it, and it was a big day. I still have the pictures. Now we have Haynsworth up for the court and coming before the Judiciary Committee, where Tunney and I are. So we were somewhat empathetic to him. He got himself caught in a very—not insignificant but not significant—jam about purchasing shares of stock in a company about which his court was making some judgments that could have an impact on their price.[8]

Q: Conflict-of-interest situation.

---

4. US Fifth Circuit Court of Appeals.

5. Edwin Meese was Reagan's attorney general.

6. The beginning of this process occurred under the Nixon administration.

7. Judge David Bazelon of the US Court of Appeals for the District of Columbia.

8. Labor and civil rights groups also opposed Haynesworth, and he suffered from a liberal Democratic backlash against Senate Republicans, who had successfully filibustered Lyndon Johnson's promotion of Abe Fortas to chief justice in 1968.

EMK: Yes. He went back to the courts and had a very distinguished career. He was a very honorable individual but got himself in a jam. Then we followed that with Carswell, who made all kinds of racist statements prior to the time he came up, denied it, and then got before the committee and was a poor witness. He was pummeled, and he was defeated. And then came Rehnquist. Rehnquist was appointed in 1971 by Nixon.[9]

Q: He had been a Republican activist, I think.

EMK: A Republican, very activist. He had gone to Stanford Law School, was number one in his class, and he had clerked for [Justice Robert H.] Jackson. Jackson served on the court when they decided *Brown v. Board of Education.* During their consideration, they had a memo that said that separate but equal was the way the court had to go because of precedent. The question was who drafted the memo? There was strong indication that it had been Rehnquist, which he denied.[10] Justice [Hugo] Black's secretary, whom he lived with for a long time and eventually married [in 1957], was . . . living in Maryland. She said she remembered very clearly that Justice Black told her that Rehnquist was the person who wrote that [memo].

Q: And it was his beliefs. It wasn't written as an expression of Jackson's views; it was Rehnquist's views.

EMK: The person who found it was Joe Rauh. The Lawyers Committee for Civil Rights heard about it, and they wanted to call her [Mrs. Black] up to testify. I spoke to her on the phone; I didn't go out to visit. She said, "Look, if you call me up it will kill me. I'll be asked about my relationship with him [Justice Black]. We eventually got married, and we had this thing which was very special, but this will absolutely kill me. I just can't go; I'd come apart."[11]

She talked to a couple of the other people on the committee, but we never could move on that. It was troublesome. We knew he [Rehnquist] wasn't telling the truth. We had eyewitness testimony that in Arizona Rehnquist would see lines of Hispanics and working poor waiting to vote, and he'd walk down

---

9. After Haynsworth's and Carswell's failed confirmations, Nixon successfully named Harry Blackmun to the Fortas seat. The president nominated William Rehnquist, from the Nixon Justice Department, in 1971. The Senate confirmed him as associate justice and would do so for chief justice when Reagan promoted him in 1986.

10. *New York Times* Supreme Court correspondent Adam Liptak wrote in 2012 that new evidence supported the view that Rehnquist's memo on *Brown* reflected his own views, not those of Justice Jackson. See "New Look at an Old Memo Casts Doubt on Rehnquist," *New York Times*, March 19, 2012, http://www.nytimes.com/1987/07/05/opinion/washington-kennedy-and-bork.html.

11. Justice Black's first wife died in 1952. Although he was a widower for five years, his marriage to his secretary, Elizabeth DeMeritte, was somewhat scandalous in 1957 Washington because he was seventy-one and his new bride, a divorcée, was forty-nine. See Roger K. Newman, *Hugo Black: A Biography* (New York: Pantheon, 1994), 460–69. The second Mrs. Black died in 1987, at age seventy-nine, of a stroke, the year after Rehnquist became chief justice.

those lines with the Constitution and say, "Can you read this Constitution? Why are you here?" An eyewitness says that as they saw him talking they'd see people bailing out and walking away. There were eyewitnesses to this kind of thing, and there was no question he had been involved in it. So I led the fight, we got thirty votes.[12]

Q: Excuse me just a minute. That was a question then, not of his competence as a lawyer, but of his ideology.

EMK: Of his ideology.

Q: He was very smart.

EMK: Oh, he's very smart; he was number one in his class. Sandra Day O'Connor was behind him by about three years, but they were very good friends. Reagan appointed Sandra Day O'Connor because Rehnquist obviously recommended her. He thought that she would be right in the same line as he was, which she wasn't, but they were very close. When Sandra was leaving, she went in and talked to Rehnquist because they thought he was leaving, too.[13] They had been very close on the court.

Q: So Rehnquist's appointment was . . . evidence of an ideological component of these decisions.

EMK: An ideological effort to reverse and change. You can go through the different appointments, but let's take the ones we have and what the courts have said. We have Rehnquist, we have Alito, we have Roberts, and we have Thomas.

Q: And Bork. Thomas, Roberts, and Alito are the next—all of whom had worked within the executive [branch].

EMK: President Reagan appointed O'Connor [in 1981]. That was the first Supreme Court nominee President Reagan had. We have all of these nominees; I don't know whether we want to bother taking them in order.

We had Scalia, who came up after Bork,[14] and everybody had been through that battle and didn't want to have to deal with all of this hard questioning

---

12. There were actually thirty-three votes against Rehnquist's confirmation as chief justice.

13. O'Connor and Rehnquist were actually in the same class at Stanford Law School, and both were considered top students. She dated Rehnquist for a time while in law school until her parents expressed disapproval over his table manners. Sandra Day met John O'Connor when they both served on the *Stanford Law Review,* and they enjoyed a long and happy marriage. While visiting Arizona, Chief Justice Warren Burger had been impressed by state judge Sandra O'Connor and recommended her to President Reagan for the US Supreme Court. In 2005, John O'Connor was suffering from Alzheimer's, and Justice O'Connor thought she should retire from the Court after one more term to care for him. She assumed that Chief Justice Rehnquist would step down in summer 2005 because of terminal thyroid cancer, and she would leave the next year. When the chief reported that he had no intention of retiring, she decided to submit her retirement letter to President George W. Bush in July 2005. Only two months later, Rehnquist died.

14. Actually, Scalia came up for confirmation after Chief Justice Rehnquist, not Bork.

again. He got in and out in about, I think, just under an hour. Mario Cuomo called me and said, "Don't worry about Scalia; he's going to be okay. He's effectively one of us." He also called Joe Biden[15] and others. So he went right on through.

What I'd rather do is take the framework. We can get into the battles on the individual justices, but the basic point is with Rehnquist and then Scalia and Alito and Roberts, all of these people had worked in the Justice Department. We had started the discussion about the *Grove City* case, and the architect of *Grove City* in the Department of Justice was Roberts. That came out during the confirmation hearing.

And this is against the background now [2005] where we have what they call the nuclear option up in the Senate. It effectively would change the rule to a [simple] majority vote in the United States Senate on judicial appointees instead of the sixty votes, which is the current rule. And it's instead of using the rules of the Senate to change the rule, which is under Article V, I believe, of the Constitution. It says that each body is going to make its own rules, and we've made our own rules, and if you're going to change the rules, you have to do it at the start of the session.

It would be a dramatic shift and change in the power of the Senate, the independence of the Senate on issues of advice and consent. The Founding Fathers had really established a pretty fair balance between the Executive and the Senate. I've read those debates at the Constitutional Convention that reflect that, and this will be a dramatic shift and change. I think it would have the very important and significant effect of diminishing the influence of the Senate.

We now have a compromise that's not terribly satisfactory.[16] I think the real question on everybody's mind—we're talking now the first of June [2005]—is whether it'll hold over any period of time. I'm hopeful that it will, because I think we're probably going to get a Supreme Court nominee fairly soon, in [late] June. Rehnquist will announce his resignation, and we'll have a nominee. My own sense is it'll be a conservative, but we'll be trading a conservative

---

15. Both Democrats, Cuomo was governor of New York, and Biden was senator from Delaware.

16. In 2005 Republican Majority Leader Bill Frist of Tennessee threatened to use the "nuclear option" to truncate Democratic-led filibusters of Bush's judicial nominees. In turn, Democrats threatened to stymie all Senate action. A so-called Gang of Fourteen, seven Democratic and seven Republican senators, created a compromise to oppose using the nuclear option, as well as filibusters of judicial nominees, except in extraordinary circumstances. A simple majority vote to confirm lower federal court nominees was adopted by Senate Democrats in 2013; Republicans adopted it for US Supreme Court nominations in 2017, in order to confirm Trump nominee Neil Gorsuch.

for a conservative, and not someone way outside even of the conservative judicial mainstream.[17]

Maybe this president [George W. Bush] wants to continue to have a struggle and a fight on this. What's happening now, of course, is the continued decline of respect for the United States Senate, which is harming the Senate in a very important way, but certainly doesn't help the president. I know he doesn't want to face the issues and is not doing it by just talking about Social Security [reform]. He'd rather talk about that than Iraq and other questions. But it would be a significant institutional shift, and I don't think the American people really have bought into it or will buy into it. But we'll have to wait and see.

Q: Yes. Do you think the [Gang of Fourteen] *compromise will extend eventually to issues other than judicial?*

EMK: Well, I think that's the clear implication of this. This is a very aggressive way of imposing will, by effectively removing the [Senate] parliamentarian, who is supposedly called according to Senate rules and precedents, and substituting this prescribed format, which is in complete conflict with the rules as they are understood and as effectively stated by the parliamentarian in these circumstances. That's radical. What we have is a radical regime, not a conservative regime, a radical regime. And it's not what Justice Harlan,[18] the great conservative, described about the preservation of institutions. This is an administration that has undermined institutions—is attempting to, obviously, in the Senate, in the intelligence agencies, and in the FBI. And they're doing it with other agencies. They're certainly doing it with the environment—putting people who don't believe in the programs and are really committed to undermining them into key positions in the administration. We've faced this at other times, in the Legal Services Program—

Q: Senator, you came out very quickly, right after Bork's name was announced by the White House. You were ready for this one, it seems.

EMK: Yes. There generally is a fairly good idea about who the four or five possible nominees are going to be. That was true with Clinton, and it was certainly true about Reagan as well. We had had a long association with Bork, going back, obviously, to the firing of Archie Cox at the time of the Saturday Night Massacre, which was notorious. He had been around writing very provocative articles on a wide range of different issues, antitrust and a lot of other kinds of issues and questions. He was, by far, the most ideological hard-liner of any of the people coming up.

---

17. Rehnquist did not resign in late June 2005, as Kennedy and many others expected him to do. Instead, O'Connor announced she would leave the court upon confirmation of her successor. John Roberts was well on his way to taking that seat when Rehnquist died, and Bush named him to the chief justiceship. Samuel Alito ultimately replaced O'Connor in January 2006.

18. John Marshall Harlan I of the US Supreme Court.

What happens in these Supreme Court battles is people say, "Let's keep our powder dry"—both the people for and against. But all the time, "keeping the powder dry" works to the advantage of the nominee to move ahead, because they unveil a whole strategy of support for these nominees—and they do it very quickly, before people who have reservations get a chance to do it.

I have to come back to that, how it's done now, in an immediate time cycle. Haynsworth and Carswell took time, weeks and months of hard work. Bork was a long time, and even Thomas took some time. But with these recent Supreme Court nominees, in the time we take a break while they go to the bathroom, senators are going out and spinning. When we say we're going to take our time, it works to their advantage because the other people are so strong in favor of it. That's why it seemed to me that it was important to say "whoa" on this [Bork's] judgeship.

Q: You got some time. You got Biden to postpone, or to not hold, hearings, I think, until the fall, which gave you the summer, additional time to do the groundwork for the hearings.

EMK: That's true, but I spoke right away on Bork—within a half hour of when he was nominated—to hold people in their place. It was a placeholder, so they had to understand that they were going to have a battle. This thing was going to be a fight, and they were going to have accountability on it. Otherwise, the rhythm of these battles flows in favor of the nominees quite strenuously, and it makes it more and more difficult.

I think Bork was honest in his views, but he just lost. They [Reagan administration] made a decision to go very hard ideologically, and then they tried, to some extent, to mask it. I think when Meese and Reagan made the decision to reverse the courts, one of the spin-offs was that there wasn't going to be consultation and compromise [with the Senate]. If you look back historically at the appointments made by different presidents at different times in the country, they had that kind of exchange and interchange in the selection of nominees. The Senate was very much involved with it.

We had new senators from the South, and most of those had won with the help of strong black constituencies. I talked to all the leaders of all the black organizations personally [about the Bork nomination]. We were very active in working with the black preachers, and the black preachers worked with churches and local communities to build grassroots organizations. We worked with editorial boards at newspapers and radio, and we worked with the political wing of the DNC[19] to get to the people who were active and would be concerned about these kinds of jurists back in people's states. It was a full-court press across the board.

---

19. Democratic National Committee.

We prepared books for all the members of the Senate and had those books tuned to relate to the interests of the various members, looking back over the kinds of things they had talked about in the course of their careers or the things they campaigned on. We delayed the hearings for some time so people had an opportunity to read them.

Once we had made the decision in early July that it wasn't going to be over until the fall, we had an unprecedented campaign, with legal experts who examined his opinions and writings and speeches. We even had commercial television, with Gregory Peck targeting the moderate senators. By August, we had organized 6,200 black elected officials, and, as I mentioned, I talked to Lowery.

They turned that summer convention into an anti-Bork organizing session. The AFL-CIO got involved, and Bill Taylor organized a lot of professors. We had 1,900 law professors in opposition, which was 40 percent of all the legal academics, and then we had Bill Coleman, Barbara Jordan, and Andy Young speak about it in the beginning, when we started in September.[20] During the course of the summer, I spent a good deal of time phoning senators and other political people.

Q: *It sounds like you didn't have a vacation.*

EMK: Well, it was a full-court press. On Bork, we had Chesterfield Smith, who was president of the [American] Bar Association, very highly regarded, and he testified in opposition. He was from the South, from Florida. Bob Meserve, who had been against Frank Morrissey,[21] came down and spoke in opposition. The ABA was very powerful; they talked about his temperament and ideology. My statement in the beginning freed the country, and then we were able to mobilize the thoughtful and respected leaders in the Bar and all of these organizations to weigh in, and they made a very powerful case.

Just a bit more on Bork. One thing I'd say in conclusion is that Bork did crystallize the sense in the country not to go back on civil rights. They didn't want to go back and fight the old rules on affirmative action and abortion. He did agree that there was a constitutional right to privacy, and all Supreme Court nominees since Bork have recognized that.

Now we can go to Thomas. With him we had a number of forces working. One was Danforth[22] himself, who had a very decent record [on the 1991] Civil

---

20. Peck was an Academy Award–winning actor for playing the iconic Atticus Finch in *To Kill a Mockingbird*, and he was a champion of liberal causes. Joseph Lowery was president of the Southern Christian Leadership Conference, Taylor the US Civil Rights Commission general counsel, Coleman the former secretary of transportation, Jordan a former Texas congresswoman, and Young the former US ambassador to the United Nations.

21. Smith and Meserve were former presidents of the American Bar Association. Meserve had opposed the 1965 nomination to the federal judiciary of Kennedy family friend Frank Morrissey, who was patently unqualified.

22. John Danforth was a Republican senator from Missouri.

Rights Act, which was coming up just about the same time. That was a dynamic that sometimes has been missed. He had a strong civil rights record, being the prime sponsor of it, and with Thomas being black, there was a basic presumption in favor of Thomas, certainly at the beginning. And Bill Coleman, who was strongly against Bork, now flipped and was supporting Thomas.

One point on Alito and Roberts. There's been a tremendous turnover in the Senate since we had some of these battles. If we had had people who were in the Senate and had gone through the Bork and Thomas battles, I'm not sure that Alito and Roberts would have gotten quite the free ride they got. I think members of the Senate who went through that period of time spent a lot of time thinking about the Supreme Court, and a lot of time thinking about who should serve and what their responsibilities were. We are some distance beyond it, and the Senate has changed very much. And with the very significant turnover, we don't have people in the Senate who have witnessed these kinds of battles. I'm not sure how our Founding Fathers would have thought about that. They're coming at it fresh, and coming at it fresh is not always advantageous. As a matter of fact, it's quite deceptive. My sense about Roberts is that he was an indispensable figure in Republican administrations going back to the very early '80s, when we had President Reagan and the Voting Rights Act and the Civil Rights Restoration Act, the solicitor general bringing cases, and all the way through. He had a very cramped view, I think, of civil rights, voting rights, and the role of the solicitor general. He was able to portray that view as being that of the administration and not really his own. And in the course of the hearings I don't think we were able to break that out at all. He just sailed right through. He's a very pleasant person. He's very smart, and he had a lot of allies here, and at Hogan and Hartson, among the Federalists,[23] and otherwise, and he was able to go right on through.

I'm basically by nature and disposition not interested in the destruction of people. I'm interested in advancing the cause of humankind rather than being judgmental. I don't relish it. I love fighting on minimum wage or health or civil rights issues, but not in terms of the destruction of people. So in any of these battles, I never got a lot of personal satisfaction from the defeat. I suppose more so with Bork at the time, for obvious reasons, the real threat that he posed. I never thought Haynsworth posed the kind of threat that Bork did, or that Thomas was going to pose.

By the end of it, I thought Carswell was kind of a buffoon. I didn't have any respect for him at all, but you couldn't help having some respect for Haynsworth. He had been an important jurist. He certainly went back and had a good career. I never really relished the thought of defeating these people.

---

23. Hogan and Hartson was a distinguished Washington law firm; the Federalist Society is a conservative interest group based at American law schools.

And as for the judiciary, I want at the end of this time that I've been in the Senate to say that I've led the fights and opposed people for the federal judiciary. But when they look back on the quality of the people I've recommended and sent, they've been the top. That's how I view that whole point. Since I'm so involved and active in the selection and ensuring that people who are going to get on the courts are going to have core commitments to the Constitution and be good judges, I have to have the best.

We've had some very sad circumstances. I failed to appoint a person recommended by Eddie Boland,[24] who, going back to 1962, made the speech for my nomination. He was the only member of the Congressional delegation in Massachusetts to support me. They didn't want to get caught between [Edward] McCormack and Kennedy.

But Eddie Boland had gone to Ireland with my brother [Jack] and was a great supporter of my brother. He agreed to support me, and that made an enormous difference. It gave me credibility right away. The [1962 state Democratic] convention was in his hometown of Springfield. It made a difference in terms of the delegates in the western part of the state who had enormous respect for him. Endorsements generally don't make a lot of difference unless people have a sense that there's some kind of connection. If they know that you're connected in some way, they'll listen to you; they'll say, "Tell a little bit, tell something about the person you're talking about."

But if you go out and endorse some person just because they're a Democrat, people don't pay you a whit's bit of attention. It maybe helps them a little bit to raise some money, but I don't think, myself, that it makes much difference. But because of the association that Boland had had with President Kennedy, that endorsement made a lot of difference. Boland was the leader in ending the war in Central America.

I offered the Boland Amendment initially in the Senate, but it took five years before Inouye[25] offered the Boland Amendment, which had been my amendment. We carried it by fifty-one [votes], and it stopped the Contras, the war there. The only thing Boland asked is that we appoint his [friend] to the federal bench. His [friend] had been recommended in the top five, but he hadn't been recommended in the top three. I took the top one, Judge Ponsor,[26] who's the judge out there now.

---

24. Edward P. Boland served as the congressman from Massachusetts's Second District from 1953 to 1989. He worked in JFK's Ohio presidential campaign and endorsed Edward Kennedy for his first Senate run in 1962. The Boland Amendment limited and ultimately banned US military aid to the Contras in Nicaragua in their attempt to overthrow the Marxist Sandinista government. Reagan administration efforts to circumvent the amendment led to the Iran-Contra scandal.

25. Senator Inouye was a Democrat from Hawaii.

26. Michael Ponsor is a federal judge in Springfield, Massachusetts.

Boland didn't speak to me again until his death. He'd say hello, but he didn't say anything else, and his family didn't until this year. I went out to Springfield, and I've been helpful to Mary Boland's son, getting him into school, and I helped another one to get a job in New York. The children feel that we ought to get beyond all of this. I've invited her to the Kennedy Library repeatedly as our guest, and she's starting to come now. Now she's fine.

Q: Did you wish you hadn't done that?

EMK: Oh, no. I thought I ought to put Ponsor on, but I got a lot of criticism. Not only was Boland upset, but all the political people who were so loyal to me and loyal to Boland couldn't understand why I wouldn't put him [Boland's friend] on [the federal court]

Q: There wasn't something else that Boland—

EMK: This was the only thing he wanted. He was a fellow named Judge Keyes, and as I said, there was a level of difference between Judge Keyes and this other fellow.[27] It wasn't just, "I'm taking the other guy just because he's a pol."

I haven't done that, I don't do that. This was a painful thing. But in any event, Ponsor is a brilliant judge out there, and he's universally admired and respected. He's eloquent, he writes, he's very highly regarded and respected.

We had one situation where I had two or three vacancies, and I had them all lined up, and there was a vacancy out in Worcester. And Slade Gorton[28] of the state of Washington wanted his brother put on. I said, "He didn't come up in the lineup." "Well," he said, "you're not getting your judges. I'm putting a hold on all your judges." So we waited, and it went on for about six or seven months. I went back and talked, personally to a lot of the people. I said, "Can his brother handle the job? I'm not going to appoint a turkey." They said, "Well, he can. He's not the brightest bulb in the chandelier, but he's competent and can do it." So, boom, I released it. It was such an interesting thing. Here's this piousness now on the nuclear option, when Slade Gorton was out there holding this up and completely supported by all the Republicans.

My own belief is the confirmation process has broken down, because the nominees are so coached in their answers. The nominees look at videotapes showing where the mistakes were made for other nominees in answering questions about the *Roe v. Wade* case. They go through that time and time and time again and see how the successful nominees got through answering it, and how the other nominees got themselves in trouble answering it. This is like the preparation for a bar exam or the SATs. These people are all bright, and they

---

27. Judge Daniel Keyes served on the Chicopee, Massachusetts, District Court. Ponsor held degrees from Harvard College, Oxford (Rhodes scholar), and Yale Law School; Keyes's undergraduate and law degrees were from Boston College.

28. Gorton was a Republican senator, originally from Massachusetts.

go on through. There are only a few of these kinds of questions that are troublesome. What we've seen, though, is from that [post-Bork] period, they've all spoken in generalities, never anything specific. They [Supreme Court nominees] say *Brown* is okay, like we saw with Roberts, but they won't get into it. *Griswold* is okay—that was on birth control—but they don't get into it. So basically, the sense you get is that the administration is looking for ideologues, but now they're looking for them without the paper trail, and they're moving on. That's the lesson you get with Bork, who had written so much, was so opinionated, was such a poor witness, and the country rejected it.

I'm going to vote only for people for the Supreme Court if they are going to make affirmative commitments to constitutional values. If they're going to leave this to be an open issue, or if there's a question about it, then I don't feel that I have a responsibility to support them. This is a lifelong job, it's extremely important, and there is too much at risk.

Perspectives

Carey Parker, Edward Kennedy's legislative director: About two hours after President Reagan announced Bork's nomination, Kennedy went to the Senate floor and gave a strong speech opposing the nomination. "Robert Bork's America," as people called it. We had a few lines in the speech like, "In Robert Bork's America," this and that will happen, in order to describe the dire consequences that would result from Bork's confirmation to the court. The brakes were slammed on, and it was clear that this would be an all-out fight. That was probably the single strongest step we took against the Reagan administration. The senator did it instantly, which has been relatively rare. Senators come out in opposition to other judges, and sometimes it takes a day or so. The administration gets the favorable publicity initially, but Senator Kennedy wanted to speak against the nomination immediately and say, basically, "Over my dead body. This nomination is not going through."

Melody Barnes, Edward Kennedy's aide and chief counsel on the Senate Judiciary Committee:

Q: So this argument that the judicial nomination process has been politicized— some people look at the Bork nomination as a turning point, and not a good turning point.

Barnes: In many ways, the Bork hearings exemplify one of the most honest confirmation exchanges. Everyone has taken Bork to mean "hide the ball." But, with Bork, you had straightforward questions, and you had straightforward answers, and the fact that he lost because his nomination fell on the weight of his answers means that we did not confirm a justice whose views were inconsistent with the views of the majority of the Senate. It doesn't mean that that was a problematic confirmation process, in my view.

Senator Alan Simpson (R-WY): Sometimes he'd come up on the Senate floor and he'd say, "You bastard, you really threw a harpoon, didn't you?" I said, "Well, you deserved it. You nailed me last week and I think you needed that." That's the way we did our business, with affection. We've never really gone at each other but we have—I told him when he did the floor speech about Bork, I said, "Ted, that was savage. That was really rat crap—abortions, back alley stuff. This is a Yale professor, for God's sake, and not some jerk with a knife." When you get him, when you nail Ted, he gets his head down to the side and cocks it. I've seen that many a time. I said, "Don't you cock your head and give me that crap." But he was passionate. He felt very strongly and driven on that one.

Laurence Tribe, Harvard Law School professor and Edward Kennedy's advisor:

Q: Where the real stakes were for him was when it got to the Supreme Court. Describe for me what Kennedy would view as being the kind of person he would want to see on the Supreme Court, recognizing that what he might want to see on the Supreme Court is going to differ from what necessarily gets nominated or proposed.

Tribe: He wanted to see people who were extremely smart and able to handle themselves in that very refined arena. It wasn't enough that they have great instincts; they had to be really well armed. He had a sense, a very good judgment of who was sufficiently articulate and powerful intellectually. And it was important that the person have a compassionate vision of human suffering and what human problems were all about, and how law intersected with them.

That's why he liked people who were fairly pragmatic and had a sense of what works in the world and what doesn't. He liked Steve Breyer a good bit, partly because Steve seemed to be compassionate and he cared about people, and for Kennedy it mattered. It's very much like [Barack] Obama. Obama cares about someone's ability to appreciate where the rubber hits the road and how doctrine actually affects people in practical terms. When, for example, Bork talked about wanting to be a justice because it was an intellectual feast—that was one of the lines that grated with Kennedy the most.

As soon as he was nominated I got calls very quickly from both Ted Kennedy and from Joe Biden. Kennedy's immediate reaction—I mean, he basically said, "Is this guy as bad as I think he is?" He had already obviously heard a lot of things about Bork's views of various things. I said, "I think he is just about as bad as you think. He's extremely smart, but I think he will put his brains to use destroying values that you care deeply about." Then we talked about it. And this was before Kennedy made his somewhat intemperate statement about . . . Robert Bork's America would have women with coat hangers. That wasn't actually as inaccurate as people may think, but it came across as dema-gogic and it probably was not the right thing to say at the right moment.

In any event, I told him I thought that the only way to oppose Bork was to be quite forthright about the way his values were not just far from the main-stream, but would generate a set of principles that would be dangerous to women and to minorities. Then I kind of elaborated, and that fit very much with what he had already heard. He had no difficulty from the very beginning thinking that Bork's mere intellect and his objective qualifications were some-what beside the point. He was a dangerous man and his views did not belong on the Supreme Court.

I had written a book a little before that, which I had shared with Kennedy and others, that had been published by Random House, called *God Save This Honorable Court*. I think maybe Kennedy actually had a blurb on it. Anyway, Kennedy had seen it. It made the case that throughout our history the Senate had in fact exercised a significant role in reviewing the ideological compo-sition of the court, and that thinking about whether a justice would move the Constitution in a fundamentally wrong-headed direction from the per-spective of whatever senator was evaluating it was an appropriate role for the Senate to play.

I think he asked me, "Well, what about all this stuff about how presidents are surprised that justices change?" [W]hen presidents have in fact carefully selected someone to carry out their vision of the Constitution, it's usually worked about the way the president expected. So there was very little reason to expect that Bork would be something other than the kind of guy that Reagan wanted him to be and assumed he would be.

I have a chapter in that book called "The Myth of the Surprised President," and I think Kennedy found that reassuring. It fit his idea that when a presi-dent selects somebody in order to move the court and the Constitution in a direction that a particular senator conscientiously thinks is wrong, the sen-ator shouldn't hesitate to oppose on that ground. In fact, it was kind of an overdetermined decision, because all of the groups that Kennedy generally listened to would have pushed him in the direction of opposing Bork. What I said gave him kind of an intellectual armature within which to fit it.

Actually, I met with him a number of times to go over some of the questions that should be asked of Bork. We went through a rehearsal: What if Bork says this? What if Bork says that? I played a role both with him and with Biden, but with Biden I went to much greater lengths and actually played the role of Bork in some murder board sessions, at Biden's house. With Kennedy it was a little less formal.

There are very few people in the Senate that I've ever seen who actually use their brains in the process of questioning. There was Moynihan, and a very small number of others. Teddy was not among those who used the interrogation process as a way of actually thinking through something. It was a rehearsed exercise in which he wanted to get certain things on the record, wanted to make sure he covered certain bases. He did it well, and he was well prepped, and he often had reasonably good follow-up questions, but that wasn't his greatest skill and that wasn't where he was at his best. He was at his best in thinking through who he needed to have on the stand, who needed to be there, what things we needed to establish. The questioning process was not one where you could see his mind at work, particularly.

Carolyn Osolinik, Edward Kennedy's chief counsel on the Senate Judiciary Committee: Just as Senator Kennedy's staking out the opposition to Robert Bork on the day he was nominated contributed to Robert Bork's defeat, I think having a campaign against Thomas on hold for the first critical few weeks contributed significantly to his being approved.

The [George H. W. Bush] administration had learned some lessons from Robert Bork, so they had all their ducks in a row before he was nominated: everything from the humble roots to issues overcome and the cadre of supporters from every which way and busing the people in from his hometown and—

Q: And he had Danforth.

Osolinik: And he had a godfather.

Q: There was no godfather for Bork in the Senate, was there?

Osolinik: No. That was part of his problem, yes. Well, not having a godfather is one thing, but having Danforth as your godfather is a whole other thing. There may be no other senator more liked and respected than Senator Danforth by members of both parties. His imprimatur on Clarence Thomas was impossible to overcome.

Senator Kennedy had excellent antennae for what was beginning to work. He could observe his colleagues and see who was troubled by what, because there were different issues for different people. In real time Kennedy would give the instructions to get more on this issue because he wanted to give it to this senator over the weekend. That was one of Senator Kennedy's tactics in all of these nominations, to . . . make it as easy as possible for these senators to understand what the problem was. He tailored those packets. They always went out on a Friday; he tailored them to individual senators' interests and had a handwritten note on every one of them.

The so-called nuclear option is one of the most complex legislative maneuvers, used by both parties to disrupt judicial nominations.

Jeffrey Blattner, Edward Kennedy's staffer and chief counsel on the Senate Judiciary Committee: There was a fight in the Senate in 2005 about the nuclear option, as it was called, which is changing the Senate rules to eliminate the filibuster of judicial nominations. That fight arose, in my view, because the Democrats overplayed their hand on filibustering court of appeals nominees. The backlash from that was what this nuclear option was. I think it would have terribly harmed the Senate had it happened. And I'm going to be partisan here: I think that the Democrats ultimately cared more about the Senate as an institution than most of the Republicans did—and that the Democrats blinked. I think that Alito was a failure of political will. The Democrats did not do a particularly good job of questioning him, generally speaking. . . .

One of the consequences of this nuclear option thing was that Reid[29] felt the need to keep the moderates from speaking out before the [Alito] hearings. The *quid* for that *quo* was muzzling Senator Kennedy and other liberals about the nomination. I thought Reid's message to the caucus, and I was involved contemporaneously in these discussions, was "Keep your powder dry." And I think that that inhibited Senator Kennedy.

The only way to beat one of these nominees is to start on day one, make the argument forcefully from the beginning, "Here is what is at stake"—do the kind of opening statement that Kennedy did . . . on Bork, to really lay out the case. You're going to take some hits in doing that. Nowadays you've got twenty-four-hour cable TV talk, and they're going to be saying bad things about you if you're a politician, if you have the guts to step out in that way. But I don't think there's any other way to do it. It is a mass education challenge, and if you cede the floor to the proponents of the nomination all the way up to the hearings, you're done.

From his seat on the US Supreme Court, Stephen Breyer looked back on Kennedy's deft guidance of his nomination.

US Supreme Court associate justice Stephen G. Breyer, First U.S. Circuit Court of Appeals judge, Edward Kennedy's counsel on the Judiciary Committee: He knows just what he's doing, and he introduces me to different people [in the Senate]. He made sure I met Senator Dale Bumpers, because Dale Bumpers is a good friend of Richard Arnold,[30] and Richard Arnold had not been appointed and probably would have been if he hadn't had serious cancer. It was terrible. Richard Arnold was a wonderful person. He really was great, as is Ruth [Bader Ginsburg]. The other people on the list are very good people. But Kennedy wants to be sure that Bumpers takes me in, once I'm nominated, and isn't sitting there being resentful. So he makes sure I have a chance to meet Bumpers. Then he takes me around to meet this person, that person, the other person.

Q: He was your sponsor?

---

29. Senator Harry Reid was a Democrat from Nevada who led his party in the Senate as majority and minority leader.

30. Arnold was an Eighth US Circuit Court of Appeals judge from Arkansas.

Breyer: Yes, yes. Absolutely. He's ratifying me, continuously, and he's trying to make certain that the others take me in, that I'm not from Mars, and that I'm a reasonable person. He knows just how to do that.

Q: Is there any one particular senator, when he took you into the senator's office that you remember particularly well?

Breyer: I'm trying to remember. He took me to Arlen Specter.[31] He [Kennedy] said, "The thing is, you listen to him, but Arlen isn't going to listen." I listened. I didn't have to say anything. Very good.

Q: Specter came out for you.

Breyer: Oh, yes. Yes, it was much easier, actually, from the confirmation point of view, than the First Circuit [nomination] had been, because there wasn't tremendous opposition.

I'll show you another example of Kennedy's reaction after I'm confirmed— I've used this over and over because it makes a very important and interesting point. I'm confirmed, I'm at Logan Airport, and I'm flying back with Senator Kennedy. We get off the airplane, and we're walking down the area there in front of the lobby, and a reporter comes up from a Jewish newspaper, and says to me, "How do you feel about two Jews being on the Supreme Court?" Kennedy sort of mutters to me, "Fine." I said, "Fine." Just like that. Fine! You know, Fine! It's not a big deal. It's fine. That's Kennedy's instant reaction.

You see, that's a political reaction, knowing precisely what to say. That also is not just that it's the right thing to say from a political point of view, but it tells you in the tone of voice a whole story of Jews in America. That's where we're trying to end up. We're trying to end up where, from the point of view of race, the point of view of religion, the point of view of national origin. Of course. Why shouldn't there be two Jews on the Supreme Court? What are you talking about? And we're approaching that with race.

You see, in that tone of voice, it's not just a political reaction, it's also a statement of a goal. And the goal is a very good thing for the country. I can use that story about him in order to tell people something about the position of race and religion in America, and the progress. I just told that to a person who is a rapporteur from Senegal for some UN Committee on Human Rights. He's investigating racism in America. We had lunch. I told him that story. He says, "You're right! That's the goal." That's Kennedy. It's good.

---

31. Specter was a Republican senator from Pennsylvania.

Edward (Teddy) Kennedy's maternal grandfather, Mayor John F. Fitzgerald (with hat over heart) and his daughter Rose (with white hat) preside over a Boston parade in 1910. Young Teddy learned about Boston's history and politics from "Honey Fitz," as the mayor was fondly called. *Courtesy JFK Presidential Library and Museum, Boston*

As the Kennedy fortune grew, Edward's parents, Joseph P. Kennedy Sr. and Rose Fitzgerald Kennedy, purchased a waterfront estate in Palm Beach, Florida. In 1937, they and their nine children spent the Christmas holiday there and assembled on its steps for a photograph, with the youngest, Teddy, in a sailor suit (front row, second from right). *Copyright © John F. Kennedy Library Foundation*

Teddy's favorite photo of himself with his dad, Joseph P. Kennedy Sr., US ambassador to the Court of St. James's, was taken at the American embassy residence in 1939, just before World War II began in Europe. As a senator, he kept the picture in a prominent spot in his Washington office. *JFK Presidential Library and Museum, Boston*

Young Teddy Kennedy, only six when the family moved to London for his father's ambassadorship, was the darling of the international press, which captured him launching his toy sailboat in a London park in 1938. *JFK Presidential Library and Museum, Boston*

Teddy Kennedy adored sailing, no more so than with his brother Jack (right) on his boat, the *Victura*, around 1946, after JFK returned a war hero from the South Pacific. *Courtesy JFK Presidential Library and Museum, Boston*

All of the Kennedy brothers played football with a passion, both in family pickup games and on college teams. Teddy (far right) made the Harvard varsity team in 1955 and scored a touchdown against Yale, earning him a coveted letter. *JFK Presidential Library and Museum, Boston*

Both Edward (far left) and Robert Kennedy (far right) graduated from the University of Virginia Law School, where Teddy won the moot court competition with future senator John Tunney. In 1958, during Teddy's second year, Robert returned to UVA for a reunion. Their brother, Senator John F. Kennedy (second from right), accompanied by his wife, Jacqueline, delivered a dinner speech to the reunion attendees. *CCBY image courtesy Virginia Law Weekly and University of Virginia Law Library*

The Kennedys' power and influence in Washington reached its peak when Edward Kennedy was elected to the Senate in 1962, joining Attorney General Robert Kennedy (left) and President John Kennedy (right) in government service. The three brothers gather outside the Oval Office in 1963. *Courtesy JFK Presidential Library and Museum, Boston*

President Kennedy applauds his brother, Senator Edward Kennedy, at the 1963 All New England Salute Dinner in Boston. There Teddy joked that he was tired of being accused of benefiting from his famous clan, so he was changing his name to "Teddy Roosevelt."
Courtesy JFK Presidential Library and Museum, Boston

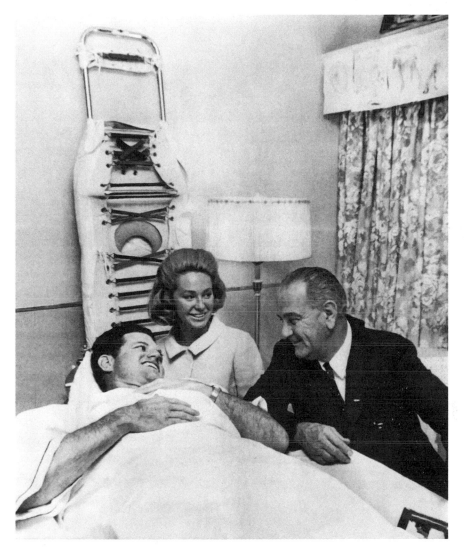

Senator Kennedy survived a near-fatal private plane crash in 1964 on his way to a Massachusetts political convention and spent the next six months hospitalized with a broken back. He and his wife, Joan, welcomed President Lyndon Johnson for a bedside visit. Unlike Bobby Kennedy, Teddy had a productive and friendly relationship with LBJ. *Everett Collection Inc/Alamy Stock Photo*

Ted Kennedy was a law student when he first met Vice President Richard Nixon while visiting his brother John on Capitol Hill. In 1969, then-President Nixon invited Kennedy to the White House for a reception for the League of Women Voters. Senator Kennedy was a staunch proponent of voting rights for all Americans eighteen and over. *Courtesy Richard Nixon Presidential Library and Museum*

As a Democratic Party outsider, Jimmy Carter (right) never fully embraced Edward Kennedy or his more liberal policies, especially on universal healthcare. Kennedy's uneasy relationship with the president was evident in a 1977 Oval Office meeting, and it grew more so when he challenged Carter for the 1980 Democratic nomination. *National Archives and Records Administration; Jimmy Carter Library*

Although President Ronald Reagan and Senator Kennedy disagreed on most policy matters, they had a cordial Oval Office meeting in 1981. *Courtesy Ronald Reagan Presidential Library*

Senator Kennedy was a masterful campaigner and attracted many votes as he visited factories throughout Massachusetts, including in Fall River, during his 1982 re-election bid. *Courtesy JFK Presidential Library and Museum, Boston*

Edward Kennedy Jr. (left) lost his right leg to cancer at age twelve. In 1984, he and his dad appeared at a rally on Capitol Hill to raise funds for cancer research. *Courtesy US Senate Historical Office*

The enduring cause of Senator Kennedy's legislative career was universal healthcare. In 1985, he appeared before a Senate committee, armed with posters to plead his case. *Courtesy US Senate Historical Office*

Starting with the Vietnam War, Senator Kennedy visited US military personnel overseas to assess their needs and determine the progress of America's armed forces. He traveled to the Persian Gulf in 1987 and met with the troops in Bahrain. *Courtesy US Senate Historical Office*

Senator Kennedy promoted economic opportunity throughout his political career by speaking in favor of job creation as a means to a better future for all Americans. *Courtesy US Senate Historical Office*

In 1993, Senator Kennedy joined forces with the Clinton administration to advocate for comprehensive healthcare reform. He and Nancy Kassebaum (left) welcomed First Lady Hillary Clinton to the Senate hearing room before she testified on behalf of the legislation. *Courtesy US Senate Historical Office*

The Kennedy family's deep Irish roots extended to Dunganstown, their ancestral hometown in County Wexford. Teddy Kennedy proudly displayed a signpost for the town in his Senate office, symbolizing his heritage and role in the Northern Ireland peace process. *Courtesy US Senate Historical Office*

Edward Kennedy sat for twenty-nine oral history interviews. He is interviewed here in his Senate office by James Sterling Young (center) and Steve Knott (right), and accompanied by his beloved dogs Sunny and Splash. *Courtesy University of Virginia Miller Center*

President Obama escorts Senator Kennedy, weakened by cancer treatment, from the Oval Office to the motorcade to a national service event at the Seed School, where the president signed the 2009 Edward M. Kennedy Serve America Act. *Courtesy Barack Obama Presidential Library*

10

Holding On to the Senate Seat: The 1994 Campaign

Except for his first run for the US Senate in 1962, when he was an untested political commodity, Edward Kennedy almost never had to worry about the outcome of his Senate election campaigns. He typically won by comfortable double-digit margins, even in 1970, the year after Chappaquiddick, when he swept to reelection by a remarkable 25 percentage points.

Yet, as 1994's Senate contest drew closer, the tide seemed to be turning against the experienced sailor. Despite the personal and professional benefits of marrying Vicki Reggie in 1992, several other factors made his victory less than a foregone conclusion. Having to testify on camera in the 1991 Palm Beach rape trial of his nephew William Kennedy Smith bolstered the narrative of prodigal Kennedy men. In addition, Senator Kennedy had spent considerable time on foreign affairs in South Africa, Latin America, and Ethiopia, and on arms control, which had less resonance with Massachusetts voters than domestic matters.

The partisan politics of 1994's congressional midterm elections also created headwinds for the senator's campaign. The Clinton presidency seemed in a downward spiral, with its faltering healthcare reform proposal and mounting scandals. Republican Newt Gingrich's insurgency in the House of Representatives was about to result in a stunning GOP takeover of the lower branch for the first time in forty years. Teddy's opponent, Mitt Romney, a devout Mormon, who was fifteen years younger than the senator, offered a straight-arrow option for Bay State voters. The scion of another wealthy political family, Romney also possessed all of the educational, experiential, and financial hallmarks of a successful candidate.

Senator Kennedy had been pulled off the campaign trail throughout the spring and summer of 1994, first by the terminal illness of his sister-in-law, Jacqueline Kennedy Onassis, who died of lymphoma in May, and then by his legislative duties as chair of the Labor Committee. Polls reflected the toll of his absence from the hustings as Romney took a slight lead.

When Kennedy could finally turn his full attention to the race, he and his seasoned staff and family spared no effort. Vicki's brilliance and aplomb on the stump, especially effective with female audiences, proved a boon. Pro-Kennedy interest groups joined the bandwagon. The senator took Romney's measure in debates, displaying his deep knowledge of issues and the legislative process. Kennedy's campaign also discovered some less flattering elements of Romney's venture capital firm, related to a plant closing in Indiana, and spread the message through strategically placed ads. The polls now turned in Kennedy's favor. Ultimately, his margin of victory in the hardest fought re-election of his long career would be an impressive 17 percent.

Yet the Democrats lost their majority in the Senate, which would test the senior Massachusetts senator's leadership.[1] As Kennedy's chief of staff Nick Littlefield observed, "The period of 1995 and 1996 in the Senate and Congress is about Ted Kennedy leading the fight against the Gingrich right-wing revolution around the core issues of jobs, education, and healthcare for working families. And even while in the minority, Kennedy in 1996 actually raised the minimum wage."

Just three weeks after the new Republican-dominated Congress gaveled to order, Senator Kennedy presided over yet another family funeral, this time for his mother and the clan's matriarch, Rose Fitzgerald Kennedy, who, at age 104, succumbed to her infirmities at the storied Hyannis Port compound. "For all of us, Dad was the spark. Mother was the light of our lives. He was our greatest fan. She was our greatest teacher," her youngest child explained in his eulogy.

EMK: [There] was a very important period when I did much more in terms of foreign policy. That changed after the '80 campaign where I went to the Labor Committee instead of staying on the Judiciary Committee because of President Reagan's attack on domestic issues and programs. My last large trip was down to South Africa, and I think the very important legislation I did with Weicker following that trip was a principal contributor to the elimination of apartheid.

But prior to that time, I'd been to Ethiopia on hunger. I took my children on that trip. I spent a good deal of time on Chile and Argentina when Pinochet[2] was in power. I took several trips to the Soviet Union on arms control. I've been to Bangladesh on two different occasions and India. And all that time I was away from Massachusetts. I think it was probably ten or fifteen years that I was not around nearly as much as I have been, say, in the last ten.

I think that the degree and the intensity probably softened up a good deal because I wasn't around as much. And also my personal life was more disruptive. I think there was still good support here, but I don't think that schedule could be continued a long time—

---

1. See Nick Littlefield and David Nexon, *Lion of the Senate: When Ted Kennedy Rallied the Democrats in a GOP Congress* (New York: Simon and Schuster, 2015).
2. General Augusto Pinochet was president of Chile.

Q: Was there a feeling that you were spending time away from—

EMK: Yes, too much time away, and also they wondered whether I was really interested in what's going on here. And they may have thought the positions I was taking weren't really quite where they were—just a general softening of the degree of support. You could take a look at some of the work of this fellow Kiley, who has polled for me since I started, and see that there are some dips. There's obviously a dip after the Florida incident with—[3]

Q: Yes.

EMK: And there was a tightening, obviously, in the race with Romney. But in my own looking back over that time, I'm conscious of the fact that I hadn't been around. I was doing things I thought were very important, and I think *were* important at the time. I think we made some important differences in Ethiopia in the hunger issues there, clearly in South Africa, and clearly in the restoration of democracy to Chile and Argentina, and also clearly with regard to the arms control agreements during the Reagan period, which was the eighties. They've been basically acknowledged by George Shultz and Max Kampelman[4] and others. But nonetheless, it took a good deal of time and preparation for the trip, it took time doing the trip, and it took time subsequent to the trip. And those were significant chunks of time as well as interest.

Q: You were also considered presidential material at that time [1970s and '80s].

EMK: That's right, and we spent a lot of time traveling in different states, spent a good deal of time campaigning for different candidates, keeping the presidential options open. So, yes, we were away from Massachusetts for an important period of time. If you look back historically, you'll see that after they've run for president, people always have a sinking spell in their state. McGovern did after his presidential campaign. Frank Church did. Bradley[5] did in New Jersey. And I certainly had some of that. We got licked [in 1980 Democratic presidential nomination contest]. People are saying, "Gee, we always thought we had the best senator around, and now we find other people don't think our guy's quite so hot. Maybe we ought to take another look at him."

You run through that kind of period. They're with you when you're running, but afterwards they're wondering, "Why did he get into that? He's been away from us a long period of time. I didn't understand why he was spending the time talking about X, Y, and Z. I'm not a bit interested. Talking all about ethanol. What's that have to do with us?"

---

3. Kennedy refers to the evening of March 30, 1991 (Good Friday), when he invited his son Patrick and nephew William Kennedy Smith to a bar in Palm Beach. Smith left the bar with a woman, who subsequently accused him of raping her at the Kennedy family's beachfront mansion. Senator Kennedy had to testify before television cameras at the trial. The jury acquitted Smith, but the senator's reputation was again sullied.

4. George Shultz was Reagan's secretary of state; Max Kampelman was a diplomat.

5. Bill Bradley was a Democratic senator from New Jersey.

Q: What's that have to do with Massachusetts?

EMK: Actually, it does have something to do, but it takes a while to explain it to them.

All of this diminishes or takes away from your base. Now [in 2005] we're probably in good shape in terms of the politics here because we've been so intensely involved again. I enjoy it, and we're current in terms of all the things that are going on. Hanscom Base is preserved, and we worked with the business communities and all of that. And the stem-cell research—which I've been on the cutting edge of in the Senate—that's gone through Massachusetts, that's very relevant today. The biotech industry; that thing is hot. Education. This is the education state. So we're current in terms of some of these things that people care about.

You put your finger on a variety of different factors: the change in the campaign, the things that are different, and the things that are the same. Some aspects of the campaign are much the same. I'm sure I've developed, and I hope become a wiser person, and been able to reflect that in the way I'm able to communicate with the people of Massachusetts from the beginning, obviously, on the basis of experience and knowledge and work.

You develop a better command of, one, the issues, but I think most importantly, a better feel for yourself and what you care about, and what motivates and drives you, what influences you, what you feel about different policy issues and questions. That evolves. Your knowledge about issues evolves. Your ability to connect with people from experience evolves, and your understanding about the institution where you're working and how you can be effective develops and evolves.

All of those are evolutionary, but there are significant shifts and changes in how you campaign in terms of the state and its issues, in terms of the changing demography of the state, the evolution of the state, the changing economy of the state, changing techniques and technology and how they're used or not used and used effectively, and how you do this. Personnel, obviously, shift and change in a very significant and dramatic way. And one of the most important and dramatic presences in my life that has affected my whole relationship with the state and with my life has been Vicki. There's been a very dramatic shift and change in terms of my own effectiveness and peace of mind and my own personal development.

There was one aspect of the campaigning [in 1994], of the registration, where we had Jesse Jackson Jr., Martin Luther King III, Bobby Kennedy Jr., and Teddy Kennedy Jr. going to colleges, and half or two-thirds of the college would show up at an auditorium with those four. And once in a while, I'd have a celebrity go in, and to hear them talk, they had to show that they were registered to vote. We got tens of thousands of students to do that.

Vicki more often than not traveled with me. She had—which we had mentioned but didn't get into it—a very effective women's group, which really kicked off when we had the five women senators who came up and spoke at a large event that was a fundraiser, but not a high cost. It was $125, bring your daughter. And we probably had twelve or fourteen hundred people. Bringing your daughter was a great idea. A lot of people couldn't because their daughters were at school or whatever, but they'd bring a mother.

Vicki had a very effective women's group. They met, they worked, and they were very much involved. They had their own literature, their own program. They had a series of speakers. I would say in the '94 campaign against Romney, the principal energy that really moved the whole campaign was women. They are an incredible energy, an incredible force, and Vicki got them really stirred up. They were very effective. We haven't done justice in describing these schedules, but I think when you talk with Vicki, she'll give you a flavor of that.

People have to have a sense that you pay attention to what's up here at home. That's why this whole thing on Hanscom is a big deal. People have a feeling that you're here, but in this state they have a sense that people who are involved in public life also have played national roles. President Kennedy is obvious, and Cabot Lodge.[6] Chris Herter was a national figure who was governor here and secretary of state. [John] Volpe was governor here and secretary of transportation. So they have a sense that people here have been involved in national politics, and they give you somewhat more leeway. But they don't want you to get to the point where you're losing touch, and I was getting close to that position, I think—

Q: *In the eighties?*

EMK: The late eighties, and that was—

Q: *Was that a factor in the '94, do you think?*

EMK: I think somewhat. I think it came back by the end. But in the beginning, I think people said, "Ted has lost touch, his politics is out." You'd see a lot of these articles, that I was gone. Probably some of that was personal lifestyle as well. All of that added up: distance, lifestyle, word got around. I think it's even as basic as losing weight. When you're losing weight, people have a sense that you're more interested in their problems. It's all these immeasurable kinds of things.

I lost thirty or forty pounds last year. I'm trying to lose another ten this year. That makes a big difference in people's minds. You're really not interested in them; it's a bowl of spaghetti or something. [*Laughter*]

Q: *Well, yes, but it's also kind of a rededication and a rethinking—*

EMK: Yes.

Q: *—which is not common among long-serving senators.*

---

6. Henry Cabot Lodge Sr. and Jr. were Republican senators from Massachusetts; the younger Lodge also served as US ambassador to South Vietnam and was the vice presidential nominee on the unsuccessful ticket headed by Richard Nixon in 1960, which lost to JFK.

EMK: That's right. Howell Heflin was from Alabama, and Howell and I got along real well. He was head of the supreme court in Alabama, and he was very good on the floor one day on what Alabama had been through on the race issue—just very eloquent. He hadn't talked like that before, and he could really talk when he needed to. We have a bell down in the Senate gym, and if you lost weight, you could ring the bell. So he said, "Teddy, I haven't heard that bell ring recently. I'll be listening in that gym for that bell to ring." [*Laughter*] He had a wonderful way of being able to take a very simple little thing and make it funny. So I said, "Well, Howell, we'll show you a thing or two." [*Laughter*] I'd lose a little weight, and I'd make sure that he heard it.

So, Splash, I thought we might have a little run, and we'll go for a little sail. Would you like to do that? Would you like to? You would? Okay. All right. You don't have to get your ball. No, you don't have to get your ball just yet.

Well, we can ramble on, but people have to get home. So now I have to get you a couple of things so you're going to be warm enough. We'll go. There's a light breeze, but it'll be kind of nice. You'll get a little sense, and it'll be nice, and then I'll get you in at the pier. It's high tide; we'll get you in by 2 or something.

Perspectives

Kennedy's in-laws had unique perspectives on the melding of the Reggie and Kennedy families.

Edmund and Doris Reggie, Edward Kennedy's parents-in-law:

Edmund Reggie: I must tell you the truth. I love him [Teddy]. He is my best friend.

Doris Reggie: The wedding was wonderful.

Edmund Reggie: It was very nice. It was a beautiful wedding.

Doris Reggie: He immediately embraced us. We had been close friends by this time. As the years evolved, we became closer and closer friends. But I guess, immediately, it was like, now we're family. And at every event we were treated with the greatest respect, as his own sister or brother or mother, because he was so, so devoted to his mother. The respect that he had for her that we saw and witnessed,

The senator's wife devoted a major portion of her interview to describing the 1994 election and the successful political partnership that she developed with her husband that helped produce a victory for him in that difficult race against Mitt Romney.

Vicki Kennedy:

Q: So, are we back to—I almost have to digest more of this. I'm telling you, it is so rich in terms of insights and emotions and all of that, and it's really wonderful stuff. Getting back a little bit to, dialing back one more time. Getting back to your relationship with him and how it grew, and recalling that you said it didn't start out as a politically connected, inspired, or even relevant, politically relevant relationship, but it came to be that.

Vicki Kennedy: Yes.

Q: So, was the 1994 election campaign the turning point or the starting point of that?

Vicki Kennedy: The starting point, maybe I'd say. I guess maybe you'd say starting point, probably the starting point. I traveled around with him. As I said, he asked me to do that, and so he was—even in '92, we were going around the state, campaigning for other candidates. He was doing a little campaigning for President Clinton, around the country, really not so much, but some, and really doing a lot in the state. He knew '94 was going to be a competitive election for him, I mean he suspected it probably would be, in Massachusetts, and was laying a lot of groundwork early. We were doing a lot of work in the state in '92, and I was just basically tagging along. As the race in '94 was evolving and developing, it became more and more necessary. Clinton was president and there was so much of the agenda that was under Teddy's committee. He was the chairman and it was exciting, and he was working, they were marking up healthcare. It was—he was so busy at work, but his race was heating up, and he needed me to be in Massachusetts, doing things for him. And then we had strategy—the Senate stayed in the session through August.

But we were having strategy meetings in the spring, and I was involved in that. I really didn't know anything about campaigning. As much as I loved politics, I had never been involved in a campaign, or I'd never been on the campaign trail. But he started needing me to go do events, and I would go to Massachusetts and do events, and so that started in '94. Then I eventually had my own schedule, and I was out there, and he and I would connect in the evenings. When he was finally on the ground, we would connect every evening and do our evening events together. We would have a different daytime schedule. I guess that really is—that was sort of the beginning. I was involved in a lot of strategic things during that time, and I think that was beginning with my getting involved kind of strategically.

Q: But it was not going well at the beginning.

Vicki Kennedy: No.

Q: [I]t seems to me, you started out helping, but you became much more central. Is that the right word?

Vicki Kennedy: I think probably that's true.

Q: As it went on, and the strategy that you are credited with bringing about, his awareness of the Ampad[7] situation.

---

7. Ampad is a paper products company owned by Mitt Romney's private equity firm, Bain Capital; it acquired and shut down a paper plant in Marion, Indiana, throwing its employees out of work and earning millions for Romney's firm.

Vicki Kennedy: Well you know, and I didn't really know about Ampad, nobody knew about Ampad, but actually, somebody actually called us from Indiana to tell us about Ampad. But what I said at a meeting, and it was just from the kind of law I practice. It was just, when they were saying, "Oh, well, he [Romney] had a business record, and he just took over companies and there's really nothing there." And I said, "Well, wait, of course there is. There are different ways to take over a company, and you've got to look." Basically, I was just saying that you can either take care of the employees or not, I mean these are choices that you make. And I was just encouraging them to look at the ways that it was done. I felt pretty strongly that Teddy's record was fair game. None of us were talking about going after anybody personally, that was never—Teddy wouldn't have done that and that was never what he did do. But his opponent was running on his business record, and that a business record was like a voting record, and that it was fair game. I just felt that he had to look at the business record.

We finally got everything—everything kind of happened, everything got on track. It was even-steven, as Teddy said, at Labor Day, which was a big shocker; that was a shocker. But it was amazing to watch Teddy during that time, amazing. He was so clear-eyed, he was so sure of who he was.

Q: That developed too. That was not the—he seems to have, when he came up to Massachusetts, he seemed to be off his game that day.

Vicki Kennedy: So off his game. I think he broke his foot, walking into the campaign party that evening, and he was just off. He was late, the plane had been canceled. They had him in a dark, awful—the campaign had put him in a terrible room, he didn't know the people there, he wasn't looking at his usual crowd. He hadn't been campaigning. He always needed time to warm up and to get his stump speech going and to get with the program, always. I mean, who doesn't? But he *really* did, and he hadn't had a primary. He didn't campaign in the month of August, and he hadn't campaigned in September because the Senate had been in session. And so here Romney wins at this primary and he's like this big rocket, and Teddy's been working on healthcare and a crime bill and everything else that he's been doing.

Q: Education.

Vicki Kennedy: Education. He comes in to this dark bar, I think is what it was; it was a bizarre room, breaks his foot going in. He didn't know he'd broken his foot, like a bone in his foot. He was just tired, he'd had a tough day, he had no opponent, so it's not like he's had this gigantic victory, he's not feeling exhilarated, and he looks at a room where he didn't know anybody in the room. It wasn't his usual suspects and it just was a flat—it was just flat. I think his back hurt, his foot hurt, it was just you know, just yuck. It was just a bad night and was a total contrast with Romney's.

Q: *Who was running the campaign at that point? Was it Michael?*[8]

Vicki Kennedy: I think it was probably Michael, but I actually don't—

Q: *But it wasn't the old hands came in.*

Vicki Kennedy: No, I think they came in shortly after that. But I don't blame Michael for that. Michael was—Teddy had always had a family member run a campaign. That had been something he'd always done, but there had always been old hands who had been there, doing the actual organizing. Michael was terrific. He could run a business, he was brilliant, but here Michael gets handed the most unbelievable race of a lifetime. So you have this great family member who comes in, and Teddy has the opponent from central casting, in this tsunami, Republican tsunami, in the year of the "Contract with America," where Newt Gingrich is talking about the welfare state, and the Clinton midterms were all going down like a ton.

Teddy's old and out of step, so they said. It was the first time in history he couldn't lose weight for an election. He said, "I just can't, I don't know why, I can't." It's the first time he didn't, it's the heaviest he was in his life, ever. For some reason Teddy's weight was always a topic, and it was the barometer to the world. "Oh, he's heavy, he must not be doing well." He was sixty, he was sixty or sixty-two. I mean it was like, "Oh, he's old." When you think back on it, it's laughable, to think that they were thinking he was old. It's just unbelievable.

Q: *Well, this is the contrast with Romney.*

Vicki Kennedy: With Romney. And Romney was just saying, "Let's give him a gold watch and send him back to Cape Cod." But Teddy found his voice, Teddy found his voice. I didn't go to debate prep or anything. I mean I would never not go now, later, you know, now. There's no—oh, how I wish there were a now. But I would never later have not gone, but then I wouldn't have dreamed of going. I mean that's how it evolved. He did debate prep every night and did that separately from my going.

Q: *Did you travel around with him?*

Vicki Kennedy: During the day we had—because we had so much territory to cover, I did different things, and then during the evenings we would connect. Because we did all day, I mean it was morning until night. Once he got out of the Senate, we worked very long days.

Q: *And Dave Burke joined.*

Vicki Kennedy: Dave Burke joined and Ranny Cooper. Everybody came back.

Q: *Were they drafted or did they volunteer?*

Vicki Kennedy: No. There were a lot of volunteers and there were also some drafts. I think no, everybody was willing. Dave Burke wrote Teddy a letter and said, "Look, what can I do?" And Teddy said, "You don't know Dave Burke."

---

8. Michael Kennedy was Robert Kennedy's son and Edward's nephew.

I said, "No, I don't know him," and he said, "Oh, he was fantastic, and I'm going to ask Dave to ride in the car with me." He said Dave was the head of this company and that company, and he was just great. Teddy just wanted a peer to be in the car with him, to give him that security blanket. I was off doing my thing during the day, and he thought Dave could handle the press. So Teddy asked Dave, and Dave I think was a little shocked—that wasn't quite what he had in mind. But Dave gave up his life for a month or whatever, six weeks, and came, moved to Boston and traveled with Teddy, and, boy, what a difference it made. What a difference it made.

Then Ranny. I remember the night Ranny came in. She took a leave of absence from her job. She understood what Teddy needed. She had been his chief of staff for so many years, and she understood how to advance him, she understood how to have press people on the ground. He needed to have his campaign run like he had his office run, and it needed to be run like a presidential campaign basically, where you had people on the ground, where he had the assets in place at events, like he's used to having.

Part of the problem was this had become an international event, and it was not being run in that way. Teddy would walk into an event and be accosted by—you've got press from all over the world, but there weren't people on the ground. So he didn't know what he was walking into, I mean it just wasn't a campaign in the way that he could or should be managed. We just needed to have a more major kind of operation.

I remember the first night that Ranny was on board, the night of the first day that Ranny came onboard, and Teddy said to me, "I'm going to sleep tonight, because Ranny's going to be worrying about it and I don't have to anymore." It was really, really very wonderful. I'm sure it wasn't for Ranny, but it really was for Teddy, it really, really was for Teddy. And then you could just—people just wanted to see him out there, they just wanted to see him out there. And I asked him if he thought he could lose. He said, "Well, I could, but I won't. I could but I won't, because I know what I have to do, and I'm going to do it." No, he never thought he'd lose, And you could see it in the way he projected himself once he got there.

Q: *Was there something called Topsfield?*

Vicki Kennedy: Topsfield Fair. Well, at Topsfield Fair—they've all written his political obituary, and you've got Japanese cameramen—I mean no, seriously, they were from everywhere in the world. The last Kennedy brother is about to go down in flames here, you know? We're walking in, and it's not a particularly happy Democratic sort of area. We walk in and there are these signs. We joked about it so much. The carpenters were magnificent, they were magnificent. They were on Teddy's side, they had these signs—these big, burly, fantastic, magnificent men, and they had these signs and as we walked into the Topsfield Fair they were going, "Ted! Ted! Ted! Ted! Ted [deep voice]!" And as we later described it, the Romney people had little bow ties, and they were going, "Mitt, Mitt, Mitt, Mitt [high pitched voice]." [*Laughter*] I mean that was the telling, that's how he described it anyway. But that was certainly the way we felt about it.

So you walk in and you've got our guys, who are all these big, gigantic, strong men, and then you had these little guys. And so we felt big, gigantic, and strong, and felt that Mitt was little and weak, and it was just the feeling of exhilaration, because of all these great supporters. There were little altercations between the Mitt men and the Ted men. This gigantic carpenter and this Mitt guy were against a chain-linked fence, and the big carpenter goes, "Officer, officer, he hit me." [*Laughs*] It was just silliness, it was silliness, just the whole thing was silly. So we walked through the Topsfield Fair, and all these people are following us around, but you could just see in Teddy's step, he just was feeling, "Okay, this is going to be good." I think part of it was just having his supporters around, and he's just starting to feel really good about it.

He gave a speech at Faneuil Hall that didn't get press at the time, but it really was great and well received, and then you later got the sense that it was—it was in October, but it really was the beginning of a real shift. I think it was about three weeks before the election, but things really shifted, were really beginning to shift at that time. And there was an interesting thing. Whenever people felt that Teddy was getting too far ahead, then the race would tighten up. So we never wanted them to know how far ahead he was, because they wanted to kick him and they wanted to teach him a lesson, but not that much. They really didn't want to lose him, but they just wanted him to know, "Look, we're really mad, we're not happy," but they just really didn't want to lose him.

Q: It was not a good economic time in Massachusetts.

Vicki Kennedy: It was a very bad economic time, we lost so many jobs. It was just really, really tough. It was a very difficult time, a very difficult time, coming out of a recession.

Q: Didn't that work against Romney?

Vicki Kennedy: No, because he was saying he's a businessman and he created ten thousand jobs, and he was the new person. Where was Kennedy? He didn't do anything, he let all these jobs leave. Teddy said, "Well, we had Republican presidents during all this time." "Oh, but you were in the Congress," and you know, so it was that kind of thing, and it was just, "Kennedy is old and tired and blah blah blah." But you could just feel it start to happen, but there were some ugly moments, where people just would not shake your hand, or they'd look the other way, and they were angry; a lot of anger out there. Then there was the first debate and that was a great moment. Again, there were labor guys, carpenters, and ironworkers and those people, out there, lining the road at Faneuil Hall and just saying, "Ted! Ted! Ted! Ted!"

Q: And he had the right podium.

Vicki Kennedy: Oh, those podiums, well, that was hilarious. I didn't even know until Eddie Martin's death, that they had switched those podiums that day. He did have the big, bulky podium, and poor little Mitt Romney was just dwarfed behind that podium and a half, it was like a double-wide I guess, a double-wide podium. It seemed perfectly sized for Teddy, and poor Mitt was just dwarfed behind it.

Q: *People on the stage, a lot of actors and actresses, as you know, speak of the audience as a person often, at least some have, and every night is different. They feel that they can read the audience. I can understand that, but it seems to me that maybe you and he also have this capacity to read an audience. Do you?*

Vicki Kennedy: Oh, yes. He absolutely had the vibe of an audience. He knew if an audience was flat; he knew if they needed quiet; he knew if they could rally to a big, roaring speech; he knew if he could get them going. He knew if it needed to be short because they were just not with it that night. Yes, absolutely. There's a personality to an audience, there's a personality to a room, and there are some rooms that just aren't conducive to doing—like that room that he was in that night of the [GOP] primary. There are just some rooms that just don't work, no matter—if you have a great audience, the room might work anyway, but there are just some rooms that, if you have an iffy audience, aren't going to help you get there. He had that sense absolutely, definitely.

You know, I just was thinking of something that I had forgotten. From the time we were engaged, not just married. From the time we were engaged, he used to push me on stage to speak at events. That would just surprise me. I don't know why, but he would do that. So, my first trade union convention, it was the garment workers, we were in Florida. We weren't married yet, we were engaged. It was around May, we were married in July. I remember walking in and they said, "Ted! Ted! Ted! Ted! Ted!" It was exhilarating and he got up, and they introduced me and he said, "Go on up, Vicki, say a few words." I said, "Ted—" And I'm thinking he has totally lost his mind, I mean what am I going to say? So he said, "Oh, tell them the story of such and such," but he just, he looked at me and said, "Go on, they want to hear from you, they'd love to hear from you." And he used to do that to me all the time. Don't you think that's funny?

Q: *Well, it can be very unnerving.*

Vicki Kennedy: I know, but I just think it's really—it was unnerving, but I would be okay of course.

Q: *You would rise to the occasion.*

Vicki Kennedy: I'd do it because he would say, "Go do it," and you can't exactly say, "No, I'm not going to do it." But he would do that to me all the time. I don't know why he did that. Until this moment, I don't know why he would do that.

Q: *Well?*

Vicki Kennedy: I don't know. I don't know, I think it's kind of funny.

Q: He had a great deal of confidence in you.

Vicki Kennedy: Well clearly, I guess he did, but he did that to me all the time. And sometimes I'd have to say, "Look, whatever you do, do not call on me, don't call on me today." And then he'd get that little devil twinkle in his eye, and he'd go call on me. Sometimes I'd look at him, "No, no, no, no." And then so he'd decide not to, but he loved to do that. I don't know, I don't know. I guess it was good practice, because it's pretty easy for me to get up now these days, but I don't know.

Q: Well, you're supposed to be part of his life.

Vicki Kennedy: Yes, so go up and speak. [*Laughter*] Wind you up and go talk. But he did that, so I guess he really was serious about the partner, the whole thing. And then just over time, I started to be a part of meetings about strategy, and then I started to be a part of prepping for Sunday shows, and then I started to be a part of editing his speeches, and then I started to be—we would be talking at breakfast about something and he'd say, "That's really great, could you just do a one-pager on that while I take my shower?" [*Laughs*] And I'd type a one-pager on that. Then they'd call from the office and say, "We've got a conference call on such and such—" They'd say, "Do you have time for a conference call with the senator and his staff on such and such," and I'd be a part of conference calls on strategy on a judicial nominee or on some other issue. And then all of a sudden, it was just this seamless, total involvement in every issue he was working on.

Q: You said all of a sudden.

Vicki Kennedy: Well, I guess it wasn't all of a sudden but somehow—

Q: Quickly.

Vicki Kennedy: Yes, but I mean I guess it wasn't as quick. At some point, I was just involved in everything. I went back to a law firm after they [Democrats] lost the Senate [in 1994]. I had left to do the campaign. I went back to a law firm, I worked back in the law firm until '97, and then it was not possible for me to do. Teddy was really very supportive of my staying in the firm, but it wasn't possible to be married to him and to have a private law practice. My clients were ending up in the newspaper, because I was married to him, and just wasn't possible.

So I think it was because I couldn't practice law any more, and I was doing other things, you know nonprofit boards and things like that, but he would start looping me into his issues. He would be doing his work after dinner, and I'd be in the library, where he would be working, and I'd read or do something, and he would start handing me memos: "What do you think about that?" or "What do you think about that?" It was a gradual thing. I can't even tell you when it really kicked in, but it did, and it started probably with speeches, almost first, where he'd say, "This speech needs some work; what do you think?"

And I would redo a speech, that kind of thing, and then it eventually became more strategy sessions, and then I was eventually involved in—

Q: In almost everything.

Vicki Kennedy: In almost everything.

Q: How did his staff take this?

Vicki Kennedy: I thought I had a great relationship with them. I'm so respectful of them. I wasn't stepping on their toes; I mean they were the experts. I was always, up to this moment, totally deferential to their expertise. It just wasn't that kind of role. It wasn't telling them what to do or stepping on their toes, and I sure hope that they felt the same way. It was just more brainstorming. Maybe from law firm experience, because we always felt that more heads were better than one, and it's just a collaborative approach, lots of ideas and thoughts. But they were the experts, they knew the policy issues and stuff, but it was just, as I say, just kind of brainstorming. And in terms of things about judgment and issues that related to him, I think I could weigh in on what might be right in terms of where do you think he should be on that—you know, positioning. Does that make political sense, that more political kind of judgment, and not in terms of substance and policy.

Q: Did you see him as stretched too thin at times?

Vicki Kennedy: Yes, and I definitely would weigh in on that, I definitely did, to the chief of staff.

Q: What to focus on?

Vicki Kennedy: No, not to that degree. I didn't get into, "Don't have him do this," but I worried about his well-being, and I worried that he was doing too much and that he needed time off. He would accept every single—"Oh, yes, that would be a good thing to do, that would be a good thing to do." Then I worried if he was having too many 7:30 breakfasts and not getting home until 7:30, I mean too many twelve-hour days, and then doing homework after dinner. Just seemed to me to not be healthy. I just didn't think it had to be like that. I thought they were wearing him out, and I thought he was getting fatigued. So that would happen from time to time, when I would get worried about his health. I'd say, "Let's think about a better schedule." I did weigh in on that, absolutely, absolutely. I kind of think that's a wife's role or should be, and they'd say, "Oh, no, but he's the one." I'd say. "That's okay just tell him; you can tell him I said so."

I can remember telling him, "Oh, your doctor called." This is early on. "Your doctor called and set up this appointment for you." He said, "Oh, really? Isn't that interesting, that my doctor called." I said, "Isn't that amazing, that your doctor set up this appointment." He knew I was lying through my teeth. He said, "That's very interesting, that the doctor would just on his own, call up." I said, "Isn't it something, how he just set up this whole stress test and just thought it would be a good time to check your blood pressure." He said, "Really, isn't that something, how kind of him." You know? "Yes, isn't that great." But he was—then he got really good at it. He didn't need me after a while to bug him about those things, because he really got very good about all that. But that was a little learning curve at the beginning, prevention. Didn't know how to prevent a brain tumor though, but he was otherwise pretty healthy.

State Senator Edward M. Kennedy Jr. (D-CT) and Congressman Patrick J. Kennedy (D-RI), Edward Kennedy's sons:

Q: Just two more brief things. I'd like you to talk a little bit about his second marriage and what difference that made, to get married again, to Vicki. I have known him only since well into that marriage, but so many people now talk about pre-Vicki Teddy and post-1992 Vicki. I'm just asking for your comment on that. That was one of the things I had in mind when I was saying, did you see any change in him? Maybe not in him but maybe in some parts of his life.

Edward M. Kennedy Jr.: I didn't think he was going to get married again, so I was surprised when he made the decision to get remarried. I thought he had—I mean, he dated a lot of wonderful women, he had wonderful friends, he had a wonderful family, loved spending time with them. So my thinking was, "Why do you need a wife, right, when you have all of that?" I don't know, that was just my thought. I do think that Vicki was really helpful to my father, especially in the last couple of years of his life. I think she really helped him work harder and focus and direct himself, I will say that.

Patrick Kennedy: I think politically, she was very—I mean clearly, vital and helping him. I think he was clearly—that [1991] Harvard speech, that was a big challenge for him. His personal life was becoming a big issue, and Vicki really was somebody who gave him some stability, if even for just his political life. She was a great source of strength and political stability, definitely, no question about it. And I think personally, there's no question that she was very helpful to him in bringing some focus, as Teddy [Jr.] was saying, back on what he loved to do so much in his work, because she was such a good person to keep that kind of sounding board and focus on it, because she came from a political family too. So she had that same interest and was there to back him up in his vital interest in life, which was politics as well.

Kennedy's chief of staff observed the relationship between the senator and President Clinton, especially during Kennedy's 1994 re-election campaign.

David Burke, Edward Kennedy's chief of staff:

Q: I would like to hear your observations on Kennedy and Clinton. The reason I got into this was, after reading the Elsa Walsh piece on Kennedy and Clinton in the New Yorker *magazine—it was mostly on Clinton—it made a great deal, not at length but in content, of Clinton helping Kennedy out in '94 and of Kennedy helping Clinton out earlier. And setting something of a background for Kennedy's relationships with Clinton on policy as president in the Senate, because that was an interesting relationship. I've tried to get into this by asking, what do you know? Where was Clinton in this '94 campaign? Or any observations that you have about the senator and Clinton at any point.*

Burke: Very little, to tell you the truth. Just to put me in the story, in '94, I was still in a financial company on Wall Street. I had just left after merging it with another company, and I was going into semi-retirement, except for staying on the board of directors and that sort of thing. I was up on the Cape when I heard about Teddy and his race. As in '93, '92, '91, '90, '89, I was not involved with Teddy on a daily basis, so I didn't know what he was or wasn't doing with Clinton.

I would have been terribly surprised if Clinton hadn't been very helpful to him in '94, and indeed he was. Hillary was too. She came to the campaign and spoke, I remember, out west, in the Mount Holyoke area and so on. The Holyoke area was Mount Holyoke College. It became quite apparent that the numbers were bad, and it looked like Teddy was going to lose to this fellow Romney, who, as we all know now, is very attractive cosmetically. He's a very attractive and terribly articulate candidate, so he was an unusual challenger for Ted Kennedy. The senator had run against people before, but they were just people, and this guy was out of central casting. I wouldn't be surprised if the Clintons took note of that and, given their ambitions for the future, were in touch with Teddy to say, "Anything I can do to help you, you let us know," because they knew they were going into a tough year.

Imagine, as we've discussed before, the surprise to the whole world when Newt Gingrich's revolution, who was the Katrina of politics in those days, blew down every tree except for one oak tree still standing, Teddy Kennedy. Who'd have believed it? I thought of that when he was making the decision this year [2008] as to whom to support. It seemed to me that he could have given Hillary more credit. But he sees something in Obama. We'll all see, won't we?

Senator Kennedy's links to his Massachusetts constituents were a key to his longevity in office, as was the crucial work of his trusted Boston office director in forging those relationships.

Barbara Souliotis, Edward Kennedy's Boston office director:

Q: To what extent is this office sort of his political eyes and ears? For instance, as 1994 approached, and there were some signs that it might be a tough race with Romney, was this office trying to get the word down to DC that there may be some trouble back home?

Souliotis: Oh, yes. They're concentrating so much on national issues, and we're concentrating more on Massachusetts and the state and what's happening up here. Yes, we knew that Romney was going to be tough. It was going to be a big push by the Republicans in saying that he'd been there too long, and it's time for somebody else. We talked to the campaign people once they set up their shop. And the Kennedy coordinators—I said we have them today in every city and town—they would be calling all the time. This is what's happening; Romney's out here campaigning. That network is very good to keep us informed of anything that's happening in their city and town. That's still ongoing today. If there's a major fire, like Malden Mills in Lawrence, I would call the senator and say, "You should come up for this because they will be needing some federal assistance."

Q: He respects your judgment on these types of things?

Souliotis: Yes. It's just experience. We've been through a lot of them and I should be able to make a judgment on when he really needs to be here. The economic effect on a city or a town can make a big difference. Many times, when the senator reads the news clips, he calls me first and says he's coming up before I even have a chance to call him. He has the best judgment of anyone on when he needs to be in Massachusetts.

Q: Somebody told us, and I don't remember who it was, that in the '94 campaign against Romney, when they were doing all these focus groups and polling and this, that, and the other thing, that he could learn more from your parents than he could from these—Have you heard this story? Have you heard him say this?

Souliotis: Yes.

Q: Does he talk to your folks?

Souliotis: Oh, yes. When he was traveling around the state, particularly after the plane crash, if he was doing a full day in the area, and he needed two or three hours to eat and relax and rest his back, he would come to my house in Haverhill. If he were in the western part of the state, he'd go to Don Dowd's house. He'd prefer to go to somebody's house than to go to a hotel. So when he was in the Merrimack Valley, he always went to my house. I think it was because of my mother's cooking. He would call them and say, "I'm coming. Is it okay if I come for dinner?" He's been up there many times for dinner. My brother, who's a dentist up there, my father was in construction, and my mother worked at Western Electric at the time, and they had twelve thousand employees. His Kennedy coordinator was the principal of the school, and they all knew a lot of people. So, at dinner, he would always ask what was happening, and they didn't hold back anything.

Q: So he doesn't have a problem with that?

Souliotis: Absolutely not.

Q: He's not sensitive to criticism?

Souliotis: No. He always wanted to find out what the people were thinking or what they thought about what was happening in the schools, with businesses, what was happening with Head Start, what was happening with the economy and healthcare, or what people thought of some particular bill he was working on. He knew he was going to get the true answer from these people. But I remember one time we had like ten or twelve people up there for dinner because *Look* magazine was following him around for a story, and there were two people from the magazine, Caroline Kennedy, and Joe Kennedy [II], the Kennedy coordinator, the driver and me, my family and some other staff. The people realize that he's just a regular guy. He played touch football out in the backyard with my nephews before coming in for dinner. He knows them all pretty well.

Running just ahead of Mitt Romney in the polls, Senator Kennedy had to give his best performances in debates to solidify the victory in 1994. His advisor, Paul Kirk, played a critical role in planning the debates.

Paul Kirk, Edward Kennedy's special assistant, attorney, and friend: Mitt Romney. Well, let's see. I was an outside advisor, and the debates were happening. Also I think I've been in other situations as co-chairman of the Commission on Presidential Debates, so perhaps the senator figured I had background experience, and I was pretty good at negotiating. What happened is the Romney campaign and the Kennedy campaign agreed to debate. Then the question is where and when and how many and all that stuff. But the issue I think Dave's referring to—I got my good friend and Senator Kennedy's former administrative assistant Eddie Martin, maybe you know he passed away this year.

He and I were the Kennedy representatives at this meeting. There was Charley Manning,[9] who represented Romney, probably a couple of other fellows whose names I forget for the moment. We were talking about the fact that it was going to be at Faneuil Hall on a certain night. Somebody brought a video of the last debate held at Faneuil Hall, which was Bill Weld, incumbent Republican governor, and Mark Roosevelt, his challenger in the last governorship race, who was a former state rep. They had a debate and at our meeting they played this tape of their debate at Faneuil Hall. Maybe it was just to give those of us in the meeting a sense of the format and how their particular format worked.

Bill Weld was a big, tall guy, about six-five, and when I was looking at this video, it looked as if Bill Weld was—you know those little elementary school desks with the inkwells? It looked like Weld was much too big for this podium. Obviously I'm thinking about our candidate, who at this point is way overweight, and all I could think of was Senator Kennedy in his then physical oversize as he would look behind these podiums. That would be at the end of the debate. So I tried not to make a big issue out of it, because if I did—

So I said something about, "Geez, that's very unfortunate that Bill Weld had such a small podium, given his height." I said, "We ought to just make sure we have an opportunity to figure out what the right structure is," or something vague like that. "Oh, yes, absolutely, we should do that," Romney's people

---

9. Manning was Romney's chief strategist.

said. "OK, so you don't mind if we get our own podium, as long as it's acceptable to you?" "No, that's fine," they said.

So whatever number of days there were between that meeting and the debate, Eddie Martin and I went out to some warehouse in Arlington, and they had some daises and podia there. We found two podia downstairs in this building, which are good size, plenty of breadth, and we had two of them brought to Faneuil Hall. Somehow Marty Nolan, formerly of the *Boston Globe*, got word of the matter, and he wrote this story about the debate. Something about, "And Kirk got these two condominiums and brought them into the hall." But in any event what was critical about it is that we didn't have to suffer this whole humiliation of sidebar stories about Senator Kennedy's size as compared to—

Q: Mitt Romney's.

Kirk: Oh, yes. Until the debate was over, and Nolan or somebody got wind of the story; I don't think the Romney folks even paid any attention to it, but then, when Marty wrote his column, they knew they'd been had afterward. By the way, that was the senator's finest hour in the toughest campaign he ever had.

Q: Yes, it was a tough one. The campaign staff had been reluctant for him to— everybody had been reluctant, hadn't they, for him to even debate?

Kirk: Senator Kennedy?

Q: Yes.

Kirk: Oh, yes.

Q: The Washington staff said, "Forget it."

Kirk: But Romney was coming on so strong. The pressure. What's happened with debates in the past campaigns, figure out when the challenging candidate gets the best attention—we'll do it on a Friday night at 6:30 p.m. on the radio in West Springfield for forty-five minutes. In other words, the less the better. You couldn't in the '94 race—here's a senator who's been in office for thirty years. He had no choice. It had to happen. I remember the day of the debate. I was out here at the Kennedy Library, and he [Senator Kennedy] came to review his notes and to reflect. It was like this is where he came to get strength, as if he was to be in the shadow of his brother's place and ask for his inspiration. Quiet. Then he put on his game face, and he was at his best. That was it. It was all over after that.

Demonstrating his knack for crossing the aisle to find some common ground with Republicans, Senator Kennedy achieved some of his most enduring policies while in the minority. His chief of staff, Nick Littlefield, explained how.

Nick Littlefield, Edward Kennedy's chief of staff for the Senate's Health, Education, and Labor Committee: Gingrich[10] took over the Congress after

---

10. Georgia congressman Newt Gingrich became Speaker of the House after Republicans won the majority in the 1994 midterm elections.

Kennedy was re-elected in '94, and the Democrats were in total disarray—Clinton was getting ready to give away the store, and the Republicans were in ascendancy. They were going to abolish the Department of Education, they were going to cut Medicare to smithereens, they were going to abolish the minimum wage. Those were three things that Gingrich wanted to do and said he was going to do. Kennedy was the single person who said from the very beginning, "No! That's not going to work; it's not going to happen. We're going to stop you. We're going to stand strong as the Democrats we are, for the people we were elected to represent who need help in these areas."

It may well be that Kennedy's greatest legislative period was when he was thrust into the minority, and Gingrich was set to take over the country and to do the things I just said. Kennedy fought in the Senate, got senators to rally 'round, to stop the Gingrich revolution. Almost none of it happened. Most importantly, to save President Clinton—who at the start was willing to triangulate[11] his way right through to the Gingrich agenda—Kennedy said, "You can't do that" and held Clinton's feet to the fire. Ultimately, Clinton vetoed the Gingrich budget, the government was shut down, and the Republicans basically lost the game at that moment. They lost seats in the next election, and Gingrich was gone two years later.

The period of 1995 and 1996 in the Senate and Congress is about Ted Kennedy leading the fight against the Gingrich right-wing revolution around the core issues of jobs, education, and healthcare for working families. And even while in the minority, Kennedy in 1996 actually raised the minimum wage. Not only did the Republicans not abolish it; he got it raised. Not only did they not cut Medicare; Kennedy got the biggest increase in federal government regulation of private health insurance in the Kennedy/Kassebaum HIPAA[12] legislation to minimize the role of preexisting-condition exclusions from healthcare and to create portability from job to job. If you lose your job you can take your healthcare. That was the biggest expansion of federal regulation of private health plans in decades. He did that in the minority.

The following year he did children's health insurance, the SCHIP[13] program which is so well regarded and celebrated now. That was a Kennedy initiative all the way. So in the minority, he took these issues of jobs, education, and

---

11. "Triangulation" referred to Bill Clinton's "third way" or "New Democrat" embrace of moderately liberal policies, between Gingrich's conservative Republicanism and Kennedy's more liberal wing of the Democratic Party. Clinton's political strategist Dick Morris coined the term "triangulate" in this political context of the mid-1990s as a path to the president's re-election in 1996.

12. Kennedy cosponsored the Health Insurance Portability and Accountability Act with Senator Nancy Kassebaum, a Republican from Kansas.

13. State Children's Health Insurance Program.

healthcare and pushed them, to get the Democrats to stand up, and to actually make progress from the minority, which is almost unheard of. He then drove Bob Dole[14] out of the Senate, where he was going to show off his leadership ability to run against Clinton. Dole threw up his hands because he couldn't deal with Kennedy and his legislation and still be a Republican. He couldn't stop these bills, and the Republicans were saying, "What's wrong with you? You can't stop these bills. You're the majority leader. Why can't you do anything?"

Kennedy took over the Senate in 1996, and that's when the Washington powers-that-be came to see Senator Kennedy as *the* great legislator. There is story after story. The leading newspapers, most of the major political journals, all wrote pieces on this theme, "My God. Kennedy is now standing atop Washington; in the minority he's running the Senate." I don't think anyone has ever had that kind of an impact with that weak a hand in terms of where he was in the Senate, in the minority.

The senator's stepchildren, Curran and Caroline Raclin, drew on their close and warm relationship with him to describe the effective political partnership between Kennedy and their mother, Vicki:

Curran Raclin, Edward Kennedy's stepson:

Q: You said earlier that the relationship between Ted and your mother was extraordinary, unique maybe.

Curran Raclin: Yes.

Q: I'd like you to talk a little bit more about that. Were they—it looks to me, and not a few other people have noticed, that it's a romance of the century. It was that romantic relationship. There's much more to it than that, didn't you think?

Curran Raclin: There is. I think why it's unique is because there are so many pieces to their relationship, and everyone else who has been in a relationship has one or some of those pieces, hopefully, at least one of those pieces, and they had all of them. That's why it's unique. They have the romance, and that's an important piece, but that's a bigger piece of it too. You can break that down more. There is an age difference there, but that was part of it. Ted's younger than his age, do you know what I mean? He was younger than his age. I think that had he been with someone his own age, there would have been issues, so that doesn't work. He needs someone closer to Mom's age. Intellectually, they had to be paired up and they are. In terms of their likes and dislikes, generally, they are. So they have the same kind of—the whole finish-each-other's-sentences-and-thoughts and know-what-each-other-wants kind of thing, that's what it is. But the fact that there was that trust that they

---

14. Dole was the Republican Senate majority leader from Kansas who ran for president in 1996.

had for each other, which was good. I don't necessarily think that that trust came easily to either of them, for their own various reasons, but they had it for each other, I think that's important.

But they weren't just husband and wife and had this incredible romantic relationship; they were best friends. They could just hang out all the time and spend time together for days at a time, alone. For their anniversary, they've gone on a ten-day sail by themselves. That is a recipe for divorce for most people. Sailing alone for ten days when the main boom breaks, when the lightning hits your boat. That could be a marriage-ender.

That's when you see people at their worst, and it wasn't. It's just, all they do is tease each other about how they reacted, and that's it. That takes a special kind of thing, and I don't know that either of them would have reacted that way with someone else. I think it was—you talk about chemistry, and we overuse the term. This was that. It took a very specific pairing to get the reaction that you get out of both of them. I think that's why it's so special. And I think that Ted's treatment of Caroline and me is a testament to that.

When you have kids, your default is to take care of them. You have to make a decision to leave them. Our parents took care of us. Even though they're divorced, they took care of us. I have a relationship with my father. But Ted did not have to take care of us. He had to make a decision to do that, and he did beyond anything that he should have been responsible for. I think that's a testament to that. There's no reason he had to do anything for that; that's a decision. When you have your own kids, you're responsible for them, that's your responsibility, but we weren't his kids. I was seven or eight years old; Caroline was four or five, six. That's a whole other package. Not that I wasn't lovely at that age, but it's still a lot of responsibility. I think that taking on that responsibility and this burden, which is essentially what—we're not good conversation pieces, so that's what we are at five and six years old, eight and nine years old. It is a big testament to his love for Mom and his love for Caroline and me.

Q: But your mother and he were also partners, weren't they, in politics?

Curran Raclin: They were. When you get into the 1994 election and you start getting into that, that's when I think—

Q: Do you remember that well?

Curran Raclin: I remember the '94 election. I don't remember the intricacies, just because I wasn't privy to how that was going, but I remember the election night very well. I remember the whole thing. I remember the lead-up to it and everything. It was stressful and it was Mom—Mom is unbelievably intelligent. If she wants to do something, she'll do it well; that's not an issue. But she enjoyed this, and working with Ted, she enjoyed it more.

Q: She becomes an advisor, a partner.

Curran Raclin: Absolutely. Very valuable in terms of insight in terms of "What do you think of this?"

Q: And a perspective. She has a perspective that he may not.

Curran Raclin: A perspective that he wasn't getting, I think. So that kind of diversity was a good thing.

Q: There are many accounts of how she became evermore a part of his political—

Curran Raclin: No, it's very true. It started from just, whether it's how to run an ad campaign in 1994, and then eventually getting into policy and the campaigning and writing speeches and doing everything else, that it became much more. She was definitely the chief advisor for him. At the end, the last several years, she's been with him all the time. It's just how it works out. She knew everybody on the staff and they knew her. I think it was easier for the staff to accept her, because she's not just the wife who is talking, she knows what she's doing. So it's easier for people who have been there for a while to say OK, because it's not just some dummy who is coming up with crazy ideas. She actually is very intelligent and knows what she's talking about, and they appeared to have worked, so that probably helps.

Caroline Raclin, Edward Kennedy's stepdaughter: Every night, without fail, he would always come home from the Senate, and we'd always have dinner at precisely 7:15. Not 7 and not 7:13, but 7:15. He was very scheduled, very on time, but it wasn't something you had to study for. They were given topics to talk about, but we weren't given topics. It was more of an informal idea. Yes, we talked a lot about what was going on in the Senate, like funny stories. "Well, what did you do today?" "Oh, I had an art project" or whatever it was, but a lot of it was like I said, based around the Senate and the nation.

Q: Politics.

Caroline Raclin: Politics, a lot of which I didn't originally appreciate, to be honest. I thought it was boring, but then I think in high school was when I got into it. Maybe because Curran went to college three years before I did, so maybe I had more one-on-one time at the dinner table and wasn't so shy. I don't know. This is the first time I thought about that, but yes, it was a lot of fun. And then after dinner, it was homework time, so Curran and I would go do our homework, or Curran would pretend to do his homework, and I would actually do my homework, and Ted would go do his homework.

He had an office in every house where we lived. The one I'm specifically thinking about is the one in our current house, 2416 Tracy Place. He would go to his little office, and he'd have his briefcase. The briefcase was an ever-present part of the life. It was like another arm. And in the briefcase he'd have all the clippings from the day and everything that happened. He'd write all the notes and he'd spend a couple hours every night at the desk doing it, and just concentrating on that. That was a good example for us, who wanted to watch TV or whatever it was. And then after that, we'd play the games that I talked about, like chess and gin and everything.

Q: Well, you said you had never seen anything like your mother's and his marriage.

Caroline Raclin: Yes.

Q: It's a romance.

Caroline Raclin: It was a romance.

Q: That grew perhaps deeper, but it was more than that, wasn't it?

Caroline Raclin: Of course. But I think, I mean they'd just rely on each other so much, and they never were apart. I guess with a lot of marriages, it seems that you maybe grow used to the person, but you might not really have the passion or whatever it was, or have the spark or have the joy or the fun, just going through the routine. It wasn't like that at all. They were dynamic.

Q: They were dynamic. She became a partner, didn't she?

Caroline Raclin: Oh, yes. Oh, 100 percent, and she was behind every single political statement, every speech she went over, as well as the office. And then they would practice every speech and he would highlight the—I don't know. I've never seen anybody else prepare for a speech other than him, so I don't know if this is common practice, but he'd go over it dozens of times, and highlight the words that he wanted and put the pauses in the speech so it became natural. Anyway, so that's just what they would do. They constantly would talk about politics and policies that he was working on and what exactly the next move would be. They were always looking into the future but still keeping the whole picture in line. She's just amazing at that by herself, so the two of them combined were like this dynamic duo, Batman and Robin.

Curran Raclin: My favorite story with him [Ted] involves—the most helpful he was ever to me was when I got in trouble, when I did something foolish in college. But the funniest story I ever had was when my sister did something foolish and got in trouble. That night she was home and she said, "What do you think I should do?" And I said, "What do you think you should do?" And she said, "Well, I guess talk to Ted." I said, "Yes, you talk to Ted before you talk to Mom. Are your crazy?" She said, "OK." I said, "In the morning, I'll distract Mom, and you pull Ted aside." She [Caroline] had gone out with some friends she wasn't supposed to go out with.

It was the night before Easter, going into Easter morning the next morning. We go to my Aunt Ethel's house for the big Easter thing at her house. So the next morning, Caroline talks to Ted, and he goes, "All right, I'll talk to your mother. She'll talk to you later, but I'll talk to her first. Just don't say anything until she talks to you or I talk to you." So, we're going to the thing [at Ethel's], and Ted goes, "We're going to take two cars. Mom's going to be late, so Mom's going to come later." So we're in the car going out there, and Ted's like, "OK, I talked to her. She's pretty upset, but I've calmed her down mostly. She's a little stressed out because she's late, and she's probably going to get upset with you on the way back, but don't worry about it, it will be OK. Everything's going to be fine. She's going to be upset, but you know your mother, she gets upset. Don't worry about it."

So we do the Easter thing at Aunt Ethel's house, and we're heading back to the car, and my Mom goes, "Caroline, come with me. Curran, go in the van with Teddy." So Caroline goes with Mom in the car, and we get into the van. Ted gets behind the driver's wheel, and I lock the door, and he goes, "Curran, my boy, there are few places and a few times in your life that you will be happier than you are right now, to be in this car, instead of that one." I said, "Boy, you said it, man." [*Laughter*] "Thank you for pointing that out." He goes, "Just remember this. When you think that it's always bad, it's not always bad. You're in the van today." I said, "Thank you."

He was always calming. He was always able to put a spin on things. I got into a little bit of trouble one evening in college, about 2 in the morning, and I called the house and explained to my mother the situation, and she said, "Well, [*sighs*] here's Teddy." I can't tell you how relieved I was to hear those—I mean, talking to Mom, I love her, but she can be frightening. She's the only person in the world who scares me.

And he said, "All right, what's going on?" And I told him, and he said, "OK, sit down, don't move. I'm calling you in six minutes." He called me back in six minutes and said, "All right, here's what you're going to do, this, this, this. Good luck, have a good night. I'm going back to bed." I said thank you. And for some reason, it's just the way he explains things. He's always like, oh, it's going to be all right. You trust him, he's relaxed, that's always the way it is. So every time anything happened, he was always relaxed; he knew what to say. Part of the advantage of that is that you feel like he's got experience. Whatever you're going through, he's been through that and worse.

Q: *And worse, but a lot worse.*

Curran Raclin: And you can talk to him and he can tell you, "Listen, you're going to come out of this." He's inspirational.

Kennedy's in-laws observed how solicitous he was toward his mother Rose, who died just after the 1994 election at age 104.

Edmund and Doris Reggie, Edward Kennedy's parents-in-law:

Q: *Could you tell us something about what you saw regarding his relationship with his mother?*

Doris Reggie: Oh, it was so—

Edmund Reggie: He would be here [on Nantucket], and we'd have a weekend together, having drinking and fun and all of that, going out and dancing to rock and all of that stuff. Then, when it started approaching mid-afternoon, "Goodbye." He had to go to the Cape because he had that piano player for his mother. They and the staff sang Irish songs to her.

Doris Reggie: It was a sing-along.

Edmund Reggie: Many times we went with him, many times. I am positive, many times she didn't understand what was going on. He would talk to her as though we're talking here, a little louder because her hearing was impaired by that time. But her favorite songs, they were mimeographed in a book. I don't know whether you saw the book or not. All of her songs that she loved. Mainly Irish songs.

Doris Reggie: [*Sings.*] "Sweet Rosie O'Grady," you know, and all these. We would spend the weekend—

Edmund Reggie: That was every afternoon.

Doris Reggie: Every Sunday.

Edmund Reggie: Every Sunday morning.

Doris Reggie: Sunday morning. He'd have a priest say Mass at his mother's home. It would be the sing-along with the pianist on Sunday evening.

Edmund Reggie: He had a priest come every Sunday.

Doris Reggie: Every Sunday morning. But we spent many weekends there when we were there for the Mass, the sing-along. But he brought his mother to table with us at times too. He put her right next to him, most beautifully coifed and in her wheelchair. He paid complete attention to her. I was so impressed.

Edmund Reggie: Complete, through the meal.

Doris Reggie: "Mother, Doris and Edmund just got back from your favorite hotel in your favorite city. And what is that?" you know, the Ritz, or something like that.

Edmund Reggie: She would just talk it out.

Doris Reggie: She would say it. And, "What do you want to eat?" Maybe it was eggs or whatever. She would mention what she felt like eating, and they would prepare it. But she was the guest of honor, and so happy. She adored him, he adored her, and it was really something to see. The devotion of the grandchildren when she passed away was unbelievable.

Edmund Reggie: It really was.

Doris Reggie: We were at the house and each of them would come in—

Q: You were at the house when—

Doris Reggie: Oh, after she died.

Q: After she passed away, when they waked her.

Doris Reggie: When they waked her.

Edmund Reggie: We did not stay long.

Doris Reggie: No no. We came for the funeral, and we were there for the wake, naturally, her children were grieving. To see the devotion of her grandchildren. They were weeping, and it was so touching.

Edmund Reggie: That family is something else. I thought we had a close family.

Doris Reggie: They adored her. She was elderly, and she was always treated with such respect. She was always an integral part of the family, regardless if she was infirm.

11

Pursuing Peace: Kennedy's Heritage and Northern Ireland

Over Senator Kennedy's long career, the centuries-old conflict in Northern Ireland became a transformational issue. Growing up in a family whose Irish heritage served as both a point of pride and as a source of discrimination gave the senator a multifaceted perspective. He was well aware of the historical oppression that Irish Catholics had suffered at the hands of the British. Yet his family paradoxically embraced many aspects of British culture during Ambassador Joseph P. Kennedy Sr.'s tenure at the American embassy in pre–World War II London. In fact, Teddy's sister, Kathleen, married English nobleman Billy Cavendish in 1944. Jack was perhaps the most Anglophilic of Teddy's brothers, admiring the urbane statesmen of Britain's upper crust. Yet just a few months before his assassination, President Kennedy made a sentimental journey to the Kennedy ancestral homestead in Dunganstown, Ireland. He told the throngs of adoring Irish citizens about his "pride [in] being of Irish descent" and how he would carry their good wishes in his heart.[1]

True to their roots, the Kennedys and Fitzgeralds strongly supported their co-religionists' cause in Northern Ireland. Indeed, some of Teddy's earliest memories were of his grandfather John F. Fitzgerald relating stories about the Emerald Isle and how one day the North and South would unite in a Catholic majoritarian republic free of discrimination. For the Kennedy clan, Irish politics was visceral. From Kennedy's initial days in the Senate, he was an outspoken critic of British policy and the treatment of Irish Catholics in Northern Ireland. In 1971, he drafted a resolution, with Senators Abraham Ribicoff and Daniel Patrick Moynihan, calling for the withdrawal of British troops from Northern Ireland and, ultimately, for a united Ireland.

---

1. Maurice N. Hennessy, *I'll Come Back in the Springtime: John F. Kennedy and the Irish* (New York: Washburn, 1966), 104–5.

Senator Kennedy's thoughts on Northern Ireland grew more nuanced starting in 1972, when he met John Hume, a moderate Irish Catholic political leader in the North. Hume cautioned against fiery rhetoric, arguing that it perpetuated the cycle of violence. He instead called for a peaceful political dialogue that was respectful of the civil rights of all groups in Northern Ireland. With Hume's encouragement, Kennedy published an article denouncing violence by any group, including the Irish Republican Army (IRA), dedicated to ending British rule of Northern Ireland, and calling for power sharing among the majority Catholics and the minority Protestants there.

In his talks with Hume, Kennedy came to realize that the flow of money and arms from the United States to Northern Ireland was a major impediment to the peace process. He began working with other prominent Irish American political leaders to urge that Americans stop providing support to the IRA.

Through these groups, Kennedy also worked to influence White House policy. He encouraged Presidents Jimmy Carter and Ronald Reagan to pressure the British government to moderate its position. The senator forged a particularly strong relationship with President Bill Clinton on the Irish question. Not only did Kennedy provide the White House with a valuable back channel to Sinn Féin (the IRA's political wing), through his former staffer Nancy Soderberg, then at the National Security Council, but Clinton named Jean Kennedy Smith, Teddy's youngest sister, ambassador to Ireland. These relationships paid dividends in 1994 when Kennedy and Ambassador Smith lobbied Clinton to approve Sinn Féin leader Gerry Adams's visa for a trip to the United States, clearing the way for a ceasefire and the start of the Good Friday negotiations.

Kennedy continued to play a role throughout the peace talks and implementation of the 1998 Good Friday Agreement, working with Clinton's special envoy, former senator George Mitchell (D-ME), as well as with key interest groups in Northern Ireland. Kennedy even refused to meet with Adams at various times in an effort to pressure the IRA to respect the ceasefire and to disarm, which illustrated how far Kennedy's position had evolved since his early days in the Senate. In 2007, the senator witnessed the culmination of his work when he traveled to Northern Ireland to attend the Stormont ceremony, inaugurating the power-sharing government of which he had long dreamed.

Q: You had made a trip to Ireland while your brother was president, but that was not for purposes of dealing with the [political] situation. We read in the briefing materials that we should start right at the beginning with your consciousness of Ireland, what you saw of it, what you saw of the Irish and Americans, what you learned of them through your grandfather Fitzgerald.

EMK: I think it's probably appropriate to start with my grandfather, John Fitzgerald, who was the son of Irish immigrants who came in the late 1840s from Ireland. He was the son who was born here. He was the first immigrant who really made it politically in this country. He was elected to Congress in 1896 and elected mayor of the city of Boston in 1906.

I'll just pick up about the point of his pride in his Irish ancestry and his deep love of Ireland. He also had an enormous thirst for knowledge and interest in people and a love of history and of the Irish tradition.

He was very sensitive to the prejudice and discrimination against the Irish, and he took steps to reduce discrimination against the Irish and other ethnic groups. He was the first Irish mayor who appointed a fire commissioner who was an Italian. Thousands of Irish appeared outside his house saying, "Appoint one of your own, Honey Fitz. Appoint one of your own."

He had this great, great love of Ireland and Irish history, Irish tradition, and he was the spokesperson for the Irish community. At that time, newspapers used to be a penny or a nickel, but most of the immigrants didn't buy papers. They'd always wait to see who Honey Fitz supported and say that was good enough for them. He was the leader of the community. So I had heard about Ireland a great deal as a child because that was something he was very much involved in and cared about.

There was a lot to do with Grandpa, but if you're talking now just about the Irish connection, I think we can leap from that to the fact that my brother [John], after he was elected to Congress in 1946, took a trip to Ireland and hitchhiked around. He went down and visited the Lismore Castle, where we had family relations from my sister Kathleen.[2] He hitchhiked to Lismore, and he had a very good time—I don't think a spectacular time, but he had a very good time, and he had stories.

I went to Ireland in 1962 before I ran for the Senate, on a brief visit. I went to Israel and Greece and Italy, and then to Ireland very briefly. I went back to the [Kennedy] homestead there just for two or three days. It was basically a political trip prior to the time I was running.

Q: *Is that where you gave your St. Patrick's Day speech that upset the British?*

EMK: I think that was when I gave my St. Patrick's Day speech. The trip was basically seeing some government officials. We were down to visit the homestead and then out to the west and Galway. I met a very interesting woman, Frances Cendell, who was the lord mayor of Limerick, and until very recently was still active in the community. We had a very nice lunch in a hotel, and she said afterwards, "There's a crowd outside who would like to talk." We went up to the second floor and out on a porch, and an extraordinary crowd had gathered. They came from all over. She gave a magnificent introduction, and I was really challenged as to what my message was. I remembered my St. Patrick's Day speech, which I gave and they loved. But it was provocative in

---

2. Lismore is the Irish estate of the Duke of Devonshire, in County Waterford, Ireland. Kathleen (Kick) Kennedy's husband, Billy Cavendish, was the heir to the dukedom but was killed in Belgium by a Nazi sniper in 1944, only four months after his marriage to Kick. She remained close to her in-laws and was buried in the family's plot, at St. Peter's Church, near their English estate, Chatsworth, after her 1948 death in a plane crash.

terms of the British. When I got back, my brother said something along the lines of it was interesting that I had my own foreign policy.

I went back in 1963 after President Kennedy's loss. I went to Europe and visited some countries in relation to the Kennedy Library. I went to government houses, I remember. To the best of my knowledge, it wasn't '63, but was shortly after that.

They did a television program with Sean Lemass and tied into a kind of international hookup. He was the taoiseach [prime minister]. It was a very brief trip. I had met Lemass when he was here at the White House [in 1963]. I went to only two official White House events: one was the evening of Sean Lemass, and one was for Tito.[3] My brother wasn't wild about me being down there, and I wasn't wild about being down there either, looking like I was a plant from the White House. He was very nice in asking. He said I ought to come down for Sean Lemass because of the Irish association and tradition. He had a dinner for him in the West Wing, and there were probably only sixty, sixty-five people there.

The idea or seed about President Kennedy going to Ireland arose. That was 1963, and he had a terrific trip. It was such a great success. The filming of it all was breathtaking. I always said that I thought it was probably the happiest time when he was president. You could see that and feel that after he talked to de Valera. He talked about the River Shannon, and she [Mrs. de Valera] quoted poetry, and he tried to go back and write it down. Interestingly, he wrote a good part of that down after the dinner, but he couldn't get it all and called back from the helicopter. They called him, and he wrote it all down and used it in his departure statement.[4] He was absolutely in touch with the country and its people, and they with him.

I think I told you, when we came back [to Hyannis Port] on that Friday night we showed the ABC/NBC/CBS films of his trip to Ireland, and all the family was there. Then Saturday night he said, "Who wants to see what film we're showing up at the house?" "What is it?" "It's the trip to Ireland." A few went over to watch it. Then Sunday night it was only my brother Jack and I who were over there watching it. By this time he knew every part of each of the half-hour films. I think I've described how we would go from one house to the other on Friday, Saturday, Sunday nights generally when he came up to the Cape—my brother Bobby's house one night, one night at his house, and one night at our house.

President Kennedy came back from Ireland [in 1963]. He'd gone to Wexford, and everything had to do with Wexford and the Kennedys, and my mother

---

3. Josip Broz Tito was president of Yugoslavia.
4. Mrs. Sinéad de Valera was the Irish president's wife. See President John F. Kennedy, "Remarks at Shannon Airport upon Leaving Ireland, 29 June 1963," https://www.jfklibrary.org/Asset-Viewer/Archives/JFKWHA-203-003.aspx.

said, "Why didn't you go where Grandpa Fitzgerald came from?" And my brother Jack said, well, when he campaigned with Grandpa around Boston, he'd go to one part of Boston and there would be [County] Kerry people, and another part would be people from Waterford, people from Wexford, people from Sligo, people from the West, and he said, "It seemed that Grandpa, when he finished talking, always left the impression he was from there. So I never knew what part of Ireland he ever came from, and he never clarified it." So my mother said, "Well, you shouldn't tell that story anymore."

I think that what we just mentioned here has had, obviously, a very important impact in terms of the Catholic population, which is almost half of the state [Massachusetts]. I think we're probably second to Rhode Island in terms of a Catholic population. Over the years, we've taken some positions—obviously, abortion—that they've been very troubled by. Aid to private schools they feel very strongly about. By and large, they are in favor of the death penalty, which I'm opposed to. So you have three rather powerful issues that they think about, and that I've had some differences with them over.

On the other hand, they know that, in terms of the abortion issue, we are a strong family, and they know I believe in family and that I'm very close to my children and my children are close to me. And we've been very close to our parents, our parents were close, the brothers and sisters are close. So they know that, in the more fundamental way, family is held in high reverence, and they also know the high degree of patriotism—every one of the four [Kennedy] brothers was in the service. This is very important to them, service is important to them. Family is important to them. Involvement in terms of community or charity, our work in terms of mental retardation is very important to them. That's something that families are affected by.

And a lot of them are interested in Northern Ireland, Irish history, Irish tradition. I've spent a lot of time on that. My sisters have been very involved in it. We've worked on Irish immigration issues and diversity issues; this is very important to them. So a lot of things that they care very deeply about, we've been very much involved in. And I think that's made a big difference.

Q: Have there been any cases where a figure of the [Catholic] Church has openly opposed or counseled voting against you for your stands? This happened to John Kerry. It's happened to other Catholic officeholders elsewhere in the country. You don't seem to have been a conspicuous target.

EMK: We had Cardinal Law[5] who said, when I was getting the annulment [of my first marriage]—it was front page in the newspapers—"Kennedy is still married and he knows the rules." He made what I considered to be inappropriate comments. "He knows the rules of the Church," and I do, and there

---

5. Bernard Law was the cardinal of Boston.

was no reason for him to go after this thing publicly in ways that were embarrassing. They have not threatened to deny me Communion.

We had a very close relationship with Cardinal Cushing before a lot of these personal things came up, and after that, we had more tension with Cardinal Law. We had Cardinal Medeiros,[6] who was not as tied in to the community. I would attend an important occasion—the particular one I'm thinking of we can locate. It was probably about five or six years ago at the cathedral in Boston. Cardinal Law was there, and he said, "We want to welcome Senator Kennedy, even though he's not right on our most important issue." That and his comments about my annulment were public, but he didn't threaten—

Q: But it was not counseling parishioners to vote against you or to go after you?

EMK: No. We had some scattered incidents that I heard about down on the South Shore—Quincy and Weymouth—in one or two of the campaigns, but isolated, not concentrated.

Q: Were these the local priests?

EMK: Local priests. And then Vicki and I went to the bishop out in Worcester.[7] He actually invited us to come to his twenty-fifth anniversary of being a priest. This was probably five or seven years ago, and there were right-to-life pickets outside. That was going to be the big story; this is the big story. He went out there and asked them not to do it, and he went out of his way to say we were welcome, very much. He went the other way. He had been the archbishop in Connecticut before that. We had a situation in the [1994] Romney campaign where the *Boston Globe* asked me about the ordination of women. That was no more an issue or a question than the man in the moon. I've never gotten asked that question anyplace, on any program, or in any community. But the *Boston Globe* said this is a very important issue. People really want to know about your position on this. And I said—we can get my exact statement—that I've always stood against every form of discrimination against women—against anyone—and certainly the teachings of the Church—and I believe that women are qualified to handle any position, civilly or as far as the Church goes. Women in the Church have been outstanding leaders, particularly in education and health, and I don't see any reason why they can't handle any position. But I said ultimately this is a decision for the Church. I'm not going to get into their teaching, and I'm not going to get into contention with them.

It's always so interesting to me about married priests because Vicki's family are Maronite, and they have married priests. I could never understand why in a press conference someone doesn't ask the pope, "You say you're against married priests. Well, you recognize married priests in the Maronites. Can you

---

6. The archbishop of Boston was Humberto Sousa Medeiros.
7. He was Daniel Patrick Riley.

explain why you recognize them there and you won't recognize them some-place else?" It's amazing that somebody doesn't ask that. I think there are a lot of very powerful positions of the Church that are troublesome, and I speak to those.

I think we have to do a good deal more in terms of these culture-of-life is-sues for women on abortion. As all of us know, these are not easy choices for women in the first place. And I think we as a political party, and probably all of us, can do a good deal more to help them avoid making difficult decisions and choices that they might not otherwise make if they had information about their activities or weren't pressed by economic forces. We don't give a high degree of support to adoption and other services. There's a whole range of different kinds of activities that I think are legitimate concerns to people, and I think just in the political world, there's much more that can be done and language that can be used that could be less confrontational. There are people who have very strong beliefs and values in this area.

Before discussing his trips to the land of his ancestors, Kennedy described the differ-ence between how people in Ireland and the United States view history.

Well, as George Mitchell said, the difference between the United States and Ireland, the trouble with Ireland is they never forget history, and the trouble with the United States is we never remember it. [*Laughter*] There's something to that. They never forget it. They never forget anything over there—particularly a grudge, I think. I described the trip that I took to Europe when I met with Seán Lemass in Ireland and did the broadcast. That was in May of '64. We have March 3, 1970, a speech at Trinity College and September 1971 is the health-care trip to Israel and the UK, and that trip is where I first met John Hume.[8] This is just in the background of what we're talking about, and then I'm also including here the '76 Democratic platform, which included the references to Ireland. It's the first time that the Democratic platform—or any platform—referred to Ireland.

Q: Do you want to tell us how that happened?

EMK: I think it was me and Morrison,[9] the congressman from Connecticut, who was very involved in Ireland and Irish affairs at that early time. We were in touch with the platform committee to see whether we could get some lan-guage in the platform—I'll have to remember who was on the committee at the time. Carter was aware of what we were doing. This was going to be dif-ferent and controversial, but we had negotiations. I can remember for one reason or another being up in Boston at the time.

---

8. John Hume is a founding member of the Social Democratic and Labor Party in Northern Ireland and holds the 1998 Nobel Peace Prize for his efforts to establish peace there.
9. Bruce Morrison was the Connecticut congressman.

Finally they accepted some language in the Democratic platform. It said: "The voice of the United States should be heard in Northern Ireland against violence and terror, against the discrimination, repression and deprivation which brought about that civil strife, and for the efforts of the parties toward a peaceful resolution of the future of Northern Ireland. Pertinent alliances such as NATO, and international organizations such as the United Nations should be fully apprised of the interests of the United States with respect to the status of Ireland in the international community of nations."

It was recognition that this was not going to be a local problem. It wasn't just a British problem; it was going to be an international problem and an international issue, and the United States was going to be involved.

Q: That was controversial?

EMK: That was very controversial, obviously, because the British were very strongly against us. Within the administration as well—it's difficult for me to characterize it. It was because there were a number of us who felt very strongly. And although I was not in a very strong personal relationship with Carter, we worked it through his staff and his people to have that included. It was the first time any political party platform had recognized that this was going to happen, that the United States as a country was going to have an interest in Ireland.

Q: So you were the prime mover?

EMK: Yes. I'd say so—with Congressman Bruce Morrison, who was also involved. At home, my mother certainly encouraged us to read the history and poetry of Ireland. [William Butler] Yeats was recognized and read, and my mother read *Trinity*, by Leon Uris, and urged us to read about the history of Ireland as we were growing up. I don't think there was a strong interest in this, but I think my focus and attention developed later in the early 1970s.

Q: That was when you really got into it, wasn't it? This would have been your second meeting with John Hume. You had met him earlier, but you hadn't discussed—

EMK: Probably in late '71, I had made a statement on the Ribicoff/Moynihan/Kennedy [Resolution] calling for the withdrawal of British troops from Northern Ireland and establishing a united Ireland. Then we went through the history of the Irish contributions, and there are a lot of parts in that speech that had a ring to them.

I got into that speech tragically, "The government of Great Britain fails to realize the presence of British troops in Ulster is compounding the violence instead of contributing to peace. Where have we heard those words, in relation to what country? Indeed, the government is moving blindly in the opposite direction, and rarely has there been a clearer example of the well-known truth that those who cannot remember the past are condemned to repeat it." I talked a little bit about what was happening in Vietnam and also what had happened in the Algerian war.

Q: That was a very strong speech, and what's interesting about is that it comes apparently before you met Hume.

EMK: That's right. That was before I met John.

Q: Was the speech your idea?

EMK: It was. There was a new British policy of internment[10] in Northern Ireland, and that triggered a good deal of reaction and resentment. Ribicoff had spoken about it, and I felt that I ought to speak about it. That's what basically triggered it at that particular time—the internment policy. I made that talk in October of '71. Well, you see, this was in September of '71. I had gone on the health [policy] trip [to Britain]. I remember at that time the people speaking to me about what was happening over in Ireland, and when I came back, I gave that talk. That probably had as much to do with what triggered it. I think that was the sequence.

Now the next thing that happened is that in January of '72, the marchers are killed,[11] and there's a dramatic escalation of violence in the North. The British dissolved the Stormont Parliament, and they would rule the North directly until a political settlement can be reached. The IRA exploded bombs in Belfast . . . and then in November of that year, I traveled to Europe and met John Hume in Bonn. I had called him—I think '72 was when de Gaulle died.[12] I was in Europe. I was coming back from the Middle East.

The trip to Bonn, I think, was for NATO. I guess I had called him several days before. I was someplace else in Europe and called him about meeting me in Bonn, and then we had a conversation. He came to Bonn, and I spent a couple of hours with him in the residence of the ambassador or the chief counselor. I think that's where John began the great education of Edward Kennedy about Northern Ireland and planted the seeds that grew and grew and grew into a wonderful relationship.

Q: He said when he got your call he didn't believe it was you. He thought it was somebody playing a joke on him. And yet he borrowed money from his savings and loan to pay for his trip, and was put up at the embassy, which is where you met him. How had you come to identify him as a person you ought to talk to?

EMK: I think he had established himself. He had certainly established himself on Bloody Sunday in Londonderry as a courageous political figure. He lay down in front of tanks—with his wife and his children standing there— and they moved to within a foot of running over and killing him. He never flinched, and that's what basically stopped it. So he was a charismatic figure who believed in nonviolence and was principled, eloquent, and profound.

---

10. Internment referred to mass arrests, without trial, of IRA members.

11. On January 30, 1972, Irish nationalists marched through Londonderry, Northern Ireland. British soldiers shot and killed thirteen of the unarmed demonstrators. The incident became known as Bloody Sunday.

12. French president Charles de Gaulle died in 1970.

I think he has always maintained those qualities, and was therefore convincing, sincere, and visionary in terms of what the future was going to bring.

You look through the different types of discussions that took place from '72 up to even now [2006], and you'll find the resonance of Hume's sense about different communities, different traditions working together based on respect and nonviolence. There were different formulations as time went along, but at the core of it was that different traditions ought to be able to work out their differences through mutual respect.

The political process rather than the bomb and the bullet. He lived that, and he was a very colorful figure as well as being enormously persuasive and eloquent. I've listened to him when he's talked to important groups, and he's eloquent and visionary. In casual or smaller groups, he has a lot of warmth and friendship. He's a delightful person. He mixes those elements to be an important political figure, and he's been recognized as such over the course of his life.

So his view of the situation, and of how progress could be made, made a very important impression on me. He certainly outlined a pathway that would offer the opportunity to help resolve the differences, and that was a pathway I basically embraced from that time on.

Q: He was a person who could see possibilities even in a bad situation.

EMK: Well, he had a bad situation with the killings in Londonderry—which are still very raw to the people there, because of the brutality and the firing on what they considered (and which I think were) truly unarmed civilians. It turned out to be more a massacre than a battle. Then the whole attempt to cover it up inflamed passions and has left them inflamed even to today. So that was 1972.

I left out the time I went to Ireland and spoke at Trinity College in 1970. I had been invited over. They hadn't had many who spoke at Trinity College because it was a bastion of conservatism. It wasn't really tied to the issues in terms of rule in the North at all. I think you get a sense from that speech that I was very interested in Ireland and what was happening there generally, but that speech was not focused on the political problems of the North.

Q: Did what John Hume told you change your views in any way?

EMK: Yes, the answer is yes. He looked at this as a political process that was going to be built upon different traditions and mutual respect. It was going to be resolved in a political evolution rather than in unilateral actions by the political parties. How that was going to be done, as I mentioned, was going to evolve—whether they were going to get into questions of counteractions or changing and altering the police and the judiciary, then seeing reductions in violence—or whether a different framework was going to be suggested later on.

A process was going to be established that he believed could move the whole debate and discussion within a nonviolent framework and could result eventually in some settlement. That's how he viewed it rather than the groups taking action. Some of us had suggested that they withdraw troops, and then there would be counteractions, movements toward unification and other kinds of actions. That was the significant change. And it certainly appeared to me that it was important to listen to someone who had suffered the way he had, and had shown the courage and determination he had shown, living on the ground as he was and experiencing the harshness he was experiencing. I believe it's important to listen to the ones who are risking their lives and are attempting to do it in a nonviolent way.

In the early days with him was a fellow, Austin Currie. [He] was a strong voice at that time. The Orangemen[13] came into his house and grabbed his twelve-year-old daughter and branded her on her breast with a hot iron, and he just boom! moved out of the area. That ended it for him, which you can readily understand. John had an innocent daughter who was supposed to be kidnapped, and they grabbed the wrong girl. These people were tough individuals who were risking everything and were still nonviolent. And it seemed to me that their cause was going to certainly be my cause, and their views were going to be very persuasive. I was going to advocate and support. That was the beginning of that whole process.

So we've been back now to '73 where I outlined a different framework in the article on foreign policy that's still referencing the major kinds of challenges that were faced. But in that article, I point out, "The violence and terror must be ended. I condemn the brutality in Northern Ireland. I condemn the violence of the IRA. I condemn the violence of the UDA.[14] I condemn the violence of the British troops. I condemn the guns and bombs. I condemn the flow of arms or any funds for arms from the United States or any country to Northern Ireland. And I share the words of [William] Cardinal Conway, who spoke eloquently about the Ulster terror in his Christmas message, 'To kill a man deliberately, snuff out, is a terrible deed, and this is true no matter who does it, no matter what side he is on.'"

This was condemnation of violence on all sides. Then I went through the difficulties and perceptions in terms of the continued internment, and also the [British] troops [in Northern Ireland].

Q: *You were consulting with or talking with Hume—or* [chief legislative assistant] *Carey Parker was—throughout this period, weren't you?*

EMK: Yes.

Q: *About major speeches.*

EMK: Well, you know, the violence continued. I quote, "As former president John Lynch of the Republic stated, 'The only solution is united by agreement in independence and Ireland in a friendly relationship with Britain, and

---

Ireland should be a member with Britain of the enlarged European community. I hold this view because I believe that there is no other way to dispose the continuing and difficult legacy history has left—certainly no way which will not compound the problem for our children.'"

That seemed to be the pathway of movement in that talk. This was a more comprehensive statement. I would say this was a refining of my views, and also a very strong plea for the rejection of violence. This is following the meeting with Hume in '72.

Q: Was it a tough sell to convince Irish Americans that they needed to—?

EMK: Yes, it was very tough, particularly as it moved on from there. This is '73–'74. We had a very strong organization called NORAID,[15] which is the Irish American group that was very supportive of the IRA in terms of finances. They didn't like the criticisms of the IRA, but their principal opposition really developed a few years later in 1977, when we brought together what we called our Four Horsemen urging Irish Americans not to provide support for the IRA or engage in violence.[16] After '76 we had a Democratic president increasing escalation or evolution of the fact that Ireland was a matter of interest to United States foreign policy. Our interest in Northern Ireland was always a source of antagonism to the British, who said that Northern Ireland was an internal British matter.

Q: Could you tell me when in the course of these events or talks with Hume the difficulties posed to the peace process by not only NORAID but the pro-IRA sentiment among the Irish Americans in the Diaspora came up as an important impediment in the eyes of the people involved in the peace process? Was that discussed at all? There came a time when the Four Horsemen, you and others, took a major role in turning that sentiment around in support of the peace process and against the support of violence by the IRA.

EMK: I think it really was in '76, the Four Horsemen, and the continued statements and comments we made in each subsequent year. A number of events were taking place at the time as pointed out in my notes: "Hume mentioned that the European Commission on Human Rights has vindicated the Catholic position on torture and inhumane conditions in the internment camps. Although proceedings for the commission have not received much publicity, Hume finds it increasingly embarrassing to British politicians."

All of this was working at one time. That didn't have much impact in terms of NORAID, and Hume was talking about a time-phased withdrawal of the British, and reform of the local police. Even Hume had talked about the phased withdrawal because they can't be there, you can't have peace while

---

15. Irish Northern Aid Committee.

16. The Four Horsemen were Irish American legislators Senators Edward Kennedy and Daniel Patrick Moynihan, Speaker of the House Thomas P. (Tip) O'Neill, and Congressman Hugh Carey.

having the troops present. And then there was the discussion about trying to find some common ground—getting away from your question—trying to find common ground and begin to try to find ways they could work together. I don't remember—until the '70s with the Irish Four Horsemen—that we really were able to take on NORAID and the strong economic support that Irish Americans were giving to the IRA. That took a good deal of time, and it was controversial. We were finding out through the Justice Department that it was beginning to have some impact and effect.

Q: The reason I ask is that practically all the people we talked to in Ireland pointed out their growing awareness—after the government of Ireland was given a role in the process—that the sentiment or the feelings in the Irish Diaspora were not being helpful to the peace process. They were very concerned not only about the position of the United States government vis-à-vis Northern Ireland, but very concerned about the state of opinion among the Irish Diaspora and the credibility it gave to the raising of arms. [T]hey talked a great deal about that, and a great deal about how the Four Horsemen—you and Tip O'Neill especially—helped turn that around? I was wondering if this was pointed out to you.

EMK: It was very clear from what Hume was pointing out to me, certainly, that if we were going to have any success with a political process, we had to stop the flow of arms and funds for arms to the IRA from the US. I did that in the '73 article. Hume felt that that was the most important thing we could do for Ireland: urge Americans who were sending the arms and money to the IRA to withhold support. I guess the figures show that about 75 percent of the IRA funds were coming from the US, and NORAID was the principal organization for all of that.

It was very apparent to me that I certainly couldn't do it alone. If it was going to be done, it would have to be with a broader-based group of prominent Irish. We were able to get Tip O'Neill—who had just been elected Speaker at the time—and it was a confluence of events. Mike Mansfield left the Senate, and we had a good friend, Charlie Ferris,[17] whom I had worked with when I worked with Mansfield, going over to the House and working with Tip. He was particularly responsible for this. And with my own conversations with Tip and Charlie Ferris—and I think with John Hume's conversations with Tip as well—Tip came on board, and after that it was easy to get Moynihan and Hugh Carey to join us.

We had a series of statements with a number of our Democratic and Republican colleagues in the Senate and with House members. But it was basically the four of us who initiated those statements, and to a great extent most of them were drafted by Carey Parker working with John Hume. We did a lot

---

17. Charles Ferris served from 1963 to 1977 as chief counsel to the US Senate majority and chief counsel to Senate Majority Leader Mike Mansfield. He also was House Speaker Thomas P. O'Neill's chief counsel in 1977.

of work on that, in later years with Trina[18] on my staff. This was getting us started on that first statement in '77. The theme was to get all organizations engaged in violence to renounce the campaign of death and destruction.

It was an obvious reference to the IRA, and I think we were getting some traction then. *Newsweek* magazine had a story about forcing Irish Americans to consider the bloody use of their guns and money. So even though the conditions in the North were not improving, at least we began the process. Then we had corresponding actions being taken on the British side. I'm not sure which year was Sunningdale.[19]

Q: *Senator, did you find that your own Irish American constituents had a romanticized view of the IRA?*

EMK: Oh, there's no question that they had a romanticized view of the IRA. There were a number of Irish who were coming in here illegally, and they depended upon the Irish community to get jobs and to develop relationships. There were thousands and thousands of Irish who came over here during this period. I saw it as the chairman of the Immigration Subcommittee. We ended up with the Donnelly visas,[20] but they tried to increase their ability to immigrate over here. So we had a force coming here illegally—some legally, but many illegally—and intersecting with the existing groups here, and that added velocity to the groups and their romanticizing about the struggle, particularly when there had been a good deal of violence in the wake of Bobby Sands and the hunger strikers.[21]

That's probably when they hit their height, and we were coming right into the teeth of the gale on this, without very much progress to show for it. I think, to the contrary, we were coming into a situation with Reagan winning in '80 and then [British prime minister] Margaret Thatcher coming in and being very tough on it. Then we had the increasing emotional feeling with regard to the injustice taking place in Northern Ireland. It wasn't clear how all this was going to work its way through.

We had all the tragedies: in '81, as I mentioned, was the hunger strike at Long Kesh. In '79 the killing of [Lord Louis] Mountbatten [by an IRA bomb] was something that really startled a lot of people, the growth of violence. It was very hot here in terms of the politics of it.

Q: *Can we talk a little about how the presidential and executive side got moved or didn't get moved to be supportive of the peace process? The first was Carter, who made*

---

18. Trina Vargo specialized in Northern Ireland policy.

19. The 1973 Sunningdale Agreement was an attempt to establish a power-sharing Northern Ireland executive and a cross-border Council of Ireland. It collapsed in 1974.

20. Donnelly visas, named for a Democratic congressman, Paul Donnelly, from Massachusetts, were a part of the 1986 immigration reforms that offered ten thousand visas by lottery each year to primarily Irish, Canadian, and British immigrants.

21. Bobby Sands, a convicted member of the IRA, died in prison in 1981 after a hunger strike to protest the conditions of his and his compatriots' imprisonment.

the first statement that seemed to be supportive. I take it Bill Shannon must have been an ambassador who was sympathetic to that, is that the case?

EMK: Yes. Bill Shannon was selected by Carter and was a very gifted and talented writer. He had followed Ireland for some time, and I think gets great credit in Ireland for his attention to policy. He was a very positive and constructive force during that period. Particular events don't stand out, but there's no question he was a positive force. I talked with him—not an enormous number of times or in great detail—but I was in touch with him during the period. The Horsemen were moving. Corresponding actions were taking place among the British during this period, and different leadership was coming on, and discussions, but I can't recall any important alterations or change. At some time—I think it was probably the first year after '80—we started having the Speaker's St. Patrick's Day lunch with Tip O'Neill. That became an important event. St. Patrick's Day began to change, and instead of just having a bowl of shamrocks given to the president, the president had to come to the Speaker's lunch.

A number of us persuaded the taoiseach that this was the time for him to come to the United States. What I'm outlining now we perfected later, but we persuaded him to come over at that time to garner greater attention. Either the taoiseach would have an opportunity to talk to the president about policy, or they'd have a chance to talk to him at the Speaker's lunch. All Reagan wanted to do was have jokes at the lunches. I don't think from '77 to '80 Jimmy Carter showed any interest. I might be wrong, but I don't believe there was any action by the administration during that time.

We had the prisons and the Iranian seizure in late '79, and I started to run in '79. I don't remember any action that was really taken or any leadership that was done. After 1980, we had President Reagan and very tough action from Margaret Thatcher, and a different phase of the relationship. We had the Speaker's luncheon, and then Reagan started to at least meet and have leaders from Northern Ireland come. They hadn't come before.

Q: *That started under Reagan.*

EMK: Yes. They started to come over themselves, and we started to get them involved with the Speaker's lunch. He could decide who he wanted, and that was worked out with the Irish.

Q: *Was that a good thing?*

EMK: Yes, it was enormously important eventually, because it gave some focus and attention to this issue. A fellow who worked under President Reagan—I guess it was William Clark[22]—was the Northern Ireland contact. He showed a good deal of interest. He had some Irish roots, and he was willing to

---

22. William P. Clark Jr. served under President Ronald Reagan as the deputy secretary of state from 1981 to 1982, national security advisor from 1982 to 1983, and secretary of the interior from 1983 to 1985.

listen. I think the president had some conversations with Margaret Thatcher to try to soften her up a little bit—at least it was always thought that she softened up a little bit—and then Tip let her speak to a joint session of Congress. I don't remember talking to Tip about that in detail. We didn't see a great deal of change or alteration—some, perhaps.

Q: *Was part of this trying to counteract the British position and the State Department's traditional position that this was an internal affair?*

EMK: That's it, and that continued all the way through President Clinton. But this was not an issue back in '81. We had the hunger strikes and people starving themselves to death. This was not an issue that was going to go away. We tried a number of different interventions with Reagan to get him to appoint a special envoy for peace, but he was not interested in that.

I introduced a resolution for a new Ireland forum to establish institutional alternatives to British control. Margaret Thatcher was very strong in her rejection of anything and everything to do with it. That was the early '80s, '80 through '84. Then in '85 Thatcher signed the Irish Agreement with Garret FitzGerald.[23]

Q: *Wasn't that a step of progress?*

EMK: Very important, and I think that was the result of a good deal of work that Garret was involved in. I don't have the year that Sunningdale was moving along and collapsed [1973–74], but there was at least an initiative on it. And then the right-wing labor groups in Belfast did a strike on that thing and ended it. I don't know what year that was, but that's an important date in this, because it showed that the leaders who were involved were at least beginning to talk about it. FitzGerald and the '85 agreement were important.

In '81 we had the Friends of Ireland,[24] so this built on the Four Horsemen issue via the Friends' annual statements, and Reagan endorsed that.

Q: *He finally came around, didn't he, more or less, in the second term?*

EMK: I think Clark had a positive influence on him. I saw Reagan on different occasions, and he would never bring up the Irish situation. We were always told when we went in to see him that we could talk only about the things we were scheduled to talk about. We were told not to get off on other things. So we didn't have a chance.

He certainly moved from just wanting to tell jokes. Over the time he was president, as he came up to those lunches, it had gradually become more substantive. The first time, everyone was told very clearly they were just to tell stories. He would tell a couple of stories, and Tip would call on people around the room to recall stories. He'd call on the Americans, Jimmy Burke[25] or others,

---

23. Garrett FitzGerald was prime minister of the Republic of Ireland from 1982 to 1987.

24. Senators Kennedy and Moynihan and House Speaker Tip O'Neill founded the Congressional Friends of Ireland in 1981 to support peace and reconciliation in Northern Ireland.

25. Burke was a Massachusetts congressman.

to tell stories. Then he gradually called on some of the Irish, and they would tell a story, but they would also make some little comments. Eventually those lunches turned into being about substantive kinds of issues—not profound, but at least the chance for people who came from different kinds of traditions to sit down at lunch.

And of course that format became the very significant and important framework where eventually, under President Clinton, all the leaders came over and stayed for three days. Most of the political leadership came to that lunch, and virtually all of those who were involved in the Good Friday Agreement were in the White House and would stay there for several hours. One evening they stayed there literally for four or five hours. The president went up to bed, and they stayed there talking and speaking on it.

So that framework was very important, and it eventually evolved that the Irish prime minister would come over and sit down and would actually have substantive talks with the president. The people who were interested in Ireland came to town for these receptions, and they would talk to people within the administration. All of this was an evolutionary process where the Irish issue became of much greater substance, and was really important and got a lot of attention.

Q: I think Garret FitzGerald and John Hume met Reagan. Maybe it was at one of the lunches.

EMK: Yes.

Q: John Hume spoke of this.

EMK: I met Garret in Ireland before he came. I visited him when he was the taoiseach. He then came down to Cape Cod.

I think during this period, the '80s, the whole question about these negotiations—the framework and reforms that were going to be necessary in the North—also included the economic component: if they're going to work out and get some progress made, we ought to have an economic component. That was going to be the sweetener, because there were a lot of hard economic times in the North, and this would be helpful and appreciated, particularly by the Protestant groups.

Q: So you were getting appropriations for an Ireland fund.

EMK: We were talking about trying to get appropriations as a sweetener to the conclusion of a framework. We went to work on President Carter to get economic assistance. Reagan had proposed $50 million for five years, but most of it was all incentive for the private sector to come in. Tip and I wanted direct aid, and when we talked to [Reagan's chief of staff] Don Regan[26] about that, he indicated he was prepared to get us the money if we were prepared to call off the dogs on the Boland Amendment, which was to end the war with the

---

26. Regan was Reagan's chief of staff.

Contras, in Nicaragua. It was sort of a quid pro quo, and we weren't going to have that.

Q: *Senator, were you involved in getting Irish American businessmen to invest in Northern Ireland?*

EMK: We tried to get some of the large American corporations, companies who had branches in Northern Ireland, to see if we could work with them in ways that would be constructive and positive. We had people like Jack Welch,[27] a whole series of successful, prominent Irish American business people, who came and we met, particularly during the Clinton period. We had a very significant number, several hundred, to try to see if we could get them to take some interest in making their various subsidiaries in the North a constructive force. We talked to the State Department and Treasury Department as well as the intelligence groups, but that never went anywhere. I think we could have done some things, but we never had any success on it.

I talked to a number of business people to see if that could be achieved, and also with some of the more conservative people. A fellow named Jopling was the minister of agriculture under Major,[28] and he's a good personal friend from years and years ago. We went over to the Ditchley conferences. He's actually a very good friend of my sister Jean's, and he was in Dublin when we went over to see her. He was very prominent in the conservative groups, and he poked around to see whether we could get any takers on this, but it just wasn't possible.

So moving along towards '88, that's when Hume told me he had been meeting secretly with the new head of Sinn Féin, Gerry Adams.[29] He [Hume] was making the argument that the violence wasn't working, and even if the British would get forced out, the Catholic community would be at the mercy of the Royal Ulster Constabulary and the eight thousand members of the [Ian] Paisley Unionist Party. So he proposed that the IRA give up the campaign of violence and agree to meet with all parties, hosted by the Irish Government, and if the settlement could be agreed upon, it would be put to a vote in both parts of Ireland, with Britain agreeing to abide by it. John's proposal, in broad terms, would eventually happen a decade later.

Q: *You're starting to hear reports that perhaps Gerry Adams is somebody who can be dealt with?*

EMK: We've gone by the visit of Garret down at the Cape.

Q: *I have it as May of '85.*

---

27. Jack Welch was CEO of General Electric.

28. Thomas Jopling served in the cabinet of British prime minister John Major.

29. Gerard Adams is president of the Sinn Féin political party in Northern Ireland, a post he has held since 1983, and he has been a member of the Northern Irish parliament since 2011. Kennedy initially opposed granting Adams a visa to visit the United States, because of his ties to the IRA, but ultimately the senator supported Adams.

EMK: May of '85. Prime Minister FitzGerald came to Cape Cod, a visit with Mrs. [Joan O'Farrell] FitzGerald. I can still remember him pushing her wheelchair across the lawn down there. As these notes reflect, he mentioned three areas: one is security, the second the judiciary—how we were going to get confidence-building in terms of the judiciary. (He had a really complex proposal there.) And then the future role of the Irish government in the North and who was going to speak for the North, those kinds of arrangements, and how much authority and how much power they were going to have.

Q: That visit was before the Anglo-Irish Agreement with Thatcher [between Britain and the Republic of Ireland in November 1985]?

EMK: He [FitzGerald] called it a very tough negotiation and said he was not at all sure how it was going to all work out.

Q: And the third issue, according to your notes, is the future role for the Irish government in the process. It appears that FitzGerald was pushing for that as a precondition, as almost a precursor for being able to do much—to have the government of Ireland accepted as a player.

EMK: In the North.

Q: In the North. When he visited you, that had not yet happened. But in November, that was allowed for the first time.

EMK: That was very significant. There was the agreement between Hume's SDLP[30] and the Irish government. One of them had to have the role, and the question was how much the role was going to be. Eventually he [FitzGerald] was able to negotiate that the Irish government was going to have a role. I don't know how the Anglo-Irish [Agreement] considered the political parties, the SDLP, how they included them. In that agreement, he also talked about the financial aspect—the importance of it—and we talked about talking with Tip O'Neill and also Albright.[31] I had talked to Democratic Senator Byrd, who was on the Senate Appropriations Committee, and I also talked with Republican Senator Hatfield about it, and they were open to helping. Without getting into the details of this, I always thought that it would have to start in the House with Tip, where we had the most leverage, and that these people were going to respond.

Q: I think it was the Anglo-Irish Agreement that FitzGerald negotiated with Thatcher. It also recognized, for the first time, consent as the basis for the government of North Ireland. That was recognized in the language of the '85 agreement, which was considered at least a breakthrough in principle, some give on the British feeling that it was, in effect, their colony.

---

30. Social Democratic and Labour Party.

31. Madeleine Albright, future US ambassador to the United Nations and secretary of state in the Clinton administration, was then on the faculty of Georgetown University and a foreign affairs advisor for the Democratic Party.

EMK: That was very significant and important. I remember Garret had spent a lot of time thinking through all of these multidimensional aspects of it and having a very good grasp of the interrelationships of these issues and what was possible. He had backup positions and a very comprehensive view. I think he deserves a lot of credit for the whole movement. It was a difficult time. Then he talked about how they were going to try to soften up the IRA with financial incentives important to the Protestants. I don't know what he was suggesting on the IRA. I guess he was talking about something to do with release of prisoners who were not involved in violence. I think that's what they were talking about and that Protestants had that interest as well.

Q: Do you have any sense of how it was that Margaret Thatcher came around? She was entrenched in the late '70s and refusing to budge an inch. But it seems at least by the mid-'80s that she's willing to make some concessions.

EMK: Not other than what Clark was able to do during this period, the general alteration and change within the administration. The longer the president [Reagan] stayed in office clearly made some difference, but I don't have any particular insight into that. There are some notes here from the St. Patrick's luncheon. The interesting part was Tip going after Garret about the Irish package. Tip said, "Cut the bullshit, Mr. Prime Minister. Is President Reagan going to go for the larger money or isn't he?"

Well, FitzGerald said, "This is a matter that's going to have to be solved here in this country." Tip was clearly irritated, and we sat down with FitzGerald and talked about his general commitment to Ireland. He tried to say that he couldn't get involved, but Tip wanted to get him very much involved. It's interesting. FitzGerald commented that Margaret Thatcher didn't have a deep sense of history.

Her lack of a sense of history. It does appear, at least from these notes, that FitzGerald said that Thatcher had been tough on the Unionists. She had become more involved in the Irish situation, and she'd seen Paisley and Molyneaux, who had been very active.[32] He [FitzGerald] said, "So you see from these that she is involved and engaged in what was happening up there in the North, and has some kind of feel." As far as her general alteration and change, it looked like she had as tense a relationship with the Unionists and Paisley as she did with the Catholics and Hume. There was always the thought that if the US was going to do something, the Europeans were going to match it, and that's what was going to make a significant amount of resources available.

I can remember that was something they hoped for—contributions from the EEC.[33] He continued to press that, and he said, "Part of the agreement supported early release for those who had been associated with terrorist acts,

---

32. Ian Paisley and James Molyneaux were leaders of the Protestant, pro-British Unionist party, which wanted Northern Ireland to remain in the United Kingdom.

33. European Economic Community.

but they themselves had not been involved in terrorism." They had indications that this could be supported by both the Protestants and the IRA because both of them had people in jail. So they're already thinking about those issues.

Q: *Did you have any direct dealings with Alec Reid or Tim Pat Coogan?*[34]

EMK: I saw Tim Pat Coogan the time I went over there to visit my sister Jean. I had lunch with him. He was very strong. I had a long lunch with him. Of course, he's a controversial figure and a provocative figure, but he has great insight into the IRA, and he was convinced that Adams was on the level about giving up violence. I've read his book on the IRA. He has real insight into that whole organization.

I didn't meet Reid, although I heard a good deal about Reid from both Reynolds[35] and Coogan and some of the other people I saw when I was over there. Yes, Reid came down for dinner at my sister's, but I didn't get a chance to talk to him in the kind of detail that Reynolds talked about. They used the church in a very important way on the violence issues, but he did not get into that this evening. Reid came to Jean's one evening for dinner, and he told me he was convinced that Adams was not going back to violence and was committed to a peaceful path, and he was satisfied with it. That made an impression upon me.

Q: *Could we talk a little bit about Jean?*

EMK: I think we probably should do that.

Q: *We're getting into the Clinton years now, and that's a big part of the story.*

EMK: In 1992 we have the election of President Clinton, and we have some interest on my sister Jean's part in being ambassador to Ireland.[36] At first I didn't know whether she was enormously serious about it, but she was. I pursued it, and we got on track fairly quickly and began to gain momentum. It was eventually accomplished.

Q: *It was controversial, wasn't it?*

---

34. Reid was a Catholic priest and peace facilitator and Coogan an Irish journalist in Northern Ireland.

35. Albert Reynolds was the Irish prime minister.

36. Elizabeth Shannon, wife of Jimmy Carter's US ambassador to Ireland William Shannon, stated in her Edward Kennedy oral history interview that she spoke to the senator after the acquittal of his nephew, William Kennedy Smith, on rape charges in Palm Beach, Florida, resulting from an outing to a bar with his Uncle Teddy. According to Mrs. Shannon, Kennedy told her, "'Jean is furious with me, because she thinks that I really dragged her son into this situation.' He [Ted] said, 'I have to make it up to her so I'm going to support her candidacy for the ambassadorship.' And he did, very strongly. He went to the president [Clinton] and said, 'I really want this to happen'; so it did." The widowed Mrs. Shannon was disappointed that Kennedy, who had courted her for three years before she ended the relationship, would not support *her* bid for the ambassadorship to Ireland, as were Tip O'Neill and the *Washington Post*. See Interview with Elizabeth Shannon, University of Virginia Miller Center, April 28, 2009, http://millercenter.org/oralhistory/interview/elizabeth.

EMK: It was somewhat, although not enormously. Brian Donnelly wanted this. He had been the author of the Irish visas, and he was from Massachusetts. There was a question about whether Tip was leaning that way. I talked to Tip, and he said, "You ought to go by and tell Brian that this is the way it's going to be, or something to that effect."

Q: This new session, on October 9, is the third time we've talked about Ireland. Jean and I thought it would be nice for you and Vicki to talk about your trip at the culmination of the Irish peace process.

EMK: The trip was on May 8, 2007. I had heard—probably five, six, eight weeks before—that this event was going to take place. I circled it on my calendar and decided to go. The event itself was important not only as the culmination of so much time and effort we'd spent on Northern Ireland, but I had missed a similar occasion in South Africa with [Nelson] Mandela. There was some Senate business going on, and it was a long way there, and I passed up that opportunity.

I had been very involved and engaged in the abandonment of apartheid in South Africa, with all the legislation we had introduced with Lowell Weicker as a result of a trip I'd taken there in the early 1980s, and Mandela's release. I'd seen Mandela back here, and he had mentioned my going over there for the ceremony. I planned on it, but it came in the middle of a lot of activities in the Senate, and it was a long trip. I missed it, and I regretted that. I wasn't going to miss this one.

Sure enough, just at the time this was going to take place, which was going to involve leaving on a Monday night—the ceremony was going to be on May 8—one of the major pieces of legislation was called up on the floor, the restructuring of the Food and Drug Administration. I was the floor manager of it. So I had to decide if I wanted to leave that night and be gone all the next day, Tuesday, and then get back Tuesday night and be around Wednesday, and miss a very important part of the whole debate. I decided to go.

The situation had frozen when we had taken it up to the floor on Monday. I couldn't see a pathway for a series of amendments. I asked the secretary, Paula Dobriansky, if she planned to leave early Monday morning to get over there at eight or nine o'clock. We'd get a night's sleep and have all these program issues. I asked if she could wait until six or seven o'clock Monday night, which she did. It was very decent of her.

I left the Senate floor and raced out there. I asked Sherrod Brown[37] if he would floor-manage the bill for me, which he agreed to do. It looked like there was going to be a series of amendments, but it worked out. I might have missed one or two insignificant votes, but all the action on the bill took place

---

37. Sherrod Brown is a Democratic senator from Ohio.

after I got back, and we were able to get it passed. It was, in retrospect, the thing to do.

I went out to Andrews Air Force Base; we were using a smaller plane, a jet. It's configured to have two fairly decent-sized chairs that face each other, and then a sofa with, probably, three seats. In the back of the plane are four seats, one of which is taken by a radio operator. There were four Air Force people on the plane, and it was a very small plane, so it was a very tight fit.

On the plane was Paula Dobriansky, undersecretary of state for democracy and global affairs. She had been on the Council of Foreign Relations. She's a very bright, smart, and very pleasant person, and very nice to me. Richard Powers was from Boston. He's a big contributor to [George W.] Bush—he made a lot of money—and he was very pleasant. Vicki was there [on the plane], and we were going to meet my sister Jean over there [in Belfast].

We arrived in Belfast at 6:30 or seven in the morning. We went to the Culloden Hotel. We changed and went directly to Stormont, to the balcony of the Stormont government room. It's made of hard wood, a light tan color. It's a very hard, cold atmosphere. The desks are very austere, the chairs are very upright. The room has a higher rise for a couple of seats, and then a rectangular space where different officers sat. Then it extended a little bit into the room. When we were up in the balcony, I sat next to Mrs. Paisley, who was a gracious and lovely person. One of his [Ian Paisley's] daughters was rather stunning, and they were extremely nice. I sat up there with Richard Powers.

Q: Is the first time you met her?

EMK: It was the first time I had met her. She was very gracious and charming, and the daughter was very personable and lovely. In another location was my sister Jean, whom we had met at the hotel. . . . Jean sat with John and Pat Hume, whom she knew, at a different place, not in the balcony. We were in the balcony. Tony Blair and Bertie Ahern[38] arrived and sat opposite us.

We had talked to the press outside briefly before going up, and then they had a series of elections for the first minister, [Ian] Paisley, and then the deputy first minister, McGuinness. They had brief nominating speeches before electing the members of the Cabinet. They probably elected ten people, but it was all done very formally. It was obviously prearranged: people were recognized and spoke briefly.

It was interesting that there was a lot of banter and joking, a good deal of laughter, the typical schmoozing done by politicians. It was much livelier than I expected and much more engaging than I anticipated—much more upbeat. It was an extraordinary, hopeful moment, but considering the tensions between the various groups, it was truly a remarkable climate and atmosphere of banter, good humor, laughter, joking—

---

38. Tony Blair and Bertie Ahern were prime ministers of Britain and Ireland, respectively.

Q: Did this include Paisley?

EMK: Yes. He was lively; he acknowledged his wife. He looked at me, but he didn't really react very much. He has a lively sense of humor. [Vicki has just come in to the interview.] Paisley smiled and engaged in the banter. It was a very typical gathering of politicians, and Mrs. Paisley was pleasant and gracious. The elections went on probably forty-five minutes or so. They made brief statements and nominee speeches, a couple of minutes long. So when that broke up, we went up to somebody's office and sat in there for a while, and they brought some party people in to meet us in a room where we made some calls back to Boston, to talk to some of the press.

We assembled at the foot of the stairs of Stormont, and at the stop of the stairs were Prime Minister Blair, Prime Minister Ahern, Paisley, and McGuinness. The staircase was probably forty stairs, I suppose, going up, and at the bottom of it, they had children afflicted with Down syndrome, half Catholic, half Protestant. They had fake instruments, but they looked semi-real. There was background music, but they were pretending they were the ones playing it. It was very moving and very emotional.

[Gerry] Adams was there. He had all of his top lieutenants there, very political—they call them "hard men"—and the Protestants' hard men, people who despised and hated each other but were forced into the process. It was an incredibly eclectic group, and they had this performance by the Down syndrome children, Protestant and Catholic. It was a surprise, but extremely well done.

There was a poignancy. People stopped talking and listened. You know, at any other occasion like this, everyone would be talking, no one would be listening. But because it was so poignant, everyone listened, and it made people think of the Troubles. People really listened and watched, and they saw these children, and they realized that if they weren't in conflict, there may be some hope for these kids.

Vicki Kennedy: Jean Smith was so deeply moved. We all were. I don't think there was a dry eye in the place when they finished. At first, as Teddy said, it was so startling, and then it was just so moving. Gerry Adams was standing right behind where we were. We had chairs because Teddy's staff people wanted to make sure he could rest his back. I felt a little bad, but we did have little chairs in the corner. Gerry Adams was right behind us. Teddy—do you remember?—he knew every one of those children.

EMK: Yes.

Vicki Kennedy: He went up to them afterward to congratulate them, and he called them by name. It was an incredible moment. They finished their first song, and then we looked up to see these four men—Tony Blair, Bertie Ahern, Martin McGuinness, and Ian Paisley—walking down those tall stairs together. It was absolutely incredible. I took some snapshots. I whipped out my little digital camera, so I have some pictures of them coming down. It was really stunning.

EMK: They came down probably a third of the way, and then they spoke. The first one was Paisley, and basically he was saying, "We're all here at Stormont. We're committed to the queen. We love Her Majesty, and I'll be a part of this government because we're going to remain respectful and in love with the queen of England. To the queen!"

I thought, "Oh my God, what's going on here?" Then up gets Martin McGuinness who says, "I'm up here as a free Irish Republican, and I'm here to tell the people of Northern Ireland, we're going to be united and free. All Ireland will be united and free!" And he stops talking, and I thought, "For crying out loud. Here are two politicians maintaining their constituency." Then Blair gets up and gives an eloquent talk about different traditions and la-di-da-di-da. Then Bertie Ahern says nice things about Blair. Blair says nice things about Ahern, and Ahern says nice things about the Kennedys.

But these first two tigers just didn't give an inch on their interpretation of the agreement. To perpetuate ties with the queen and England: that's why they were there. And the other one was there because Ireland will finally be united and free, and a republic. We were just waiting for the gunmen to come out and start shooting. [*Laughter*]

Vicki Kennedy: Teddy's taking it to an extreme, but that really is basically what happened. It was an unbelievable thing.

EMK: We were going to meet with Blair over in Hillsborough. So we went over there. Blair was just in the process of leaving as prime minister. He had a week more to go, and this was the high point of his term. He came over, and we were in one of the waiting rooms. Hillsborough is a lovely place. It had been the British royal family's home for years. We waited while he was saying goodbye to all the people who had been part of the team: the negotiators, the home secretary team, and the servants. It was very nice.

Blair was very funny. I told him we had just seen the movie *The Queen*, and he rolled his eyes. Then I mentioned how Vicki and I had gone up to Chatsworth, the great home of the Devonshires, and Charles was there. They didn't tell us Charles was going to be there. We had a wonderful lunch, and he was very good company, very interesting, lively and charming. Then Debo, the Duchess of Devonshire,[39] said, "Don't you think the crown ought to give Charles a place where can walk his dogs? He can't walk his dogs in any of his estates, and he loves to walk the dogs. And the crown ought to; don't you think so, Teddy?"

---

39. Charles refers to the Prince of Wales and Debo was Deborah Freeman-Mitford, who was the sister-in-law of Edward Kennedy's sister Kathleen.

I mentioned this to Blair, and he said, "They just don't get it, do they?" He asked if I had met the queen, and I said, "Yes, before the war I went to the tea dances, and I danced with Elizabeth." He said, "You did?" I said, "Yes, I didn't dance very well, but I danced with Margaret,[40] and I danced with the [future] queen." He said, "I shall remind her the next time I see her, Teddy, and I'll let you know what she says about it." He was quick, sharp as a tack.

And then we sat down and people asked him a few questions. I asked him why he thought this agreement would stick when others broke apart. He said it was really amazing. He said, "When I make a speech and talk about reconciliation, I can look out at my audience and people are nodding. It's entirely different from any other time I've ever talked about reconciliation. I'm completely confident that this time it will take."

It was an interesting observation about the significance of the agreement and the fact that, as one who had spent a lot of time with the parties—and knowing the groups that had been supporting these parties—he believed it was going to hold and was going to take. After that meeting, we went back to Stormont for a meeting I was supposed to have with Paisley and Martin McGuinness. Blair had taken more time, and the afternoon had gone on, so we were about an hour-and-a-half late getting back there. McGuinness was there and Paisley's son was there, and he extended apologies for his father's not being there. He said his father had had a big day and it had gotten very late—which was true.

He's very impressive. He's very smart, very tough, very shrewd. He has a wry sense of humor, laughs at his own jokes. He'd say things and then laugh at them and himself, to try to make a point. The basic point he and McGuinness were talking about was the funding that was going to come from London—it wasn't going to be enough. As a result of the Troubles, there had been a very significant deterioration in the infrastructure in Belfast, and they needed a peace dividend.

They felt that the only way they were going to be able to convince people on the ground that this agreement and renouncing violence were going to hold was to get a peace dividend. They said the United States ought to participate in the peace dividend by helping them with their deteriorated infrastructure.

They both could agree on that. They made the pitch about what they thought they were going to get from London and what they thought they could get, and about their needs, and about the important responsibility of the United States. They wanted to be candid with us about it.

My comment was, "Welcome to the political world. That's what we worry about, water rates. We had this problem in Boston, cleaning up Boston Harbor.

---

40. As a boy, during his father's ambassadorship to England, Edward Kennedy danced with Princess Elizabeth, now the queen, and her sister, Princess Margaret.

Water rates all went up, from $120 up to $800. This is what politics—" They didn't think that was terribly interesting or very funny.

Then they switched to the investment conference. They were going to try to have an investment conference, to get people over there to invest. They asked if we would help. Everybody was aboard on that, and that's in process now. I talked to the Irish foreign minister the other day. Powers is very much involved in having a significant conference—in Boston, and also in Chicago and Washington—trying to get people over there to invest.

The overwhelming conclusion on this—and particularly in the climate and atmosphere of the world community now—is that this worked in Northern Ireland. This has now taken hold, and everyone has benefited, and they didn't have to have success at the expense of one of the parties; each of the parties benefited. That was John Hume's great theme in the very earliest days, at the start of this whole process—that everyone could benefit and not at the expense of the other. That's been the theme that has kept those negotiations positive and constructive and open: if everyone holds hands and moves together, everyone benefits.

That's in contrast with so much that's going on in politics, both in terms of the United States Senate, which we just finished talking about regarding immigration, where the Democrats are saying, "We can't do this because we have to have hard votes, and let's let them not get cloture and blame it on the Republicans." It's getting into the blame game, which is so common and has permeated our politics now to a much greater degree than it had when this country was at its best. It's so much a part of what's going on in other parts of the world.

Vicki Kennedy: One of the interesting things people were talking about was the change that brought Ian Paisley to the table. In all the conversations we had with people, it was that his wife turned to him at one point and said, "Okay, Ian, you have to do this for the children and grandchildren. We have to make peace here."

John Hume, Pat Hume, his wife, and other people were pretty consistent in saying that she had had a big impact on him. We had been in Northern Ireland probably ten years before, and the feeling and the atmosphere were so dramatically different this time. This time, we'd go into Belfast and we could see cranes everywhere. It was a moving, hopping place. When we were there before, we had to go through checkpoints to get to Northern Ireland. I remember we had to have guards sitting outside our bedroom door at night. It was the threat of violence. This time it was a whole different atmosphere of things on the move.

Teddy, you had gone to Hillsborough and met with lots of the leaders when we were there ten years ago, but I don't remember that Ian Paisley would meet.

EMK: No, he wouldn't meet.

Vicki Kennedy: You met with Trimble[41] and Gerry Adams and with others in other parties, but I didn't recall that—I thought he wouldn't meet. He was so hard line, and to think that now he and Martin McGuinness were going to be together was quite something.

And I think you also had mentioned that this was Tony Blair's last week in office. And this is really important—Teddy, you were so instrumental in getting President Clinton to give Gerry Adams his visa all those years ago. That really started the peace process. They had a lot of fits and starts and fits and starts, even after the Good Friday Agreement, but in the last couple of years you refused to meet on that one occasion with Adams because of the bank robbery and the killing of Robert McCartney [allegedly by IRA members].

You met with his sisters, and Adams came to town and you said no. They were in that "no snitching" mode, and no one who had been close to it would talk about it, and Teddy refused to meet with Gerry Adams. It was a huge slap in the face, I think they felt, but actually it was an enormous positive message for everybody. I personally believe—and people have written it, and I think it's going to be more and more understood—that that was a catalyst for pushing toward this last time.

They'd lost you. You had always been anti-violence and had been very strong against the IRA's use of violence, but after having championed the visa, your refusal to meet with Gerry Adams that time was a very powerful message.

EMK: Yes, that was a big deal. I think we described in our earlier meetings the role of the White House as a meeting place, where they all could come together. In Ireland, everybody was watching everybody, and if they had a meeting in a hotel, someone would always be seeing and snitching on them. Here, although they were reluctant, they could all go into the White House. They'd all sit in different parts of the room, but they could talk, and then they could meet at the hotels. . . . They couldn't say no, because people back home would say, "Why are you turning down the White House?" They had to go. It's the political dynamic of the United States and the political dynamic of positive reinforcement of political initiatives, all of which are available and which worked in this case.

If you look back on this, what made a difference to the people on the hard right was their visits to South Africa. The Afrikaners had been big supporters. When they went down there and saw that there was beginning to be some reconciliation in South Africa, that made a big difference.

Adams was trying to get me to get involved with the Basques, to see if we could try to get some reconciliation between the Basque leadership and the Spanish. I looked into it, but there wasn't the political—. . . there wasn't

---

41. David Trimble was the leader of the Ulster Unionist Party.

any—at least we couldn't see where the—That was very loaded and dangerous because there are some very bad people there.

There are some bad people in the IRA too, but Reynolds said that from the time Adams said they had given up violence, they couldn't find a single instance where he violated that commitment, that pledge. He said, "The British Intelligence can't find it, we can't find it, and your people can't find it, so he can be believed." That's the big deal: we had that kind of assurance from the prime minister of a country, saying that about somebody. But we couldn't get anything close to that with the Basques. We inquired about it, but I never got beyond the point of inquiry.

Q: *Was Hume noticed or acknowledged* [at the 2007 Stormont ceremony]?

EMK: Yes. He was acknowledged, but never as much as he deserved.

Vicki Kennedy: I thought that was the one sad note of the whole thing. After all he suffered and fought for, he was treated in a very secondary way. Here's this man from the middle, who was against violence from the beginning, and the two extremists, McGuinness and Paisley, were honored while Hume was shuffled very much to the background. Maybe one person mentioned him. I think he's not well, and it was just sad. That was the one sad note.

Albert Reynolds was there. He was happy, of course; he'd been from the south, but it was the other people who had played external, very tangential roles, who seemed to be more in the thick of things. Hume seemed isolated and very sad. I think he's suffering great depression anyway. It was difficult.

But just back up and say this one thing about Paula Dobriansky. What a gracious and lovely person she is. I don't know if Teddy said at the beginning that she held the plane for his work in the Senate. More than that, she gave up the seat of honor in the plane and sat in a less comfortable seat.

EMK: On the way back.

Vicki Kennedy: Actually on the way there, too. She sat and visited with you for a while, but there was one bench that was the only conceivable place anybody could lie down, and she gave that to Teddy: that was the respect she showed. . . . She was very respectful and very nice, even though she was the president's [Bush] representative. She treated Teddy as the senior person on the trip who had done so much for this peace process. She was enormously gracious and very nice.

Q: *So, one of the other fathers of the historic event was you. You were mentioned?*

Vicki Kennedy: By Bertie, certainly, and Blair might have mentioned the Kennedy family.

Q: *They did, right.*

Vicki Kennedy: I think Blair did as well, in the public place. Yes, that was very nice.

Q: *Do you share Blair's sense of confidence that this is going to work now?*

EMK: Yes. This is going to stay. I think we had a pretty good indication that Adams and his group had made the decision to go for it. The others are troublemakers. They're criminals, the Loyalists, and a lot of them are still in groups over there.

Q: Both sides?

EMK: No. The IRA have given up their arms. What's happening, according to the foreign minister I saw last week [October 2007], is that increasingly Catholics are going into the police force, and they're becoming increasingly effective, and they're beginning to isolate more of these criminal elements, and that thing is beginning to take. That was the last area, the policing power.

Q: You were pressing this too, for them to get into the policing?

EMK: Yes, get into the police.

Q: So that the police are not all on the inside.

EMK: Adams always wanted to leave something out, so we could always go to 10 Downing Street and get a picture that he was negotiating with Tony Blair. He never wanted to settle everything. He always wanted to leave something out, and he did that with great success. He kept going up and up. The SDLP [Social Democratic and Labour Party] was John Hume's party, and it kept going down.

Vicki Kennedy: As a last point, it's in every way such a contrast from being there before, and that's a positive thing, the whole feeling of the people, but also the movement and building and go, go. Teddy, where did you make your big speech [in January 1998]?

EMK: In Derry.[42]

Vicki Kennedy: They were supposed to have metal detectors. It was the whole thing, bulletproof vests and so on. It was a big deal there before, and such a different feeling now. They were supposed to have metal detectors to go in, and Chris Doherty, a lawyer who used to be on Teddy's staff, had advanced the whole thing. He's in Washington. We assumed everybody had gone through metal detectors, but somehow they couldn't get the metal detectors there in time, and he said they told him, "Don't worry. Everybody's armed in the room, but we know who they are." Teddy was making a speech to an armed crowd.

EMK: They all have their guns, but we know who they are. [*Laughter*]

Vicki Kennedy: We found that out on the trip home. It was such a different—

EMK: They wouldn't let somebody in there that they didn't know. That's their task. It isn't that they're carrying heat; it's just if you don't know him—

Vicki Kennedy: Don't worry, we know who they are. They have their guns. When Teddy spoke then, he had Protestant and Catholic parents who had lost

---

42. In January 1998, Senator Kennedy delivered a major speech, urging peace, at the University of Ulster, in Derry, Northern Ireland, to both Unionists and Republicans, who had been engaged in armed civil unrest, known as "the Troubles," since 1969.

children in the Troubles, who talked about coming together and healing. All those important symbols and people were out there. Think about the change that happened over ten years.[43]

Q: *Well, it must be something that you* [Senator Kennedy] *take a lot of pride in, because without you it couldn't have come about.*

Perspectives

Carey Parker, Edward Kennedy's chief legislative assistant: In October 1971, a month after his return from Europe, he signed on to a resolution that Senator Abe Ribicoff and Congressman Hugh Carey, who was a member of the House at the time, introduced in Congress calling for immediate British withdrawal from Northern Ireland and the reunification of Ireland.

That was what the American Irish wanted to hear, but as John Hume indicated to some friends of ours in Ireland, "We can understand your frustration, but that's not the way the crisis in Northern Ireland will be resolved." He wanted to talk to the senator, and the senator said, "I have to go see John Hume."

John Hume, founding member of the Social Democratic and Labor Party in Northern Ireland: Senator Ted Kennedy is one of the greatest public figures outside of Ireland who played a major role in our peace process and in the program for peace and justice in Northern Ireland. I'll never forget when I first met him. I was just a young elected representative in 1972 and received a phone call; I was so astonished at receiving it that I thought it was somebody conning me. A voice in the phone said, "This is Ted Kennedy. I'm going to Europe and I would like to meet you to get fully briefed on how you see the situation on Northern Ireland." I was amazed, but I knew it was him because it was his voice.

Senator Kennedy has been at the forefront in the United States of changing traditional American thinking, particularly traditional Irish American thinking, about the future of Ireland. He's done this by totally opposing violence, because violence has no role to play in solving the problem of a divided people, but instead in supporting, socially and economically, the coming together of both sections of the community and of the British and Irish governments.

You see, it's now taken for granted that the British and Irish governments worked together to solve the Northern Ireland problem, but until then, the British government always refused to talk to the Irish government, saying it's an integral part of the United Kingdom, Northern Ireland, therefore, it's none

---

43. Between the Derry speech in 1998 and the Stormont ceremony of reconciliation and government formation in 2008.

of your business. Similarly, to get pressure put on the British government to do it, we were looking for foreign assistance, for assistance from the United States; Ted Kennedy and Tip O'Neill and Pat Moynihan and Hugh Carey agreed to support us to get the British and Irish governments to work together. But until then, no president of the United States would make a statement interfering with the internal affairs of Britain. . . .

But finally, on St. Patrick's Day, 1977—go back and look again and you'll see—President Jimmy Carter made the first-ever statement on Northern Ireland made by a president. That will go down in history as a very historic statement. He was persuaded to make the statement and the statement was drafted by the Four Horsemen: Ted Kennedy, Tip O'Neill, Pat Moynihan, and Hugh Carey, in consultation with myself. "The time has come," Jimmy Carter said, "for the British and Irish governments to work together to solve the Northern Ireland problem. If they do so, we will support you economically."

Carey Parker: Reagan did intervene in 1985 to urge Thatcher to accept a role for Ireland on Northern Ireland. Kennedy and Tip O'Neill urged Reagan to do so, and he agreed to. The result was the Anglo-Irish Agreement of 1985, which gave Ireland a voice on Northern Ireland issues. In general, though, the Reagan Administration was willing to go along with anything that the British Government was willing to accept, and there was a lot of pressure on the British Government from Irish America. Our feeling was that British policy, by and large, was controlled by the [Ian] Paisleys and the hard-line Protestant community in Northern Ireland. Their effort was not so much to try to reach reconciliation between the two sides as it was to end the violence, and they treated it as a war that they had to win, not as a peace they could negotiate.

It took a major effort over more than a decade to get to the point where the Catholic community in Northern Ireland felt that the John Hume SDLP view was the path of the future, not the Gerry Adams IRA view.

We weren't able to make much of a difference until Gerry Adams decided in the 1990s that he was interested in pursuing peace negotiations. That revelation came to us partly through John Hume and partly when the Senator's sister, Jean, became ambassador to Ireland under President Clinton. She picked up Adams's shift very quickly, and she was very influential in convincing Senator Kennedy that it was genuine. The British government was absolutely unconvinced. They felt that Adams was an out-and-out terrorist and that he should, under no circumstances, be accommodated.

The issue came to a head when Adams sought to visit the United States. The British government was adamantly opposed to such a visit, and the State Department initially opposed it. But it seemed to be very important to Senator Kennedy that if Adams was genuinely interested in making a shift toward reconciliation, he should be allowed to come here and be able to talk to the Irish American community, so that they would understand the direction that the party was heading in and so that there would be an end, once and for all, to American support for the violence.

Trina Vargo, Edward Kennedy's foreign policy adviser and founder of US-Ireland Alliance: [Niall O'Dowd] is a publisher of an Irish American newspaper. He came to me because he knew that it would take Kennedy to make this [the Adams visa] happen because Kennedy had always been opposed to the IRA, and he would first have to be convinced if there was to be any hope with the president. That's one of those things that many people don't know or understand. In the tabloids in Britain they'd often suggest Kennedy was an IRA supporter, when in fact he was opposed to the IRA. People who cared about this knew that you had to get Kennedy on board; it was an absolute must to make it happen.

They were coming to me because—I don't know if by statute or just by practice—they couldn't speak to the White House. Nancy Soderberg wouldn't talk to O'Dowd at that stage. But they also knew that they needed a go-between, and that was me, on a daily basis. . . . It suited everybody if I was in the middle and Kennedy was in the middle, him in the big picture, me in the day-to-day, because if anybody tried to be cute, and not live up to the commitment, then I could say, "No, that's not what was agreed." I would also be able to mediate between both sides by making it clear to each party what the other side could or could not accept.

Nancy Soderberg, Clinton National Security Council official and former foreign policy advisor to Edward Kennedy:
Q: Clinton says there was a bigger fight over that [the Adams visa] *in the Cabinet than anything else early in the administration. Is that fair?*
Soderberg: It was huge. Yes, Louis Freeh was apoplectic. Janet Reno was apoplectic. Warren Christopher.[44] Opposed to it, both—Louis Freeh was anti-terrorism, and Janet Reno the same thing. "You can't do this; it will send a message to our anti-terrorist allies." Warren Christopher was saying that it would ruin our relationship with Britain; they'd stop cooperating with us on Bosnia and Iraq. I said, "No, they're not. They're not doing that as a favor to us. It's in their interest to cooperate on those two issues." As far as the terrorism message goes, I wasn't worried about Adams coming here and blowing up anything. I thought, actually, in the long run, if he came here and the president of the United States stuck his neck out for him, and he didn't deliver a cease-fire, it would enable us to go to the Irish Americans and say, "See? This guy's a

---

44. Freeh was FBI director, Reno attorney general, and Christopher secretary of state in the Clinton administration.

fraud. Quit sending him money," and undermine him further. It was that kind of win-win logic that convinced Clinton to do it.

Without Clinton, it [peaceful negotiations] probably would have happened, but probably only about now [2008]. I think he sped it up by a decade—he provided the confidence. He enabled both sides to talk with each other with a modicum of trust that just was not there without the United States. They trusted what they told us, but not each other. So that enabled them to have a conversation and move things forward in a way that was not possible before. Clinton instinctively wanted to get it done from day one. He wanted to get involved, see where we could use it. But I wouldn't underestimate electoral politics. He wouldn't have done it had it been wrong from a foreign policy perspective. I literally never saw Clinton make a foreign policy decision for anything but policy reasons. But in this case, you get the added benefit of all the electoral votes. It's not just Massachusetts; it's all the Catholics around the world. There are forty million in America, and a lot of them are in the swing states of the Midwest. There are a lot of Irish in this country.

Gerry Adams, president of the Sinn Féin political party in Northern Ireland: We made a formal request for a visa. We had just had this conference that Bill [Clinton] and his friends had organized, and Jean Kennedy Smith wrote a letter of endorsement, endorsing the visa, but senior officials in her department, in her office wrote objecting to the visa.

So here you have the ambassador being supportive and her own staff, who presumably would be subordinate to her, were taking a different position. Teddy then starts to come into the fray because John Hume clearly had been briefing him all along in the course of the process. Some of the main people in the Clinton administration were people who had worked with Teddy Kennedy, Nancy Soderberg, for example, and others. But certainly Nancy would be the most prominent of those. So I just presumed that there were all sorts of back channels going on. If somebody got a formalization from source A, then the Nancys of this world would go on to Teddy and Teddy could go on to John Hume, or Teddy could go on to Jean Kennedy Smith and Jean Kennedy Smith could go on to Father Reid, and so on.

I think the president's instinct was right on this, but he himself will tell you that a quiet word from Teddy Kennedy, what you should do, Mr. President. Chris Dodd[45] also, who was a very big buddy of Teddy's, made the same call. So the president called it against the advice of his senior officials and also against some powerful others, like Tom Foley, who was the Speaker of the House.

Teddy was nonviolent. He had lost two brothers to violent actions. He was a supporter of John Hume. He never pretended to be a supporter of Sinn Féin;

---

45. Senator Dodd was a Connecticut Democrat.

he was always a supporter of John Hume. He and I got on well, but that's aside. For him then to come out in the wake of this huge blast in London and to say there should be talks, the British government should be talking to the Republicans. And he stuck with that. Even though it was all heaped on top of him, that he was a supporter of "terrorism." He wouldn't have become a figure of vilification in the States but certainly here, this was pointed up as a terrible thing for this man to be. But he was right.

Elizabeth Shannon, wife of US Ambassador to Ireland William Shannon, Edward Kennedy's friends:

Shannon: He [Ted] loves his Irish heritage. I think he loves his *Boston* Irish heritage more than his Irish heritage. Once I gave him a beautiful book of poetry that I had Seamus Heaney[46] autograph for him, and he really treasured that and loved it, and he used to like to read it. So he loves the art and the literature of Ireland, but his heart isn't there like it is with some people. His heart is here [in Boston].

My husband was the same way. He always said, after we went to Ireland, that I got more involved and interested and wrote more on Ireland rather than the Irish Americans. But he was interested in Irish America and so was Ted. They loved those stories and they'd tell the same old stories again and again and again, and scream with laughter at them. And they always related to the Boston Irish and the Boston pols, what they tried to do and where they came from and how they accomplished what they did and so on, more than Ireland itself.

---

46. Heaney was the Irish Nobel laureate.

12

Shaping Immigration

Only three generations separated Edward Kennedy from the mid-nineteenth-century potato famine that took the lives of one million Irish peasants and prompted another million inhabitants of the Emerald Isle to flee for their lives. Boston was the nearest Cunard ship terminus and offered the cheapest passage. Upward of 10 percent died in steerage on what aptly came to be called "coffin ships." More than half of those who survived to start a new life in the New World were illiterate, three-quarters of them had no trade, and starvation was common among the immigrants. They now constituted one-quarter of Boston's population. The Kennedy and Fitzgerald clans descended from these Irish refugees.

Both of Ted Kennedy's paternal grandparents had died by his birth in 1932, but his close relationship with his maternal grandfather, Honey Fitz Fitzgerald, the first Irish American mayor of Boston, ensured that the youngest of Joe and Rose Kennedy's children would be imbued with the family's Irish history. "In my family, we were vividly aware of the immigrant stories of our great-grandparents," he wrote in 2006. From his downtown Boston office window, Senator Kennedy could gaze at the building where his forebears arrived from Ireland in the late 1840s. "All found the American dream, and I have been one of its fortunate beneficiaries," he observed.[1]

The fight for fair immigration policy and his struggle for healthcare reform constituted the two most visceral concerns of his nearly half-century in public life. Upon arriving in the Senate, Kennedy asked to serve on the Judiciary Committee's Immigration Subcommittee, despite its low prestige and paltry budget. There he worked on the Immigration Act of 1965, which represented a poignant legislative tribute to his late brother, President Kennedy, who had proposed immigration equality as a senator in the late 1950s. Celebrating passage of the law was his newly elected Senate colleague, brother Robert, representing the Empire State. They both looked on as President Lyndon Johnson signed the legislation on New York's Liberty Island. The policy removed the decades-old discrimination against Asians, Africans, and Greeks, who had minuscule quotas, in contrast to favored immigrants from Britain, Germany, and Ireland.

---

1. Edward M. Kennedy, *America Back on Track* (New York: Viking, 2006), 171.

Not surprisingly, given his family's roots, Edward Kennedy maintained a sustained effort to engineer national policies that opened the nation's borders to refugees fleeing strife around the world. He chaired the Judiciary Committee's Refugee and Escapees Subcommittee, where he began making the case for providing sanctuary for those fleeing war-torn Vietnam, particularly Vietnamese spouses and children of American military personnel and those who had aided the United States in its unsuccessful struggle against communist takeover of South Vietnam.[2] Kennedy traveled the world, promoting democracy, and meeting with refugees in India and the Soviet Union. He held hearings on the victims of civil strife in Biafra and, with his two eldest children, Kara and Teddy Jr., undertook a fact-finding mission to Ethiopia and Sudan to see firsthand the causes of humanitarian crises there. The 1980 Refugee Act resulted from his efforts.

The senator could often find bipartisan support, especially with his friend, Republican senator Alan Simpson of Wyoming, in working on immigration policy.[3] But the increasing partisanship of the 1990s spilled over into the early 2000s and stymied Senator Kennedy's last major immigration battle, when he teamed with colleague John McCain to try to guide comprehensive reform through the Senate. Their attempts to find a common-sense compromise, in 2006 and 2007, between securing the nation's borders and finding a way to citizenship for illegals already in the country failed. Kennedy became increasingly disappointed by the lack of commitment on the part of Democratic leadership in the Senate and what he considered racist GOP policies, like building a wall between the United States and Mexico. Kennedy had worked productively with George W. Bush on education reform, but the senator found the president less "engaged, accessible, and available" on immigration issues. "In this age of terrorism we must obviously be vigilant about our immigration policy. But we can strengthen our security without weakening our proud heritage as a nation of immigrants," Kennedy asserted in 2006.[4]

EMK: If you take the events from the 1960s, the Portuguese, the Italians, the thing that they were principally concerned about was immigration, the national origin quotas, and the Greeks. And I was able to get something done with that. This was discrimination against them, which was very real. It was great to have the ability in the Senate to get something done that was very much for them. That was important, the fact that I was so warmly embraced and treated and received and supported in that, and then was able to do something that was right for them, and right in terms of the country as well as a source of satisfaction. A lot of them still remember a lot of that.

---

2. Vincent Bzdek, *The Kennedy Legacy: Jack, Bobby, and Ted and a Family Dream Fulfilled* (New York: St. Martin's Griffin, 2010), 172.

3. Nick Littlefield and David Nexon, *Lion of the Senate: When Ted Kennedy Rallied the Democrats in a GOP Congress* (New York: Simon and Schuster, 2015), 348.

4. Kennedy, *America Back on Track*, 172.

Q: *Are immigration issues still present* [in 2005]?

EMK: Still very similar.

Q: *But the ethnography of it has changed?*

EMK: It's changed very much. At that time, it was Italian, Portuguese, Greek, Middle Eastern, Lebanese, still some Armenian, and a handful of Asians, who had been very much squeezed out. Now their systems have been regularized. We went through a period where the Irish were still coming here, and that was a big issue, but now great numbers of them are going back. Now it's the Hispanic, Cambodian, Dominicans, Brazilians who are coming on in, and Central Americans.

Q: *Arabs? Any Arab issues—*

EMK: Some Arabs, some Muslim, probably not as many as in some other communities. There's always the distinction between an Arab, because there's a great number of Christians within the Arabs, and the Muslims. A lot of the Muslims aren't Arabs. There are still the Pakistanis and Indians.

Q: *Is that population looming any larger in your—*

EMK: Well, the Indian population is, certainly. You see the most, probably, in California, but there's an important population here [in Massachusetts].

Q: *But not a significant effect on your work or campaigning?*

EMK: Well, they're involved, they're very professional and also a lot in the medical services, biotech professional groups, doctors, professionals. They care a lot about their families, family unification. We've been working on that for years.

Q: *Right. It's less working class, more professional.*

EMK: More professional, that's right. We've seen that. That's been very different. We're working now [2005] with McCain on the immigration issue. That's had a continuing resonance because there's been a lot of injustice in the way people are treated. We have a sizeable Haitian population, and they treat the Haitians differently from the Cubans, the Haitians are different from Nicaraguans—and the Cubans differently from the Nicaraguans. I'm familiar with all those distinctions. You can gain asylum, you can be *given* asylum and still be kept in jail if you're Haitian, but not if you're from Nicaragua or El Salvador; you're released. And just that fact is a burning fact in terms of the community. It's a small one, but I follow these and keep after and have kept after these distinctions. And then some countries have the visa waiver programs, which are very important.

So for a lot of the older communities, there are still a lot of these kinds of issues; their older families care about them. There are whole new communities in Massachusetts. There's been a very dramatic—which we can come to—shift from a manufacturing society to a much more high-tech society. So there's a big demographic change and shift in that area that we can come to. And this other kind of base has obviously shrunk. But I've always maintained, and continue to maintain, the close associations with the older base, and they care a lot about it. They're still an important part of our community.

Conceptually, that's what we're trying—I have to spend a little time in getting back—I've gotten away from it, you know—to have a chance to get back into it. I'm going to do *Meet the Press* on that Sunday.

Q: This coming Sunday?

EMK: No. This coming one I'm going to do *Face the Nation*, but it's going to be on immigration because we're going to do that immigration bill markup [in 2006]. The Senate is going to be debating that immigration bill so I'm going to do that, but they'll get into other stuff.

Q: Well, you did get into immigration.

EMK: Yes, they probably got a little bit more than they were looking for, but it's rather interesting, the dimensions of that kind of thing.

Q: There's a real lack of guidance of people getting that picture about immigration. What they hear about is this fight, or that fight.

EMK: Lou Dobbs,[5] evidently they get Lou Dobbs down there. He's just so wrong on it.

Q: It's sort of conceptual pollution so that people can't get a picture. Presidents used to give that picture.

EMK: Yes. They're the ones who are supposed to be doing it, and they're the ones who have the luxury to be able to look down the road and get the best people, the task forces, persuading the people. The great senators can't because for the most part we're firemen. We're putting out fires, you know. The government lost its engine, and I've got to be doing the pension issue here now. So I spend all my time getting geared up on that or the immigration issue. I'll get geared up for that.

The idea that you're looking and have the chance to look further on out is a very limited kind of capability that most people don't have—I mean, we do a fair amount of that but it's something that's not generally done, and that's what the executive branch is supposed to be doing. If they don't do it, it doesn't get done.

Q: Well, maybe not, but it takes a new sort of campaign to get public understanding of this. It's very discouraging to be on the receiving end of all this in terms of information.

EMK: I don't know what the programming is down in New Orleans, down in Louisiana. They don't get *Meet the Press*. They don't get *Face the Nation*. They just get Fox. Rush Limbaugh, they get that part. They don't get the other things. They don't get the *New York Times*. It's not distributed down there. That's what they get and it's just unbelievable. It's not good.

---

5. Lou Dobbs was then the host of a CNN news program; he moved to the Fox Business Network in 2011 and is a noted opponent of immigration.

Senator Kennedy spoke about his grandfather Honey Fitz's stand on immigration issues.

EMK: The literacy test was one thing he had to oppose. He also had a dust-up with Cabot Lodge about the types of people who were coming in. So this was real in his mind, and he was very active and very involved. When he had the dust-up with Cabot Lodge, he went to see President Cleveland about it. I'm not sure how much progress he made, but this was in the '20s[6] when there was a good deal of both racial and ethnic tension. At the turn of the century, there was what they called the "yellow peril" in the West.

The Dillingham Commission was established and made recommendations about the types of America we should be in the '20s, and affirmed that we wanted to retain restrictions and maintain a closed-door policy. The Founding Fathers, as we all know, had a very open-door policy, and were welcoming. And obviously the Statue of Liberty and those marvelous quotes from Lazarus[7] are about welcoming the poorest of the poor into the United States. That was a different tradition than we saw both in the '20s[8] and then expressed most dramatically in the 1950s in the McCarran-Walter immigration law that established quotas based on place of birth and put restrictions on the place of birth.

There were other restrictions prior to that in other immigration bills, but these were probably the most notorious. They restricted the numbers of immigrants to just a small fraction of what the numbers had been before the real flow of immigrants began. I think the Portuguese got maybe four or five hundred. The Greeks got three or four hundred, the Italians maybe a thousand, and the Irish had thirty thousand. The Scandinavian countries were virtually unlimited. So it was very targeted.

The conversations that my grandpa had with my brother Jack at that time obviously had a very important influence on him, because one of the first books he [Jack] wrote was *Nation of Immigrants*, which is very well done, and talks about prejudice and discrimination against immigrants. It was published in the 1950s and outlined an alternative immigration policy that advocated knocking down the walls of discrimination and emphasized

---

6. Actually 1890s.

7. Emma Lazarus was a nineteenth-century American poet whose famous lines are enshrined at the based of the Statue of Liberty:

Give me your tired, your poor,
Your huddled masses yearning to breathe free,
The wretched refuse of your teeming shore.
Send these, the homeless, tempest-tost to me,
I lift my lamp beside the golden door!

8. The 1924 Immigration Act.

family reunification, special skills, and refugees. It's interesting that those themes keep coming back up, in the Hesburgh Commission and the Jordan Commission[9] later on.

Q: I think another thing in that book was what immigration contributes to the country. It wasn't just over the barriers that were put up. That was a pro-immigrant and pro-immigration policy, that we needed these people.

EMK: He [JFK] pointed out that whether you're talking about the church or music or the arts or culture or politics, children of immigrants have made an extraordinary contribution over the history of the country. Back at the time of Bunker Hill, more O'Briens died than anybody else. There were Irish immigrants during that period, even before the Revolution. Grandpa always had these little tidbits and stories.

The point we're trying to review is that we had a sense about discrimination against the Irish, discrimination against ethnic groups, and that there were laws that perpetuated it. There was this sense from Grandpa about the unfairness and injustice of those laws, and he could see them up front in Boston and could see, as he traveled, the increasing offense it gave in terms of our country being truly a democratic country. That was something that was evident in my early life. I still have one of those window signs from Grandpa's time in the House in Washington, "No Irish need apply."

There are lessons from my observations about my brother's experience in the Senate and about how he worked with other people, and that comes back to how I've worked on immigration. I always try to work in a very strong bipartisan way. This morning I was thinking about the indicators that contributed to that viewpoint, and it was the observation I had about my brother Jack working with Saltonstall.

They had a New England Senate group, and my brother was very involved in that when he was first elected to the Senate. His maiden speech was on how to develop Massachusetts and the New England economy. He worked with Senator Saltonstall rather closely, and he by nature and disposition was rather a positive politician in terms of looking for opportunities to move ahead and make progress. He worked with other senators, and it was a different kind of tradition than the harsh politics where you can't get ahead unless you push someone else down. He understood that people could move together and have a positive outcome—even if others made progress, even if your adversaries made progress, there could be a positive outcome. That was a lesson, certainly eventually in Northern Ireland, but it was a lesson he brought to the Senate, an important lesson.

---

9. Father Theodore Hesburgh was the president of Notre Dame when appointed by President Eisenhower to head the Civil Rights Commission in 1957. The US Commission on Immigration Reform, chaired by Texas congresswoman Barbara Jordan, was established by Congress in 1990.

I remember, right after I won the Senate seat, getting a card from Eddie McCormack, who I ran against in a very hotly contested [1962 Democratic] primary. I beat him. It was a very tough primary. So I had just gotten into the Senate, and I got this card about Eddie McCormack returning to law. I remember bringing that down and showing it to my brother, and I said, "You know that Eddie McCormack. I'll never forget how tough and mean he was to me."

My brother just laughed and said, "I'll tell you what you do. For the rest of time you're in the Senate, just at election time, have a successful fundraiser, and then call Eddie McCormack and ask him if he'll do a fundraiser for you, and leak how much you expect from him. Then, when he has that fundraiser, raises that money for you, when you pick up all the checks and walk out, you can smile. That will be the best way to get back at Eddie McCormack." He was thinking in those terms rather than going after someone with spikes and knees and the rest.

Now we arrive in the Senate [in 1962]. I was elected to the Senate, and President Kennedy had been interested in immigration and wrote that book, as I pointed out, and had been involved in it in a tangential way when he was in the Senate. And when Bobby [Kennedy] was attorney general, he was involved. They made a presentation about that time, '63, before the Judiciary Committee. So it was going to be an issue.

It was obviously a civil rights issue, and although the civil rights issues as we think of them are rooted in a different tradition, when you look at this, the basic fundamental elements of hostility and bigotry and prejudice and discrimination were evidenced in terms of the ethnic politics of Massachusetts and most of the industrial states. So you had the elements of the civil rights movement and also the elements of discrimination and bigotry that existed in immigration and in immigration policy. We saw what had happened here in the United States during World War II, with the Japanese internment. This is all very much a part of the evolution of our democratic liberties.

When I arrived in the Senate, I was appointed to the Judiciary Committee and the Labor Committee. We're all appointed to what they call two "A committees." The Judiciary Committee was chaired by Jim Eastland and he asked me, as the only new member on that Judiciary Committee, to think about what subcommittees I wanted. He said for me to come to see him the first part of the following week. So I thought long and hard and talked to different friends about the committees.

The subcommittee I was very much interested in was the Immigration Subcommittee, which was a rather sleepy subcommittee, but it seemed to me that this offered an opportunity to be even more involved and engaged in the immigration issue. Its focus was immigration and refugees. It was the least desirable of the subcommittees because of both the subject matter generally and it had the smallest budget. I think it had a budget of $100,000 or so.

You got only one staffer if you took that assignment. If you got one of the other committees, like Administrative Practice or another one, if you got to be chairman of it, you got additional kinds of resources. We didn't have many staff people at that time, so there was always a lot of jockeying around to see who could try to get ahead in that field.

Q: Could you talk a little bit about why you wanted to be on such an unprestigious committee, such a sleepy committee, not just in terms of your and your brothers' and your family's interest in immigration, but did you have something in mind by doing that? Did you believe you could really make a difference?

EMK: Well, this was an issue I was interested in, and I knew I could be involved in, and there was a real absence of much leadership in the Senate on it. I knew that my brothers were going to address this issue, so it seemed to me a great opportunity, an opening, in terms of having some impact on public policy issues.

Q: So you had obviously given some thought—you may not remember all this, but you had made up your mind by '63 that those were what you wanted. I think it's very interesting that that was your choice.

EMK: Those were the areas I was interested in and wanted to work on.

Q: Immigration came first, didn't it? That was your first?

EMK: Immigration was the first one, and I became chairman of that subcommittee rapidly, I think within a year. It was a small subcommittee, but I became the chairman of it, and I was on the other committees. This is where the action was. Legislation had been introduced, sent to the Congress by my brothers.

Q: In July of '63 he [President Kennedy] submitted an immigration bill. And I think Hart and Celler drafted it. Did you have a hand in the drafting of that? You were brand new.

EMK: Probably not. When you're in the Senate, you have one legislative assistant, one administrative assistant. So unless your legislative assistant knew an awful lot about the subject matter, they are just basically worked out through the administration. I think more likely than not it was drafted by the Justice Department, and they got people to draft different sections of the bill and put people on it. It's somewhat different now, but that was certainly the way it was done.

Q: So, the bill went nowhere.

EMK: No. The bill didn't go any place at all. That was July '63. In the latter part of '63, I lost my brother. Then the major effort on civil rights came up in '64, which was Johnson, which got all the focus and attention in '64 and took an incredible amount of time and energy. Then until we got that conference in June or July of '64, and then I had my plane crash and was in the hospital for seven months. But when I was in the hospital, I worked on immigration. I read a lot about immigration. People came in and talked to me about immigration.

I used to have, particularly the last three months I was in the hospital, hour-long seminars.

Q: Johnson, I believe in his State of the Union in early '65, came out very strongly for a policy change, immigration reform, and he picked up the bill, the Hart-Celler bill idea that your brother had inspired. There's an account of a meeting he called at the White House at that time. It was a snowy day in January of '65, just before or just after the State of the Union, in which he—you were there. Do I have this right? Were you back in the Senate?

EMK: Yes.

Q: You were there, a lot of congressmen were there, and various immigration groups were there. This was written up in the New York Times. *Johnson said, "This is something we're going to do and we're behind on it and we're going to get it done." That's when immigration reform really got pretty high on the agenda, and you got very much involved in it. It was your first putting together of a coalition in the Senate, wasn't it?*

EMK: That's right, yes. It was my first major piece of legislation, both in terms of shaping it and conducting the hearings on it, and getting it through the committee, and getting it to the floor, and effectively floor-managing it. Johnson said that he wanted public accommodations in the Civil Rights Act. He had three or four major issues that my brother had been interested in, and he included this one, which was the green light and got the priority, got the notice from the leadership that the House was going to do the hearings and we were too.

Q: You gave a fairly full account of what the opposition was and the way you went about this; it was a very workmanlike job. Do you have any personal recollections?

EMK: The real issue at the time, which has resonated over the years, is the element of the discrimination that already exists in this country. And the second thing is the immigration bill itself. But the important thing was the issue of illegal immigration, and how people tied immigration with illegal immigration, and mixed those up. It was very important that if you were going to get an immigration bill, they had to be separated. You were going to have an immigration bill that was going to deal with the parts that were unfair and unjust. And you're also going to be busy with the illegal aspects of it.

People were very strongly against immigration because they think only of illegal immigration, but you have to separate those two issues and have people understand that you're serious about addressing the illegal immigration issues. Then they'll listen to you about fixing the legal immigration issues. That was one of the very important points, and it's still the key aspect today. The last bills [I worked on with John McCain in 2005–6] were defeated because of all the focus on the illegal immigration issues. When that becomes paramount, you lose the argument in terms of trying to do something about having a responsible legal immigration policy.

The second part, which was very evident to me, is the role of the economy: if the economy's going to be shaky, even if you're able to separate the legal from the illegal immigration issues, you're going to have a lot of difficulty because you're talking about the dangers of individuals replacing either your jobs or taking your home, threatening your existence, and there's always fear of the unknown. If the economy is expanding and growing it is different—but you remember, in the early '60s it was flat.

President Kennedy had put in to cut taxes [to stimulate the economy], but the time when we began to hit the [immigration] issue in '65, the economy began to grow. So we saw the difference in terms of the atmosphere and the climate, the willingness of people to try to deal with the issue, because it was an expanding and growing economy. What you have at another time, at the current time [2007], is enormous uncertainty in terms of the middle class, and that's reflected in apprehension about what's going to happen on the other side.

Q: It seems in retrospect, comparatively, that it was easy to put together a coalition that would make this major reform in immigration policy. The fly in the ointment was what you had to give to get the national origins quota system out and to strengthen family reunification. The opponents came up with the idea of a cap on Western Hemisphere immigration. You fought that and did not win that, in '65, but you kept at it. That had to do with Mexican immigration.

EMK: Mexican and the West Indies.

Q: And maybe Cuba.

EMK: That came up towards the end of the debate. They put the limitation, although there hadn't been a limitation before that time.

Q: That's right.

EMK: So you would have had people coming from these areas—other regions, in any event. They appointed a Western Hemisphere Commission, and the only way we could override the limitations was if the commission made a recommendation that was adopted. Then they would lift the—

Q: Right. And you were on that commission.

EMK: Yes, but we knew they weren't going to let that thing go. It was interesting. Bobby recommended to me that we ought to let it go, that we shouldn't pass the '65 Act. He recommended that we let the thing slip. He said, "It will be a bigger deal next year. If you get a focus on it, it will be a bigger deal next year. You'll win it next year, but you can't win it now."

I said, "I think we ought to try and take it now," which we ended up doing. I remember talking with him about the Western Hemisphere restrictions on the bill—it wasn't a big cloud because there was so much interest in abolishing the national origin quota and the Asian Pacific Triangle.[10]

Q: There was a lot of local interest.

---

10. "An individual with one or more Asian parent, born anywhere in the world and possessing the citizenship of any nation, would be counted under the national quota of the Asian nation of his or her ethnicity or against a generic quota for the 'Asian Pacific Triangle.' Low quota numbers and a uniquely racial construction for how to apply them ensured that total Asian immigration after 1952 would remain very limited." See "The Immigration and

EMK: An enormous amount. It was a big deal.

Q: That was the focus there. In a sense that's the start of what became the big illegal problem, crossing the border, because there was pretty free passage across the border until a cap of 120,000 from the Western Hemisphere was instituted. That meant that if there was a draw of jobs over here, they would cross illegally.

EMK: It did, but you had that magnet effect happening. It was as much a product of the times as it was the legislation. It's the movement of people, and you see the movements and migration now in other parts of the world. The border was virtually open, even though, if you look back at the time, in the legislation, we doubled or tripled the border security. But it still didn't make much of a difference.

Although you have to remember that one of the elements of immigration evident during this period was the Bracero Program [1942–64]. This was, outside of slavery, the most heinous policy the government has supported and tolerated. It first permitted significant numbers—hundreds of thousands— of [Mexican] agriculture workers to come in and work in California and the western states under subhuman conditions, and the program paid the workers through the banks back in Mexico. A good many of them never got paid, and it exploited these individuals in the most intolerable way. This was an issue that was bubbling up as well during that period. Actually, the Bracero Program was ended just about—

Q: Sixty-four.

EMK: —this time as well, although the elements of it continued, exploitation of these workers. But the rest of the program itself stopped. When the program itself stopped, more people began to flow in here. When they had the Bracero Program, the total numbers were moderated, but my own sense is that the explosion of these numbers is related to the conditions in Mexico. The dramatic expansion of their population, dramatic expansion of the American economy, demand, our move west and south, and the failure of Mexico to try to develop any kind of program to deal with these individuals.

Q: I'm glad you're mentioning this, because when the big immigration reform of '65 came out—and there's been a lot written about it and what happened by almost everybody—very few people made any mention of the Western Hemisphere cap or the Mexican problem, which was not solved by that immigration reform. In fact, from their point of view, it was like putting a national origins quota on, though it set a Western Hemisphere quota. While you're taking away all the others, you're putting a cap across the border. It does seem to me today that problem has just returned and returned and returned until it's the dominant issue.

Nationality Act of 1952 (The McCarran-Walter Act), in "Milestones in the History of US Foreign Relations—1945–52," U.S. Department of State, Office of the Historian, https:// history.state.gov/milestones/1945-1952/immigration-act.

EMK: I think Bracero ended as a program, but these extraordinary conditions still remained. We went down to Texas and did some hearings in the summer of '67. We talked about the Texas Rangers being the enforcers of this program and how they still exploited migrant workers in the fields.

This is something my brother Bobby picked up in '66 with César Chávez, and was very much involved in, in terms of economic justice. After the Bracero Program ended, all the workers who were still left here had to fend for themselves. They continued to be exploited, although there weren't as many moving back and forth. We were helping them get organized and exercise their rights. There was extraordinary conflict between the growers and the workers.

I compare the hostility between them to the situation three days ago when I was in a meeting in Dianne Feinstein's[11] office with four of the principal growers, the head of the Growers Association and Arturo Rodriguez, who is head of the United Farm Workers union. They were all sitting together and going over names in the United States Senate, for a bill that both of them are supporting. It will bring the workers good wages, health benefits, housing, and will permit them to organize but guarantee a workforce for the growers.

This is an incredible transition in terms of atmosphere and climate—what they call the AgJOBS Bill, which we may or may not get passed.[12] It's an incredible legacy from that period, which has eventually turned out to be somewhat more hopeful out of necessity, because now, with the increased border security and patrols on the southwest border, it's slowed down, in a very important way, the movement of people from Mexico to work in agribusiness. So now a lot of the growers are actually moving to Mexico and buying land down there where they don't have the hiring problems, and it's having a very significant impact on the growers in California.

Q: I think I can follow the transition here, from when you get into the '80s. You and Hart and Javits were working together on this in the Senate, and you were successful with the compromise you struck on Western Hemisphere migration principle. But you got the other things. In 1980, you did the Refugee Bill. I don't know whether you remember that, but it took the refugee problem out of the standard immigration policy and made a separate system of it. Do you have anything to say about that?

EMK: Well, yes. The problems with refugees, the most notable one, the Vietnamese refugees, were increasing. But also, there were other kinds of refugees from the Middle East. There had been turmoil in the mid-'70s. Even in Lebanon and Africa.

Q: Eastern Europe also.

---

11. Feinstein is a Democratic senator from California.

12. Congress did not pass the Agriculture Job Opportunities, Benefits, and Security bill, which would have established a process for earned legalization for undocumented farm workers and implemented reforms of the agricultural guest-worker program.

EMK: They were still coming from Eastern Europe. In Eastern Europe in '56 there was the Hungarian Revolution. The Hesburgh Commission was initially set up to look at refugees from communist countries, and then we took it and moved to look into refugees generally. In the '70s we had the refugees from Bangladesh. Bangladesh got independence, and they had ten million refugees. As I mentioned, the real challenge was what we were going to do with refugees from Southeast Asia. It was very clear. We were willing to take some refugees, but we had no clear policy about how we were going to treat them. We basically took recommendations from the Hesburgh Commission.

Q: The Hesburgh Commission recommended that, but before they submitted their report, we got a refugee bill.

EMK: We had a refugee bill that had to respect and use the definition of refugees that was accepted internationally. There were different phases. We had the migrant health bill in the early '70s, and that was really a result of hearings I had done down in Florida and in other places. We found out that these migrant worker women had four times the number of stillborn deaths because of all the pesticides and herbicides and insecticides they were inhaling. The health conditions, particularly of women and children, were just abhorrent, and we passed migrant health legislation.

So we had different bits and pieces of legislation all during this period, and then we had the refugee bill. I went over [1971] and walked along the border between India and Bangladesh in a couple of days. I saw all these small Indian villages accepting the Bengalis, although the villagers were terribly poor. They accepted all these refugees. We shaped a refugee bill under President Ford, in '76 or so, '77, about Vietnamese refugees.

We eventually took about eight or nine hundred thousand Vietnamese. The first people who got on the boat had been down in a place they called Vung Tau in Vietnam, where the people who had done contracting with Americans all came from. They left there and got out very early, but we didn't take in the people who had really worked with the Americans, a situation like we have at the present time with the translators in Iraq. We didn't take in those individuals, but we didn't have large bloodbaths. There was some personal recrimination in the communities, but they never had big bloodbaths in Vietnam.

A lot of the people who had been very loyal to the United States went to re-education camps for five, maybe seven or eight years. So after we took these seven or eight hundred thousand refugees, we got tired of taking them, and we cut back on Vietnamese refugees at a time when many of these people who had been loyal to us were just getting out of prison. We had a lot of trouble getting some of those people who really deserved to be taken in, because they had risked everything for Americans and American lives.

We were interested in a lot of these ancillary kinds of issues in terms of refugees. We were also interested in a number from South Africa, and what was happening with apartheid. This was becoming an increasing issue and problem, which eventually resulted in my going down there. But that's another issue for another time. The '80 [United States Refugee] Act was a good act.

Q: It was a breakthrough. It was the first time we had a policy.

EMK: A humane policy. It was very good.

Q: And it separated refugees from issues of immigration policy. Otherwise, you would have had a much, much more—

EMK: It was interesting because we obviously had differences with [Jimmy] Carter on a lot of issues, but on human rights he did well. You have to give the president his due and credit for that. A lot of it was the fact that he had Cy Vance,[13] who was very interested in human rights, and a very active State Department that was very involved in human rights issues. I think during that period we got probably support from the Justice Department down there as well. This was the end, you know, before the '80 election.

Q: Homelessness surged among these international people during this period, because of both violence and disruption, and this is the almost purely humanitarian, not the economic consequence. I think that this aspect has not been sufficiently noticed. It was a real triumph, I felt, in 1980 to do that.

EMK: We would take in probably seventy thousand to eighty thousand refugees every year in the United States. It's incredible. The last years since 9/11, we're down to about forty thousand because of all the difficulty in the processing. We have taken groups of refugees—it's amazing. We've gotten them settled, and it's like no other country. Even with the numbers cut back, we're still far, far, far ahead, and most of that goes back to that '80 Act.

Q: Getting back to immigration, we could move ahead.

EMK: There were several parts of my maiden speech in the Senate in 1964, which was on civil rights. The last part of it deals with the Civil Rights Act itself and why that ought to be supported, and relates to the circumstances we had in Massachusetts. But the earlier part talks a good deal about the issues of assimilation in the state, and how 40 percent of the population in Massachusetts was not native-born—the largest percent of any state in the country—and about how a Catholic, in 1780, couldn't vote in Massachusetts, and how a Jew couldn't get a place to stay in the Berkshires. And the blacks were locked into their own education system because of the failure in housing.

It talks about some of the ethnic conditions that existed in the state at that time and the fact that Massachusetts moved ahead in working through those circumstances, for the most part—not all, but for the most part—and became a better, fairer place. And using that as an example of assimilation, it could do it as well with regard to Negroes (as they were referred to then; referred now to as blacks) because we've had lessons from our experience in immigration.

---

13. Cyrus Vance was secretary of state.

The second major part was the reliance on bringing the people of faith to enlighten public policy. There were moral issues that were related to this whole issue and question, and here, just as men and women of faith can inform and enlighten in terms of public policy—the morality of war and peace and poverty and the death penalty—they can enlighten with regard to discrimination and bigotry and prejudice. That's the enlightened aspect of religion: bringing a moral perspective to public policy issues, as distinguished from the interference of religion in terms of personal morality, which is what we've seen today.

I think the fact of Cardinal Cushing speaking about immigration and immigration reform, leaders of the Episcopal Church speaking about it, the Jewish community speaking about it as well, gave this debate a moral tone about how we're going to treat each other and that we're all God's children, so to speak. That same kind of tone was what we tried to do in the more recent immigration, not as successfully as previously—we can come back to why when we talk about that period.

This was a very important aspect, the importance of this issue in relationship to the fundamental values of our country and what "American" stands for in terms of valuing individuals—paraphrasing Dr. King—valuing them for the content of their character and not the color of their skin. And I think that this is an important factor in terms of the general immigration issue historically that too frequently is missed.

Q: Yes. And that was there from the beginning. The Catholic Conference of Bishops in '65 was a major voice for immigration—and the National Council of Churches and Jewish organizations as well. Then you have on the other side the Daughters of the American Revolution, the patriotic societies, the American Legion, and so on. Behind the coalition for reform is this moral—doing what's right and doing what's best for the country.

EMK: So, here we are in '65. We had had the strong support within the administration. We had been working hard; '64 had been a big year in terms of the Civil Rights Act. And 1965 was the big year for the Voting Rights Act. I was chairman of the Refugee Subcommittee, conducting the hearings, putting together the strategy, and working with our colleagues on the Judiciary Committee. We were also reaching out to the House side, where Cellar and Rodino[14] were the principal figures.

When we got to the floor on the immigration reform bill, as I mentioned earlier, the one big stumbling block was the group of southerner and westerner Senators who wanted to get more control of immigration through a limitation of the Western Hemisphere flow. That delayed the bill a few days, and for a short period of time it made its passage somewhat uncertain. Eventually

---

14. New Jersey congressman Peter Rodino was a Democrat.

we were able to get an agreement taking this amendment, which put a limitation on the Western Hemisphere flow.

We were able to get it passed by a vote that was very similar to the final votes on the civil rights bill, somewhere around seventy-three or seventy-four to eighteen. They had a signing ceremony at the Statue of Liberty.

Q: Of those three—the eighteen-year-old vote, the poll tax, and immigration—as you look back on it, which of those was the most far-reaching?

EMK: I think the immigration bill, because of the really egregious aspects of the immigration law that was so discriminatory in its form and substance and shape. The poll tax was too, to some extent, but they both were rooted in denying people participation in the democratic process. These were all important measures, but obviously the immigration issue was at the heart, and my first major legislative undertaking and success. I guess the eighteen-year-old vote was probably later on, as I remember it now. It went back to 1970.

Q: We're talking about the problems in the current century, today [2007], and we start out with President [George W.] Bush and Vicente Fox[15] pledging to work together to solve the Mexican immigration problem or the illegal immigration problem, and that seems to be going well, right up until the moment of 9/11. And then immigration drops off the radar. Then, in 2004, you start talking with McCain, and it looks like there are possibilities for a bipartisan effort to address the perceived problems about immigration, so-called illegal immigration. Do you want to talk about your conversations with McCain and why you thought it was a promising moment?

EMK: McCain from Arizona, a border state, had started working on some immigration legislation, and had mentioned in casual conversations to me—I think probably in 2004, that maybe we could find a way of working together. I believe sometime in late 2004 we sat down and had our staffs sit down to go over some general concepts. It seemed like there was a real possibility. We had some important differences, particularly with regard to workers' rights, avoiding worker exploitation, and some other provisions, but nonetheless we were able to work at the staff level and work very well with him on the McCain-Kennedy legislation, which we eventually introduced, and which eventually, in one form or another, got to the floor.

It recognized what I considered to be the most important feature, the fact that we have twelve million people here, and that that number is growing constantly, and that they are living in fear, fear of deportation, fear of prosecution, fear in terms of their own future. He was very interested in a temporary worker program, and business was interested, and the Chamber of Commerce was interested in a temporary worker program. I was concerned about workers' rights. Workers' rights meant not only the prevailing wage issues and protection from

---

15. Fox was Mexico's president.

exploitation, but the most important was that the workers would be able to move toward earned citizenship.

They could either be petitioned by their employer, or they could become permanent residents through self-petitioning. We had a similar kind of feature in what they call the H-1B program, which are the high-tech workers. There were all kinds of issues. Should families be able to come with temporary workers? What were the annual numbers going to be? How long were they going to be able to work here? What would be the working conditions? There were a lot of very complex and difficult issues to be worked through.

In any event, we worked through most of them. The feature that was most important in this whole effort was that we had a very strong nucleus of Republicans and a very strong nucleus of Democrats. We met every morning and at least once more during the course of the day, when we had this legislation up before the committee. With the Republicans, we had McCain, who cared about this issue and was knowledgeable about it, and we had Martinez,[16] from Florida, who also understood the issue and had a good deal of emotion involved in the issue, as a former refugee.

We had Lindsey Graham, who was learning about it and glad to learn about it. He got sort of a kick out of being part of the whole process. We had Hagel, who had some background. He had his own legislation and was interested in the subject matter. He had worked with Senator Daschle previously on some legislation. Brownback, a new person, was brought on by McCain, but was concerned about the exploitation of workers and the human and divided family aspects of immigration. Then there was Specter, who was on the Judiciary Committee and had some interest from a long time in the past. We went through a series of meetings ourselves. That was on the first bill, and we were able to get it passed in the Senate.[17]

In 2007, the second time we dealt with immigration, we had a group that included McCain, but he was running for president, so he was not around very much. We had Martinez, but by that year he was the chairman of the Republican National Committee, so he couldn't involve himself as much as he wanted to earlier. We had Hagel, who was in the process of leaving the Senate, and who had lost a good deal of interest in immigration. We had Brownback, who was running for president and switched his position, and we had Lindsey Graham, who was up for re-election and who stayed the course pretty well. They were replaced by other Republicans. And we had Specter, but he's hot and cold on this issue and unable to deliver.

---

16. Senator Melquiades Martinez was a Republican.

17. Senators Graham, Charles Hagel, Brownback, and Specter were all Republicans, from South Carolina, Iowa, Kansas, and Pennsylvania, respectively. Tom Daschle was a South Dakota Democrat and leader of his party in the Senate.

They were replaced by Kyl,[18] who was strongly against any kind of immigration reform in the first 2006 bill, and who we had to deal with in the second bill in 2007. He was knowledgeable and was forceful, and had the White House on his side. So this is the genesis of the dramatic shift between the first bill and the second bill, the strength of the team.

As to Democrats, the 2007 group was basically me and Salazar, who was terrific all the way through. Menendez[19] was part of the team in the beginning but then fell off because of the point system and the fact that we had included provisions to end "chain migration." He did not really feel strongly about it. Durbin, who was most interested in the DREAM[20] Act, his own proposal, was somewhat interested in the total bill, but not nearly as strong as he was certainly in the first 2006 efforts, until the very end of the second 2007 effort. We had Barack,[21] who was somewhat interested in it the first effort in 2006 and then was not around the second time because he was also running for president.

So the basic architecture of all this really fell to Salazar and me on the Democratic side, and a very weak Republican team. On the Republican side, even though Kyl was with us on this compromise, he was unable to bring anyone with him and was backed by the White House— Chertoff and Gutierrez— who sat in all the meetings, and Joel Kaplan, who was also a staffer.[22]

They would bring a raft of lawyers from either the White House or the Justice Department who supported their positions on the bill we were drafting. Cornyn[23] was very troublesome and sat through many, many of the meetings in support of Kyl and continued to pull him away from the bill. So the dynamics of what had been a very strong effort the first time in 2006 had shifted and changed dramatically and significantly, and it was a most important shift. Plus we had effectively lost the high ground, the high ground being that in the first bill we were addressing national security concerns, because we were looking at the great numbers of people coming into this country, the four, five, six hundred thousand coming in, and we couldn't have a border that was open like that in a time when we had national security concerns.

We were also addressing the relationship with Mexico, and we were addressing the moral issue, how we were going to treat each other. You had the Catholic Cardinal Mahoney,[24] who was very involved in both the first

---

18. Jon Kyl was a Republican senator from Arizona.
19. Senators Kenneth Salazar and Robert Menendez were from Colorado and New Jersey, respectively.
20. Development, Relief, and Education for Alien Minors.
21. Obama was then a Democratic senator from Illinois.
22. Michael Chertoff was secretary of homeland security, Carlos Gutierrez secretary of commerce, and Kaplan White House deputy chief of staff for policy.
23. John Cornyn is a Republican senator from Texas.
24. Richard Mahoney was the cardinal of Los Angeles.

and the second efforts, but primarily the first. We were addressing the fact that even those who were coming here on a temporary basis were going to be treated fairly and were going to have an opportunity to obtain citizenship. That quieted labor, whose support we didn't have the second time, so we had a very tough time in 2007.

Q: Labor pulled away?

EMK: Labor was strongly against the 2007 bill, with the exception of a couple of unions. In 2006 there was the series of mistakes in the management of the legislation as a result of the leadership, in working the bill on the floor. Before the 2006 bill came to the floor, it had gone through a Judiciary Committee markup, and Frist had indicated that he was going to call up his own bill, which was a very bad bill. It didn't have the components for dealing with twelve million people, and was basically a Chamber of Commerce bill.

With the first bill we went through the Judiciary Committee for markup, and Specter introduced his substitute, which in effect included a great many of the bad provisions in the House legislation. The House legislation had in it what they call Title II, a lot of provisions denying rights and protections to immigrant workers that had initially been developed by Gingrich years before, and had been part of a right-wing bank of ideas about how to short-change or undermine refugee rights and liberties. So Specter introduced his proposal that had the essentials of the McCain-Kennedy bill but put in a lot of the bad provisions. Specter indicated that he'd be willing to take many of those out between the time it got out of committee to the time we got to the floor.

Q: Many of the bad things?

EMK: Many of the bad things, what they call the Title II provisions, which are the notorious provisions eliminating discretion of judges and providing for deportations without appeal, holding people for a long period of time without sharing evidence—a lot of very harsh provisions. I talked to the head of the American Bar Association, and they said they'd be glad to review these provisions with Specter, and Specter said he'd sit down with the head of the Bar Association. It was never done. Specter never did any of that. He basically just stiffed us.

We had a long markup, the last day starting at 9 o'clock in the morning and ending at 6 o'clock at night, and I thought at 4:30 or 5 o'clock, "We're never going to end the markup." We were supposed to have a cloture vote on the Frist bill in the middle of the week, unless we got something out of our committee, and then finally late, late in the day, Sessions let the bill come out of committee and it got put on the floor.

In the markup, we were able to make some very small changes in the particularly harsh language we had inherited from the House bill written by Sensenbrenner. The other provisions of the bill stayed in there. Then we had a series of different floor amendments, but the harshest amendments, the meanest amendments, were the ones offered by Ensign[25] and Sessions. They said that if an immigrant was on his way to becoming a citizen, fulfilling all the requirements—which is that they demonstrate a work record, pay their taxes, are willing to pay the fines, are learning English—they would become a citizen over a long period of time. At that time I think it was twelve years to become a citizen, under that bill. Even then they would never be able to get the earned income tax credit for their children, which was a purely punitive and discriminatory provision.

People who got out of prison for rape or for armed robbery or for murder or whatever would be able to get earned income tax for their children, but immigrants couldn't. They were going to take away the savings of immigrants if they had paid into Social Security, effectively take away all of their savings so that they couldn't be used in terms of any retirement program. It was a series of absolutely punitive, mean-spirited, and basically racist amendments that passed the Senate.

I've said at other times that the three issues that bring out the worst in terms of the functions of the Senate are civil rights, the debates on gay rights, and immigration. All one has to do is go back and look at the first debates on Ryan White, and the amendments that Jesse Helms put in, and the mean-spiritedness of that debate. Immigration starts out as reasonably sanitized, and then—as we have seen recently, in 2006 and 2007—basically deteriorates into racist amendments and racism on the floor of the Senate. It's been dressed a different way, but I've said that it's the same music we heard in the early '60s with different words. It's blatant and flagrant, and it's basically from the same states that elected senators who were the last to accept the progress we made with the civil rights bills.

Now in the Senate, under the leadership of Reid, we had a sense that bills have to be completed within a certain period of time. This is a newer phenomenon of modern times. When we had the civil rights bills in '64, it was weeks or months before we finally got to conclusions on them. Even before President Bush, we had about a six- or seven-week debate on the Elementary and Secondary Education Bill. We've been weeks on different proposals. We had the '76 tax bill. There are six different sections, and we took six weeks to conclude.

After about five days, Harry Reid wants to conclude the floor debate, and there is building—among some of the Republicans and even some Democrats—increasing anxiety about this bill, and the number of amendments. There wasn't an agreement on the number of amendments. We were hearing different numbers, and Harry Reid was saying that these numbers of Republican

---

25. Congressman James Sensenbrenner was a Wisconsin Republican; Senator John Ensign was a Republican from Nevada.

amendments were twenty, and that he couldn't go ahead with floor debate. I'd hear from the Republicans who were working with us that they could bring it down to maybe six or eight amendments, and that we ought to go ahead with votes.

We had a situation where, as we were moving through some of these amendments, we were getting some amendments that were particularly bad, as I've just outlined here. They had a fence amendment, to put a big fence along the border. Chertoff had briefed all of us and said there are areas where there ought to be fencing, but there are other areas that are a waste of time and money and energy to fence. But they had a long, long fence, and I think we had only sixteen or eighteen people who voted against that amendment.

You could see increasingly on the floor of the Senate, the increasing apprehension and fear: what have we got ourselves into? We saw that in our Democratic caucus with a number of senators wondering why we were considering this immigration bill. We ought to be doing energy or some other kinds of things.

I remember very clearly that two of the really excellent statements and speeches in support of the immigration bill were Lieberman and Biden on the first bill in 2006. Then on the second bill, a year later, Salazar made a floor speech that was just breathtaking. He talked about immigration, how his family has lived here for four hundred years, within a 250-mile radius. They lived down in New Mexico, and it was part of Spain and Mexico, and then they moved up to Colorado, eight generations ago. He talked about how his family has been looking at the mountains and the rivers and the streams for eight generations, and he asked why he shouldn't be able to be valued on his own.

It had a really dramatic impact in terms of the Democratic caucus. It just quieted things down. This was on the '07 bill. He was just a giant. His statement was about English and the English language, whether it's going to be a national language or whether we ought to have it as a unifying language. You have these individuals like Inhofe,[26] who were interested in undermining the bill, stressing and emphasizing that English will be the national language. Salazar would get everyone talking, and the Inhofe amendment carried about sixty-five to thirty-five.[27] Then we had an amendment by Salazar saying that English should be a unifying language, and that carried about fifty-two or fifty-three to thirty-five.[28] So they both passed and it softened the impact, but it was just the power of his own history.

There was an amendment about permitting local police to pick up suspected troublemakers if they had reason to believe the people they were picking up may have committed a crime. This was rather interesting. Just at that moment,

---

26. James Inhofe was a Republican senator from Oklahoma.
27. Actually 64 to 33.
28. Actually 58 to 39.

I was standing down in the well, where the floor manager stands, and a page came running up to Menendez and said, "Senator Martinez, here's a note for you. Call your office." And Menendez said, "We all look alike, don't we?" He took the note and went back and gave a rip-roaring speech. He gave a talk and just said, "We all look alike, don't we?" It was what it's all about, just to illustrate the point. The poor page didn't know. Someone said, "It's that fellow out there on the floor."

But as I mentioned, there was an amazing amount of emotion and feeling and passion out there, exhibited by both the people who were for the bill and the people who were against it. You read through those discussions and debates, and you just see that. As a result, you have these global politics. You have the global politics now, as we're coming into elections, into '07. We had it coming into '06 as well, with the Democrats saying, "Why are we doing immigration?" This was Schumer and Reid, and to some extent Durbin.

They said, "If we do immigration, our people are going to have a lot of tough votes, a lot of hard votes that they're going to have a tough time explaining. It will make them more vulnerable, particularly if we're going to try to win. We're going to end up in conference. We'll probably get snookered"—and they use the word snookered over there—"if we get a conference, and we'll end up with a bad bill, and then we'll be stuck with it."

This was the first point: "Let's not have a bill come out, and then not get cloture on the Frist bill and blame the Republicans, and pick up the pieces with the Hispanics. That's what it's there for." I said, "It's because the Hispanics are much smarter than you think. If you think Hispanics are going to buy into that and not see through it, we don't understand politics. They're going to see through this thing, and they're not going to understand. When finally we have a Democratic majority, Hispanics are not going to understand why we're not trying to get immigration reform passed. They're not going to understand it. Maybe you can explain it. Maybe these fellows can tell Reid, and maybe he can explain it, but I'm not going to be able to explain it." And that was the dichotomy.

Q: *Within the Democrats.*

EMK: The Democrats. This is the failure of leadership to say, "We have to start, and this is it. I say we have to go to the wall. If we don't make it, we're going to have done our best; it's going to be the right thing to have done; it's going to be the right thing from a political point of view. Sure, there are going to be some tough votes, but that's what we get paid for here." But they were tentative, constantly tentative. We want to do this enough so that we can get the Hispanic votes, but not enough so that we get our people caught in it.

Q: *So it was really gaming the whole issue.*

EMK: Gaming the whole issue. It was the principal tentativeness that undermined the whole legislative process. It started with the leaders, with Reid and Schumer. I don't think Durbin was a very big part of it. Even Schumer, in the Democratic caucus, before we passed the bill in '06, was saying we were going to have a tough time with the Republicans.

Finally, at the end of last year, 2007, Reid manufactured a cloture vote on the bill. We just took the bill up on the Thursday. No votes Friday, no votes Monday, and he was going to have a cloture vote on Tuesday, thinking that we have the Republicans and Democrats together and everybody's going to stay together. Some of the Republican senators we needed said we have to be able to vote on a half a dozen of these things, no matter how they come out.

Q: Amendments.

EMK: Amendments. And then we can support the bill, but we have to have an opportunity to vote for half a dozen of these amendments, which is the way life goes in the Senate. And if you're not going to give them the opportunity to vote, then they're not going to vote for cloture. So when Reid talked to me on Tuesday and said, "We're going to have the cloture vote," even though I said, "Well, Harry, we haven't voted on Friday, we haven't voted on Monday. How can you have the cloture vote on Tuesday now?" "Well," he said, "I filled the tree."[29]

I said, "You can't. We're going to lose this vote, that's the end of it." He said, "Well, I'll give you until Wednesday." And he set the vote for Wednesday, got the consent on it, but the atmosphere had been polluted.

Then he tried to get the cloture vote over for Thursday, and the Republicans said no. So there was a preliminary cloture vote, and we lost badly. But the idea was that we might be able to pick up their support if we have more votes on amendments. On Wednesday evening, we had sixteen or eighteen votes; we stayed in until midnight, and that in Senate terms is when our people basically give up. They said, "We'll have six votes at six o'clock, and we'll divide the three hours evenly between now and six."

When they do that, when they don't take their two hours on one amendment, it means they've given up, and I have to control the time. When they said we'll vote five votes, three hours divided on it, it means they're not serious. And that happened at six o'clock, and we had, what? six votes? Then at midnight we had six more votes, and our people were off in their hideaways drinking wine. They had basically given up. You had to drive it on Thursday and Friday, probably, to keep the Senate in there, but we would have passed that bill. We would have passed the bill.

What happened is, on that Thursday afternoon, Reid went over and forced the Republicans and said, "We have to be entitled to our votes, too." We had to let them vote. If you want to get the bill passed in the Senate, it's about

---

29. In the Senate "filling the tree" means that a bill has all of its possible amendments added by the majority leader. The term refers to a diagram where the tree trunk represents the bill, and the branches are amendments added to it.

letting them vote on their amendments. You're going to have to cover your own people with some votes on their amendments, but you don't have to have one-for-one votes. And if you're insisting, as Reid did, "We have to have one-for-one," you're putting yourselves in an impossible position. You're setting yourself up for failure. And then he went over in the afternoon and just antagonized Sessions and two or three others, so we went five hours without any voting, and it was done, finished.

Q: *Was it his insistence on cloture vote that was hostile?*

EMK: He was stopping the Senate. Whatever the atmosphere of the Senate, he was stopping the Senate from voting, to try and suggest to the public that the Republicans were basically stopping the Senate, and it was their fault that we were not considering amendments, when we had it all moving along the night before. Any serious student of the Senate would say that this was moving, and I believe, quite frankly, we would have gotten the bill passed.

We would have had fifteen more votes on Friday and ten more on Saturday, and it would have been done. But he went out to manufacture a situation to antagonize Republicans, to try to blame them, so there'd be a blame game going on, and stop consideration of the bill. Then what happened is, everyone agreed to have one more vote on Friday, and I knew it was all over. People who had been with us left us, and we ended up with something like a forty-one to fifty vote. We lost.

Q: *You came that close.*

EMK: If we had continued the bill on the floor of the Senate, I'm convinced we would have passed it.

Q: *So behind all the gaming, the party was not unified about doing it.*

EMK: They weren't serious. The leadership was not serious about doing it. It's very controversial and comes back to the controversy.

Q: *Were the Republicans playing the same game, the blame game?*

EMK: They were, yes.

Q: *Was it Frist and McConnell?*[30]

EMK: Yes, but we opened ourselves up. Each side was trying to blame the other, and Reid got blamed the first time he pulled it down. That's why he came and brought the bill back again to the floor in 2007. So he got some credit for bringing the bill back up, but there's no question in my mind that that was the opportunity that was missed. In this second round on the floor, Reid let Dorgan[31] get a vote on an amendment.

The Dorgan amendment that labor wanted was to cut back the temporary worker program, and they knew that if we eliminated the temporary worker program, Kyl was going to get off the bill. So they reduced the temporary

---

30. Senator Mitch McConnell is a Kentucky Republican.
31. Byron Dorgan was a Republican senator from North Dakota.

worker annual numbers from 400,000 to 200,000. I told Kyl that that was going to happen before we got in there, and it did, because it had happened on the previous bill in 2006.

Then Dorgan tried to eliminate the temporary worker program with the idea that that would sink the bill. He lost by one vote the first time, and then he got another opportunity to offer. He went over and got some of the Republicans who were against the bill and said, "Look, if you stick with us, we're going to sink the bill," and he won it by one vote the next time. But clearly the leadership gave him the green light to do that, because there were other senators who hadn't had an opportunity to offer their amendments. That happened on the 2007 deal.

The point I'm basically underlining is the dichotomy that existed in the Democratic leadership. That was very real, and I think it probably cost us the opportunity to get the bill passed. Perhaps not, but I think it did.

Q: Well, when you have a bipartisan effort and initiative, and then you turn it into a partisan game, it's not an issue that can be handled in a partisan way, is it? From the very beginning, bipartisanship is required.

EMK: We're mixing a lot of different elements here. You had Mitch McConnell, who is the Republican leader, sitting down with Harry Reid and me, talking about how to reach an agreement on this proposal. Mitch McConnell was sitting in our meeting and nodding and nodding, and leaving, and having absolutely no intention of doing anything but sinking the bill. He sat through that meeting and didn't talk. That was the way he operated.

But you had Harry Reid, who shifted from not caring about this bill to thinking it was an ordinary bill and speeding it up on the floor. If you can't speed it up, pull it. Then he found all the emotion that went into this bill, and so he had to bring it back to the floor again. Then we eventually finished it, and he's glad that it's finished, but we have to come back and revisit it. He announced, in 2007, that this was going to be one of the leadership bills, and he announced that he was going to bring it to the floor just before the summer break. He announced that.

He was never really interested in it until the very end, and at the very end it was too late. The Senate is a chemical place. There's a lot of emotion, there's feeling, there's a timeliness in how the Senate works, and if you lose the rhythm and lose the balance, you lose in a tough and difficult fight, and that's what was lost at the time. You can go back and look at this string here and that string there, but that's what was lost.

The Democratic leadership bears a big part of the responsibility for it. The basic concept is that with the exception of the provision in the legislation that dealt with the safety and security of the twelve million people, it was a Republican bill, and the challenge was for me to hold all the Democrats, and for Kyl—with a Republican bill—to bring enough Republicans to get the cloture. That was the overall basic strategy.

We held three-quarters of the Democrats, but the Republicans couldn't deliver anyone besides Kyl. Their leadership didn't, Mitch McConnell didn't. Trent Lott[32] was pretty good on this issue. I'd say that McCain was very courageous all the way through and never hesitated on his support, and took a real pasting and dropped enormously in terms of the presidential campaign. Lindsey Graham dropped in terms of his re-election. He's been sputtering to try to come back by offering amendments on the fence and all the rest of it. Brownback has left the issue.

One of the interesting little sidebars is the tension between Cornyn, who's from Texas, and John McCain. In the first bill in 2006, Cornyn worked out with me an amendment on temporary workers. But then as soon as he went back to Texas, he disowned it. He offered an amendment on the floor on the first bill, where McCain was around. McCain was very good on the floor debating, and Hagel was terrific when he was there. Hagel rarely spoke in the Senate, but he was good when he did on this issue. Cornyn came up to me and McCain and said he was going to offer this amendment, and McCain said, "That's a bullshit amendment," and I was rather surprised to hear him use that word. He said, "And we don't want any more of your bullshit amendments. You're going to sink the Republican Party. You're going to antagonize all the Hispanics, and your amendments are all bullshit."

Then they both turned red, but Cornyn went back. I couldn't believe that Cornyn would take all that, but he did. So that was that. I think Cornyn offered one more, that I think was defeated.

On the 2007 bill, we had the final meeting before we had the announcement on a Thursday morning. The Wednesday evening we had—

Vicki Kennedy: You mean before it came up to the floor.

EMK: Before it came to the floor.

Vicki Kennedy: Before the thing they called the "grand compromise." I think that's important to do when you're planning to—

EMK: We reached an agreement, what they called a "grand compromise," and people interpreted more into it than was agreed to, although I stayed with the agreement all the way through. But we were still working out particular amendments to the compromise, and you could see that the window for introducing the bill and bring it to the floor was shrinking because of the time on the calendar. We had other bills coming up for floor consideration, and we had to get this compromise finished. We thought we were going to wind it up on a Wednesday night, and it didn't get wound up. So we said, "We'll meet on Thursday morning over in the Rules Committee room." I was over there, and I think Cornyn showed up. But nobody else showed up.

Q: "We" being the committee?

---

32. Lott was a Republican senator from Mississippi.

EMK: I'm talking about the principals, our team of Republicans and team of Democrats working on the compromise. I heard there was going to be a floor vote at 10:30, eleven o'clock, and people had gone over there to vote. We come to the meeting, and I could see, if we didn't get this compromise settled, it wasn't going to happen. So there was a vote, and I said, "Why don't we go back to the Vice President's Room and we'll sit down and see?"

Into the Vice President's Room now comes Leahy; I hadn't seen him the whole time. Leahy says, "I thought they took my amendment on farmers, but I don't see it. How are my farmers going to be treated under this bill? We have small farms and we have large farms and we have medium-sized farms, and our farms are different from the farms in Wisconsin. There are some sheepherder problems, too. I'm not going to agree to anything until I have a good chance to go through this. I'm going to go through this over the weekend; I'm going to just take my time to go through it." I said, "Well, I think this thing has been handled." He said, "No, I'm not going to be rushed; I'm not going to be stampeded." So up he gets and walks out.

And in comes McCain and there's Cornyn, and Chertoff is in there, Specter's there, I'm there, and some of the staff are in there. Cornyn says, "I have three or four amendments I want to offer on this," and McCain just explodes and says, "John, we're not going to listen to any more of your bullshit amendments." Cornyn says, "Wait a minute, John. I've been part of this whole process, and I've been waiting and waiting. I was there last night, and I didn't get a chance to offer mine." "Well," McCain says, "we're tired, we're finished, we're wound up. You're not going to be getting any more." And then Cornyn says, "Look, John, I've been working on this while you've been out campaigning in the national."

And McCain snaps back and says, "I was working on this before you ever got to the Senate, and we're sick and tired of you." Boom! Up gets Cornyn, out he goes, and then we say, "Are there any more amendments? No more amendments? Close it down, and we'll have the press conference at two o'clock." We had the press conference announcing the compromise at two o'clock. Kyl came to it, which meant Cornyn could go screw himself. He attended the meeting; that's all we needed. McCain came and I came, and that's all we needed to announce the compromise. That's what you had going into it. That's why it's going to take another forty-five years for someone else to get this thing passed.

Q: So that's the personal chemistry that comes into it.

EMK: We had the negotiation meetings. We had ten or eleven meetings every week in 2007 over in [Vice President Richard] Cheney's room. It's on the second floor of the Dirksen building, and whoever wanted to come could come talk to our group. If somebody knew somebody who had an amendment, they could come over and talk about it. So people would come over and talk about their amendments; we'd sit around and talk about them.

The Wednesday night before this, Cornyn still had four amendments, and little Esther[33] said, "Every one of them is bad, just bad." I said, "Esther, you know what we're going to do? We're going to take two of his amendments, whichever two he wants. We're going to take them, and we're going to say, 'The other two we're not going to negotiate if he wants us to take two.'" He said fine. So we put two of the bad ones in the compromise, they negotiated, and that's when he came around with another one the next day. Poor Esther was in tears when I said, "You're going to take these two amendments or this thing isn't going to happen."

That was the problem at the end with Kyl: he didn't know when to finalize a deal. Because he had the family issue with Menendez that we could have worked out that would have permitted some of the families in the backlog to obtain their green cards, and it didn't make any difference. Kyl had said yes, but not unless he did better on the temporary worker issue. I said, "We'll take care of you on the temporary worker, Jon. You have to stay with this thing. We have to stay in here, and I give you assurance that the bill won't come out of here without a temporary worker program in it." Otherwise he would have walked as soon as the temporary worker program was gone. I said, "Stay in there. We'll give you assurance that we won't have a bill unless it has a temporary worker program."

If Kyl was going to have a temporary worker, Menendez was going to have to get something. If only Menendez had stayed in that coalition and had been able to make a deal. He had made several speeches against the compromise because of the changes to family immigration, and that bothered Democrats. They were concerned about the family point system and the change we made in family priorities that was cockamamie. That's something you probably have to do globally. But the way we did it was not a terribly efficient way of doing it.

Q: So by this point, time was against you. The window was shrinking. Is that right?

EMK: That's it. It was shrinking. The legislation was very close, whether you accept it or not. I remember meeting with Frank Sharry—a very good fellow at the National Immigration Forum and a good friend and very knowledgeable, very tough—and Cecilia Munoz,[34] who was terrific with this issue. She said, "I want you to know that out there in this city there are five hundred mimeograph machines all ready to say, 'Kennedy sold us out.'" That's when I said to them, "Well, make sure they spell Salazar right."

Then they laughed and said, "All right, we'll give you one more crack at it." But the bill was right at the border, in terms of my own support. I thought if we had gotten this thing passed through with the House, eventually it would have increased the power of the president, and we would have been able to say,

---

33. Olavarria was a counsel to Kennedy and the Judiciary Committee.
34. Munoz represented the National Council of La Raza.

"Look, this is what we need at the very end. He's going to sign it, and it's going to be a big deal for him, but we need to get these points." When you're going that far and you're that close to the end, I think we probably could have gotten parts of the bill fixed. There would be too much for the president not to risk trying. He would have seen that thing enacted.

You could say, "No he won't, he'll screw you." It was going be as big for him, getting rapped—he got rapped more for not getting this through. I got rapped too, but he got a pretty good rap for being ineffective. I think if you'd done something on the family aspect of the bill. And the other part was if we had passed this bill, you elect a Democratic president, you have the twelve million people in place, twelve million people who are safe and secure. In this bill was also the AgJOBS bill, which would have covered 800,000 to 900,000 workers. You had the DREAM Act in there, and I think we could have been able to work out compromises on the other particularly harsh provisions, the Title II provisions. We're going to have to restore democracy in any case, with regard to a lot of civil liberties issues.

I think the last part on this whole feature, this issue about safety for the people, was so well illustrated by a raid in New Bedford [Massachusetts] in March. ICE[35] raided a factory down there, 360 people who were working on a defense contract, making some materials for the military. They went in and pulled probably 300 or so people out of the plant and separated these families. The biggest percent of the workers arrested were women. A lot of them had children at home, children in school, small children. Some of them were single moms, living in apartments with the children, and the mothers were being taken and shipped out to detention centers, and the children were coming home to no mother. No mother to pick them up at school, no mother to pick them up at daycare.

This was one of the most barbaric actions I've ever seen in this country regarding people. I think outside property and certainly slavery, the most barbaric that I've personally witnessed.

Q: You went up there?

EMK: I went up there on the following Sunday. I went down in a basement of a church, pulled up a chair and sat down and listened. I heard the most extraordinary stories: a father with two children saying the children haven't slept all week, and their mother is in a Dartmouth prison just a few miles from here. Could I take them over so the children can see their mother? I'll go in the prison. Let them see their mother and let the mother come out, and I'll come back, just so they can sleep. This is happening here. It was just the most extraordinary—nursing mothers. Their children were taken to hospitals.

---

35. Immigration and Customs Enforcement.

This was being done in New Bedford, Massachusetts, here—it was a Chertoff operation. This was the most inhumane, indecent, Gestapo-like—I used the word Gestapo-like—activity. I told Chertoff this. He had tried to work with Bill Delahunt, a Congressman from the Cape district, an old prosecutor, to try to find a fair way of treating women and the children. I mean, if the people have violated the immigration law, they violated the immigration law, but you don't treat them inhumanely here in the United States. We've been unable to do it, and a part of this bill was going to do that, if I had ever gotten it far enough down. I'm going to have to try to amend another legislation, which I will do.

But in this instance, they shipped people up to Fort Devens and airlifted them to places in Texas and New Mexico, where they were denied attorneys; their attorneys couldn't find them. They even deported American citizens they can't find now. Some of these people were American citizens and had foreign names, and they sent them back to Guatemala, and now they can't find them. The contrast with this law we did not pass! They all came down to me and said, "Can't you do something?" With this law, these people would have been able to stay here. It would have guaranteed they would stay here unless they'd come here in the last six or eight months. That's a big deal.

Q: Does Chertoff care?

EMK: No, he doesn't. We've had very tough exchanges on this thing. The lawyers, this is the lawyers. Chertoff would say, "We notify; we follow procedures. We notify the Department of Health in these states afterwards, and we're sensitive to humanitarian needs" and all the rest of it—it's just baloney. ICE ought to have a protocol in every one of these raids.

The federal judge here finally issued a restraining order. It took him three days, but the lawyers representing the workers got a restraining order saying they couldn't deport any of the workers until they could speak to their lawyers. It needed a federal judge.

Just a last point: the interesting dichotomy on the issue of immigration with the undocumented is that you have two things. One is the politics, but there's a more substantive issue. In the House, all the Republicans were very strong anti-immigrant. In the Senate, it was divided between Republicans who aligned with the Chamber of Commerce, understood that the farmers and the growers and companies needed workers, we need workers for an expanding economy, and therefore we ought to bring more workers in the country. But they're temporary workers, so we're going to send them back, and that's fine. The Republicans in the House say, "We're not going to have lawbreakers." It's a values issue as well, divided between the Republicans who are interested in the economic benefit and who deplore immigration—at least they say, "We're not going to be sympathetic to undocumented illegals." But a lot of that is the racism.

The issue I see is on the one hand you ask, what are the values Americans really admire? They admire people who work hard. They admire people who look after their families and care about their families. They admire people who look after their parents. This is a big issue, particularly in this immigrant population. They're also willing to join the military and the armed forces. We have seventy thousand now who have served in Afghanistan and Iraq; seventy thousand immigrants have served who have been permanent residents. The individuals work, work, work, work. Forty billion dollars is being sent back to Central and South America this year. They care about their families. They're not just coming here for a free ride.

More of them are churchgoers, and they take more care of their parents. What we have on our side is that magnet of jobs over here. And while this anti-immigrant crowd is just burning this other side of the issue because these people are violating the law by coming in here, we have that magnet of jobs. We have the cash register blinking, blinking, blinking, blinking, while the immigrants are caring about their starving kids, wives, and families. We're so morally superior to that because the immigrants are viewed as lawbreakers, and they're doing nothing other than just growing our economy. It's something Americans don't think much about when they're thinking about the issue—or a lot of them don't.

Q: Or it's something they don't hear much about.

EMK: They don't hear about it.

Q: When you look at the talk shows and all the stuff that's—

EMK: You can't get away from the fact that we just can't have open borders. I agree there's a role for legal immigration, and you have to deal with the illegal immigration. But if you're going to deal with the illegal immigration issue, what we were saying in this legislation is the undocumented are going to come in. You can't build a wall because the wall's not going to be high enough. Janet Napolitano[36] said if you build a wall forty feet tall, they'll have a ladder forty-one feet. Or they'll dig underneath it. So what are we going to do, put something down into the ground, or so high they can't climb over? It's 1,800 miles on the southern border, and we have 4,200 on the northern border, and you have the coastline.

The idea is they don't press, they stop at San Diego. Only 30 percent of the people will come in at San Diego, but it's 250 percent at the other end of the border. It only takes common sense to understand what's going to happen. There should be a legal way for the people to come in and out of the country. We'll say, "Okay, you can come in, and you know what else we're going to do? You're going to get a card, so if you're here, you'll be able to go back

---

36. Napolitano was attorney general and then governor of Arizona and would serve as secretary of homeland security under President Obama.

home"—which they can't do now. The twelve million can't go home. A lot of people would welcome the chance to go home, but they can't, so what do they do? They get married and stay here, and this is a problem.

The concept was that we channel these people here illegally through a process, and then open up the process so a lot of people can return, which will bring less pressure, and try to develop a process where they're going to have economic development in Mexico. A third of the money the undocumented return is to spend in their local communities for water wells and other things. It's interesting. They want it to go to their family, but they also want a little economic development. We should have worked that with the Mexican government, to do something, because the demographic flow over the next thirty years begins to shift and change.

The other day I was talking to the foreign minister of Ireland, and he said, "We had a fair, and we had thousands of Irish in the United States who want to go to Ireland and work. Americans want to go over there. We're not able to deal with them because of the economic prosperity." If you look over the demographic issues in this country with Mexico, over a period of time properly done, you have some different patterns. But, you know, it was always to try to get them to do some things in their country, in Mexico.

Q: Two things. You haven't mentioned [President George W. Bush]. *You mentioned Chertoff. Where was he in all of this? Was he helpful?*

EMK: Well, Bush wanted to get a bill, but he's completely ineffective in trying to influence people. He spoke to me on a couple of different occasions. I went down to see him this year about funding for No Child Left Behind, and he asked me to remain behind. I had gone down there with George Miller and Enzi and Buck McKeon.[37] He said, "Can we get a bill?" and he was interested in doing it [immigration reform].

Then I saw him at a St. Patrick's Day lunch, and he said, "What can I do?" I said, "You ought to talk to Specter of the Judiciary Committee, and Leahy." Leahy bears a part of the burden on this bill, too, because we had the first meeting with Leahy and the White House. Leahy said, "I'm not going to report out a bill that the president doesn't agree to, that the president won't indicate he's going to support."

Well, we knew what the elements of the bill were; you know who is going to sponsor it. I knew what they were. So Leahy said no, no, he wasn't going to do it, and he was very assertive about that. When we started to work on

---

37. A signature legislative victory for the early George W. Bush presidency, the No Child Left Behind law resulted from a bipartisan collaboration among President Bush, Senator Kennedy, California congressman George Miller, and Republican senator Judd Gregg of New Hampshire. This effort created reforms for American public education in 2002. Senator Michael Enzi represents Wyoming, and Howard McKeon was a congressman from California; both are Republicans.

the immigration bill, it was the time of the flap over the US attorneys; the US attorneys were being politicized. The attorney general [Alberto Gonzales] was replacing US attorneys who were not political enough, and it was a real flap in the Justice Department.

And so Leahy would have nothing to do with our ability to have a markup in our Judiciary Committee. We never marked up our bill in the Judiciary Committee. We went straight to the floor, bypassed the Judiciary Committee, and there was always a sense that if we'd gone to that committee—I always said, "We marked it up last year. We've had umpteen hearings on it. We've marked it up effectively. You don't have to go through the committee, but we've been able to mark it up and take a little time on that." Three days, I think, could have made some difference.

With Bush, towards the end on this '07 bill is when I saw the difficulties. I wanted to go down and see the president, to ask him, to say we needed to have some compromises on the bill—to get Menendez on board, try and make some adjustment on these family provisions. It was basically the green card provisions. The argument I can never understand with Kyl is he says we can't increase the total number of green cards, the cards that permit people to work and allow them to move on the path towards citizenship. But he was going to make sure, of the twelve million who were here—this was the deal—that all of them were going to get on the path to citizenship, all of them. It was going to take some time, but every one of them could get on the path. That's a big deal for all the undocumented. They're going to have to pay fines, but they're all going to have to get on the path, a big deal.

Towards the end, there were different compromises I thought Kyl had to make, and I asked to see the president. They wouldn't let me: Chertoff and [White House Chief of Staff] Josh Bolten[38] wouldn't let me talk to him. So I went down and talked to Chertoff and Bolten and told them exactly what was going to happen, and it did. I went down two or three times in that last ten days and said, "Unless you move toward a compromise, unless you do this compromise, unless you do that, this is where we're headed. I'm just giving you the straight scoop on it."

Q: So it wasn't a case of his trying and not being effective at the right moment.

EMK: The president wasn't involved, and I think they thought he wouldn't know. Listen, I'm a pro. I don't expect him to understand the details. What you know is that you have to have a compromise. The president says to Chertoff, "Kennedy says we have to give Menendez 200,000 green cards." He'll say, "I think we can do it for 120,000 green cards"—or something like that. And then he looks at you and says, "Will you take 140,000 green cards?" and I say yes

---

38. Josh Bolten was also former OMB director.

or no, good. The president doesn't have to know the nitty-gritty on this stuff. But that didn't happen.

So, in retrospect, the president has a part of it too. If only he had been engaged, accessible, and available. It was in contrast to the No Child Left Behind bill. When we ran into a stone wall, I said, "We can't have vouchers." And the president said, "Okay, I'll take the vouchers out, but I'm going to offer them on the DC approach." I said, "That's fine, we'll fight it there, and we'll go onto the other issues." He was involved in that, but not this one.

Q: Are you going to have another chance with the bill, the reform?

EMK: Yes. The fact is, these issues are not going to go away, and you see them now in the raids they're having with labor, as I told the building trades. All the heads of the building trades came in and said this bill was a disaster, absolute disaster. I said, "Well, let me tell you something, you have undocumented now who are all working in the building trades down in Miami, in San Diego, and LA. They're not paying workman's compensation; they're not paying their insurance. If they get sick, you're double paying for these people. Why not make them safe here? Then you can organize them. You're not going to organize them if they're undocumented. Why not make them safe here and then go out and organize them?"

They said, "Oh no, you're going to have other undocumented people coming in." I said, "I just don't get it." I was over with the head of the ironworkers, a fellow named [Joseph] Hunt, who's a pretty good fellow. I did an event for Howard Dean,[39] and Hunt came, although the other trades urged the building trades not to go because I was going. But Hunt came over and said, "Any more immigration bills, Kennedy?" I said, "Let me just go over this one more time so you know." He said, "Okay, okay."

I said, "They're undocumented, so you ought to be bringing a RICO[40] charge against these contractors, because they're all using suitcases full of money out of these banks in Miami. They're paying these people cash, and everybody knows it. You get treble damages, and you're not doing that and you're not organizing the workers. I don't see how that's a path for the benefit of your workers. I just don't get it. I might be missing something, but I don't think I am."

My hope is that we'll probably make some progress. We've gotten this thing into the final stages, but I was absolutely convinced that we were going to elect a Democrat, and we would be a lot further down the road if we were adjusting and changing this bill instead of starting over again. We're going to have to start over again with a new president. We're going to have to start dealing with

39. Dean was former Democratic governor of Vermont and presidential candidate.
40. Racketeer Influenced and Corrupt Organizations Act.

this bill again. I think there are ways. I think the next time we're going to come from a hard Democratic side of it, a workers' rights side.

Q: Do you think the Democrats will behave differently?

EMK: I would hope so, with a Democratic president.[41]

Q: This is a continuation of yesterday's session on immigration. This is October 9 [2007]. Vicki Kennedy is with us.

EMK: I thought we'd just look at immigration globally, from '80 through the late '90s, because some important things happened, both in terms of the substance and in terms of the process. I think it's probably worth mentioning, without getting into the details of the particular legislation, which I think can be looked into by those who want to.

The recommendations in 1980 are really a result of the Hesburgh Commission, and the actions that were taken by the Senate took place after 1980, maybe '82, '84, but they weren't successful in getting through both the House and the Senate. The first bill of substance that marked an important difference was the '86 Act that was called IRCA.[42] The most significant part of that legislation was that it provided amnesty for many of those who were here illegally. They had to be here for a period of time. I think it was four or five years, which is interesting because later on, when we passed legislation—or tried to this last year or two—we're always searching for how far we ought to go back. I believe that the '86 Act went back about four years. We might have modified it and moved it forward a bit, but that was a pretty significant difference, because a lot of other people came into the country in the meantime.

The '86 Act also proposed employer sanctions. That was a new proposal, because up to this time, employers were never really held accountable at all. All the focus and attention were always on the workers. If there were raids, it was always the workers who were deported, and the employers never had really any penalty at all. This Act reversed that practice and established some penalties for employers. But the way the provisions were established raised substantial concern, particularly among the Hispanics, that they'd be used to discriminate against Hispanics and against American workers because of the issues of documentation. Anybody who looked Hispanic or looked foreign would not get the job, or if they had the job, they would be dismissed. That's a fairly general theme that I've seen over the time: if there were provisions in immigration acts that permitted discrimination, they resulted in discrimination, and that has been the history.

This legislation was heavily debated and passed. Only a few voted against it. I was one who voted against it because of the employer sanction provisions

---

41. Kennedy got a Democratic president with the election of his colleague and candidate Senator Barack Obama in 2008. But EMK died in August 2009 before he could work on another immigration bill.

42. Immigration Reform and Control Act.

and the fear of discrimination. There was the ability for three million of the undocumented to adjust their status to permanent resident aliens, and then become citizens over a period of months and years in the future.

One interesting point was amnesty. Forgiveness was somewhat of an issue, but not an important one during that period. I don't believe the '86 Act had the extensive penalties for people. It was the recognition that we were going to have people with second-class status in this country. This was the beginning of that debate: if we had people with second-class status who were going to be subject to exploitation, it was going to have a negative impact on society. We had to deal with enhanced border security, and we were giving increasing focus and attention to skilled workers. But the central mark of the '86 Act was the amnesty.

We had the next major legislation in 1990, when we wrestled with Simpson in our Judiciary Committee was about green card numbers and skilled workers and the border patrol, and also, again, about some employer sanction provisions. There was a debate about what the numbers of green cards were going to be, whether we were going to have an increase in the total number of individuals receiving green cards. I think at that time we added a diversity program to represent some of the countries that historically contributed immigrants but were gradually getting squeezed out because of the way the other legislation was going.

I think Jack Brooks[43] was there. He was a very colorful figure. When we sat down in conference, he'd start off the discussion, "Does Senator Kennedy have his Irish? Are the Irish in this draft?" I'd cringe and go on to the other provisions. He was a very colorful Texan and a bit of a rogue, but a delightful personality.

The '90 Act was a very good bill. I think there were only three or four votes against it, and it got even better on the floor of the Senate. Some unusual amnesty provisions provided additional protections for people seeking asylum. They won narrowly. It was a very good bill, although Simpson was very concerned because the Democrats controlled the House. The bill provided some expansion for legal immigration, and he thought if that bill went to the House, it would be taken over by the Democrats and made a good deal more liberal. He refused to permit the Senate to finish consideration of the bill.

I made an agreement with Simpson that what we would effectively do was pre-conference the bill. That means that we'd finish all the amendments, and then before what they call the third reading of the bill on the floor, which preceded passage (and which meant no more amendments could be taken up), the leader would effectively pull the bill, and we would consider it in conference. The House had a bill, we would have a bill, and I told Simpson that

---

43. Brooks was a Democratic congressman from Texas.

unless he was satisfied with the bill that was worked out in this pre-conference, I wouldn't sign the conference report. There wouldn't be a bill. And on that basis he agreed.

We had long sessions in the Capitol at night on the bill, and there was great pressure to make it more liberal and more progressive. We had to resist those, and several times it looked like the legislation was going to fall apart. Eventually we worked out our agreements. It was still a good bill, very good legislation. We began to provide some help to local communities and beefed up the border, had skilled worker provisions. The provisions about employer sanctions had been for the most part pretty well straightened out, and they kept faith with the Hesburgh Commission. Then we brought it back to the floor, and within half an hour we passed the bill and passed the conference report effectively together by the same margin.

The next serious legislation was in 1996, when the Republicans had taken over. There's always the tension between the legal immigration and the illegal immigration issues, and the Republicans were picking more and more on the illegal immigration and making it an issue. We had a situation where Republicans under Gingrich passed an extremely harsh piece of legislation that was enormously detrimental to immigrant rights and civil liberties, cutting back on asylum, on notification of immigrants, on the flexibility of judges by cutting back on appeals, cutting back on representation—just cutting back on all the rights. A very bad bill came out of our committee, but we hoped it might be made better. I'm not sure how I actually voted on the '96 Act.[44]

In any event, the bill went to a conference, and Gingrich put it into the continuing resolution with all of its bad provisions. [President] Clinton was able to get some of those provisions out—not many of them, but it was just a very bad bill that had Republican support. The House Republicans circumvented the whole process, all the rules. It was bad, but we couldn't vote on it as an individual bill. I'm not sure if I voted on the omnibus budget bill. I spoke in opposition to it, but we couldn't restrict it or restrain it. That was the beginning of the festering in the House of Representatives for legislation that would be bigoted and harsh and discriminatory towards immigrants.

Q: Did the House refuse to negotiate with the Senate on this? They were obviously drawing a line in the sand and setting it up for failure. They refused to conference with the Senate on it at all, and when they did, it was already a done deal. Clinton threatened to veto it if it passed, and you and Simpson were adamantly opposed to it. You said you would filibuster if that bill came to the floor. It was pretty awful. It had the provision saying people can't be treated for AIDS; states were permitted to deny public education. It was really bad. It was an awful bill.

---

44. Kennedy voted for the Senate version of the bill, which passed 96–3. Only Democratic Senators Paul Simon, Russ Feingold, and Bob Graham voted against it.

EMK: But they put it in the omnibus budget bill and got it through. Clinton made some adjustments to the immigration provisions, but it was still a very bad bill. That's the atmosphere that continued to dominate the House of Representatives as we came to 2001 and 9/11—that same climate, same atmosphere, the same views among the Republicans.

And we saw it expressed in the battle on immigration bills in more recent times, and also expressed in the PATRIOT Act, which has some particularly discriminatory aspects towards immigrants. The most dramatic policy was what they call the NSEERS,[45] which required the fingerprinting of all Arab and Middle Eastern people, fingerprinting and photographing everyone, which of course created an enormous stir and raised important constitutional issues and antagonized broad communities.

Q: That was very quickly after 9/11.

EMK: That was under Ashcroft,[46] and it was the most dramatic policy, I think, but it was typical of the provisions he included in the PATRIOT Act, and their view towards immigration.

Q: The border crossing from the south didn't get much attention right after 9/11. The president had been saying he wanted to work something out with Fox to solve that problem, including a guest worker program, but that all stopped in its tracks with 9/11. Now it's coming back.

EMK: So now we find ourselves at the point where the dichotomy is still evident: people viewing the person next door very positively, the hard worker, the industrious worker, and admiring the student and admiring the church-goer and admiring the people trying to make it. But they have this very intense hostility towards the undocumented person and are not able to distinguish between the two. So they're ambivalent about this issue. When considered as people coming and following a tradition—and all Americans know we're a nation of immigrants—people have positive views, but when they have the sense that it's done illegally, then they have a different view.

Q: Where are we with immigration now [October 2007]? Where are we going?

EMK: At the present time, we're going to try to draw lessons from this experience and what the prospects are in terms of the future. On the one hand, in the United States Senate we're considering trying to do some immigration reform by piecemeal bills. We're looking at the AgJOBS Bill, the DREAM Act, what they call H-1B, which is the skilled worker program, and H-2B, the unskilled worker program. There's a general sense that if you put all of those bills together, there might be some support for this approach, but underneath it all would be a recognition that you're basically selling out the twelve million

---

45. National Security Entry-Exit Registration System.
46. John Ashcroft was the attorney general.

people who are here, and their safety and security, because these bills are the engines that help get the immigration reform bill through.

If you start taking out the goodies and leave behind the other aspects of it, it will do a real disservice to immigration reform. That's what a number of the Hispanics feel, although they're caught in a difficult position because they favor some of these provisions very strenuously. They favor the provisions dealing with AgJOBS and the DREAM Act. They're less interested in the high-skilled workers, the H-1Bs, and the less-skilled workers in the H-2Bs. The H-2Bs are the ones who work in resorts in Massachusetts. The H-1Bs are the ones who work in Microsoft, and they have rather special privileges because they can bring their families over. H-2Bs can bring their families over, but they don't generally, and the H-2Bs return to their countries because they can travel back and forth.

Probably a fairly interesting indicator in terms of the undocumented would be if you regularized their return to their community, there would be a lot of people who would go back. There's no question that a lot of them stay here because they don't think they can get back, and because they stay here, then they put their roots down here; they get married and start living here whereas otherwise, they might have just gone back if they could have gone back and forth and stayed in their community. That's called circular migration, and if you have an effective immigration system, there's no question there would be a lot less pressure. People would return, and that solves some people's problems. But you can't get there unless you have a comprehensive reform bill.

So, at the current time, as we're meeting now, there's some life in trying to get the AgJOBS bill, which is the bill that Larry Craig[47] and I initially introduced. I let Dianne Feinstein take it over because she was back and forth in her support on the immigration reform bill, and once she got the AgJOBS bill, which is a big deal in California, she signed on to the immigration reform bill. She's still looking to see if we can try to figure out how to pass an AgJOBS bill. Durbin is working on the DREAM Act, which says that if a child was here at the age of fifteen and brought here, after they've been here for five years and continued their education, or they could choose to go into the military, they could get on a path towards permanent residency and then eventually citizenship.[48]

So those are still out there in the Congress. The chance of those bills passing as a group, I think, is unlikely. There's a possibility of bits and pieces of them

---

47. Craig was a Republican senator from Idaho.

48. The DREAM Act failed in Congress, but President Obama issued two executive orders to implement some of the Act's provisions. Courts stymied one of the orders, and the Trump administration rescinded the other, although it did not cancel work permits granted by the Obama administration to so-called Dreamers, undocumented aliens brought to the United States as children.

passing, but I don't believe there's the will to do it, because the other groups will get into it to get their bills passed.

There's some sentiment in the wake of the 2007 bill that we ought to try to pass legislation that would maintain the safety and security of the twelve million, and not give them the path towards citizenship. The Hispanic groups would accept that, but they wouldn't have until we lost the 2007 effort. It is certainly my impression that that would be perceived as being amnesty. The people violated the law and we're letting them stay, and we'd be right back in the debate again. The atmosphere is so poisoned now that it doesn't seem to make a great deal of sense to do that, although it might be worthwhile doing some hearings later in the year on this whole issue.

So we're in a situation where the federal government is involved in increasing what they call the ICE raids, immigration customs raids, and we've seen, in the last weeks, a series of them. They cause enormous disruption in local communities, incredible fear, not just among the people apprehended, but in the whole community if there's a sizeable immigrant population. The raids are taking place in different parts of the country, and Chertoff was on the national news last week saying that he's going to continue them. He has the law, he has to enforce the law, and he's going to continue to do it. We've seen a dramatic increase in the number of deportations every year. I think we're up to three hundred thousand deportations, and he said this is what the law is and he's going to enforce it.

There's tremendous fear over this. It's going to drive the undocumented people underground, and you're going to enhance the underground economy, and it's going to put undocumented people more and more in the shadows. It's going to drive them to the criminal element. There's no question, because they're not going to be able to survive otherwise. That's what will happen.

A second, broader issue is that the Department of Homeland Security has absorbed all of the immigration services. The immigration service has historically been of two parts of the immigration structure. One component is service to people who are immigrants, and the other component is enforcement. But they have been two very important components, and they've worked closely together when it's run well and effectively, and there are services for immigrants.

Now it has all been tied into the Department of Homeland Security, so effectively the process has lost all the service aspects and is just punitive. It's badly bureaucratic. The morale of the whole agency is deteriorated and broken, and the delays, the time, the mistakes, the whole process has taken a very bad turn. That's part of the reality now. It's more and more difficult getting foreign students here and more difficult getting immigrant families reunified. Some of the able or more gifted foreign students are going to other places around the world, and we're losing a lot of them. It has affected some industries, tourist industries and the rest. A lot of people would otherwise want to come to the United States because the value of the dollar has gone down and they can get terrific deals here. That's a secondary aspect to this problem.

A third part of the administration's policies has been what they call the "no match rule," which is requiring employers to verify with Social Security whether there's a match between the records of the Social Security Administration and those of employers and the employees to try and catch undocumented workers. At the present time, the numbers of mistakes that are made, just by Social Security, are identifiable, and they review their documents. They re-review these Social Security documents every year, and they find out that of the seventeen or eighteen million Social Security numbers, three to four million are mistaken, and among immigrants who have become citizens, it's up to 30 percent. So what's happening with this is you're going to have Americans who are legitimate workers being fired because their names are maybe spelled differently. And you're going to find that immigrants who are legal workers here are going to suffer extensively, and employers are going to try to find ways of not hiring people who may present problems in the future.

Q: *They would be liable.*

EMK: They would be liable. There's very serious accountability if they make mistakes. At the present time, that law is suspended because of a court case, but we don't know where it's going to eventually come down in the future. Some of us were thinking that this might cause sufficient disruption among employers to change their attitude about immigration reform and they might turn out to be allies for us.

The fact is, in the immigration debate, the Chamber of Commerce did virtually nothing for us. Employers did virtually nothing. The growers did some things, but the other employers did virtually nothing in terms of the support for immigration reform this time. They had done some things previously. So you have these ICE raids, this "no match rule," and also the increasing involvement of state and local police in apprehending immigrants. There were limited provisions that existed in the current immigration law, where if states wanted to send their people to the Department of Justice, they could have a six- or seven-week training program to learn a bit about immigration laws, and then the states can go ahead and involve their police in immigration enforcement.

Alabama was a state that did it, and what they found out in Alabama was that the amount of racial profiling went up 30 or 40 percent. The police went out and thought they had had their training, and they started pulling people over as they were passing through Alabama, and caused enormous disruption. The reaction from the immigration groups is that they are no longer supporting and working with local police on drug busts, guns, and crime.

Q: *And gangs more recently.*

EMK: And gangs. They're halting and stopping their cooperation because of this. So these are some of the conclusions. We tried, with Congressman Delahunt, to work out guidelines to ensure that detainees' humanitarian circumstances were addressed and those with humanitarian circumstances are released.

Q: This was after the New Bedford raids.

EMK: After New Bedford. We're committed to doing that, but we haven't been able to get this done. I would say in broad strokes, on the future of immigration, the country can't tolerate the current conditions. We need to have a program that's going to deal with the undocumented here and the borders. We have to have some kind of confidence. The American people have to have some kind of confidence we can do it, but to get there, you're going to have to be more creative and imaginative.

Q: The problem is not going to go away.

EMK: It's not going to go away, and you need much broader, more comprehensive initiatives that involve other countries in the hemisphere in this effort, not just us. We have to make it a matter of national security as well as national pride and humanitarianism.

Q: Do you think the path we're on now is moving toward the European way of bringing immigrants in: not to become English, not to become French, not to become German, not to assimilate?

EMK: Well, what we have learned now is that these cells being used by al-Qaeda in a number of the European countries are individuals who have been denied assimilation in these nations and who have been isolated, discriminated against, and denied basic, fundamental human rights and justice. As a result they've developed a very hostile attitude toward the community they're in, and to the government and to the basic values of these societies, and therefore are fertile grounds for recruiting by dangerous people who will threaten the United States.

That's all out there and will be out there now, as we're going to find if we continue on this path of harsh, cruel treatment of this population. The variety of different things this administration is involved in is going to sow the seeds of real danger for this country and society in the years to come. The echoes of what we heard during the Hesburgh Commission about the sons and daughters of these immigrants having such an intense degree of hostility is very real. There's a sense that immigrants themselves who have broken the law, have come here, who are trying to make it, are spending all of their time, for the most part, working hard, looking out after their children. But if their children see their parents, who are working hard, playing by the rules, trying to be good citizens, and doing all the things this country is supposedly standing for—if they see them ultimately cast aside, punished, exploited, discriminated—

Q: Or deported.

EMK: And deported—the rage that's going to come from these . . . people is going to be dramatic. Part of the challenge for our society is to reduce the pressures and tensions, whether they're ethnic, racial, gender, or whatever. But we're just creating hotbeds of churning and rage, and that's very dangerous for this country over the long term.

Q: The problem is going to get worse, and the collateral damage, so to speak, is going to get worse. Are you a pessimist? Or do you just think we have to have a change of administration, a change in thinking, or a cooling down in some way, of the essentially racist or anti-ethnic feeling?

EMK: I think the forces aligned or arrayed against this have to be dealt with. I don't think they can be ignored. I think there are answers to it, but it requires leadership. We don't have leadership on this, certainly from the president at this time. He's incapacitated and incapable of providing strong national moral and effective leadership. The failure of the whole business community to even try to be of any kind of help whatsoever in this effort is just a catastrophic failure. The president was just missing in action in this. He's pleasant enough, and he can say the words, but he was isolated and not engaged or involved. Even when he made some speeches, he was unable to have an influence on his own party in a very important and significant way.

My own view is that there's reason for hope and some reason for optimism, even given what's happened to him, and that's because of the political realities. As we move through the elections, we're going to find, as we did the last time, those who took the harshest positions and were the most negative actually were defeated.[49]

That's not lost on politicians. The voting groups out there, this whole movement and trend, is going to be stronger and more involved in the future. There will still be the voices of the know-nothings, which has been part of the American tradition since the birth of the country. But my own sense is that people of goodwill and vision can fashion and shape legislation that will address the most fundamental challenges, and they can, over a period of time, work on the different features of this proposal. It may take several different bites at the apple, but I think it can and has to be addressed and will be addressed. That's really the future.

Q: Don't misinterpret the question, but you mentioned the president is missing in action. A president wasn't missing in action in '65, and the times were different and all that, but—I don't want to bring Iraq into this, though it may be the most important thing—how would you envision, if you were the next president? What would you see from that vantage point, rather than the vantage point of a senator, that a president could do to get us back on the right track?

---

49. Senator Kennedy did not foresee the Trump phenomenon.

EMK: Well, it seems to me that you'd have to galvanize the base and your supporters in an important way. You may look for different kinds of alliances, and then obviously try to minimize and isolate those in opposition. It may very well come to the point where you have to develop broad support. There's still some division within the Hispanic community. You have to make sure you have all those people on board. I'm not sure we did get all of those on board quite the way we could have and should have, because some of the groups were outside. You have to make sure you get all the church groups. Some were still on the outside.

You can galvanize labor if they have a feeling that these people could be part of the legalization program and aren't going to be subject to exploitation. We're going to get labor. There's no reason not to have that, because that's also in the interest of the business community. They want them to work for a period of time. I don't think that's really inconsistent. What we had the last time was enough to keep them on board. There's enough support out there to be put together, but it would have to be put together in a different way.

I think, finally, people have to understand that this is a major defining issue for our time, and we have to deal with it or we're going to reap the [whirl]wind. This is an important national challenge, and we need a president who's going to be willing to take this thing on and be an inspiring leader, and say, "These are the things we have to do. This is an issue for our country. We have to deal with this, and deal with it." I think people will have to get into that. There are other issues, obviously, out there that people want to focus on, but they have to put this right up there too.

Q: *Right now it seems that the people who are standing up, who have the bullhorns, the Lou Dobbs and other people like that, are trying to take back our America, and we've lost our way. It seems that the bully pulpit is a place where it would be quite effective to doubt that theme, but say what we really are and why we should be true to the kind of people we are and the traditions we have.*

EMK: Well, it's the naysayers. You need to have the positive message, the inspirational message, the uplifting message. We should point out who's paying Lou Dobbs. That's an interesting thing. If they find out he's getting paid by these ultra right-wingers—he's paying them and they're paying the system—they're not in the country's interest. You have to play it with inspiration as well as hardball with these people.

Q: *Well, you're not despairing.*

EMK: No. I know what it takes. We have to get about the business of pulling all aspects of support together, and it's going to take strong presidential leadership. They have to feel it, understand it, be committed, and get about the business of doing it. It's a defining issue for our country, our society, and our future, and we have to get a handle on it.

Perspectives

David Burke, Edward Kennedy's chief of staff: Our immigration policy at that time [before 1965] was so skewed, and so openly biased—it was just openly and shamelessly—we had an Asian-Pacific Triangle. If you're Asian, you can't come in here. We only let a handful in every year. And you're lucky to get that. I mean, why? The Irish have a quota, a number—why can't we have something like that? Why are they favored? Why are the Irish so favored? And something has to be done about that. No, how is this son of Irish immigrants going to handle the cutback on Irish numbers, to cut back the number of Irish individuals in this country, in fact? Remember, we're talking families and reunification and so on. Why do we have to get into this and—? But he [Kennedy] took it on. It just was not right. I think that that was my first surprise with him, that there were certain things that he is deaf on, and one is political advice like, "I'd stay away from that issue, that's a killer." That's not a good way to open a conversation with him. He just looks at you sort of with a wonderment, like why are you—it's just not fair.

Nicolas Katzenbach, US attorney general during the Johnson administration: There was a good deal of pressure from some senators—I think they were probably southern senators—on immigration controls, particularly from Mexico for the border. . . . It was perfectly all right to change a lot of the quotas as far as Europe and so forth was concerned. It was all right to open it up to some extent in Asia, but the real problem in the Senate, and the House, I guess, was always with the Latin American countries, and particularly with Mexico. They wanted strict limits on the number of immigrants.

Carey Parker, Edward Kennedy's chief legislative assistant: Immigrants were welcomed into this country for hundreds of years, because we needed them. There certainly was no such thing as illegal Irish immigrants coming into Boston when the senator's ancestors arrived here in the nineteenth century. In fact, Kennedy was a leader in the enactment of one of the first immigration reform bills in modern times, the Immigration Reform Act of 1965. It had a different rationale: to end what was called the Asian-Pacific Triangle, which was very discriminatory against immigrants from Asia. Interestingly, I've seen comments in recent years that not enough credit has been given to the 1965 Act as a milestone of civil rights.

Q: It abolished national quotas.

Parker: Yes. The feeling has long been that the Civil Rights Act of '64, the Voting Rights Act of '65, and the Fair Housing Act of '68 were the big three civil rights bills in the '60s, obviously because they all had so much to do with segregation. But historians are now are saying that the Immigration Act of '65 deserves to be one of the big four civil rights bills of that decade. It's interesting that it passed in the same year as the original Voting Rights Act, which was a huge achievement by President Johnson.

Senator Alan Simpson (R-WY):

Q: Let's just talk for a minute about the 1990 bill because Kennedy voted against the '86 bill.

Simpson: He told me he would do that. But he said, "I think you've done a great job," and he made remarks after the bill passed. There were a lot of remarks made. It passed the Senate eighty-three to seventeen, I think. His remarks are in the *Congressional Record*. It was gracious. He knew what I had done and he told me honestly, "I can't vote for it. God, they'll tear me to bits."

Q: But then when you got to the 1990 bill, on everything leading up to that you worked very closely with him and you both did vote for it. What made the difference? That was a very different bill.

Simpson: Well, it was—and that's where we hung together, and Jack Brooks (congressman and chairman of House Judiciary Committee) was over there waiting for us with his cigar! What he didn't know was that Ted and I had made a pact, and that we were going to stick, and that the House could never take this away from us in the conference. Old Jack's sitting there tapping his cigar, "Well, Teddy, we're here for you. We're going to help you all we can!" Boy, he could take you through the coals. He was bragging and telling Texas stories. He was a fun and tough Democrat.

He said, "Well, we're not going to have any of that part right there," and we said, "Oh yes, we are. We're going to have all that." "Oh no," he said. "I know you and Kennedy don't agree on that." We said, "Oh yes, we do," and his jaw flew open and then we put it all in—stuck right with it. It was terrible in one way because he got beat in the next election because his constituents felt he had sold out or something. He was holding on for the Texas proviso kind of thing, which meant it was legal to hire an illegal but illegal for the illegal to work. That was the Texas proviso and that was originally the work of Brooks and company!

Esther Olavarria, counsel to Edward Kennedy and the Judiciary Committee:

Q: [T]ell us how you first met Senator Kennedy and how you came to hold the position that you have.

Olavarria: Well, it was back in the summer of '98. I had been an immigration attorney in Miami for about nine years and was looking to move to DC, and actually just through word of mouth heard of the position and was lucky that he—from what I understood in the interview—he was looking for someone who knew immigration law, and he didn't necessarily care that the person didn't have Hill experience. Often at other offices, they want the Hill experience.

So I went through the interview process and made it, I guess, to one of the finalists and sat down with him one afternoon for the meeting in his office. I was a little nervous, and I went and sat down on his chair and he says, "No, that's my chair." [*Laughs*] So, nice start. I'm going to get this job. But it went really well. He was very gracious. He wanted to know about my background. I was born in Cuba, so he was interested in that, and we talked about that.

Q: *You've been with the Senator since 1998 working strictly on immigration-related issues?*

Olavarria: Immigration, refugee issues. From time to time, I dabble in some other things like the Supreme Court nominations and things like that, but almost exclusively immigration, refugee.

Q: *Can you give us some sense of what aspects of the immigration issue Senator Kennedy seems most engaged with?*

Olavarria: Yes. Historically, he has been interested in refugee issues and I know, well before I started with him, he had those interests and traveled extensively. Others that you'll probably interview on the staff can tell you about that, but that interest continues to this day. For example, the committee has jurisdiction over refugee resettlement and once a year will meet with the secretary of state to determine what the refugee levels, numbers will be, the numbers we'll admit. He authored the Refugee Act of 1980 that started this whole process. So he's continued to be very interested in that throughout and whenever there are crises—for example, the Lebanon war that just happened now. He was very interested, very concerned, about the plight of the internally displaced and refugees in that situation. Now Iraq and Kosovo.

Q: *Has your relationship changed with him over time? I'm assuming your comfort level has grown over time.*

Olavarria: Very much so, yes. It takes a while to figure out exactly how to best serve him in the process and getting to feel comfortable with his needs, and I've gotten to the point where I feel like I am—especially, I guess, over the last three or so years when we've been working on comprehensive immigration reform, where I've been with him for long periods of time.

Q: *Are you frequently at his side in hearings and so forth? You would be the person to sit by his side?*

Olavarria: I would be the point person when he leans back and asks the questions at the hearings.

Q: *How often does he lean back and ask you questions?*

Olavarria: During hearings, all the time. He is really engaged. Sometimes it's just a comment about some remark somebody has said, or sometimes it's a question. He always manages to ask you the question that you're not prepared for. You'll bring binders and folders full of materials, and he'll always ask me at least one question each time that I need to—

Q: *And if you're stumped, how do you react?*

Olavarria: Well, I'll tell him. I've gotten to the point where I can tell him, "Senator, I don't know the answer to that question. Let me find out for you." So you find somebody in the audience who is an expert, or you get on the phone and get back to him.

Q: *The first time you had to do that, was that a nerve-wracking experience?*

Olavarria: Oh yes, absolutely.

Q: *And the first time you had to tell him you didn't know an answer to anything was—?*

Olavarria: He took it well. I think he prefers for you to tell him that than to try to bullshit him.

Q: *Is he somebody who ever gets irritated with staff?*

Olavarria: Oh sure. Compared to others, he doesn't have that kind of reputation, but he does. It's interesting to see that he's been doing this for so long, and he still sometimes gets nervous about an event, some place where he's going to speak or a hearing or an amendment on the floor. At that time, then he's, "Well, what am I going to say about this? What about this?" And he plays devil's advocate. Or when he thinks that the explanation you're giving him is just too long, that it's not something that he's going to be able to regurgitate and talk about on the floor or at a hearing and so forth, and he gets a little testy, a little irritated, you've just got to say, "Okay, Senator, let's start all over."

Q: *Do you think the nervousness comes, in part, from this—we keep hearing about how he studies really hard and he does his homework, and he wants to be the master of the facts in that room. Is that part of it?*

Olavarria: I think so, and he knows that people are expecting him to play that role.

Q: *Could you talk a little bit about that relationship [between Senator Kennedy and Senator McCain] from what you've seen?*

Olavarria: It's a really fascinating relationship. They're very different personalities. McCain can be very abrupt and abrasive and aggressive, and Senator Kennedy knows how to deal with that and counter it when he has to—but also stroke McCain when he has to. I think they've become quite close.

Q: *We're talking to you in August of 2006. There has been a tremendous amount of debate on an immigration bill over the last—I'm not sure when this all began—nine months?*

Olavarria: Even longer than that. I mean, they started working together on this bill in December '04.

Q: *I understand why Senator McCain, coming from Arizona, would have a strong interest in immigration. Could you try to explain to somebody who might be reading this transcript fifty to a hundred years from now why Senator Kennedy has an interest in this issue?*

Olavarria: I've heard him tell the story a bunch of times, and it is basically dating back to his family. His great-great-great grandparents—I can't remember how many great-greats there are but—came from Ireland during, I want to say during the time of the potato famine, and they were able to work hard and make it in this country quite successfully. Because of that history and also because of, I guess, his brother's concern about immigrants. I mean, President [John F.] Kennedy's book, *A Nation of Immigrants*, and so forth. He felt very strongly about this issue.

Senator John McCain (R-AZ):

Q: I'm going to ask you—lots has been written about immigration, so we'll get to that at this time.

McCain: Oh, yes. That was a classic example of Ted Kennedy, because he had to take positions that in no way impacted the whole principle and effort for immigration reform, but at the same time he realized that in order to get a sufficient number of votes, he had to make a concession. I guess one of the biggest areas, the best example of that, is the issue of a legal temporary worker program. Now, the unions have always been opposed to legal temporary worker programs, and we all know the reasons behind that, and I respect those views. Ted had that position as well, but he knew in order to get a sufficient number of Republicans that he had to support that for the greater good. The greater good here is so important. Ted was very aware people die in the desert every day, people are exploited, young women are mistreated and have no recourse. The problems with illegal immigration in this country are so huge, and everything about his humanitarian spirit was appealed to, and that's why he made it such a high priority and the reason why we kept going back at it. So Ted not only took a position, but cast votes against his stand on a specific aspect of the legislation.

Every morning we would get together at 8:30 in the President's Room off the floor of the Senate. That happens to be the place where Lyndon Johnson signed the Civil Rights Act,[50] a very historic room and a beautiful room, and he and I would talk first for a little while and then we'd bring in the other senators, including Senator Obama, not frequently, but he would sometimes come, and we would plot out the strategy for the day.

We would sometimes have very spirited discussions about what we should do and how we should handle a certain amendment. But most importantly, Ted would say to Democrats and I would say to Republicans, "You've got to vote against this amendment, even though if it was stand-alone, you would vote for it." Because there were efforts from both left and right—admittedly, stronger from the right, but also from the left—to destroy this legislation. He

---

50. Actually the 1965 Voting Rights Act.

would do it with humor. Sometimes he would speak as sternly to a senator as I have ever seen one senator talk to another senator in front of a group of senators. We almost made it. I think that we were on the verge of it, and we went into a ten- or twelve-day recess, and unfortunately we lost a lot of the momentum. But I've never been prouder of an effort that he made on that issue.

13

Escaping a Quagmire: The Iraq War

The lessons Edward Kennedy learned from Vietnam informed his views on the use of military force in Iraq. In the wake of the September 11, 2001, terror attacks on the United States, however, he kept an open mind and listened carefully to witnesses before the Armed Services Committee. High-ranking military leaders opposed the rush to war in Iraq, and Senator Kennedy found them particularly persuasive. Drawing from the writings of Saints Augustine and Thomas Aquinas, Kennedy believed that certain criteria must be met before he could support going to war. Although, in the aftermath of the 9/11 attack, the senator asserted that the United States was justified in striking its perpetrators, al-Qaeda, and their patrons, the Taliban, in Afghanistan, he did not believe the criteria for a just war had been met in Iraq. The George W. Bush administration's rationales for removing Iraqi dictator Saddam Hussein by force remained unconvincing to Kennedy.[1] Moreover, he was dubious that Iraqi regime change would produce peace in a country riven by ancient religious and tribal strife. Kennedy thought the United States would be better served by turning its attention toward limiting North Korea's rogue dictator and his nuclear ambitions.

Kennedy opposed the 2002 Authorization of the Use of Military Force (AUMF) in Iraq, as he had in 1991's Gulf War, to expel Saddam from Kuwait. A total of twenty-three senators voted nay on the AUMF. Kennedy, along with his senior colleague Robert Byrd (D-WV) argued vociferously that the Founding Fathers intended that the decision to go to war be a joint one taken by the executive and legislative branches. Senator Kennedy also believed that the Bush administration should have created a genuine multinational force, as had President George H. W. Bush in the first Gulf War. Once more, Kennedy became the national leader of an antiwar movement. He even received a call from George W. Bush's chief of staff Andy Card, who asked the

---

1. The Bush Doctrine, associated with the forty-third president, called for preemptive military strikes to protect American security and justified their use for regime change in Iraq, arguing that brutal dictator Saddam Hussein had supported terrorists, including al-Qaeda; used chemical weapons on Iraqi Kurds; ignored UN resolutions; and possessed weapons of mass destruction, including nuclear capabilities.

senator to tone down his attacks on the president. Former president George H. W. Bush made the same request of Kennedy. "Be nice to my kid, will ya?" the elder Bush chided the senator at a public dinner in Texas.

Unable to prevent the invasion of Iraq in March 2003, Kennedy turned his attention to ending the war. Labeling Iraq "Bush's Vietnam," the senator fought to pass a timetable for the drawdown of US combat forces. Kennedy also called for the Bush administration to keep Congress fully informed and to adopt specific criteria for measuring progress in the war. At the same time, Senator Kennedy proposed expenditures to protect US troops in Iraq more effectively. In 2005 Kennedy worked with the Hart family, who had lost their son in the war, to promote funding for "up-armored" troop vehicles to defend service personnel from deadly improvised explosive devices placed along roadways.

Kennedy reported in his oral history that the Iraq war had only facilitated recruitment of terrorists, empowered Iran, destabilized the entire Middle East (leading to the Syrian conflict), displaced millions of refugees, and stretched American military forces "to the breaking point." Kennedy worried that the nation's emphasis on foreign wars meant the diminution of domestic policy, which made the Senate seem less relevant to Americans. "[T]here's so much uncertainly out there about where we're going in this country and as a society and institutionally that they're looking at least to some political figures for some direction and leadership. And we are obviously trying to provide it." Edward Kennedy's principled opposition to the wars in Vietnam and Iraq defined his legacy, both as a senator and as a national leader.

Q: This is an interview with Senator Kennedy, December 9, 2007, in Washington. Vicki is with us. We're going to talk about war, with specific reference to the Middle Eastern conflicts: the short [1991] war in Iraq and some of its antecedents, Afghanistan, and the current ongoing war in Iraq.

EMK: To understand my view about the Iraq conflict and my hesitancy about the involvement of the United States, I think it's only fair to look at both the immediate and the historic background. Both are very important. The immediate background is the fact that it was al-Qaeda and the Taliban that attacked us on 9/11. They were the adversaries, and Iraq was a diversion that echoed and resonated with the American people as we were coming into the administration's rush to war with Iraq.

We have to understand that going to war is the most important decision a legislator makes. Clearly it is for a president, but certainly the votes we cast to bring a country to conflict, into war are the most important. I think even with this Iraq situation, it's important that we look at some of the experiences of the immediate and the historic past.

The past experience for me was not just Afghanistan, which I'll come to, but if you look back further, it was the Vietnam War and the great conflicts we faced in World War II—when everyone signed up and was aboard. We had been attacked, just like we were on 9/11. The other series of conflicts we've gotten into sprang from the tension we had with the Soviet Union in the post–World War II period—the anti-communist period, the surge by the communists to expand their influence, and the tensions that brought.

I've been a student of the anti-colonial period. It was a period President Kennedy had been very much involved in, and it's something I watched very closely and learned from. I had been in law school, and he suggested I go down to see the Algerian conflict. This was after Morocco and Tunisia had freed themselves from the colonial powers; and Africa was moving away from the colonial powers.

President Kennedy looked at the great strife between the Soviet Union and the West as represented by India, which had freed itself from the British. Which way was India going to go? Were they going to go with democracy or were they going to go with communism? He was very active in supporting India for that reason. He thought, coming out of World War II, as these countries were freeing themselves from colonialism, they were also open to the strife between communism and capitalism and Western democracy.

He had gone to Southeast Asia and had been there just before, or at the time of, Dien Bien Phu.[2] He had watched the Algerian situation develop. So he had some sense—which I certainly observed, because it was something that was discussed—of the movement of people to free themselves from colonialism, and the strife that "occupiers" had to endure in some instances—the French in Algeria and in Southeast Asia, the British in Malaysia—to hold on to their countries, and the internal conflicts that were taking place. This obviously spilled over into Vietnam.

The Vietnam experience developed in the post–Dien Bien Phu period, where they had actually gotten a peace treaty. [President] Eisenhower signed onto it, but the breakdown and deterioration of that agreement began because the communists and Viet Cong were pressing it, and the involvement of the United States began to escalate. I think we've gone over my own transformation in Vietnam.

So we've seen where the United States had gotten into the conflict in Vietnam with all the extraordinary misrepresentations, the lies, the loss of American lives, the billions of dollars spent, the failure to level with the American people about the impossible situation of westernizing Vietnam. So there's a resonance.

We've been involved in a lot of other conflicts that I took strong positions on—one with regard to Contra aid [in Nicaragua]. That's a somewhat different phenomenon, but it's an important one, and we were very much involved and

---

2. Dien Bien Phu was the site of the Vietnamese communists' 1954 defeat of the French colonial army.

engaged working with Congressman Boland trying to end that conflict. I played a role in that. Then we have other incidents of executive authority: Panama, Grenada, and a different situation, obviously, in Korea.

One has to be cautioned about the ability of the United States to resolve political conflicts with military solutions. I think there was a healthy kind of skepticism about that. But there was also a recognition that the United States had to be prepared to involve itself in areas where we had strong interests. We were slow in responding to Bosnia, though the Dayton Accords were a success. We didn't get into Rwanda, despite the [genocidal] killings that took place there. I think history will have to judge our unwillingness to do that. We were slow getting involved in Kosovo, which eventually, with American leadership, turned out in a satisfactory way.

We clearly have an interest in being involved abroad, but the emphasis should always lie in diplomacy first—the economic, social, political initiatives that can be made—and in a military approach last. That's still certainly something we're guided by now.

In the first Gulf War, I agreed with Mitchell and Sam Nunn[3] that we had not given economic sanctions available to the United States enough time to work to get Saddam out of Kuwait. I had seen sanctions work, and work very effectively, particularly in South Africa. Within four years of sanctions being imposed on South Africa, Nelson Mandela was out of jail, and they had a change in the government there.

The reason they worked is that they were comprehensive. All of Europe was involved in the economic sanctions, and when the United States got involved in it, it had a dramatic economic impact on South Africa. It seemed to me that we ought to seek first to use sanctions to achieve our interests in that part of the world [Iraq] without getting into a military conflict. I thought it ought to be given a try, and it hadn't been. That was my reservation about it.

What we learned from the Gulf War is that [President George H. W.] Bush built international support for a military operation rather than taking unilateral action, and, most importantly, understood the limitations of American forces going into and occupying Baghdad. That's been noted and discussed and debated. The neocons[4] felt that they should have gone into Baghdad, but

---

3. Senators George Mitchell and Sam Nunn were Democrats from Maine and Georgia, respectively.

4. "Neocons," or neoconservatives, arose initially among American Marxists who opposed the Stalinist regime's excesses in the Soviet Union. By the 1960s they no longer felt at home in the Democratic Party, which drifted toward the New Left. As promoters of American interests abroad and the use of military force to protect them, neocons became increasingly disillusioned with President Jimmy Carter's foreign policy failures. Many joined Ronald Reagan's conservative movement. Jewish American neocons were particularly aghast at Saddam Hussein's atrocities and compared him to Adolf Hitler. Paul Wolfowitz, Douglas Feith, Elliott Abrams, Eliot Cohen, and Richard Perle, who all served during the

Scowcroft[5] and Bush cleverly decided not to go in militarily to overthrow Saddam or to occupy Baghdad. They saw the dangers of trying to occupy the country and remembered how the British had been driven out in the 1920s when they tried to cobble together the Sunnis and the Shi'a and the Kurds into a country.

They made a wise judgment in terms of restraint and focused military objectives, and that was enormously important. The cooperation we had from the international community was evident by the thirty-four-country coalition that included Arab states—even those who didn't join, like Germany and Japan, contributed almost $17 billion. So the important lessons learned were the limitations of military power and unilateral action, particularly with regard to the Middle East, and particularly with regard to Iraq. That was very important.

Q: *There was also the fact that Kuwait had been invaded by another country, and so the limited US objectives that Bush sought were to get Saddam out of Kuwait and restore Kuwait's sovereignty.*

EMK: And that effectively happened. The Iraqis were not prepared to fight the American forces. They had a low morale, and all the rest that we've learned historically. Saddam Hussein claimed Kuwait as part of Iraq. However, Kuwaitis felt invaded and occupied. It's a dicey part of the world in terms of drafting various boundary lines through the whole region. They were really drafted during the colonial period, but nonetheless, that was the purpose and the reason for the conflict, and when the Iraqis withdrew from those areas, the United States ended its effective presence, although we maintained these zones—the northern zone and the southern zone.

Q: *The no-fly.*

EMK: The no-fly zones. Later, incidents of terrorism took place: the Khobar Towers and US embassies in Africa blown up, and the bombing of the USS *Cole*, the navy ship being refueled in Yemen.[6] We had acts of violence and terrorism taking place, and the limited response by President Clinton, that's been pointed out historically.

Q: *Was the period you're talking about now the time when terrorism first appeared on the radar screen? Saddam's invasion of another country was the impetus for the Gulf War. Was this the period when you and the government and others became aware that there was something else going on?*

George W. Bush administration, were instrumental in advocating that the United States invade Iraq to remove Saddam Hussein from power.

5. General Brent Scowcroft was George H. W. Bush's national security advisor.

6. Kennedy was referring to terrorist bombings of Khobar Towers in Saudi Arabia (1996), US embassies in East Africa (1998), and the USS *Cole* (2000), which were aimed at US military and civilian personnel. He then cites the first World Trade Center bombing in 1993.

EMK: I think so. There were these series of different events in the early '90s, the [first] attack on the World Trade Center, and then the embassies in Tanzania and Kenya, and then the USS *Cole* in Yemen. Those were the most dramatic and notorious events. Even though those took place, I don't think there was much of an effort to tie them together and see it as growth and the dangers of terrorism.

Now as to 9/11, President [George W.] Bush wins the election—a controversial election. We have learned from Suskind's book on Paul O'Neill,[7] President Bush's secretary of treasury, that from the earliest days of the administration, going into January of 2001—this is several months, obviously, before 9/11— the administration had been fascinated by Saddam Hussein and was trying to build a case against him.

This was brought out by O'Neill and by Suskind, in the book, which addressed Cabinet meetings on the topic at that time. It was a theme reiterated by O'Neill and Suskind in that book, and it's been authenticated by others. The administration and President Bush, Cheney, Wolfowitz, and Rumsfeld,[8] all had their eye on Saddam Hussein and were looking for the opportunity to topple him. They believed it would be easy to bring changes that would be useful to spread the United States' interests in the Middle East. They scoffed at the diplomatic efforts made by President Clinton—which had been significant—towards the end of his terms, and they were very engaged in thinking about how they were going to topple and defeat Saddam Hussein in his own country. Planning had taken place.

Q: *Looking back, how would you explain this—I don't know whether to call it an obsession or what. How should people understand what motivated the administration to adopt this goal?*

EMK: I think the first evidence of it was the strong, strong dissent that was heard when President [George H. W.] Bush decided not to go into Baghdad during the first Gulf War. That decision was strongly criticized by the neocons, Perle and others outside of government, in the advisory capacity, who continued to raise it after the war. They were saying that this had been a very significant and great mistake, that the United States should have gone into Baghdad, and that it would have made a major difference in terms of our interests in the Middle East.

This argument was carried forward in public letters, documents, and papers that were widely circulated. It became a rather acceptable concept in

---

7. Ron Suskind, *The Price of Loyalty: George W. Bush, the White House, and the Education of Paul O'Neill* (New York: Simon and Schuster, 2004).

8. Bush's advisors included Vice President Richard Cheney, Deputy Secretary of Defense Paul Wolfowitz, and Secretary of Defense Donald Rumsfeld, all of whom supported invading Iraq in 2003.

conservative circles that we should have taken the actions then, and that it would have changed the Middle East for the better. It was a theory that was out there—at least a theory that was held by the neocons—and it was discussed and debated among them and acceptable to them, although I don't think it had general support.

Many who shared this view came into government with Bush II in responsible positions, mostly in the Defense Department. In any event, that was the climate and atmosphere in the administration after January and through the summer, although I don't think people outside the administration had much sense about it.

Now we come to 9/11. I think I've described the drama of that with Laura Bush.[9]

Q: No, we have not.

EMK: On September 11, Laura Bush was coming up to testify on early education before our Education, Health, and Labor Committee. We had been working with her on issues of literacy and early education. We had a conference in Georgetown with her on early education. This was the idea that the earlier the intervention, the better it is for the children.

There was dispute and questions about the idea, how significant the impact was going to be, and also whether we were going to be able to get resources to do it. Laura Bush had been involved in reading programs, and I had attended reading programs with her. I do it with a reading program called Everyone Wins at the Brent School here in the District of Columbia. I've done it for twelve years or so. Laura Bush has been involved in reading programs, and we had attended programs together and had spoken at events. She agreed to come up to the Hill and testify in favor of early education on this particular day—9/11.

I was in my office. The hearing was at ten o'clock. She was going to come in around 9:15 and meet me and Judd Gregg, and then, about fifteen or twenty minutes later, the other members of the committee were going to come in and meet her. We were all going to go to the Senate Caucus Room from my office, which is on the third floor of the Russell Building, 318, opposite the Caucus Room, and she would testify at 10.

I arrived at the office probably around 8:30 or quarter to nine. We were preparing for the hearing and for Laura Bush when Beth[10] came in and said that Vicki was on the phone and that there had been a crash of a plane into one of the [World Trade Center] towers. It was very alarming. I think you were the first one to call in. I forget the time.

Vicki Kennedy: 8:45, 8:50, something like that.

---

9. Laura was George W. Bush's wife and First Lady.
10. Beth Hoagland was a Kennedy staffer.

EMK: I was alerted, but I didn't believe this was a terrorist attack. It just didn't sink in. And then probably twenty or twenty-five minutes later, the second plane hit. Vicki had called in about that, and it was quite evident that something was happening, something was going on, some kind of attack.

This was the time Laura Bush was supposed to arrive. I went and spoke to the staff and said we'd better find out and cancel the hearing and notify Mrs. Bush. They said, "She's already left the car downstairs." So I went out of my office and to the car, and I saw her walking down. She was completely unaware; she was walking by herself. She had an aide behind her, and then behind her were the Secret Service. She was walking down rather elegantly, a poised person, completely unaware of what was happening at that time.

She came into the office. Judd Gregg had just arrived, and we filled her in as to what was happening. Then probably the security gave her some fill-in, although they were rather mystified by it all. They didn't really know what it all meant. They were in a holding pattern. I started going around the room, showing her different things in my office. I thought rather than just sitting there I ought to try to occupy her thoughts. She was interested and inquisitive. At some time in here, there was information that the Pentagon had been struck.

Vicki Kennedy: I was involved; I was here on the phone, calling into the office, and I know at some point, you and Mrs. Bush had a press conference canceling [the hearing]. I had been calling your office, and then the office was evacuated, and then you called me, and I was very eager that you get out of there. But you wouldn't leave Mrs. Bush. You said, "No, I'm here with Laura Bush," and you felt an obligation to stay with her, very gentlemanly and very kind.

I was somewhat crazed, wanting you out of there. But you said, "The Secret Service is here; don't worry." I said, "Well, they can't stop a plane. They've hit the Pentagon." And you said, "Oh? Where did you hear that?" I said, "It's on CNN, and you can see the smoke from upstairs in our bedroom. You can see it coming across the river. So you'll have to get out of there."

You hung up to go talk to them, but the Secret Service was unaware—you all were unaware that the plane had hit the Pentagon, and there were other planes still in the air at that time.

EMK: Just at this time, we went over to the Caucus Room, and it was absolutely packed. I spoke about what was happening and then Laura Bush spoke, which she did very well. I have it written down, but I can't tell you exactly what I said at the time. The point was that there had been some conflict or attack, and we were not going to have the hearing. We would do it later on.

Then she talked briefly, and we went back into my office. The Secret Service was going to take her out. We walked down the corridor towards the east side of the building where there are some elevators. The Secret Service said, "We'd better hold." They were looking around to find an office to go into, and Judd Gregg's office was there, so we went into his office and stayed there. The Secret Service was outside.

At that time, they said that there were seven or eight other planes, and they didn't know where they were going, whether they were going to go to the Capitol or to office buildings, or what they were going to do. So they made a decision they weren't going to move her. That's when I suggested that she call the president. At that time, he had not called her, nor had she called him, nor had the Secret Service. She had not called her children. So she went into the room, and we went out, and she tried to get him. It took a long, long time, twenty or thirty minutes before she was able to get him. But I'd say for an hour and a half there hadn't been any communication whatsoever between the two of them, or with the children, which I thought was rather interesting.

She came out and said she had talked to the president and her daughters, and then the Secret Service took her, and we came out. All the phones were down, and people were out on the grassy areas outside the Capitol. I got in the car to come home, and of course the roads were absolutely jammed. Everybody was trying to get their kids out of school, but the authorities said it was probably better to leave them in school where they could get information. They were located, they were safe and secure rather than being home. Some parents were home, but some couldn't get home. They wouldn't be able to get in at some places. The idea that you drop the kids off at home was kind of interesting; people were adjusting to this. Your kids couldn't come home.

Vicki Kennedy: Curran was a freshman at college, but Caroline[11] was at school, and we had been talking a lot that morning. Teddy said, "I think it's safer for her to stay at school," and I agreed. Remember, you called me when you finally got in the car, and you said, "Traffic isn't moving, I'm going to get in the subway." I said, "No!" I was terrified of the idea of the subway, because who knew what was going on—there might be a bomb.

You stayed in the car, and it took you forever to get in, but then Caroline managed to get through on the phone, and she was hysterical. I said, "No, Teddy and I have discussed it, and you'll stay at school, and I'll get you when things are quiet." She said, "Come get me right now. I want to come home. I need you to come get me." I said, "Okay, but it's going to take me a while." She said, "That's okay." School is five minutes from here, and it did take a while, but I picked her up with a friend of hers who was there and couldn't get a parent to pick him up. I brought him here too. We waited and then Teddy got here. We kept the TV off so they wouldn't see it, but then when they finally did see it, it was just a pretty traumatic day, to say the least.

Q: *And during this time, it wasn't known what else was on the way.*

---

11. Curran and Caroline Raclin were Kennedy's stepchildren.

EMK: No.

Vicki Kennedy: No. There were missing planes that were still in the air.

EMK: There were missing planes. They finally made the judgment—it was probably early afternoon—that there were no more planes. One was the Pennsylvania plane.[12] It was going out west and then turned around, and they didn't know where that was going to go. They changed from seven or eight, and then after the Pentagon and that one in Pennsylvania, they realized they had all the planes down. That night, we went back into the Senate. It was eight o'clock. I talked to [Thomas] Daschle, to urge him to go back in—to have the Senate go back into session. We all went back in and the House went back in—

Vicki Kennedy: To show that terrorists weren't going to stop us.

EMK: Yes, they weren't going to stop the functioning of government. Then they had the anthrax scare that closed the Senate Hart Building. They didn't know how many people were being targeted, and whether we were about to be. This was coming at us through the mail. So we had these two very dramatic moments, and it was heightened, clearly for me, because of the fact that Laura Bush was there, the First Lady—her presence, and the drama of these horrific assaults and attacks on these buildings—the people going out those windows. That will remain in my memory forever. The horrific aspects of this were just emblazoned in people's minds—the smoke at the Pentagon. But through all this, people believed that Saddam Hussein was behind it. I think there's no question they did.

Q: Does this include your colleagues in the Senate?

EMK: Well, it was pretty broad, pretty widespread. I remember going to the briefing, that afternoon or the next morning, and they said it was al-Qaeda. The briefers said they believed that was it, but there was a good deal of skepticism. I remember telling Vicki they pretty much knew who these people were, but there was a lot of talk.

Q: They were mostly Saudis.

EMK: Yes, they were Saudis.

Q: The briefing was by whom?

EMK: The briefing was from CIA.

Vicki Kennedy: But they said it was Bin Laden,[13] right?

EMK: Osama bin Laden, yes.

Q: Not Saddam.

EMK: Not Saddam. The American people certainly believed it was Saddam, and the political leadership let it go on. All the polls reflect that. You get it even now: half of the American people still think it was Saddam Hussein, even though it's been completely debunked. Certainly during all the debate

---

12. That plane was crashed by terrorists in Shanksville, Pennsylvania, as passengers rushed the cockpit.

13. Bin Laden was the Saudi leader of al-Qaeda.

and discussion, people thought it was Saddam, even though the members had been briefed. So, there was a universal condemnation of Osama bin Laden and the Taliban, and al-Qaeda, not only by everyone here in the United States or Congress, but also by the American people and the world. We were unified.

French newspapers said, "Today we're all Americans." It was just an overwhelming, complete, thoroughly unified response—assault and go after al-Qaeda in Afghanistan, and we did. Americans came together, with a unified purpose, an understanding of the reasons for the commitment of American forces, and the establishment of a goal that was going to be achievable. That was when the United States went to war, and that was when it made sense in terms of bringing everyone together. Of course it brought Europeans together. Even the Iranians were helpful, when they get the—

Q: On the border.

EMK: On the border, and when they set up Karzai[14] at the end, they had the Bonn Conference, and all the Muslim countries were very supportive. It was a worldwide, unified effort to deal with the challenge of the time. Of course, that dissipated almost overnight with the Iraq War. It's difficult to capture the dramatic, horrific, and sobering reaction to 9/11 in terms of its impact on all of us as individuals, and also the country. This is really the Pearl Harbor in this generation—that was an assault on military targets, and this was an assault on individuals and civilian targets. It was just incredibly powerful. The unified response now was Afghanistan.

So, we're at the end of 2001. The Senate has passed a unanimous vote, 98–0, on the Afghanistan war,[15] and we're moving into 2002. I think as history shows, there was increasing anxiety about the steps being taken by the administration that were divisive in terms of the country—the PATRIOT Act and the issue of civil liberties, the Axis of Evil speech, which was a condemnation not only of Iraq, but also Iran and North Korea. And there was the Cheney speech in August. So what you had is the increasing pressure and increasing loss of support worldwide, in terms of actions that were taken by the United States; cracking down on individual rights, the way we were dealing with these issues at home. Then there was, as we've seen, the move towards the conflict with Iraq in the fall of 2002.

Q: And there was also in there the announcement of the [Bush] doctrine of preventive war or preemptive war. All of these things were coming head on heels.

EMK: You're absolutely right, and I made a statement on that at Harvard that it would be useful to have flagged here, in preparation for this debate. I was admitted to the faculty of arts and sciences at Harvard, and spoke about this. It was a brief speech, probably eight or ten minutes, but a very good one,

---

14. Hamid Karzai was the president of Afghanistan.
15. The Afghanistan war to depose the Taliban and capture al-Qaeda forces.

about the difference between preemption and prevention. It was just at this time, at the beginning of the debate on the Iraq War.

Vicki Kennedy: I think you made that speech in early September of 2002.

EMK: September 2002. Now the drumbeat starts about the necessity of doing something about Iraq. We had the beginning of the escalation of rhetoric on Iraq. Over the course of the summer, when we were up in Massachusetts in August and early September, we had a sense that the administration was going to move towards opening up a front with Iraq.

I can remember talking with friends in Boston about the increasing likelihood that it was going to take place, and I was honest about it, but I indicated that I was going to wait until we had some hearings. We had an incredibly important and powerful hearing in the Armed Services Committee on September 23. We had General Shalikashvili; Wes Clark; General Hoar of the Marines; General Nash, who was a commander in Bosnia; and General McInerney.[16]

A number of those had retired, but all are very distinguished military officers on a panel addressing the challenges of going to war in Iraq. They were virtually unanimous in cautioning against going to war with Iraq, and particularly going to war without the international community. General Hoar is from Massachusetts. He said that if we did go to war with Iraq, it would end up being an urban war. He pointed out that all the advantages the United States has in terms of technology, firepower, and all the rest, would be lost because it would end up in a street fight, which would be just soldier versus soldier, and it would look like the last fifteen minutes of *Saving Private Ryan*.

It was a very powerful presentation, and we had the best of the best in terms of military leaders. All of them had seen a good deal of conflict in Vietnam and some in the Gulf War. They were virtually unanimous in cautioning against going to war, and that had a very important impact on me. I gave a speech in opposition to the war shortly thereafter at what's called the SAIS[17] at Johns Hopkins.

The other very important hearing we had was an intelligence hearing. Rumsfeld had used these words in a public hearing. When he was asked where the weapons of mass destruction were, he said, "They're in the area around Tikrit and Baghdad and east, west of Sadr, and north somewhat." I think he said about 127 different locations.

Levin[18] said, "Well, if they're there, why don't we send the [international weapons] inspectors in, point them out, and identify those eight or ten different areas?" Rumsfeld said, "The inspection teams are all penetrated, and if we do that, they'll move them."

---

16. Generals John Shalikashvili, Wesley Clark, Joseph Hoar, William Nash, and Thomas McInerney all appeared before the committee.

17. School of Advanced International Studies.

18. Senator Carl Levin was a Democrat from Michigan.

Then Levin said, "Why can't we get cameras and watch them move them?" And Rumsfeld turned around to Tenet[19] and said, "Okay, we'll give them eight or ten locations." He told Levin, at different times, that they were continuously giving the locations of these centers to the inspection team, and then after the war got started, they got a report from the inspectors that they never got any of them. They never gave them any locations whatsoever. I thought the reluctance and resistance to give the inspection teams the locations was a rather fierce indictment that this wasn't for real. I thought this added up to the fact that we were just getting the drumbeat of harsh rhetoric [to invade Iraq].

Take that sense, and then add to it the rhetoric that was starting about the mushroom cloud. You had Cheney saying that without question Iraq did have weapons of mass destruction, and you had the president using similar kinds of words. There's a whole sequence of these kinds of hot-button words they were using that had been carefully designed to build public support for the invasion.

In the summertime (we're backing up to 2002), I had talked to [former] President Clinton, who had spoken at a labor conference outside London. He indicated that he had noticed this rhetoric building up, but said we should not get all worked up about it. He told me this confidentially—because Blair had convinced Bush to go to the United Nations, and he thought the United Nations would put some common sense into the two of them. I remember that conversation. We took notes on it. I don't know where those notes are from that summer.

I also had Gordon Brown,[20] who had been up at the Cape that summer, over for lunch. He didn't get into much of a discussion about the British position, but I got a very clear sense from our conversation that he knew Blair was aboard and that Blair had convinced the president that they ought to go to the UN before taking action. There was no question when we had the resolution in the Senate[21]—and this is one of the most important historic points—that the administration wanted action and wanted it immediately. They had a faltering economy and faltering polls. Those were the realities. President Bush wanted to have the vote prior to the [midterm] election, there's no question about it, particularly in contrast to his father, who waited until after the election to get the vote on the first Gulf War. There was a clear path he could have taken, but he didn't take that path. There was an absolute drive to get this done and get it done rapidly.

On the Friday before the vote, which I think ended up being on Wednesday or Thursday, Bob Byrd asked me to come down to his office, and we had a

---

19. George Tenet was CIA director.
20. Brown was British chancellor of the exchequer.
21. The resolution to which Kennedy refers is the October 2002 Authorization of the Use of Military Force in Iraq.

meeting with three or four senators who were like-minded in opposition to war. We had figured out we had eight votes against it—although we said we had ten—and we thought we were increasing. But we had effectively eight votes against it.

Q: Against authorization?

EMK: Against authorization for going to war. Then on that Monday it opened up somewhat, and probably eight or ten senators came on. Carl Levin was in that group, Barbara Boxer was in it, as was Corzine.[22] A number of people were with us on that Monday. It built a little bit. When we were going in to vote, we thought it was about eighteen votes. I think we got up to twenty-two or twenty-three.

Q: Twenty-three.

EMK: Twenty-three votes on it. I had a conversation with my colleague John Kerry. He was sort of torn about what to do, and I mentioned to him that he ought to vote against it. I think you vote the substance, then the politics of it. On the politics, I thought if he voted for the war and they had a great success, he wasn't going to get any credit for it, but if he voted against it and it didn't go right, he was going to get some credit. Besides, considering what I thought to be the substance of it, to vote the politics was bad.

Since I mentioned John, just historically, I was reminded that after 2005, I delivered another big speech on the war, and it was about getting out, setting the timeframe to get out of Iraq. John was on *Meet the Press.* Tim Russert said, "Do you agree with Kennedy that there should be a specific timetable of withdrawal for American troops?" He said no. I had forgotten about that.

In any event, historically, I think Senator Byrd deserves an enormous amount of credit. He was very eloquent through all of this, and right on the button about who brings a country to war. The nation has to be brought to war. It has to be a shared power, a shared responsibility. This was a unilateral action, and it was going to be a great mistake. Of course, he was absolutely right on all points. It was a lonely position during that time. Those who took a different position were roundly criticized and condemned readily and repeatedly.

Q: For what?

EMK: For having a different position, for saying that the attack of 9/11 was by Osama bin Laden—not Saddam Hussein—and we ought to keep our eye on battling him [bin Laden]. We ought to keep our eye on battling al-Qaeda. They were the threat to the United States. They were the ones who had attacked us. We were involved in diverting the resources from the battle against al-Qaeda in Afghanistan. It had been demonstrated most basically and fundamentally

---

22. Senators Barbara Boxer and Jon Corzine were Democrats from California and New Jersey, respectively.

that Iraq did not present a clear and present danger, an imminent threat to the United States. Nowhere could they demonstrate that Iraq was an imminent threat to the United States or to our national security—and this is ultimately the criterion that has to be used in deciding to use force to protect the United States. They failed to meet that criterion and that measurement. They took their eye off the ball in terms of who the perpetrators were on 9/11, and with this action, we saw the collapse of the support of the international community for the United States' position in fighting al-Qaeda and the Taliban and Osama bin Laden.

Q: The administration's argument was, by then, that al-Qaeda and Iraq were basically the same enemy.

EMK: That's right.

Q: That is, Iraq made the attacks possible. I thought they had two arguments: one was to justify the war on Iraq as a war against al-Qaeda. Didn't they try to do that?

Vicki Kennedy: I thought they said we have the lessons of 9/11. They kept talking about the lessons of 9/11; we have to get them before they get us. We have to get Iraq, because we've learned the lesson of 9/11. And then they kept conflating it, to make it seem as though Iraq had been involved in 9/11.

Q: Yes, that's right.

Vicki Kennedy: Without letting people think they hadn't been.

EMK: The president indicated that many meetings took place between al-Qaeda and the Iraqis, which was completely untrue. Cheney did the same thing. Then, in the State of the Union, the president talked about the yellow-cake[23] and the building of the nuclear weapons, which was also completely untrue.

Q: [Quoting from Bush's State of the Union address] "The British Government has learned—"

EMK: —learned that the Iraqis were importing this material that could be used for the development of enriched uranium. There was no question that at the highest levels—Cheney, Rumsfeld, Condi Rice,[24] and the president—there were distortions, misrepresentations, and mistruths. That was true with Tenet as well. And that all created a climate that built very broad support for going to war, which we did [in March 2003].

We went to war with a military that wasn't properly equipped to deal with the type of conflict they were going to face: our Humvees did not have proper armor, so our soldiers didn't have the right equipment. The administration went to war without a plan to secure the peace and made repeated errors in

---

23. Yellowcake is a form of uranium oxide that that can be processed for use in nuclear weapons. President Bush did not use the term "yellowcake" in his 2003 State of the Union Address, but he stated that "[t]he British Government has learned that Saddam Hussein recently sought significant quantities of uranium from Africa."

24. Condoleezza Rice was Bush's national security advisor and then secretary of state.

terms of the administration of the war effort. They went to war without a plan about how to eventually get out of Iraq. They continued to mislead the American people. Wolfowitz stated that we would be treated as liberators, that we would be able to use Iraqi resources and money to offset costs and pay for the war.

And we were constantly given rosy scenarios, all the way through the conflict, right up to the very end—for four-and-a-half years. We had this incredible mad search for weapons of mass destruction that weren't there. We spent hundreds of millions of dollars searching for them; the administration kept saying they were there and were being hidden. We used American troops as police. They never made an effort to involve the Italian *carabinieri*,[25] the Spanish police, and British police—all highly professional and good at police work. Instead, they used American troops. This was a catastrophic failure. We were completely unprepared to deal with the kind of military threat we faced from the insurgency, including the blowing up of the Humvees by IEDs.[26]

I had raised the issue of the postwar humanitarian effort. We finally got John Warner,[27] who was chairman of the Armed Services Committee at the time, to have one hearing on it. It was the most pitiful hearing—certainly one of the most pitiful I've ever attended. It was basically all slogans and clichés about how different organizations were coordinating and working together, how they were going to deal with all the problems related to the flow of people and refugees in the postwar period. It was insulting in terms of its blandness and lack of substance.

Of course, when we saw the invasion, none of that was there initially, but it came later. We've taken the political heat for it with the growing escalation of hatred and distrust by the Iraqi people, and it's been enormously costly.

Q: Do you have any recollection, first of all, about when you fully realized that the die was cast—this is before the votes were taken—that the administration was determined to do this come what may? Second, when did you begin to realize that there was a lot of lying and deception practiced by the administration? In retrospect, the pattern becomes pretty clear, particularly now. But I wonder if you have any thoughts or any memories of when you—Was it that summer, for example, August of 2002, that you began to realize that Bush was going to do this regardless of the rationale?

EMK: I mentioned that it was in the summer of 2002 when my antennae really went up in terms of where we were, where the administration was leading us. Cheney spoke to the Veterans of Foreign Wars, and I had given several speeches before we went to war. We had al-Qaeda and Osama bin Laden in Afghanistan. We also were not taking into consideration Iran, which was

---

25. Paramilitary police.
26. Improvised explosive devices.
27. Warner was a Republican senator from Virginia.

dangerous, and North Korea. North Korea has now dimmed, at least today, despite the fact that this administration almost got us in conflict there.

We weren't taking into consideration those two significant forces. We weren't finishing the job in Afghanistan; we were going into Iraq, and it made no sense. I don't know when I had the interview in Boston where I said this was a "fraud cooked up in Texas."

Vicki Kennedy: That was later, after the invasion. It was September 2003.

EMK: By early summer, certainly, and then by September, early fall, it was increasingly clear. Bush gave a speech in Ohio in October 2002, before the war, where he overstated the case. They telegraphed all of this pretty well in a series of speeches by Bush and Cheney and others. They were telegraphing and escalating it fairly quickly.

This is a classic example of ideology over policy. The ideology and the viewpoint were from Gulf I and Bush I, when the neocons said they should have gone into Baghdad. Their view at that particular time remained a tenet of their Middle Eastern policy. Bush gets elected and puts these people into positions of responsibility. They've never forgotten that we didn't go into Baghdad, and they're working it tirelessly right from the very beginning, building and using 9/11 as an excuse to carry that forward. That's the scenario. It was an ideological view, rather than a public view.

They did this not only with an ideological view, but also with incredible incompetence. It was gross incompetence: a policy based on the ideology of rosy scenarios; blank checks provided for funding—with no accountability; distortions and misrepresentations; failure to accurately and truthfully characterize the circumstances in Iraq; and denial that Iraq had slipped into a civil war. We had misrepresentations and distortions getting us into the war, existing while we're there, and continuing all the way through—including the fundamental mischaracterization that democratic institutions and values can be imposed from the top down rather than built from the bottom up.

This past week [December 2007], I had a meeting with Reverend Ian Paisley and Martin McGuinness. It was their first trip to the US since they took power in Northern Ireland in May of last year. They sat in a room in the Capitol. We had probably eight or ten senators—Lindsey Graham, Gordon Smith, Susan Collins,[28] Dick Durbin, Schumer, Jack Reed, Leahy—and they talked about economic development. They said there was no chance for them to go back to an earlier time of the bomb and the bullet.

Lindsey Graham came in at the tail end of the meeting and said, "I'm here to try and get lower golf fees at the golf course in Northern Ireland," whatever golf course is up there. I thought, "What kind of a comment is that?" But they laughed. Graham said "We're still going to be able to have peace in the North,

---

28. Smith and Collins are Republicans from Oregon and Maine, respectively.

so I can play golf." They laughed and I thought, "Oh my God, how did we get"—Then he said, "What was it, anyway, that let you two guys get together?" Ian Paisley picked it up—he never would have talked before—and said, "The recognition that you cannot impose it on us. You can't impose peace on us."

He said, "Blair—he's my friend and I admire and like him, and he's been a great help on this—never understood it until the very end. He always thought he knew how we could get peace, but he didn't. It was only when he showed enough respect for us to be able to negotiate this thing that we were able to do it."

And that was true with regard to Martin McGuinness as well. They said, "You just cannot put these benchmarks—like the benchmarks we have in Iraq—deadlines. It has to be on the local people. They have to be trusted. They have to be helped along the way, but they have to do it themselves, because otherwise it will never, never go."

As he listened, we transitioned to Iraq. You could hear what they were saying, and see how in conflict it was with the administration's policy. It was breathtaking, with Reverend Paisley and Martin McGuinness completely agreeing. Martin said he'd been up in Helsinki for four days and nights with the Shiites and the Sunnis, and he said he finally put one word out: leadership. He said leadership has to come locally, but you can't impose any of these conditions on the locals. He said, "It's never going to work."

This crowd, these neocons, had a policy and a zealousness about Iraq and Saddam Hussein and have basically undermined and destroyed, temporarily, America's standing in the world. They've pursued the war with an ideological commitment, incompetence, misrepresentation and distortion, rosy pictures, and open-endedness. They've failed to give the servicemen proper equipment and the support they need. In the meantime, look at what the lessons have been.

The lessons are that today the Taliban are stronger than ever, and al-Qaeda is growing. You have a greater recruitment for al-Qaeda than they ever had—since 9/11, al-Qaeda's ability to recruit and maintain and train people has grown. Iran's power has increased, and it poses more of a threat now than it did prior to the Iraqi conflict. There are four million people displaced, both in Iraq and in the Middle East, and they are increasing instability in Jordan, in Lebanon, and in Syria. Our army has been stretched to the breaking point, and thirty-odd thousand wounded Americans are going to be reminders of this failed policy in a most dramatic way. It's cataclysmic in terms of its significance.

I addressed those issues in series of talks and speeches from the beginning. Now I am arguing for the closing down of this war, with a recognition that—at least I believe—for the Iraqis to be able to make a judgment and decision themselves, they have to be convinced that the United States is going to change and alter its policy and get out. That is still the key to getting them to make the decisions for reconciliation in the north. That's still what's necessary.

What you don't have, even with the surge today, is some military progress. Basically it's in areas that have been ethnically cleansed, for the most part, but you don't have the reconciliation. And you need reconciliation, because even as the military figures have said, you have to have the military, but you have to have reconciliation. My own view is that the Iraqi political leadership is effectively holding American military personnel hostage until they're going to have political reconciliation and settlement. We are spilling American blood and spilling resources over there, while they're dithering and refusing to make the tough judgments and decisions that have to be the basis for political reconciliation, as they did in Northern Ireland.

Q: Do you think we've passed the point of no return?

EMK: My own sense, from listening to people I respect over there, is that it's a very hard slog for these people to make the tough judgments and decisions. Hopefully they will, but it's very hard for the parties to be willing to make those kinds of judgments. It sure doesn't appear to be going on now.

Q: But as General Petraeus[29] used to say, you have to have pacification before you can get reconciliation in order not to have violence. It looks like it's the horns of a dilemma.

EMK: It is, but not for five years. They had a military budget of $4 billion. They had $4 billion. We now have $400 billion a year, and they're continuing to go to a country of twenty-five million that had been beaten ten years ago, completely militarily destroyed. At some time you have to say the military has done everything they can. I think after four-and-a-half years, you say the military has done everything it can. They've gone and done everything they've been asked to do, and if this crowd isn't going to do it, then why are we going to continue at this?

They don't have large weapons, so what are they going to sweep through the whole Middle East, this military? They're all small arms. The other countries are so worked up about it that they're taking a pass on it. Destabilization in the Gulf. Those countries are all sitting back. Everyone's saying, "They're going to have chaos over there." Well, if they're going to have chaos, you'd think the countries in the region would be somewhat worried. Hello? What we're doing is continuing to see the loss of lives and deterioration. We need a big change.

Q: A change in the White House, you mean?

EMK: Well, we need change in the White House, but we need a change in policy. I think you can get other countries in on it. The US *ought* to get other countries involved and have very aggressive policy changes. I'm all for that,

---

29. General David Patraeus was the commander of the Multi-National Force—Iraq and developed strategies for counterinsurgency and surge of forces to stabilize the war-torn country.

but I just don't think that what's happening now, continuing along, is going to work.

Q: *Has the time passed for diplomacy?*

EMK: There are probably diplomats who can be helpful and useful, and who should be called on to do it. It's certainly worth it.

Q: *With the majority of the American people apparently finding the course of action or the current state of affairs unacceptable, why the inability of their representatives in the Senate and Congress to do anything about it?*

EMK: I think they're caught by two factors. One is that this new threat of terrorism is something they don't quite understand, and they're very concerned about. Security is an inherent need people have; they react inherently to it. That's why we honor people who are so courageous, who risk their own security for others. We admire people who do things when they're not being called on, jump into rivers to save people, for example, when they're not in the military. What they're doing is noble, and we give great recognition to it. So security is number one. Secondly, Americans have bought into the politics that we have to support this war because we have to support our soldiers.

That's different from Vietnam. That was not there. It was a great mistake for Democrats to buy into the theory that we have to support our soldiers, and therefore we have to appropriate more money. That has slowed the whole process of ending this conflict. No one believes we're going to leave American servicemen without bullets to defend themselves. They don't really think so, but they're not sure about it, and when—

Q: *And when the president says that's exactly what they're up to—*

EMK: —exactly what they're up to, as he has misrepresented other things. People say, "You ought to be able to change the policy without risking my son over there." We were at the airport not long ago, and a captain of a US airline came up and said, "Don't you ever vote for stopping the funding over there, so my boys over there are left not being able to defend themselves. Don't you ever do that."

Here's a well-educated person who actually believes we would leave people over there to be butchered because we're not going to let them defend themselves. It's absolutely ridiculous, but the Republicans were very clever in getting that as a test, and Democrats bought into it. And once they bought into it, it slowed the effort to end the war in a very important and significant way. It's a big mistake. Now, all of our Democratic resolutions say we'll do whatever it takes to defend the boys.

Carl Levin says he's for a more sensible and responsible policy, but when he was asked on a television program last week, he said, "We're going to take care of the service members; you can be sure. You've heard that from me; we're going to make sure they have what they need." And once you buy into that kind of thing, you're in a very different circumstance.

If you read back through the debates on Vietnam, that wasn't the case. It wasn't that we were ending the war and drawing down and therefore exposing our boys to more danger. That was not the argument we used. I think we've bought a pig in a poke on this one, and that has slowed this down incredibly.

Q: So it's disarmed the Democrats—

EMK: In a very important way. One of the things that I'm proudest of is the series of six or seven speeches I gave. They were major: I argued that before going to war the points we've outlined, that we've talked about here, should be addressed.

One was we should internationalize the effort. I pointed out how the war was all cooked up by the administration and that we were being manipulated with the intelligence, how the intelligence was being used to distort it. I talked about how the war has made us less safe, which I think it has, and then about how we have to disengage so the Iraqis will stand up and take responsibility. That was in '05, and they still haven't taken responsibility.

And then finally, how the AUMF resolution no longer applies. And at the National Press Corps in January '07, on the issue of the surge, I said we ought to have a reauthorization of the conflict. Those are the major benchmarks.

Any consideration of this whole period of time—we haven't gotten into it much this morning—has to look into the detainees, what's happened with the detainees.[30] This is an element of this whole Iraq situation, and it's not unrelated, obviously, to Afghanistan. But it has really come to an extraordinary moment in American history, where we find now, even while we're talking about this, reports in the national newspapers that the recordings of the torturing of certain individuals—and I guess filming aspects of it—have been destroyed.

We're told now that the president didn't know anything about that, and we're told that the president knew nothing about the national intelligence report that the Iranians' nuclear program was at a much slower rate than they anticipated in terms of driving towards nuclear weapons. He didn't know about that either.

This destruction of material is really something. The refusal of the administration to let witnesses come before the Judiciary [Committee] and investigation committees is something. The threat that the administration has given the Intelligence Committee who said they're going to insist that the code that's been accepted by the Department of Defense for treatment of prisoners—which

---

30. Detainees refer to captured al-Qaeda fighters, particularly those held at the US naval base in Guantánamo Bay, Cuba. President Bush declared that the Geneva Conventions did not apply to them because they were non-state terrorists, not POWs. "Enhanced interrogation techniques," such as waterboarding, approved by the US Department of Justice, were used on some of these detainees to acquire intelligence that might prevent future terror attacks and help to decapitate al-Qaeda by finding and killing bin Laden, which the Obama administration accomplished in 2011.

is consistent with the Geneva Accords—will also apply to the CIA. Now the president has indicated that he's going to veto that measure.

The president said sixty or seventy times that Congress had the same information he had in going to war. We've asked for the Presidential Daily Briefs to find out whether that's so. He made them available to the 9/11 Commission, but he won't make them available to the Intelligence Committee. The administration said they'll veto that legislation I wrote requiring that the documents be shared, but we have to get those, of course.

This whole government secrecy is a monumental shift in terms of executive leadership. It's basically saying that he, as chief executive, has all power on war-related subject matter and that he will exercise it any way he wants to. It's an extraordinary byproduct of this whole period and something that's so inconsistent with the Constitution, the Founding Fathers' view about the shared power. That's very evident in the Founding Fathers' writing about war-making powers: the commander in chief is on the one side, and the ability to declare war is on the other, with Congress. They obviously wanted that as a shared power.

But this executive has usurped all power dealing with the war to itself. We've gone through—which we didn't get into today—the War Powers Act[31] that came after the Vietnam War. What the country understood at that time, Republicans and Democrats, was that going to war is a shared responsibility. We're back to what we talked about at the opening: nothing is more important for a member of Congress to do than to cast a vote about war and peace.

We saw how the president ran off with that authority in the Vietnam War, and we needed the War Powers Act to try to reclaim it and have it a shared responsibility. We have not learned from history. We have the same experience now—we have the wars both in Iraq and Afghanistan. This president has usurped power for himself and to his administration—and he has a Supreme Court that's dangerously close to just rubber-stamping it.

Right now, while we're visiting, they're considering the case about whether those who have been held for six years in Guantánamo have any habeas corpus rights when they're absolutely contained by American forces. That's an interesting issue. Vicki and I had the opportunity to go to the Supreme Court and listen in to that discussion [oral argument] just this last week. It will be enormously interesting to see where they come out.[32]

---

31. Passed by Congress over President Nixon's veto in 1973, the War Powers Act attempted to limit the president's commitment of troops to foreign conflicts without congressional approval.

32. In *Boumediene v. Bush*, 553 U.S. 723 (2008), the US Supreme Court decided by a vote of five to four that foreign terrorism suspects held at the Guantánamo Bay Naval Base in Cuba have a constitutional right to challenge in US courts their detention.

Q: Why do you suppose President Bush has not tried to bring the country and other countries together, when he was handed a unified country and a unified sympathetic world after 9/11? This is a real puzzle for future historians: why, with that enormous asset and benefit—which rarely comes to presidents in Cold War days and otherwise— why he has not built on that to try to keep the country together and build support for his views? It seems to me he's not done that with Congress, never tried to. Has he tried to do that with other countries?

EMK: I think he actually believes in a "coalition of the willing." He actually believes they have an international coalition over there in Iraq. He keeps repeating it. He thinks they have the people—the British who are in with us— the forty-eight countries, including Fiji and Estonia and Latvia. He talks about it. We get 93 percent of the casualties, but he talks about the "coalition of the willing."

Q: But he has much rhetoric that says we'll do it unilaterally. "You're for us or against us"—That was the opening speech. And we're prepared to do it unilaterally if we don't get support. The coalition his father built for the Gulf War was real.

EMK: That's right, but I think he feels he has the—What did he say, "I'm the decider"? I think he believes he has his coalition over there now, and he's very—

Q: Surely he doesn't think he has the country behind him on this.

EMK: No, but he thinks history will treat him right. I don't think I'm saying anything new. He's bullheaded, and he's certain in his viewpoint. He doesn't sweat alternatives or varying positions. I saw Zbigniew Brzezinski the other day at breakfast—four months or so ago—and he said Rumsfeld used to have him in every three months. He has a strong position in opposition to it [the Iraq War], but he [Rumsfeld] used to come in and listen to him [Brzezinski]. I don't think that President Bush has any of that kind of thing, none. There are some very good people who are very loyal to him—Scowcroft, for example, was incredibly loyal to his father [George H. W. Bush], his best friend. He is very knowledgeable about defense, very smart, and could get two or three people together, give them a pathway, and get out of there. But he's completely isolated, completely isolated.

Q: You haven't mentioned the Iraq Study Group. [33]

EMK: I thought it was generally useful. There are different stories about it. Jim Baker was told that the president was going to buy into that, and that was the reason he stayed with it. And then they didn't, and he was all upset at the end of it. It reaffirmed the importance of internationalizing it, reaching

---

33. Congress appointed the ten-person bipartisan Iraq Study Group in March 2006 to review the war in Iraq and offer policy recommendations. Released at the end of 2006, the Group's report suggested a phased withdrawal of US forces, along with diplomatic overtures to Iran and Syria, among its findings. Republican James Baker III, former secretary of state, and Democrat Lee Hamilton, former Indiana congressman, served as co-chairs.

out to these other countries, talking to countries. President Bush has a basic position that he's not going to speak to these countries—he refuses to speak to Syria. Jim Baker went to Syria twenty-three times. And now you have an administration that won't talk to Syria, won't talk to Iran, and wouldn't talk to North Korea.

I had briefings prior to voting on the Iraq war with [William] Perry—who had been [President Clinton's] secretary of defense and did the negotiations on North Korea. He pointed out that the dangers North Korea poses are so much greater than those posed by Iraq, that North Korea was producing this rich uranium, and that the dangers of it going to terrorist countries are so real. How could we discount them? That thing was enormously significant and important.

Vicki Kennedy: My timing might be off on this—but I don't think it is— North Korea apparently admitted in the summer of 2002 that they were producing a nuclear weapon, and the administration discussed it with Japan and countries in the region, but didn't reveal it publicly or to Congress until after the vote to go to Iraq.

EMK: Yes, that's right. This point is very important. If they had revealed that prior to the vote, people would have been more focused on North Korea. But they kept all that quiet so we wouldn't remain focused on where the real danger was, with Osama bin Laden and the North Koreans and the Iranians. That's the type of manipulation they were so much involved in.

Q: *The Iraq Study Group offered this president a way out when he was up to here in trouble, a way to bail out. I think it's astonishing that he didn't avail himself in some way of that opening. I don't know how to interpret it. What about your personal relations with Bush in all this? I've seen some notes of Andy Card's visit to you, about going easier.*

EMK: I had a call from at some time during this period of two or three years, a couple of years. I think there were two occasions. One was Andy Card's call, saying why didn't I let up on Bush and not be so tough. That was after I said, "This is a fraud made up in Texas." I said, "My general response is that this war is very tough and very important, and bad things are happening, and you have to expect people to talk." That was my response to Card. Then I went down to Texas.

Q: *That was 2003.*

EMK: Yes.

Q: *When you got the* [George Bush Excellence in Public Service] *award.*

EMK: Then Bush Sr. wrote me, because he thought I was too tough. I don't know where that letter is. I thought a long time about whether I ought to write him back, and then I eventually called him. That was after I had been down in Texas. I remember calling him from the Cape; it was a reasonable conversation—I appreciated his letter. I could understand why he felt that way, and I'd certainly give it thought in the future. We talked about some other things, and that was about it.

Q: I think you also pointed out in one of these conversations your willingness to work with him [George W. Bush] on other issues like education. Were you saying it's not personal, it's principled?

EMK: Yes. I had worked with him on both education and immigration.

Q: He pulled the rug out from under you on education, didn't he?

EMK: He didn't do the funding. You can say that the standards-based education is a concept, so that "every child" makes some sense. There are all kinds of problems with the "No Child [Left Behind]" concept, but the idea of every individual child being measured at least, and finding out what they need— what they now call standards-based—is a worthwhile and valuable effort. We have our differences with "No Child."

Q: Do you want to say a little bit about your award from the Bush Foundation, and your visit down there with the family to receive the award, what that was like? I think some people on the other side were very much opposed to it, to put it mildly. I saw the film of it, by the way. It was very interesting, and it went largely unreported in the press.

Vicki Kennedy: This was 2003. The war had started, but he [President Bush I] wrote and asked you to receive this award.

Q: It was in February of 2003; then in March the invasion started.

Vicki Kennedy: But then, after you accepted and set the time for October of 2003, you stepped up your criticism of the war and of President Bush 43. You offered not to go, but he said he wouldn't—no. I'm sure President Bush 41 was very hesitant, but he wouldn't think of your—I don't remember that exactly. Maybe somebody thought you shouldn't go. I don't remember.

EMK: That's right. He was nice enough to ask, and then I made two talks that were tough on the war. I believe I got hold of Simpson[34] and told him to check with him, and if he wanted to let it go, we'd take a pass on it. Simpson called me back and said no, he wanted to go ahead with it.

I called him [Bush I] and told him we were looking forward to coming down. I went over to see Scowcroft about what he was most satisfied with in terms of his presidency, and what we could talk about that he would be interested in. He was very helpful. I took a lot of his suggestions that were consistent with my thinking and put them in a context I was comfortable with and that fit in with where I was.

That made some difference, because I think Scowcroft called him up and said, "Kennedy's down here and wants to do this—do it right and do it well." That changed the atmosphere too. Then Scowcroft said, "Put on your armor, because you're going to get quite a reception down there, and I hope it's going

---

34. Senator Alan Simpson, a Wyoming Republican, was Kennedy's friend.

to be all right." He warned us about how we were going to be treated down there. He was concerned about it, but it went very well. The president, Bush I, gave me an introduction that mentioned all the things I had said about him, which, of course, I'd forgotten—that I got up and walked off, you know. We played around with it.[35]

Q: *"Where's George?"*[36]

EMK: "Where's George?" He's very engaging and personable and interested in people, [George H. W.] Bush is more of a public figure than the other one.

Vicki Kennedy: He and Barbara Bush were very gracious to us. All of our children were there. Teddy's sisters were there, Ethel was there, and I think Caroline Kennedy was there. My parents were there. So we had a big family contingent. My sister was there. It was a big Kennedy/Reggie family group there, and the Bushes could not have been more gracious. The reception was very good.

I remember there was a heckler or two in the audience. I was sitting next to Barbara Bush, and she was just horrified. I said, "Don't worry. Teddy can handle that." She said, "We just don't do that here; that's really impolite. Our [Texas A&M] students are just not like that." So they took the person out, and it was enormously well received. President Bush was so funny, saying how Teddy had said, "Who does he think he is, King George?" He set the mood, teasing Teddy, and Teddy was very respectful—true to himself, but very gracious. It was very nice—politics at its best, I think.

Q: *Yes, I thought so. An object lesson that's lost in the media today, that you can have all of these differences but also civility and recognition that you're not 100 percent right all the time.*

Vicki Kennedy: Exactly.

Q: *I loved your stories about Bush saying that whenever he wanted to give the crowd some red meat, he'd bring your name into it. And your stories about some of the Texans who went after you were very good. I think this Iraq situation just has endless permutations.*

EMK: Yes, that's right.

Q: *And it will be a long time before history sorts everything out. But there are some things you've helped with here.*

EMK: I think one of the moments was when I went up to Boston. I think it was in the late fall of probably 2002—

---

35. The charming word play between President Bush 41 and Senator Kennedy can be watched at this link: https://www.c-span.org/video/?179023-1/excellence-public-service-award. The former president ended the event with these words to the senator, "Be nice to my kid, will ya?" In 2014 the John F. Kennedy Library Foundation bestowed the Profile in Courage Award on the first President Bush, and his granddaughter, Lauren Bush, accepted for him.

36. Kennedy used this taunt against Vice President Bush at the 1988 Democratic Convention.

Vicki Kennedy: I think it was probably '03, after the war began.

EMK: It was relatively short notice, and I said, "Are there any events going on I can go over?" Barbara Souliotis said, "The AP person always likes to talk to you." She meant a fellow named [Edward] Bell, a very good person up there. So I said, "Okay, why don't I put him on for a half an hour?" When I went over to talk to him, he said, "Rather than me asking you a lot of questions about Iraq, why don't you just tell me what's on your mind about it?"

So he leaned back, and I just talked, and boom! When I got out, I didn't even realize what I had said. I was in Framingham, at a press conference. I think it was on the base closings. My staff came up and said, "Oh, my God. It's all over the wire and all over this and all over that, what you've said. People are going to ask for your explanation and your rationale and the proof of all this." We were bobbing and weaving there for about two or three days. Then the Suskind book about Paul O'Neill came out in January, and I said, "Amen." And then there was the fellow who was head of the Council on Foreign Relations.

Q: Haass?

EMK: Yes, Richard Haass, who was quoted as saying that he ran into Condi Rice in August and she said, "Don't waste your breath; the decision [to invade Iraq] is made." They had cooked that thing up in Texas during his August recess. So I was right on the button, but I had eaten more bird feathers—

Vicki Kennedy: Ted, I think this is important. I was in Washington watching CNN, and I saw a crawl, "Kennedy says that Iraq war is a fraud made up in Texas." I called Barbara Souliotis and said, "Barbara, have you eaten lunch? What is he saying?" She said, "Oh, this is really a big thing. They were supposed to talk about fishing rights. They were talking about fishing and suddenly it was about this."

That's when Andy Card called you. But what was really interesting about your response is that you didn't back down at all. You said no, that really is what it is. That impressed me enormously; you just kept going right at it. I think you said to Andy Card, who's a really good fellow, "Andy, show me why it wasn't. You talked about 'rolling out a product; you don't do it in August, you do it in September.'"

EMK: Rove[37] spoke to the Republican National Committee in February or March, out in Austin, out West, where he talked about the conflict in Iraq. That part was public, and the Haass thing was around. He had talked at a Republican Committee meeting, where Andy Card said, "You don't roll it out in August." Remember? So they knew.

What I knew at that time—I had read those papers that had the descriptions of Perle talking about going into Baghdad, differing with Bush [I] on the Gulf War. I had read all of that, and it was in my mind, that they were already

---

37. Karl Rove was Bush's senior advisor.

cooking this thing up. So I knew this thing was going on. I would have had difficulty putting my finger right on it, but I knew this was going on. Although it did come back at me pretty fast, with wanting evidence on it. It took a little while to get those pieces of evidence.

Also on this, it's tangential, but on this [Justice Department] torture[38] memorandum: we were very much involved in Gonzales, when he came up for attorney general. At that time, there had been in effect what they called the Bybee Memorandum. The Bybee Memorandum had been in effect for two years, and this Bybee[39] is now on the Ninth Circuit [US Court of Appeals]. He was approved because none of us on the Judiciary had any idea that he had written a memorandum that permitted torture.

It said that unless a prosecutor could prove specific intent, that the person torturing the victim was interested primarily in hurting the person rather than gaining information, there would be no prosecution. The CIA was therefore immunized, because they were all in there to get information, not sadistically just trying to torture. You would have to demonstrate that the person was sadistically trying to hurt the person in order to prosecute the act. It gave all of them immunity. We had really blown that up, and an awful lot of that material we had gotten from the fellow from the ACLU.[40] Not the head but—

Vicki Kennedy: Anthony Romero.

EMK: Romero. We led the fight on the Judiciary Committee, and Gonzales then repealed it [the memo] and put out this other part that applied only to the Defense Department, not to the CIA. It permitted them to continue. The torture goes back—interest in torture, to the event that Vicki mentioned some time ago, a dinner we had at Jim Wolfensohn's house. Rumsfeld and his wife were there, Kofi Annan was there, and Chuck Hagel and Jay Rockefeller and their wives were there.[41] That was in what, February or March?

Vicki Kennedy: That was in either January or February of 2002. I remember because we had your seventieth birthday party here, and I had invited the Rumsfelds. So this must have been February. Maybe ten days after that, they were here. Jim Wolfensohn had a dinner party for Kofi Annan, and he and his wife were there, and Rumsfeld and his wife, as you said, and a lot of press people like Jim Lehrer and his wife. Andrea Mitchell was there and some other people from the World Bank.[42]

---

38. The official term was "enhanced interrogation techniques."

39. Assistant Attorney General Jay Bybee was head of the DOJ Office of Legal Counsel.

40. American Civil Liberties Union.

41. James Wolfensohn was president of the World Bank, Kofi Annan was UN secretary-general, and Jay Rockefeller was a Democratic senator from West Virginia.

42. Rumsfeld's wife is Joyce. Jim Lehrer was a PBS news anchor, whose wife is Kate. Mitchell is an NBC news correspondent and host of her own shown.

We were all at one big table in Wolfensohn's dining room, and Jim asked Kofi Annan and Don Rumsfeld, "What do you think is the biggest challenge facing our world right now?" Rumsfeld made a meaningless little quip, and then Kofi Annan said, "Well, I think the big problem is Afghanistan, and whether Afghanistan is going to be able to survive through June." Then he said, "I also worry about the image of the United States when the world"— exactly what you all were talking about earlier—"was with the United States after 9/11, but there's now a division."

Then he said, just hypothetically speaking, without being too direct—but he was very direct—"The issue of prisoners of war and the Geneva Conventions are very concerning to the world community." Rumsfeld stepped in suddenly, he was going to be serious, and he made some defense of why the Geneva Conventions didn't apply.

That continuing issue of treatment of prisoners and torture still resonates even now.

Q: *And the worst is yet to come, probably, in terms of revelations.*

EMK: I think that's right: rendition.[43] What's very important during this period that we haven't gone through are each of those speeches. They really say what was on my mind at the time. There's no sense in going through those, but they—the speech before we got into the war, why we shouldn't get into the war, why the war was all cooked up, all the things. The importance of internationalizing and getting in were two very important speeches about how the war was cooked up and how intelligence was manipulated and how the world was less safe as a result. Three major speeches in those areas, and then about how we disengage, and also about how the president ought to come back for additional authority because the Constitution requires it. I think they lay things out about as well as I could.

Q: *Those are an extraordinary series.*

EMK: When you talk about the war and these conversations, you're talking about the framework for these speeches: the reasons I felt strongly about going into war, what the background was of going to war, and also about the implications. Also—which we didn't get into—the other issues about torture are certainly tangential to this whole process, but one enormously important in terms of where we are.

Q: *But they're part of the costs.*

EMK: Part of the whole cost.

Q: *The collateral damage, the whole erosion of civil liberties.*

EMK: It's interesting why there weren't more people. It's interesting why we didn't have more opposition to the war. I was against it, but Byrd was really

---

43. In this context, rendition means sending a terrorist suspect covertly to be interrogated in a country with lower standards of criminal rights than the United States.

the very significant voice against it, and a rather lonely figure there for a while. There were only a few of us, a handful, who were against it. Why weren't there more against the war? On the other side, you had this massive public opinion. For any review of this period, people ought to get the polls to see where the public was, and the impending [2002 midterm] election. And of course the results were successful for the administration because they diverted attention away from the economy and Bush's sliding poll numbers. People ought to have his numbers and where the economy was, and why they necessitated going through this, and then how his numbers came bubbling back up, and how they picked up a lot of seats in both the House and the Senate. They gained control of the Senate. So it paid off politically and dynamically.

Then there is one last worthwhile point we haven't been able to hammer, although I think it's enormously interesting. I'm waiting for the opportunity to do it. That is, Bush's father—Bush [I]—said that he went to war with fifty-two votes in the Senate, effectively. I think it was fifty-three to forty-seven on a proposal and then the actual vote was fifty-two to forty-eight. So a majority of fifty-two to forty-eight voted to go to war.

Now we had fifty votes to halt the war, to get the timetable, but Bush [II] said no, no, no. You need to have more than sixty. So fifty-two votes was good enough for Bush [I] to go to war, and it was even good enough—they said he had the majority—but in order to halt the war now—or to get a timetable— this crowd is saying fifty-three, a majority, isn't enough.

It was enough to take us to war. They say no, no, it's not enough to halt the war. They're saying that you have to have the other aspects, manipulating effectively, the rules of the Senate. They were prepared to play by one set of rules, but when it was going to work the other way, they weren't going to play by that set of rules.

Q: What's holding more Republicans back from getting on the right side of this issue and against the president?

EMK: It's what I mentioned earlier: we have to support the troops. We want to honor those people over there fighting who have been suffering, and we're not going to cut and run on those people. They've worked too hard, they've lost their colleagues, and we're going to honor the memory of those who have died before them, gallantly, and bravely, we're going to honor them by continuing to give them the support they deserve.

And we say, we honor their memory best by getting the policy right. They dropped our hate crimes proviso from our Defense Authorization Bill the other day because the pro-war Democrats were going to vote against the Defense Authorization Bill, even though we have the hate crimes in it, and the growth of hate crimes. We've been trying for years to get it approved.

They have another vehicle. They have the defense appropriations legislation, they can vote against the war, and moveon.org would give them a pass on it. But the liberal Democrats are going to vote against it. So Nancy Pelosi pulled the hate crimes out of it.

Senator Kennedy's frustration with the Bush administration policy on the Iraq is evident as he discusses the aftermath of the 2004 presidential election in which his Massachusetts colleague Senator John Kerry lost to Bush.

EMK: Well, we already saw, in the day after the election, the press conference he [President Bush] had—we watched up in Boston—at 1:00. It was the most ambivalent press conference, because he was combative and kind of arrogant in one sense and sort of conceding in the other sense, but there was no sense of alteration or change or sort of willingness to embrace the new paradigm. When we watched that, it sort of looked like we were in for a period of continued confusion, when they're really not sure where they want to go. We've sort of seen that in the recent weeks. And of course, just to say a final point on this, you see this dramatic contrast on Iraq, where they were just talking about the military aspects for the last, really three years, and during the course of the campaign and now suddenly it's all diplomatic. They used the hard military aspects of it and the politics of fear for the election and delayed all of the efforts to try the diplomatic approach. I think we probably have lost what opportunity there was there, to try and have a diplomatic solution.

I mean, I think it's—my own sense at this time is that it's fairly well lost [2006]. We'll have to wait and see. Obviously, a diplomatic effort should be put together if there are enough elements out there to do it, but I think it's been so clumsily handled. Secondly, I think they don't have the backup team of competent operatives to really—to pull in the Democrats and say look, we really want to get—let's give it a try, give us an opportunity to try and do a diplomatic kind of thing and indicate that to other countries and really put some leverage on it. The United States has still got tremendous power and influence.

Q: Is it the Baker-Hamilton [Iraq Study Group] *thing?*

EMK: Well, I think it will ebb some, but I think they don't have the capability of really implementing a lot of these initiatives, the skill to try to do it. I just don't think they've got the people in place to follow through on it and do the backup kind of things that are necessary. I mean, Condi Rice has that capability. Cheney certainly doesn't, and it certainly looks like the others don't, but Gates[44] is coming up now. I'm not sure that's going to work. It's a massive disaster from the first.

Kennedy believed the electorate in 2005 was growing more unsettled about the Iraq war and domestic issues. He feared that the Senate's failure to address these problems would render it irrelevant.

EMK: I think in this climate and atmosphere, for some reason, there's a lot of political uncertainty, and I'm a known quantity. It's difficult for me to look

---

44. Robert Gates replaced Rumsfeld as Bush's secretary of defense.

at it from their point of view. They may differ or not differ, but I'm a known quantity in a time of a lot of uncertainty—the uncertainty of where we are in Iraq, the uncertainty in education, in their jobs, are they going to keep their health insurance, and where they're going to go next, their kids. I hope we're talking about things that are important in their lives, but I think they may be giving more focus and attention to what's happening.

The flip side of this is I think the Senate has become less relevant to their lives. In the '60s we were passing Medicare, which affected people's lives. We passed aid to education; it affected people's lives, real people on every block around Massachusetts. Now we're not doing things that are very relevant to them, and so the Senate becomes less relevant. But still there's so much uncertainty out there about where we're going in this country and as a society and institutionally that they're looking at least to some political figures for some direction and leadership. And we are obviously trying to provide it.

Q: Do you have a lot of support for your views on Iraq? Or is that a problem for you?

EMK: I don't consider it a problem. I've never considered it a problem because I was so absolutely convinced right from the very beginning about it. I think historically we're going to be reaffirmed in our position. It isn't so much getting in. You have the issue, the mistake of getting in there. The real question is how you're going to deal with this thing now. That's what people want to know, and that's where we're going to have some suggestions and ideas. Now's the time when I have to reformulate that. I'd hoped to get to that during this break, and I have my staff working. I've told them who I want them to talk to get the ideas for when I get back. I think it needs a new reformulation.

The very relevant aspect of this is the abhorrent treatment of the prisoners. We've been after that in the Armed Services and in the Judiciary Committees. We haven't been able to get to it in the Armed Services Committee the way we should have. But we have McCain and Lindsey Graham—who should have been natural allies in it. The administration feels that it'll be just Kennedy trying to go after the administration because I have such a strong position on the war. But when we have the defense authorization, we're going to have Jack Reed offer these amendments on how to deal with the problems of the prisoners, which is going to make it—

I watched this on the Judiciary [Committee]. I helped lead the fight on Gonzales, because he was involved in this. But they have one nominee, Haynes, who's the general counsel,[45] and I have my eye on him for his involvement in the torture issue. We've tried to do something on that, but have not been able to get off the dime, which I'm disappointed in.

At other times in his Senate career when Kennedy took more interest in global issues, some of his Massachusetts constituents believed he was neglecting policies in his

---

45. William J. Haynes II was general counsel of the Department of Defense.

home state (as in the period leading up to the 1994 re-election campaign). In light of the senator's becoming a leading opponent of the Iraq war, he explains how he continued to maintain an active role in issues that affected the Bay State. Particularly through new technology and supporting local projects, Kennedy continued to forge links to his constituents and created a balance between domestic and foreign affairs.

Q: *Well, you referred to the uncertainty of where we're going. I'm trying to get a sense of whether these changes—the technology, the demography, the economic base of Massachusetts—have tended to make national issues of this kind and 9/11 more important in the thinking of your constituents than they used to be. Do you have more latitude? Do you feel less latitude in taking positions on national issues that resonate with your Massachusetts folks?*

EMK: I feel broader latitude in being able to stake out positions. I try to have well-informed, well-thought-out positions. And I'm trying to be ahead of the curve on these public policy questions. I don't just look for some way-out issue. I look at what we're facing now and realize that we're not addressing the core—

Q: *Let me put it a different way. Do you feel that you're well enough established in this new world of technology and terror that you have sufficient latitude in terms of your standing in Massachusetts to be free to take positions, including unpopular ones, on these national and global issues? Or has the technology tended to get more people on your back with more single issues and reduce the time, thought, or latitude you might have on these big issues? I don't know whether the changes over time since '62 or '64 have affected the campaigning and the constituent relations.*

EMK: Well, that's a very comprehensive inquiry. Times change, and so programs change. But what don't change are values. And what doesn't change is basically your approach to these issues. Obviously, you're hopeful that you become more experienced and wiser and profound on issues, and that you're willing to take positions that perhaps others might not. But you're conditioned by some parameters. You have some disposition by nature, the areas that you're personally interested in; that's one. But secondly, you're somewhat conditioned by what you've experienced in the Senate.

I'm on committees that deal with civil rights, with human rights, with civil liberties, with immigration, and I'm on the Armed Services Committee that deals with foreign policy and national security, and on the Human Resource Committee—the Labor Committee, which is health and education and elderly issues, a pretty broad scope. My basic approach in terms of economic and social justice is still very deep, and that's an opportunity for people. I have a commitment to being a voice for the voiceless—all of those are out there. You have to pick and choose your fights.

And you have to decide where you're going to try to be effective, and being effective in the Senate means prioritizing. You have to prioritize and spend a lot of time, and you can't spend time on things that you might very well like to. I've always said that every day in the Senate I could be three people: to go to the hearings I want to, the preparation, and to be able to speak to these kinds of issues. And there's another, different kind of issue—how the Senate has changed, how I relate to the institution, and how it becomes more difficult to become effective.

But I don't feel conditioned by the changes in Massachusetts, the demography, the technology. On the contrary, I feel probably more comfortable than ever about positions I've taken and the reasons for them. It's true I've been a strong supporter of working families, and there are fewer numbers of union members and more high-tech workers now. I've spent a lot of time on economic and social justice issues, which this group may be less interested in. And they may have a different opinion about me. But I would think, over a reasonable period of time that we're catching up with them on some of these items. I'm not *the* leader, but I'm among the leaders in the Senate on the environment, which people care about. In that whole area of high-tech, we're very much involved.

Q: I guess this was just really a question about how you are a national leader; you're recognized on national issues. You're outspoken on national and global issues.

EMK: Yes.

Q: And you are also a very hard-working senator as a representative of the people of Massachusetts. You don't find many people in the Senate who have that national stature, that national engagement, that range of national issues, and who are so attentive at the same time. You say you're having to spend more time in Massachusetts, in your home state, than you used to be able to spend.

EMK: Yes.

Q: But this is not a conflict for you.

EMK: No. So much of it is enjoyable—rebuilding the lighthouse on Nantucket. I care about the sea, I care about Nantucket, I care about our history. Or the Salem Partnership.

Q: I don't know it.

EMK: Oh, that's big here. That's very significant. Salem was the one city that was open to world trade in the American Revolutionary War, so it has an incredible American history. The wharves there go back to the American Revolution. Seventy percent of the money for the Louisiana Purchase was taken from the Customs House in Salem, Massachusetts.

It has this extraordinary history, let alone the writers—Hawthorne and *The House of the Seven Gables*, the witch trials, all of this. And we developed over a long period of time a partnership between the public and private—the business community, labor, and the public—for the restoration of Salem. We also had a Heritage Corridor for Essex County, which is now being replicated in other parts of the country. All of these little isolated communities are absolute treasure troves of Americana, all of which are being identified, located, and exhibited on certain days, what they call

Heritage Days. People go visit, and it's an incredible concept, and it's all being replicated. We got some federal funds to keep that moving. It's enormously interesting. Next year I might bring you up there when we do a topping-off of one of these events.

The restoration in New Bedford of New Bedford Park, which was all Melville, and the old [seamen's] Bethel, was great. There's a very interesting story that eventually we'll come to about how that thing got worked out with Dole's Park.[46] There's John Adams's house, the Quincy House. There are these droplets all through the state that we've been very much involved with locally, and that have given us a lot of satisfaction.

So I hope that people feel that I've been around and taken an interest in what they're interested in locally as well as nationally. Yes, the Lawrence River, Reviviendo, which is their development. The major one was the Big Dig.[47] We were able to get that last vote even though it was being filibustered. We got the Senate to turn around. And the financial community understands that. It's had its problems, but cleaning up Boston Harbor was absolutely essential. So people who would be normally against it—because they don't like my minimum wage or something—know what Boston Harbor has meant for developers down there—

Q: Yes. I think that the Massachusetts projects you have been involved in are a very important aspect to get into the oral history record. That's what I was trying to drive at, in a clumsy way—that you're well engaged in many products in your home state, and doing the other at the same time, which I think is important. Sometimes they intersect; sometimes they're separate.

EMK: That's right.

Shifting back to the War on Terror in the aftermath of 9/11, Kennedy commented on Afghan president Hamid Karzai and what EMK considered the Bush administration's failed policy toward his country.

EMK: I'm a great personal admirer of Karzai. I think the administration has left them high and dry over there [Afghanistan], and it's becoming the drug capital of the world. He's tried, as reported, to have a voice about where troops were going to be, and that's been all rejected by the administration. He has incredible credibility—of course, his father was killed.[48] He has enormous personal courage. I'm an admirer of his. It's difficult when you admire the person, but you're critical of the policy.

---

46. Senator Robert Dole was instrumental in creating Nicodemus National Historical Site in Kansas to commemorate the only remaining western town founded by freed African Americans during Reconstruction after the Civil War.

47. A project that placed Boston's main highway underground. The resulting ribbon of parks above it is now called the Rose Kennedy Greenway, named for the senator's mother.

48. The Taliban assassinated Karzai's father, Abdul, an Afghan politician and head of the Pashtun tribe, in 1999.

It's the same sort of thing when you admire these servicemen and are critical of the Iraqi policy. I'm trying to get this wonderful Hart family who lost a boy.[49] The boy wrote, "If we don't get armor on my Humvee in the next month, I won't live." And, boom, he got killed, and his father's been very committed to it. I've been very involved and active on it. He's been down listening to me talk and be critical of Iraq, and he's come to accept that position. It's difficult, because they don't want their son, obviously, to die in vain. All these servicemen, as far as I'm concerned, are heroes. They're doing what their country has asked them to do. It's just that the country's policy is wrong. But it takes a little while to get that—

Q: Have there been many casualties from Massachusetts?

EMK: Thirty-five boys killed, about four hundred wounded, about one hundred without arms and legs [as of June 2005]. We're very involved in working with the health agencies, the veterans' agencies. I sponsored a terrific conference to get them into schools and colleges and get training, and also getting all the major employers to employ them. We've had our first meeting, and we're going to have a second one beginning in the fall. They want to go to school, they'd like to go. They're busy getting rehab. You have to have almost an advocate for them. I had an advocate for all of the 187 families from 9/11.

Q: I was going to ask. In Massachusetts 187 families were affected?

EMK: Yes. I called all the people who had lost loved ones and met with them in a group at an organized session on a Saturday. They all came in and heard about the different kinds of things available to them. One of the families got up and said, "Senator, I have twenty phone numbers to call for twenty different things. I can't get out of bed in the morning. And I want to tell you, when I call, I get a busy signal or I get someone who can't help. Is it asking too much for someone to be a helper for each of us?" I was going to get students to do this, twenty students from each of the colleges.

And then I was having dinner with Nick Littlefield[50] that night, and he said, "That's what social workers do, and I'm a social worker." So he got hold of the social workers, and they assigned a person to each of the families. And about every four months, we get them together over at Pier 4 and have a little wine and beer and hors d'oeuvres just to thank them. These are people who are making $35,000 a year, and they're just making all the difference. And, quite frankly, the needs of these people are even greater now than they were at the time of 9/11. They've just run out of steam. They have such terrible troubles.

Q: Does your Boston office coordinate these things?

EMK: Yes, we do that. I'm very active with the group. They have a society, and I attend all their meetings. We were very helpful to them, raising money

---

49. Pfc. John Hart was killed in Iraq.
50. Littlefield was staff director of Kennedy's Health, Education, and Labor Committee.

for their memorial in Boston, in the Garden. It's very nice, very simple, very well done. So that's a continuing element. When you were talking about home senator, that had a resonance.

Q: Someday, some historians are going, I hope, to look at Vietnam in the context of what happened in American politics and American public life during that period and compare it with Iraq.

EMK: Oh, absolutely.

Q: And the way this is playing out.

EMK: Oh, I don't think there's any question.

Q: There's a noticeable absence right now of the kind of peace movement and agitation that there was then.

EMK: That's right.

Q: I'm not going to ask you to comment on that unless you wish to, but the parallels are considerable in terms of—

EMK: Oh, absolutely.

Q: —the comparability of events and what's happening now and what was happening then on the domestic side, what it was doing to the lives of people. The economics of it are similar.

EMK: Truth was the first casualty in Vietnam, and the whole escalation, the dramatic escalation in terms of the war, the attack on the United States, and the resolution. What did we call it?

Q: Tonkin?

EMK: The Tonkin Gulf Resolution.[51] And the complete manipulation of the truth in this war, demonstrated again by the Downing Street memo that says that the Brits concluded that this president decided to go to war in July [2002]. July! This is what we got criticized so much for, when I said the decision had been made in the summertime. I said cooked up in Texas. I missed it by a little bit. It's step by step, both incompetence and failed accountability and denial, the basic overall concept that there's a military solution for political problems when history shows that there isn't. We're just getting set in there and paying a fearsome price for all of this. I think people draw the separations, and you can

---

51. In August 1964 an engagement between a US destroyer and North Vietnamese torpedo boats in the Gulf of Tonkin prompted President Lyndon Johnson to ask Congress for a resolution that allowed him to commit conventional military forces in Southeast Asia, without a formal declaration of war. By a quirk of historical fate, Senator Kennedy missed the vote because of his severe injuries suffered in a plane crash the previous month. When the senator called the president from his hospital room in Massachusetts to discuss the Kennedy family's role in the upcoming Democratic convention, EMK concluded the conversation by congratulating LBJ on passing the Tonkin Gulf Resolution. Listen to the conversation on the Miller Center website, "Lyndon B. Johnson Presidential Recordings: Johnson Conversation with Edward Kennedy on Aug 13, 1964 (WH6408.19)," http://archive.millercenter.org/presidentialrecordings/lbj-wh6408.19-4908.

do it, and I think history is going to show exactly where it's going to be. The numbers are so much more dramatic over there [Vietnam].

We're 1,700 there;[52] they were at that time in '68, 25,000.[53] The numbers are just very considerable. Look at the Boland Amendment [to stop funding the Contras in Nicaragua]. It took us five years to stop that. The first time I offered the Boland Amendment in the Senate, we got twenty-four or twenty-five votes, and it took five years. Then Inouye offered the exact same amendment and was successful with fifty-one votes. That stopped all the funding. It took five years to do that.

It won't take that long now, the way this is moving in Iraq. It may take until this thing bubbles up, and we have an antiwar candidate. There'll always be the question of a somewhat different framework, because we have still the overlay of terrorism, which is an uncertain factor in people's minds. Then [Vietnam era] they were just faced with the fact that this was not a military solution for a political problem.

Now they still have in the back of their minds the terrorism, and whoever talks about getting out of there [Iraq] faces the threat that we may leave a terrorist state that will form some kind of a danger for us. We have to get through that aspect and the aspect that in a chaos, we're just cutting and running. But I don't think the American people are going to hold on with this much longer, myself, nor do I believe they should.

Q: *Comparisons have also been made between the then–secretary of defense and the current secretary of defense* [Rumsfeld], *and the way they moved. McNamara was getting very skeptical and second-thinking—*

EMK: That's right.

Q: *Exactly the opposite direction of movement, it seems, here with Rumsfeld.*

EMK: And you always wonder, at the end of the day, how much of this thing is really driven by the hard line, Cheney and all the rest.

Perspectives

Carey Parker, Edward Kennedy's legislative director: In some ways the situation [in Vietnam] seemed to repeat itself when [George W.] Bush went into Iraq, in a similar way to how Johnson used the Gulf of Tonkin episode as an excuse to launch the war in Vietnam. Hindsight is a lot clearer than foresight. Many members of Congress who voted on Iraq remembered the Gulf of Tonkin Resolution, and they said, "We think it's the wrong move. We're not going to acquiesce just because the president says it's the right move."

People who had been through the Gulf of Tonkin debate were more than ready to pause and ask why. When they didn't get a good answer for going into

---

52. American casualties in Iraq, as of June 2005.
53. American casualties in Vietnam.

Iraq, they voted against the resolution. There was nowhere near a majority, but it still was a substantial minority against it. Those issues were so inflammatory and so widespread across the country that you couldn't be a senator and not somehow be involved in such issues.

Senator John Tunney (D-CA), Edward Kennedy's University of Virginia Law School classmate and friend: The thing that I respected about Teddy so much was that he learned the lessons of Vietnam and applied them to Iraq. What it shows me about a guy like Kennedy, who made the same mistake that I made about Vietnam, not understanding the history of Vietnam, not understanding the culture of Vietnam, not understanding what was going on for centuries before the French got involved, not understanding the colonial period. But he learned from that and applied those lessons to Iraq by learning something about the Muslim religion, learning something about the history of the Middle East, the pre–Ottoman Empire, going right back to the early stages. Teddy understood that, and he did the right thing, and, boy, do I give him credit for that. I think that it was a defining point for our country, a defining point for him.

This idea that we could go into Iraq and in two weeks finish 'em off and that was going to be the end of it, is to me just mind-boggling. I can forgive the leader, perhaps, if he's getting that kind of information fed to him all the time, but I cannot forgive the people around him, who supposedly were experts, military experts, experts about the region, who would go along with it. To me, the idea that—it's almost as though because everybody was saying the same thing to each other, there was no independent thinking at all. And that's why, again, you get back to somebody like Bobby Byrd and Ted Kennedy, who were willing to say something that was out of sync with the general conclusion of what had been agreed to at the highest levels of government, that that was so important.

In a democracy you need real debate, and particularly when it comes time to go to war. I don't think Ted is a pacifist at all. I think he's just the exact opposite of what I would call being a pacifist. He really feels that you have got to take responsibility for trying to bring a better way of life to people around the world who are incapable of providing the resources themselves, and his interest in refugees, his interest in foreign aid, and all the things that I think you would expect somebody of his background to be in favor of.

Sharon Waxman, Edward Kennedy's national security advisor: 9/11 happens, and the focus was initially on Afghanistan. He [Senator Kennedy] supported the military operation in Afghanistan. America had just been attacked; of course we had to respond. When did it begin to change with Iraq? It was in the summer of 2002, and it was very sudden. Vice President Cheney delivered a speech at the Veterans of Foreign Wars. Brent Scowcroft wrote a piece in the *Washington Post* or the *New York Times*.[54] He [Senator Kennedy] called me. It was a Friday afternoon before a holiday weekend, so it must have been just before the end of the summer. Somehow he had connected these dots and he was very worried that something big was coming. I don't know who he had been talking to. He did not tell me at the time, but he was obviously right. I remember this so clearly because it was a holiday weekend. He called me, and he said, "Maybe I should give a speech." You know, about the UN [United Nations], and about this and that, and if there really was a threat. He wanted a draft on Tuesday. My first reaction was anger. "Are you serious? Why didn't you call me August 1st and tell me you wanted me to look into this massive policy issue, and then I could have spent three weeks really being thoughtful about it. Why did you wait until Friday before a holiday weekend?" I thought it, but I didn't say it, and then I said, "Of course. Let me get right on it."

I hung up the phone, and then I took a deep breath. I panicked a little bit because he was serious. I wasn't panicking because I couldn't do this; I was panicking because it was five o'clock. I had to write something sensible over the weekend, and everyone had left for the holiday. How, I wondered, was I going to get any information? I thought, "OK, how am I going to do this?" I don't know where the thought came from, but it occurred to me that the best way to make the case was to go right back to the administration's statements.

I hung up the phone and I called a friend of mine who works on the Intelligence Committee, Don Mitchell. He'd done a lot of Middle East work. I called him and I said, "Don, Senator Kennedy just called me. Here's the policy argument I want to make: Hussein is a terrible threat, but he's not the kind of threat that justifies war. In fact, the real threat is al-Qaeda. Do you have some documents maybe from the global threats hearings to support this argument?" The Intelligence Committee and the Armed Services Committees hold hearings every year on the global threats that America face. I knew he would know whether the statements existed and also have a copy if I could reach him so late on a Friday.

Q: *Were you also thinking about the piece of, "He's a threat but he's contained," or did that piece flip in later?*

Waxman: It was all part of the same argument. He's a threat, but he's not al-Qaeda, and, regardless, Iraq is not the kind of threat that justifies war. I called Don and I said, "Can you help me? Are there documents?" And he said, "Yes." I thought, "So there is a God." That's why I brought these. Don pulled them for

---

54. Cheney's VFW speech provided the case against Saddam Hussein: "Vice President Speaks at VFW 103rd National Convention," President George W. Bush White House, August 26, 2002, https://georgewbush-whitehouse.archives.gov/news/releases/2002/08/20020826.html. Brent Scowcroft's op-ed against the Iraq war actually appeared in the *Wall Street Journal*: "Don't Attack Saddam," *Wall Street Journal*, August 15, 2002, https://www.wsj.com/articles/SB1029371773228069195.

me. You can see, that's SSCI;[55] that's the Intelligence Committee. Don was so fabulous. He went through his files, and he found the documents.

Q: The administration's statements?

Waxman: The administration's statements. Here's one from George Tenet dated February of 2002, and it says, "Last year I told you that Osama bin Laden and the al-Qaeda network were the most immediate and serious threat this country faced. This remains true today, despite the progress we have made in Afghanistan and in disrupting the networks elsewhere." Bingo! The focus and threat were al-Qaeda and Afghanistan. Nothing about Iraq. And there were a lot more of these. This was only one piece of what I needed to write, but it was Friday at 5:00, and I was really scrambling. So Don Mitchell has forever a really special place in my heart.

You know, you can make an argument. You can say Iraq is not a threat. But the argument is always stronger when other people say the same thing, especially when you're Ted Kennedy and when you can use the administration's own words. I just knew instinctively that I could build a strong case using the administration's own testimony. Kennedy also wanted a UN component. I spent some time pulling together statements from credible sources to build an argument.

Q: And your initial concept, to make this clear for the speech, is that the war on terror is one thing, Iraq is quite another. And Saddam Hussein is a threat, but he isn't the threat that justifies war. The real threat is al-Qaeda. That's what Tenet said, that is what the record shows, and that's where we should stay focused, in Afghanistan. That was your first thought.

Waxman: That was my first thought and that's where I thought Kennedy should focus when making the public argument.

I don't think anyone really thought we should be going to war, but the environment was so political. It was just before an election. People were really scared. [Thomas] Daschle was running for his political life, and the Democrats felt like they had been on the wrong side of the last Iraq war. Afghanistan was going pretty well. People believed Saddam Hussein was behind the attack on 9/11. He wasn't. But they thought he was. I had staff look at the public opinion polls. People really believed, after 9/11, that Saddam was behind it. It was really interesting to me. Whether they believed it just because he had been the bogeyman for so many years, or because the administration was spinning up—

Q: Oh, I think it was clearly the latter.

Waxman: The American people really believed it, and it was very hard to take the other side. I don't think anyone really understood what we were getting into, and, based on the intelligence, the case just wasn't there.

---

55. Senate Select Committee on Intelligence.

Q: Did they believe it or were they using that as the argument to make the case for what they wanted to do anyway, which apparently Cheney just admitted this past week.

Waxman: Are you talking about the members [of Congress] or the administration?

Q: The administration.

Waxman: Oh, the administration. It was cooked up. They were going to go to war in Iraq regardless, and this was their excuse.

9/11 was very fresh. It was still raw. It was a scary time in America. I was scared. Who wasn't scared? I stood on my office balcony and saw a plume of smoke over the Pentagon, and I knew that the last plane might have been coming to the Capitol. Then there was the anthrax scare and the sniper [who terrorized the DC area]. It was a really scary time, and the American people were feeling very vulnerable. I don't know if there ever was a time, certainly in my lifetime, where people felt so vulnerable. What the administration did was cynical. To put members of Congress in the position of having to say no in that environment was very cynical and just wrong.

Q: There are certain parallels to the Gulf of Tonkin Resolution and the escalation of war there [Vietnam]. Senator Kennedy, at the passage of the resolution, was not here, because he was flat on his back, but he expressed support for the resolution.

Waxman: He just wasn't convinced. He thought it [an Iraq War] *was* wrong. It was cynical. It was not a war we had to fight. We couldn't use the containment word, as I said before, but [Saddam] Hussein was contained. The "no-fly zone" was costing us a lot of money, but it was nothing compared to the huge, huge, huge strategic blunder that this war has proven to be. So the senator was absolutely right.

The thing about the whole war period that really struck me was how personal it was for him, how passionate and how intensely focused he was on really trying to stop it. To your point, I have wondered if there was a bit of Vietnam in it, like maybe, "I wish I had done more to stop the Vietnam War. Maybe I waited too long." I really don't know. I wasn't here for Vietnam. But I felt the Vietnam War was always in the room.

The great thing about Ted Kennedy is that he always believes he can make a difference. "We've got to go out there. We have to try." He doesn't want to dance around the issue. We would talk about the hardest arguments to address from the supporters of the war, and he would look at me and say, "I want to go right to the heart of their strongest argument."

Q: What did he see as their strongest argument at that point?

Waxman: I think the whole terrorism idea: "If you don't get them there, they'll get us here."

Q: When Bush shifted his argument to "weapons of mass destruction," what was Kennedy's response?

Waxman: He [Kennedy] believed the real issue was nuclear weapons. Chemical and biological weapons are part of the discussion about weapons of mass destruction, but the real issue is nuclear weapons. Senator Kennedy separated the issues. He did not believe we would go to war over chemical and biological weapons and that nuclear weapons were the real issues—

Q: Well, but also wasn't it, "Let's let the inspectors do their job"?

Waxman: That is right. That was his argument: "It's not al-Qaeda. The focus is Afghanistan, and the inspectors are on the ground. Let's let them do their job. This is not about chem and bio; to the extent that it's about weapons of mass destruction, it's about nuclear weapons."

I always knew that Senator Kennedy had a great strong argument when the administration came after him. It was a great sign. Every time he gave a speech and the RNC[56] would issue a statement saying, "He's not a patriot," or "defeat and retreat," or whatever their talking points were, I knew we were really getting to them. Kennedy went out to the Council on Foreign Relations and gave a speech in which he basically indicted them for—he didn't say "lying," but really just—

Q: He used the word "fraud" or "fraudulent."

Waxman: Fraudulent, distorting, misrepresenting the intelligence, and it was all a prelude to CIA director Tenet's hearing in the Armed Services Committee. The Republicans sent Jon Kyl out to refute him point by point, and I thought, "That's great. We must be right, because they're not going to bother if they think they can just dismiss it." Kennedy gave a speech in January of 2005 saying, "We need a political military strategy that gets us out of this country, where they take responsibility for their own future. We broke it, but they have to fix it. And part of that strategy has to be some sort of timeframe, and we should put them on notice that next spring—"which would have been 2006, so about eighteen months—"we're going to begin to withdraw."

You know, Kennedy used the "timetable" word or "timeframe," and the Senate went crazy. I was getting phone calls from other staff, "Oh, my God, you are not going to make us vote on that, are you?" People on national television were being asked—"Do you agree with him?" Carl Levin was great about the policy. John Kerry said "no." He later came to the same position as did others in the party.

But the point is not who said it first. The point is that there were very lonely times. He disagreed with the administration, and he was isolated from many in his own party. He and I would tussle over whether it was productive to force his colleagues' vote on these proposals, and I rarely thought it was. He sometimes tended to think, "Well, gee, we should be on record, and we should be clear." I'd think, "You're on record, you're clear, the speech is clear, the policy

---

56. Republican National Committee.

is crystal-clear. Introduce an amendment in if you want, but why push it to a vote and go down in flames? All you do is help the administration with a failed amendment, and then you put your colleagues in a terrible position." Let the policy ripen over time. This was perfectly rational advice, and I know he would normally agree with that, but on this issue he didn't want to hear it. He did not want to hear any analysis that might have suggested holding back. It's not easy disagreeing with Ted Kennedy.

Brian and Alma Hart, parents of fallen soldier in Iraq War, PFC John Hart:

Brian Hart: John said that they were being ambushed on these roads and that he had body armor on because they were sharing it. They called it hot swapping. He had been assigned to an assault squad, with a squad assault weapon, but they needed armor on their Humvees or else they would get killed on the road. He said it was just a matter of time before that happened to him. He was very matter-of-fact.

It wasn't long after John's death that we decided, "They can't do anything worse to him. We can piss off anybody we have to."

The funeral procession was all lined up outside, and Senator Kennedy asked to come, and we were pleased that he came. We told Senator Kennedy what we knew, that they essentially were running out of ammunition and tourniquets, that they had no blood-clotting agents, that there were five armored Humvees in northern Iraq, and that there was a chronic shortage that enlisted personnel certainly knew about but that somehow wasn't being reported up the chain of command. We talked for about a half hour, and Senator Kennedy said that this was the first factual information he had heard, and he was on the Senate Armed Services Committee. It was confirming rumors that he had heard from Jack Reed and from some of the National Guard families whose sons had been killed in August.

I had found out that the military had been lying about the production rates at the plant [that makes armored Humvees]. I knew but I couldn't figure out why. I was approached by a person in the audience who had ties to the manufacturing plant, who told me that the purchase orders had not been received, even though the Pentagon was telling the Congress, as late as mid-December, that the plants had received the orders and were running full out. They actually were running at about 25 percent capacity.

Q: What did you conclude about why the situation was the way it was?

Brian Hart: It was about the money.

Alma Hart: And the election coming up.

Brian Hart: And the election. I found out that the plant had not received the production orders. This was months after generals told Congress in November that they had but the plant was in fact running at only about

25 percent capacity. We started to relay this information to Representative Marty Meehan[57] and to Kennedy.

So we formed a strange relationship with Senator Kennedy that grew into a strong bond and friendship. As Alma and I would find out information from all kinds of sources—like soldiers' family members calling us anonymously with information—we would pass it to the Senate. Senator Kennedy would ask the questions [at congressional hearings], and the generals would usually be more than happy to answer, because they were the ones being shorted equipment. That's how we formed a five-year working relationship with Senator Kennedy, and that's how all the troops, six months after those hearings, got body armor, when a third of them hadn't had it in October '03. By 2005 every vehicle that left a base in Iraq was an armored factory-built Humvee or MRAP.[58] That's how this happened.

---

57. Meehan was a Democratic congressman from Massachusetts.
58. Mine Resistant Ambush Protected.

14

Fighting for Universal Healthcare: A Goal Fulfilled

Walking toward the Edward M. Kennedy Institute for the United States Senate, on Columbia Point, in South Boston, a visitor might notice a neat, modest building housing the Geiger-Gibson Community Health Center. Named for two Tufts University doctors who developed the concept of neighborhood-based medical care for low-income residents, the center was conceived at a 1965 policy dinner held by Senator Edward Kennedy. Inspired by the innovative idea, the senator soon introduced and guided legislation that eventually resulted in funding of similar health centers across the country. By the dawn of the twenty-first century, nearly twenty million poor Americans received healthcare in such centers, thanks to Senator Kennedy.

The origins of his interest in healthcare, however, are traceable to experiences throughout his life, with severe medical conditions befalling him and his family. As a young lawyer, Teddy worked in the Massachusetts Cancer Crusade, raising funds to battle a disease that would eventually take a heavy toll on his loved ones and, ultimately, take his life. Senator Kennedy had learned at an early age the importance of receiving healthcare, a point that was undoubtedly reinforced after he broke his back and sustained other serious injuries in a 1964 plane crash during his first Senate term.

Through six months of convalescence and recuperation, Kennedy recognized that he enjoyed certain advantages unavailable to less fortunate Americans. He witnessed firsthand the unfairness of the health insurance system while his son Teddy Jr. endured arduous treatment for bone cancer in the early 1970s. Senator Kennedy learned that the parents of other children in similar situations could not afford the same level of successful treatment that his son received under the health insurance policy provided to members of Congress and their families. Moreover, Kennedy could take time away from his job to care for his son, a luxury many parents did not enjoy. So the senator successfully fought for the Family and Medical Leave Act, signed into law by President Bill Clinton in 1993.

Fighting for disadvantaged groups who lacked access to quality healthcare quickly moved to a prominent place on the senator's legislative agenda. As Sheila Burke, chief of staff to Republican Senator Robert Dole observed, "I think Kennedy thought that the government should help solve problems that people couldn't otherwise solve and that it should always support those who were least capable of solving their problems." When Democrats held power in Washington, Kennedy seized the initiative, passing a host of landmark legislation, including COBRA (giving workers access to group health benefits after a change in job status), the Ryan White CARE Act (offering treatment to HIV/AIDS patients), HIPAA (establishing health insurance portability and protecting patients' privacy), and SCHIP (providing health insurance for children).

When Republicans controlled the White House or Congress, Kennedy fought to scale back healthcare budget cuts proposed by President Ronald Reagan and, subsequently, House Speaker Newt Gingrich. Yet Senator Kennedy knew the value of reaching across the aisle to work with Republicans, such as Senators Nancy Kassebaum, Robert Dole, Orrin Hatch, and John McCain, on major pieces of healthcare legislation. When Kassebaum disagreed with her Democratic colleague, she still appreciated Kennedy's institutional memory and his desire to find a way for Congress to succeed as a crucial component of the three governmental branches.

Kennedy's battle to reform what he saw as a broken and unfair system led him back repeatedly to one of the defining issues of his career—universal healthcare insurance. In the early 1970s, he held private negotiations on the issue with the Nixon White House. Kennedy ultimately broke with President Jimmy Carter over how to approach healthcare policy, and affordable medical care for all Americans became the central theme of Teddy's unsuccessful 1980 presidential nomination campaign. In the early 1990s, Senator Kennedy worked closely with President Bill Clinton and First Lady Hillary Clinton on trying to pass national health insurance legislation, but the administration's bypassing of Congress in developing the policy ultimately doomed it. Teddy's collaboration with President Barack Obama on the Patient Protection and Affordable Care Act (PPACA), which passed in 2010, seven months after the senator's death, appropriately made it the crowning achievement of his Senate career.

At the White House bill-signing ceremony, attended by Senator Kennedy's widow, Vicki Kennedy, his son, Congressman Patrick Kennedy, and his niece, Caroline Kennedy, President Obama observed, "I remember seeing Ted walk through that door in a summit in this room a year ago, one of his last public appearances, and it was hard for him to make it, but he was confident that we would do the right thing."

To Edward Kennedy, access to affordable healthcare was a right, not a privilege. No issue was more important to him than working to ensure that all Americans had access to quality medical treatment. His son Patrick, named for the first of the Kennedy clan to arrive on US shores in the midst of the 1840s Irish potato famine, placed a poignant note on his father's Arlington grave immediately after passage of the PPACA. It read: "Dad, the unfinished business is done."

Q: This is the March 28th [2008] session¹ in Washington with Senator Kennedy. The subject today is healthcare, and Vicki Kennedy is with us once again, thankfully.

EMK: And Splash and Sunny will join us soon.

Q: They will join us soon. They have business in the kitchen or somewhere.

EMK: I thought maybe I'd start off initially with my association with the health issue and also the family's association with the health issue and why it was a central force in my life growing up, and with my early days in the United States Senate—how the opportunity to become involved in it from a policy point of view, in many respects, goes back to my own observations about the importance of health in a personal way, but also in a way that exposed me as a young person to the policy considerations, and the impact that it had on me.

I have commented, probably earlier in our discussions, about the fact that my sister Rosemary was mentally and intellectually challenged, and how she always was considered special in our family. As a small child, I found that I could play with children that were my age, or in many instances I would find that she was both available, acceptable, and desiring to play ball with me. We'd take a soccer ball and either play soccer, or bounce a lighter ball, like a beach ball, and play tag with it, or other children's games. She always seemed to be willing to spend more time with me than the others, who were always distracted in playing other games.

I noticed that she had some special kinds of needs. I observed that early as a child. I didn't understand it in the early years, and it took a while, obviously, to grasp the full dimensions of that, but I noticed that that was different. The regular kinds of childhood activities with childhood accidents when I was growing up were probably not different from other kinds of activities of large families.

I suppose the first major challenge that I saw was in 1961 when my father had the very serious stroke, which really disabled him in a very important way. He lived on for a number of years afterwards, but I saw the enormous— I was exposed to the dramatic moments of the time right after he had that stroke, about whether he was going to live or die, and also to the whole issue of being significantly disabled, and the corresponding actions of incredible care and loving attention that he was able to receive. The dedication of nurses and healthcare personnel, and the patience and the love and commitment of so many of those who worked with him, took an immense amount of time. Attention to this was a very powerful factor in terms of my whole observation of this part of my life.

---

1. Unbeknownst to the trio, this session would be the last of twenty-nine interviews with Senator Kennedy, for only seven weeks later he would suffer a seizure at Hyannis Port, receive a diagnosis of terminal brain cancer, and spend the last fifteen months of his life battling the disease. The senator and Professor Jim Young had planned additional interviews, including some on video (instead of audio), before fate intervened.

He eventually went to the Rusk Institute in New York and got specialized attention from this fellow, Henry Betts, who is still alive and now runs an institute in Chicago. Betts was a junior figure to Rusk,[2] who was the national leader in rehabilitation. This was a first dramatic opening in my life, other than Rosemary.

I was elected to the Senate, and in the early years as my family arrived I was exposed to the power of asthma with a small child, Patrick [Kennedy]. We detected when he was two that he was a chronic asthmatic. He had the test that is given to children, where they have pinpricks along their arm—I think it's twenty-four pinpricks—of different kinds of allergies. His arm looked like a nuclear meltdown; it just absolutely reddened, all of it. He was allergic to everything. My brother Jack Kennedy was allergic to cat fur, and my sister Pat had allergies, and maybe the others had some, but I certainly noticed those as they were growing up. My brother Jack would come back to the Cape and would go into his room, and he'd come out about an hour later, storming mad, wondering who let the cat sleep in the bed while he had been away, or some cat had come on in. He'd be battling the allergies for the next several hours.

When Patrick developed it, we brought in medical experts at least once a year and sometimes twice a year, from around the country. They came in at nighttime. They would examine Patrick and talk with him, and then they would go off by themselves and have a meeting at a hotel, and then they would come over in the morning and brief me on their understanding of his condition, and their recommendations. Since he was chronic, there was a whole series of different types of medications that they would talk about, and the advantages and disadvantages of each. That continued all the way up through his graduation from Andover, even in his last year at Andover.

The last meeting was at the Parker House in Boston. He had some time off, and my son Teddy was going to take some time off, so the three of us were going to go away, and the doctor said, "Don't go further than thirty-five or forty minutes from a hospital." So we went down to Key Biscayne, because we were thirty-five minutes away from the hospitals down in Miami. So, it was a major factor and a force as he was growing.

Later, in the early '70s, we were faced with the health challenges that Teddy was facing with cancer of the leg. I always thought it was osteosarcoma, but I've been told it may have been chondrosarcoma. I remember very clearly his talking about and complaining about a bump on his leg, and how it wasn't getting any better, and it was getting sorer.

One morning I was headed to Boston and I was getting briefed about the various health meetings I was having in Boston. One of the staff people, Phil

---

2. Dr. Henry Betts, who worked with Dr. Howard Rusk, treated Joseph P. Kennedy after his stroke.

Caper, was also a doctor, and I had mentioned to Phil about the swelling. He examined Teddy and said, "You've got to get an X-ray on it right away." I remember hearing later in the morning when I was up in Boston, about how they looked at the X-ray and saw the cancer, and that this was just enormously serious—life-threatening. It was going to take immediate and dramatic action, which presented a wide range of both emotional and real decisions about the removal of his leg—the conversation prior to that time and the conversation after that time.

At the same time, my niece was getting married, Kathleen. So this was a very emotional, roller-coaster period in my life. And then much later, my daughter Kara found out that she had lung cancer. That was as a result of a picture that had been taken of her lung after—She had pain in her shoulder and was under medical attention for stenosis, and the very good doctor—

Vicki Kennedy: Dr. Wiseman. This was her internist.[3]

EMK: —suggested that they take a picture of the shoulder. They found that she had lung cancer, and we had to move within a matter of hours. We went, later that afternoon, up to Johns Hopkins and had discussions up there with their medical team, which were very unsatisfactory. Then we had medical consultations with some experts and made a decision to follow a different route, which was surgery, which has worked out very successfully. She's now four or five years free from any cancer.[4]

So healthcare was something that had a real powerful impact. Also, in 1962, I remember the incident when my brother [Jack] lost a baby to hyaline membrane disease. The child lived three days and then died at the Children's Hospital in Boston.[5] The interesting factor and force of all of this is that, if the child had been born two years later, it would have survived. The progress that was made in medical research would have permitted the child to survive. Here was the person who was the president of the United States, with all of the assets that he could have, and still was unable to see a positive outcome of this.

Within all of that, financial security was certainly present. It was present also in 1964 when I had the plane crash we've described earlier. I was able to get medical attention, initially up at the Cooley Dickenson Hospital, and then later at the Lahey Clinic that was located in Boston, before it moved down outside of Boston in later years.

I was exposed to the most extraordinary groups of doctors and nurses at the Lahey Clinic. Dr. Adams,[6] who was the head doctor up there—there may

---

3. Dr. Jon Wiseman was Kara's physician.

4. At age fifty-one, Kara Kennedy succumbed to a heart attack, in 2011, only two years after her father's death.

5. President and Mrs. Kennedy's son, Patrick Bouvier Kennedy, was born prematurely in August 1963 and lived only thirty-nine hours.

6. Dr. Herbert Adams treated Kennedy.

have been a day when he didn't come in and see me, but I don't remember it. This included Christmas Day, New Year's Day, the whole time I was up there. The commitment and the dedication of the doctors and the nurses, and the support systems and the professionals, were just breathtaking. I think it probably led me to the very strong commitment that I've always had, politically, to strong support for nurses, for support personnel, because I always recognized their indispensable role. The doctors, yes, but the support personnel for their patience and their time.

During the period when Teddy—Now we're probably into '74, so we'll have to come back to how this intersected with the policy judgments and decisions. It was all within a few years of each other—the dramatic time that I had in the Dana-Farber Institute in Boston with my son Teddy. He had a treatment, and we found out that he had this leg cancer that required the loss of his leg, and that's a special circumstance that we can get into.

After we made a judgment about which regime we were going to follow—there had been several recommendations, and we spent hours trying to make a decision. What was interesting was that there were alternative ways of proceeding, and when the final decision was made, which I made, those who had different regimes were all very supportive. There was a real coming together of people who were all looking for a common resolution and solution to the challenges they were involved in. They all had different pathways, but nonetheless, once the judgment was made, they all were incredibly supportive.

It required that Teddy spend three days every three weeks at the Children's Hospital in Boston, taking methotrexate, which is a medication that helps kill cancer cells, and this other medication[7] that helps to alleviate some of the adverse effects of methotrexate. That involved me giving him shots, which I did, both before he came on up to Boston and then right after he had finished the immediate treatment—for the next couple of days intensively, and in the night a couple of times, and then periodically, every four or five days after that.

What happened was, after two or three months, the NIH took this off the list of regimes that they were supporting for experimental research. The whole regime had been completed. NIH had enough material to wind up their conclusions. When we had started, my best impression was that there had been less than a hundred children that had completed the regime, but they had had—

Q: *This was on an experimental research basis?*

---

7. Citrovorum.

EMK: Experimental research basis by the NIH. There were probably less than a hundred that had gone through it, but they had had positive numbers on that. Before that, it was very tough; the survival rate was not good, you know, 15 to 20 percent. But after this it was 85 or 90 percent. So that was enormously encouraging.

After about three months of my being involved in it, they had completed the whole regime for it. While it's an experimental drug, it's paid for by the company or whoever is producing it. But once it's stopped, the payment stops, and these families had to pick it up. Since it's an experiment, none of the insurance would cover it, except mine, which is Senate insurance, federal employees' insurance. The cost is $2,700 a treatment.

These parents would be in the waiting room—they had sold their house for $20,000 or $30,000, or mortgaged it completely, eating up all their savings, and they could only fund their treatment for six months, or eight months, or a year—and they were asking the doctor what chance their child had if they could only do half the treatment. Did they have a 50 percent chance of survival? A 60 percent chance of survival?

This was a very powerful presentation, in terms of starkness, about health and health insurance and coverage, and basically the moral issue presented here. We were all in the same circumstance. This is a very rare disease that could have happened to anybody. It happened to a United States senator; it happened to children of working families. There was nothing that they could do about it, and they were being put through this kind of system. This is about as stark as you can get, in terms of the compelling aspects of this issue.

A secondary issue that came up that's related to the public policy is family and medical leave. I'd have to leave the Senate on Friday, and I could go and tell [Senate Majority Leader] Mike Mansfield that I wasn't going to be there. Just in terms of the votes, I wasn't going to be there. It wasn't a question about me not—I should be with my son, and I was going to be with him, but I wasn't going to lose my job because I was leaving, and I was getting paid for it while I was gone. I was getting paid leave on this.

At the time that we were debating family and medical leave, these families would lose their jobs if they didn't show up, let alone get paid for it, you know? They would either lose their job for not showing up, or at least lose their pay, because they didn't have the kind of coverage that we had in the United States Senate. That was at the same time that we were debating the family medical leave, and here you had about the most stark—the decision that parents have to make about whether to be with a child or—to have the job that they need, or the job that they love. I didn't use the example of Teddy, really, during the debate, until the very end, during the final windup.

After President [George H. W.] Bush vetoed it in 1992, I sort of pulled out the stops on it.[8]

Q: *The experience with Teddy—the way I hear you talking about it is it really brought it home to you, personally. This is your first personal experience with that kind of situation, you know, with people having to spend themselves into poverty in order to end up—the choices.*

EMK: Yes, the families in that setting, and talking about that, and seeing and feeling their emotion. The situation you could grasp very easily, but the emotion of that was something that was enduring and continuing, and I still remember it very clearly. I talk about it occasionally when I talk about healthcare, even now.

I spent six months in the hospital and five months in a Stryker frame—six months in all—when my back was broken [in the 1964 plane crash], and I saw the dedication of the people. I knew it was costing a chunk of change for the insurance companies to cover my health insurance on it, but it didn't present itself—the starkness, the compelling aspects—

Q: *Pocketbook issues.*

EMK: —about the pocketbook. And that has never left me. That aspect of it I've been constantly exposed to in the time that I've been in the United States Senate, and I go back to it on many different occasions, on the different hearings or things that follow this. One very important set of hearings that I had in the Senate were the hearings in the—We're getting ahead a little bit but it's probably worthwhile pointing out because it's close to this subject matter.

In '78, when we took the committee across the country, we tried to match up, in the hearing, the panel that we'd have. We'd have one panel and we'd have probably ten witnesses, but we'd group them so that there were five subject matters. We would have the way that the United States covered the particular illness, and the way the Canadians covered it, just to present to the American people the difference, you know, how the systems were in terms of real-life circumstances. We'd have what were common experiences in the particular areas that families would be affected.

One of the most dramatic that I still remember so clearly was in Chicago. It was two families that had children who had spina bifida. In the US family the mother was a schoolteacher and the husband was a construction worker, and they made a good chunk of change and had a very good life. There was one other child in the family. Then the mother had to stop teaching school to take care of the child because it got sicker and sicker. And then, because the mother got run down, the husband quit his job. They went through all their

---

8. Congress passed the Family and Medical Leave legislation again in 1993, and President Bill Clinton signed it into law two weeks after his first inauguration.

savings looking after this child, and the result was that the state was going to take away the child because the parents could no longer take care of this child. You had the mother and the father completely distraught about this. This was out in Chicago.

Then—this was very interesting—in Canada, the family with the spina bifida child, and they were taking care of it. While the mother had the spina bifida child, she had a family of four: three of them had graduated from high school and were out. She had one left, and she went and adopted three children who were disabled, and the governmental system paid for taking care of them—the food and the clothing and a stipend for the housing. You'd ask the mother why she took in these children and the mother's response was, "I want to teach this child what love is all about."

You had this dramatic contrast between the system that was just wringing the last ounce of humanity out of a family, and this other system that was dealing with it in a humane and decent way, and a more economical way in terms of the whole process. I mean that was just one—I can remember it just as clearly as I'm here. You know, these things don't leave you.

And they are just as much out there today. You could have that same hearing today in Chicago, and you could have it in any city in America, and have the exact same results on it, and that part has even grown, because you've got so many more—I mean, I use the example of the parents that hear a child cry in the night and wonder whether they are $485 sick, because that's what it costs to go to an emergency room. They listen to the child. Is the child getting better or sicker? They wait until the child finally goes to sleep and wonder whether the child is going to be worse in the morning, because they can't afford the $500. Or they take that $500 that they put aside to educate their kids, and it's gone. And that is what's happening all across the country.

So this aspect of health and the coverage and the rest of the policy issues are all rooted in a very early association and personal attachment. Finally, the policy issues come and attach themselves in different ways, and we can talk about that. You can talk about how people who have a preexisting condition— Even Teddy [Jr.], who has had cancer—even though he's forty-seven-years old, he could not get an individual insurance policy today, because he's had cancer, even though he's as healthy and strong as can be. He could not go out and buy, in the United States, an individual policy. That's the way it is. That's the way the system works on this.

Obviously, he's in a group—but then, if he left that group, could he still carry on through? You didn't used to be able to, but you've got the Kassebaum bill now that says that they can't discriminate against [a pre-existing condition]—if he's gotten into the system, they can't knock him out. But that's sort of a feature of the policy. We can go back now to a time when we got started in the health policy issues, but I think it's at least of some importance and consequence how we got into it.

Q: *Before you go into that, while you're still on the injustice and the suffering, did you feel, at those hearings or at any time during your career, that when you pointed this out—the actual human condition that people face and families face—that people paid a lot of attention to that? Did it get traction, as they say? Or did people say, "Well, how unfortunate," and then go their own way?*

EMK: I think people understand it. A continuing aspect is that people are very fair, and they're rather empathetic and sympathetic about their neighbors. This is something that they understand and they feel, and they appreciate. The question—you can continue to say, "Well, they may feel that, but if they're going to be up against the wall and have to pay another big chunk of change, how long are they going to feel it?" I think there's that kind of issue and question, and if the negative aspects are presented to them, in a way, they'll be influenced by that as well.

The idea of fairness in this country still has a ring to it that's sort of overwhelming, such as when you're talking about increasing the minimum wage, even among people who all do better than that. People understand it, and they're empathetic and go for it. People understand this. And what's interesting is that every family knows somebody who has had the circumstances that I've talked about, and they feel strongly about it. They are wary.

There are ways of trying to undermine that, which the opposition is very clever at. I find that the arguments are old and they're tired, but they still have a ring to them: the idea that you're going to have a bureaucrat in every hospital who will be making medical decisions, the idea that hospitals will close, that doctors will leave, that the expenses will go on up through the roof, that you'll have socialized medicine. All of these features can be manipulated in ways that can impact and affect people's fundamental decency.

So, I suppose we can go to where we got into the policy issues and questions, if you think this is the place.

Q: *OK. You got into this very early, and there are many people who have talked about Walter Reuther and the Committee of 100.[9] Reuther apparently approached you to serve on the committee, and they had kind of a lobby to push for this at that particular moment. Is this how you really got into it in the policy way?*

EMK: Well the support for—I'm on the Health Committee and also on the Education Committee. The way the system works, obviously, is whoever is the senior one gets the choice of the different committees. It appeared to me that Claiborne Pell[10] was going to take the Health Committee, and I was going to be on the Education Committee. I liked Senator Pell.

---

9. Reuther was president of the United Auto Workers, and the Committee of 100 supported national health insurance.

10. Senator Claiborne Pell was a Democrat from Rhode Island.

I had been in the Senate for five years, and although that sounds like a long time, in time of the Senate it was a short time, and I'd been out a good chunk of that time because of the plane crash in '64—I'd spent '64 out of it, and '63 was a difficult year. Then we had the '68 campaign and that was a difficult year as well. But now, in '69, we're looking at both the committees and where I'm going to spend time and how I can be the most useful and productive.

That was the time of Walter Reuther, whom I had known from the time he had been supporting my brother [Jack]. He was very significant and a major figure, and highly regarded and respected. The UAW had been a union that had supported my brothers, as well, so there was a good association with that. In a meeting up in Boston—and I don't remember who had set this up, probably one of our supporters from the UAW set it up in Boston at one of the hotels—I had an extensive meeting with Walter Reuther about their proposals for developing a national health insurance movement. Would I be willing to be involved, active and help lead it?

That sounded like a great opportunity to me. They had demonstrated both effectiveness and commitment, and this was something that was enormously important and could make a large difference. We were coming out of the period of the mid-'60s, where we had passed Medicare, in '64 or '65. We actually completed it in '65, but there had been discussion, even in the Medicare, that this was only a part of the whole movement of comprehensive coverage.

I was aware of Harry Truman's '48 effort to try to get universal healthcare, and his disappointment, and that at least Roosevelt had looked at it in the '30s and decided to go with Social Security rather than the health issue, and that it went back to Teddy Roosevelt's progressive period, where he tried to move it along. So I knew the concept of the issue of national health insurance. I had heard enough, having been in the Senate during the '64 battle, and in '65, to know that we had taken a chunk of this but we hadn't done the whole job. I had seen the success that they had had in '64 and '65 and thought that this was both a great opportunity and an area of very important need.

So, we had Reuther, and I was able to get a number of people who were cosponsors of it, Democrats, and only one Republican. The one Republican was John Sherman Cooper,[11] who was not a liberal Republican. I never could quite understand what that was really all about. I was a great pal of John Cooper. He was closest to my brother Jack, and a dear, dear, valued friend in the Senate. I've told the stories about John Cooper and the respect people had for him. But when we put in the bill the first time, we had one Republican, and it was John Sherman Cooper. People sort of gasped.

On the Democratic side, we had a good chunk—I don't know, probably thirty to thirty senators on there, and we were on our way. I put it in with a

---

11. Senator Cooper represented Kentucky.

congressman who was on the Ways and Means Committee, Jim Corman,[12] who was a very bright, smart person, who had worked with Reuther and had been for comprehensive, single payer.[13] This is basically the single-payer program [which was defeated].

Now we're into the period of the '70s, and we're trying to think about how to go through—We go through a whole series of different maneuvers over a very considerable period of time. We're trying to see how we can build a coalition and how we can expand the breadth of our support.

One interesting phenomenon during this period of time is that Wilbur Mills[14] who was the chairman of the Ways and Means Committee, an enormously powerful position, was interested in running for president. No one gave him much of a chance, but he thought that the way to do it was to be for national health insurance, and so this opened up—To have the chairman of the Ways and Means Committee being your ally on this was a very significant and important opportunity.

He and I got along fine. I had never been all that close to him, but he respected my brother Jack, and they had some mutual friends. So we had this sort of dance, trying to get him into the program. He wouldn't go for the single-payer program and through all of this period, we're sort of adjusting and changing. The Republicans, even when they came our way later on, were always sort of holding back and always tipping the tide to the industry—and the industries that were most effective were the insurance industries and hospitals—during the series of debates.

We suffered a very serious setback as we started to move ahead in the early '70s, with the loss of—Walter Reuther was killed in an airplane crash. And also by the fact that Wilbur Mills got himself in trouble [with personal indiscretions].

Q: Well, labor pulled out?

EMK: When we went with Wilbur Mills, they thought, in the '74 period, '76 period, that they were going to have a veto-proof Congress. They said, "Why are we making accommodations and adjustments now to try and get a bill, when we can wait, and we're going to pick up all kinds of seats in the House and the Senate, have a veto-proof, and therefore, we'll be able to get a much better bill?" It's always the classic kind of circumstances, where you're holding out for the perfect, rather than dealing with the good. This was the first example.

The next example—and we may not want to get ahead of ourselves—was during the period where Nixon was just getting started on Watergate, and

---

12. Cornan was a California Democrat.
13. In a single-payer system, like Medicare, the government covers most medical expenses, via tax revenues, of all residents.
14. Mills was an Arkansas Democrat.

getting impeached—the process of threatening for the impeachment. Mel Laird,[15] who was very close to President Nixon, and had also been on the Ways and Means Committee or Appropriations Committee, was a very smart person and had talked to Nixon. They believed that if this was such a powerful issue and one with such popularity, that it might even save Nixon from impeachment.

We had conversations with Mel Laird about how we were going to proceed. He had basically the concept of pay-or-play, which we would grab today if we had that opportunity, which meant that you either have an insurance program for your people or you pay into a fund. That concept is used in Europe in their industry, not only for health but also for training programs. They have training programs with the requirement that you either have to train a certain percentage of your workers in a continuing training program, or you have to pay into a fund that will continue to train them, and so you have an ongoing and continuing training program.

That was what we called the school-to-work program, which we actually implemented here during the Clinton administration. But the only way we could get it passed was if we sunsetted it, and we sunsetted it, and the Republicans wouldn't vote to continue it, which was a good program. Now we're into the '70s, where Nixon gets impeached,[16] and so that whole effort collapses.

Q: *How close do you feel it was? You had mentioned early about trying to get a coalition together that could push it through. You got give on the part of the Nixon people, or at least there was an expression of some interest because it might help him out in a time when he needed it. But labor had sort of stood aside. Does that mean the coalition never withstood in the first place?*

EMK: Well, it really never came enough together, because when labor sort of took a walk on this, that was a setback. I thought we still might be able to get it pulled together with the Republicans and enough Democrats on it, although labor was teed off at it. There was some division within the labor movement on it.

You know, it was always very interesting with labor, because there was a great dichotomy. You had industrial unions that wanted it, because a third of all of their premiums that are paid are being used to cover somebody else. So those are lost wages. They understand that their economic interest is in getting universal coverage, because then they weren't going to be picking up and paying for people who didn't have it. So that made sense. They were going

---

15. Melvin Laird was Nixon's secretary of defense.

16. The House Judiciary Committee approved three articles of impeachment against Nixon, but he resigned from the presidency before the full House of Representatives could consider them.

to increase their wages and have a stronger position, and it was sort of the right thing to do for other workers. They liked it. That's one part of it.

The other part of labor said that they don't want any part of this program for universal coverage, because they want to be able to deliver it as part of their organizing. They want to be able to go out and say, "Join my union because we're going to give you health insurance." They're not as interested in universal coverage, because that's going to take away a major kind of an appeal that they would have.

So you had lip service. You had some who were very strongly for it—the industrial unions; others who said they were for it and really were not; and others who basically sat on their hands because they said, "Why are we going along with this Kennedy proposal when we can use this as an organizing tool? We're losing members, and we're losing support in terms of working—this is a key way of getting it. It's got a lot of grassroots support, and we use it as an organizing tool." Of course they didn't use it as an organizing tool. They didn't do the follow-up on it. Andy Biemiller[17] and Meany and the other follow-on leaders were not interested really, in following—

Vicki Kennedy: Kirkland.

EMK: Lane Kirkland. Lane Kirkland was more interested in the international labor movement. I mean, he was somewhat interested in Solidarity [the anti-Soviet Polish labor movement]. He did do some good work in terms of the support of international, but he wasn't really interested in this. We had a hard time keeping all of that moving.

Q: This jumps ahead too much, but has labor's position fundamentally changed from what it was then—their circumstances from then to now? Do they still have that—?

EMK: They still have that dichotomy. You know, it depends on the unions, about where they are. Some of them have got other issues that are as important, if not more important, in terms of the narrow labor issues. All of the railroad unions were concerned about Amtrak—that's thirty-one of the unions who were all concerned about—that's their particular part of it. The building trades were concerned about independent contracting. And they're worried about immigration and this kind of thing that they get on the health.

The number one issue for labor today is the Employee Free Choice Act, to permit them to have card check-offs for organizing. That's really the most powerful, although you still—this is one of the four or five issues that they'll list, but they've got other issues as well.

In a number of areas there is a heightened interest on the part of labor, because in an increasing number of these negotiations they are losing ground because they are having to pay higher co-pays and higher deductibles. Therefore, it's becoming more of an issue at the bargaining table, where it was sort off the

---

17. Biemiller was the AFL-CIO's chief lobbyist, and Kirkland its president.

bargaining table for years. Even in the UAW, it was never—all they would do is continue to make progress in coverage, and now they're in a gradual kind of retreat.

They made this macro deal recently, where they developed a foundation to offload some of the expenses—a rather complicated financial deal that helped them get out from some of the legacy costs on it. But I'd say that now, in many more union disputes, healthcare is front and center, but they still care about some of these other issues.

We could go on in terms of where we are in the '70s. We've gone through pretty much on Nixon.

Q: Were you getting Republicans coming aboard at all during some stages of that? Was Weinberger[18] *seriously interested?*

EMK: He was a spokesman and secretary, but he really was strongly against doing anything that was going to deal with the payroll tax. That issue had been somewhat opened, about whether we would raise the limits in terms of the people who were paying or not, as a source of both health insurance or long-term care. He took a very strong position that they wouldn't do anything at all on that, which meant that we weren't going to be able to get revenues on it. So it was basically put off and put over.

Q: So the possibility of a compromise on the play-or-pay lost you labor, and then stopped things with the Republicans, so that sort of left you high and dry.

EMK: Yes. I think that's probably where we were in the mid-'70s. The next time we come back to this is with Carter.

Q: What's the story there?

EMK: Well, basically, in the '76 campaign, the candidates who were running then—Udall was running—

Q: Was Jackson involved?

EMK: Jackson in '76. Three of them were strong for universal comprehensive coverage, effectively a single-payer or universal coverage, except Carter.[19] Carter refused, during the whole course of the campaign, to take that position. He had reasons that I don't know. I guess he wanted to do everything on his own on this thing. He sort of relished the idea that he didn't have to make a commitment on universal comprehensive coverage. He had stated, in the course of the convention—The convention in '76 had a good plank for universal coverage, which he claimed to support and which was written mostly by the people that supported—by the UAW people, and Leonard Woodcock and Corman, Woodcock being the head of the UAW then.

But whenever he [Carter] was asked about it—he talked about healthcare; he talked about coverage; and he talked his way around it. You know, he used

---

18. Caspar Weinberger was secretary of health, education, and welfare.
19. Senator Henry Jackson was a Democrat from the state of Washington; Jimmy Carter was the Democratic governor of Georgia.

artful words all the way through this. I campaigned for him and appeared with him on a number of occasions, but he was never—When he got the nomination in '76, I think it's probably the only convention I didn't speak at. He wasn't all that interested in me speaking at it. He wanted to be separated and clear from the Kennedys, and he made that somewhat clear.

Q: I don't understand that. Can you shed any light on that?

EMK: I don't quite understand that either.

Q: Was it a feeling of competition?

EMK: It just didn't make a lot of sense. When he got elected, the question was—he had given certain indications that he was going to be for it, but that he wasn't going to be for the bill that I supported and the Democratic left supported. Then the question came about what the timing was going to be. As we were moving along during that time, he kept delaying putting forward a proposal, and it developed that he was going to put forth principles but wasn't going to put forward legislation.

He talked about doing cost containment. Health planning was going to be first, and then he was going to try and do cost containment next, before we had coverage. Then it eventually kind of deteriorated, where he was getting caught up with the high rates of inflation, economic challenges, and he was going to support a step-by-step program in healthcare, where he could take a step, and if other economic indicators didn't come out quite right, he could either delay or pause before they'd take the next step.

Congress was going to have to take action again for the second step, so what we were faced with was that we were going to have not just one battle, but a series of battles for the next four or six years, and passing every two years an add-on in terms of health, which was a nonstarter.

Q: Political, I guess.

EMK: That is, effectively, where he was going. And that was effectively what the debate was about, and that was effectively the reason for the division. It was couched in a lot of different ways. You read through the notes and the exchanges, and he is saying you can do this step-by-step in different ways. You can say, well, we'll step it up but it will have to be a vote of disapproval rather than approval, trying to change it.

So we were talking about all of these intricacies about how to do it, but what was happening was that time was going by. The people who were concerned about the economy were catching his ear. He had said that he was going to try to do an energy bill first, and then when that didn't go through, he still was back to these principles, and that was the real delay. So we failed.

Q: Do you know if—Stu Eizenstat was his domestic advisor at that time. What I wondered was, do you think the idea was ever floated to him to go for the principles and leave it to you and the others who are for this, to try to see what you could get with his endorsement, rather than try to manage the details of how we're going to do this?

EMK: I don't think he was into it. The problem was he didn't really want to stand up on it, and you couldn't—there's a difference if you've got somebody who wants to, someone who is serious about giving certain principles and support to those as it moves on along. He wasn't. He was completely ambiguous about it and resentful of the pressure that was being put on him for doing this. The little sidebar on this is that he eventually fired Califano,[20] which halted any of the progress that we were beginning to make.

Q: You had some very direct exchanges with Carter.

EMK: Well, let me come back to what I was going to say about Califano. Califano and I both went to the Holy Trinity Church here [in Washington] when our children were small, and part of the service was that, after nine or ten o'clock Mass, the children would go down for Sunday school, and they would have a discussion there for the grownups. They'd have one of the Jesuits who would come over and lead the discussion, and they were always enormously interesting, very interesting, very gifted, talented lecturers. There were always a couple hundred people who were there with their children, and then, at whatever time, an hour later, you would break up and hook up with your children and drive them home.

Carter found out that Califano and I were going to the same meeting, and he heard that they were just talking in general terms, and he became enormously suspicious of Califano. Califano never trimmed on Jimmy Carter's principles. Wherever Carter came down, he stayed. You'd talk a little bit about it here and there, trying to glad-hand your bid on some of these kinds of things, which I understood. But he never trimmed, never played a game on that thing, and he stayed absolutely consistent.

Carter fired him because he thought he was becoming too friendly with me on this; there's no real question. And once he left—I mean, he was the only one who really understood the healthcare issue—it was gone. Eizenstat was, I thought, a positive. He wanted to be helpful in trying to bridge the gap. Califano didn't want to have a split. It's kind of interesting, in these notes,[21] the extent that Jimmy Carter said that he didn't want to have a split with us.

He mentions in these notes that he didn't want to split with us, but there was no question. This is Carter speaking: "I want to work with you. I know that we are not going to have a chance to get any bill passed unless we have your help and your support, but I'm facing serious problems with this. What I would like to do is to talk to Stu first thing in the morning and get back to

---

20. Joseph Califano was Carter's secretary of health, education, and welfare.

21. Senator Kennedy was a habitual note-taker, particularly after meeting with presidents, when he would write down or dictate his memory of the conversations. Throughout the oral history interviews, he used these archived notes and his diaries to spur his recollections. They are archived in the John F. Kennedy Presidential Library but not yet open.

you, to ask you to come down here and explain why it is in the interest that we do this before the [1980] election."

He's demonstrating—but he had made the judgment and the decision that health was going to be put aside, and that was after we had gone all the way through all of this part, and after he made several commitments to us on that part. He was just backing out of that. I mean, he was facing extraordinary challenges on this, but he just wouldn't move on it, just wouldn't go on it.

Q: *I think by that time—they got after him for overpromising, and he says in some of those notes, "I can't take on another major commitment at this time." But it is an interesting exchange in that memo. So now you don't have—so he's another Nixon?*

EMK: The basic point where it broke down was—He used the technique of saying that he had announced principles and that would be their commitment, and then he'd move on from there. But you have to announce as part of the principles whether you were going to have one bill or several bills, and he would not make it clear that it was going to be one bill, and he wouldn't make it clear that, even if it was going to be one bill—We talked about, well, then it's going to have to take the Congress to unwrap it. He wouldn't go that far.

We gave him that kind of alternative to preserve it, but he wouldn't go there. He would only say, "We'll get one bill and if we meet the economic points test further on down, then we'll submit it so that it can have a second phase, and a third phase, and a fourth phase." And that was the break. That was just completely unacceptable, in spite of the fact that we had a lot of conversation about how to do it and when to do it.

We had the attention, obviously, of Carter. He understood that the spending on healthcare was not unrelated to the spending on inflation. But there's a way of dealing with both of those, and he wasn't prepared to do that.

Q: *How was the coalition at the time you were trying to get Carter to move?*

EMK: We were together then.

Q: *Was it pretty good? Was labor there?*

EMK: Labor was back with us, because they had been instrumental in writing the Democratic plank, and Carter committed to the Democratic plank. They had the expectation—and I was very happy with the Democratic plank, so it looked like we were all back on the same wavelength. Then there were these series of different meetings with Leonard Woodcock and Carter. Woodcock would say, "He's equivocating," and then Carter would say, "I'm going to put out the principles," and then he wouldn't put out the principles, and then the principles that he announced were not adequate. So labor lost interest and basically gave up on it.

Q: *Was it at all bipartisan support then in the Congress, or was it still basically a Democratic [initiative]?*

EMK: Basically a Democratic. At that time we were—I forget, but we had an overwhelming majority.

Q: *A very large majority.*

EMK: A very large majority. There were probably three or four Republicans who had some interest in it. Bob Dole was sort of—and Chafee had some interest in this, but when it came down to trying to work this thing, they basically abandoned their positions pretty quickly on this. It became pretty clear that Republicans didn't want to—and the various groupings in the Republicans were against it, so they opposed it.

Q: *Then [Ronald] Reagan comes in. Did you have more on Carter?*

EMK: No. I was just thinking about Moynihan and the Finance Committee, but the real tension that we had with them was later on.

Q: *Yes, that was with Clinton. When the idea got nowhere with Carter, and Reagan was then elected, did you think, "It's dead for the next four to eight years?" Was that your feeling? "It's the last chance until another time long away?"*

EMK: Yes. There was going to be no real opportunity to move it during the Reagan period. That's when, as you might remember, I went from the Judiciary Committee back to the Labor Committee because there was going to be massive assault on all the domestic programs. And, at that time, there was going to be the consolidation of all the block-granting[22]—all of these programs, some of which were block-granted.

It seemed to me that it was just going to be important then to try to hold on to where you were in terms of all of the domestic programs, and that's primarily what we were engaged in. We were involved and active in other issues then. We went to South Africa, and also we had Chile, and we had the arms control issues where there was some of the back-channeling with Reagan. But on the domestic, we weren't going to get anyplace at all, and that was very apparent to me. What happened is he continued to have the continuing loss of coverage in health insurance and continuing increased [health] expenditures. The indicators were still going the wrong way.

We did have, in '67—we've gone way past that, but we did neighborhood health centers. That was passed. That was a big deal. It was about $35 million. I don't know whether we've covered that.

Q: *You've mentioned it before but haven't really talked about it.*

EMK: That was a major health issue, and it's even bigger now because it's about $2.5 billion a year and about seventeen to nineteen million poor people get healthcare through the neighborhood health centers. It started out with two centers: one in Columbia Point, Massachusetts, and one in Mound Bayou, Mississippi, in the poverty program. It was initiated by two doctors from Tufts: a fellow named Jack Geiger and a fellow named Count Gibson. I went with them out to the Columbia Point system and later on to Mississippi.

---

22. Block grants are federal government allocations to regional governments to use for a wide variety of projects. Because they offer more discretion to local governments, conservatives prefer them over funding that includes more specific federal parameters.

At the Columbia Point system I became convinced about the possibilities for the neighborhood health centers, and offered this as an amendment on one of the pieces of legislation that was coming through—I can't quite remember—some health bill that was coming through. It got to the [House-Senate] conference [committee], and Adam Clayton Powell was the chairman of the conference, and he said, "Well, the last item on the agenda is this program by Senator Kennedy, who is over here now. What's that about? We want to wind this conference up." So I explained what the health centers were about, and he said, "Well, how much money is in there now?" I said, "There's enough money for three of them." And he said, "Write in the legislation to put one in my district, and you can put the other two wherever you want. Is there any objection on it? Have we wound up the business of our committee? The conference is ended."

And that was the beginning of the health centers, and that program we've stayed after. I think I've spoken at every one of their annual meetings since that time. They've just done amazingly well. One of the principal reasons that it has done so well is because of the makeup of the advisory committees for each of the boards. The makeup is between consumers and providers, and the balance is such that it's reflective of what they want in that community. So, in the South End, they want AIDS treatment and testing, and in the North End of Boston, they want dental care, because the water is bad, or whatever it is. They've got sufficient flexibility within that, but it still maintains a comprehensive range of services. Now they've got associations with these hospitals, which have strengthened all of them in a very important and significant way, and there's sufficient flexibility so they can do that. It has all been welcomed.

We were facing a period, when Reagan got in, that they were going to be put into a block grant on the preventive healthcare. Orrin Hatch was supposed to be the negotiator for the Republicans, and he just wasn't interested. You had to go over and sit for about twelve hours, and go over each health plan and figure out where it was going to be put in—enormously tedious work, which we did. Baker finally took it over because Orrin Hatch wouldn't do it, and he said, "We've got to end this whole process. We could be here for another week."

So I said, "Well, I'll tell you what we'll do. Instead of having the four block grants, say that there's nine block grants, or ten block grants, and I'll say, 'This is a victory for Ronald Reagan because he's got these things block-granted, but we've been able to preserve—' and you can say the exact same thing: 'We wanted to block-grant it; we've got it block-granted; and we did have to have a few more block grants to take in.'" And that was basically the architecture of the press conference that we had. One of the things that we saved were the neighborhood health centers.

That was in '80. I don't know where we want to go—

Q: *Let's start with the Cancer Act.*

EMK: In Massachusetts, in 1961, I was asked to be the chairman of the Cancer Crusade in the state. I had not been very much involved and interested in cancer, but I had been involved or engaged in Massachusetts, in this proposal. They had a very distinguished group, including a fellow named Sidney Farber, who the Farber aspect of the Dana-Farber Institute is named after, and he is a leading researcher. He's a very inspiring figure. And they had a leading Republican state chair, who is a very decent fellow. We traveled for probably forty nights, meeting these volunteers.

It had been suggested that this would be interesting, but it would be enormously valuable and worthwhile in terms of the politics of it because you're meeting these groups and meeting them under very good circumstances. I traveled all over Massachusetts, meeting all of the people who were involved in the Cancer Crusade, and they were just a very impressive group of people who were very emotionally involved in that.

After I was elected and came to Washington and was on the Health Committee for a very short time, Mary Lasker, a distinguished woman philanthropist of the Lasker Foundation, spoke to me about doing a "war on cancer." She said that we had to redo the whole Cancer Institute to make it more effective in dealing with the challenges of cancer; to have their own budget, for example, and their own administrative way of proceeding, and being able to target more resources to clinical research.

They had a number of other recommendations, and they had these recommendations as a result of a panel that had been set up by Mary Lasker, that was made up of very distinguished individuals. It became what was known as the "war on cancer." The *New York Times* was strongly opposed to it, thought we were targeting too much of the money, and that you couldn't just legislate solutions to cancer. So it was lively and controversial, but I thought we had a strong case. We wanted to get this passed, and it looked like we had a good chance of getting it passed. Nixon was really the figure that was blocking it, and it was entirely personal; he would not do it if the bill had my name on it.

One of the people who was very involved in this effort was a fellow named Benno Schmidt, a very successful financier from Texas. He had handled several different fortunes and had been very successful. He was enormously committed and very knowledgeable about the cancer issues, and he was a very strong supporter of Nixon. He went down and talked with Nixon, and finally he called me and said that if I took my name off it, Nixon would sign it.

It was an interesting phone call that he had had previously with Jake Javits, who was the principal co-sponsor. Benno said, "Jake, Nixon will sign it if you and Kennedy take your names off it." And Javits reportedly said, "I'm not going to do that, because I wouldn't do it to my friend Ted." Well, he *would* have done it to me at the time, but he didn't want to have to drop his name off there too. I'm not sure whether he dropped his name or not. He may have still been able to stay.

I told Benno, "That that's fine with me," and with that, they put Peter Dominick's[23] name on there as the prime sponsor, who hadn't been interested in it, hadn't shown up for any hearings on it, had been rather cool to the whole idea, and it got passed. We had a signing down at the White House. At that time there weren't many people that—the people on the inside were aware of what had happened, and one of the nice things is that Benno Schmidt wrote this all down in an essay that's in the archives of the National Cancer Institute, in very considerable detail, about his conversations with Nixon and the rest. That was an interesting health sidebar.

One other small item in more recent times, in 2004, was the Family Opportunity Act. The Family Opportunity Act was legislation that I introduced with Grassley and Congressman Sessions,[24] who is the most conservative member of the House. He's from Dallas, Texas, and he has a disabled son.

Under the current system, in order for a person to get services for a child, they have to work at the Medicaid level. If they work above that, they don't get the services. You have people who are enormously talented, who've got skills and families, but they still have to sacrifice and work at the Medicaid level in order to get these services for their child. It's enormously unfair.

This legislation permitted them to increase their salaries and still get their services. You pay more taxes, but it had a step-up so they could get several thousand dollars more and still maintain—and if they moved up, they gradually had a reduction in terms of the money that they got. So this was a winner for the families; it was a winner for the whole Medicaid because it reduced the amounts that were being drawn as these people made more money; and it increased the money for the federal revenue, so the taxpayers were greater protected. Except, under the budget it cost $6 or $8 billion, and you had to get that money—for what reason? You know, under the budget restrictions, so that slowed it down.

It was interesting that 90 percent of the heads of households that have these children are women, and there are about six hundred thousand in the country. The men leave and the women are the ones who take care of the children that are in the greatest—One of the very powerful arguments that we had on this is that it applied to people in the military. They couldn't earn whatever—if you could imagine that, and the military wasn't quick enough to make the adjustments on it. When people found out that this was happening to people in the military, they let this thing go—We never had a hearing in the House or the Senate; it was just done in the budget, passed in the reserve fund and

---

23. Senator Dominick was a Republican from Colorado.
24. Senator Charles Grassley and Congressman Pete Sessions served Iowa and Texas, respectively.

money allocated within the budget, and it's in effect at this time now. It made a difference to—

. . . And that took probably five years, six years, to get that thing finally done. It's not an insignificant part in these—coming out of order—we have two that are probably out of order: One was the program called SCHIP,[25] initially the CHIP Program, the Children's Health Insurance Program. This was modeled after the Children's Health Insurance Program that was passed in Massachusetts, where a fellow named John McDonough was a [state] representative and very much involved in it. It was successfully passed in Massachusetts, where they used the money that was part of the big tobacco settlement to designate it for health insurance for children.

I worked out legislation with Orrin Hatch, and the basic compromises on the legislation that were put in are why the opposition of President [George W.] Bush at this time makes very little sense: one, I wanted to have Medicaid standard for healthcare coverage for children, which is very extensive coverage because it has a lot of prenatal care. Well, it has not only the prenatal care, but it also has a good deal of preventive care. Hatch wouldn't go for that. He said, "What we are going to have to do is describe the services, and we'll say that the state has to provide a certain number of them, but we're not going to require some." Some of the ones that he wouldn't require were dental care and eye care. We left it as an option in terms of prenatal care, I believe.

The second big compromise is we said that it would all be administered by private insurance companies, within a certain context. So he got the privatization and he got states making the judgment decision on the benefit part: the two big, big compromises, from our point of view, which is the compromise with the Republicans. He would be able to say this was a state program. And then they changed it from Hatch-Kennedy to—the Republicans had insisted that they call it a *state* children's health insurance, to make sure it wasn't going to be a federal program. State, SCHIP, they insisted on it and that was eventually dropped.

That had a lot of complications to it because the Clinton administration opposed it because it had budget implications. President Clinton had made an agreement with the Republicans—Trent Lott—on the budget, and Trent Lott wasn't going to support the alterations and change, so they resisted and resisted and resisted it. It was effectively defeated once, and then we were able to save it at the very end. At the very end we had everyone pulling for it, including Senator Clinton. By that time we had Marian Edelman,[26] who had been rather cool to it in the beginning. They thought we were going to draw money away from Head Start and other kinds of programs, and they

---

25. State Children's Health Insurance Program.
26. Marian Wright Edelman was president of the Children's Defense Fund.

weren't—Hatch and I went around and spoke to all of these organizations here in Washington, together, putting in a very considerable amount of time and effort and energy to get that moving.

They had a very tumultuous meeting in the Finance Committee. I called up Orrin and laid into him that I thought he was selling out. He's never forgotten this thing. Eventually, as the result of the meeting, they did save it, but they had to cut back on it a bit. But he has never forgotten my conversation with him.

Part of the problem now is that there are three or four states where they have given waivers on the CHIP program for parents to be involved, and there are some states that have more parents than they do children. That's a criticism. The [George W. Bush] administration wants to cut all those out. The compromise, from the Democratic point of view, has been that they would change the match so the states had to pay more, but not to drop them.

The reason that the parents had come on is because they had been given a waiver by the Republican administration. The Republicans had given them waivers to let them to do these parents, and now the Republicans, including George Bush, are using that as an excuse not to support and fund the program. I mean it's the most—and in spite of the fact that George Bush had said down in Texas—When they put the program in place, he was claiming all the credit in the world for it, and saying that he was going to double it in Texas if he was reelected.

So that is one of the very important health programs that we've been able to—

Q: How many would that add—a ballpark?

EMK: Seven million.

Q: Seven million more?

EMK: Well, seven million, and they had probably, if we took the additional—In the Democratic proposal they had about four million, and there would still be probably four million that would be left out. The question is at what income level do you cut people off? At what percent? The Republicans wanted it at 200 percent of poverty. We have probably five or six states, including Massachusetts, that have gone up to 300 percent of poverty. You know, you need to get it up to—300 percent of poverty is about $35,000 a year for a family of four; 200 percent is $22,000 or $23,000; and 400 percent is probably $50,000 in Massachusetts. But you're still looking at a family that is hard-pressed.

Q: So this was done in what—'96, '97?

EMK: This was done in '97.

Q: After the collapse of the major initiative.

EMK: That's right. This was done right after we also passed the Kassebaum-Kennedy bill [in 1996].[27] In the wake of the collapse of the Clinton [health-care] program, we were looking for targets of opportunity. Senator Kassebaum

---

27. The Kennedy-Kassebaum bill became the Health Insurance Portability and

showed some interest in passing legislation that said that if people had some disability and had insurance and were part of a group, that they could move and take their insurance with them, and they couldn't have another group require that they drop their health insurance in the future. We had quite a go-around on that, because when it came to the floor the Republicans were opposed to it. We had a very tense period with Dole on this and accused him of refusing to call this up and went after him quite extensively on the floor.

Q: He was running or thinking of running for president [in 1996] at that time.

EMK: Thinking of running. One of the techniques that we used is that the majority leader would come out and talk about what the agenda was, and one of the things I did constantly was when he came out, I would challenge him and say, "Will you yield?" Well, he has to; he's on the floor. He has to yield, and you'd say, "Why aren't we taking up this bill? It's bipartisan. Why aren't we doing this? Why aren't we doing that?" I just kept after him and after him and after him on this, all the times that he was doing this. Eventually, you build up—I did it on the minimum wage, with Dole, and he eventually receded on that. And I did it on this, and he eventually went along with this and added rather a dangerous provision.

Q: Savings.

EMK: The health savings account, which is a way of permitting high deductibles for people. It doesn't help low- and medium-income working families. It's only against catastrophic injury. But it obviously helps the very wealthy because they can afford the deductible, and if they have a serious illness then they are effectively covered. It's enormously profitable to companies, and these companies tend to be all Republican.

They added a provision on the floor of the Senate in order to get our legislation through. I had to work out the resolution of it with Congressman Archer[28] from Texas in the House of Representatives, who was chairman of the Ways and Means Committee. We had a number of meetings on it. He was a very principled and committed figure, very conservative. We had this sort of go-around where his mother was fascinated with my mother, so my mother signed a book for him, and he was very tickled with that. We enjoyed a warm personal kind of relationship and there's no question that it made a difference. He retired from the House.

Vicki Kennedy: I think you gave him your mother's book.[29]

EMK: I did.

Accountability Act (HIPAA) of 1996, which provided health coverage for workers who lose or change jobs, limited insurance denial based on preexisting medical conditions, and protected the confidentiality of patients' medical records.

28. William Reynolds Archer Jr. was a Texas Democrat who switched to the Republican Party.

29. Rose Kennedy published *Times to Remember* in 1974; it was released in 1995.

Vicki Kennedy: I don't think your mother signed it; maybe you signed it.

EMK: That's probably right. In any event, that was basically the Kassebaum-Kennedy thing. So we can go to Clinton now.

Q: This is I guess the third in your career to date.

EMK: Unsuccessful.

Q: The third major effort [to pass comprehensive healthcare legislation].

EMK: The third major effort.

Q: A window of opportunity, or whatever you want to call it. People are going to do a lot of comparison between Kennedy on this one and Kennedy on the other two—not just Kennedy, but the whole idea. You know, there are a number of people who say that this was just the death knell of the whole idea, that it's not going to come again, but I'll leave that aside. Didn't you have very high hopes for getting this thing across under Clinton? What went wrong?

EMK: There was a great sense of anticipation and a great sense of hope that we'd finally have healthcare legislation that was worthy of its name. It was clear that he was for it, and that this was an important issue in the course of the campaign. It certainly appeared at the start of the administration that we were on track to get healthcare, but that hope gradually deteriorated and fizzled for a number of reasons.

Q: When he committed himself in the campaign—I'm thinking of Carter, who had committed himself rhetorically to it. Had you been advising Clinton on this during the campaign or earlier? I'm trying to get your impression of his degree of commitment to this, coming into office.

EMK: It's difficult to measure. I didn't know Clinton all that well, other than the casual political relationship with him. I mean, I campaigned with him. We started with a very warm relationship with the Clintons, starting really right in the beginning. We went out and visited the [Arlington] gravesite of my brothers with the members of the family, and he was certainly very responsive to—

Vicki Kennedy: Can I say something here? I had an experience with him because I sat at his table before he was inaugurated, after he was elected, at Katharine Graham's house. You were at a different table, and I was at Katharine Graham's table where he was. Taylor Branch[30] was there, and there were several other people there. He proceeded to talk about healthcare that night, and he was very specific. I remember it like it was yesterday. He said if he couldn't get healthcare reform, he didn't deserve to be president. That's what he said. This was like December of '92. There was no doubt, I thought after that, that this was a deep commitment of his.

EMK: So this is sort of the start, and there were just a variety of different things that affected the whole effort in terms of the success of the proposal.

---

30. Taylor Branch is a Pulitzer Prize–winning historian.

First of all, there was the extraordinary amount of time it took for them to develop their particular proposal. Rather than taking any of the existing proposals and modifying them slightly and moving ahead, they wanted to do their own kind of healthcare proposal, and to take into consideration a lot of different suggestions and ideas. So they developed the task forces that were set up to try to sift through various ideas and suggestions.

They had constant meetings, and they had a coordinator whose name was Ira Magaziner, an enormously gifted and talented person, a close personal friend of the president, a Rhodes scholar, and very successful person in the private sector, and very committed to this, as sort of a central coordinator. He was very friendly with us, and we had a warm relationship with him, but nonetheless there was the establishment of these task forces, and that delayed the—

Q: *There's a reference in there to a boat ride with Ira Magaziner.*

EMK: That was at the Cape. That was up at the Cape during the summertime. We took him out and his family out, his children out.

Vicki Kennedy: Yes, we went to have a picnic. Didn't we go to Great Island [near Hyannis]?

EMK: Yes. They had a picnic, and it was all to find out what was in that task force. [*Laughing*] Ira was very judicious. We found out what we needed to find out, which was whether we were going to get squeezed out in terms of jurisdiction. It wasn't in their interest to squeeze us out, and he understood that, but he had to maintain his security of the plan. He couldn't have us come steaming along and be chortling that the jurisdiction was going to be in our committee rather than the others. He was very helpful in terms of making sure that we had a foothold in that. That was really the result of that trip. He knew what that was about, and we knew what it was about, and it was enormously important. Otherwise, we couldn't have been nearly as effective.

In the spring and the summer [of 1993] . . . you had Whitewater, the White House firings, the commodities trading, and Ken Starr getting started.[31] And during the spring and summer, this was when the big organizations, the NFIB and HIAA[32] began to get geared up in terms of their "Harry and Louise" ads.[33]

---

31. Distracting stories in the early Clinton White House included Travelgate, about the firing of the Travel Office staff; Mrs. Clinton's pre–White House commodities investments; Assistant White House Counsel Vince Foster's suicide; Whitewater, about the Clintons' pre-presidency real estate deals in Arkansas, which led to the eventual appointment of special prosecutor, Kenneth Starr; and revelation of the Monica Lewinsky affair. The latter resulted in the president's 1998 impeachment.

32. National Federation of Independent Business and Health Insurance Association of America.

33. "Harry and Louise" ads refer to a $14–$20 million 1993–94 television campaign funded by the Health Insurance Association of America—a health insurance industry lobby group, that opposed the Clinton healthcare reform proposals. Named for the actors featured in the ads, the spots portrayed a prototypical middle-class couple discussing how government-run healthcare insurance would destroy Americans' cherished freedom in the

Then in September the president presents it to the Congress, and in the fall we get a significant role, and then it comes in, in '94. Rostenkowski gets charges of embezzlement and the House committees barely get theirs through, and it was just in deterioration at that time, although our committee got it through. Then the real sad thing was that at the very end, we never even got a vote on it, which we should have.

Q: It was defeated without ever being put to a vote on the floor.

EMK: Yes.

Q: That's remarkable.

EMK: We had no accountability. People didn't want to get—it was typical for the Congress, which doesn't want to get caught up one way or the other, in voting for it or voting against it. "Don't make us vote on it." So the public had no idea where we were. The public didn't know who was for them and who was against them. They defeated it without getting their hands caught.

Q: Without ever having a public debate on it on the floor.

EMK: And the administration was just as happy about it, they were in such disarray at that time.

Q: Why did they—?

EMK: I don't know why they decided to go to a different proposal rather than taking what they had. They insisted that they wanted to bring people who had ideas about how to develop a better proposal. I think we had had good suggestions and ideas. There was a range of different options out there, but they wanted to have it very specific all the way through, rather than leaving some of these issues and questions for further development.

Q: And wanted to start it de novo, *from scratch.*

EMK: Yes, and they wanted to be very detailed about the particular functions of these different kinds of groups and pools, purchasing pools. They wanted a description of the size and the shape and what they were going to have in terms of different regions of the country, what they were going to do. The details of this proposal they wanted to master and to have outlined, and that becomes enormously complicated very quickly.

Q: Instead of starting—

EMK: They could have started any way. There were a lot of different ways you could have started. You could have said, "These details we're going to leave to a board; these details we're going to leave to different agencies to make descriptions"—which are suggestions now that are out there, in Tom Daschle's book,[34] and other kinds of things. They wanted to spell it out in detail, what

---

medical field. The ads encouraged viewers to make their opposition known to members of Congress.

34. Tom Daschle, Scott S. Greenberger, and Jeanne M. Lambrew, *Critical: What We Can Do about the Health Care Crisis* (New York: Thomas Dunne Books, 2008).

they were going to do. That's the way they thought was the best way to go, so that's the way that they went.

I can't give you what went on with the president in terms of why he made that kind of judgment rather than something else. I can't give you that part. It was just that they were going to have the comprehensive universal, and they were going to develop their own proposal, and they were going to hear the people who were very good on it, which they did, and they were going to have that kind of a proposal. I think everybody understands now that that was a catastrophic mistake.

Q: Yes. Was there any consultation about this strategy with people in the Congress?

EMK: No.

Q: They just went ahead and did it?

EMK: They thought that they could get it done in a timely way. They underestimated the complexity of it, and then they were faced with a variety of other kinds of issues that came up during this period of time, which diverted the focus and attention away from it.

Q: Dan Rostenkowski gave an oral history interview.

EMK: Yes.

Q: Not to me but to somebody else, and he relates a conversation about that with the president, before Hillary was appointed to do this. Dan's version of that was, "I told the president he's making a huge mistake; that he ought to approach this—I said, 'First of all, you're a politician. Think about what you can get through and start from there. Let's get something and get the people involved in Congress, rather than turn it over to [what he referred to as] a bunch of academics.' " Was that the impression created in Congress?

EMK: I'm not sure people saw it quite that clearly at the time, but that's obviously, in retrospect, clearly what happened. You know, there are different approaches and ways of dealing. Sometimes people just send up ideas and let the other—but sometimes if they do that, they lose control over where it goes, so they don't like to do it.

They made the judgment decision to be more specific. They had very able, gifted, talented people, very knowledgeable, and they were going to get it and get it right, and get the best people to try and get that right and do it in a timely way. But the time slipped. It became disjointed, it became un-coordinated, and there were a number of other factors that interceded and became important, and moved and shifted the calendar back on it, and that caused an unraveling of the whole process. And as the process deteriorated, the groups that were focused in opposition became stronger and stronger, and their ability to influence became greater, and they had very considerable success.

We missed the opportunity, at a key time in this development, to move this whole process into what we would call the budget resolution, which would have permitted us to expedite the process, and you would have had the legislation in March instead of in October. Senator Byrd refused to do it. It would have been massaging the budget process, certainly, to get it to have an inclusive kind of program, such a massive program, but its implications in terms of the budget are massive. We're talking about a healthcare system now of $2 trillion, so its implications in terms of the budget are massive.

But we were unable to get that done, and once we were unable to get that done, which was a major setback, we had mistake after mistake. Although, I have to give it to Senator Clinton—She mastered the details of this [as First Lady], appeared before our committee and other committees, answered all the questions, and they were complicated and difficult questions. She understood it and she was an effective spokesperson for it.

Q: In mastering the substance. But what about the politics?

EMK: The politics was that Phil Gramm[35] and the Republicans decided not to let anything pass. This could have been healthcare, it could have been education, it could have been the environment, it could have been tax policy. They recognized, you have a Democratic president, a Democratic House and Senate, and the best way to undermine that is to show they are ineffective, and what came tripping down the pathway was healthcare—I think it could have been anything else—and he said, "We're not going to let this thing go through."

They had people who had been interested in healthcare who were prepared to move ahead, and they blew the whistle—Gingrich blew the whistle—and said, "We're not going to pass anything on through," and these lemmings just followed. The record is there on it. They had a unified front in opposition to it. There was a small group of Republicans that tried to work with a group of Democrats at the very end of it, but it wasn't a serious kind of effort. Bob Kerrey[36] was involved in it, but it wasn't a serious effort.

They [Republicans] made a judgment decision in this process—this was about '94—that they weren't going to let it go through. They made a calculated political judgment on it, and they were right, and Democrats lost, big time, in House and Senate [in the midterm elections]. They served their special interests in terms of the insurance companies, in terms of the drug companies, in terms of the health industry professionals. They got massive contributions from them. Those groups got set up and were very effective, and it just ended the whole effort with a whimper.

We had Travelgate, Whitewater, and then we had the divisions in the Senate between our [Labor and Human Resources] committee and Moynihan,[37] with Moynihan wanting to do welfare reform, which is what he's always been interested in. Therefore, we had meetings in the White House where the president said, "I want to do healthcare," and Moynihan said, "No, we're going

---

35. Senator Gramm was a Texas Republican.
36. Senator Kerrey was a Democrat from Nebraska.
37. Senator Daniel Patrick Moynihan was chair of the Senate Finance Committee.

to do welfare, and we're not going to do it." He was completely uncooperative. And O'Donnell,[38] who is still around now doing these television shows like *West Wing*, was the [Moynihan] staffer, and just would undermine any of the efforts that our committee had in trying to move this whole process. Moynihan undermined the whole process in terms of moving toward it.

So everything was delayed, and it isn't difficult to delay things in the Senate. It isn't a master plan, it's just a whole process about how this delay took place, and with that delay, the corresponding actions that took place from the other side just became so overwhelming and so powerful that they effectively sank it.

Clinton went down in terms of public opinion. The administration was divided as to what ought to come up next. With his popularity down, they thought, "Well, we'll move ahead with NAFTA,"[39] and that antagonized labor, which was trying to be of some help to us, so they took a walk. And you have the other kinds of activities that he was involved in, as I said: Travelgate, Whitewater, and other issues that undermined him.

Q: And deficit reduction came.

EMK: The deficit reduction.

Q: It came ahead of the budget.

EMK: The whole budget debate, which took a lot of effort and energy from the administration. It was decided by a single vote in the early summer [of 1993], and healthcare was off to the side.

At the end of the day—we had markups in our committee, which were enormously interesting, very well attended, and we get a bill out of our committee, which was a very good bill, very close to what the administration wanted, but it was too rich for the Senate. Then Mitchell redrafted and reshaped his own bill, which was very good and very clever. We have this debate today [March 2008] between Hillary and Barack about whether it [health insurance] has to be mandated or not mandated. All Mitchell said in there is, "Under our proposal, we're going to get to 95 percent, and if we don't get to 95 percent, Congress then can go ahead and mandate it." They'll have to pass something. So he left it off the—but put it out there so we voted, and he could say, "We're not mandating anything," to move on through.

He had a lot of other very good simplifications and proposals: a lot of biomedical research programs, and long-term care, which people were very interested in and committed to. He had a lot of different features in that program at the end, which made it—and it would be today—a strong, strong program.

Q: So was this a presidential failure, basically, in the timing?

---

38. Lawrence O'Donnell Jr. went on to host MSNBC's *The Last Word*.
39. North American Free Trade Agreement.

EMK: It's basically a miscalculation on their part, an obsession with the details. In one sense you had to sort of admire the fact that they were trying to give as much information and get this information out. On the other hand, just strategically, in retrospect, it should have been done in another way. But you can't take away from the fact that they were trying to get this out. The problem that they had was the secrecy, and that caused a lot of backlash—because it lasted so long.

It was a combination of different elements, but the basic blame, clearly, I would give to the Republicans. I mean, we deal with other complicated issues up there. The other day, someone took the administration's position on Pfizer, and they did the charts and all of that, and they were all saying that it looked just like Hillary's health plan, you know, what the appeals are, and where they go on through, and put all the boxes up there, and the intelligence agency, and who has access to what. They did a chart up there just to show how ridiculous—I mean, you can do that virtually on any piece of legislation.

They lost. They had a basic failure in terms of giving the urgency and the time, although he was committed and she was committed to it. It was just too much information. And you had very powerful groups on the other side, very powerful forces that understand that they're going to lose out on a lot of money.

Q: It just seemed very difficult for the people outside to get a sense of what's going on. It sounded so complicated. Maybe it was just the reporting, but everything that would come out—the consumer maybe gets afraid to change anything. "What does this really mean?"

EMK: Oh, that's right.

Q: And then you have the opposition with its bullhorns out there telling you to not trust any of it.

EMK: Well, it's difficult in doing the comprehensive. We had internal battles. We reported the bill out without the provisions in it that would have given jurisdiction to the Finance Committee. That upset the Finance Committee, so they put a hold on our bill, and so therefore we put a hold on their bill. Now we have internal squabbling among ourselves on it. But Moynihan never really cared about it.

Q: No. He said, "There is no crisis." He said, "It's an insurance crisis, it's not a healthcare crisis."

EMK: So, Mitchell took command of it, and he was very easy to work with. Daschle was very involved in it, and myself. It was whoever was interested in it. Mitchell would say, "Whoever is interested, come to these meetings," and they gradually just ended up being Mitchell, Daschle, and myself. Harry Reid came a bit to do some of the routine things. That's how he got his start on it. But others didn't care much about it.

I think it's important, probably, in the discussion, to think about what is out there now in terms of the future, and I think this: On the plus side, you have the fact that there's pretty much an agreement about what is going to be in the bill, which is a lot different. Between Barack and Hillary, there's pretty much agreement on it. There are some tweaks and changes, but there's a pretty good common understanding about the details of it. People would know how to draft that very easily, very quickly, if they were going that way.

Secondly, I think there is a much better understanding and awareness, because many of the states have already debated these issues now. Massachusetts has debated it, California has debated it, the state of Washington has, Maine has, Vermont has. There are a number of states that have gone through these discussions and debates.

And the language has altered and changed. I was always against individual mandates, but Massachusetts got an individual mandate, and I can live with that today. There are people who had locked on the positions that, "We are not going to have a mandate on companies and corporations." Well they have—the Republicans went along with that in Massachusetts. They're not as worked up about that aspect of it. They call it something different. I'm not as worked up about individual mandates. The philosophical and ideological differences that were out there, that put people at people's throats, have been in a very important way adjusted and modified, and—not melted away, but—that's two.

Thirdly, I think the business community understands, in terms of globalization, that they're going to have to deal with this. It is such a weight in terms of their ability to deal with the globalization.

Q: You mean the competitive?

EMK: International competition, competitiveness. This thing is a big deal for them and it's not going to go away. And there's a greater involvement of the population because over the period of these recent years there have been more and more of these negotiations between workers and others, about co-pays and deductibles, than we ever had previously. That really wasn't on the table. We'd deal with the issue on the basis of theory—whether you're covered or not covered.

These labor disputes that are going on are, by and large, healthcare disputes. And by and large it's about coverage, and by and large, in many instances it's about retirement. So the population as a whole has a much better understanding and awareness of the significance of these theories and of these issues than they had before. All of that is out there in ways that can help the process move forward.

On the other side, the other side knows how to—you have an increasing hostility towards government and government solutions and resolutions to problems, and this is going to have to take a governmental hand. You can have the private sector very much involved in it, and you ought to have that, but it's going to have a governmental framework. This increasing hostility towards anything that appears—There's enormous ambivalence.

Everybody's crying for food safety. We're going to have a good food safety bill, and that's going to mean that government is going to—you're going to have to have registration; you're going to have to have inspection; you're going to have to have the power of recall in that. And yet, people on the one hand all want much safer food, and on the other hand they don't want government involved. There's this incredible dichotomy that's going to make it somewhat more difficult.

Secondly, it used to be more for the coverage on healthcare; now, it's the cost. It's much more cost now than coverage, even though you've got a large number of people that aren't covered. The cost is the thing. If you look through your polls in there, that's the thing that is of most concern. People don't want to pay any more. They think we're paying too much, so they don't want to pay any more. In these programs—Barack's is fifty and Hillary's is a hundred—they're going to have to be able to show how they're going to be able to deal with this. There are going to be a lot of people whose ox is going to get gored in this, who are going to lose out on money, and there are going to be people who are going to be unemployed, and that's going to create a lot of problems. Those are going to be in specific areas where—We're talking about the general good. And this is complex. It's enormously complex.

Q: *In any reform at this point, would it not mean that people in the private sector involved in the health industry are going to lose their jobs or lose their business, or not lose it but they're not going to get as much? I mean, the thing is profit. It's for profit.*

EMK: Sure. Yes, that's right.

Q: *You know, the bottom line.*

EMK: But you can at least—if you put the hold on this thing now, in terms of future expenditures you're going to be a lot better off. You've still got forty million [Americans] who aren't covered—so you may have to use those people to, just in the administration, to get those forty million people covered. You'll have to take a look at some of this.

We were out at the Mayo Clinic. They are treating, doing the Medicare at 30 percent less than they're paying Medicare. This fellow that I was talking to, who was doing health policy out there, talks about Intermountain Corporation in Utah. They're doing it at 40 percent less. And this fellow was telling me that there are fifteen or eighteen states that are doing it at less than any of the European countries that are doing it, and getting better results than any of the Europeans. So he said, "Why aren't we providing incentives for the ones that are doing it right, and disincentives for the others?" Building on these things.

You know, there are different ways of doing a lot of this. You're going to have to have case management. You're going to have to have preventive care. Information technology can save you $140 million a year. There's ways of getting to it. Americans understand that these people do it, and they do it more efficiently, and they do it for a lot less. Shouldn't they get rewarded? Americans will say yes. On the other hand, you'll have the people who will say, "We're all going to get thrown out of our jobs." I think it's going to have to be worth the effort.

Q: *So you take the private systems and ideas that are working, and you give those incentives.*

EMK: You've got evidence-based medicine; that's the other big hot item now. What works best: If I operate on you, or I give you drugs, or that I have some other kind of treatment that will make you healthy? Why aren't we evaluating the principal operations and finding out which one of these does the best, and say that we'll have reimbursement for those rather than the others? Well, the industry will get all worked up about that.

They found out that 70 percent of the pills that people take have no effect on them whatsoever. People don't know, because—But you're going to go to individualized medicine because you're going to be able to take the genes and the proteins of different people and find out how they're going to react to different kinds of medicines, and all the people that are going to be able to do that will have much more effective results and use half the treatment and half the medicines. All of that is out there now. That's the kind of outside stuff that Barack and Hillary—that's the stuff, rather than just the routine stuff now.

Q: *So you're an optimist?*

EMK: You have to be on this. Let me give this one more try, and then we'll let somebody else worry about it. [*Laughs*]

We started out today just talking about the human aspects of it. We don't want to get away from those aspects we've been talking about, you know, the central drive for my own interest in this. You had mentioned that we had talked earlier—and these are just some reminders about what was happening right after President Clinton was elected. He tasked his task force to have legislation within a hundred days.

Q: *A hundred days.*

EMK: We went to a big retreat in Jamestown. Do you remember that? Remember Dianne Feinstein getting up?

Vicki Kennedy: Oh, my goodness, do I ever.

EMK: She got up and said, "What is this business about healthcare? Take my name off," or whatever it was.

Vicki Kennedy: Is that when Pat Moynihan was also on a panel, or was that at the next retreat?

If you remember, Hillary's father died during that period of time when they were supposed to get healthcare out, so she was at his bedside and then he passed away. So I think it was delayed. That's my recollection. It maybe didn't happen in those hundred days, or if she did get it out, it was rushed. She's working on healthcare and her father is dying at the same time.

Q: At some points, I've thought about Carter's first year, and the energy bill, which came first, and that was prepared in secret by Jim Schlesinger. He wouldn't even let Stu Eizenstat know what was going on. He didn't present it to Congress, and you know what happened then. Well, he didn't bring anybody into it but he had it all worked out, what should be done. You know, Tip O'Neill and others helped him, but it was this very complicated piece of legislation in terms of getting it through—which committees had jurisdiction, and so forth. I guess they retrieved something out of it, but he didn't get the comprehensive reform that he was looking for. It just raises the academic question as to whether comprehensive reform of anything these days is possible when you have a very complicated system to deal with. So, you think there's a chance for this [healthcare reform]?

EMK: Yes. I think there is an increasing understanding and appreciation. You have to change the mix. You'll have to spin off. This evidence-based medicine—you'll have to give that to a board that people have confidence in. We can't decide that, but that solves that problem.

You have to categorize the issues that you want, and put time limits on it. It's like the base closing commission saying, "We'll resolve this within a certain period of time. Each side gets eight or ten amendments." We do that with trade agreements. We do it with BCRC;[40] it goes up or down and you either accept it or reject it, and the administration has to live with it. If it's a disaster, they take the heat on it. Unless you're able to work that kind of a process out, I don't think you can do it, and that's going to take a big deal. Everybody will want a part of it.

We had this information technology that we passed, which I didn't mention before, the information technology, which was an Enzi-Kennedy-Frist-Clinton [initiative]. This was an interesting little story with Hillary. Enzi was not familiar with information technology, and I went over and talked to him and briefed him, and then he understood it and he said fine. Now Hillary calls me up and says, "Ted, I've got the bill on information technology."

I've been heading it for four years already, and she has just arrived in the Senate. "I've got the bill, and we'd like to get it reported out. It's a Frist-Clinton bill." I said, "We're working on our bill." "Well, Ted, I don't like to do this, but Frist says that if you don't report it out, he'll put our bill on the calendar and then call it up as majority leader. So that will be embarrassing." I said, "Let me just find out more about it."

I go and talk to Enzi, and Enzi said, "That's not going to happen, Ted. If Bill Frist calls that bill up, I'll publicly oppose it on the floor of the United States Senate, and I've told him that." Ring, ring, ring. "Hello, Ted? This is Hillary.

40. Defense Base Closure and Realignment Commission.

Ted, could you put our bill as an amendment to yours, when you report out yours?" I said yes. "And could I be, then, a principal co-sponsor?" I said, "That's fine. It will be Enzi-Kennedy-Frist-Clinton." "Thank you very much." Boom, the press release was out that afternoon. Isn't that an interesting little tidbit? The time on that was probably three or four years ago.

Q: Interesting on the Senate and interesting on the people.

EMK: The other part, which gets back to the more important discussion you were having, is that it goes over to the House and it dies over there. This was the last year with Nancy Johnson, Barton, and Tauzin.[41] I had gone over to see them all about it, but they all wanted a piece. It's become so hot now, information technology; everybody's interested in it. They all wanted to have a big piece on that. It's just motherhood. They all wanted—and as a result, nothing came out of it. Nancy Johnson was defeated, and Barton doesn't really care about it.

It's being held up on our side now by Pat Leahy,[42] and the reason he's holding it up is because I'm holding up a gun bill, what they call LEOSA,[43] which permits concealable weapons to be available to retired police officers, even though local jurisdictions forbid it or state jurisdictions forbid them carrying them into certain places. This will override it. So if a community— Charlottesville—said, "No concealable weapons in bars or in churches," this will override it. If you've been a retired policeman, you'll be able to pack your heat in a bar, or in church, down there. This overrides local communities.

No training requirements.

Vicki Kennedy: No vision requirements, no mental capacity requirements.

Q: And Leahy wants this?

EMK: Yes, because the Fraternal Order of Police all want it. I'm going to trade it off for micro-stamping.

Vicki Kennedy: Micro-stamping of the ammunition.

EMK: Yes. I've checked with all of the gun people and they said, "If you can get a vote on that, it's worth letting this thing go. That's more important." So that's a deal I'm going to—all of the good people say that that's a worthwhile swap if you can get it.

---

41. Representatives Johnson, Joe Barton, and Billy Tauzin were Republicans from Connecticut, Texas, and Louisiana, respectively.

42. Ultimately, Congress passed the Health Information Technology for Economic and Clinical Health (HITECH) Act of 2009, which "provides the Department of Health and Human Services with the authority to establish programs to improve health care quality, safety, and efficiency through the promotion of health IT, including electronic health records and private and secure electronic health information exchange." "Health IT Legislation and Regulations," https://www.healthit.gov/policy-researchers-implementers/health-it-legislation.

43. Law Enforcement Officers Safety Act.

On the gun stuff, there's several in there that they don't want to face. They sell guns to people who were on the terrorist list. They had forty-eight people who were on the terrorist list and were able to buy guns. So, I have the amendment to prohibit them from buying guns, and the terrible cry—you would have thought the Senate was coming to an end! They don't want to vote on that. The NRA[44] wants them to be able to buy guns, and these people didn't want to get caught up in it. Or, being able to have .50-caliber—That can shoot down a helicopter. Terrorists could use that. They don't want restrictions on .50-caliber rifles.

Vicki Kennedy: Or the ammunition. You could go on eBay right now and get .50 caliber. You know, it's unbelievable what you can find online right now. At my gun board, gun violence prevention meetings, they handed out .50-caliber shells, empty, you know, nothing in them. So I gave it to Teddy. He was going to show it on the floor of the Senate, but then it was a prop you couldn't use, or something.

EMK: Oh no, I could, but they thought it was a little inflammatory.

Vicki Kennedy: A little inflammatory. So tell him how you were going to the airport—

EMK: So I stuck it [the shell] in my pocket, and I'm headed to Boston, and I'm going through the [metal detector] machines. I've got my shoes off, my jacket up, I'm bumbling over, and I reach into my pocket, and there's that .50-caliber [shell]. And I'm looking at the Homeland Security guys right up here. I've got this brand new [staff] guy traveling with me—who was it?

Vicki Kennedy: Derek, or something.

EMK: Derek, who was—you know, it was just about his third day on the job. I said, "Derek, come over here." He said, "Yes, sir?" And I reached in and I said, "Keep your hand closed." He goes down and—

Vicki Kennedy: He's like, "Pass the chalk." [*Laughing*]

EMK: His eyes are as big as the side of that wall over there, and he takes off outside the airport.

Vicki Kennedy: That was really funny.

Q: All right.

EMK: I think we got a lot of material down.

Q: Yes, we did.

Perspectives
S. Philip Caper, physician and staffer on Edward Kennedy's Senate Health Subcommittee:

Kennedy staffers and White House officials recalled the decades-long debate over national health insurance.

---

44. National Rifle Association.

Caper: [Richard Nixon] had what today looks like a very progressive healthcare package, including national health insurance. Nixon, at that point, was in big trouble. And he was looking for a win, which is one of the things that motivated us to start talking to him and to try to get this, because the administration was very much a part of the negotiations on the Kennedy-Mills [national health insurance] legislation. I think people did think it was inevitable, or at least in 1971, '72, '73. I think the first time that we really realized that it wasn't inevitable is when we lost the vote in the House. It was a committee vote, in the Ways and Means Committee, on the Kennedy-Mills bill. That went down to defeat fairly narrowly in that committee.

I remember Kennedy was there for the committee vote, was there in the House in the committee room. He went over to watch it, and he came back afterwards and said, "You have no idea how powerful these insurance guys are. They've just begun to flex their muscles. . . ." In the end the insurance industry and the lack of dedicated support on the labor side killed it. That's the closest we've come [until the Obama Patient Protection and Affordable Care Act].

Stuart Eizenstat, President Carter's domestic policy advisor: This debate, in the context of a potential, looming Kennedy challenge [in 1980], happened as Carter's popularity was dropping. Polls were showing that Kennedy would win the nomination if he ran. I argued with the political people—with Hamilton and Jody and Jerry Rafshoon[45] and others—that the best way to forestall a Kennedy challenge was to agree with him on health insurance, because if we did, there would be no rationale for his running. This was the big enchilada. Many of the other issues were—mixing metaphors—icing on the cake, but the cake was national health insurance. That was the core. That was the big social program. That was the issue that the party stood for and that the liberal wing wanted.

I'm convinced that when the negotiation failed, that convinced Kennedy that he should run and had to run. It wasn't long afterward that he did. No one can prove it, but it would have been difficult for him if we had reached an agreement. What rationale would he have had to run if we were working together on this [healthcare] program? I would posit that with all the difficulties we had—the [Iranian] hostage crisis that came later, with inflation, with high interest rates—that it was the Kennedy challenge, splitting the party, that was certainly a significant factor, if not the central ingredient in all of this. It wasn't the single ingredient; there were the external circumstances—but it was debilitating, it was divisive, and it certainly was a factor in electing Reagan.

---

45. Chief of Staff Hamilton Jordan, Press Secretary Jody Powell, and Communications Director Gerald Rafshoon were President Jimmy Carter's political advisors.

Kennedy worked closely with the director of the NIH on HIV/AIDS policies to promote research and treatment.

Anthony Fauci, physician and AIDS researcher, director of the National Institute of Allergy and Infectious Diseases, National Institutes of Health: The Kennedy connection is that Ted had always been very open-minded about gay men, about people who were disenfranchised, any people who didn't have good health coverage, whether you were an injection drug user, or whatever. It was very clear that he was very empathetic towards people in need. And that's the reason why I think, early on, he rose as the champion of helping us in so many different ways. The fact that Kennedy was out there pushing that concept [expanding clinical trials] made it much easier for me, during a more conservative administration, to do it. I think that was the beginning of a very special relationship with Kennedy, because I don't think anybody would screw around with me if he was very favorably disposed to the things that I was trying to do.

David Blumenthal, Edward Kennedy's staffer on his Senate Subcommittee on Health and Scientific Research:
The Clinton national health insurance proposal was yet another failure in Edward Kennedy's battle to pass universal healthcare.

Q: Was it [special] *interests that killed it* [universal healthcare] *under Clinton?*

Blumenthal: I take a different view. I know that there are people who think that it was either the HIAA, Harry and Louise, or Clinton's incompetence, all of which were important. But as I look at—and I'm not a political scientist—but as I look back at the forces you need to change something as massive and as complicated and as politically fraught as healthcare, I think you need a constituency that favors it. I mean, you can't get something through our legislative process unless someone's lobbying for it, and who was lobbying for it?

Caper: I think one of the biggest mistakes that Clinton made was to come up with something that was so damn complicated nobody could explain it, and nobody could understand it. I mean, that's a recipe for legislative gridlock automatically. And the fact that they didn't understand that was astounding to me. Then the process they went through with all the secrecy and all the—it heightens everybody's paranoia. It was just mishandled.

John Hilley, President Clinton's director of the White House Office of Legislative Affairs:
Q: During the Clinton national health insurance, why did there seem to be a moment of opportunity? There had been twenty years in which nothing had happened. Why did this seem to be a moment of opportunity under Clinton?

Hilley: My opinion is very different. It was never a moment of opportunity, absolutely not.

Boy, from where I sat, it seemed like hell, to tell you the truth. Two things were happening. The administration was not far enough along to understand how to do this properly—and that's all part of the public record, and I'm sure it will resurface here in 2008—so they were way too green to be able to do this properly. But on the other hand, the Republicans, because of the complexity of the issue and the opportunities that had been created by the White House's mishandling of it, were just out to kill. There was no way Dole and his guys were going to do anything in that year because they saw that it was too important electorally as an issue. So for all that we went through, there was never a real chance. In fact, in the late summer of '94, when we had this bipartisan group that was trying to revive it after it had melted, that bipartisan group was a sham. There was no way that Dole and the leadership of the Republicans were going to let that take life either. So, on the first, second, or third bounce, it was dead.

The politics weren't lined up right nationally either. I mean, you had business lined up against it. I don't have to repeat all that, but there was not an opportunity. Now, Kennedy played a very constructive role. I would like to have seen him much more involved. In other words, we basically had this thing conjured up and said, "Here it is, here's this way to do this national healthcare," when the proper approach would have been to gather a Kennedy and a Mitchell, people like that, and say, "OK, here's our goal, what's the best we can do," rather than, "Here's this immaculate conception, do it." That just doesn't work.

Senator Tom Daschle (D-SD):

Q: Can you recall some of those issues in which both of you were intensely involved? We know healthcare was—Would it be fair to say that that was the first issue that brought you together as working colleagues on an issue?

Daschle: Yes, we worked very closely together. I was on the Finance Committee. I was chairman of the Policy Committee in '93, and as chairman of the [Democratic] Policy Committee, the then majority leader, Mitchell, had asked if I would coordinate the [Democratic] Caucus healthcare effort. That meant working very closely with Teddy and one of his staff at the time, Nick Littlefield, who also became a good friend.

Teddy was obviously the primary motivator and the primary architect of our caucus healthcare policy. Of course, he worked very closely with Hillary, but he was in his prime at that time. He had the seniority; he had the clout; he had the respect. Nobody challenged his credentials. But, unfortunately, he didn't have the committee assignment. You would think that that committee assignment would be the key, but there was the Finance

Committee, and, unfortunately, there was a difference of opinion with regard to how we should approach this between many of us and the chairman of the Senate Finance Committee at the time, Pat Moynihan, so things got substantially delayed. Ultimately, in part because of the delay and because it languished for so long, we ended up on the defensive, and it was unsuccessfully concluded. It was a very significant learning experience for me, to say the least. That was probably the first time that I worked in depth with Teddy on a project.

Q: Were you George Mitchell's point person for healthcare?

Daschle: I was, right.

Q: And with the Finance Committee, it's the money that matters, I guess. To his committee, it was less that; it was the program and the policy goal, not the accounting. Has that gap been bridged yet, do you think?

Daschle: Yes, I think it has. First, just out of complete respect for Ted's contribution to health policy these four decades, I don't think there's any doubt that this is probably the best working relationship that the HELP [Health, Education, Labor, & Pensions] Committee and the Finance Committee have ever had. I give credit to Max Baucus,[46] as well, for his attitude and for the way he's gone about this, from what I can tell. I'm not nearly as plugged in to that on a daily basis as others, but from my perspective, it certainly would appear that they're working pretty closely together and they've vowed—vowed may be a strong word—but promised or committed to a one-bill strategy on the floor, and that's also very encouraging.

Q: Would you say that he has learned any lessons from the 1993 experience? You've observed and worked with him on both of these occasions, getting ready for the next push. Has he ever mentioned any lessons he's learned? We're not going to do that again, or something?

Daschle: First of all, he [Kennedy] wasn't calling the shots, unfortunately. If he had been calling the shots, we'd probably have healthcare reform today, but he wasn't. He was *one* of those calling the shots, but he was only one. The Clintons were the primary architects of the strategy as well as the policy. George Mitchell, Pat Moynihan, and to a certain extent Bob Dole were all key participants. Ted Kennedy was one of those at the table, but again, not in nearly as dominant a role.

Looking back, the best lesson one could have used in that experience would be simply to have said to Senator Kennedy, "Look, work something out and we'll support the product." That blind assignment would have worked extremely well, because he would have salvaged it had he had the opportunity. But there are a lot of lessons to be learned and I've given a lot of speeches over

---

46. Senator Baucus was a Montana Democrat.

the years, talking about what those lessons are. To a certain extent President Obama has applied those lessons so far.

Q: You worked closely with the White House as the Democratic leader, or you've had to. Did Ted have an independent relationship with the Clintons, working on policy issues that the party would be concerned with in the Senate?

Daschle: He did, because he's such an icon and because he was viewed as such a legislative giant, especially in the '90s. He had a lot to do with many of the key questions that we faced at the time. He obviously is very deeply interested in health, but he's also interested in issues involving working people. He was very involved in the welfare reform debate with President Clinton at the time. He has an interest in foreign policy, and the war in Bosnia was an issue upon which he spent a good deal of time.

Senator Nancy Landon Kassebaum (R-KS): I really enjoyed being ranking member [of the Labor and Human Resources Committee] through the debate on the Clinton healthcare reform. Senator Kennedy held extensive hearings, which I always said were wise because it was an education on healthcare. They were extensive hearings, and that's when I first gained a real admiration for his willingness, when he cared about a legislative issue, to spend time, to work on it, to really make an effort to achieve some success in getting people together and to understand. It just never really—there was not enough that either of us could do to get enough support. I think neither of us agreed enough, either, to come together in support of that bill as it stood.

Q: But neither did any of the rest of the Senate.

Kassebaum: No.

Q: Or the House.

Kassebaum: Yes, well clearly not the House, and there was not even that kind of support in the Senate. But it was an important hearing at the time to try to help people understand some of the intricacies of healthcare, and how reform was not going to be just something you could say, "Let's do it, and wave a wand."

That was my first impression [of Senator Kennedy]. A part of it is that a lot of people said, "Oh, Kennedy doesn't really pay much attention in the Senate. He just has a good time and he goes off and he doesn't care." He really, in my mind—and I feel like I am not a person who could comment that well on it—grew in a seriousness towards the Senate and the legislative process. For those who like history, who have a sense of history and politics, I've come to believe that longevity has a role as well, because once you lose people like that, you've lost an institutional memory. And that's going pretty fast now.

While you could disagree with him, at the end of the day he wanted the institution to succeed, and he believed strongly in the importance of three strong bodies of government: the executive, the legislative and the judicial [branches]. While you might sometimes hear him rant and rail, he was not going to ever want to see that change. That's my own personal view, and that's what I think guided him on a lot of issues the longer he served.

Q: Why do you think that HIPAA got through when healthcare reform hadn't?

Kassebaum: Senator Kennedy played a huge role in getting that through. There's where I saw him really be able to go to the House side and negotiate. He knew where to make a call and do a bit of joshing to get it done. The House wanted medical savings accounts. We had reached an agreement, Senator Kennedy and I, that once we got it through committee, where we thought we had all the votes lined up on both sides—my side got a little shaky in some instances—that no amendments would be added on the floor, and both of us tried to keep them off, even ones that both of us cared a lot about, like mental health coverage. We were fairly successful. But health savings accounts became a huge issue when we were in conference [committee].

Q: Senator Dole wanted them too.

Kassebaum: Yes.

Q: Did he want them at that point for—This was, after all, close to an election year. Was it simply a factor for him in election?

Kassebaum: I don't know. Some of the Republicans, you know—I don't really know, but I do know that we had some real meetings on the House side. I don't know quite the sequence of it all, but the person who was able to bridge a decision on that was Senator Kennedy with Bill Archer, and that was huge, because Archer was strong. He had a lot of pressure on the House side. Plus, I have always given a lot of credit to Dennis Hastert[47] on the House side, to try to get it moving along.

Sheila Burke, chief of staff to Senator Robert Dole (R-KS): Any solution [on universal healthcare] that didn't involve the financing committees was not likely to be a realistic one. There was no great love between many of the Finance Committee Democrats and Kennedy, and certainly not with the Republicans on the Finance Committee at the time. Even with the Democrats, there was tension, and certainly on the House side.

Q: What were the principles that you saw in him that undergirded his approach to healthcare?

Burke: Equity, that there was an inherent unfairness in the system, that he should help people who could not otherwise fight for themselves. I think Kennedy thought that the government should help solve problems that people couldn't otherwise solve and that it should always support those who were least capable of solving their problems. I always had a sense that it was about the unfairness in the system. The coverage of children, the disabled, the

---

47. Congressman Hastert of Illinois was then the chief deputy whip for House Republicans.

engagements were all about those least capable of caring for themselves. I had a sense that Kennedy as a person of extraordinary wealth and extraordinary gifts felt the obligation to care for those least cared for.

Congressman Patrick J. Kennedy (D-RI), Edward Kennedy's son:
Patrick Kennedy: The thing I think that's so misunderstood about his politics is that he was for justice. There's this terrible mischaracterization, that's politically motivated by the right, to make Democrats out to be for some redistribution of wealth, kind of paternalistic, let's help the poor people, let's help the minorities, let's help—My dad was for making sure there was justice, and that people started at the same starting line, so that if they didn't have the same backgrounds and same place where people could get to that same starting line, that that was where society owed them an education to get them there, owed them support of services, social, childcare, human services, whatever, to get them there. That this was about justice. I think that's the appeal that unfortunately we've lost, in terms of how that's gotten across, because it's not about—I think it's a principle everybody agrees with, that nobody's getting anything other than justice, which is just allowing them to have the same opportunities that others have. Unfortunately, it's been mischaracterized as they're getting something that someone else isn't getting, at someone else's expense. And my dad was all about making sure that people who didn't have the same opportunities were given the same opportunities. It's a whole different way of looking at things, but it's an important different way of looking at things, that justifies the work that he did in a very powerful way.

Q: I think that will be more and more understood as study and reflection distances itself from the ideological and political struggles of the moment. You're not the only one who has made this observation in the oral history, so I think that will also come out very much in the oral history.

Patrick Kennedy: The human dignity part, we saw it when he brought us around to the hearings on healthcare and the like. He was so intent on people not being dissed, if they didn't get the healthcare. I mean, he was really enraged. . . . I think he had this sense of identification with people that he would not want to be in that position where he was put out just because he belonged to the wrong group of society, and then was denied because he was discriminated against. He had this sense of, I don't know, empathy or compassion or whatever it is, of putting yourself in someone else's shoes that was very strong.

15

Coming Home to Port

By the start of the twenty-first century, Senator Kennedy had produced an admirable legislative record. Expanding civil rights, lowering the voting age to eighteen, abolishing poll taxes, liberalizing immigration laws, fighting for universal healthcare, ending the draft, supporting peace initiatives throughout the world, creating education opportunities, establishing public service projects, and leading the charge against conservative judicial appointees were all part of his portfolio. He had long ago accepted that he would never become president and that he would continue to make his mark on history through the legislative process. Although the Republican Party vilified him as a means for raising funds, GOP members of Congress appreciated Kennedy's personal concern for them and would work with him when they found common ground. He continued to organize policy dinners at his Northern Virginia home and, just as his mother had taught him, supervised every detail to make the event perfect.

As he moved closer to the Senate's longevity record, Kennedy would be crowned by the New York Times's *Adam Clymer as "the leading senator of his time" and "one of the greats in history, wise in the workings of this singular institution, especially its demand to be more than partisan to accomplish much."[1] By 2008, his Republican colleague John McCain labeled Kennedy "the last lion of the Senate. . . . He remains the single most effective member of the Senate if you want to get results."[2] Yet Kennedy worried that "anti-democratic" forces were corrupting the Senate in an attempt to stymie legislative results.*

Joined by his niece Caroline Kennedy, Teddy anointed his young Senate colleague, Barack Obama, as the rightful heir to Jack's and Bobby's legacies. For the chamber he loved, Kennedy labored over the new president's domestic centerpiece, the Patient Protection and Affordable Care Act, until brain cancer overtook the seventy-seven-year-old senator from Massachusetts on August 25, 2009. Like his mother and father before him, Teddy passed away at the family's famed Hyannis Port compound. Joe and Rose were returned to their roots and buried in the Boston suburb of Brookline, where

---

1. Adam Clymer, *Edward M. Kennedy: A Biography* (New York: William Morrow, 1999), 609.

2. Peter S. Canellos, ed., *Last Lion: The Fall and Rise of Ted Kennedy* (New York: Simon and Schuster, 2009), ix.

they had lived as newlyweds and begun their family. Their youngest child, however, was laid to rest with his brothers, Jack and Bobby, at Arlington National Cemetery, overlooking the nation's capital and the Senate, which he had mastered in his nearly half-century tenure there.

EMK: People are basically unchallenged today [2005]. The country is unchallenged, we as a nation. We always do best when we're challenged. We did best when we came out of the Depression. We did best in World War II. Fifteen million Americans had to get jobs. We brought the economy back, in time. We were faced with the challenges on race: we tried to deal with people who had strong feelings; we tried to work our way through. Churches were involved, people involved, businesses involved. People felt a part of trying to stop the war in Vietnam; they were a part of something and tied to society.

Now we're here, we've had four tax cuts, and we're having two wars, and people are confused. They're seeing our respect around the world diminish. They're less sure about whether we're the rising tide of power or whether it's going to go to China and India. They're feeling restless about where they're going to end up, their health, their jobs, their families, their kids. People are less involved and participating less. There's a frustration out there, and I think an awful lot of people come in and pick up and play on that kind of atmosphere—and are doing it very successfully.

People are spending less time with their children; the children are less predictable, less certain. There's more concern with parents. They're looking for outs. It's an unchallenged nation at this time, and our tradition—at least in terms of the appeal of President Kennedy and the rest—was to challenge people. It wasn't a set of promises; it was a set of challenges. Then we all do better. That's the sort of politics I believe in and I think the country responds to. It's a very important element in terms of American society and in terms of all of us as individuals. We've all seen it in different aspects of our own lives.

Q: Well, the challenge that the [George W. Bush] *administration talks about is the challenge of terrorism, which seems to get the biggest play in the media.*

EMK: But we're not personally involved. I went last night to—the mayor is trying to get companies to give him some help to beautify little communities, neighborhoods, streets. It's the tenth anniversary of the program, and last night I went to it. They must have had a couple of thousand people. All the neighborhoods asked their favorite restaurants, and they all came in and had different food tables. Phoom!—people were turned on. They were doing something within their community.

The mayor had asked the companies to provide some resources. It's not a lot. [*Splash barks.*] Come here, Splash! And I saw people in all these different communities, gals from Brighton, [Massachusetts,] saying, I live just down the street from Joe. He's a great neighbor. I see him at church. It's tying into this kind of thing. These kids are feeling a part of something.

No one is feeling a part. It gets back to what we talked about earlier, about our presence versus the communications, money, and television. In the early sixties in Bedford-Stuyvesant, Bobby had a program where they provided, I think, $1,000 if they got 85 percent of the residents of the streets to say that they'd fix up their front yard. Each would get $150 to put the garbage cans out and straighten up the gates and do other things. But they had to get 85 percent of the people on these streets. The first time they were in a gymnasium in Bedford-Stuyvesant, and Bobby had to have all of his staff go out to get five streets to qualify, to get the 85 percent. He had everybody who worked on his campaign go; otherwise, nobody was going to show.

Two years later, they had a thousand streets. They had the drawing in a big, enormous auditorium. There were about five or six thousand people in there, and they were picking the streets. They had other streets that qualified. The whole place was just turned on in a community that had absolutely lost all hope. I think there's this idea that all you have to do is find—I don't disdain the concept that at some time in your life you have to find Jesus and everything else is saved. But his life was a life of service.

This is fundamental. We're not going to get into a theological discussion, but I don't think you have to go very far to see this, that there's nothing you really ever have to do except have this. It gives you an excuse that can lead you in a lot of different directions.

Q: *What you're saying about people getting involved in things that are—*

EMK: A higher purpose.

Q: *Getting involved in a higher purpose, but also getting involved in something they can do something about—*

EMK: That's it.

Q: *—which is, right now, the local community. I see this tremendous activism about schools, about all these local issues. But the people who are involved in that are not connecting with national. They're tuning out, it seems to me.*

EMK: I agree with that.

Q: *And when you say as a nation we're not really challenged, I think a lot of people are turning their activism and their engagement to things they can do something about.*

EMK: I agree with that. You see it in the most recent polls and the studies at the Institute of Politics.[3] Eighty percent of the kids are involved in some kind of community service, and there's an increase in this mid-career program where they can get skills and go to work in nonprofits. That's just exploded, the

---

3. The John F. Kennedy Institute of Politics at Harvard was founded after the president's death.

numbers have gone up. All these indicators are that they've turned off politics and turned to service. I think a big part of that is that they can get some immediate payback and satisfaction.

I might have told you this story before. I went to the twenty-fifth anniversary of the Peace Corps, and I sat at the table and asked why they'd volunteered. And effectively, they all gave the same answer: This is the first time that anyone had asked us to do anything for somebody else. Well, that's an indictment of the society.

So you have the Peace Corps that does this, and you have the Legal Service Corps, and the lawyers can do something, and in the National Health Service Corps, doctors can do something. You can bring the Constitution to people; the Domestic Corps you could do, an American Service Corps you could do, so people can actually do some things.

One of the key parts of the whole service program that I like is Learn and Serve America, which they have in the school. They get a very small grant, and they have to try to turn the academic course into a service learning course. So they have a school down here—and about $50–60 million a year, it's nickels . . . it's one that I'm particularly interested in. They'll titrate water that they're getting in their ponds to show the increasing incidence of nitrates as a result of the oil-fired and coal-fired plants out in Ohio. So they have to know what dioxins are, so it has a science component, and it has a hands-on component, and they write the essays, and they write to the newspaper.

They turn them into environmentalists. Think what it is on the earth, the changes in the dirt, and what's happening in lead paint poisoning. Why is lead bad? What other things are bad? They can do that, but it takes a science teacher who can translate this kind of thing. So they need some grants, and what they find out is they get one or two of these courses going, and the kids flock to them, and they do well in them, and they're so interested in it, it puts pressure on them to get other courses like them going.

Q: You get a multiplier effect.

EMK: A multiplier effect, and interest in it. So that's what's out there. Yesterday we went to a program where they're doing math and science in disadvantaged high schools. They had only forty to eighty kids; they're going to three hundred next year. It has had an incredible success, what they have them doing. The way they get them interested is they have one of these fellows who's a top researcher at MIT. He has five hundred patents, but he started as a teacher in the Cambridge schools, and he still goes over there and teaches. And he devised these plans just to get the kids interested.

There's a little picture in the *Boston Globe* of me blowing in to measure my lungs. I looked at this mouthpiece. It had been chewed; it had been used by about forty people before me. [*Laughter*] All the cameras are going, and I say, "Well, hope I'm alive tomorrow," and bang! They found that my lungs are not as good as some. I said, "Well, I'm not as full of hot air as some other politicians."

We're doing absolutely nothing in the United States Senate that's relevant to anybody's life. We passed a class action bill. January, February, March, April, the end of May [2005]—five months, and we have passed a class action bill that has no relevance except to keep workers at Wal-Mart from being able to bring their cases; and a bankruptcy bill that just makes bankruptcy courts collecting agents for the credit card companies. We took ten days on the supplemental for Iraq, and we've had probably four days on a highway bill that really is pretty standard stuff in terms of impact. It's basically a continuation of what we do every year since we started the highway bill under President Eisenhower. Now that is what the United States Senate has been doing—and the debate on the nuclear option to curtail filibusters on judicial nominations.

It's basically five months of having absolutely nothing to do with anything that anybody, any family, is concerned about. They're concerned about the costs of prescription drugs, whether they're going to be able to keep their healthcare. They're concerned about what's happening in their schools; the tuitions are going up. The costs of housing—are they going to be able to buy a house? In all these kinds of things, there's nothing. We're not doing anything that is in any way, shape or—

The disaster over in Iraq, we're not even talking about it. We're not talking about accountability for people who've been involved in the most egregious torture that has offended people's souls. We're not talking about that.

It's really the abdication of political leadership in a very dramatic and significant way. If someone tells me about the growth of another phenomenon to fill in this emptiness in people's lives, I'm not surprised. I don't want to oversimplify. That's separate from how you appeal to people. I do think we have to talk with people in a different way than the more traditional ways about a series of programs. There has to be a different conversation. Words have different meanings—now we're talking about a different phenomenon, the rise of the Republican Party and how they use words effectively and better than we do.

Q: *The Senate was a very different place* [early in Kennedy's career]?

EMK: Take, first of all, the structure of the work. From the time of civil rights through the Vietnam War, we were working virtually twelve months of the year. . . . [T]he Senate was starting on Monday at 9:30 or 10. Everyone showed up for those, the markups [of bills]. They showed up for all of the days. We were in a good number of the evenings and nighttime. Everyone stayed around during the week. For social events, there might have been a few traditional dinners or the White House press or radio correspondents' dinner, on occasion. But Monday, Tuesday, Wednesday, and Thursday we were in [session] through the evenings.

I can remember having my children in. In the summertime, the military bands used to play on the steps between the Senate and the front steps of the Capitol, and they rotated. They would play from 7:30 to 9. So I used to have my children come down, and we'd picnic. I'd offer my amendments, and we'd play in the field out there. There were several other senators with young children, and we would sit out there and have a picnic and listen to that music. The children would all go on home when the band stopped at nine, 9:30. We'd go home at ten at night, 10:30.

People listened to each other, and they took the action. That's nonexistent today. Ninety-five percent is done by staff, and people come what I call parachuting into the Senate on Tuesdays, listen to the lunch discussion, go back to their office and see people, because they're so far behind. They're out the door for fundraisers every night—Tuesday, Wednesday. They want to be out of there Thursday night. We don't have serious votes on Friday. If we have a vote, it's at 9:30 in the morning with no debate.

We never permitted what they call stacked votes, so you had two votes. You always had the debate and then the vote. The idea that you stack these things, you could be in Peoria, you're going back, and Tuesday there are four stacked votes. You lose the whole essence of what the Senate is, about your involvement in it, your relationship with people, and what the purpose is, which is the exchange of ideas.

This has been the corruption of the Senate, which has been driven by two factors, I think. One is the forces that don't want the Senate to meet and be very active. If we're not active, it's much easier to slow legislation down. There are people, primarily Republicans, who don't want us to deal with these issues. It's difficult enough to get things through over a period of time, but if you don't meet that often—

Now we are what they call three weeks on and a week off. That was Howard Baker saying: Look, we're here now just Tuesday, Wednesday, and Thursday. I'm going to suggest that everyone stay around when we're here and use your time off. Every three weeks, we'll give you a week off to do your fundraising and all the rest. Now you have the worst of both worlds. You have the week off, and they're still not around.

So the ability of forces to paralyze the Senate has been enhanced immeasurably, and those are basically antidemocratic forces. Those are institutional forces. Those are financial interests. Those are special interests of every form and shape. That has happened institutionally. We have the deadlock between the Republicans and the rest, which is philosophical, which is the way the country has voted. So that's different.

Now people can come back and say, "Well, my God, you had filibusters all during that time." That's true. We had the filibusters all during the early time. We had that, but eventually they were—I remember very clearly how the

'64 one [on the Civil Rights Bill] was broken. I think I described it earlier to you—being in [Everett] Dirksen's office for eight or nine hours with just one staff and members of the Judiciary Committee and going over those aspects of public accommodations which Republicans—Dirksen and Katzenbach—had worked out. Everybody agreed that we wouldn't support amendments to it, but we could do amendments to other provisions.

We stayed in that room and did that. I tried to do that afterwards when we had the *Grove City* case, and people won't sit in the room. They won't stay. They make the agreement. They have to go back and redefine it. People don't have the confidence that they can do it, and they have to clear it with the special groups that are out there now. The bed-check interest groups have been enhanced by their power and their influence on members. And you see a major diminution and contrast in the body itself. Part of it is the money, people's requirement to raise the resources for campaigns.

Although, I think we're reminded in the recent times—or I was—with Paul Wellstone,[4] the person who had the least resources. By the time he died, which was just a couple of weeks before the [2002] election, he had more money than anybody. It started all coming in by the internet, an entirely new way that opens up new kinds of opportunities for members to be independent and spend less time fundraising. It lets us tap into real people with real interests, the public interest, and circumvent special interests and get people back to doing what they should be. That's a hopeful sign.

Q: *On the internet?*

EMK: On the internet.

Q: *When did you establish your website?*

EMK: We were the first ones, because I hired a fellow named Chris Casey. He was from Massachusetts, and he came down and talked to me about it. It sounded fabulous, and Chris was a very gifted, talented person. We were the first ones on it. And then he went to the Democratic Policy Committee and got other senators on and has written a book.

Q: *Is that a significant source of information for you?*

EMK: It is good.

Q: *People write in?*

EMK: People write in and communicate, and we've stepped up a lot. Splash, did you have your supper? See? Look. See, he comes back in now. That's okay. Sit down.

For people who've used it skillfully and well, it's had a major—I don't think I have used it as much as I might have. Vicki is enormously computer-literate,

---

4. Senator Paul Wellstone was a Minnesota Democrat who died in a plane crash. Kennedy had been campaigning for Wellstone and was asked to accompany him on the flight but declined. Observing that the weather conditions were poor for flying and remembering his own crash in 1964, EMK's caution saved his life.

and she spotted this thing in the last campaign. We didn't do it nearly to the extent that we should have. Now we're on top of it. We have our bloggers in place, and we're very high-powered.

Q: Do you sense in the communications that come via the internet that this is a way of reconnecting?

EMK: Reconnecting, absolutely, and there's a new way of talking with them, too, that takes some doing, takes new thinking. There's a different dialogue in terms of the national debate and discussion—how you talk about issues—because of the way people are getting their information, which is a lot different from the way it was before.

Q: Do you have some examples?

EMK: Well, the most dramatic was the one used by Doris Goodwin. She said when Franklin Roosevelt made his fireside chats, someone could be out walking down a main street for the evening, and all the windows would be open, and he or she wouldn't miss a word, because everyone was listening to it. As compared to now—

Q: It's noise—

EMK: The noise or the clatter of the numbers of stations that are on and the difficulties of getting through—that's an obvious contrast. We're just beginning to use both the internet much more effectively and the blogging, and our lists are increasing. I haven't used it to raise funds, but I've heard incredible stories about how people use it. People have to learn about it. The principal people say, "You don't just send them your speech on Iraq and then three weeks later say, 'Send me $25.'" You have to engage them in terms of having them feel that they're actually involved in what's happening. They want to get inside of what's going on in the Senate. You have to think it through, and you have to be a part of it, which is understandable. That's what people want to do; it's the involvement. This is what I was mentioning about neighborhoods.

It's a different way to reach a different group of people out here doing this kind of business. And it's the issues of communication, the questions. It's what Grandpa in terms of people trusting him, because he lived by his heart. Well, it's a different world, a different time, but a similar sense, that people feel you're listening to them or you've listened to them or they have common purpose with you, and you're going to act in ways that they have confidence in or would want you to act. We have to be clever enough to be able to do that. Once you're elected to the United States Senate, just by definition, you're apart. There's always some respect for that office, but automatically there's a separateness, and you have to understand that as an elected official. I have to be conscious of the fact that people consider because I'm an elected official, I'm separate from them. I have to make sure that separation is just in name and title and doesn't become a real separation in terms of their view about me. We've worked hard at it, and we've had some success.

I've been very fortunate with the deep roots that other members of the family have had here in Massachusetts. My grandfather's roots were very real and very deep and affected families in Boston for years. Obviously, now I don't hear as much about it as I did in the early years, but they were very deep and very real. And my mother, who went to school in Boston, taught Sunday school in Boston, and had a group, the Ace of Clubs, was a very significant presence in the greater Boston area. She was highly regarded and universally respected all the way through until her death.

The activities of my parents were important in terms of their outreach in their charities, their commitment, and the relationship with church leaders. My father had a very strong personal relationship with Cardinal Cushing, which was very significant and important. Clearly, President Kennedy had an enormous hold on the people of Massachusetts, legitimately so. The great sense of pride that people felt when he was elected was very important.

So I've been blessed with a very powerful tradition, and that has been an extraordinary, unbelievable asset. The central challenge is to maintain and to try my best to enhance it, which means living up to high standards established by my brothers and parents and grandparents.

[T]he difference in the institution [of the Senate] is interesting. I think among Republicans, the principal difference is that the people entering the Senate when I first got there had been successful in other fields. Chuck Percy had been president for thirty-two years at Bell & Howell. So he comes in there, and he's a very significant figure. He has views about how business works. He knows something about this. Jake Javits came through politics, as an attorney general, but he was a multidimensional figure in terms of the arts and of a broad range of issues. He's not going to listen to somebody tell him how he's going to vote. Cliff Case,[5] I think, came from a law firm background. You had others. Cooper came to the Senate after being a [state] circuit judge, but he hadn't come up through the House. He was an independent figure in Kentucky. He was conservative, but he was a very important figure on civil rights, on ending the war in Vietnam. He was an independent figure with leadership.

Now the ones coming in there are this crowd from the House, where they've been so disciplined, and they think the Senate is just like that, and they just follow and fall in line. They don't exercise their independence. They're not willing to buck any kind of leadership. You could get a Hatfield.[6] He's been out now probably twenty years, but in the time of the nuclear freeze, Hatfield was willing to co-sponsor a measure, the nuclear freeze, with me. I'm not on the Foreign Relations Committee; I'm not on the Armed Services Committee.

---

5. Senator Clifford Case was a New Jersey Republican.
6. Senator Mark Hatfield was a Republican from Oregon.

Some people would say, "What is Kennedy doing here? Hatfield's the same way! He's on the Appropriations Committee. What's he doing? Why are they having a hearing on arms control?"

But because Hatfield and Kennedy were in that Senate Caucus Room, we must have had fifty cameras in there. We had Carl Sagan, the great scientist of the nuclear winter. We had Bartov, who was the principal advisor for the Soviet Union on arms, coming over here, talking about the nuclear winter. We had the two people, all three networks, all night.

Hatfield would do that with me on milk. We had the big scandal about the milk in Third World countries, the European producer—Nestlé. The question was whether we were going to have international standards, and the United States was the one country that vetoed this thing. Hatfield and I had the same view at that time. But these were independent people. President Nixon spoke to an elderly group at the Capitol Hilton, and I listened to him. He said, "We have to get nutrition to our elderly people. The elderly people are entitled to this kind of nutrition." I called Chuck Percy[7] and said, "Why don't we put this program for the elderly people on? What are you thinking about?" He said, "A $100 million this afternoon on appropriations." I said, "Glad to co-sponsor it with you. Put me on." Boom! It went through in the afternoon, the beginning of the Meals on Wheels Program. It wasn't, "I have to check with my leader on this thing." I believe in a political party, and people can't be going off [independently] all the time. But this place has stagnated. And it wasn't at that time. We were controlled, obviously. The civil rights struggle was long and painful. We were slow ending the [Vietnam] war, everybody knows—

Q: Was this true when Bob Dole was leader? Or has it changed?

EMK: It's changed somewhat, but Bob, as in the [1996] presidential campaign, was cranky at times. And a bit bitter at times.

Q: Was the [party] discipline like it is [now]?

EMK: Not quite like it is, although he was a tougher personality than Frist. But they didn't have probably the White House cracking the whip.

Q: The Democrats are not that way?

EMK: Well, they've stayed fairly together over the last two or three years [2002–5], but that's a result of the fact that a lot of the stuff has been watered down. We don't have a Democratic position on the [Iraq] war now. Individuals have a position, but we don't have one on the large, overarching issues. You can get them to vote for increased funding on education, Pell grants, and things like that, but a single position on major kinds of questions of war and peace and the economy, it's not there.

Having said all that about the Senate in the early sixties, there were those who weren't always working. You had people who spent their mornings out

7. Senator Charles Percy was an Illinois Republican.

playing golf, and coming in and eating lunch and signing their mail, giving a short speech, and going over to Jim Eastland's office to decide what judges they were going to put through or not put through, where they were going to go. They'd settle that business and have drinks in the afternoon. There was some of that. I think there was much more of that before I got there [in 1962].

Q: They were not worried about being re-elected?

EMK: Yes.

Q: Or didn't spend as much—

EMK: Some of them didn't spend as much time at it. As you read through Caro's book,[8] the Senate was different. There are fluctuations in times about when it plays a role and when it's on cruise control. Finally in '57 you had that Civil Rights Act, but in the fifties it was pretty much cruise control, I think. In the sixties, the civil rights and the war got it going, and then Johnson with Medicare and education and all that.

Those [budget] decisions ought to be made by members [of the Senate], not by staff. Those things are at the heart. You might say, "We're going to try to get more money. We're not going to leave it there; we'll have a new program." But you're dealing with real people, real lives, real consequences of your actions.

But in these judgmental kinds of issues about who's going to get the [budget] allocations . . . it's mean, because you have poor people struggling over crumbs, and that's the worst aspect of it. There's no question about it. It's bad, bad choices and no good solution. But those are at least judgment. Basically, we're supposed to be prioritizing. That's what we do: we prioritize for the country.

Perspectives

Supreme Court associate justice Stephen G. Breyer, Edward Kennedy's counsel on the Judiciary Committee: Well, it's an attitude. It's a certain attitude towards life. If you grew up—When Jack Kennedy is president, 1963, I'm twenty-five years old, and that whole period is very important in a person's life. I worked for Arthur Goldberg[9] after that, and that symbolizes a—it's not just a symbol. It's a certain attitude. It's a practical attitude. When you're around Senator Kennedy, you sense that. It's fun. You talk to him for a while, and it's fun. It's interesting. And you're trying to—it's pragmatic.

Q: And it's hopeful.

Breyer: Yes, hopeful. Always, always, always. That's Arthur Goldberg, too. I use that quite a lot in a talk, but it's so truthful. "So, I'm writing a dissent [on the Supreme Court]? Next time it won't be a dissent." I write my dissent. Go complain? What's to complain about? Please! Write another one. I go back

---

8. Robert A. Caro is the author of a multivolume biography of Lyndon Johnson. His *Master of the Senate* (New York: Alfred A. Knopf, 2002) won the Pulitzer Prize.

9. Arthur Goldberg was a Supreme Court associate justice for whom Breyer clerked.

and tell Joanna,[10] "I've written something, and this time everybody's going to agree." And she says, "I've heard that one before." So, they don't agree. Then we'll do another one. That is Kennedy.

The people in my life, in those positions, who have influenced me: Kennedy, Goldberg, Archie Cox. Did they have influence? They have every influence! I think why people are so unhappy now [2008]—We were a part of something. We were a part of something that's larger than ourselves, something that's working for a varied series of objectives. It sees people not as enemies; it sees people as people to work with, and bring them along, and listen to their problems, and do your best, and keep going. That's what he's [Kennedy] like. I think, "He's quite sick now, and then he won't be there. That'll be like—" he's not our father, but he's a figure. He's the column there that's supporting this, so it's hard.

Archbishop Desmond Tutu, South African anti-apartheid activist: I did want to say too, I think in 1990 or so we went to stay at Hyannis Port. We went to stay at Robert Kennedy's and then later on Ted and the family arrived. We went sailing. But the thing that I do want to underline is it was a very touching thing. His mother was still alive but bedridden. He took me to meet his mother, and I get so upset when the general media are negative about some of the things that have happened, and I say no one—maybe because no one knows about it but no one has reported. Of course, he would sit by his mother, and they would be singing Irish ditties together. And then he would spend time reading to his mom. I mean, it isn't something that you could have called up [the media] and said, "Yes, I may have made mistakes, but I also am a good son to my ailing mother," and I would want that to be put down as one of the things that I'd want to say about him, that he had proved to be a caring and a loving son.

Laurence Tribe, Harvard Law School professor and Edward Kennedy's advisor: What I admire most about him is the extraordinary way—how much he made of what he had. He's not a brilliant guy. He's bright but he's not brilliant. But he is so serious and so dedicated. It's really impressive. And the way he would really think through things, even though he didn't necessarily have the raw intellectual horsepower to make them easy. He really was serious and thoughtful and worked at issues with a dedication that I've just not seen other people do.

What's impressive to me is how perfect an example of the leader he is. He could so easily have been lazy intellectually or morally, could so easily have rested on his laurels or just had a good social life. Instead, he was so serious

---

10. Joanna is Breyer's wife.

about trying to figure out what really matters in people's lives, what will effect important change in the direction of the country's constitutional trajectory, and then translating those insights into serious decisions about staffing and priorities and energy. It's the translation of the vision about what matters into a strategy for what should be done, and carrying it all out without having necessarily the intellectual horsepower somebody else might have. It was so impressive. I mean, someone like Moynihan, who is quicksilver smart but drunk in the middle of the day—that's just a very different model.

Kennedy took the abilities that he had and deployed them with such persistent effect and, over the years, caring about the same issues deeply. He didn't just drop issues he cared about. Part of what I did, for example, occasionally would have to do with healthcare. Healthcare would sometimes intersect with constitutional issues. There are things he cared about that he just never dropped: civil rights, civil liberties, human dignity, healthcare, certain ideas of equality. That kind of commitment over that long a career, in a way that built coalitions and actually got stuff done, deserves a lot of respect.

Thomas Oliphant, *Boston Globe* reporter and columnist: My experience with Kennedy has been that he screws up when the stakes aren't very high, but he's a pretty reliable workhorse when the stakes are high. In fact, if I look back over the whole career, I don't think I can recall seeing him screw up when the stakes were high. He's a meticulous preparer. You keep thinking of the images: the weight; the appearance; the way he speaks extemporaneously; maybe throw in a little drinking and all the rest of it. What it masks is the attention to detail that characterizes his work.

Something that has been a hallmark of his entire Senate career. Before he gets going on something—the meetings, the arguments, the planning that goes into something. I kidded him—I remember saying to him once, "You do these things as if you were a Republican." . . .

Q: Were his brothers like that, do you know?

Oliphant: It was a very meticulous [1960] presidential campaign, and it was a very meticulous administration. For example, this examination and re-examination and et cetera, the staffing process during the Cuban Missile Crisis—in a process like that, that's not seat-of-the-pants, that's the setting in which the idea of the blockade [of Soviet ships to Cuba] emerged. Otherwise it never would have; no one would have ever thought of it. Bob Kennedy was a little bit more improvisational. And it had often more to do with feelings than with content.

But [Edward] Kennedy, ideologically, is an extremely eclectic politician; catholic with a small c; very, almost, experimental when it comes to means, anything that works. He is not a knee-jerk liberal in all respects. There are aspects of his political philosophy that are anything but—and believing, as they all do, that politics is the grace that enables things to happen, that also inculcates a willingness to bend and even to have your positions change. Only somebody like that could have tried to referee this impossible effort to rewrite the criminal code. Because maybe you had to take things in the bill that the liberals were going to hate. I mean, in the [1980] presidential campaign, he got guff all the time from audiences because of compromises he had made with Eastland and Thurmond and people like that.

He's a fanatical believer in a strong, vibrant presidency because of the weakness of the office. A true believer in all the new theories and everything that had so influenced his brother.

He [Ted] had completely made his peace by then [1988 that he would not be president]. The line that he uses in speaking—he's at the Hospital Association of Missouri or something, and he's introduced by the president of the Hospital Association, who acknowledges in the audience, there's also the president of the Iowa Hospital Association, et cetera. And Kennedy will get to the microphone and say, "My God, what a rough thing to put me through. Everybody here is a president except me." There are many other ways that he does it as well, and you wonder sometimes. But it gradually became apparent, to me anyway, that he had mastered legislation and advocacy of positions inside his party and was becoming very happy at the success he could have.

Q: Truly comfortable with that?

Oliphant: Yes. Now, there would be moments. I think of Dukakis insisting on taking ten days off in the Berkshires after the [1988] Democratic Convention. It's like Kerry windsurfing in Nantucket all those years later [2004] or not doing anything when this whisper campaign about going to the shrink after '78 started—things that offend Kennedy's sense of how you do politics. But that's separate from resentments. And of course it all ultimately had its climax in what I still think is one of the most astonishingly selfless acts I have ever seen a politician commit, and that was to free up his two top aides, his chief of staff and his communications director,[11] to go and work for John Kerry when it looked like Kerry would lose, didn't have a chance. I have never seen a politician do that for another politician.

Mary Beth came right out of Kennedy's hive. And Stephanie Cutter is one of the best, and she was in charge of the whole communications operation for Kennedy at the time. And of course Shrum eventually became, first of all, almost like a son, and then, eventually, almost like a brother. He got Shrum to Kerry to save his ass in '96 in the Weld fight in Massachusetts.[12] And Shrum was, of course, present from the word go with Kerry. But for a politician to give

11. Mary Beth Cahill was Kennedy's chief of staff, and Stephanie Cutter his communications director.

12. Robert Shrum was Kennedy's speechwriter; William Weld was a Republican governor of Massachusetts who ran against Senator John Kerry in 1996.

another one his chief of staff and his communications director, I think, tells me how Kennedy keeps his ego in check. Ten days out from the Iowa caucuses in 2004, Kennedy's weekend-long trip through eastern, meaning Catholic, Iowa is all you need to know about what he was willing to do to help a guy [Kerry] he didn't know all that well.

There have been a couple of times when I have sensed a certain exasperation on Kennedy's part with Kerry's work habits, which are somewhat different from his. There were a couple of times when I have seen him tell Kerry things about Massachusetts that he quite obviously didn't know, which to Kennedy's way of thinking is an unforgivable sin. It's unthinkable. But all that said and done, look at how clean his skirts are just in terms of what his behavior was. And those things he did in 2004 are so beyond what politicians do for each other.

Nick Littlefield, Edward Kennedy's chief of staff for the Health, Education, and Labor Committee: What did happen in the first two years of the [George H. W.] Bush administration is that more legislation was enacted through the Labor Committee in the areas of health, education, jobs, labor, the arts, than in any time since the Great Society, when the Labor Committee had been responsible for higher education loan programs, elementary and secondary school aid, issues affecting low-income Americans participating in the healthcare issues. The 1960s was, of course, until the Vietnam War dragged the Democrats down, a very progressive time. There had been nothing like it for the twenty-five years since then, and those first two years of the Bush administration were enormously productive. But I was talking about the bipartisan tradition of the Labor Committee, which is very important, because that's what enabled us to get so much done, to work with Bush so effectively. I learned about that tradition early on. We knew we couldn't really do anything big if it wasn't bipartisan, particularly when we had a Republican president. Senator Kennedy made working with the members of the committee one of the top orders of business.

Each year, at the beginning of the year—we talked about the dinners we had for experts on substantive issues—we also had a dinner at Kennedy's house for the members of the Labor Committee. We would have a Democrats-only dinner, and then we would have a Democrats and Republicans dinner, and sometimes we would have a Republicans-only dinner. Again, everyone would come because of the pleasure of going out to McLean for a Kennedy dinner. Being part of the Kennedy aura and charm and hospitality and compassion and generosity and friendship was something people enjoyed.

I have great tales of what went on at these dinners, the Republicans and the Democrats all sitting together, and Senator Kennedy tending to every detail of the dinner himself. He would pick the menu. He would decide which china, which silverware, who would sit where, the name tags, the place settings, everything, because he wanted to make it perfect. It's all part of his tending of his relationships with the other senators.

It's in his nature as a person to be kind and thoughtful and to reach out to people; that's who he is. He's the youngest child in a family of ten [nine children], and he spent a lot of time with his mother, and I always thought she was the one saying, "Teddy, you have to be kind to this person. Teddy, you have to write a thank-you note to this person. Teddy, this person is sick; you have to call and visit him in the hospital." I'm sure his mother, with her social skills and thoughtfulness and generosity, was very much a part of the senator learning this. He was incredibly committed to building these relationships. He understood that's how relationships get built and how things get done. But it was also with Senator Kennedy much more than that. It was who he was— treating people with respect and being generous and hospitable was second nature to him.

So while on the one hand the Republicans would demonize Senator Kennedy to raise money in their campaigns and to make political points, to a man, to a woman, they enjoyed him, and they were grateful for their friendship with him, and they appreciated his bigger-than-life personality and warmth and his sense of humor and joviality and how seriously he took his work.

They respected him for reaching out to them. He would reach out to them when a member of their family was sick. He would be in touch with them and offer to help and bring them up to Boston to be treated at the Dana-Farber or at Mass General.[13] He would reach out to them when one of their kids was going to graduate from school. His reaching out to his colleagues was way beyond the norm. But this conduct was not strategic, pragmatic—this was who he was.

He has enormous respect for people in public service. He has enormous respect for people who run and win elections, and he was going to treat them with appropriate respect. Of course he had enormous respect for the White House and the office of the presidency. This was an outgrowth in part of his love and respect for his brother, President Kennedy. No matter how much he disagreed with the White House, he would never diminish it. And the same was true with his colleagues. We'll talk about the individual relationships.

If you look at his legislative record, starting in 1989, which is what I know about, up until the time I left ten years later and certainly since then, each of his major legislative accomplishments was in partnership with one or more Republicans. The spectrum of Republicans that he made deals with crosses the entire range of Republican ideology, from Lauch Faircloth to Nancy Kassebaum and Jim Jeffords, from the most conservative to the most liberal Republicans or moderate Republicans. He told me from the very beginning,

13. Dana-Farber Cancer Institute and Massachusetts General Hospital.

"Everything has to be done bipartisan at this point," and that's what we did. The story of how he worked on these relationships is a crucial part of understanding how he's been as successful as he's been.

Theodore Sorensen, John F. Kennedy's speechwriter and special counsel: I think of the three John was more intellectual, more scholarly. I think of the three Robert was more emotional, wore his emotions more on his sleeve; he was perhaps a little more, because of that emotion, a little more passionately committed on certain issues and on his views of people, whom he loved or hated. Whereas John was more likely to take people as they were, for better or worse.

And I think Edward has been the best senator of all of them. He knows how to work with other senators. He knows how to work the process. He knows— he's had a superb team at all times. And he has made the most of that. He has certainly been the leader of the liberal Democrats in the Senate and in the party.

I think in many ways he's a more relaxed, genial campaigner than the others. Bobby's passion would sometimes characterize his campaign appearances, almost raising the level of intensity. And Jack was certainly an excellent campaigner—and superb on television—but probably not the same easy style on the platform as Edward. The most important quality to note about all three of them is the extent to which each of them evolved and developed over years of public life, dramatic change in all three cases.

Lee Fentress, assistant US attorney, Robert Kennedy's staffer, Edward Kennedy's friend: Jean said something very interesting to me in Florida, when we were down there at his birthday in February [2009]. Jean said, just as an aside, "You know, I now really appreciate how lonely Teddy must have been through the years, after losing all of his brothers, because I feel that way, having just lost Pat; and Eunice is sick and not herself any more. I feel lonely and can only imagine how he's felt all these years."

We had a wonderful weekend night a couple of weeks before the end with the senator, at the Cape with Vicki; Nick Littlefield and his wife, Jenny; Vince and Alicia Wolfington. We had a piano player, and we sang. It was really a wonderful dinner. Boy, I'm telling you, you could look at those penetrating eyes, and if he couldn't articulate everything that was on his mind at that point, there was a message there, and it was strong, you know? A sense of friendship. Everybody was so blessed to be able to have that last night with him, that last weekend, a couple of weeks before.

Q: Yes. How he spent the final chapter, once he knew it was the final chapter.

Fentress: Sure, and he knew. The last couple of times you'd see him, and look at him, he would look at you and not say anything, but there was a message in his penetrating eyes.

John Kenneth Galbraith, founder of Americans for Democratic Action, President Kennedy's advisor and ambassador to India, Harvard professor of economics: Those of us who were reasonably close to the issues of the time came to understand how extremely important his [Edward Kennedy's] role was. It affected anything with a Massachusetts overtone, but it also had a strong effect on anything that was important with a decent liberal reputation of the party. He had an instinct for both. One was compelled by being senator; the other was compelled by a wide-ranging intelligence that made him one of the most prominent liberal Democrats of his time.

Q: *Do you think of Ted Kennedy as the champion of liberalism in modern American politics? Is that an appropriate title for him, other than yourself?*

Galbraith: I don't regard myself quite in that league. I would say that Edward Kennedy has been the most reliable voice for liberalism in the Senate. I say that not with any sense of originality, but because that is also believed by a large number of informed people. He was not a man confined to the big issues. He had an eye for anything that was important. That was always something that surprised me. He would come up with something of urgency in Massachusetts, which I would say to myself, "Galbraith, you should have thought of that yourself."

Elizabeth Shannon, wife of Ambassador to Ireland William Shannon, Edward Kennedy's friend: For the next nearly three years,[14] we saw one another, and he couldn't have been a sweeter, kinder suitor. We did a lot of things together.

We just had a very nice time, but it was clear that I wasn't right for that family. I was far too independent, and that family kind of takes you and envelops you. So in the end we parted, but he was very sweet and very kind and very fun to be with and full of jokes and full of good times.

He had some bad habits—Don't we all? And I thought those were not such a good example for my own sons. I'm glad he found a good wife, he needed a wife to stabilize him. My youngest son was only fifteen when Bill died. They were still teenagers at home, and I just didn't want to bring another man into their life at that time, particularly one that would have really changed their lifestyle so much.

So, putting all of that together, a future didn't work out for us, but I always have the fondest of memories of that period with him and think that he's basically an enormously kind and good-hearted man who has made some bad mistakes in his life, but has done so much for his family and this country. He'll go down, obviously, as one of the great senators. We saw eye-to-eye on

---

14. After William Shannon's 1988 death, Elizabeth Shannon and Edward Kennedy dated from 1989 to 1991.

every political issue. Maybe I was even more liberal than he, and I would really love to see him live long enough to see a healthcare program in this country. (Obviously, that didn't happen.)

And most of his bad habits are self-inflicted wounds. He's never done anything bad that I know of to anyone else. Chappaquiddick was a bad thing, but it was an accident. I don't think he has knowingly ever, that I ever saw or knew or heard of, been bad or cruel to people. And the good that he's done for people, both in small individual personal ways and in big, broad sweeps of playing his role as a senator representing them and representing his state and his country—I think he's been fabulous. I really think he's been a giant in that.

Q: And the individual, thoughtful gestures—

Shannon: Endless.

And he certainly has learned, as none of the rest of them [Jack and Bobby] did, because they just weren't there, how to make the Senate his platform. He also has this enormous quality that sadly doesn't exist in the Senate any more, of being collegial with his opponents.

His mother's funeral, which I went to, was in the North End in St. Stephen's Church, and I was just looking at the men coming down the aisle when it was over, and I thought to myself, there are more Republicans than Democrats here. He walked out of the church with Orrin Hatch. He knows that's how you have to work with people.

In thinking about him and his life thereto, I get cross with some of the people who were his friends, not congressional colleagues or people in politics, but his personal friends, because he is kind and fun and generous. Some of them were not good friends to him. I remember having a conversation once with several of them who were at Hyannis at the end of the party. He had gone to bed. Anyway, he wasn't there, and I was saying, "Instead of encouraging him in some of this drinking and other things, you should really be the ones to be a good big brother." They clearly weren't going to play that role at all because if they did they thought they might not be the ones that he would then choose for his best friends. He was badly served by some of them.

He was fabulously served by his staff, who did everything they could for him, and to make his role—He owes them a lot, he knows he does, for the staff work that they did, but he himself chose them, and he chose really good people. That's important in a career, you know, who you get to work for you.

Melody Miller, Edward Kennedy's senior aide and spokesperson: On top of these responsibilities, which would be a full-time job for anybody, he was also a target of death threats. I kept a person on the phone—for forty-five minutes so the FBI could trace it—who was going to kill him, and we caught him. I know of people who were captured on the edges of crowds during 1980, who had weapons on them, and the Secret Service got them. I know of an apartment in Philadelphia that they raided and found motorcade routes and everything about getting Edward Kennedy, plastered on the walls, and they disrupted that. There were people who came to his house. We had to have the Fairfax plainclothes police keep an eye on his home. We used to have to have the police car sit in the driveway until we caught the guys who were after him, tracked them down. We had vicious mail, vicious phone calls. There's nothing that I have not heard in my left ear, in terms of profanity and hate spewed at him, from jealousy or as a result of Chappaquiddick—and I do want to talk about that.

When you have been with somebody in a car and a backfire happens in a car, either the one you're in or next to it, and you see him dive down and throw his briefcase over his head, you know that he is living with fear. Every time he took a step outside of his house, he never knew whether there was going to be somebody behind a tree trying to knock off the last Kennedy brother. He fully expected it to happen. He told me once, as he told, I think, a number of people, that he didn't want to live his life looking over his shoulder, so he made a decision to simply go forward, not to be surrounded by security, because that just reminded him of this problem. Dave Burke once told me that when he's not running for president, when we get past that, then he's not so much in the bullseye. Whenever he was presidential and that was being talked about—every one of those four years, from '68 on—then he was in the center of the bullseye, and our death threats and death mail would pick up.

He's carried an extraordinary burden, a burden that would have made anyone else crumble; they would have been crushed by it. But he not only carried it and survived, he triumphed, and that inner fortitude is absolutely extraordinary. He's done it, and now he's doing it again, with all flags flying and thumbs up, trying to manage dying in front of everybody, from a brain cancer tumor, and do it with class, like he's always tried to do everything that required courage. He's doing this with courage too. I ache for him. I ache for all of us who love him. I hope that he's going to have a few more years, because we have a lot to do still. We have this oral history to finish; we have his book to finish; and we have his [Edward Kennedy] Institute to build, so that we can carry on so much of what he started. If we can get health insurance legislation, if he could tie that up with a ribbon before he leaves the Senate, that would be absolutely wonderful, just wonderful.

Senator Robert Dole (R-KS), Republican majority leader: The [Senate] atmosphere has changed a little. The best examples I can think of are when President Clinton nominated Justice Ginsburg and then a member of Kennedy's staff, Stephen Breyer. I was Republican leader, so Clinton called me and said, "I'm going to send up Ruth Ginsburg." I said, "OK. I don't agree with her philosophy," but it never occurred to us that we ought to have a filibuster or that we ought to require them to have sixty votes. I think Breyer received ninety-six to two[15] or something and Mrs. Ginsburg about the same. That's a pretty stark difference between what was happening then and what's happening now [2006, with John Roberts and Samuel Alito], at least in that area.

Again, I don't want to be another Al Simpson here and start kicking Congress around, because I was a part of it for thirty-five-and-a-half years and enjoyed most of it. But it does seem a little more personal, a little more confrontational. You can see what they do on immigration and some of these issues that ought to be resolved on a bipartisan basis. Bipartisanship and compromise are pretty good words. President Reagan used to say, "If I can't get 100 percent, give me 90 percent or 80 percent, or maybe even 70 percent, and I'll get the rest later." Kennedy was in that mold. He came from a different view, but you could talk to him and work out differences, as the [oral history] briefing book showed that we did many times.

That seems to be the one difference now. It's sort of a daily gridlock. You never know whether you're going to get anything done or not until you get there. We had gridlock. We had times we couldn't move, but just looking back, without being too specific, in most cases we'd reach some agreement. We'd have a vote or we'd decide not to have a vote. We'd modify the measure or accept, say, a Kennedy amendment, knowing we'd probably work it out in conference. There has been that change and that would probably apply to both parties. It takes two to tango.

Kennedy understood how the Senate works. You don't get much done unless you have some relationship with the leaders, not only your own, but on the other side. I imagine there were times we had our differences. I can't remember what issue, but sometimes we were pretty vocal about it. When I'd see Kennedy get up in the back, I knew we were in for something. Then he'd start screaming and shouting, and I knew this must be more than I thought. But then he'd calm down. There are theatrics up there on both sides. If you go back and catalog the different bills that Kennedy's had input in, it would be a pretty big pile. As the leader, I was generally involved in some way, whether it was the Voting Rights Act or Americans with Disabilities Act.

There was a lot of healthcare. One thing that Kennedy was right on about was the minimum wage. We had trouble getting—Even though I supported my presidents, I have a different view. I don't think it is conservative to say you can live on $6 an hour. That doesn't make sense to me. Of course, as I said, he was smart and had this great staff. They knew parliamentary procedure, and if you didn't watch—I think I made a slip or two where he got something in I wasn't counting on. No question about it, from his philosophical viewpoint,

---

15. Actually eighty-seven to nine. Ginsburg's confirmation vote was ninety-six to three.

he's probably the outstanding senator up there on their side of the aisle and has been for a decade or so.

Vicki Kennedy: A gift for people but a political gut. Even in the last year of his life as he got sicker, he didn't lose his political gut. It was quite wonderful. He just intuitively had that political instinct about just—we would talk about healthcare or there would be some strategy. He kept that sense, it was wonderful.

Curran Raclin, Edward Kennedy's stepson: Well, it was difficult, because the decline at the very end was so quick. The lead-up to that was not. You'd talk to him, and he can't remember a name. Well, names haven't always been his strong suit, so it's hard to remember he's sick. It's hard to accept that there was a problem because he used pronouns with no antecedents, but he's been doing that since I've known him. It was never his strong point. So that was a little difficult, but there were times that he had a bad day, and it was really difficult. I didn't want to see him like that.

Q: Soon after the diagnosis, though, he really started doing a lot of work on this book, on True Compass. *That became one of his priority projects.*

Curran Raclin: Well, the man's got dedication. Except for healthcare, I think he accomplished everything he wanted to do. I mean, everything he did. But, yes, I'm really glad that he finished the book. I wish he had been able to see it, but I'm really glad he finished it.

Q: So I meant up to that time, here he is dying, in effect. He's not giving up, he's got at least two things he wants to do.

Curran Raclin: He definitely was keeping busy. He was at the house, but he's making calls, he's doing work, he's got the videoconference set up, so committee meetings by videoconference, this giant camera in the room. His work ethic is ridiculous. I really don't understand how he could work so much, take so much time for family, and still sleep. I don't know where he got the hours. It doesn't make any sense to me.

It was hard, just because you're talking about a guy who doesn't complain ever and never shows pain. Just by watching him walk, you could know he has pain, his back is a mess. To see him struggle, it must have been really something. So I think that was difficult.

Caroline Raclin, Edward Kennedy's stepdaughter: On the Cape, he was very—He loved the nature of it. The house is right on the beach, and because of that, you can look out to the ocean and you can—In his and Mom's room, they had a wind meter, telling them where the direction of the wind was coming and how many knots it was, and the tide charts and everything were always out. He was very aware of what was going on, on the ocean, always.

Their room used to be Grandma's [Rose Kennedy] room, his mom's room, and it's on the corner. It's on the southeast corner of the house, and it looks right out onto Hyannis Port Harbor. So you have the breakwater right there and you have the pier right there, and you can see *Mya*.[16] It's perfect. There was this pair of ospreys, large sea birds that live really close to the house. He was obsessed with the ospreys. I think they lived there since I've lived there, so twenty years or however long. And every time he'd say, "Those are the ospreys. Look at them go. He's hunting, you can see him hunt. Oh, he's diving!" Then you pass the nest, "Those are the baby ospreys." The little heads sticking out. He just loved them. I guess he never lost his sense of wonder, or he never took them for granted, I guess is a better way of putting that. It proves, because he pointed the ospreys out to you.

Actually, speaking of singing, this past year, especially this past summer at the Cape, when he was sick, we were trying to find things to lighten the mood. Well, first of all, he was always the one who would first lighten the mood. You know, all of us would get pensive or depressed, and he would be the one to think of something funny. It really should have been the other way around, but I guess that's who he was.

But at dinner, we still obviously had dinner every night, and he would be sitting there at the head of the table, and Mom would be sitting right there, to the right of him, and I would be sitting there, right next to Mom. Kara was there a lot, and so she would be sitting just to the left of him. It was all these positions, and Aunt Jean [Kennedy Smith] would be sitting right next to Kara, so it was a nice little dinner. We would have—well, I guess it started as what we called spontaneous song syndrome, with Mom just singing show tunes. She really liked show tunes and Motown and stuff like that. So singing. Then it got to this point where every night, we would have to have something prepared. You were expected to sing or perform or do something. It was generally singing. Aunt Jean had the famous "The White Cliffs of Dover." I think she recited it. I didn't even know it was a song.

Q: *Oh, it was.*

Caroline Raclin: Oh, was it? Maybe she was trying to sing and I just thought she was reciting it.

Q: *"There'll be bluebirds over the white cliffs of Dover someday." This was a World War II song.*

Caroline Raclin: Oh, that's funny. Anyway, she would sing that almost every night.

Q: *It was a very sentimental song.*

Caroline Raclin: But she made it funny, because that's what she does. Aunt Jean is one of the funniest people I've ever met. And the two of them, Ted and Aunt Jean together, are just a pair. Oh, my God, it's unbelievable. It's just

---

16. *Mya* was Kennedy's sailboat.

constant. They just crack each other up, too, and nobody else understands what on earth they're talking about. It was so funny, because she—They loved imitating British accents, I guess from when they lived in England, I don't know, but it's always been this thing. And so, especially this past summer, she would just be like [*imitates accent*], "Oh, Teddy." I can't do a British accent but, "Oh, Teddy, what are you doing over there, sitting in your chair?" He would retort, "Oh, I'm just looking at you. " And they would go back and forth. I don't even know how to describe it, but it was so funny. [*Laughter*]

Q: *She stayed up there, didn't she?*

Caroline Raclin: She stayed up there, yes. She came up, and she rented a house for weeks and weeks, and even when that expired or whatever, she stayed at the house. Yes, she was always there. She made him so happy, you know? Even just sitting. He really wanted to be outside a lot, so he'd sit on the porch, and he'd have his little chair. He had two spots on the porch that he liked, both of course looking out to the ocean, and he would just like to sit with people. You didn't really have to talk. [*Chokes up*] Have you ever heard the word, ruff-tuff-'em?

Q: *No.*

Caroline Raclin: I'm the first one to tell you about ruff-tuff-'em?

Q: *Yes, tell it.*

Caroline Raclin: Oh, my. That was one of his favorite words. Ruff-tuff-'em. He made it up, obviously. Basically, if you were complaining about something, he'd say, "Don't you want to be a ruff-tuff-'em? I'm a ruff-tuff-'em, he's a ruff-tuff-'em, let's go all be ruff-tuff-'ems." Like "oh, I don't want to go in the water, it's too cold." "Be a ruff-tuff-'em." It was constant, throughout the whole thing. Actually, one of the last conversations I had with him was very funny, because I was whispering in his ear, and I said, "You're a ruff-tuff-'em." He just laughed; it was so funny because he hadn't laughed that day or whatever, or that I'd seen. He is a ruff-tuff-'em.

I didn't even talk about the dogs at all. Now is my chance. There's nothing really new, I mean Splash was right there next to the briefcase.

Q: *Did he have these dogs when your mother married him?*

Caroline Raclin: Oh, no. They came after. We got Splash after we moved into Tracy Place. I don't know when that was. I think he's thirteen years old right now, twelve or thirteen, and he was two when we got him, so ten years ago approximately. They've been married for seventeen years. So, yes, we got him when he was an adolescent. It was so funny because they went to a breeder in Virginia looking for a puppy, and they knew they wanted a Portuguese water dog, they researched it. Believe me, they researched it. They researched everything. And they went and they didn't really connect with any of the puppies.

But there was Splash, and Ted was just automatically drawn to Splash. And it was, "Oh, this dog is not for sale, sir. He's a show dog, and we're training him to be a show dog, and he's been in a couple of shows," or whatever it was. But he was dreaming, I'm convinced, of Splash and visions of sugarplums dancing in his head with the dog. And so I don't know how they convinced him or what they did, but they got the dog, and they were just inseparable. It's unbelievable. I mean, Splash would go everywhere with him, to the office, on political campaigns during campaign season, just everywhere. He's a very well-behaved dog.

And then Sunny came, and she was a rascal. We got her when she was a puppy, and she just wreaked havoc with the best of them. She was supposed to be my mom's dog, and of course that didn't happen because she just automatically gravitated toward Ted. So then they both became his dogs. And then we got Cappy, again in the hope that he would be my mother's dog. I think this one might have succeeded. He's still a puppy. I think he's around a year old now.

Q: Sunny and Splash are audible in almost all the interviews.

Caroline Raclin: I'm sure. I mean, they're everywhere. What did everybody else have to say about them is the question, because I know my grandfather, my mom's dad, is not a fan of dogs.

Q: Well, I didn't know that. But yes. I can't help but wonder what people two generations hence are going to think when they hear Ted saying, "Splash, what are you doing?" Right in the tape. "Come over here."

Caroline Raclin: "That's a good boy." They're like, well, who is he talking to?

Q: And then the barks.

Caroline Raclin: Oh, yes. Are those in the written transcript as well?

Q: You've got your ear-shattering moments, because they're right next to the microphone.

Caroline Raclin: Why would they bark?

Q: Somebody comes up at Hyannis Port, somebody comes in the drive.

Caroline Raclin: Oh, yes. No, they're very protective of him. Splash is very protective of him. Yes, I guess you guys would sit in the sun room at the Cape, wouldn't you?

We were just talking about your interviews with Ted, and it reminded me of something. Ted and Mom would always have huge, raucous dinner parties. And everybody would be having a good time, et cetera. But he would get tired. He'd take a little glance at his watch. Then, in the middle of a sentence, as somebody else was talking, he'd say, "Well, it was so great to see you. Thank you so much for coming." [*Laughing*] And everybody was just, if they had just met him, "Okay, this is very interesting." But if you knew him, you understood that he wasn't being rude. And he wasn't being socially awkward or obtuse or anything like that. That was just what he did. "Thank you for coming. Good night." Then they'd slowly get their coats and leave. The end.

Vicki Kennedy: So then you go back, what was the constant? The Cape, the Cape. He was there when he found out that his brother Joe had been killed, and so you've got that sadness, and obviously his father died there, and you go through all of the rituals of sadness. His mother later, much later in his adulthood, died there. You go on and on, but it still was the place that he found solace, always. I mean *he* died there. This is where he spent his last month. There is no place he would have rather been than there.

He absolutely was a man of the Senate. He had a senatorial temperament. I am so thankful, in retrospect. You know, I had times of wondering, maybe he should retire and go off and live life and let's go sail and let's go—you know, I've wondered. I'm so thankful that he lived the last days as a senator, because that is so—it was more than his job. It really was who he was, and it was really important; it was important. He loved it. He was honored to be the senator from Massachusetts, really honored. He always said that it was the greatest honor of his life. He did it well, and I'm glad he got to do it.

Q: Did he ever talk to you about the things he was proudest of, or that meant the most to him?

Vicki Kennedy: It always came down to his family, I mean, it was always about his children. Nothing else ever came close.

Q: Not any of the stuff in the Senate?

Vicki Kennedy: No. I mean if it's family or achievement, his children were the most important, the legacy of how they turned out, and the grandchildren, they were number one no matter what, no question about it, no question about it.

Q: So he still wouldn't talk about himself and his accomplishments in that way.

Vicki Kennedy: No. He never—

Q: I've seen this so often, the "what are you proudest of." "The children." He said that at the Miller Center, he says it any number of times, and is that just the modesty showing?

Vicki Kennedy: No. I think he thinks that the most lasting thing on earth are his children and his grandchildren, the world he leaves behind. I think then if you put another category, so now say which Senate accomplishment were you most proud of? You have to put it in another—you have to phrase it differently. So what Senate accomplishment was he most proud of? I think his work on civil rights, his work on civil rights. He thought it was the great unfinished business of this country.

Congressman Patrick J. Kennedy (D-RI): I will say this much. I think that in light of all the negativity of politics and politicians today, my dad's funeral tributes and the spontaneity of the turnout for him ran contrary to everything in politics today, about what people say about politicians and what they think about them. It says a lot about him, because there was no political figure in modern life who was subject to more ridicule and right-wing bashing than my dad. And yet, people got to see through it, got to see him as an effective—and in the totality of his life and contributions—and an amazing political figure who accomplished enormous social progress for this country.

That is an amazing testament to my dad, but also to the fact that people can see through all of the hype of modern political discourse that's often really deflected from the reality of what someone is doing in their life, and that we often think doesn't take into account what people are really up to. People got to see what my dad's real work was about after all. When we were listening to what people were saying, they knew what he had done for them in a lot of respects. It was very reassuring to all of us that it wasn't just the tabloids people were reading. They really knew what an effective guy he was.

Epilogue: Observations on Oral History

Two years before his passing in August 2013, Professor James (Jim) Sterling Young told a *Roll Call* reporter, "So much of history is written from the ivory tower looking down, and it's amazing how much is written about politics from people who have never met a politician. You get a much better feel for the human element, and you get a much better understanding of the connection between the personalities and the choice-making" from the recollections of those who made history. Systematizing the gathering of such stories fills the gaps in memoirs, letters, media, and documents, which are often unavailable to scholars and the public for decades after they are generated.

Yet an oral history project provides insightful material for those interstices only if it is methodologically sound. The University of Virginia's Miller Center, home of the Presidential Oral History Program, has honed its approaches to elite interviewing over four decades of practice, starting with the comprehensive Jimmy Carter Presidential Oral History Project in the early 1980s.

The Miller Center operates with clear philosophical and methodological guidelines:

- Clear understanding with cooperating partners that a project's integrity flows from absolute independence for the Miller Center's scholars and their colleagues who conduct the interviews. Partners, who join project advisory panels, can provide guidance on those to be interviewed and encourage participation, and they can offer fruitful directions and topics for conversations, but they must not establish parameters for subjects or lines of questioning. No persons, issues, or events should be off limits.
- The Miller Center follows the laws and protocols of oral history, recognizing that interviewees own their words until cleared by a deed of gift, which may contain any stipulations the signers specify.
- As with the presidential oral histories conducted by the Miller Center (from Jimmy Carter through George W. Bush), Kennedy Project interviewees were presented with lightly edited transcripts shortly after their interviews and were given the opportunity to make any changes

they wished before settling on the final version of their interview, which became the authoritative record of the conversation.

- All interviews were conducted under a strict veil of confidentiality, and no information shared during an interview could be revealed by the interview panel unless and until the interviewee provided clearance through a legally executed deed of gift. Even then, the Miller Center traditionally does not release interviews until the project's rollout, typically five to ten years after interviews commence. We have found that these procedures promote maximum candor. Interviewees are encouraged not to edit themselves into the recorder but, rather, speak truth to history, with the option of expunging, redacting, or placing stipulations on a released transcript. Fortunately, the Kennedy Project, which, in total transcripts, exceeds the Carter through Bush II interviews combined, had an unsurpassed record of clearing interviews for use in the fall 2015 rollout. More have been released since then.

- The Miller Center employs a staff of professional researchers who prepare extensive briefing books for each interview, which include biographical information about the interviewee, a timeline of the events in each president's or senator's administration/career, journalistic accounts involving the interviewee, media interviews with the subject, memoir and secondary literature excerpts, and public documents. These briefing books are shared with both the interview panel and the interviewee. Public domain sections of these briefing materials are posted on the Miller Center website once the project is released.

- The Miller Center typically does not conduct "critical oral histories" that are marked by adversarial exchanges more similar to those in a courtroom. Instead, its resident scholars, and those chosen from the University of Virginia and beyond for their expertise in a particular subject matter, prompt the interviewee with informed queries that result in revealing dialogues.

Conducting the oral history of such a celebrated figure as Edward Kennedy presented both opportunities and challenges. As Young told Ted Sorensen, "I'm sort of a veteran in this field with politicians, and I've never encountered one who is so committed and so understanding of the idea of oral history and the importance of it." Another benefit of working with the senator included having access to a massive archive of his notes, documents, speeches, diary entries, and memos, collected over his life and career. The senator's army of advisors and staffers (former and contemporary) could not have been more forthcoming with their recollections and briefing materials for interviews.

One of Senator Kennedy's admirable traits, frequently noted by friends and foes alike, was his commitment to preparation. Renowned Harvard law professor Laurence Tribe observed that what Kennedy lacked in native intellect he accounted for by mastery of subjects through sheer hard work. Ironically, this workmanlike approach weakened the initial interviews, as the senator provided rehearsed answers and tried to include every possible detail. As he became more comfortable with the process and developed a friendship with Jim Young, the senator relaxed and let the conversations develop naturally and, therefore, more fruitfully.

Forging trust between the oral historian and the interviewee is crucial to promoting candor and producing the most revealing descriptions of people, decisions, and events. The reader can see this trust developing over the first half of the released interviews in the Kennedy project. For instance, as the senator apparently becomes tearful when recalling President Kennedy's assassination, he, in characteristic Kennedy fashion, does not remark on the revealed emotion, but Professor Young alerts us that he, too, has welled up over memories of the tragedy.

In Jim's own interview for the project, he explains that he earned the senator's trust by letting him talk about his childhood in the initial informal conversations. Kennedy shared with Young a story he had written as a schoolboy about a student who is so unhappy at boarding school that he tries, unsuccessfully, to flee. Jim did not press the senator to explain whether the youthful narrative described his own lonely childhood. After the senator's death, Young related that by not remarking on the sad revelation, he gradually garnered Kennedy's confidence.

Yet the interlocutor must take care to maintain a professional boundary between himself and the respondent. By the time Young and Kennedy discussed Chappaquiddick, nearly two years into the project, it becomes apparent from the transcript that the professor steps over that self-described line. The interviewer is not supposed to join in the telling of history, Jim observes, but he does in this instance, expressing a sympathetic psychological analysis of Kennedy's behavior. Nevertheless, perhaps the senator would not have discussed the event at all if he had felt uncomfortable doing so with an untrustworthy questioner. The developing connection between the two men actually reveals a key Kennedy personality trait, frequently identified in the interviews of colleagues, staffers, and family, that the senator was a natural extravert who formed warm relations, which facilitated his effective navigation of the legislative process.

Jim Young was no Kennedy sycophant. In fact, when asked if he had been among the hordes of Kennedy family admirers, particularly in the political science professoriate, he answered with typical Youngian bluntness that he was not, despite his mentorship by JFK devotee Professor Richard Neustadt. Thus, Jim began the project with an admirable objectivity that may well have escaped many Camelot acolytes.

In addition, the two other primary interviewers, Professor Stephen F. Knott and Senior Research Associate Janet Heininger, who led most of the other spoken histories with Kennedy associates, were free to mine conversations for the senator's strengths and weaknesses, successes and failures.[1]

Perspectives

Elizabeth Shannon, wife of U.S. Ambassador to Ireland William Shannon, Edward Kennedy's friend: So it was a lonely childhood, and he did want to tell that story. I don't know how much of it will be in this new book that's out about him. Have you seen that?

Heininger: I just have been told about it a couple of days ago, so I have not seen it yet.

Shannon: I haven't seen it either. I didn't even know. I just saw an ad for it in the paper the other day. I think people feel like, "Ooh, another Kennedy book." But there are things still—

Heininger: There is much that's not told, in part because the stories can be very polished.

Shannon: Right, and honed and made to fit the image. Certainly Ted, like all the Kennedys, wants that image to be the image that the world sees and the public sees, although I'm a little surprised that he's doing this [oral history] and telling everybody just to say what they want to say, because I'm sure that if they really do that, some of his men friends, one or two of his real pals, could tell some hairy stories, stories that would debunk the myth.

Heininger: He's very much of a historian. He has very much of a historical sense. As you say, the Boston Irish milieu of this is understanding where the past comes from or where it's led to. He recognizes that he is a historical figure and an important historical figure, and there is much more there than just what is going to be written down. He's been very explicit with us: "Please ask people to be candid. I really want that."

Shannon: Does he want them to be candid about his womanizing?

Heininger: You know, we said when we went into the project, "We can't do this if there are certain subjects that are going to be off limits." And he said, "Nothing is off limits." Much of it is out there in the press, anyway.

Shannon: Yes, it is. It's all been written about. That one book by one of his former staff members—of course they got that off the shelves in a hurry— there was a lot of gossip in that.

Heininger: Our sense is that he really wants the fullest story told, and it's a real risk, as you say. When you undertake oral history and you cede the control over it to someone else, it takes a lot of trust to be able to do that. And to give explicit instructions: "Please tell everyone to be candid. I want the real story told."

---

1. Having noted how different interviewers approached the Kennedy project, this epilogue on the oral history process includes their names.

Shannon: It is. He is enough of a historian and the keeper of the family's role in life to want that, because you want the full man. You don't want—

Heininger: The airbrushed image is not a picture that's reality, and I think he understands that.

Shannon: I think so too. He also understands that if life around him had not been such a soap opera, if he hadn't lost his brothers and sister, his own life would have shot off on a different trajectory and it might be different. But this is the way it is and this is the way it's been, and that's what life has handed him and handed his family, and so it's important just to tell the story.

Heininger: And from an objective observer's standpoint you could say, "Look at the crucible out of which he came, and look at what he's accomplished." We all have frailties and foibles and bad habits and bad behavior, but if you weigh it all, where is the balance going to come?

Shannon: That's right . . . and it's best to get it—to have the straight story instead of the innuendo. A lot of people I know, I mean hundreds of people who were just on the verge of Ted's life, tell stories and write stories, and they think they've got something interesting to say, or juicy to say, or something about it, and it's based on half-truths or partial truth. If you can go to all the people who really have been close to him, you get the truth, and that's not a totally whole—You know, he's not St. Francis in his garden with his animals, but at least you get the good.

James Sterling Young, director, Edward Kennedy Oral History Project, University of Virginia Miller Center professor of government:[2] The oral history got off on the right foot. It was the time for the senator to do it, and that was by his decision. It was certainly the time in my career when I had the time to do it and wanted to do it. It got off on the right foot in part because the way we do oral history was known to the senator. He understood it, and we were on the same wavelength about how this would be conducted and what the objective was.

The objective was to give future generations the benefit of the knowledge and experience that he had acquired over the years, and in this way give future generations a sense of not only who this towering figure was as a man and as a person, but how the history played out as he saw it and shaped it over an extraordinary period of time in the Senate. This is a one-of-a-kind oral history.

I decided to start out the interviews with him. He was the first to be interviewed after the project was launched, and I don't think that was accidental. I think he wanted to start. We decided to begin by starting out where he started out in life. To tell you the truth, I was dreading starting out with

---

2. Somewhat reluctantly at the end of the project, Jim Young allowed himself to be interviewed by Edward Kennedy's advisor and friend, Lee Fentress, who had worked closely with Jim and the Kennedy family in launching the project.

healthcare or immigration or something, and I really didn't know how this would be received, but I felt that was the easiest and the best way, and there was a certain logic to it. So it was growing up and his later life before he went into the Senate. I think he was somewhat surprised, but he was very serious, going back to his earliest memories.

I didn't have a whole list of questions to ask, but I asked: "What are your earliest memories?" He got started on that, and, in a very curious way, he started telling a lot of stories from his childhood and his memories about his experiences and coming back, living in New York. He got into his early schooling and the interview went quite well. We didn't know each other at all. I think we both felt that this was a safe and a good thing to talk about, knowing that the big stuff was to come later.

We were going to have a two-day interview, and the second day I went there, and he called me over to his desk in his Senate office and said, "You might be interested in this." There were some old schoolbooks of his, and I could tell by the scent that they had been in an attic or a basement somewhere. They were his workbooks. They had his papers, his exams from when he was a very young boy. And I said, "Yes, this is very interesting." He said, "You see, this is what I was trying to do, this is what the question was." And then he flipped over to the next page and I could see this struggling handwriting and all of this. He was going through the book and was telling me a little bit about this. Then he came to a fairly lengthy—a page-and-a-half of writing—of a test that he had been given. I saw the teacher's grade up at the top and I said, "Well, you did well on that one, you got an E." He said, "Oh, no. Oh, no. E is next to F." [*Laughter*]

So he went through a little bit more and then he said, "This is a story I wrote." I started reading it, and it was a story about a boy at school who was very sad and who didn't like it at school. He was just so sad, and he wanted to run away, and he got his little bag together and tried to run away. They caught him, and all the things in his bag spilled off and rolled down the hill. So then we were beginning the interview.

Lee Fentress: That's marvelous. Of course the little boy is him, correct?

Young: Yes. I didn't know that, but I wondered. I was so astonished; I was prepared to talk—

Fentress: It is very personal, the first interview.[3]

Young: Yes, very early.

Fentress: Showing you these papers.

---

3. The first two interviews with Senator Kennedy on his early life have not yet been cleared by his estate, but his memoir, *True Compass*, published after his death, contains intimate stories of his peripatetic life in boarding school, as well as fond memories of summers on Cape Cod.

Young: Yes. It took me a while to absorb that message, and then to see what he was telling me about himself. Maybe it was a test, I don't know, trusting me with something that was very personal, but it wasn't treated as something about himself. This was something that I guess might be, and I didn't want to ask him. I was too gingerly about it at the time, but it turned out to be a very good way to start. I had my doubts as to whether we'd do this, because it allowed him to start talking about his family and his father. That's the way we got started into it. He became very anxious at some point. He said, "Well, now you know; we've got to get to the issues here. We've got to get to the issues."

Milton Gwirtzman would help him get briefed. Milton would produce the story and then all the backup about the issues, and that was the most challenging, really, time in the project, because he worked so hard at it, and I saw how important it was for him to be prepared. And I knew that what I was seeing was the senator being prepared and not wanting to have to say, "I don't know or I don't remember," which he was able to say later on, after we got over this. It was a real challenge for me, because the depth and complexity of some of these issues, like immigration, to go through the years, not to speak of healthcare.

The Judiciary Committee business was more straightforward and easier, but the thing was, he had to get it all in, and I began to see that we were never going to finish this up if we went into this amount of detail, and, furthermore, there was a problem here, that he was talking beyond his memory. He was talking about past events, blow-by-blow, I called it, accounts of things he had read about in the briefing book, but it was as though he was not talking from his own memory. So the challenge then became with him to get him to talk from his memory, and this meant to get him to look at me and engage with me, rather than have the briefing book. That happened. It was a long haul.

Fentress: But it didn't happen immediately.

Young: No, it did not happen immediately. Then the briefing books began to be more systematized and there was a regular procedure, and I thought I'd see my whole life as reading briefing books. So I talked with Vicki about this, and we both agreed. I said to her that people are going to understand that he's reading from something when they hear the oral history if he does a lot of this, though he was very good at it. But fortunately he would pause sometimes in this, and I would get in a question that had little to do with what he'd been talking about. I'd say, "Did you do this?" And so forth. He said yes. He said, "Actually, that's rather interesting." I said, "Well, tell me about it." It was a diversion. The [briefing] book is let alone; he starts talking. So this is the way he came to understand, as a conversationalist, that he didn't have to tell everything. He didn't have to go blow-by-blow with everything. Most of it was going to be on the record anyway. Healthcare, immigration, is going to be heavily documented.

I told him one time after the interview, "You know, at this rate, we're going to be going on for a long time, and I've got to tell you I've got a few years on you." [*Laughter*] Which was kind of a shock to him, I think. Anyway, this was part of the evolution of him getting to see oral history more nearly for what it was, that it wasn't everything but it's what stands out in his memory that's important, it's not everything that happened. The best way into that was when he would remember a scene, an episode, a person or an event related to that issue or something. That's what made it easier and that's what made it really good oral history.

Once my heart got into the project, in addition to my mind being involved, I talked to him about the importance—I did this fairly early on—the importance of letting himself show his person and his personal life. I said, "I don't mean to pry, but my point is that people should know the kind of person you are, your thinking. I happen to see you as a person of enormous inner resources. I have no idea what those resources are, but this is an extraordinary thing the way you have conducted your career, stuck with it despite every possible discouragement to you and setback and adversity and tragedies." And I said, "What I want the future generations to know is what it took, the kind of inner strength you had that kept you going and doing this kind of thing. If it's not there, I fear that people will make it up for you if you don't have anything to say about it." I gave that little talk two or three times, and the first time I did he said, "I agree with you. I'm just not ready yet."

And this was early on in the project. I said, "Any time you're ready I'll do it any way you want, any time you want. It will be just me in the room if that's what you want. You just let me know." And so we had that conversation a few more times. The latest, the last one, up at the Cape, once when I was up there, sitting before the fire and Vicki was there. Vicki said, "Jim, what is it you really want to get out of this personal life?" And I guess I had become pretty articulate by that point, in my little pitch. Ted is sitting over there listening, listening, so I gave my little spiel and she said, "Well, I'm very glad to hear that, because I think that's just the right thing and that's just the right reason to do it. Teddy?" And Teddy said, "Yes, I think we can do that now."

I said fine, thinking it would be a little while off that we would do it. So I said, "OK, if you want to use somebody to transcribe it, I'll play by your rules with this and we won't do it through our editors or our transcribers or anything. It will just be me." He said, "That's fine. We'll have Barbs [Souliotis] do the transcript," and I said, "That's fine." So we went in to dinner. This was the night before. I think the interview was going to be on the Clinton impeachment.

Fentress: The next day, was it?

Young: Yes. So we sat down and he said, "So, all right, why don't we just do this tomorrow?" And I said, "Well, sure, but you know, senator, I'm not thinking of just one shot. I think it will take several sessions." And he said,

"All right, so what do you want to talk about tomorrow?" The food was getting cold, and I couldn't eat, and I said, "I've kind of wondered whether what was really bothering you was the Chappaquiddick thing, and I just wondered if that's something you just want to get off your chest so we can go on to other things."

Vicki said, "Oh, Teddy, I don't think that's the best idea." Teddy said, "Well, it's up to Jim." I said, "I agree with you. I don't think it's the best idea. I think there are a lot more important things than that, but I just wondered whether this was something you just had to get out of the way." So he said, "OK, so what are we going to talk about tomorrow?"

I'm thinking, and I said, "All right—religion, politics, and you. You know, I don't even know whether you're an observant Catholic or not. I don't know what your faith means to you, if anything. I think you need to talk about that. I do remember your brother, before he was president, went out to Texas [in September 1960] to assure people that he believed in the separation of church and state and that his decisions as president would not be instructed by the hierarchy." And I said, "I'm looking today at people who seem to think it's necessary to declare your religion and make your religion known to the public. That's the politics part of it. You've lived through all of this, from that time to this. How's that for a subject?" He said, "Fine, fine." Vicki said, "Great."

Fentress: And off we go.

Young: And it went off and there was no briefing book, nothing.

So that was the first window, and I was just in awe of what he said. Vicki said, "I've never heard him talk like that before." It was remarkable.

I think it was after that that I went up to the Cape another time. He was out on the front porch when I came up, and he said, "Hello, my friend," and that's when the friendship began.

That time on the porch [at Hyannis], and it was not just the Catholic Church, religion. There was a cosmos here that was all intertwined with the religion. It was in the evening, we were having a glass of wine out on the front porch. It was growing dusk, and we sat at the table, and he said, "Come outside." So we sat there. He said, "Do you hear that? Listen to that." It was the waves breaking up against the jetty, and he started making these sounds [*Imitates the wind*]. He said, "You know the sea, it's talking, it's talking to us." These were just remarkable moments. Anyway, that's part of the closeness and the friendship that grew on top of, not in lieu of, the professional work, the serious work we were doing.

We had other sessions—quite painful for him, but he did it and he did it in his own way—about his losses, personal losses in the family, about Chappaquiddick. This was just extremely difficult for him, and he organized it in his own way. It was very moving for me, but I was just letting him do the talking. That cemented our closeness again. He felt so good after that was over, it was done.

We talked about his father's grief and his mother's anger, anger at God. This is all part of the religion. So it evolved to the point that we were very comfortable with each other. [I]t changed my mind a bit about oral history in the sense of how it's done. The original idea I had when I started it up, when I did the Carter White House, which was my first oral history project, was to get these people—and these were people who had been in office, who are not still in office—that was another different thing about it—the idea was to get them away, to sit down and have a day or two of reflection in the company of a select group of scholars.

I've come to see that that's not always the best oral history, because not everybody needs a day or a day-and-a-half, even if they can give it. And the idea of getting a president in a room and trying to find out—trying to do an oral history in a day, I've come to see, well, how did you ever get that data? I think I was scared they couldn't get any more time with them, and here was Senator Kennedy, who would make a long-term commitment. So I think do it in short bites, do it in a manageable manner, because then you learn as you go. You don't do that with one shot—

And you build as you go, you learn more things, and it works much better this way.

Caroline Raclin, Edward Kennedy's stepdaughter:
Young: She [Vicki Kennedy] *gave him* [Edward Kennedy] *advice too.*
Caroline Raclin: Yes. I think a lot of his decisions had—
Young: I don't know whether that was there from the beginning, but by the time this project started.
Caroline Raclin: When did this project start? Years ago.
Young: The first interview I did with him was in January of 2005. I think your mother was a major supporter or originator of the whole idea of doing the oral history. I think she had a lot to do with it, and she was an enormous help to me in interviewing him. I did a lot of interviews with him over the years. You know, he wasn't an easy person to interview.
Caroline Raclin: Because he never talked about himself.
Young: That's right. But he came to. I think that was in part because he came to trust me and started calling me a friend, but in part it was because your mother had the right idea too, and knew how to bring him out and how to move him.

Maybe you've already said it, but why don't you take a shot at putting yourself in the position of somebody two generations hence, somebody who is looking back, trying to understand Ted, his time, and his life. Sometimes it's very hard to get a picture of that when you—Historians tend to look at documents, and some of those documents, it's necessary, and some of those documents are very revealing, his own notes and everything.

Caroline Raclin: Oh, he always wrote notes.

Young: But here's a guy who doesn't talk about himself very much, who relatively few people really knew, and you're one of them. So, how would you help people, say of your age even, studying politics and trying to understand this man, this time? What kind of person was he?

Caroline Raclin: He was—That's a strangely broad and difficult question. He was a hard worker, jovial, fun-loving. I guess there were two sides of him, or primarily two sides, if I wanted to go into that. There's one side of him that was his personal side, the side that loved costume parties and dressed up as Barney, for God's sake, at the Christmas party at the Senate, and loved to tell stories and jokes. Always a happy person, despite everything that he had been through before.

And then you have the worker part of him, with all the behind-the-scenes work. Yes, you have all the documents telling everybody these are his accomplishments, but there's so much work that went behind that. He always did his homework, and we had all the clippings come in every morning and he would read them, hundreds of papers of clippings.

He always wanted to know every angle of everything, whether it was related to work or related to us or related to anything. Very compassionate, didn't really—He just cared about other people. He definitely sacrificed himself. I'm not saying Jesus here, but I'm saying he spent a lot of time helping other people, when it might have been more beneficial—more selfish, more beneficial to himself—to spend that time on him. He wore himself thin. I don't think anybody else could really do all of those accomplishments.

For instance, when they resected his tumor, he had brain surgery. Since I work with people who have brain surgeries for various reasons, and then I see them that day and the next day and the next day, I know for a fact that they don't get up and walk, they're not able to, that's it. He got up and he walked, you know? He's just disciplined. It's creepy. "I am going to do this, and I am going to get better." His will—I can only aspire to do that.

And then, yes, he had this amazing ability, and I keep referring to it, but again, to go through so much terrible hardship and then come out of it. He gives himself a little bit of time to mourn or be pensive or whatever it is, but then he comes out of it, and he'd say, "OK, well, that's OK and I'm going to continue." And whether that was healthy or not, whether he should have given himself more time is a question that I ask. But there is a lesson to be learned by it because now, with his passing, I have a much bigger tendency than he did to get sad and depressed and pensive and whatever you want to call it. But because of his lesson and because of everything, basically the way he lived, you say, "OK, that's true, I'm going to use this and I'm going to continue to be productive, and I'm going to continue to live my life." And this is what Ted would want, this is what Ted would do. "What would Ted do?" We should make bracelets.

Curran Raclin, Edward Kennedy's stepson:

Young: The oral history is going to have a very long shelf life, in perpetuity, in fact, and if you think about the next generation, the generation after you, people who have not had a chance to know him personally, but they will listen to people talking about him and get a sense, and they'll listen to him talk in the oral history. He gave many hours to this. So, what would be your message to people way down the pipe, from your own experience, about what kind of man he was or what he meant to you or how he touched your life?

Caroline Raclin: That's a tough thing to answer.

Young: What could they learn? What did you learn from him that they might be able to learn through you? Does that make it easier?

Caroline Raclin: I think the important thing, or maybe there are a few things, because there are a lot of things you see and hear about him, both good and bad, and I don't think that either gives you a necessarily accurate portrayal of him. I think there are some things that you hear that are positive, that seem unrealistic, and they're not. When you hear certain things about his dedication or his perseverance, it seems superhuman, that he could take onto his shoulders his entire family, and just keep taking more, and it's not. He did. I've seen, I've met, I've talked to, I've spent time with the family that relies on him, and they all absolutely do. They all look to him as a father. He just wants to give, that's all it is. He just wants to give of himself, and professionally, he does that in the Senate. He does that with his social justice and his healthcare, supporting immigrants, the poor, that's what he does there, just giving what he can give, in the Senate.

Personally, it's to those around him. It's to his family. I guess the one thing you can't get over is—and you don't believe it until you actually see it yourself, and it's unfortunate because I didn't even believe it until I saw it myself is that everybody has a Ted Kennedy story, where he did something for them individually, to the point of almost absurdity. I can't tell you how many people I've met at random events. Last week, I was in Washington for a UN event, and this random person says, "Oh, he wrote me a letter when my mother died." What? "Oh, yes, he sent me a card when my brother died." These are just random people, they just guessed because they are supporters of refugee reform. Everyone has something, he wrote me a letter or he gave me a call. It's unreal.

No one does that; that's not the norm. People will call certain people, but he called everyone, and he really cared. He didn't do it because he had to. He could not have made those calls and gotten re-elected in 2000, with 80 percent of the vote or whatever it was. It was not a make or break. He did not do this to win. He did it because he cares. And he has this genuine concern for people, and that's all it is. I think that it's important to see that he does not tell people about those, because he never cared about the credit.

Young: He's not seeking credit.

Caroline Raclin: It's not about the credit; it's not about the glory. It's just about doing the right thing to help other people, and the rest will work itself out. That's really what it was. He didn't care about other people knowing, that's not why he did these things. You know how many things he did that were never—the press wasn't invited or they didn't tell anybody, because he didn't want people to know. Meeting with wounded veterans or whatever it was, he doesn't want the press there because it's uncomfortable for the vets. He doesn't care about a photo opportunity. He's gotten his picture taken a hundred times, he doesn't care about that. So I think that's the important thing to care about, he was not about the credit or about getting press. He was all about just doing what he felt was the right thing to do.[4]

Young: Helping people.

Caroline Raclin: Helping people the way he thought was best to help, and helping individuals.

Young: None of this is in the legislative record.

Caroline Raclin: Because you can't legislate individuals. You can't say, "We're passing SR-1001 to help Bill, because his dad couldn't get insurance." You know? There are no bills like that. That's constituent care, but that's him taking care of everyone he can, and that's really important.

Young: And it's not just for people in Massachusetts.

Caroline Raclin: No, it's everywhere. It's just whatever he can do to help. That was the right thing to do, and he wasn't going to limit himself. He did the broad scheme in the Senate. He knew that on broad strokes, he could help large groups—minimum wage laws, for example. He could help large groups of people, but specifically, he knew he could do other things for individuals, and he probably only would wish that he could help more, but physically, you run out of time. But that's really what he did, and that's the important thing about it; all he did was give of himself.

I will tell you a story, though. I thought of this just now because I was talking about giving. When I was in high school, I went to the Senate almost every day during the summer, and I loved it. I could just watch the Senate in session all day. But I used to walk around the Capitol sometimes too, and

---

4. I once witnessed one of these "do the right thing" episodes. As a Supreme Court fellow in 1994–95, I assisted in planning the funeral of former chief justice Warren Burger, who lay in repose in the court's Great Hall. As I left work late one evening, through a side entrance came Senator Kennedy, by himself, with no staff, to pay his respects during visitation hours. No press, no public to impress, just stopping by the court after a long day at the office to say farewell to "the Chief"—whose ideology certainly didn't match Kennedy's. I recall thinking at the time, "What a decent thing to do."

I used to go down and get lunch with him on occasion. One time he said, "Curran, come on. I'm going to give you a tour." I said, "OK." So we go around the Capitol, and he starts giving me a tour of the Capitol.

The man knows more history than any tour guide. He has more knowledge. He's forgotten more than I will ever know. So pretty soon, we've got other people noticing that Ted Kennedy is walking around the Capitol talking, so they start following. By the end of the thirty minutes we're walking around, we've got thirty people following us. He's giving a tour to everyone, answering questions. I've taken a picture of him and everyone, but it's hilarious to watch him walk around the Capitol, pointing up at the paintings, talking about them, the walls, with this entire tour group behind him. You'd have security, going places you normally don't go. They'd go, "Oh, Senator, sure come on in," you know, a little restricted access. But he loved that; there's nothing that made him happier.

He had patience, I can tell you. He got stopped in the airport for his photograph, whatever it was, thousands of times. Multiple times, every time he used to go to the airport. I've taken more pictures of him with every model of camera, with more strangers, than any other person in life. My uncle is a photographer, and I've taken more pictures than he has. It's ridiculous. He always said, "Curran knows how to work that machine. Curran, come take this picture." So I'd always take the picture. He never got tired, "Sure, we've got time." Whatever it was, he would say, "Of course we've got time." He's never going to say no; he's just like, "No, we've got time, come on. Come over here, you take the picture. Curran, take the picture; you come over here too." He always wanted to get other people.

Young: He wanted you to get in the picture.

Caroline Raclin: Exactly, everybody come in. He was like, "Give me a pen, I'll sign something." He always wanted to give something else. He knew what it meant. Somebody came up to him in the airport once, this little old lady goes, "Has anyone ever told you that you look like Ted Kennedy?" And he said, "Yes, I've heard that before." But no, he really just enjoyed it, like he really—it made him happy. He didn't even want the thanks. That wasn't why he was doing it. He felt it was his duty to help other people. It was his responsibility to help other people, because he felt he had been so fortunate, he was supposed to help other people, and he liked it. He did it because he felt it was his duty, but he liked it.

Young: Because he was. There are a number of commentaries on him that picture him as a person who is driven, almost to the limit of endurance, sort of in an effort to ban some demons or for some kind of redemption, or some kind of compulsion. Did you see that in him at all?

Caroline Raclin: No, I don't. I can't speak to whether that was it, but I never saw that. It really didn't seem like he felt like he was trying to right wrongs, or he was trying to redeem anything. That's never an implication. It was always just he felt like—I don't think he felt that he could ever make up for the mistakes he'd made, so I don't think that he was trying. I don't think he was going to forgive himself. I don't want to speculate on that, but I really don't think that's what drove him. I think what drove him was that he felt that, as I said before, it was his duty to help other people. And I think if he hadn't made mistakes, these well-documented mistakes in the past, he would be exactly the same in that aspect. He would still be that same kind of driven-to-help-other-people kind of person.

Exactly, but it wasn't even—just helping people. If someone was grumpy, and he helped them, and they were still upset but their lives have been improved, that would make him happy. He wasn't looking for a thank you. He wasn't looking for a favor back. I think he got happiness out of it, but he also felt that he owed it to society, to people, to help them, because he had been fortunate growing up as well, and he knew it. He was spoiled as a child, as I certainly was, but I think that he felt that he had to make up for that, and maybe if there is any kind of redeeming for that, it might have been in that sense. He said, "Well, I've been very fortunate, but not everyone has been. I need to help them." So I think that's part of it.

Lee Fentress, assistant US attorney, Robert Kennedy's staffer, Edward Kennedy's friend and advisor:

Young: That's right, and so it's caring for the future generations as he's cared for his own generation. I came to see these oral histories that we do as basically an enduring project of public education, so that the experiences and the knowledge that don't get written into books, or written down in papers, can be communicated directly to the next generation, and to generations after that, which means you learn from what I've learned, or learn from what I did and failed to do, and learn about how it was done. I can understand the sense the Kennedy Institute makes, because that's what it's doing. I just thought it was a marvelous idea when I heard about it, that it's not a mausoleum for papers.

Fentress: It sort of evolved when the senator was in his fortieth year [in the Senate], trying to figure out what to do with those papers, commemoration of what he would do. Ed Schlossberg[5] played a role in establishing this vision.

I must say, Jim, these histories wouldn't be taking place were it not for you, my friend. Early on in this process, everybody sensed, when the decision was made to come to the University of Virginia and the Miller Center, it was in very large part because of your professionalism and your real sense of history, and that's to a large part why we're here. Our choice has been reinforced every day.

Young: Well, that's wonderful to hear. It's really the last and best project in my life. It's an incomparable experience, to have this opportunity and to get to know somebody

---

5. Ed Schlossberg is Caroline Kennedy's husband.

by doing oral history with them. It was just an amazing experience for me. I wrote to Vicki once that this project has always been uppermost in my mind, in my work, but now it's also in my heart. You can't avoid that. The more you know, and the more you get to know the real people, the more impressed you are.

Fentress: It's hard to keep your distance, it really is.

Young: Yes, but for me it's the first time—It's important to pretend to be the historian of the future. You've got to ask what people—

Fentress: But you have in every sense.

Young: But then for that professional inquiry. It worked in the first instance because he was interested in history, and I knew something about it too, and was also interested in the future of this. You don't get into oral history unless you're concerned about the future.

Fentress: Right.

Young: You're not in it to write your own books. But in the second instance, because we became friends in this process, and this is something that just doesn't happen.

Fentress: Without question. I got three or four phone calls at the end of different interviews, from Vicki and the senator, saying, "We just finished with Jim, and it was wonderful. Here's what we covered." I would be in a car somewhere driving, and I'd just get this call right out of the blue. I think Teddy would say, "Let's call. I want to share this."

First of all, I was obviously flattered, but the point was that they enjoyed it, and it was a wonderful experience. They felt they were doing something very important. And that was, in large part, the way they were conducted, obviously, and the tenor and the trust. That can't be overemphasized.

Young: I sense that, and I feel really blessed to have a professional endeavor, which I've dedicated a lot of my life to, but in this last project of mine, to have it turn into something so extraordinary, and to really be able to see and perceive and be a friend of Ted Kennedy—Words just fail me. The personal and the professional experience, together, is just something most academicians never experience.

Fentress: Right. Well, that's the nice thing about oral histories.

Young: It is.

Fentress: And how wonderful this is, that we're not going to have to be chasing letters and those dictated remarks, that you have his words, and you have all of his contemporaries' words on a nonpartisan basis. It's wonderful.

Young: Well, it's meant a lot to me. I told Vicki that I feel doubly blessed. I was a stranger who got to know him just by doing oral history with him and who at some point became a friend. That's a double blessing, and I don't think this would have happened if it hadn't been for you.

Fentress: Well, I don't know.

Young: You and Vicki were the movers here.

Fentress: I had lunch with him. We were sitting up in Maine, talking, and he said, "Lee, what are you doing? What do you want to do?" And I said, "I don't know. I'd like to be doing something, because I'd throttled back from my

[law] firm." He said, "I've got some ideas. Why don't you think about applying for the job as the president of the JFK Library?" I said, "Well, I don't think— No, I don't see that. I don't think I'm qualified. I don't have enough—I didn't know the president."

The next thing I know, we're in Washington having lunch alone on a Friday afternoon. I meet him at a restaurant there. Of course, I get lost and he's sitting there waiting for me for fifteen minutes, and I know that being late, for him, is verboten. He was very nice. He outlined a broad concept of doing an extensive oral history that would take several years. I remember driving home thinking, "What's he asked me to do?" It turned out that he had asked me to take over the project, to interview the different entities doing oral histories, and make a recommendation of how to proceed.

So that we did. We went around and looked at all of them, and saw presentations from each of the institutions. It became clear that the Miller Center and the University of Virginia had a different approach to oral histories, much more elaborate, but it was clearly—It was an art, and it was a science. They had taken it to higher levels than the other groups, and most importantly, we began to sense the real interest that you had in the project, and felt very early on that everybody wanted to work with you, and we could trust you. I wrote a long memo to both the senator and Vicki, giving the strong points about each, and, finally, with a recommendation. We were all unanimous. Then we had a couple of trips down here to talk about proceeding.

Young: Oh, I remember you visited and then you said, "Let me have Vicki come out." I remember sitting around that little table. I hadn't made a study of Kennedy in particular, and I said, "I just think of him as a self-made man. That's just my image of him when I think about him. He was born a Kennedy, he was this, and he was all those things, but he was, above all, a person who made something of himself, who had made what he is."

Appendix: Edward M. Kennedy Oral History Project Interviews

Gerry Adams, November 11, 2010, Belfast, Northern Ireland; James Sterling Young, Russell L. Riley

Bertie Ahern, November 8, 2010, Dublin, Ireland; James Sterling Young, Russell L. Riley

Dermot Ahern, September 30, 2005, Dundalk, Ireland; James Sterling Young, Stephen F. Knott

*Stuart Altman, March 14, 2007, Arlington, VA; Janet E. Heininger

*Nan Aron, January 26, 2007, Washington, DC; Stephen F. Knott

Melody Barnes, August 16, 2006, Washington, DC; Stephen F. Knott

*William G. Barry, April 23, 2010, New City, NY; Janet E. Heininger

Robert Bates, May 8, 2007, Friendship, MD; Paul Martin

Robert Bates, July 26, 2007, Washington, DC; James Sterling Young

Birch Bayh, September 10, 2009, Washington, DC; Janet E. Heininger

Samuel Beer, February 17, 2005, Washington, DC; Stephen F. Knott

*Joseph Biden Jr., May 26, 2010, Washington, DC; James Sterling Young, Janet E. Heininger

Jeffrey H. Blattner, March 30, 2007, Washington, DC; Stephen F. Knott

David Blumenthal, March 20, 2007, Boston, MA; Janet E. Heininger, James Sterling Young

David Boies, September 23, 2008, New York, NY; James Sterling Young

Stephen Breyer, June 17, 2008, Cambridge, MA; James Sterling Young

Stephen Breyer, September 28, 2008, Washington, DC; James Sterling Young

David Broder, December 1, 2006, Washington, DC; Stephen F. Knott

Edward Brooke, August 16, 2006, Washington, DC; Stephen F. Knott

David Burke, June 19, 2007, Eastham, MA; James Sterling Young

David Burke, April 9, 2008, Washington, DC; James Sterling Young

Sheila Burke, July 27, 2007, Washington, DC; Janet E. Heininger, James Sterling Young

Robert C. Byrd, June 5, 2006, Washington, DC; James Sterling Young, Russell L. Riley

*Mary Beth Cahill, March 24, 2009, Washington, DC; Janet E. Heininger

*Joseph Califano, January 23, 2008, New York, NY; Janet E. Heininger

Philip Caper, March 20, 2007, Boston, MA; James Sterling Young, Janet E. Heininger

Richard Clasby, October 11, 2005, Milton, MA; Stephen F. Knott

Adam Clymer, July 12, 2006, Washington, DC; Stephen F. Knott, Paul Martin

Thad Cochran, September 19, 2006, Washington, DC; Stephen F. Knott Janet E. Heininger

*Ranny Cooper, December 14, 2007, New York, NY; James Sterling Young, Janet E. Heininger

*Ranny Cooper, February 25, 2008, New York, NY; James Sterling Young, Janet E. Heininger

Thomas Costin, September 15, 2006, Nahant, MA; Stephen F. Knott

Greg Craig, July 13, 2010, Washington, DC; James Sterling Young

John Culver, March 31, 2005, Washington, DC; Stephen F. Knott, Gregg Lindskog, Paul Martin

John Culver, June 5, 2007, Washington, DC; James Sterling Young

John Culver, September 22, 2009, Washington, DC; James Sterling Young

*Stephanie Cutter, November 10, 2009, Boston, MA; Janet E. Heininger

John Danforth, October 25, 2005, St. Louis, MO; Janet E. Heininger, James Sterling Young, Paul Martin

Thomas A. Daschle, April 29, 2009, Washington, DC; James Sterling Young
*Dale de Haan, October 2, 2006, Washington, DC; Stephen F. Knott, Darby Morrisroe
Eugene Dellea, August 9, 2005, Pittsfield, MA; Stephen F. Knott
John Dingell, June 16, 2005, Washington, DC; Stephen F. Knott, Paul Martin
*E. J. Dionne, February 20, 2007, Washington, DC, Stephen F. Knott, Paul Martin
Gerard Doherty, October 10, 2005, Boston, MA; Stephen F. Knott
Robert Dole, May 15, 2006, Washington, DC; James Sterling Young, Janet E. Heininger
*Paul Donovan, February 17, 2009, Natick, MA; Janet E. Heininger
John Douglas, November 30, 2005, Washington, DC; Stephen F. Knott, Robert Martin
Donald Dowd, August 9, 2005, West Springfield, MA; Stephen F. Knott
Michael Dukakis, November 9, 2009, Boston, MA; Janet E. Heininger
*Thomas Eagleton, October 24, 2005, St. Louis, MO; James Sterling Young, Janet E. Heininger, Paul Martin
Stuart Eizenstat, July 26, 2007, Washington, DC; Janet E. Heininger
Michael Enzi, September 19, 2006, Washington, DC; Stephen F. Knott, Janet E. Heininger
David Espo, March 25, 2010, Washington, DC; James Sterling Young
John Farrell, July 13, 2006, Washington, DC; Stephen F. Knott, Paul Martin
Anthony Fauci, September 10, 2007, Bethesda, MD; Janet E. Heininger
Judy Feder, July 5, 2007, Washington, DC; Janet E. Heininger
Rashi Fein, March 21, 2007, Boston, MA; Janet E. Heininger, James Sterling Young
Kenneth Feinberg, July 8, 2008, Washington, DC; James Sterling Young
Dan H. Fenn Jr., November 4, 2004, Charlottesville, VA; Stephen F. Knott
Lee Fentress, October 16, 2009, Charlottesville, VA; James Sterling Young
Charles Ferris, June 29, 2006, Washington, DC; Stephen F. Knott
Max Fine, May 25, 2007, Bethesda, MD; Janet E. Heininger
Alice Fitzgerald, Patricia Hagan, July 13, 2005, Cambridge, MA; Stephen F. Knott
Garret Fitzgerald, Michael Lillis, Sean Donlon, September 28, 2005, Dublin, Ireland; James Sterling Young, Stephen F. Knott,
Robert P. Fitzgerald Sr., June 18, 2009, Boston, MA; James Sterling Young
*James Flug, November 27, 2007, Washington, DC; James Sterling Young, Janet E. Heininger
*James Flug, December 4, 2007, Washington, DC; James Sterling Young, Janet E. Heininger
*James Flug, December 18, 2007, Washington, DC; Janet E. Heininger
Wyche Fowler, November 9, 2009, Washington, DC; James Sterling Young
Mary Frackleton, July 8, 2005, Hampton, NH; Stephen F. Knott
*Michael J. Frazier, March 29, 2007, Washington, DC; Stephen F. Knott
John Kenneth Galbraith, August 15, 2005, Cambridge, MA; Stephen F. Knott
Ann Gargan (King), October 11, 2005, Milton, MA; Stephen F. Knott
*Joseph Gargan, August 11, 2005, Hyannis Port, MA; Stephen F. Knott
*Joseph Gargan, October 31, 2005, Charlottesville, VA; Stephen F. Knott
*Connie Garner, December 16, 2008, Washington, DC; Janet E. Heininger
*Connie Garner, May 27, 2010, Washington, DC; Janet E. Heininger
K. Dun Gifford, July 13, 2005, Boston, MA; Stephen F. Knott
Lee Goldman, May 5, 2007, Flat Rock, NC; Janet E. Heininger
Willis D. Gradison Jr., September 11, 2007, Washington, DC; Janet E. Heininger
Marcia Greenberger, February 21, 2007, Washington, DC; Stephen F. Knott, Janet E. Heininger
Ellen Guiney, March 24, 2008, Boston, MA; Janet E. Heininger
Milton Gwirtzman, May 29, 2009, Washington, DC; Janet E. Heininger
Milton Gwirtzman, August 5, 2009, Bethesda, MD; Janet E. Heininger
Charles Haar, October 10, 2005, Cambridge, MA; Stephen F. Knott
Timothy A. Hanan, May 7, 2009, Washington, DC; James Sterling Young
Alma and Brian T. Hart, February 18, 2009, Bedford, MA; Janet E. Heininger
Terry Hartle, April 11, 2008, Washington, DC; Janet E. Heininger
*Orrin Hatch, May 24, 2006, Washington, DC; Stephen F. Knott, Paul Martin

*Health Care Roundtable: Michael Myers, Mark Childress, David Bowen, April 29, 2010, Washington, DC; James Sterling Young, Janet E. Heininger

Robert Healy, August 10, 2005, Scituate, MA; Stephen F. Knott

Antonia Hernandez, March 22, 2007, New York, NY; Stephen F. Knott

John Hilley, September 21, 2007, Great Falls, VA; Janet E. Heininger

*Claude Hooton Jr., December 16, 2009, San Antonio, TX; Janet E. Heininger

*Larry Horowitz, April 16, 2008, Atherton, CA; James Sterling Young, Janet E. Heininger

*Larry Horowitz, April 17, 2008, Atherton, CA; James Sterling Young, Janet E. Heininger

*Larry Horowitz, May 3, 2010, San Francisco, CA; James Sterling Young

John Hume, September 29, 2005, Dublin, Ireland; James Sterling Young, Stephen F. Knott

Robert E. Hunter, February 11, 2009, Arlington, VA; Janet E. Heininger

Lester Hyman, October 6, 2008, Washington, DC; James Sterling Young

*Michael Iskowitz, November 5, 2007, Washington, DC; Janet E. Heininger

*Michael Iskowitz, April 21, 2008, Sedona, AZ; Janet E. Heininger

Christopher Jennings, July 13, 2007, Washington, DC; Janet E. Heininger

John F. (Jack) Jennings, May 21, 2008, Washington, DC; Janet E. Heininger

Olatunde (Olati) Johnson, March 22, 2007, New York, NY; Stephen F. Knott

Stanley Jones, March 9, 2007, Washington, DC; Janet E. Heininger

Stanley Jones, September 14, 2007, Washington, DC; Janet E. Heininger

Jan Kaliki, March 18, 2009, Washington, DC; Janet E. Heininger

Nancy Kassebaum (Baker), April 6, 2009, Washington, DC; Janet E. Heininger

Natalya and Boris Katz, February 15, 2009, Cambridge, MA; James Sterling Young

Nicholas Katzenbach, November 29, 2005, Princeton, NJ; Stephen F. Knott, Kent Germany, Paul Martin

*Edward M. Kennedy, Interview 1, January 21, 2005, Washington, DC; James Sterling Young, Stephen F. Knott

*Edward M. Kennedy, Interview 2, February 18–19, 2005, Washington, DC; James Sterling Young, Stephen F. Knott

Edward M. Kennedy, Interview 3, March, 23–24, 2005, Washington, DC; James Sterling Young, Stephen F. Knott

Edward M. Kennedy, Interview 4, June 3–4, 2005, Hyannis Port, MA; James Sterling Young

Edward M. Kennedy, Interview 5, June 17, 2005, Washington, DC; James Sterling Young, Stephen F. Knott

*Edward M. Kennedy, Victoria Reggie Kennedy, Interview 6, August 2, 2005, Hyannis Port, MA; James Sterling Young, Stephen F. Knott

Edward M. Kennedy, Interview 7, October 14, 2005, Hyannis Port, MA; James Sterling Young, Stephen F. Knott

*Edward M. Kennedy, Victoria Reggie Kennedy, Interview 8, December 19, 2005, Washington, DC; James Sterling Young, Stephen F. Knott

Edward M. Kennedy, Interview 9, February 27, 2006, Washington, DC; James Sterling Young, Stephen F. Knott

Edward M. Kennedy, Interview 10, March 20, 2006, Washington, DC; James Sterling Young

Edward M. Kennedy, Interview 11, May 8, 2006, Washington, DC; James Sterling Young

*Edward M. Kennedy, Victoria Reggie Kennedy, Interview 12, August 14, 2006, Hyannis Port, MA; James Sterling Young

Edward M. Kennedy, Victoria Reggie Kennedy, Interview 13, August 15, 2006, Hyannis Port, MA; James Sterling Young

Edward M. Kennedy, Victoria Reggie Kennedy, Interview 14, November 29, 2006, Washington, DC; James Sterling Young

Edward M. Kennedy, Victoria Reggie Kennedy, Interview 15, December 1, 2006, Washington, DC; James Sterling Young

Edward M. Kennedy, Interview 16, January 6, 2007, Washington, DC; James Sterling Young

Edward M. Kennedy, Interview 17, February 12, 2007, Washington, DC; James Sterling Young, Stephen F. Knott

Edward M. Kennedy, Interview 18, April 3, 2007, Hyannis Port, MA; James Sterling Young

Edward M. Kennedy, Interview 19, May 30, 2007, Hyannis Port, MA; James Sterling Young
Edward M. Kennedy, Interview 20, May 31, 2007, Hyannis Port, MA; James Sterling Young
Edward M. Kennedy, Interview 21, August 7, 2007, Hyannis Port, MA; James Sterling Young
Edward M. Kennedy, Interview 22, August 8, 2007, Hyannis Port, MA; James Sterling Young
*Edward M. Kennedy, Interview 23, October 8–9, 2007, Hyannis Port, MA; James Sterling Young
Edward M. Kennedy, Interview 24, October 9, 2007, Hyannis Port, MA; James Sterling Young
Edward M. Kennedy, Interview 25, December 9, 2007, Washington, DC; James Sterling Young
*Edward M. Kennedy, Victoria Reggie Kennedy, Interview 26, January 7, 2008, Washington, DC; James Sterling Young
Edward M. Kennedy, Interview 27, January 7, 2008, Washington, DC; James Sterling Young
*Edward M. Kennedy, Interview 28, February 19, 2008, Washington, DC; James Sterling Young
Edward M. Kennedy, Interview 29, March 28, 2008, Washington, DC; James Sterling Young
*Kara Kennedy, Edward Kennedy Jr., Patrick Kennedy, December 9, 2009, Washington, DC; James Sterling Young
Victoria Reggie Kennedy, April 8, 2010, Washington, DC; James Sterling Young
John Kerry, June 21, 2010, Washington, DC; Janet E. Heininger
David Kessler, March 9, 2008, San Francisco, CA; Janet E. Heininger
*James King, March 23, 2007, Gloucester, MA; Stephen F. Knott
Paul Kirk, November 23, 2005, Boston, MA; Stephen F. Knott, Paul Martin
Paul Kirk, June 20, 2007, Boston, MA; James Sterling Young
*C. Everett Koop, September 25, 2007, Hanover, NH; Janet E. Heininger
Sandy (B. Alexander) Kress, July 2, 2008, Austin, TX; Janet E. Heininger
*Mathilde Krim, December 12, 2007, New York, NY; Janet E. Heininger
Kathy Kruse, December 8, 2008, Washington, DC; Janet E. Heininger
Barbara Lahage, May 8, 2008, Hull, MA; Janet E. Heininger
Patrick Leahy, August 5, 2009, Washington, DC; Janet E. Heininger
Anthony Lewis, June 18, 2009, Cambridge, MA; James Sterling Young
John Lewis, December 4, 2006, Washington, DC; Janet E. Heininger
Judith Lichtman, February 21, 2007, Washington, DC; Janet E. Heininger, Stephen F. Knott
Nick Littlefield, May 3, 2008, Boston, MA; James Sterling Young
Nick Littlefield, May 4, 2008, Boston, MA; James Sterling Young
Nick Littlefield, June 30, 2008, Boston, MA; James Sterling Young
Nick Littlefield, July 1, 2008, Boston, MA; James Sterling Young
Nick Littlefield, February 14, 2009, Boston; James Sterling Young
Nick Littlefield, February 15, 2009, Boston, MA; James Sterling Young
George Cabot Lodge, July 8, 2005, Boston, MA; Stephen F. Knott
Trent Lott, July 22, 2008, Washington, DC; Janet E. Heininger
Richard G. Lugar, March 6, 2009, Washington, DC; Janet E. Heininger
Nance Lyons, May 9, 2008, Boston, MA; Janet E. Heininger
Neil MacNeil, May 9, 2006, Bethesda, MD; Paul Martin, Charles O. Jones
*Ira Magaziner, November 19, 2007, Quincy, MA; Janet E. Heininger
James Manley, September 28, 2009, Washington, DC; Janet E. Heininger
Thurgood Marshall Jr., July 26, 2007, Washington, DC; Janet E. Heininger
Edward Martin, April 20, 2005, Dennisport, MA; James Sterling Young, Stephen F. Knott
Charles Mathias, March 10, 2006, Washington, DC; Stephen F. Knott, Paul Martin
John McCain, October 16, 2009, Washington, DC; Janet E. Heininger
Paul R. McDaniel, November 6, 2008, Gainesville, FL; Janet E. Heininger
Cindy McGinty, April 22, 2010, Bloomfield, CT; Janet E. Heininger
Alice McGoff, August 7, 2007, Charlestown, MA; Beatriz Swerdlow
George McGovern, March 22, 2006, Charlottesville, VA; Stephen F. Knott, Kent Germany, Paul Martin
Barbara Mikulski, September 26, 2006, Washington, DC; Stephen F. Knott, Janet E. Heininger

George Miller, October 13, 2009, Washington, DC; Janet E. Heininger
Melody Miller, July 15, 2008, Washington, DC; Janet E. Heininger
Melody Miller, October 7, 2008, Arlington, VA; Janet E. Heininger
Melvin Miller, August 7, 2007, South Boston, MA; Beatriz Swerdlow
George Mitchell, September 6, 2011, New York, NY; James Sterling Young
Walter Mondale, March 20, 2006, Minneapolis, MN; Stephen F. Knott, Paul Martin
James J. Mongan, May 9, 2007, Washington, DC; Janet E. Heininger
Ellis Mottur, October 17, 2006, Charlottesville, VA; Stephen F. Knott
Ellis Mottur, November 20, 2006, North Bethesda, MD; Stephen F. Knott
Michael Myers, August 28, 2006, Washington, DC; Janet E. Heininger, Stephen F. Knott
*Michael Myers, October 16, 2009, Washington, DC; Janet E. Heininger
*Ralph Neas, January 26, 2007, Washington, DC; Stephen F. Knott, Paul Martin
David Nexon, June 27, 2007, Washington, DC; Janet E. Heininger
Martin Nolan, September 14, 2006, Cambridge, MA; Stephen F. Knott
*Barack Obama, May 17, 2010, Washington, DC; James Sterling Young
Niall O'Dowd, November 18, 2010, New York, NY; James Sterling Young
Sean O'Huiginn, November 8, 2010, Dublin, Ireland; James Sterling Young, Russell L. Riley
Esther Olavarria, August 28, 2006, Washington, DC; Stephen F. Knott
Thomas Oliphant, November 15, 2006, Charlottesville, VA; Stephen F. Knott, Darby Morrisroe
Thomas Oliphant, March 14, 2007, Charlottesville, VA; Stephen F. Knott
Carolyn Osolinik, March 27, 2007, Washington, DC; James Sterling Young
*Joel Packer, May 20, 2008, Washington, DC; Janet E. Heininger
*Peter Parham, March 28, 2007, Washington, Stephen F. Knott
Carey Parker, September 22, 2008, Washington, DC; James Sterling Young
Carey Parker, October 6, 2008, Washington, DC; James Sterling Young
Carey Parker, October 13, 2008, Washington, DC; James Sterling Young
Carey Parker, October 20, 2008, Washington, DC; James Sterling Young
Carey Parker, October 27, 2008, Washington, DC; James Sterling Young
Carey Parker, November 10, 2008, Washington, DC; James Sterling Young
Carey Parker, November 17, 2008, Washington, DC; James Sterling Young
Carey Parker, December 1, 2008, Washington, DC; James Sterling Young
Thomas Payzant, March 25, 2008, Boston, MA; Janet E. Heininger
Nancy Pelosi, April 30, 2010, Washington, DC; James Sterling Young
Danica Petroshius, May 13, 2008, Washington, DC; Janet E. Heininger
Elizabeth Philipps, July 7, 2009, Boston, MA; Janet E. Heininger
Caroline Raclin, November 11, 2009, Washington, DC; James Sterling Young
Curran Raclin, November 10, 2009, Cambridge, MA; James Sterling Young
Ken Regan, July 8, 2009, New York, NY; James Sterling Young
Edmund and Doris Reggie, August 8, 2005, Nantucket, MA; Stephen F. Knott
Edmund and Doris Reggie, December 16, 2008, Lafayette, LA; James Sterling Young
*Harry Reid, June 18, 2010, Washington, DC; Janet E. Heininger
*Albert Reynolds, September 27, 2005, Dublin, Ireland; James Sterling Young, Stephen F. Knott
*Donald Riegle, July 8, 2008, Washington, DC; James Sterling Young, Janet E. Heininger
*Donald Riegle, September 1, 2009, Washington, DC; James Sterling Young
Richard Riley, September 8, 2008, Greenville, SC; Janet E. Heininger
Terri Robinson, July 22, 2009, Washington, DC; Janet E. Heininger
Terri Robinson, August 25, 2009, Washington, DC; Janet E. Heininger
Thomas M. Rollins, March 10, 2009, McLean, VA; Janet E. Heininger
Thomas M. Rollins, April 22, 2009, McLean, VA; Janet E. Heininger
Thomas M. Rollins, May 12, 2009, McLean, VA; Janet E. Heininger
Thomas M. Rollins, May 14, 2009, McLean, VA; Janet E. Heininger
Warren Rudman, May 16, 2006, Washington, DC; Stephen F. Knott, Janet E. Heininger
Mona Sarfaty, July 16, 2008, Philadelphia, PA; Janet E. Heininger

Patti B. Saris, September 25, 2007, Boston, MA; Janet E. Heininger
James Sasser, May 25, 2006, Washington, DC; Stephen F. Knott, Janet E. Heininger
*Arthur Schlesinger Jr., July 20, 2005, New York, NY; James Sterling Young
Mark L. Schneider, February 2, 2009, Washington, DC; Janet E. Heininger
Mark L. Schneider, February 4, 2009, Washington, DC; Janet E. Heininger
Elizabeth Shannon, April 28, 2009, Boston, MA; Janet E. Heininger
Stuart H. Shapiro, April 3, 2009, Bala Cynwyd, PA; Janet E. Heininger
Stuart H. Shapiro, May 15, 2009, Bala Cynwyd, PA; Janet E. Heininger
Robert S. Shriver III, Maria Shriver, January 29, 2010, Santa Monica, CA; Janet E. Heininger
Robert Shrum, July 6, 2009, Sagamore Beach, MA; Janet E. Heininger
Robert Shrum, July 7, 2009, Sagamore Beach, MA; Janet E. Heininger
*John Siegenthaler, June 5, 2007, Washington, DC; James Sterling Young
Alan Simpson, May 10, 2006, Washington, DC; Stephen F. Knott, Janet E. Heininger
*Marshall (Mike) Smith, April 14, 2008, Palo Alto, CA; Janet E. Heininger
Nancy E. Soderberg, October 9, 2008, Jacksonville, FL; Janet E. Heininger
Theodore Sorensen, May 19, 2005, New York, NY; James Sterling Young
Theodore Sorensen, December 7, 2006, New York, NY; James Sterling Young
Barbara Souliotis, July 12, 2005, Boston, MA; Stephen F. Knott
Barbara Souliotis, November 9, 2009, Boston, MA; Janet E. Heininger
Margaret Spellings, August 27, 2008, Washington, DC; Janet E. Heininger
Clayton Spencer, March 25, 2008, Cambridge, MA; Janet E. Heininger
Anne Strauss, April 10, 2008, New York, NY; Janet E. Heininger
Thomas Susman, May 23, 2007, Washington, DC; Paul Martin
David Sutphen, March 29, 2007, Washington, DC; Stephen F. Knott
William Taylor, January 25, 2007, Washington, DC; Stephen F. Knott
William Taylor, February 20, 2007, Washington, DC; Stephen F. Knott
Betty Taymor, July 8, 2005, Boston, MA; Stephen F. Knott
Charles Tretter, August 8, 2005, Boston, MA; Stephen F. Knott
Laurence H. Tribe, April 27, 2009, Boston, MA; Janet E. Heininger
John Tunney, May 3, 2007, New York, NY; Stephen F. Knott, James Sterling Young
John Tunney, October 12, 2009, New York, NY; James Sterling Young
Desmond Tutu, May 13, 2006, Williamsburg, VA; James Sterling Young, Stephen F. Knott
William J. vanden Heuvel, July 19, 2005, New York, NY; James Sterling Young
William J. vanden Heuvel, December 7, 2006, New York, NY; James Sterling Young
Trina Vargo, November 7, 2008, Arlington, VA; Janet E. Heininger, James Sterling Young
Galina Veremkroit, February 17, 2009, Arlington, MA; Janet E. Heininger
*John W. Warner, May 6, 2009, Washington, DC; James Sterling Young
*Henry Waxman, February 18, 2010, Los Angeles, CA; Janet E. Heininger
Sharon L. Waxman, December 19, 2008, Washington, DC; Janet E. Heininger, James Sterling Young
Sharon L. Waxman, May 11, 2009, Washington, DC; James Sterling Young
Ronald Weich, March 30, 2007, Washington, DC; Stephen F. Knott
Lowell P. Weicker Jr., June 19, 2009, Charlottesville, VA; Janet E. Heininger
*Burton V. Wides, February 2, 2007, Washington, DC; Stephen F. Knott
*Angela Williams, March 7, 2008, Chicago, IL; Janet E. Heininger
James Sterling Young, October 16, 2009, Charlottesville, VA; Lee Fentress

*Not released as of press time

Index